CHILTON'S
REPAIR MANUAL

NISSAN STANZA/ 200SX/240SX 1982–92

All U.S. and Canadian models

Sr. Vice President	Ronald A. Hoxter
Publisher and Editor-In-Chief	Kerry A. Freeman, S.A.E.
Managing Editors	Peter M. Conti, Jr. □ W. Calvin Settle, Jr., S.A.E.
Assistant Managing Editor	Nick D'Andrea
Senior Editors	Richard J. Rivele, S.A.E. □ Ron Webb
Director of Manufacturing	Mike D'Imperio
Manager of Manufacturing	John F. Butler
Editor	Anthony Tortorici, A.S.E., S.A.E.

CHILTON BOOK COMPANY

ONE OF THE DIVERSIFIED PUBLISHING COMPANIES,
A PART OF CAPITAL CITIES/ABC, INC.

CONTENTS

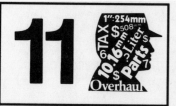

SAFETY NOTICE

Proper service and repair procedures are vital to the safe, reliable operation of all motor vehicles, as well as the safety of those performing repairs. This book outlines procedures for servicing and repairing vehicles using safe effective methods. The procedures contain many NOTES, CAUTIONS and WARNINGS which should be followed along with standard safety procedures to eliminate the possibility of personal injury or improper service which could damage the vehicle or compromise its safety.

It is important to note that repair procedures and techniques, tools and parts for servicing motor vehicles, as well as the skill and experience of the individual performing the work vary widely. It is not possible to anticipate all of the conceivable ways or conditions under which vehicles may be serviced, or to provide cautions as to all of the possible hazards that may result. Standard and accepted safety precautions and equipment should be used during cutting, grinding, chiseling, prying, or any other process that can cause material removal or projectiles.

Some procedures require the use of tools specially designed for a specific purpose. Before substituting another tool or procedure, you must be completely satisfied that neither your personal safety, nor the performance of the vehicle will be endangered.

Although the information in this guide is based on industry sources and is as complete as possible at the time of publication, the possibility exists that the manufacturer made later changes which could not be included here. While striving for total accuracy, Chilton Book Company cannot assume responsibility for any errors, changes, or omissions that may occur in the compilation of this data.

PART NUMBERS

Part numbers listed in this reference are not recommendations by Chilton for any product by brand name. They are references that can be used with interchange manuals and aftermarket supplier catalogs to locate each brand supplier's discrete part number.

SPECIAL TOOLS

Special tools are recommended by the vehicle manufacturer to perform their specific job. Use has been kept to a minimum, but where absolutely necessary, they are referred to in the text by the part number of the tool manufacturer. These tools can be purchased, under the appropriate part number, from your Nissan dealer or regional distributor or an equivalent tool can be purchased locally from a tool supplier or parts outlet. Before substituting any tool for the one recommended, read the SAFETY NOTICE at the top of this page.

ACKNOWLEDGEMENTS

Chilton Book Company expresses its appreciation to Nissan Motor Corp.; U.S.A., Carson, Calif. for their generous assistance.

General Information and Maintenance

HOW TO USE THIS BOOK

Chilton's Repair Manual for Datsun/Nissan 200SX, 240SX and Stanza cars is intended to help you learn more about the inner workings of your vehicle and save you money on its up-keep and operation.

The first two Chapters will be the most used, since they contain maintenance and tune-up information and procedures. Studies have shown that a properly tuned and maintained car can get at least 10% better gas mileage than an out-of-tune car. The other Chapters deal with the more complex systems of your car. Operating systems from engine through brakes are covered to the extent that the average do-it-yourselfer becomes mechanically involved. It will give you detailed instructions to help you change your own brake pads and shoes, replace spark plugs, belts, hoses etc. and do many more jobs that will save you money, give you personal satisfaction, and help you avoid expensive problems.

A secondary purpose of this book is a reference for owners who want to understand their car and/or their mechanics better. In this case, no tools at all are required.

Before removing any bolts, read through the entire procedure and review all necessary illustrations. This will give you the overall view of what tools and supplies will be required. There is nothing more frustrating than having to walk to the bus stop on Monday morning because you were short one bolt on Sunday afternoon. So read ahead and plan ahead. Each operation should be approached logically and all procedures thoroughly understood before attempting any work. Some special tools that may be required can often be rented from local automotive stores.

All Chapters contain adjustments, maintenance, removal and installation procedures, and repair or overhaul procedures. When repair is not considered practical, we tell you how to remove the part and then how to install the new or rebuilt replacement. In this way, you at least save the labor costs. Backyard repair of such components as the alternator is just not practical.

Two basic mechanic's rules should be mentioned here. One, whenever the LEFT side of the car or engine is referred to, it is meant to specify the DRIVER'S side of the car. Conversely, the RIGHT side of the car means the PAS-SENGER'S side. Secondly, MOST screws and bolt are removed by turning counterclockwise, and tightened by turning clockwise.

SAFETY IS ALWAYS THE MOST IMPORTANT RULE. Constantly be aware of the dangers involved in working on an automobile and take the proper precautions. (See the heading Servicing Your Vehicle Safely and the SAFETY NOTICE on the acknowledgement page.)

Pay attention to the instructions provided. There are 3 common mistakes in mechanical work:

1. Incorrect order of assembly, disassembly or adjustment. When taking something apart or putting it together, doing things in the wrong order usually just costs you extra time; however, it CAN break something. Read the entire procedure before beginning disassembly. Do everything in the order in which the instructions say you should do it, even if you can't immediately see a reason for it. When you're taking apart something that is very intricate (for example, a carburetor), you might want to draw a picture of how it looks when assembled at one point in order to make sure you get everything back in its proper position. (We will supply exploded views whenever possible). When making adjustments, especially tune-up adjustments, do them in order; often, one adjustment affects another, and you cannot expect even satisfac-

tory results unless each adjustment is made only when it cannot be changed by any order.

2. Overtorquing (or undertorquing). While it is more common for over-torquing to cause damage, undertorquing can cause a fastener to vibrate loose causing serious damage. Especially when dealing with aluminum parts, pay attention to torque specifications and utilize a torque wrench in assembly. If a torque figure is not available, remember that if you are using the right tool to do the job, you will probably not have to strain yourself to get a fastener tight enough. The pitch of most threads is so slight that the tension you put on the wrench will be multiplied many, many times in actual force on what you are tightening. A good example of how critical torque is can be seen in the case of spark plug installation, especially where you are putting the plug into an aluminum cylinder head. Too little torque can fail to crush the gasket, causing leakage of combustion gases and consequent overheating of the plug and engine parts. Too much torque can damage the threads, or distort the plug which changes the spark gap.

There are many commercial products available for ensuring that fasteners won't come loose, even if they are not torqued just right (a very common brand is Loctite®). If you're worried about getting something together tight enough to hold, but loose enough to avoid mechanical damage during assembly, one of these products might offer substantial insurance. Read the label on the package and make sure the products is compatible with the materials, fluids, etc. involved before choosing one.

3. Crossthreading. This occurs when a part such as a bolt is screwed into a nut or casting at the wrong angle and forced. Cross threading is more likely to occur if access is difficult. It helps to clean and lubricate fasteners, and to start threading with the part to be installed going straight in. Then, start the bolt, spark plug, etc. with your fingers. If you encounter resistance, unscrew the part and start over again at a different angle until it can be inserted and turned several turns without much effort. Keep in mind that many parts, especially spark plugs, used tapered threads so that gentle turning will automatically bring the part you're treading to the proper angle if you don't force it or resist a change in angle. Don't put a wrench on the part until its's been turned a couple of turns by hand. If you suddenly encounter resistance, and the part has not seated fully, don't force it. Pull it back out and make sure it's clean and threading properly.

Always take your time and be patient; once you have some experience, working on your car will become an enjoyable hobby.

TOOLS AND EQUIPMENT

The service procedures in this book pre-suppose a familiarity with hand tools and their proper use. However, it is possible that you may have a limited amount of experience with the sort of equipment needed to work on an automobile. This Chapter is designed to help you assemble a basic set of tools that will handle most of the jobs you may undertake.

In addition to the normal assortment of screwdrivers and pliers, automotive service work requires an investment in wrenches, sockets and the handles needed to drive them, plus various measuring tools such as torque wrenches and feeler gauges.

You will find that virtually every nut and bolt on your vehicle is Metric. Therefore, despite a few close size similarities, standard inch-size tools will not fit and must not be used. You will need a set of metric wrenches as your most basic tool kit, ranging from about 6–22mm in size. High quality forged wrenches are available in three styles: open end, box end and combination open/box end. The combination tools are generally the most desirable as a starter set; the wrenches shown in the accompanying illustration are of the combination type.

The other set of tools inevitably required is a ratchet handle and socket set. This set should have the same size range as your wrench set. The ratchet, extensions and flex drives for the sockets are available in many sizes; it is advisable to choose a ⅜ in. drive set initially. One break in the inch/metric sizing war is that metric sized sockets sold in the U.S. have inch-sized drive (¼ in., ⅜ in., ½ in. and etc.). Thus, if you already have an inch-sized socket set, you need only buy new metric sockets in the sizes needed. Sockets are available in 6- and 12-point versions; six point types are stronger and are a good choice for a first set. The choice of a drive handle for the sockets should be made with some care. If this is your first set, take the plunge and invest in a flex-head ratchet; it will get into many places otherwise accessible only through a long chain of universal joints, extensions and adapters. An alternative is a flex handle, which lacks the ratcheting feature but has a head which pivots 180°; such a tool is shown below the ratchet handle in the illustration. In addition to the range of sockets mentioned, a rubber lined spark plug socket should be purchased.

The most important thing to consider when purchasing hand tools is quality. Don't be misled by the low cost of bargain tools. Forged wrenches, tempered screwdriver blades and fine-toothed ratchets are much better investments than their less expensive counterparts.

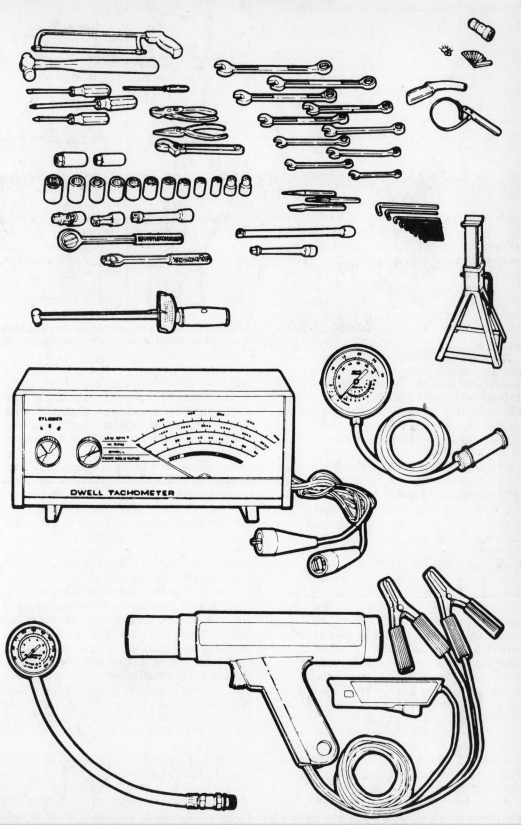

The tools and equipment shown here will handle the majority of the maintenance on a car

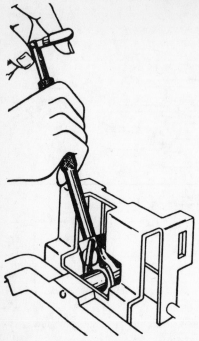

A new design speedwrench—for easy removal of retaining nuts

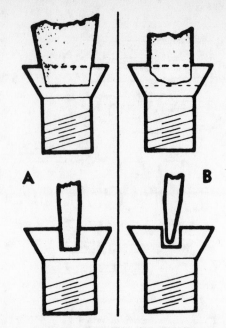

Keep screwdriver tips in good shape. They should fit in the slot as shown in "A". If they look like those in "B" they need replacing.

The skinned knuckles and frustration inflicted by poor quality tools make any job an unhappy chore. Another consideration is that quality tools come with an unbeatable replacement guarantee; if the tool breaks, you get a new one, no questions asked.

Most jobs can be accomplished using the tools on the accompanying lists. There will be an occasional need for a special tool, such as snap ring pliers; that need will be mentioned in the text. It would not be wise to buy a large assortment of tools on the premise that someday they will be needed. Instead, the tools should be acquired one at a time, each for a specific job, both to avoid unnecessary expense and to be certain that you have the right tool.

The tools needed for basic maintenance jobs, in addition to the wrenches and sockets mentioned, include:

1. Jackstands, for support.
2. Oil filter wrench.
3. Oil filter spout or funnel.
4. Grease gun.
5. Battery post and clamp cleaner.
6. Container for draining oil.
7. Many rags for the inevitable spills.

In addition to these items there are several others which are not absolutely necessary but handy to have around. These include a transmission funnel and filler tube, a drop (trouble) light on a long cord, an adjustable (crescent) wrench and slip joint pliers.

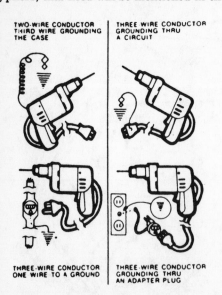

When using electric tools make sure they are properly grounded

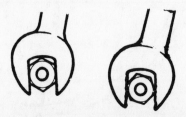

If you are using an open end wrench, use the correct size and position it properly on the nut or bolt

A more advanced list of tools, suitable for tune-up work, can be drawn up easily. While the tools are slightly more sophisticated, they need not be outrageously expensive. The key to these purchases is to make them with an eye towards adaptability and wide range. A basic list of tune-up tools could include:

1. Tachometer/dwell meter.
2. Spark plug gauge and gapping tool.
3. Feeler gauges.
4. Timing light.

You will need both the wire type (spark plugs) and the flat type (valves) feeler gauges. The choice of a timing light should be made carefully. A light which works on the DC current supplied by the vehicle battery is the best choice; it should have a xenon tube for brightness. Since most of the vehicles have electronic ignition or will have it in the future, the light should have an inductive pickup which clamps around the No. 1 spark plug cable (the timing light illustrated has one of these pickups).

In addition to these basic tools, there are several other tools and gauges which you may find useful. These include:

1. A compression gauge. The screw-in type is slower to use but eliminates the possibility of faulty reading due to escaping pressure.
2. A manifold vacuum gauge.
3. A test light.
4. A combination volt/ohmmeter.
5. An induction meter, used to determine whether or not there is current flowing in a wire, an extremely helpful tool for electrical troubleshooting.

Finally, you will find a torque wrench necessary for all but the most basic of work. The beam type models are perfectly adequate. The newer click type (breakaway) torque wrenches are more accurate but are much more expensive and must be periodically recalibrated.

Special Tools

Special tools are available from:
Kent-Moore Corporation
29784 Little Mack
Roseville, Michigan 48066

In Canada:
Kent-Moore of Canada, Ltd.,
2395 Cawthra
Mississauga, Ontario
Canada L5A 3P2

SERVICING YOUR CAR SAFELY

It is virtually impossible to anticipate all of the hazards involved with automotive mainte-nance and service, but care and common sense will prevent most accidents.

The rules of safety for mechanics range from don't smoke around gasoline, to use the proper tool for the job. The trick to avoiding injuries is to develop safe work habits and take every possible precaution. Always think through what you do before doing it!

Dos

● Do keep a fire extinguisher and first aid kit within easy reach.

● Do wear safety glasses or goggles when cutting, drilling, grinding or prying, even if you have 20/20 vision. If you wear glasses for the sake of vision, they should be made of hardened glass that can serve also as safety glasses, or wear safety goggles over your regular glasses.

● Do shield your eyes whenever you work around the battery. Batteries contain sulphuric acid. In case of contact with the eyes or skin, flush the area with water or a mixture of water and baking soda and get medical attention immediately.

● Do use safety stands for any undercar service. Jacks are for raising vehicles; safety stands are for making sure the vehicle stays raised until you want it to come down. Whenever the car is raised, block the wheels remaining on the ground and set the parking brake.

● Do use a hydraulic floor jack of at least 1½ ton capacity when working on your Datsun or Nissan. That little jack supplied with the car is only designed for changing tires out on the road.

● Do use adequate ventilation when working with any chemicals or hazardous materials. Like carbon monoxide, the asbestos dust resulting from brake lining wear can be poisonous in sufficient quantities.

● Do disconnect the negative battery cable when working on the electrical system. The secondary ignition system can contain up to 40,000 volts.

● Do follow manufacturer's directions when-

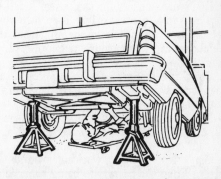

Always support the vehicle when working under it

ever working with potentially hazardous materials. Both brake fluid and antifreeze are poisonous if taken internally.

• Do properly maintain your tools. Loose hammerheads, mushroomed punches and chisels, frayed or poorly grounded electrical cords, excessively worn screwdrivers, spread wrenches (open end), cracked sockets, slipping ratchets, or faulty droplight sockets can cause accidents.

• Do use the proper size and type of tool for the job being done.

• Do when possible, pull on a wrench handle rather than push on it, and adjust your stance to prevent a fall.

• Do be sure that adjustable wrenches are tightly closed on the nut or bolt and pulled so that the face is on the side of the fixed jaw.

• Do select a wrench or socket that fits the nut or bolt. The wrench or socket should sit straight, not cocked.

• Do strike squarely with a hammer. Avoid glancing blows.

• Do set the parking brake and block the drive wheels if the work requires the engine running.

Don'ts

• Don't run an engine in a garage or anywhere else without proper ventilation—EVER! Carbon monoxide is poisonous. It takes a long time to leave the human body and you can build up a deadly supply of it in your system by simply breathing in a little every day. You may not realize you are slowly poisoning yourself. Always use power vents, windows, fans or open the garage doors.

• Don't work around moving parts while wearing a necktie or other loose clothing. Short sleeves are much safer than long, loose sleeves. Hard-toed shoes with neoprene soles protect your toes and give a better grip on slippery surfaces. Jewelry such as watches, fancy belt buckles, beads or body adornment of any kind is not safe working around a car. Long hair should be hidden under a hat or cap.

• Don't use pockets for toolboxes. A fall or bump can drive a screwdriver deep into your body. Even a wiping cloth hanging from the back pocket can wrap around a spinning shaft or fan.

• Don't use cinderblocks to support a car! When you get the car jacked up (with a hydraulic floor jack), support it with jackstands.

• Don't smoke when working around gasoline, cleaning solvent or other flammable material.

• Don't smoke when working around the battery. When the battery is being charged, it gives off explosive hydrogen gas.

• Don't use gasoline to wash your hands. There are excellent soaps available. Gasoline may contain lead, and lead can enter the body through a cut, accumulating in the body until you are very ill. Gasoline also removes all the natural oils from the skin so that bone dry hands will suck up oil and grease.

• Don't service the air conditioning system unless you are equipped with the necessary tools and training. The refrigerant, R-12, is compressed and in liquid form, and when released into the air will instantly freeze any surface it contacts, including your eyes. Although the refrigerant is normally non-toxic, R-12 becomes a deadly poisonous gas (phosgene) in the presence of an open flame. One good whiff of the vapors from burning refrigerant can be fatal.

SERIAL NUMBER IDENTIFICATION

Chassis

The chassis number is on the firewall under the hood on all models. All vehicles also have the chassis number (also known as the Vehicle Identification Number) on a plate attached to the top of the instrument panel on the driver's side, visible through the windshield. The chassis serial number is preceded by the model designation. All models have an Emission Control information label on the firewall or on the underside of the hood.

Vehicle Identification Plate

The vehicle identification plate is attached to the right-side of the firewall. This plate gives the vehicle type, identification number, model, body color code, trim color code, engine model and displacement, transmission/transaxle model and axle model.

Engine
200SX And 240SX

On the 1982–83 200SX engine (Z20, Z22 engines) serial numbers are stamped on the left side top edge of the cylinder block when viewed from the the driver's seat. The 1984–88 200SX models (CA20, CA18ET engines) engine serial numbers are stamped on the left side rear edge of the block, next to the bellhousing when viewed from the the driver's seat.

On the 1989–90 240SX engine (KA24E engine) serial number is stamped on the left side top edge of the cylinder block when viewed from the the driver's seat between No. 2 and No. 3 cylinders.

On the 1990–92 240SX engine (KA24DE engine) serial number is stamped on the left side top edge of the cylinder block (near bellhousing) when viewed from the the driver's seat.

STANZA

The CA20, CA20S and CA20E engine serial number is stamped on the right side top edge of the cylinder block when view from outside the

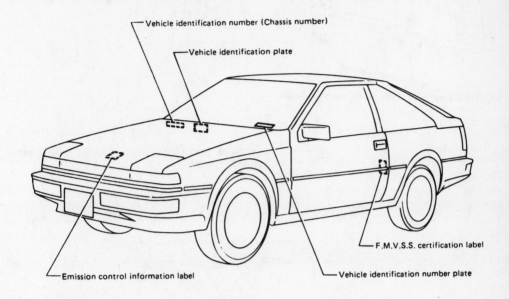

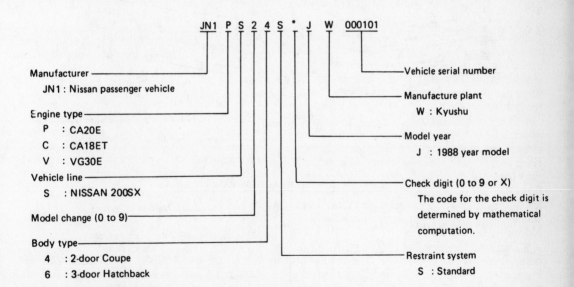

The production of the 1988 NISSAN 200SX starts with the following vehicle identification numbers:

JN1PS24S*JW000001
JN1PS26S*JW000001
JN1CS26S*JW000001
JN1VS26S*JW000001

* : Check digit (0 to 9 or X)

Vehicle identification number arrangement

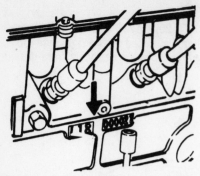

1982–83 200SX Z-series engine serial number location

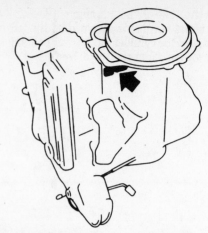

1984–88 200SX CA20E and CA18ET engine serial number location

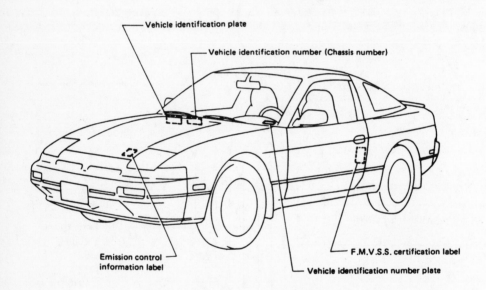

Vehicle identification plate

Vehicle identification number (Chassis number)

Emission control information label

F.M.V.S.S. certification label

Vehicle identification number plate

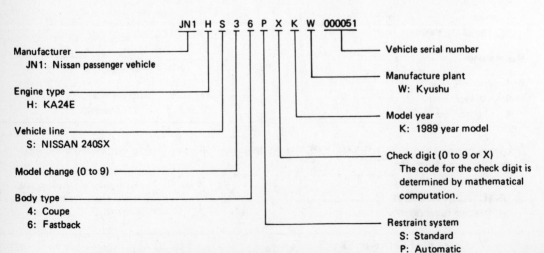

JN1 H S 3 6 P X K W 000051

Manufacturer
JN1: Nissan passenger vehicle

Engine type
H: KA24E

Vehicle line
S: NISSAN 240SX

Model change (0 to 9)

Body type
4: Coupe
6: Fastback

Vehicle serial number

Manufacture plant
W: Kyushu

Model year
K: 1989 year model

Check digit (0 to 9 or X)
The code for the check digit is
determined by mathematical
computation.

Restraint system
S: Standard
P: Automatic

Vehicle identification number arrangement

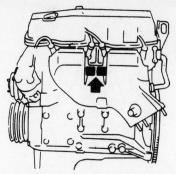

1989–90 240SX KA24E engine serial number location

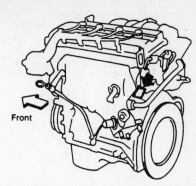

Front

1990–92 240SX KA24DE engine serial number location

car looking into the engine compartment on Stanza 1982–89 models.

On the 1990–92 Stanza (KA24E engine) engine serial number is stamped on top edge of the cylinder block between No. 2 and No. 3 cylinders when view from outside the car looking into the engine compartment.

Transaxle

For all applications, the transaxle number is stamped on the upper area of the transaxle (see illusrations) or attached to the clutch withdrawal lever (some manual applications).

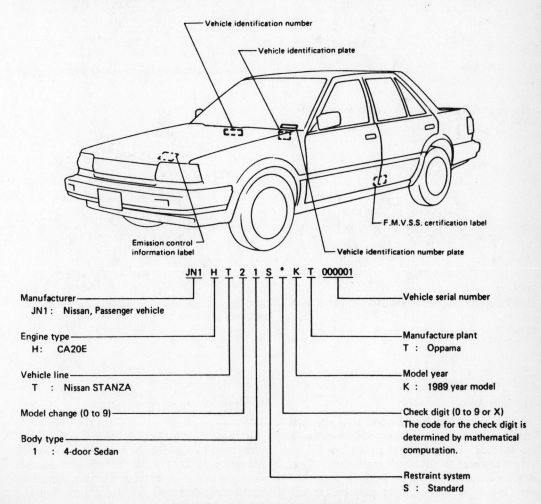

— Vehicle identification number

— Vehicle identification plate

— F.M.V.S.S. certification label

Emission control information label

— Vehicle identification number plate

JN1 H T 2 1 S * K T 000001

Manufacturer
JN1 : Nissan, Passenger vehicle

Engine type
H : CA20E

Vehicle line
T : Nissan STANZA

Model change (0 to 9)

Body type
1 : 4-door Sedan

Vehicle serial number

Manufacture plant
T : Oppama

Model year
K : 1989 year model

Check digit (0 to 9 or X)
The code for the check digit is determined by mathematical computation.

Restraint system
S : Standard

Vehicle identification number arrangement

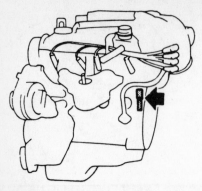

1982–89 Stanza CA20 series engine serial number location

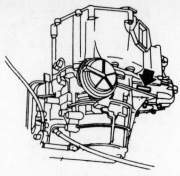

1985 Stanza automatic transaxle serial number location

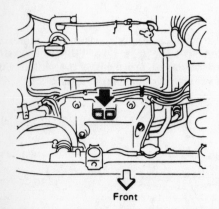

1990–92 Stanza KA24E series engine serial number location

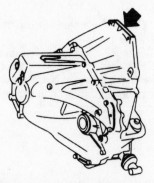

1992 Stanza manual transaxle serial number location

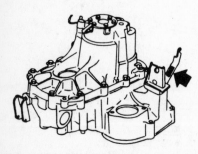

1985 Stanza manual transaxle serial number location

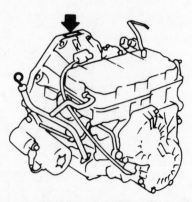

1992 Stanza automatic transaxle serial number location

Transmission

The transmission serial number is stamped on the front upper face of the transmission case on manual transmissions, or on the lower right side of the case on automatic transmissions except for the 240SX model (automatic transmission) which is on the right side but in the tailshaft area.

ROUTINE MAINTENANCE

Routine maintenance is the self-explanatory term used to describe the sort of periodic work necessary to keep a car in safe and reliable working order. A regular program aimed at monitoring essential systems ensure that the car's components are functioning correctly

UNIT NUMBER

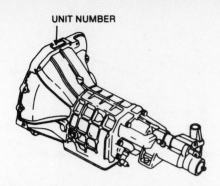

Location of the manual transmission serial number—200SX model

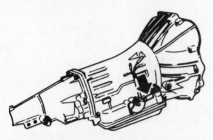

Location of the automatic transmission serial number—200SX model

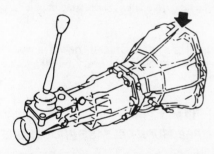

240SX manual transmission serial number location

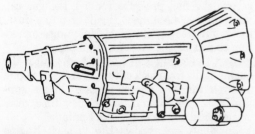

240SX automatic transmission serial number location

(and will continue to do so until the next inspection, one hopes), and can prevent small problems from developing into major headaches. Routine maintenance also pays big dividends in keeping major repair costs at a minimum, extending the life of the car, and enhancing resale value.

A definite maintenance schedule is provided by Datsun/Nissan, and must be followed, not only to keep the new car warranty in effect, but also to keep the car working properly. The "Maintenance Interval Chart" in this Chapter outlines the routine maintenance which must be performed according to intervals based on either accumulated mileage or time. Your car also came with a maintenance schedule provided by Datsun/Nissan. Adherence to these schedules will result in a longer life for your car, and will, over the long run, save you money and time.

The checks and adjustments in the following Chapters generally require only a few minutes of attention every few weeks. The services to be performed can be easily accomplished in a morning. The most important part of any maintenance program is regularity. The few minutes or occasional morning spent on these seemingly trivial tasks will forestall or eliminate major problems later.

Air Cleaner

NOTE: *The air cleaner assembly also functions as a flame arrester if the engine should backfire. It should be installed at all times when operating the vehicle.*

An air cleaner and element is used to keep airborne dirt and dust out of the air flowing through the engine. Proper maintenance is vital, as a clogged element will undesirably enrich the fuel mixture, restrict air flow and power, and allow excessive contamination of the oil with abrasives.

All models covered in this book are equipped with a disposable, paper cartridge air cleaner element. The filter should be checked at every tune-up (sooner if the car is operated in a dusty area). Loose dust can sometimes be removed by striking the filter against a hard surface several times or by blowing through it with compressed air. The filter should be replaced every 30,000 miles or every 24 months.

To remove the filter, unscrew the wing nut(s), lift off the housing cover and remove the filter element. There are thumb latches which will also have to be released before removing the housing cover. Before installing the original or the replacement filter, wipe out the inside of the housing with a clean rag or paper towel. Install the paper air cleaner filter, seat the top cover on the bottom housing and tighten the wing nut(s). Clip on the thumb latches if so equipped.

NOTE: *All models utilize a flat, cartridge-type air cleaner element. Although removal and installation procedures for these models are the same as for those with round air cleaners, make sure that the word UP is*

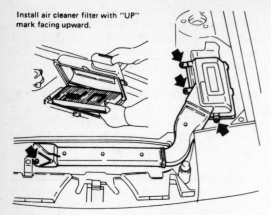

Install air cleaner filter with "UP" mark facing upward.

Install the air filter with "UP" mark facing upward

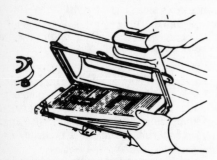

Replacing the air filter element Stanza model

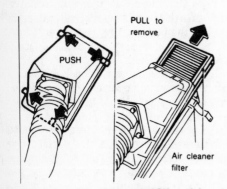

PULL to remove

PUSH

Air cleaner filter

Replacing the air filter element 240SX model

facing up when you install the air filter element.

Air Induction Valve Filter

Certain later models use an air induction valve filter. It is located in the side of the air cleaner housing and is easily replaced. Unscrew the mounting screws and remove the valve filter case. Pull the air induction valve out and remove the filter that lies underneath it. Install the new filter and then the valve. Pay particular attention to which way the valve is facing so that the exhaust gases will not flow backward

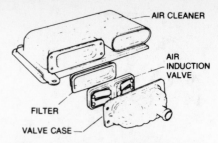

AIR CLEANER

AIR INDUCTION VALVE

FILTER

VALVE CASE

Air induction valve filter—fuel injected engine

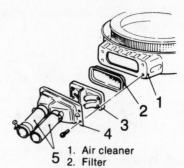

1
2
3
4
5

1. Air cleaner
2. Filter
3. Air induction valve
4. Air induction valve case
5. Rubber hose

Air induction valve filter—carbureted engine

through the system. Install the valve case. Replacement intervals are every 30,000 miles or 24 months.

Fuel Filter

FUEL PRESSURE RELEASE PROCEDURE

The fuel pressure must be released on fuel injected models before removing the fuel filter. To relieve the fuel pressure remove the gas cap then remove/disconnect the fuel pump fuse, fuel pump relay or electrical fuel pump connection to disable the electrical fuel pump.

Start the engine and run it at idle; after the engine stalls from lack of fuel, crank the engine a couple times to release pressure. Turn ignition switch OFF and install/connect fuse, relay or electrical connection to fuel pump.

On some late models the "Check Engine Light" will stay on after installation is completed. The memory code in the control unit must be erased. To erase the code disconnect the battery cable for 1 minute then reconnect after installation of fuel filter. Refer to Chapter 4 and 5 for more information.

REMOVAL AND INSTALLATION

Datsun/Nissan recommends that if the vehicle is operated under extremely adverse weath-

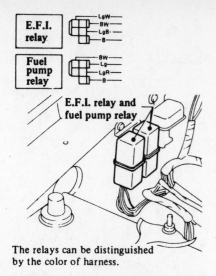

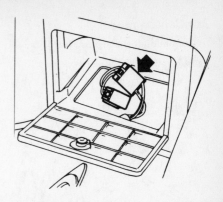

The relays can be distinguished
by the color of harness.

Fuel pump relay location—1982 200SX model

The fuel pump harness connector is in the tool box
on the rear right-hand side on the 1984 and later 200SX
models

er conditions or in areas of extreme high or low
ambient temperatures the fuel filter may become clogged. If so, replace the fuel filter immediately. The fuel filter and fuel lines should be

inspected 30,000 mile or 24 months. Check fuel
lines and fuel tank assembly for proper attachment to the vehicle. Check fuel lines and filter
for leaks, cracks, damage or loose connections.

The fuel filter on all models is a disposable or
replaceable unit if necessary. Most models the
fuel filter is located in the engine compartment
on the right inner fender well. On the Stanza

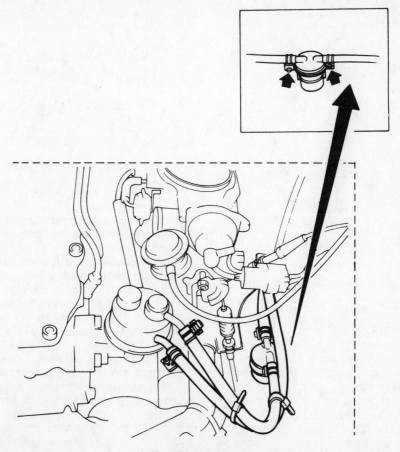

Fuel filter location

For Canada model

Carburetor, fuel pump and fuel filter

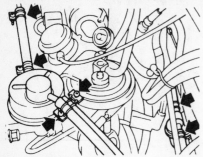

Replacing fuel filter—1985 Stanza

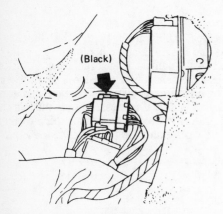

Reducing fuel pressure—1985 Stanza

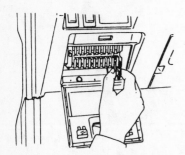

Removing the fuel pump fuse—1987 Stanza

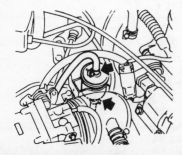

Fuel filter location—1987 Stanza

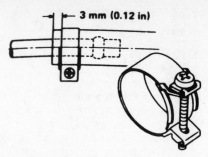

Install fuel line clamps

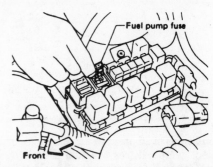

Removing the fuel pump fuse—1990 240SX model

Fuel filter location—1990 240SX model

4×4 Wagon, the fuel filter is found inline, outside the vehicle under the floor, near the fuel pump assembly.

A dirty fuel filter will starve the engine and cause poor running!

CAUTION: *If equipped with an Electronic Fuel Injected (EFI) engine, refer to the "Fuel Pressure Release Procedure" in this Chapter and release the fuel pressure before removing filter. OBSERVE ALL NECESSARY SAFETY PRECAUTIONS. Read the COMPLETE service procedure before starting this repair.*

1. Release the fuel pressure. Disconnect the negative battery cable. Locate fuel filter on right side of the engine compartment and place a container under the filter to catch the excess fuel.

NOTE: *On the Stanza 4×4 Wagon, the fuel*

filter is found inline, under the floor, near the fuel pump.

2. Disconnect the inlet and outlet hoses from the fuel filter. Make certain that the inlet hose (bottom) doesn't fall below the fuel tank level or the gasoline will drain out.

3. Remove the fuel filter from its clip and replace the assembly.

To install:

4. Replace the inlet and outlet gas hose lines if necessary. Install the fuel filter assembly in place, always replace the gas hose clamps on EFI models. Tighten hose clamp so that clamp end is 3mm from the hose end.

NOTE: *Insure that the screw does not contact adjacent parts.*

5. Start the engine and check for fuel leaks. On late models the "Check Engine Light" will stay on after installation is completed. The memory code in the control unit must be erased. To erase the code disconnect the battery cable for 1 minute then reconnect. Refer to Chapter 4 if necessary.

Positive Crankcase Ventilation Valve
REMOVAL AND INSTALLATION

The PCV valve feeds crankcase blow-by gases into the intake manifold to be burned with the normal air/fuel mixture. The PCV valve, hose and connections should be inspected every 30,000 miles or 24 months. Make sure that all PCV connections are tight. Check that the connecting hoses are clear and not clogged. Replace any brittle or broken hoses.

To check the valve's operation, remove the valve's ventilation hose with the engine idling. If the valve is working, a hissing noise will be heard as air passes through the valve, and a strong vacuum will be felt when you place a finger over the valve opening.

On all Stanza models with a carburetor CA20 and CA20S engines a PCV filter is used. To replace this filter just remove the wing nut from the air cleaner lid and remove lid, gently lift out the filter which is mounted on the side of the air cleaner. This filter is usually about 4 in. (102mm) long.

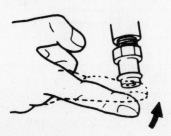

Inspection of PCV valve

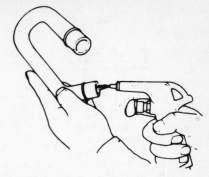

Inspection of PCV valve hose

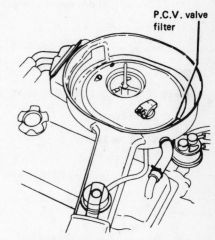

PCV valve filter location

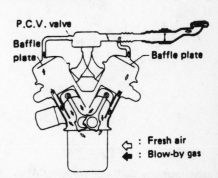

PCV valve location—200SX model with VG30E engine

To replace the valve, which is located in the side or bottom of the intake manifold:

1. Squeeze the hose retaining clamp with pliers and remove the hose.

2. Using a wrench, unscrew the PCV valve and remove the valve.

3. Disconnect the ventilation hose and flush with solvent or clean as necessary.

4. Install the new PCV valve and replace the hoses and clamp.

NOTE: *On the 240SX model the PCV valve is located on the side or front of the intake col-*

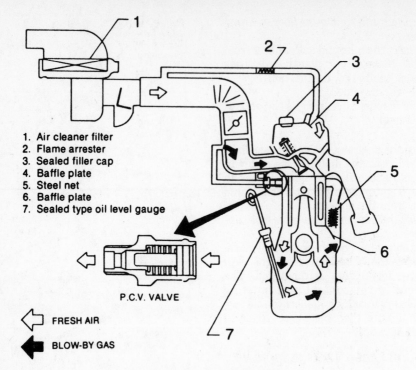

1. Air cleaner filter
2. Flame arrester
3. Sealed filler cap
4. Baffle plate
5. Steel net
6. Baffle plate
7. Sealed type oil level gauge

P.C.V. VALVE

⬅ FRESH AIR

⬅ BLOW-BY GAS

PCV valve location—1982 200SX model

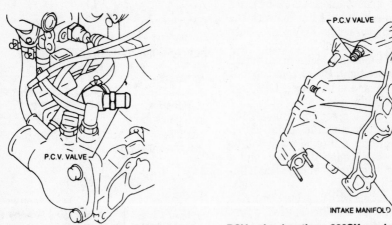

P.C.V. VALVE

PCV valve location—200SX model with CA18ET engine

P.C.V VALVE

INTAKE MANIFOLD

PCV valve location—200SX model with CA20E engine

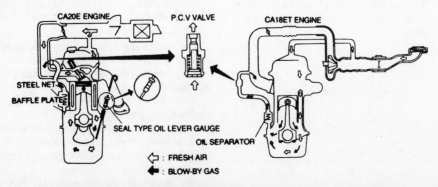

CA20E ENGINE

P.C.V VALVE

STEEL NET

BAFFLE PLATE

SEAL TYPE OIL LEVER GAUGE

CA18ET ENGINE

OIL SEPARATOR

⬅ : FRESH AIR

⬅ : BLOW-BY GAS

PCV valve system, 1984 and later 200SX model—turbo engine on right

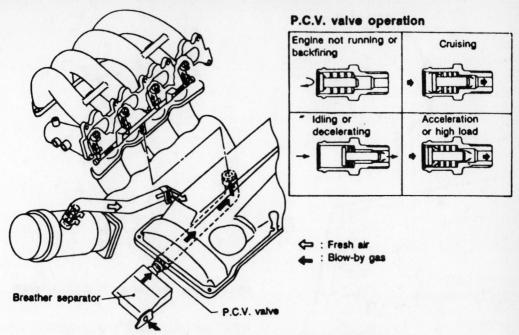

P.C.V. valve operation

Engine not running or backfiring	Cruising
Idling or decelerating	Acceleration or high load

⇦ : Fresh air
⬅ : Blow-by gas

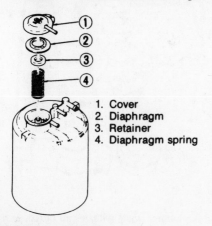

Breather separator

P.C.V. valve

PCV valve location—240SX model with KA24DE engine

lector assembly. On the 200SX VG30E engine the PCV valve is located in the end of the ventilation hose coming from the rocker cover.

Evaporative Emission Control System
SERVICING

The Emission Control System (canister and hoses) should be inspected every 30,000 miles or 24 months to inspect system make sure that all vapor hose connections are tight. Check that vapor hoses are not cracked. Replace any brittle or broken vapor hoses. No further service should be necessary.

A carbon filled canister stores fuel vapors until the engine is started and the vapors are

1. Cover
2. Diaphragm
3. Retainer
4. Diaphragm spring

Vapor canister assembly

drawn into the combustion chambers and burned. To check the operation (if necessary) of the carbon canister purge control valve, disconnect the rubber hose between the canister control valve and the T-fitting, at the T-fitting. Apply vacuum to the hose leading to the control valve. The vacuum condition should be maintained indefinitely. If the control valve leaks, remove the top cover of the valve and check for a dislocated or cracked diaphragm. If the diaphragm is damaged, a repair kit containing a new diaphragm, retainer and spring is available and should be installed.

Battery
SPECIFIC GRAVITY (EXCEPT MAINTENANCE FREE BATTERIES)

At least once a year, check the specific gravity of the battery. It should be between 1.20–1.26 at room temperature.

The specific gravity can be checked with the use of a hydrometer; an inexpensive instrument available from many sources, including auto parts stores. The hydrometer has a squeeze bulb at one end and a nozzle at the other. Battery electrolyte is sucked into the hydrometer until the float is lifted from its seat. The specific gravity is then read by noting the position of the float. Generally, if after charging, the specific gravity between any two cells varies more than 50 points (0.050), the battery is bad and should be replaced.

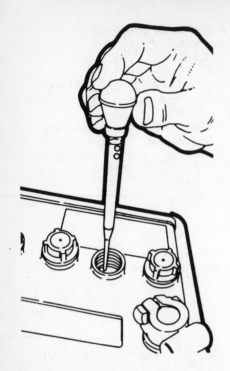

Specific gravity can be checked with a hydrometer

NOTE: *If the battery level is low, add distilled water then operate vehicle for about an hour. Retest the specific gravity.*

It is not possible to check the specific gravity in this manner on sealed (maintenance free) batteries. Instead, the indicator built into the top of the case must be relied on to display any signs of battery deterioration. If the indicator is dark, the battery can be assumed to be OK. If the indicator is light, the specific gravity is low, and the battery should be charged or replaced.

CABLES AND CLAMPS

Once a year, the battery terminals and the cable clamps should be cleaned. Loosen the clamps and remove the cables, negative cable first. On batteries with posts on top, the use of a puller made for the purpose is recommended.

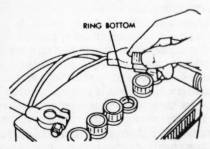

Fill battery cell to the bottom of the split ring with water

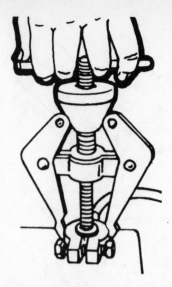

Special pullers make battery clamp removal easier

These are inexpensive, and available in auto parts stores. Side terminal battery cables are secured with a bolt.

Clean the cable clamps and the battery terminal with a wire brush, until all corrosion, grease, etc., is removed and the metal is shiny. It is especially important to clean the inside of

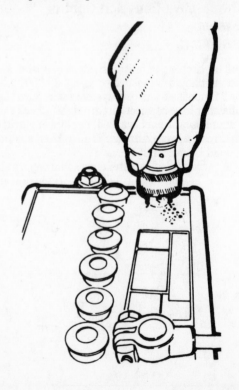

Clean the battery posts with a wire brush, or a terminal cleaner made for that purpose (shown)

Clean the inside of the clamps with a wire brush, or the special tool

the clamp thoroughly, since a small deposit of foreign material or oxidation there will prevent a sound electrical connection and inhibit either starting or charging. Special tools are available for cleaning these parts, one type for conventional batteries and another type for side terminal batteries.

Before installing the cables, loosen the battery holddown clamp or strap, remove the battery and check the battery tray. Clear it of any debris, and check it for soundness. Rust should be wire brushed away, and the metal given a coat of anti-rust paint. Replace the battery and tighten the holddown clamp or strap securely. Be careful not to overtighten, which will crack the battery case.

After the clamps and terminals are clean, reinstall the cables, negative cable last. Do not hammer on the clamps to install. Tighten the clamps securely, but do not distort them. Give

the clamps and terminals a thin external coat of grease after installation, to retard corrosion.

Check the cables at the same time that the terminals are cleaned. If the cable insulation is cracked or broken, or if the ends are frayed, the cable should be replaced with a new cable of the same length and gauge.

NOTE: *Keep flame or sparks away from the battery. It gives off explosive hydrogen gas. Battery electrolyte contains sulphuric acid. If you should splash any on your skin or in your eyes, flush the affected area with plenty of clear water. If it lands in your eyes, get medical help immediately.*

REPLACEMENT

When it becomes necessary to replace the battery, select a battery with a rating equal to or greater than the battery originally installed. Deterioration, embrittlement and just plain aging of the battery cables, starter motor, and associated wires makes the battery's job harder in successive years. The slow increase in electrical resistance over time makes it prudent to install a new battery with a greater capacity than the old. Details on battery removal and installation are covered in Chapter 3.

Belts
INSPECTION AND ADJUSTING

Inspect drive belt deflections when engine is COLD. If engine is HOT, check deflections after waiting 30 minutes or more.

Check and inspect the belts driving the fan, power steering pump, air conditioning compressor, and the alternator for cracks, fraying, wear, and tension every 12 months or 15,000 miles after 60, 000 miles or 48 months of vehicle use. Replace as necessary.

In general, used belt deflection at the midpoint of the longest span between pulleys should be less than ½ in. (13mm) with 22 lbs. (10kg) of pressure applied to the used belt. New belt deflection at the midpoint of the longest span between pulleys should be less than ⅓ in. (8mm) with 22 lbs. (10kg) of pressure applied to the new belt.

Identify how the component must be adjusted. To adjust the tension on a component without an idler pulley adjustment or adjusting bolt, loosen the pivot and mounting bolts of the component which the belt is driving, then, using a wooden lever, pry the component toward or away from the engine until the proper tension is achieved. Tighten the component mounting bolts securely.

NOTE: *An overly tight belt will wear out the pulley bearings on the assorted components.*

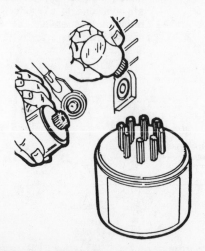

Special tools are available for cleaning the posts and clamps on side terminal batteries

JUMP STARTING A DEAD BATTERY

The chemical reaction in a battery produces explosive hydrogen gas. This is the safe way to jump start a dead battery, reducing the chances of an accidental spark that could cause an explosion.

Jump Starting Precautions

1. Be sure both batteries are of the same voltage.
2. Be sure both batteries are of the same polarity (have the same grounded terminal).
3. Be sure the vehicles are not touching.
4. Be sure the vent cap holes are not obstructed.
5. Do not smoke or allow sparks around the battery.
6. In cold weather, check for frozen electrolyte in the battery.
7. Do not allow electrolyte on your skin or clothing.
8. Be sure the electrolyte is not frozen.

Jump Starting Procedure

1. Determine voltages of the two batteries; they must be the same.
2. Bring the starting vehicle close (they must not touch) so that the batteries can be reached easily.
3. Turn off all accessories and both engines. Put both cars in Neutral or Park and set the handbrake.
4. Cover the cell caps with a rag—do not cover terminals.
5. If the terminals on the run-down battery are heavily corroded, clean them.
6. Identify the positive and negative posts on both batteries and connect the cables in the order shown.
7. Start the engine of the starting vehicle and run it at fast idle. Try to start the car with the dead battery. Crank it for no more than 10 seconds at a time and let it cool off for 20 seconds in between tries.
8. If it doesn't start in 3 tries, there is something else wrong.
9. Disconnect the cables in the reverse order.
10. Replace the cell covers and dispose of the rags.

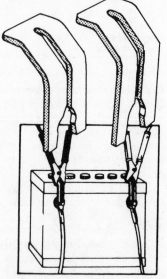

Side terminal batteries occasionally pose a problem when connecting jumper cables. There frequently isn't enough room to clamp the cables without touching sheet metal. Side terminal adaptors are available to alleviate this problem and should be removed after use.

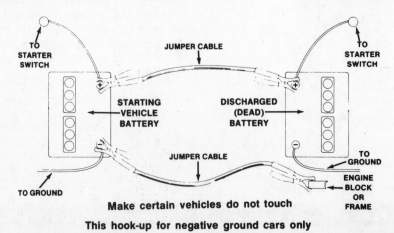

Make certain vehicles do not touch

This hook-up for negative ground cars only

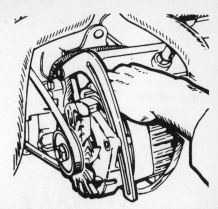

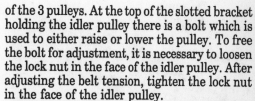

Pull outward on the component while you tighten the mounting bolts. Make sure the belt has the proper adjustment

To adjust the belt tension or replace the belts, first loosen the component's mounting and adjusting bolts slightly

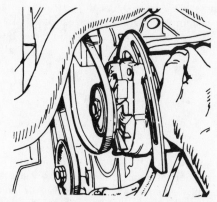

Next, push the component in and slip off the belt

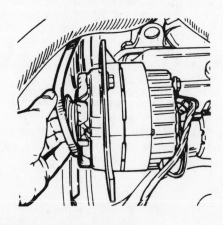

Slip the new belt over the pulleys

If a new belt is installed, recheck the tension after driving about 1,000 miles.

Belt tension adjustments for the factory installed air conditioning compressor and some other components may be made at the idler pulley adjustment. The idler pulley is the smallest of the 3 pulleys. At the top of the slotted bracket holding the idler pulley there is a bolt which is used to either raise or lower the pulley. To free the bolt for adjustment, it is necessary to loosen the lock nut in the face of the idler pulley. After adjusting the belt tension, tighten the lock nut in the face of the idler pulley.

Belt tension adjustments for the power steering oil pump (and some alternator applications) are made at the pump or component adjusting bolt. Loosen the power steering oil pump or component adjusting lock bolt and its securing bolt. Adjust the adjusting bolt until the belt deflection is correct. Tighten the adjusting bolt lock bolt and oil pump or component securing bolt securely.

REMOVAL AND INSTALLATION

The replacement of the inner belt on multi-belted engines may require the removal of the outer belts. To replace a drive belt, loosen the pivot and mounting bolts of the component which the belt is driving; then, using a wooden lever or equivalent pry the component inward to relieve the tension on the drive belt. Always be careful where you locate the pry bar not to damage the component. Slip the belt off the component pulley, match up the new belt with the old belt for length and width, these measurement must be the same or problems will occur when adjustomg the new belt. After new belt is installed correctly adjust the tension of the new belt.

NOTE: *When replacing more than one belt, it is a good idea to make note or mark what belt goes around what pulley. This will make installation fast and easy.*

On air conditioning compressor and power steering pump belt replacements, loosen the lock bolt for the adjusting bolt on idler pulley or power steering pump and then loosen the ad-

HOW TO SPOT WORN V-BELTS

V-Belts are vital to efficient engine operation—they drive the fan, water pump and other accessories. They require little maintenance (occasional tightening) but they will not last forever. Slipping or failure of the V-belt will lead to overheating. If your V-belt looks like any of these, it should be replaced.

This belt has deep cracks, which cause it to flex. Too much flexing leads to heat build-up and premature failure. These cracks can be caused by using the belt on a pulley that is too small. Notched belts are available for small diameter pulleys.

Cracking or weathering

Oil and grease on a belt can cause the belt's rubber compounds to soften and separate from the reinforcing cords that hold the belt together. The belt will first slip, then finally fail altogether.

Softening (grease and oil)

Glazing is caused by a belt that is slipping. A slipping belt can cause a run-down battery, erratic power steering, overheating or poor accessory performance. The more the belt slips, the more glazing will be built up on the surface of the belt. The more the belt is glazed, the more it will slip. If the glazing is light, tighten the belt.

Glazing

The cover of this belt is worn off and is peeling away. The reinforcing cords will begin to wear and the belt will shortly break. When the belt cover wears in spots or has a rough jagged appearance, check the pulley grooves for roughness.

Worn cover

This belt is on the verge of breaking and leaving you stranded. The layers of the belt are separating and the reinforcing cords are exposed. It's just a matter of time before it breaks completely.

Separation

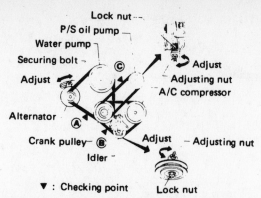

▼ : Checking point

Drive belts—200SX with CA20E and CA18ET engines

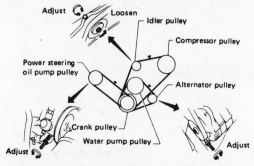

Drive belts—200SX with VG30E engine

justing bolt. Pry pulley or pump inward to relieve the tension on the drive belt, always be careful where you locate the pry bar not to damage the component or pulley.

Hoses

REMOVAL AND INSTALLATION

The upper and lower radiator hoses and all heater hoses should be checked for deterioration, leaks and loose hose clamps every 15,000 miles or 12 months. Check the front of the radiator and clean off any dirt, insects, leaves etc., that may have accumulated.

CAUTION: *When draining the coolant, keep in mind that cats and dogs are attracted by the ethylene glycol antifreeze, and are quite likely to drink any that is left in an uncovered container or in puddles on the ground. This will prove fatal in sufficient quantity. Always drain the coolant into a sealable container. Coolant should be reused unless it is contaminated or several years old.*

After engine is COLD, remove the radiator cap and drain the radiator into a clean pan if you are going to reuse the old coolant. Remove the hose clamps and remove the hose by either cutting it off or twisting it to break its seal on

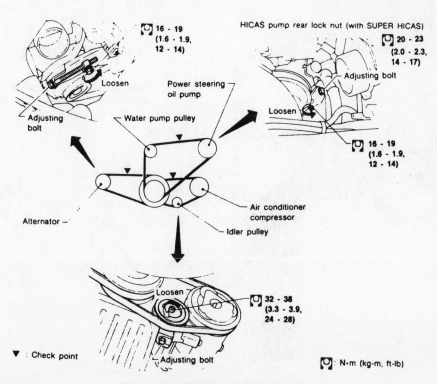

▼ : Check point

Drive belts—240SX with KA24DE engine

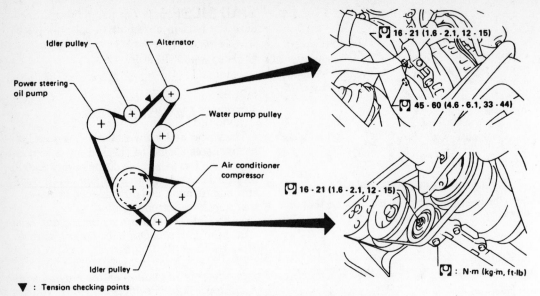

Idler pulley — Alternator

Power steering oil pump

Water pump pulley

Air conditioner compressor

16 - 21 (1.6 - 2.1, 12 - 15)

45 - 60 (4.6 - 6.1, 33 - 44)

16 - 21 (1.6 - 2.1, 12 - 15)

Idler pulley

: N·m (kg-m, ft-lb)

▼ : Tension checking points

Drive belts—Stanza with KA24E engine

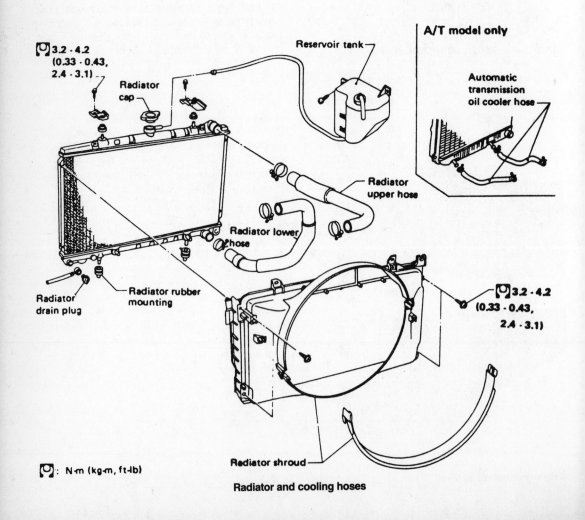

3.2 - 4.2 (0.33 - 0.43, 2.4 - 3.1)

Radiator cap

Reservoir tank

A/T model only

Automatic transmission oil cooler hose

Radiator upper hose

Radiator lower hose

Radiator drain plug

Radiator rubber mounting

3.2 - 4.2 (0.33 - 0.43, 2.4 - 3.1)

Radiator shroud

: N·m (kg-m, ft-lb)

Radiator and cooling hoses

HOW TO SPOT BAD HOSES

Both the upper and lower radiator hoses are called upon to perform difficult jobs in an inhospitable environment. They are subject to nearly 18 psi at under hood temperatures often over 280°F., and must circulate nearly 7500 gallons of coolant an hour—3 good reasons to have good hoses.

A good test for any hose is to feel it for soft or spongy spots. Frequently these will appear as swollen areas of the hose. The most likely cause is oil soaking. This hose could burst at any time, when hot or under pressure.

Swollen hose

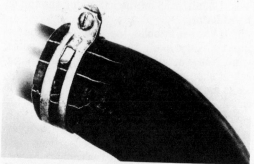

Cracked hoses can usually be seen but feel the hoses to be sure they have not hardened; a prime cause of cracking. This hose has cracked down to the reinforcing cords and could split at any of the cracks.

Cracked hose

Weakened clamps frequently are the cause of hose and cooling system failure. The connection between the pipe and hose has deteriorated enough to allow coolant to escape when the engine is hot.

Frayed hose end (due to weak clamp)

Debris, rust and scale in the cooling system can cause the inside of a hose to weaken. This can usually be felt on the outside of the hose as soft or thinner areas.

Debris in cooling system

the radiator and engine coolant inlets. When installing the new hose, do not overtighten the hose clamps or you might cut the hose or destroy the neck of the radiator. Refill the radiator with coolant, run the engine with the radiator cap on and then recheck the coolant level after engine has reached operating temperature, about 5–7 minutes.

NOTE: *It always is good idea to replace hose clamps when replacing radiator hoses.*

Air Conditioning System

SAFETY WARNINGS

Extreme care must be exercised when working on or around air conditioning lines and components.

1. Avoid contact with a charged refrigeration system, even when working on another part of the air conditioning system or vehicle. If a heavy tool comes into contact with a section of A/C line, it can easily cause the relatively soft material to rupture.

2. When it is necessary to apply force to a fitting which contains refrigerant, as when checking that all system couplings are securely tightened, use a wrench on both parts of the fitting involved, if possible. This will avoid putting torque on refrigerant tubing. (It is advisable, when possible, to use tube or line wrenches when tightening these flare nut fittings.

3. Be aware of the presence of leaking refrigerant. A breath of the gas can exclude oxygen and act as an anesthesia. When leak testing or soldering, this is particularly important, as toxic gas is formed when R-12 contacts any flame.

4. Avoid applying heat to any refrigerant line or storage vessel.

5. Always wear goggles when working on a system to protect the eyes. If refrigerant contacts the eye, it is advisable in all cases to see a physician as soon as possible.

6. Frostbite from liquid refrigerant should be treated by first gradually warming the area with cool water, and then gently applying petroleum jelly. A physician should be consulted.

SYSTEM INSPECTION

CAUTION: *The compressed refrigerant used in the air conditioning system expands into the atmosphere at a temperature of −2°F (−19°C) or lower. This will freeze any surface, including your eyes, that it contacts. In addition, the refrigerant decomposes into a poisonous gas in the presence of a flame. Do not open or disconnect any part of the air conditioning system.*

Sight Glass Check

You can safely make a few simple checks to determine if your air conditioning system needs service. The tests work best if the temperature is warm — about 70°F (21°C).

NOTE: *If your vehicle is equipped with an aftermarket air conditioner, the following system check may not apply. You should contact the manufacturer of the unit for instructions on systems checks.*

1. Place the automatic transaxle/transmission in **PARK** or the manual transaxle/transmission in **NEUTRAL**. Set the parking brake.

2. Run the engine at a fast idle (about 1,500 rpm) either with the help of a friend or by temporarily readjusting the idle speed screw.

3. Set the controls for maximum cold with the blower on High.

4. Locate the sight glass in one of the system lines. Usually it is on the left, along the top of the radiator.

5. If you see bubbles, the system must be recharged. Very likely there is a leak at some point. If it is determined that the system has a leak, it should be corrected as soon as possible. Leaks may allow moisture to enter and cause a very expensive rust problem.

6. If there are no bubbles, there is either no refrigerant at all or the system is fully charged. Feel the 2 hoses going to the belt-driven compressor. If they are both at the same temperature, the system is empty and must be recharged.

7. If one hose (high-pressure) is warm and the other (low-pressure) is cold, the system may be all right.

8. Have an assistant turn the A/C control and fan switch on and off to operate the compressor clutch. Watch the sight glass.

9. If bubbles appear when the clutch is disengaged and disappear when it is engaged, the system is properly charged.

10. If the refrigerant takes more than 45 seconds to bubble when the clutch is disengaged,

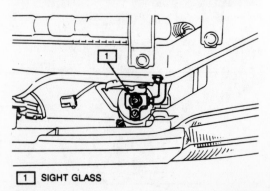

☐1 SIGHT GLASS

The sight glass is located in the head of the receiver-dryer

the system is overcharged. This usually causes poor cooling at low speeds.

NOTE: *Run the air conditioner for a few minutes, every 2 weeks or so, during the cold months. This avoids the possibility of the compressor seals drying out from lack of lubrication.*

Windshield Wipers

For maximum effectiveness and longest element life, the windshield and wiper blades should be kept clean. Dirt, tree sap, road tar and so on will cause streaking, smearing and blade deterioration if left on the glass. It is advisable to wash the windshield carefully with a commercial glass cleaner at least once a month. Wipe off the rubber blades with the wet rag afterwards. Do not attempt to move the wipers back and forth by hand; damage to the motor and drive mechanism will result.

If the blades are found to be cracked, broken or torn, they should be replaced immediately. Replacement intervals will vary with usuage, although ozone deterioration usually limits blade life to about 1 year at the most. If the wip-

er pattern is smeared or streaked, or if the blade chatters across the glass, the blades should be replaced. It is easiest and most sensible to replace them in pairs.

There are three different types of wiper blade refills, which differ in their method of replacement. One type has two release buttons, approximately one-third of the way up from the ends of the blade frame. Pushing the buttons down releases a lock and allows the rubber blade to be removed from the frame. The new blade slides back into the frame and locks in place.

The second type of refill has two metal tabs which are unlocked by squeezing them together. The rubber blade can then be withdrawn from the frame jaws. A new one is installed by inserting it into the front frame jaws and sliding it rearward to engage the remaining frame jaws. There are usually four jaws. Be certain when installing that the refill is engaged in all of them. At the end of its travel, the tabs will lock into place on the front jaws of the wiper blade frame.

The third type is a refill made from polycar-

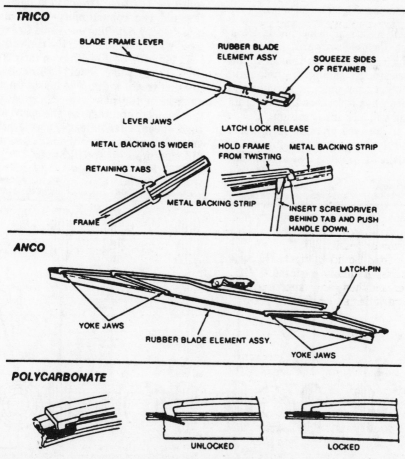

The three types of wiper blade retention

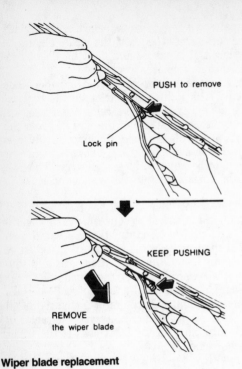

PUSH to remove

Lock pin

KEEP PUSHING

REMOVE
the wiper blade

Wiper blade replacement

bonate. The refill has a simple locking device at one end which flexes downward out of the groove into which the jaws of the holder fit, allowing easy release. By sliding the new refill through all the jaws and pushing through the slight resistance when it reaches the end of its travel, the refill will lock into position.

Regardless of the type of refill used, make sure that all of the frame jaws are engaged as the refill is pushed into place and locked. The metal blade holder and frame will scratch the glass if allowed to touch it.

Tire and Wheels

TIRE ROTATION

Tires should be rotated every 15,000 miles on once year (on later models every 7,500 miles or 6 months is recommended by Datsun/Nissan) to get the maximum tread lift available. A good time to do this is when changing over from regular tires to snow tires. If front end problems are suspected, have them corrected before rotating the tires.

NOTE: *Mark the wheel position or direction of rotation on radial, or studded snow tires before removing them.*

Avoid overtightening the lug nuts to prevent damage to the brake disc or drum. Alloy wheels can be cracked by overtightening. Tighten the lug nuts in a criss-cross sequence.

TIRE DESIGN

All 4 tires should be of the same construction type. Radial, bias, or bias-belted tires should not be mixed. The wheels must be the correct width for the tire. Tire dealers have charts of tire and rim compatibility. A mismatch can cause sloppy handling and rapid tire wear. The tread width should match the rim width (inside bead to inside bead) within an inch. For radial tires, the rim width should be 80% or less of the tire (not tread) width. The height (mounted diameter) of the new tires can greatly change speedometer accuracy, engine speed at a given road speed, fuel mileage, acceleration, and ground clearance. Tire manufacturers furnish full measurement specifications.

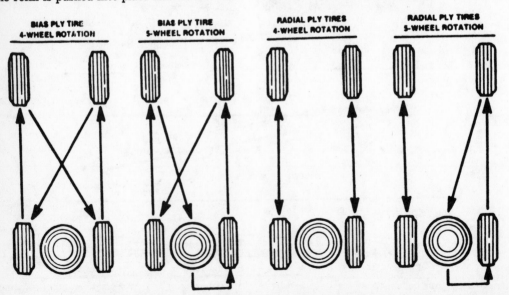

| BIAS PLY TIRE 4-WHEEL ROTATION | BIAS PLY TIRE 5-WHEEL ROTATION | RADIAL PLY TIRES 4-WHEEL ROTATION | RADIAL PLY TIRES 5-WHEEL ROTATION |

Tire rotation diagrams; note that radial tires should not be cross-switched

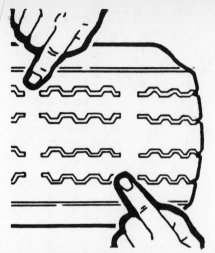

Tread wear indicators will appear when tire is worn out

A penny works as well for checking tire tread depth; when you can see the top of Lincoln's head, it's time for a new tire

TIRE STORAGE

Store the tires at the proper inflation pressure if they are mounted on wheels. Keep them in a cool dry place. If the tires are stored in the garage or basement, do not let them stand on a concrete floor; set them on stripe of wood or equivalent.

TIRE INFLATION

The tires should be checked frequently for proper air pressure. Make sure that the tires are cool, as you will get a false reading when the tires are heated because air pressure increases with temperature. A chart in the glove compartment or on the driver's door pillar gives the recommended inflation pressure. Maximum fuel economy and tire life will result if pressure is maintained at the highest figure given on chart. When checking pressures, do not neglect the spare tire. The tires should be checked before driving since pressure can increase as much as 6 pounds per square inch (psi) due to heat buildup.

NOTE: *Some spare tires require pressures considerably higher than those used in other tires.*

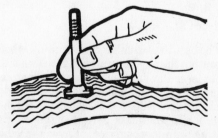

Tread depth can be checked with an inexpensive gauge

While you are checking the tire pressure, take a look at the tread. The tread should be wearing evenly across the tire. Excessive wear in the center of the tread could indicate over-inflation. Excessive wear on the outer edges could indicate underinflation. An irregular wear pattern is usually a sign of incorrect front wheel alignment or wheel balance. A front end that is out of alignment will usually pull the car to one side of a flat road when the steering wheel is released. Incorrect wheel balance will produce vibration in the steering wheel, while unbalanced rear wheels will result in floor or trunk vibration.

It is a good idea to have your own accurate gauge, and to check pressures weekly. Not all gauges on service station air pumps can be trusted.

Tires should be replaced when a tread wear indicator appears as a solid band across the tread.

CARE OF SPECIAL WHEELS

Aluminum wheels should be cleaned and waxed regularly. Do not use abrasive cleaners, as they could damage the protective coating. Inspect wheel rims regularly for dents or corrosion, which may cause loss of pressure, damage the tire bead, or sudden wheel failure.

FLUIDS AND LUBRICANTS

Fuel Recommendations

All engines covered in this book have been designed to run on unleaded fuel. The minimum octane requirement is 91 RON (Research Octane Nunber) or 87 AKI (Anti-Knock Index); all unleaded fuels sold in the U.S. are required to meet this minimum octane rating.

The use of a fuel too low in octane (a measurement of anti-knock quality) will result in spark knock. Since many factors such as altitude, terrain, air temperature and humidity affect the operating efficiency, knocking may result even though the recommended fuel is being used. If persistent knocking occurs, it may be necessary to switch to a higher grade of fuel. Continuous or heavy knocking may result in engine damage.

NOTE: *Your engine's fuel requirement can change with time, mainly due to carbon buildup, which will in turn change the compression ratio. If your engine pings, knocks or runs on, switch to a higher grade of fuel. Sometimes just changing brands will cure the problem. If it becomes necessary to retard the timing from the specifications, don't change it more than a few degrees. Retarded timing will reduce power output and fuel mileage, in addition to increasing the engine temperature.*

Engine Oil Recommendations

Oil must be selected with regard to the anticipated temperatures during the period before the next oil change. When buying oil for your vehicle select the oil viscosity for the lowest expected temperature and you will be assured of easy cold starting and sufficient engine protection. The oil you pour into your engine should have the designation "SG" marked on the top of its container.

SYNTHETIC OIL

There are many excellent synthetic and fuel-efficient oils currently available that can provide better gas mileage, longer service life, and in some cases better engine protection. These benefits do not come without a few hitches, however — the main one being the price of synthetic oils, which is 3 or 4 times the price per quart of conventional oil.

Synthetic oil is not for every car and every type of driving, so you should consider your engine's condition and your type of driving. Also, check your car's warranty guidelines at the dealership that you purchased the car from, regarding the use of synthetic oils and your powertrain and or extended warranty.

Both brand new engines and older, high mileage engines are the wrong candidates for synthetic oil. The synthetic oils are so slippery that they can prevent the proper break-in of new engines; most manufacturers recommend that you wait until the engine is properly broken in (5,000 miles) until using synthetic oil. Older engines with wear have a different problem with synthetics: they use (consume during operation) more oil as they age. Slippery synthetic oils get past these worn parts easily. If your engine is using conventional oil, it will use syn-

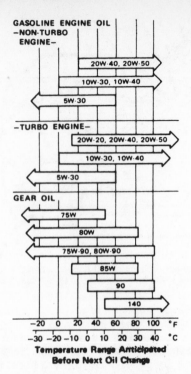

Engine oil and gear oil recommendations—use as a guide

thetics much faster. Also, if your car is leaking oil past old seals you'll have a much greater leak problem with synthetics.

Cars used under harder circumstances, such as stop-and-go, city type driving, short trips, or extended idling, should be serviced more frequently. For the engines in these cars, the much greater cost of synthetic or fuel-efficient oils may not be worth the investment. Internal wear increases much quicker on these cars, causing greater oil consumption and leakage.

NOTE: *The mixing of conventional and synthetic oils is not recommended. If you are using synthetic oil, it might be wise to carry 2 or 3 quarts with you no matter where you drive, as not all service stations carry this type of lubricant.*

Engine
OIL LEVEL CHECK

The best time to check the engine oil is before operating the engine or after it has been sitting for at least 10 minutes in order to gain an accurate reading. This will allow the oil to drain back into the crankcase or oil pan. To check the engine oil level, make sure that the vehicle is resting on a level surface, remove the oil dipstick, wipe it clean and reinsert the stick firmly for an accurate reading. The oil dipstick has two

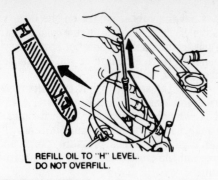

REFILL OIL TO "H" LEVEL.
DO NOT OVERFILL.

Oil dipstick markings

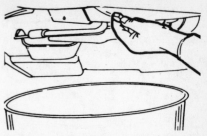

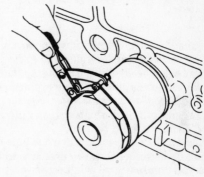

By keeping an inward pressure on the plug as you unscrew it, oil won't escape past the threads

marks to indicate high and low oil level. If the oil is at or below the "low level" mark on the dipstick, oil should be added as necessary. The oil level should be maintained in the safety margin, neither going above the "high level" mark or below the "low level" mark.

NOTE: *It is normal to add some oil between oil maintenance intervals or during break-in period, depending on the operating conditions.*

OIL AND FILTER CHANGE

The Datsun/Nissan factory maintenance intervals (every 7,500 miles or 6 months until 1989 models and every 3,750 miles or 3 months for 1990–92 models) specify changing the oil filter at every second oil change after the initial service. We recommend replacing the oil filter with every oil change. For the small price of an oil filter, it's cheap insurance to replace the filter at every oil change. One of the larger filter manufacturers points out in its advertisements that not changing the filter leaves about 1 quart of dirty oil in the engine.

NOTE: *On turbocharged engines factory maintenance intervals are every 5,000 miles or 6 months.*

1. Run the engine until it reaches normal operating temperature, then shut the engine off.

2. Jack up the front of the car and support it on safety stands to gain access to the filter.

Remove the oil filter with a strap wrench

Coat the new oil filter gasket with clean oil

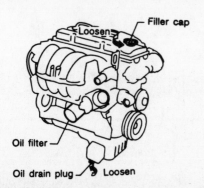

Filler cap

Loosen

Oil filter

Oil drain plug — Loosen

Oil drain plug and filter location

Install the new oil filter

3. Slide a drain pan of at least 6 quarts capacity under the oil pan.

CAUTION: *The EPA warns that prolonged contact with used engine oil may cause a number of skin disorders, including cancer!*

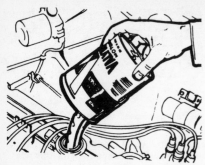

Add oil through the capped opening in the camshaft (valve) cover

You should make every effort to minimize your exposure to used engine oil. Protective gloves should be worn when changing the oil. Wash your hands and any other exposed skin areas as soon as possible after exposure to used engine oil. Soap and water, or waterless hand cleaner should be used.

4. Loosen the drain plug. Turn the plug out by hand. By keeping an inward pressure on the plug as you unscrew it, oil won't escape past the threads and you can remove it without being burned by hot oil.

5. Allow the oil to drain completely and then install the drain plug. Don't overtighten the plug or you'll be buying a new pan or a replacement plug for damaged threads.

6. Using a strap wrench, remove the oil filter. Keep in mind that it's holding about one quart of dirty, hot oil.

7. Empty the old filter into the drain pan and dispose of the filter and old oil.

NOTE: *One ecologically desirable solution to the used oil disposal problem is to find a cooperative gas station owner who will allow you to dump your used oil into his tank or take the oil to a reclamation center.*

8. Using a clean rag, wipe off the filter adapter on the engine block. Be sure that the rag doesn't leave any lint which could clog an oil passage.

9. Coat the rubber gasket on the filter with fresh oil. Spin it onto the engine *by hand*; when the gasket touches the adapter surface give it another ⅔ turn. No more or you'll squash the gasket and it will leak.

10. Refill the engine with the correct amount of fresh oil. See the Capacities chart.

11. Crank the engine over several times and then start it. If the oil pressure indicator light doesn't go out or the pressure gauge shows zero, shut the engine down and find out what's wrong.

12. If the oil pressure is OK and there are no leaks, shut the engine off and lower the car. Check oil level.

Manual Transmission/Transaxle
FLUID RECOMMENDATION

For manual transmission/transaxles be sure to use fluid with an API GL-4 rating.

LEVEL CHECK

You should inspect the manual transmission gear oil at 12 months or 15,000 miles at this point you should correct the level or replace the oil as necessary. The lubricant level should be even with the bottom of the filler hole. Hold in the filler plug when unscrewing it. When you are sure that all of the threads of the plug are free of the transaxle case, move the plug away from the case slightly. If lubricant begins to flow out of the transmission, then you know it is full. If not, add the correct gear oil as necessary

Inspect the manual transaxle gear oil at 12 months or 15,000 miles; at this point you should also correct the level. To check the oil level in the manual transaxle you have to remove the filler plug to determine the fluid level. The lubricant level should be even with the bottom of the filler hole.

DRAIN AND REFILL

NOTE: *It is recommended that the manual transmission/transaxle fluid be changed ev-*

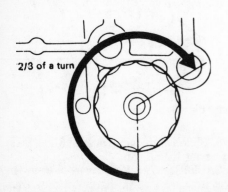

2/3 of a turn

Installing the oil filter

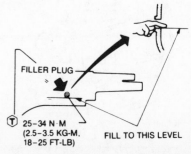

FILLER PLUG

25–34 N·M
(2.5–3.5 KG-M,
18–25 FT-LB) FILL TO THIS LEVEL

Transmission oil should be level with the bottom of the filler plug on manual transmissions

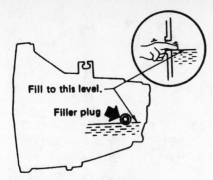

Checking oil level—manual transaxle

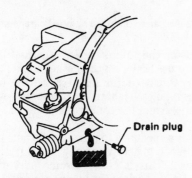

Drain plug location—manual transaxle

ery 30,000 miles or 24 months if the vehicle is used in severe service, towing a trailer and or using a camper or a car-top carrier.

1. Run the engine until it reaches normal operating temperature then turn key to the **OFF** position.

2. Jack up the front of the car and support it on safety stands level, if necessary to gain access.

3. Remove the filler plug from the left-side of the transmission/transaxle to provide a vent.

4. The drain plug is located on the bottom of the transmission/transaxle case. Place a pan under the drain plug and remove it.

CAUTION: *The oil will be HOT! Push up against the threads as you unscrew the plug to prevent leakage.*

5. Allow the oil to drain completely. Clean off the plug and replace it. DO NOT OVERTIGHTEN PLUG.

6. Fill the transmission/transaxle with gear oil through the filler plug hole. Use API service GL-4 gear oil of the proper viscosity. This oil usually comes in a squeeze bottle with a long nozzle. If yours doesn't, use a plastic squeeze bottle (the type used in the kitchen). Refer to the "Capacities" chart for the amount of oil needed.

7. The oil level should come up to the edge of the filler hole. You can stick your finger in to verify this. Watch out for sharp threads.

8. Replace the filler plug. Lower the vehicle, dispose of the old oil in the same manner as old engine oil.

9. Test drive the vehicle, stop and check for leaks.

Automatic Transmission/Transaxle

FLUID RECOMMENDATIONS

All automatic transmission/transaxle, use Dexron® ATF (automatic transmission fluid)

LEVEL CHECK

The fluid level in the automatic transmission/transaxle should be checked every 6 months or 7,500 miles whichever comes first. The transmission/transaxle has a dipstick for fluid level checks.

1. Drive the car until it is at normal operating temperature. The level should not be checked immediately after the car has been driven for a long time at high speed, or in city traffic in hot weather. In those cases, the transaxle should be given a half hour to cool down.

2. Stop the car, apply the parking brake, then shift slowly through all gear positions, ending in Park. Let the engine idle for about five minutes with the transmission/transaxle in Park. The car should be on a level surface.

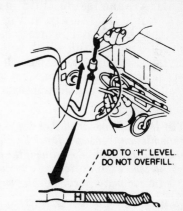

ADD TO "H" LEVEL. DO NOT OVERFILL.

Remove the automatic transmission dipstick with the engine warm and idling in Park

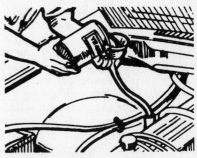

Add automatic transmission fluid through the transmission dipstick tube—use a funnel

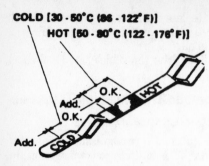

COLD [30 - 50°C (86 - 122°F)]

HOT [50 - 80°C (122 - 176°F)]

Dipstick from late model automatic transaxle

3. With the engine still running, remove the dipstick, wipe it clean, then reinsert it, pushing it fully home.

4. Pull the dipstick again and, holding it horizontally, read the fluid level.

5. Cautiously feel the end of the dipstick to determine the temperature. Note that on Datsuns/Nissans there is a scale on each side, HOT on one, COLD on the other. If the fluid level is not in the correct area, more will have to be added.

6. Fluid is added through the dipstick tube. You will probably need the aid of a spout or a long necked funnel. Be sure that whatever you pour through is perfectly clean and dry. Use an automatic transmission fluid marked DEXRON®. Add fluid slowly, and in small amounts, checking the level frequently between additions. Do not overfill, which will cause foaming, fluid loss, slippage, and possible transmission damage. It takes only one pint to raise the level from L to H when the transaxle is hot.

DRAIN AND REFILL

NOTE: *It is recommended that the automatic transmission/transaxle fluid be changed every 30,000 miles or 24 months if the vehicle is used in severe service, towing a trailer and or using a camper or a car-top carrier.*

Transmission

1. There is no drain plug. The fluid pan must be removed. Partially remove the pan screws until the pan can be pulled down at one corner. Place a container under the transmission, lower a rear corner of the pan, and allow the fluid to drain.

2. After draining, remove the pan screws completely, and remove the pan and gasket.

3. Clean the pan thoroughly and allow it to air dry. If you wipe it out with a rag you risk leaving bits of lint in the pan which will clog the tiny hydraulic passages in the transmission.

NOTE: *It is very important to clean the old gasket from the oil pan, to prevent leaks upon installation. A razor blade does a excellent job at this.*

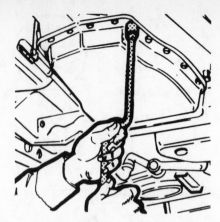

Remove the pan to drain the automatic transmission

4. Install the pan using a new gasket. If you decide to use sealer on the gasket apply it only in a very thin bead running to the outside of the pan screw holes. Tighten the pan screws evenly in rotation from the center outwards, to 36–60 inch lbs.

5. It is a good idea to measure the amount of fluid drained to determine how much fresh fluid to add. This is because some part of the transmission, such as the torque converter, will not drain completely, and using the dry refill amount specified in the Capacities chart may lead to overfilling. Fluid is added through the dipstick tube. Make sure that the funnel, hose, or whatever you are using is completely clean and dry before pouring transmission fluid through it. Use DEXRON® automatic transmission fluid.

6. Replace the dipstick after filling. Start the engine and allow it to idle. Do NOT race the engine. Check the installation of the new pan gasket for leaks.

7. After the engine has idled for a few minutes, shift the transmission slowly through the gears, then return the lever to Park. With the engine idling, check the fluid level on the dipstick. It should be between the **H** and **L** marks. If below **L**, add sufficient fluid to raise the level to between the marks.

8. Drive the car until it is at operating tem-

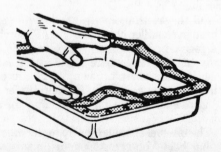

Install a pan gasket—automatic transmission

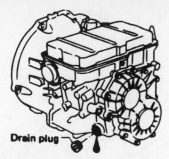

Drain plug location automatic transaxle

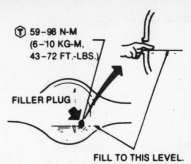

FILL TO THIS LEVEL.

Checking the fluid level in the differential on models with a solid rear axle assembly

perature. The fluid should be at the **H** mark. If not, add sufficient fluid until this is the case. Be careful not to overfill. Overfilling causes slippage, overheating, and seal damage.

NOTE: *If the drained fluid is discolored (brown or black), thick, or smells burnt, serious transmission problems due to overheating should be suspected. Your car's transmission should be inspected by a transmission specialist to determine the cause.*

Transaxle

To change the the transaxle fluid on early models, the transaxle fluid oil pan must be removed and the gasket must be replaced. This procedure is similar to the transmission procedure with the exception of the oil pan location.

On late models there is a drain plug located on the side of the transaxle case. Remove the drain plug and allow the fluid to drain then refill with new fluid, start engine and correct the fluid level as necessary. Before attempting this service read the complete section above on "DRAIN AND RFILL" procedure.

Rear Drive Axle

FLUID RECOMMENDATIONS

Use only standard GL-5 hypoid type gear oil: SAE 80W or SAE 80W/90.

LEVEL CHECK

The oil in the differential should be checked at least every 15,000 miles or 12 months.

1. With the car on a level surface, remove the filler plug from the back side of the differential.

2. If the oil begins to trickle out of the hole, there is enough. Otherwise, carefully insert your finger (watch out for sharp threads) into the hole and check that the oil is up to the bottom edge of the filler hole.

3. If not, add oil through the hole until the level is at the edge of the hole. Most gear oils come in a plastic squeeze bottle with a nozzle; making additions simple. You can also use a

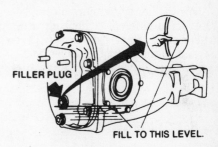

FILL TO THIS LEVEL.

Checking the fluid level in the differential on models with independent rear suspension

common kitchen baster. Use only the specified fluid.

4. Replace the plug and check for leaks.

DRAIN AND REFILL

NOTE: *It is recommended that the rear drive axle fluid be changed every 30,000 miles or 24 months if the vehicle is used in severe service, towing a trailer and or using a camper or a car-top carrier.*

1. Park the car on a level surface. Place a pan of at least two quarts capacity underneath the drain plug. The drain plug is located on the center rear of the differential carrier, just below the filler plug on some models, on others it can be found at the bottom of the carrier. Remove the drain plug.

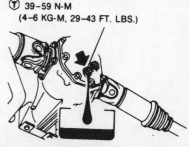

Draining the differential fluid on models with independent rear suspension

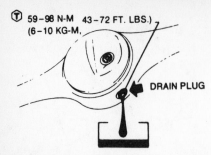

Draining the fluid in the differential on models with a solid rear axle assembly

2. Allow the lubricant to drain completely.

3. Refill the differential housing with API GL-5 gear oil of the proper viscosity. The correct level is to the edge of the filler hole.

4. Install the filler plug. Tighten to 29–43 ft. lbs.

Cooling System

FLUID RECOMMENDATION

The cooling fluid or antifreeze, should be changed every 30,000 miles or 24 months on all vehicles except the 1991–92 240SX with KA24DE engine on these vehicles change at 60,000 miles or 48 months then every 30,000 miles or 24 months. When replacing the fluid, use a mixture of 50% water and 50% ethylene glycol antifreeze.

Check the freezing protection rating at least once a year, preferably just before the winter sets in. This can be done with an antifreeze tester (most service stations will have one on hand and will probably check it for you. If not, inexpensive testers are available at an auto parts store). Maintain a protection rating of at least −20°F (−29°C) to prevent engine damage as a result of freezing and to assure the proper engine operating temperature.

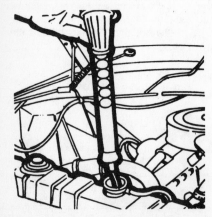

Coolant protection can be checked with float type tester

The cooling system should be pressure tested at least once a year

It is also a good idea to have the the cooling system checked for leaks. A pressure test gauge is available to perform such a task. Checking and repairing a coolant leak in the early stages while save time and money.

LEVEL CHECK

Check the coolant level every 3,000 miles or once a month. In hot weather operation, it may be a good idea to check the level once a week. Check for loose connections and signs of deterioration of the coolant hoses. Maintain the coolant level ¾–1¼ in. (19–32mm) below the level of the filler neck when the engine is cold.

Check the coolant level in the coolant recovery bottle when the engine is cold, the level should be up to the MAX mark. If the bottle is empty, check the level in the radiator and refill as necessary, then fill the bottle up to the MAX level.

CAUTION: *Never remove the radiator cap when the vehicle is hot or overheated. Wait until it has cooled. Place a thick cloth over the radiator cap to shield yourself from the heat and turn the radiator cap, SLIGHTLY, until the sound of escaping pressure can be heard. DO NOT turn any more; allow the pressure to release gradually. When no more pressure can be heard escaping, remove the cap with the heavy cloth, CAUTIOUSLY.*

NOTE: *Never add cold water to an overheated engine while the engine is not running.*

After filling the radiator, run the engine until it reaches normal operating temperature, to make sure that the thermostat has opened and all the air is bled from the system.

DRAIN AND REFILL

To drain the cooling system, allow the engine to cool down **BEFORE ATTEMPTING TO REMOVE THE RADIATOR CAP.** Then turn the cap until it hisses. Wait until all pressure is off the cap before removing it completely.

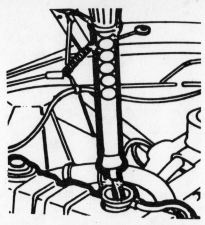

If the engine is HOT, cover the radiator cap with a rag

Some type radiator caps have pressure release levers

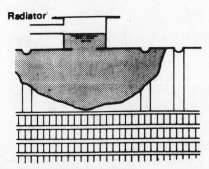

Checking coolant level in radiator

CAUTION: *To avoid burns and scalding, always handle a warm radiator cap with a heavy rag.*

1. At the dash, set the heater TEMP control lever to the fully HOT position.

2. With the radiator cap removed, drain the radiator by loosening the petcock at the bottom of the radiator.

NOTE: *On the 1982–86 Stanza models, remove the heater inlet hose from the connector*

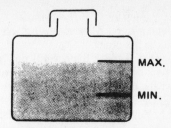

Checking coolant level in recovery bottle

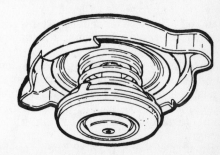

Always check the gasket in the radiator cap when checking coolant level

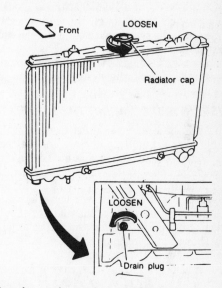

Changing engine coolant—240SX model

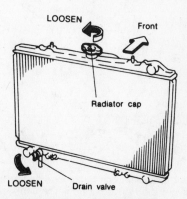

Changing engine coolant—Stanza model

pipe at the left rear of the cylinder block to drain completely. After draining, reconnect the hose to the pipe.

3. Close the petcock (be careful not to damage the petcock when closing), then refill the system with a 50/50 mix of ethylene glycol antifreeze; fill the system to ¾–1¼ in. (19–32mm) from the bottom of the filler neck. Reinstall the radiator cap.

NOTE: *If equipped with a fluid reservoir tank, fill it up to the MAX level.*

4. If you have replaced or repaired any cooling system component the cooling system must be bled as outlined:

• On 1982–86 Stanza models insert a 3mm pin into the 3-way valve, located at the firewall, and push it in as far as it will go. While pushing in on the pin, fill the radiator up to the filler opening. Replace the radiator cap and fill the reservoir.

• On all 200SX and 1987–89 Stanza models slowly pour coolant through the filler neck to release air in the system.

• On all 240SX and 1990–92 Stanza models slowly pour coolant through the filler neck to release air in the system with the air relief bolt or plug loosened.

5. Operate the engine to normal operating temperature. Check the system for signs of leaks and for the correct level.

FLUSHING AND CLEANING THE SYSTEM

To flush the system you must first drain the cooling system but do not close the petcock valve on the bottom of the radiator. You can insert a garden hose, in the filler neck, turn the water pressure on moderately then start the engine. After about 5 minutes or less the water coming out of the bottom of the radiator should be clear. Shut off the engine and water supply, allow the radiator to drain and then refill and bleed the system as necessary.

NOTE: *DO NOT allow the engine to overheat. The supply of water going in the top*

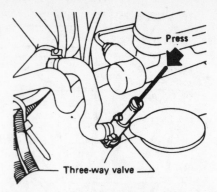

Using the 3-way valve to bleed the cooling system 1982–86 Stanza

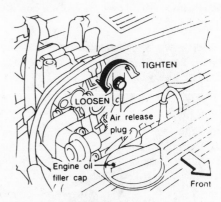

Air release plug 1990–92 Stanza

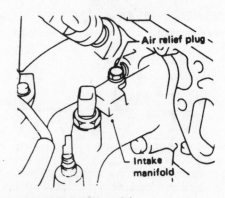

Air release plug 240SX model

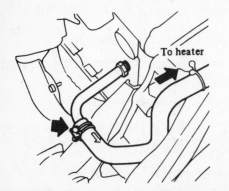

Removing the inlet hose from the connector pipe 1982–86 Stanza

must be equal in amount to the water draining from the bottom. The radiator will always be full when the engine us running.

Usually flushing the radiator using water is all that is necessary to maintain the proper condition in the cooling system.

Radiator flush is the only cleaning agent that can be used to clean the internal portion of the radiator. Radiator flush can be purchased at any auto supply store. Follow the directions on the label.

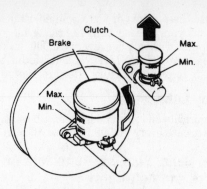

Brake and clutch fluid master cylinders

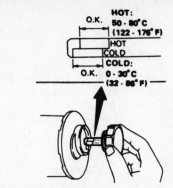

Checking power steering

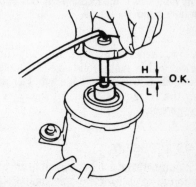

Checking power steering

Brake and Clutch Master Cylinder

FLUID RECOMMENDATION

When adding or changing the fluid in the systems, use a quality brake fluid of DOT 3 specifications.

NOTE: *Never reuse old brake fluid.*

LEVEL CHECK

The brake and clutch master cylinders are located under the hood, in the left rear section of the engine compartment. They are made of translucent plastic so that the levels may be checked (check fluid level periodically) without removing the tops. The fluid level in both reservoirs must be checked at least every 15,000 miles or 12 months. The fluid level should be maintained at the upper most mark on the side of the reservoir. Any sudden decrease in the level indicates a possible leak in the system and should be checked immediately.

NOTE: *Some models may have two reservoirs for the brake master cylinder, while other models (those with an automatic transmission/transaxle) will not have a clutch master cylinder at all.*

When making additions of brake fluid, use only fresh, uncontaminated brake fluid meeting or exceeding DOT 3 standards. Be careful not to spill any brake fluid on painted surfaces, as it eats the paint. Do not allow the brake fluid container or the master cylinder reservoir to remain open any longer than necessary. Brake fluid absorbs moisture from the air, reducing its effectiveness and causing corrosion in the lines.

Power Steering System

FLUID RECOMMENDATION

When adding or changing the power steering fluid, use Dexron® ATF (Automatic Transmission Fluid).

LEVEL CHECK

The power steering hydraulic fluid level is checked with a dipstick inserted into the pump reservoir. The level can be checked (check fluid level periodically) with the fluid either warm or cold. The car should be parked on a level surface. Check the fluid level every 12 months or 15,000 miles, whichever comes first.

1. With the engine OFF, unscrew the dipstick and check the level. If the engine is warm, the level should be within the proper range on the HOT scale. If the engine is cold, the level should be within the proper range on the COLD scale (see illustrations).

2. If the level is low, add DEXRON® ATF until correct. Be careful not to overfill, which will cause fluid loss and seal damage.

Steering Gear Box Except Rack and Pinion Type

FLUID RECOMMENDATIONS

When fill the steering gear box use only standard GL-4 hypoid type gear oil, SAE 80W or SAE 80W/90.

LEVEL CHECK

Check the level of the lubricant in the steering gear every 15,000 miles or 12 months. If the

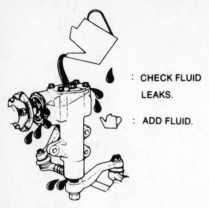

: CHECK FLUID
 LEAKS.

: ADD FLUID.

Check the fluid level in the steering gearbox through the filler hole in top

level is low, check for leakage. Any oily film is not considered a leak; solid grease must be present. The lubricant is added and checked through the filler plug hole in the top of the steering gearbox.

Chassis Greasing

The manufacturer doesn't install lubrication fittings in lube points on the steering linkage or suspension. On some replacement part applications you can buy metric threaded fittings to

grease these points or use a pointed, rubber tip end on your grease gun. Lubricate all joints equipped with a plug, every 15,000 miles or once a year with NLGI No. 2 (Lithium base) grease. Replace the plugs after lubrication.

Body Lubrication

Lubricate all locks and hinges with multipurpose grease every 15,000 miles or 12 months.

Seat Belts, Buckles, Retractors Anchors and Adjusters

All seat belt assemblies, including retractors and attaching hardware should be inspected for proper operation every 15,000 miles or 12 months or after any collision.

If the condition of any component of a seat belt assembly is questionable, do not repair the seat belt, but replace the assembly. If webbing is cut, frayed or damaged, replace belt assembly. Never oil tongue and buckle.

Wheel Bearings
REMOVAL, PACKING AND INSTALLATION
Rear Wheel Drive Vehicles
200SX and 240SX MODELS

Clean, inspect and repack wheel front wheel bearings every 30,000 miles or 24 months on

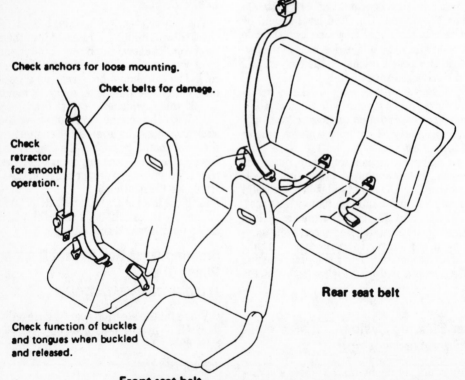

Check anchors for loose mounting.

Check belts for damage.

Check retractor for smooth operation.

Check function of buckles and tongues when buckled and released.

Front seat belt

Rear seat belt

Lubricating locks, hinges and hood latches

1982–88 200SX rear wheel drive models. The 1989–92 240SX rear wheel drive models uses a one-piece style front wheel bearing assembly no maintenance is required.

In order to clean and repack the front wheel bearings on the 200SX rear wheel drive models, the wheel bearings must be removed from the wheel hub. You should also check that the wheel bearings operate smoothly and there is no excess amount of play (looseness) in the bearing assemnbly before removing the wheel bearing. To remove, install and adjust the wheel bearings and for all other service procedures for "Front Wheel Bearings" (rear wheel drive vehicles) refer to Chapter 8 in this manual.

Front Wheel Drive Vehicles

STANZA MODELS

On front wheel drive vehicles, the front wheel bearings are different than on rear wheel drive vehicles and no normal maintenance is required. Service procedures (removal and installation) for the front wheel bearings of front wheel drive vehicles are given in Chapter 8.

The rear wheel bearings on front wheel drive vehicles are similar to the front bearings on rear wheel drive vehicles. In order to clean and repack the rear wheel bearings on the Stanza front wheel drive models the wheel bearings must be removed from the wheel hub. Clean, inspect and repack wheel rear wheel bearings every 60,000 miles or 48 months. To remove, install and adjust the rear wheel bearings and for all other service procedures for "Rear Wheel Bearings" front wheel drive vehicles refer to Chapter 8 in this manual.

TRAILER TOWING

General Recommendations

Your car was primarily designed to carry passengers and cargo. It is important to remember that towing a trailer will place additional loads on your vehicle's engine, drive train, steering, braking and other systems. However, if you find it necessary to tow a trailer, using the proper equipment is a must.

Local laws may require specific equipment such as trailer brakes or fender mounted mirrors. Check your local laws.

NOTE: *A trailering brochure with information on trailer towing, special equipment required and optional equipment available can be obtained from your Datsun/Nissan dealer*

Trailer Weight

Never allow the total trailer load to exceed 1,000 lbs. The total trailer load equals trailer weight plus its cargo weight.

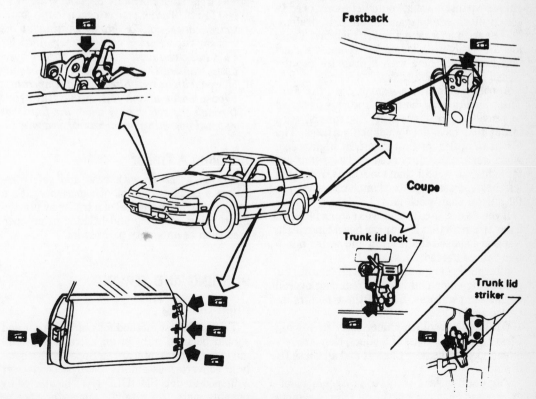

Seat belt assemblies

Hitch Weight

Figure the hitch weight to select a proper hitch. Hitch weight is usually 9–11% of the trailer gross weight and should be measured with the trailer loaded. Hitches fall into three types: those that mount on the frame and rear bumper or the bolt-on or weld-on distribution type used for larger trailers. Axle mounted or clamp-on bumper hitches should never be used.

Check the gross weight rating of your trailer. Tongue weight is usually figured as 10% of gross trailer weight. Therefore, a trailer with a maximum gross weight of 1,000 lb. will have a maximum tongue weight of 100 lb. Class I trailers fall into this category.

When you've determined the hitch that you'll need, follow the manufacturer's installation instructions, exactly, especially when it comes to fastener torques. The hitch will subjected to a lot of stress and good hitches come with hardened bolts. Never substitute an inferior bolt for a hardened bolt.

Cooling

ENGINE

One of the most common, if not THE most common, problems associated with trailer towing is engine overheating.

If you have a standard cooling system, without an expansion tank, you'll definitely need to get an aftermarket expansion tank kit, preferably one with at least a 2 quart capacity. These kits are easily installed on the radiator's overflow hose, and come with a pressure cap designed for expansion tanks.

Another helpful accessory is a Flex Fan. These fan are large diameter units are designed to provide more airflow at low speeds, with blades that have deeply cupped surfaces. The blades then flex, or flatten out, at high speed, when less cooling air is needed. These fans are far lighter in weight than stock fans, requiring less horsepower to drive them. Also, they are far quieter than stock fans.

If you do decide to replace your stock fan with a flex fan, note that if your car has a fan clutch, a spacer between the flex fan and water pump hub will be needed.

Aftermarket engine oil coolers are helpful for prolonging engine oil life and reducing overall engine temperatures. Both of these factors increase engine life.

While not absolutely necessary in towing Class I and some Class II trailers, they are recommended for heavier Class II and all Class III towing.

Engine oil cooler systems consist of an adapter, screwed on in place of the oil filter, a remote filter mounting and a multi-tube, finned heat exchanger, which is mounted in front of the radiator or air conditioning condenser.

TRANSMISSION

An automatic transmission is usually recommended for trailer towing. Modern automatics have proven reliable and, of course, easy to operate, in trailer towing.

The increased load of a trailer, however, causes an increase in the temperature of the automatic transmission fluid. Heat is the worst enemy of an automatic transmission. As the temperature of the fluid increases, the life of the fluid decreases.

It is essential, therefore, that you install an automatic transmission cooler.

The cooler, which consists of a multi-tube, finned heat exchanger, is usually installed in front of the radiator or air conditioning compressor, and hooked inline with the transmission cooler tank inlet line. Follow the cooler manufacturer's installation instructions.

Select a cooler of at least adequate capacity, based upon the combined gross weights of the car and trailer.

Cooler manufacturers recommend that you use an aftermarket cooler in addition to, and not instead of, the present cooling tank in your radiator. If you do want to use it in place of the radiator cooling tank, get a cooler at least two sizes larger than normally necessary.

NOTE: *A transmission cooler can, sometimes, cause slow or harsh shifting in the transmission during cold weather, until the fluid has a chance to come up to normal operating temperature. Some coolers can be purchased with or retrofitted with a temperature bypass valve which will allow fluid flow through the cooler only when the fluid has reached operating temperature, or above.*

Handling A Trailer

Towing a trailer with ease and safety requires a certain amount of experience. It's a good idea to learn the feel of a trailer by practicing turning, stopping and backing in an open area such as an empty parking lot.

PUSHING AND TOWING

Push Starting

This is the last method for starting a car and should be used only in an extreme case. All models in this manual are equipped with a catalytic converter assembly. Catalytic converter equipped models SHOULD NOT be started by pushing since the catalytic converter may be damaged.

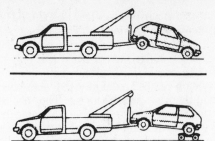

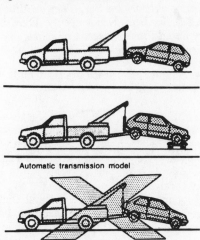

Towing—rear wheel drive models

Automatic transmission model

Towing—front wheel drive models

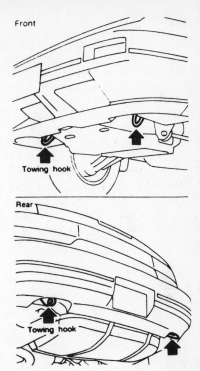

Tow hook locations—rear wheel drive models

Towing

On rear wheel drive vehicles, the car can be flat-towed safely (with the transmission in Neutral – ignition key OFF – see note below) from the front at speeds of 30 mph or less (no more than 40 miles distance). The car must either be towed with the rear drive wheels off the ground or the driveshaft disconnected if: towing speeds are to be over 30 mph, or towing distance is over 40 miles, or transmission or rear axle problems exist.

NOTE: *When towing rear wheel drive vehicle with the front wheels on the ground secure the steering wheel in a straight-ahead position with a rope or similar device. Never place the ignition key in the LOCK postion. This will result in damage to the steering lock mechanism.*

When towing from the front of the vehicle, make sure that the transmission, axles, steering system and power train are in working condition. If any unit is damaged, a dolly under the rear wheels must be used.

On front wheel drive vehicles never tow with rear wheels raised (with front drive wheels on the ground) as this may cause serious and expensive damage to the the transaxle. On front wheel drive models Datsun/Nissan recom-

mends that the vehicle be towed with the driving (front) wheels off the ground using proper equipment.

On all models there are towing hooks under the vehicle to attact tow hooks. If any question concerning towing are in doubt, check the"Towing Procedure Manual" at your local Datsun/Nissan dealer.

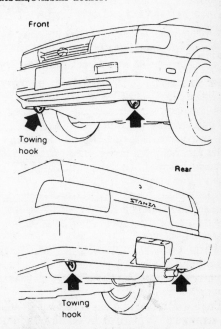

Two hook locations—front wheel drive models

JACKING

Never use the tire changing jack (the little jack supplied with the car) for anything other than changing a flat out on the road. These jacks are simply not safe enough for any type of vehicle service except tire changing!

The service operations in this manual often require that one end or the other, or both, of the car be raised and safely supported. For this reason a hydraulic floor jack of at least 1½ ton capacity is as necessary as a spark plug socket to you, the do-it-yourself owner/mechanic. The cost of these jacks (invest in a good quality unit) is actually quite reasonable considering how they pay for themselves again and again over the years.

Along with a hydraulic floor jack should be at least two sturdy jackstands. These are a necessity if you intend to work underneath the car. Never work under the car when it is only supported by a jack!

Drive-on ramps are an alternative method of raising the front end of the car. They are commercially available or can be fabricated from heavy lumber or steel. Be sure to always block the wheels when using ramps.

CAUTION: *NEVER use concrete or cinder blocks to support the car. They are likely to break if the load is not evenly distributed. They should never be trusted when you are underneath the car!*

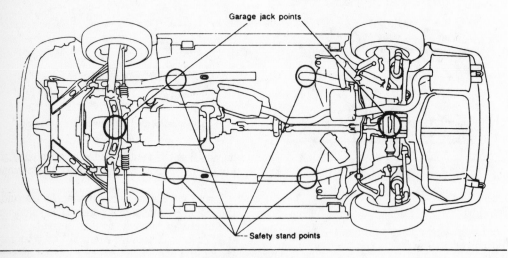

Garage jack points

Safety stand points

2-pole Lift

WARNING:
When lifting the vehicle, open the lift arms as wide as possible and ensure that the front and rear of the vehicle are well balanced.

When setting the lift arm, do not allow the arm to contact the brake tubes and fuel lines.

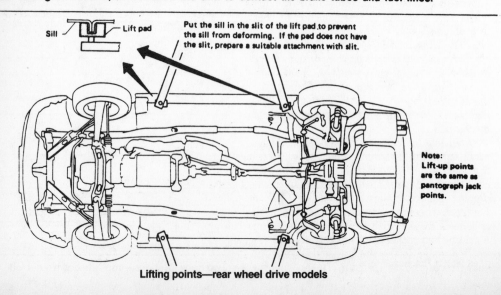

Sill — Lift pad

Put the sill in the slit of the lift pad to prevent the sill from deforming. If the pad does not have the slit, prepare a suitable attachment with slit.

Note:
Lift-up points are the same as pantograph jack points.

Lifting points—rear wheel drive models

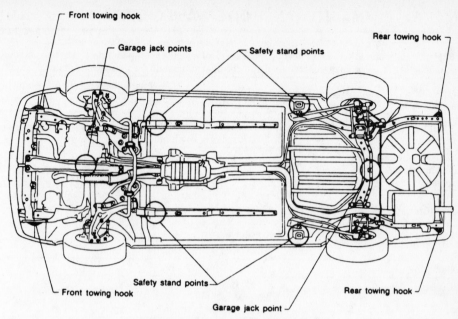

Lifting points—front wheel drive models

CAPACITIES CHART

Year	Model	Engine ID/VIN	Engine Displacement liter	Engine Crankcase with Filter	Transmission (pts.) 4-Spd	Transmission (pts.) 5-Spd	Transmission (pts.) Auto.	Transfer case (pts.)	Drive Axle Front (pts.)	Drive Axle Rear (pts.)	Fuel Tank (gal.)	Cooling System (qts.)
1982–83	200SX	222E	2.2L	4.5	—	4¼	12	—	—	2⅛	14①	10⅛
	Stanza	CA20	2.0L	4.0	—	5¾	—	—	—	—	14¼	7¾
1984–85	200SX	CA20E	2.0L	4.0	—	4½	15	—	—	2½	14	9⅛
		CA18ET (Turbo)	1.8L	4.0	—	4½	15	—	—	2½	14	9⅛
	Stanza	CA20, CA20E	2.0L	4.0	—	5¾	14	—	—	—	14¼	7½
1986	200SX	CA20E	2.0L	4.0	—	4½	15	—	—	2½	14	9⅛
		CA18ET (Turbo)	1.8L	4.0	—	4½	15	—	—	2½	14	9⅛
	Stanza	CA20E	2.0L	4.0	—	5¾	14	—	—	—	14¼	7½
	Stanza Wagon (2WD)	CA20E	2.0L	4.0	—	10	14	—	—	—	15⅞	7⅛
	Stanza Wagon (4WD)	CA20E	2.0L	4.0	—	10	14	3	—	2⅛	15⅞	7⅛
1987–88	200SX	VG30E	3.0L	4.5	—	4¼	15	—	—	2½	14	9⅝
		CA20E	2.0L	4.0	—	4¼	15	—	—	2½	14	9⅛
		CA18ET	1.8L	4.0	—	4¼	15	—	—	2½	14	9⅛
	Stanza	CA20E	2.0L	4.0	—	10	14	—	—	—	15⅞	7¾
	Stanza Wagon (2WD)	CA20E	2.0L	4.0	—	10	14	—	—	—	15⅞	7⅛
	Stanza Wagon (4WD)	CA20E	2.0L	4.0	—	10	14	3	—	2⅛	13¼	7⅛
1989	240SX	KA24E	2.4L	4.0	—	5⅛	17	—	—	2¾	15⅞	7⅛
	Stanza	CA20E	2.0L	4.0	—	10	14	—	—	—	15⅞	7¾
1990	240SX	KA24E	2.4L	4.0	—	5⅛	17	—	—	4	15⅞	7⅛
	Stanza	KA24E	2.4L	4.0	—	10	15	—	—	—	16⅜	7⅞
1991–92	240SX	KA24DE	2.4L	4.0	—	5⅛	17	—	—	4	15⅞	7⅛
	Stanza	KA24E	2.4L	4.0	—	10	15	—	—	—	16⅜	7⅞

① 1982 200SX Hatchback 15⅞ gal.

MAINTENANCE INTERVALS CHART

Intervals are for number of months or thousands of miles, whichever comes first.
NOTE: Heavy-duty operation (trailer towing, prolonged idling, severe stop and start driving) should be accompanied by a 50% increase in maintenance. Cut the intervals in half for these conditions. Refer to text.

Maintenance	Service Interval
Air Cleaner (Replace)	30,000 miles or 24 months
Air Induction Valve Filter (Replace) ①	30,000 miles or 24 months
PCV Valve (Inspect)	30,000 miles or 24 months
Evaporative Emissions System Check Fuel/Vapor Lines Carbon Canister	30,000 miles or 24 months

Battery
  Fluid Level (Check)
  Specific Gravity (Check)
  Cables and Clamps (Check)
	
	Once a Month
	Once a Year
	Once a Year

Belt Tension (Inspect)	15,000 miles or 12 months
Hoses (Check)	15,000 miles or 12 months

Radiator Coolant
  Check
  Change
	
	Weekly
	24 months or 30,000 miles

Engine Oil and Filter
  Check Oil Level
  Change
	
	Weekly
	6 months or 7,500 miles (3,750 miles or 3 months 1990–92)
	6 months or 5,000 miles (Turbocharged Engine)

Manual Transmission/Transaxle
  Check
  Change
	
	12 months or 15,000 miles
	24 months or 30,000 miles (Heavy Duty Operation)

Automatic Transmission/Transaxle
  Check
  Change
	
	6 months or 7,500 miles
	30,000 miles or 24 months (Heavy Duty Operation)

Brake and Clutch Fluid Check	 15,000 miles or 12 months

Rear Axle
  Check
  Change
	
	12 months or 15,000 miles
	30,000 miles Heavy Duty Operation

Steering Gear Check	 15,000 miles or 12 months
Power Steering Fluid Check	 12 months or 15,000 miles
Power Steering Lines and Hoses	12 months or 15,000 miles
Tires Rotate	 7,500 miles or 6 months 15,000 miles or 12 months
Fuel Filter (Inspect)	30,000 miles or 24 months ②

Chassis Lubrication
  Lubricate
  Inspect seals
	
	12 months or 15,000 miles

① On models so equipped
② Change the filter as soon as there is any indication of clogging by abnormal dirt in the fuel

Engine Performance and Tune-Up

2

GASOLINE-ENGINE TUNE-UP SPECIFICATIONS

Year	Engine ID/VIN	Engine Displacement Liters	Spark Plugs Gap (in.)	Ignition Timing (deg.) MT	Ignition Timing (deg.) AT	Fuel Pump (psi)	Idle Speed (rpm) MT	Idle Speed (rpm) AT	Valve Clearance In.	Valve Clearance Ex.
1982	222E	2.2L	0.031–0.035	8B	8B	37	750	700	0.012	0.012
	CA20	2.0L	0.039–0.043	0	0	3.8	650	—	0.012	0.012
1983	222E	2.2L	0.031–0.035	8B	8B	37	750	700	0.012	0.012
	CA20	2.0L	0.039–0.043	0	0	3.8	650	650	0.012	0.012
1984	CA20E	2.0L	0.039–0.043	0	0	37	750	700	0.012	0.012
	CA18ET	1.8L	0.039–0.043	15B	15B	37	750	700	0.012	0.012
1985	CA20E	2.0L	0.039–0.043	4B	0	37	750	700	0.012	0.012
	CA18ET	1.8L	0.039–0.043	15B	—	37	750	—	0.012	0.012
1986	CA20E	2.0L	0.039–0.043	4B	0①	37	750	700	0.012	0.012
	CA18ET	1.8L	0.039–0.043	15B	—	37	750	—	0.012	0.012
1987	CA20E	2.0L	0.039–0.043	15B	15B	37	750	700	NA②	NA②
	CA18ET	1.8L	0.039–0.043	15B	—	37	750	—	0.012	0.012
	VG30E	3.0L	0.039–0.043	20B	20B	37	700	700	NA	NA
1988	CA20E	2.0L	0.039–0.043	15B	15B	37	750	750	NA②	NA②
	CA18ET	1.8L	0.039–0.043	15B	—	37	750	—	0.012	0.012
	VG30E	3.0L	0.039–0.043	20B	20B	37	700	700	NA	NA
1989	KA24E	2.4L	0.039–0.043	15B	15B	37	750	750	NA	NA
	CA20E	2.0L	0.039–0.043	15B	15B	37	750	700	NA	NA
1990	KA24E	2.4L	0.039–0.043	15B	15B	37	750	750	NA	NA
1991	KA24DE	2.4L	0.039–0.043	20B	20B	37	700	700	0.012–0.015	0.013–0.016
	KA24E	2.4L	0.039–0.043	15B	15B	37	750	750	NA	NA
1992	KA24DE	2.4L	0.039–0.043	20B	20B	37	700	700	0.012–0.015	0.013–0.016
	KA24E	2.4L	0.039–0.043	15B	15B	37	750	750	NA	NA

NOTE: The lowest cylinder pressure should be within 75% of the highest cylinder pressure reading. For example, if the highest cylinder is 134 psi, the lowest should be 101. Engine should be at normal operating temperature with throttle valve in the wide open position.

The underhood specifications sticker often refects tune-up specification changes in production. Sticker figures must be used if they disagree with those in this chart.

NA—Non adjustable

① 4B—1986 2WD and 4WD Wagons

② Valve clearance intake and exhaust 0.012—1987 Stanza Wagon only

TUNE-UP PROCEDURES

In order to extract the full measure of performance and economy from your engine it is essential that it is properly tuned at regular intervals. A regular tune-up will keep your Datsun/Nissan engine running smoothly and will prevent the annoying breakdowns and poor performance often associated with an unmaintained engine.

On all 1982–92 models covered in this manual the spark plug replacement interval is 30,000 miles or 24 months.

This interval should be halved if the car is operated under severe conditions such as trailer towing, prolonged idling, start-and-stop driving, or if starting or running problems are noticed. It is assumed that the routine maintenance described in Chapter 1 has been kept up, as this will have a decided effect on the results of a tune-up. All of the applicable steps of a tune-up should be followed in order, as the result is a cumulative one.

If the specifications on the underhood tune-up sticker in the engine compartment of your car disagree with the "Tune-Up Specifications Chart" in this Chapter, the figures on the sticker must be used. The sticker often reflects changes made during the production run.

A tune-up should consist of replacing the spark plugs and checking spark plug wires, distributor cap and rotor. If necesary replace the air filter, gas and all other emission filters. All vacuum lines and hoses should also be checked and all necessary engine adjustments should also be made at this time. It might be noted that the tune-up is a good time to take a look around the engine compartment for problems in the making, such as oil and fuel leaks, deteriorating radiator or heater hoses, loose and/or frayed fan belts and etc.

Spark Plugs

A typical spark plug consists of a metal shell surrounding a ceramic insulator. A metal electrode extends downward through the center of the insulator and protrudes a small distance. Located at the end of the plug and attached to the side of the outer metal shell is the side electrode. This side electrode bends in a 90° so its tip is even with, parallel to, the tip of the center electrode. The distance between these two electrodes is called spark plug gap. The spark plug in no way produces a spark but merely provides a gap across which the current can arc. The coil produces 20,000–25,000 V (transistorized ignition produces considerably more voltage than the standard type, approximately 50,000 volts), which travels to the distributor where it is sent

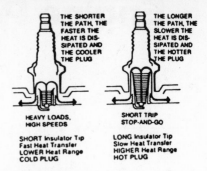

Spark plug heat range

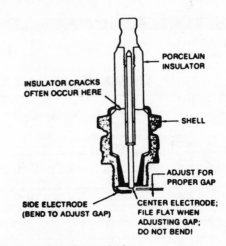

Cross section of a spark plug

through the spark plug wires to the plugs. The current passes along the center electrode and jumps the gap to the side electrode and, in so doing, ignites the air/fuel mixture in the combustion chamber. All plugs used in Datsun/Nissan have a resistor built into the center electrode to reduce interference to any nearby radio and television receivers. The resistor also cuts down on erosion of plug electrodes caused by excessively long sparking. Resistor spark plug wiring is original equipment on all Datsuns andNissans.

Spark plug life and efficiency depend upon the condition of the engine and the temperatures to which the plug is exposed. Combustion chamber temperatures are affected by many factors such as compression ratio of the engine, fuel/air mixtures, exhaust emission equipment, and the type of driving you do. Spark plugs are designed and classified by number according to the heat range at which they will operate most efficiently. The amount of heat that the plug absorbs is determined by the length of the lower insulator. The longer the insulator (it extends farther into the engine), the hotter the plug will operate. A plug that has a short path for heat transfer and remains too cool will quickly accumulate deposits of oil and carbon since it is not hot enough to burn them off. This leads to plug fouling and consequently to misfiring. A plug that has a long path for heat transfer will have no deposits but, due to the excessive heat, the electrodes will burn away quickly and, in some instances, pre-ignition may result.

Preignition takes place when plug tips get so hot that they glow sufficiently to ignite the fuel/air mixture before the spark does. This early ignition will usually cause a pinging during low speeds and heavy loads. In sever cases, the heat may become enough to start the fuel/air mixture burning throughout the combustion chamber rather than just to the front of the plug as in normal operation. At this time, the piston is rising in the cylinder making its compression stroke. The burning mass is compressed and an explosion results producing tremendous pressure. Something has to give, and it does. Pistons are often damaged. Obviously, this detonation (explosion) is a destructive condition that can be avoided by installed a spark plug designed and specified for your particular engine.

A set of spark plugs usually requires replacement after 30,000 miles (48,000 km) for all 1982 and later models. The electrode on a new spark plug has a sharp edge but, with use, this edge becomes rounded by erosion causing the plug gap to increase. In normal operation, plug gap increases about 0.001 in. (0.025mm) in every 1,000–2,000 miles (1,600–3,200 km). As the gap increases, the plug's voltage requirement also increases. It requires a greater voltage to jump the wider gap and about two to three times as much voltage to fire a plug at high speeds and acceleration than at idle.

Worn plugs become obvious during acceleration. Voltage requirement is greatest during acceleration and a plug with an enlarged gap may require more voltage than the coil is able to produce. As a result, the engine misses and sputters until acceleration is reduced. Reducing acceleration reduces the plug's voltage requirement and the engine runs smoother. Slow, city driving is hard on plugs. The long periods of idle experienced in traffic creates an overly rich gas mixture. The engine isn't running fast enough to completely burn the gas and, consequently, the plugs are fouled with gas deposits and engine idle becomes rough. In many cases driving under right conditions can effectively clean these fouled plugs.

In some cases, dirty, fouled plugs may be cleaned by sandblasting. Many shops have a spark plug sandblaster. After sandblasting, the electrode should be filed to a sharp, square shape and then gapped to specifications. Gap-

ping a plug too close will produce rough idle while gapping it too wide will increase its voltage requirement and cause missing at high speeds and during acceleration.

REMOVAL

NOTE: *Some engines have 2 plugs for each cylinder. All eight plugs should be replaced at every tune-up for maximum fuel efficiency and power. Read the complete service procedure before starting this repair.*

When you're removing spark plugs, you should work on one at a time. Don't start by removing the plug wires all at once because unless you number them, they're going to get mixed up. On some models, though, it will be more convenient for you to remove all the wires before you start to work on the plugs. If this is necessary, take a minute before you begin and number the wires (mark the distributor cap also for correct installation) with tape before you take them off. The time you spend here will pay off later on.

1. Twist the spark plug boot and remove the boot from the plug. You may also use a plug wire removal tool designed especially for this purpose. Do not pull on the wire itself. When the wire has been removed, take a wire brush and clean around the plug. Make sure that all the grime is removed so that none will enter the cylinder after the plug has been removed.

2. Remove the plug using the proper size spark plug socket, extensions, and universals as necessary. The Datsun/Nissan cylinder head is aluminum, which is easily stripped. Remove plugs ONLY when the engine is cold.

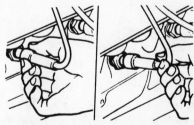

Twist and pull on the rubber boot to remove the spark plug wire—never pull on the wire itself

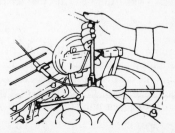

Plugs are removed using the proper combination of socket wrench, universals and extensions

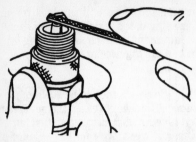

Plugs that are in good condition can be filed and reused

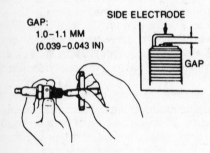

Adjust the electrode gap by bending the side electrode

GAP:
1.0–1.1 MM
(0.039–0.043 IN)

SIDE ELECTRODE

GAP

Spark plug gap adjustment

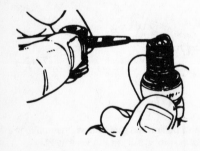

Always use a wire gauge to check the electrode gap

3. If removing the plug is difficult, drip some penetrating oil on the plug threads, allow it to work, then remove the plug. Also, be sure that the socket is straight on the plug, especially on those hard to reach plugs.

INSPECTION

Check the plugs for deposits and wear. If they are not going to be replaced, clean the plugs thoroughly. Remember that any kind of deposit will decrease the efficiency of the plug. Plugs can be cleaned on a spark plug cleaning machine, which can sometimes be found in service stations, or you can do an acceptable job of cleaning with a stiff brush. If the plugs are cleaned, the electrodes must be filed flat. Use an ignition points file, not an emery board or the like, which will leave deposits. The electrodes must be filed perfectly flat with sharp edges. Rounded edges reduce the spark plug voltage by as much as 50%.

Check the spark plug gap before installation. The ground electrode (the L-shaped one connected to the body of the plug) must be parallel to the center electrode and the specified size wire gauge (see Tune-Up Specifications) should pass through the gap with a slight drag. Always check the spark plug gap on new spark plugs. They are not always set correctly at the factory. Wire gapping tools usually have a bending tool attached. Use that to adjust the side electrode until the proper distance is obtained. Absolutely never bend the center electrode. Also, be careful not to bend the side electrode too far or too often. It may weaken and break off within the engine, requiring removal of the cylinder head to retrieve it.

INSTALLATION

1. Lubricate the threads of the spark plugs with drop of oil. Install the plugs and tighten them hand tight. Take care not to crossthread them.

2. Tighten the spark plugs with the socket. Do not apply the same amount of force you would use for a bolt; just snug them in. If a torque wrench is available, tighten all 1982–83 models to 11–15 ft. lbs. On all models from 1984 to 1992 tighten spark plugs to 14–22 ft. lbs.

3. Install the wires on their respective plugs. Make sure the wires are firmly connected. You will be able to feel them click into place.

Spark Plug Wires
REPLACING AND TESTING

On every tune-up or 30 months/24,000 miles inspect the spark plug wires for burns, cuts, or breaks in the insulation. Check the boots and the nipples on the distributor cap. Replace any damaged wiring.

Every 45,000 miles (3 years) or so, the resistance of the wires should be checked with an ohmmeter. Wires with excessive resistance will cause misfiring, and may make the engine difficult to start in damp weather. Generally, the useful life of the cables is 45,000–60,000 miles.

To check resistance, remove the distributor cap, leaving the wires in place. Connect one lead

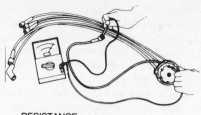

RESISTANCE:
LESS THAN 30,000 OHMS

Checking the spark plug wire resistance

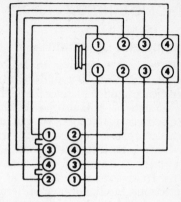

CA20E engine
Firing order: 1-3-4-2
Distributor rotation: counterclockwise

of an ohmmeter to an electrode within the cap. Connect the other lead to the corresponding spark plug terminal (remove it from the spark plug for this test). Replace any wire which shows a resistance over 30,000Ω. Resistance should not be over 25,000Ω, and 30,000Ω must be considered the outer limit of acceptability. Also measure the resistance of the wires while shaking them to check for intermittent breaks.

It should be remembered that resistance is also a function of length; the longer the wire, the greater the resistance. Thus, if the wires on your car are longer than the factory originals, resistance will be higher, quite possibly outside these limits.

When installing new wires, replace them one at a time to avoid mixups. Start by replacing the longest one first. Install the boot firmly over the spark plug. Route the wire over the same path as the original. Insert the nipple firmly onto the tower on the distributor cap, then install the cap cover and latches to secure the wires.

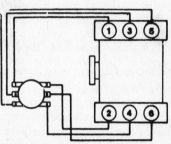

VG30E engine
Firing order: 1-2-3-4-5-6
Distributor rotation: counterclockwise

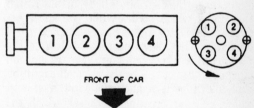

FRONT OF CAR

KA24E engine (Stanza FWD)
Firing order: 1-3-4-2
Distributor rotation: counterclockwise

FIRING ORDERS

NOTE: *To avoid confusion, remove and tag the wires one at a time, for replacement.*

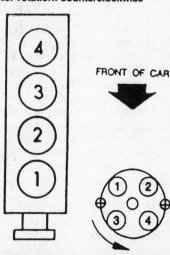

FRONT OF CAR

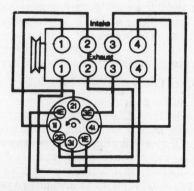

Z-series engines
Firing order: 1-3-4-2
Distributor rotation: counterclockwise

KA24E and KA24DE engines (240SX RWD)
Firing order: 1-3-4-2
Distributor rotation: counterclockwise

ELECTRONIC IGNITION

Description and Operation

In 1975, in order to comply with California's tougher emission laws, Datsun/Nissan introduced electronic ignition systems for all models sold in that state. Since that time, the Datsun/Nissan electronic ignition system has undergone a metamorphosis from a standard transistorized circuit to an Integrated Circuit system (IC), and later to the special dual spark plug system used with some models.

The electronic ignition system differs from the conventional breaker points system in form only. Its function is exactly the same: to supply a spark to the spark plugs at precisely the right moment to ignite the compressed gas in the cylinders and create mechanical movement.

NOTE: *On some late model vehicles a crankangle sensor mounted in the distributor is the basic component of the entire E.C.C.S. (Electronic Concentrated Control System). There are no adjustments necessary.*

Located in the distributor, in addition to the normal rotor cap, is a spoked rotor (reluctor) which fits on the distributor shaft where the breaker points cam is found on nonelectronic ignitions. The rotor (reluctor) revolves with the top rotor cap and, as it passes a pickup coil or stator inside the distributor body, breaks a high flux phase which occurs while the space between the reluctor spokes passes the pickup coil or stator. This allows current to flow to the pickup coil or IC ignition unit. Primary ignition current is then cut off by the electronic ignition unit, allowing the magnetic field in the ignition coil to collapse, creating the spark which the distributor passes on to the spark plug.

The dual spark plug ignition system uses two ignition coils and each cylinder has two spark plugs which fire simultaneously. In this manner the engine is able to consume large quantities of recirculated exhaust gas which would cause a single spark plug cylinder to misfire and idle roughly.

Some later models use a crankangle sensor. This sensor monitors engine speed and piston position and sends to the computer signals on which the controls of the fuel injection, ignition timing and other functions are based. No maintenance is required but inspect and replace, if necessary, the spark plug wires, rotor head and the distributor cap every 30, 000 miles or 24 months.

Service on electronic ignition systems consist of inspection of the distributor cap, rotor and ignition wires replacing them when necessary. Check the ignition wires for cracking of exterior insulation and for proper fit on the distributor cap and spark plugs. These parts can be expected to last for at least 40,000 miles but you should inspect these parts every 2 years or 30,000 miles. In addition, the reluctor air gap should be checked periodically if the system has no crankangle sensor.

NOTE: *All models without a crankangle sensor type ignition system use IC ignition unit and no pickup coil. Measure the air gap between the reluctor and stator assembly. If not within specifications (0.30–0.50mm), loosen stator retaining screws and adjust. Refer to the necessary service procedure.*

Diagnosis and Testing
IC IGNITION TYPE SYSTEM

All diagnosis and testing should be perform in order according to the service charts below. Perform all test in the order stated by the diagnosis charts. Battery voltage must be 11.5–12.5 volts before starting all test procedures.

Adjustment

The adjustment service consists of inspection of the distributor cap, rotor, and ignition wires, replacing when necessary. In addition, the reluctor air gap should be check periodically.

1. The distributor cap is held on by 2 spring clips. Release them with a screwdriver and lift the cap straight up and off, with the wires attached.

2. Remove the rotor retaining screw. Pull the rotor head (not the spoked reluctor) straight up to remove it.

3. Rotate the engine until a reluctor spoke is aligned with the stator. Bump the engine around with the starter or turn it with a wrench on the crankshaft pulley bolt for this correct position. Check the reluctor air gap by using a non-magnetic feeler gauge.

4. Measure the air gap between the reluctor and stator. If not within specifications 0.012–0.020 in. (0.30–0.50mm), loosen stator retaining screws and adjust. Always properly center stator and reluctor assembly before tightening after adjustment procedure.

Parts Replacement
RELUCTOR AND IC IGNITION UNIT

NOTE:If the distributor assembly must be removed from the engine, the distributor must be marked for correct installation. Refer to Chapter 3 for the necessary service procedures before starting this repair.

1. Remove the distributor cap and rotor. The rotor is held to the distributor shaft by a retaining screw, which must be removed.

2. Remove the wiring harness and the vacuum controller from the housing.

3. Using 2 flat bladed screwdrivers, place one on each side of the reluctor and pry it from the distributor shaft.

NOTE: *When removing the reluctor, be careful not to damage or distort the teeth.*

4. Remove the roll pin from the reluctor.

NOTE: *To remove the IC unit, mark and remove the breaker plate assembly and separate*

IC IGNITION SYSTEM TROUBLE-SHOOTING

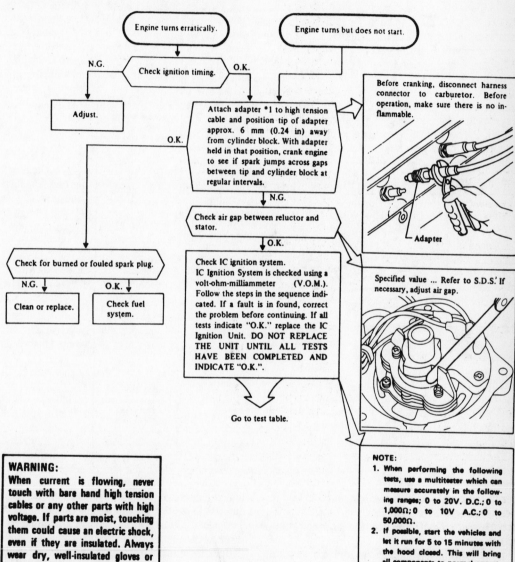

Engine turns erratically.

Engine turns but does not start.

Check ignition timing. — N.G. — Adjust.

O.K.

Attach adapter *1 to high tension cable and position tip of adapter approx. 6 mm (0.24 in) away from cylinder block. With adapter held in that position, crank engine to see if spark jumps across gaps between tip and cylinder block at regular intervals.

Before cranking, disconnect harness connector to carburetor. Before operation, make sure there is no inflammable.

Adapter

N.G.

Check air gap between reluctor and stator.

O.K.

Check for burned or fouled spark plug.

N.G. — Clean or replace.

O.K. — Check fuel system.

Check IC ignition system.
IC Ignition System is checked using a volt-ohm-milliammeter (V.O.M.). Follow the steps in the sequence indicated. If a fault is in found, correct the problem before continuing. If all tests indicate "O.K." replace the IC Ignition Unit. DO NOT REPLACE THE UNIT UNTIL ALL TESTS HAVE BEEN COMPLETED AND INDICATE "O.K.".

Specified value ... Refer to S.D.S. If necessary, adjust air gap.

Go to test table.

WARNING:
When current is flowing, never touch with bare hand high tension cables or any other parts with high voltage. If parts are moist, touching them could cause an electric shock, even if they are insulated. Always wear dry, well-insulated gloves or wrap affected parts with dry cloth before handling.

NOTE:
1. When performing the following tests, use a multitester which can measure accurately in the following ranges; 0 to 20V. D.C.; 0 to 1,000Ω; 0 to 10V A.C.; 0 to 50,000Ω.
2. If possible, start the vehicles and let it run for 5 to 15 minutes with the hood closed. This will bring all components to normal operating temperature, and will make it easier to diagnose intermittent problems.
3. It is not necessary to disconnect the harness connectors when performing the tests which follow. Simply insert the meter probes into the back of appropriate connector cavity.

*1:
Preparation of spark plug for checking Many things can be utilized as an adapter. However, it is recommended that a used spark plug whose threaded portion has been half cut off as shown in the figure be utilized.

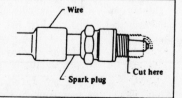

Wire

Spark plug

Cut here

Ignition system diagnosis chart

TEST TABLE

TEST	TEST METHOD	CONDITIONS	RESULT	ACTION
1. Battery Voltage (no load)		1. Ignition key in "OFF" position.	11.5 - 12.5 volts	Proceed to Step 2.
		2. Connect voltmeter as illustrated and set to appropriate scale.		Battery, charging system or starting system – Faulty.
		3. Read and record battery voltage reading. Battery voltage ☐	Below 11.5 volts	
2. Battery Cranking Voltage		1. Connect voltmeter as illustrated and set to appropriate scale.	Voltage reading greater than 9.6 volts	Battery O.K. Proceed to Step 3.
		2. Remove coil wire from distributor cap and ground it.	Voltage reading less than 9.6 volts	Battery, charging system or starting system – Faulty.
		3. Read voltmeter while cranking engine for approximately 15 seconds.		
		4. Record voltage reading. Battery cranking voltage ☐		
3. Secondary Wiring		1. Connect ohmmeter as illustrated and measure the resistance of each high tension cable.	Resistance readings less than 30,000 ohms	Distributor cap and high tension cables – O.K. Proceed to Step 4.
			Resistance readings greater than 30,000 ohms	Replace high tension cable(s) and/or distributor cap as required.
4. Ignition Coil Secondary Circuit		1. Ignition key in "OFF" position.	8,200 - 12,400 ohms	Ignition coil secondary windings – O.K. Proceed to step 5 for California
		2. Coil wire removed from coil.		
		3. Connect ohmmeter as illustrated. Check both coils.	Resistance reading not between 8,200 - 12,400 ohms	Faulty ignition coil – replace

Ignition system diagnosis chart

the IC unit from it. Be careful not to lose the spacers when you remove the IC unit.

5. Install the IC unit to the breaker plate assembly.

6. Install the wiring harness and the vacuum controller to the distributor housing. When you install the roll pin into the reluctor position the cutout direction of the roll pin in parallel with the notch in the rotor shaft. Make sure that the harness to the IC ignition unit is tightly secured, then adjust the air gap between the reluctor and the stator to 0.30–0.50mm.

IGNITION TIMING

Ignition timing is the measurement in degrees of crankshaft rotation, of the point at which the spark plugs fire in each of the cylinders. It is measured in degrees before or after Top Dead Center (TDC) of the compression stroke.

Because it takes a fraction of a second for the spark plug to ignite the mixture in the cylinder, the spark plug must fire a little before the piston reaches TDC. Otherwise, the mixture will not be completely ignited as the piston passes TDC and the full power of the explosion will not be used by the engine.

The timing measurement is given in degrees of crankshaft rotation before the piston reaches TDC (BTDC). If the setting for the ignition timing is 5° BTDC, the spark plug must fire 5° before each piston reaches TDC. All of this only holds true, however, when the engine is at idle speed.

TEST	TEST METHOD	CONDITIONS	RESULT	ACTION
5. Power Supply Circuit	IC Ignition unit / Housing / Voltmeter / "B" Terminal (Black/white wire)	1. Connect voltmeter as illustrated and set to appropriate scale.	11.5 - 12.5 volts	Proceed to Step 6.
		2. Turn ignition key to "ON" position.	Below 11.5 volts	Check wiring from ignition switch to IC unit.
6. Power Supply Circuit (Cranking)	IC Ignition unit / Housing / Voltmeter / "B" Terminal (Black/white wire)	1. Connect voltmeter as illustrated and set to appropriate scale. 2. Pull out coil wire from distributor cap and ground it.	Voltage reading is less than 1 volt below battery cranking voltage and is greater than 8.6 volts.	Proceed to Step 7-A.
		3. Turn key to "START" position and observe voltmeter while engine is cranking.	Voltage reading is more than 1 volt below battery cranking voltage and/or is below 8.6 volts.	Check ignition switch and wiring from switch to IC unit.
7-A. Ignition Primary Circuit	IC Ignition unit / Housing / Voltmeter / "I" Terminal (Red wire)	1. Connect voltmeter as illustrated and set to appropriate scale.	11.5 - 12.5 volts	Proceed to Step 7-B.
		2. Ignition key in "ON" position.	Below 11.5 volts	Proceed to Step 8.
7-B. Ignition Primary Circuit	IC Ignition unit / Housing / Voltmeter / "E" Terminal (Blue wire)	1. Connect voltmeter as illustrated and set to appropriate scale.	11.5 - 12.5 volts	Proceed to Step 9.
		2. Ignition key in "ON" position.	Below 11.5 volts	Proceed to Step 8.
8. Ignition Coil Primary Circuit	Resistance: × 1 range	1. Ignition key in "OFF" position. 2. Coil wire removed from coil. 3. Connect ohmmeter as illustrated. Check both coils.	0.84 - 1.02 ohms	Ignition coil primary winding O.K. / Check ignition switch and wiring from ignition switch to coil and IC unit.
			Resistance reading not between 0.84 - 1.02 ohms	Faulty ignition coil – replace.
9. I.C. Unit Ground Circuit	Battery (On vehicle) / Voltmeter	1. Connect voltmeter as illustrated and set to appropriate scale. 2. Pull out coil wire from distributor cap and ground it.	0.5 volts or less	Replace IC ignition unit assembly.
		3. Turn key to "START" position and observe voltmeter while engine is cranking.	More than 0.5 volts	Check distributor ground, wiring from chassis ground to battery including battery cable connections.

Ignition system diagnosis chart

As the engine speed increases, the pistons go faster. The spark plugs have to ignite the fuel even sooner if it is to be completely ignited when the piston reaches TDC. To do this, the distributor has two means to advance the timing of the spark as the engine speed increases: a set of centrifugal weights within the distributor, and a vacuum diaphragm, mounted on the side of the distributor.

NOTE: *In late model 200SX (all turbo versions and 3.0L engine), 240SX and late model Stanza a crankangle sensor in the distributor is used. This sensor controls ignition timing and has other engine control functions. There is no vacuum or centrifugal advance; all timing settings are controlled by the E.C.U.*

If the ignition is set too far advanced (BTDC), the ignition and expansion of the fuel in the cylinder will occur too soon and tend to force the

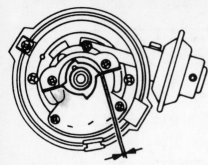

Checking the air gap

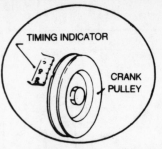

Typical timing indicator to pulley relationship

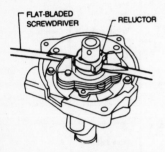

Removing reluctor from the rotor shaft

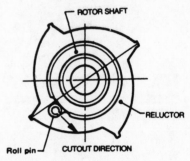

View of reluctor, roll pin, and distributor shaft

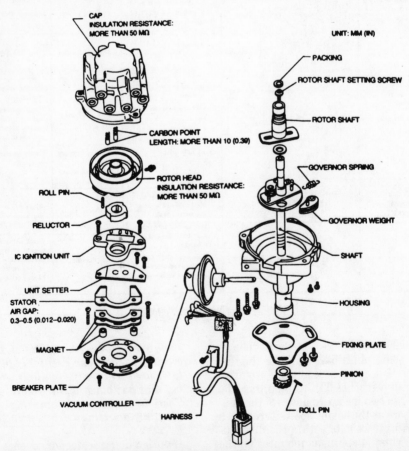

Exploded view of IC ignition type distributor

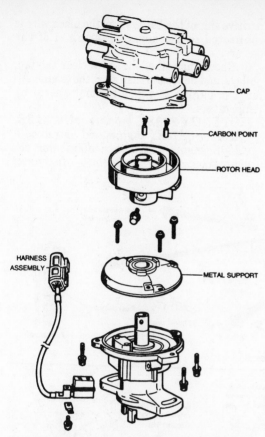

CAP

CARBON POINT

ROTOR HEAD

HARNESS ASSEMBLY

METAL SUPPORT

Exploded view of crank angle sensor type distributor

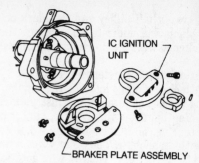

IC IGNITION UNIT

BRAKER PLATE ASSEMBLY

IC ignition unit removal

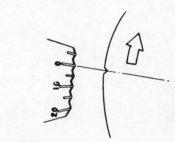

Timing marks

piston down while it is still traveling up. This causes engine ping. If the ignition spark is set too far retarded, after TDC (ATDC), the piston will have already passed TDC and started on its way down when the fuel is ignited. This will cause the piston to be forced down for only a portion of its travel. This will result in poor engine performance and lack of power.

Timing marks consist of a notch on the rim of the crankshaft pulley and a scale of degrees attached to the front of the engine. The notch corresponds to the position of the piston in the number 1 cylinder. A stroboscopic (dynamic) timing light is used, which is hooked into the circuit of the No. 1 cylinder spark plug. Every time the spark plug fires, the timing light flashes. By aiming the timing light at the timing marks, the exact position of the piston within the cylinder can be read, since the stroboscopic flash makes the mark on the pulley appear to be standing still. Proper timing is indicated when the notch is aligned with the correct number on the scale.

There are three basic types of timing lights available. The first is a simple neon bulb with two wire connections (one for the spark plug and one for the plug wire, connecting the light

in series). This type of light is quite dim, and must be held closely to the marks to be seen, but it is inexpensive. The second type of light operates from the car battery. Two alligator clips connect to the battery terminals, while a third wire connects to the spark plug with an adapter. This type of light is more expensive, but the xenon bulb provides a nice bright flash which can even be seen in sunlight. The third type replaces the battery source with 110 volt house current. Some timing lights have other functions built into them, such as dwell meters, tachometers, or remote starting switches. These are convenient, in that they reduce the tangle of wires under the hood, but may duplicate the functions of tools you already have.

You should use a timing light with an inductive pickup. This pickup simply clamps onto the No. 1 plug wire, eliminating the adapter. It is not prone to crossfiring or false triggering, which may occur with a conventional light, due to the greater voltages produced by electronic ignition.

ADJUSTMENT

NOTE: *Always refer to the underhood specifications sticker for any additional applicable procedures. Identify the type engine in the vehicle, read the service procedure and use the correct procedure for your engine.*

1. Locate the timing marks on the crankshaft pulley and the front of the engine.

2. Clean off the timing marks, so that you can see them.

3. Use chalk or white paint to color the mark

on the crankshaft pulley and the mark on the scale which will indicate the correct timing when aligned with the notch on the crankshaft pulley.

4. Attach a tachometer to the engine.

5. Attach a timing light to the engine, according to the manufacturer's instructions. If the timing light has three wires, one, usually green or blue, is attached to the No. 1 spark plug with an adapter. The other wires are connected to the battery. The red wire goes to the positive side of the battery and the black wire is connected to the negative terminal of the battery.

6. Check that all of the wires clear the fan, pulleys, and belts, and then start the engine. Allow the engine to reach normal operating temperature.

NOTE: *On 200SX models with Z22E, CA20E or CA18ET engines and Stanza with CA20E engine and with a distributor advance vacuum hose stop engine — disconnect*

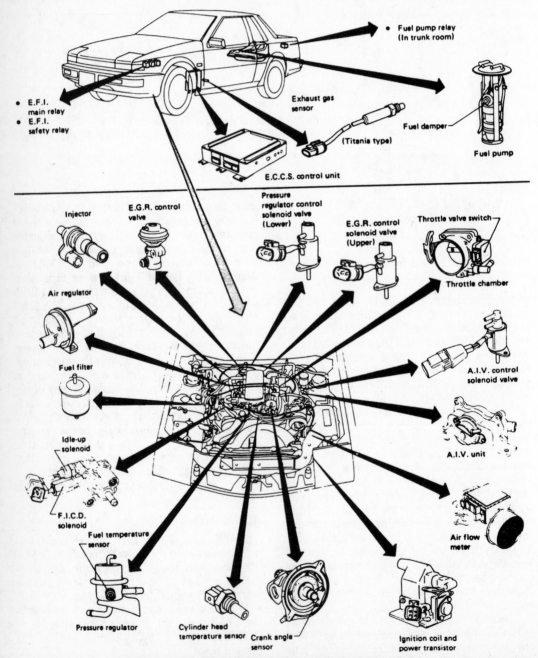

Engine and emission parts location—200SX (CA20E engine)

distributor advance vacuum hose (if so equipped) from the distributor and plug hose.

7. Check or adjust the idle speed to the correct setting. See the Idle Speed service procedures in this Chapter.

8. Aim the timing light at the timing marks. If the marks which you put on the pulley and the engine are aligned when the light flashes, the timing is correct. Turn off the engine and remove the tachometer and the timing light. If the marks are not in alignment, proceed with the following steps.

NOTE: *On 200SX and Stanza models with a CA20E engine and no distributor advance vacuum hose stop engine — disconnect auxiliary air control (A.A.C.) valve harness connector which is part of idle air adjusting unit (I.A.A.) unit and throttle valve switch then follow Step 9.*

On 200SX models with a VG30E engine stop engine — disconnect idle up solenoid harness connector then follow Step 9.

On 240SX and Stanza with KA24E and KA24DE engines stop engine — discon-

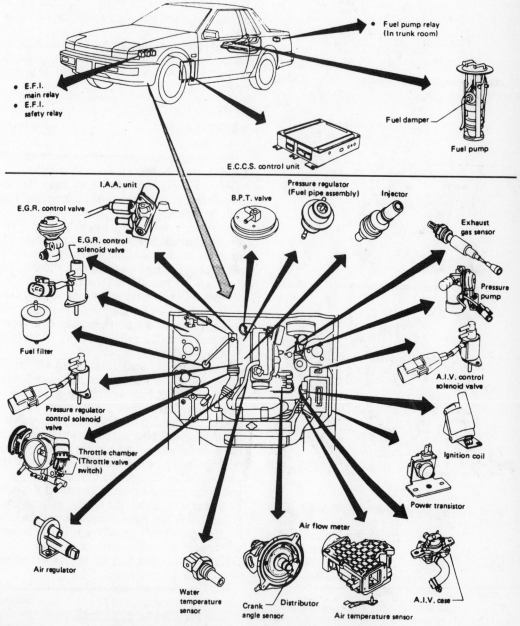

Engine and emission parts location—200SX (VG30E engine)

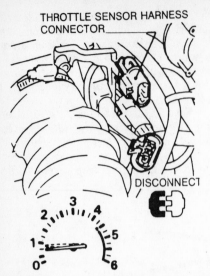

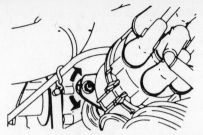

Loosen the distributor lockbolt and turn the distributor slightly to adjust timing

Throttle harness connector location—Stanza (KA24E engine)

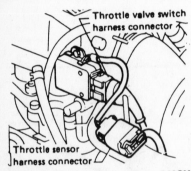

Throttle harness connector location—240SX (KA24E and KA24DE engines)

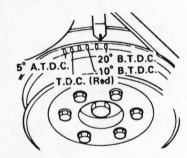

Ignition timing marks

the spark, and in the opposite direction of rotor rotation to advance the spark. Align the marks on the pulley and the engine with the flashes of the timing light.

12. Tighten the distributor lockbolt and recheck the timing. Reconnect all lines or electrical connections. Roadtest the vehicle for proper operation.

VALVE LASH

The maintenance intervals for valve adjustment is every 15,000 miles or 12 months.

Valve adjustment determines how far the valves enter the cylinder and how long they stay open or closed.

If the valve clearance is too large, part of the lift of the camshaft will be used in removing the excessive clearance. Consequently, the valve will not be opening for as long as it should. This condition has two effects: the valve train components will emit a tapping sound as they take up the excessive clearance and the engine will perform poorly because the valves don't open fully and allow the proper amount of gases to flow into and out of the engine.

If the valve clearance is too small, the intake valves and the exhaust valves will open too far and they will not fully seat on the cylinder head when they close. When a valve seats itself on the cylinder head, it does two things: it seals the combustion chamber so that one of the gases in the cylinder escape and it cools itself by transferring some of the heat it absorbs from the combustion in the cylinder to the cylinder head and to the engine's cooling system. If the valve clearance is too small, the engine will run poorly because of the gases escaping from the combustion chamber. The valves will also become overheated and will warp, since they cannot transfer heat unless they are touching the valve seat in the cylinder head.

NOTE: *While all valve adjustments must be made as accurately as possible, it is better to have the valve adjustment slightly loose than slightly tight, as a burned valve may result*

nect throttle sensor harness connector then follow step 9.

9. Loosen the distributor lockbolt just enough that the distributor can be turned with little effort.

10. Start the engine. Keep the wires of the timing light clear of the fan.

11. With the timing light aimed at the pulley and the marks on the engine, turn the distributor in the direction of rotor rotation to retard

from overly tight adjustments. Read the complete service prcodeure — then refer to the correct model and year for your vehicle.

ADJUSTMENT

1982–83 200SX
Twin Plug Engines – Z series engine

1. The valves must be adjusted with the engine WARM, so start the car and run the engine until the needle on the temperature gauge reaches the middle of the gauge. After the engine is warm, shut it off.

2. Purchase either a new gasket or some silicone gasket sealer before removing the camshaft cover. Counting on the old gasket to be in good shape is a losing proposition. Always use new gaskets. Note the location of any wires and hoses which may interfere with cam cover removal, disconnect them and move them to one side. Remove the bolts holding the cover in place and remove the cover. Remember, the engine will be hot, so be careful.

3. Place a wrench on the crankshaft pulley bolt and turn the engine over until the first cam lobe behind the camshaft timing chain sprocket is pointing straight down.

NOTE: *If you decide to turn the engine by bumping it with the starter, be sure to disconnect the high tension wire from the coil(s) to prevent the engine from accidentally starting and spewing oil all over the engine compart-*

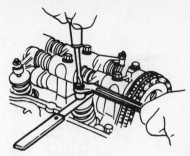

Loosen the locknut and turn the adjusting screw to adjust the valve clearance

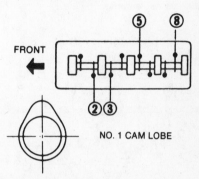

Secondary valve adjustment, No. 1 cam lobe pointing up—200SX (Z series engine)

ment. Never attempt to turn the engine by using a wrench on the camshaft sprocket bolt. There is a one to two turning ratio between the camshaft and the crankshaft which will put a tremendous strain on the timing chain.

4. See the illustration for primary adjustment and check the clearance of valves (1), (4), (6), and (7) using a flat bladed feeler gauge. The feeler gauge should pass between the valve stem end and the rocker arm screw with a very slight drag. Insert the feeler gauge straight, not at an angle.

5. If the clearance is not within specified value (0.012 in.) 0.30mm, loosen the rocker arm lock nut and turn the rocker arm screw to obtain the proper clearance. After correct clearance is obtained, tighten the lock nut.

6. Turn the engine over so that the first cam lobe behind the camshaft timing chain sprocket is pointing straight up and check the clearance of the valves marked (2), (3), (5), and (8) in the secondary adjustment illustration. They, too, should be adjusted to specifications as in Step 5.

7. Install the cam cover gasket, the cam cover and any wires and hoses which were removed.

1984–88 200SX
CA20E, CA18ET and VG30E Engines

NOTE: *Starting in mid-year 1986, the CA20E engine in the 200SX model valves are*

Checking the valve clearance—200 SX (Z series engine)

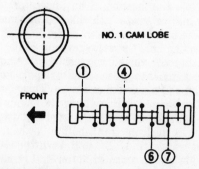

Primary valve adjustment, No. 1 cam lobe pointing down—200SX (Z series engine)

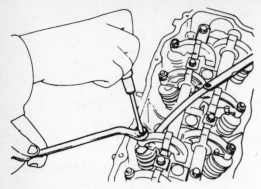

Adjusting valve clearance

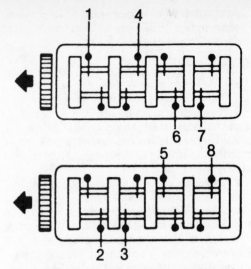

Valve adjustment sequence—Stanza (1982 only)

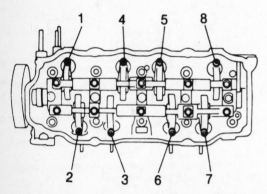

Valve location, 1984 and later 200SX (CA20E and CA18ET engines)—See text for procedure

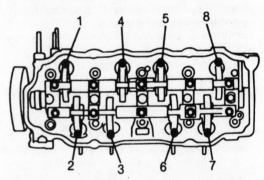

CA20E valve location/for sequence see text—Stanza

non-adjustable. On V6 equipped 200SX models the valves are also non-adjustable. Refer to Valve Clearance column in the Tune-Up Specifications Chart.

Valve adjustment should be made while engine is warm but not running. Follow the procedure above for 1982–83 models, with the following exceptions: on Step 4, check and adjust the clearance valves 1, 2, 4 and 6 as shown in the accompanying illustration. This is with No. 1 cylinder at TDC on compression. On Step 6, check and adjust the clearance on valves 3, 5, 7 and 8 with the No. 4 cylinder at TDC on compression.

1982–92 Stanza
CA20, CA20E And KA24E Engines

NOTE: *On Stanza models from 1987–92 (except 1986–88 station wagons) no routine valve adjustment is necessary or possible. These models are equipped with hydraulic lash adjusters, which continually take up excess clearance in the valve train.*

For other vehicles, Datsun/Nissan recommends that valve adjustment should be done every 12 months or 15,000 miles.

1. Run the engine until it reaches normal operating temperature. Oil temperature, not water temperature, is critical to valve adjustment.

With this in mind, make sure the engine is fully warmed up since this is the only way to make sure the parts have reached their full expansion. Generally speaking, this takes around 15 minutes. After the engine has reached normal operating temperature, shut it off.

2. Purchase a new valve cover gasket before removing the valve cover. The new silicone gasket sealers are just as good or better if you can't find a gasket.

3. Note the location of any hoses or wires which may interfere with valve cover removal, disconnect and move them aside. Remove the bolts which hold the valve cover in place.

4. After the valve cover has been removed, the next step is to get the number one piston at TDC on the compression stroke. There are at least two ways to do this: Bump the engine over with the starter or turn it over by using a wrench on the front crankshaft pulley bolt. The easiest way to find TDC is to turn the engine over slowly with a wrench (after first removing No. 1 plug) until the piston is at the top of its stroke and the TDC timing mark on the crank-

shaft pulley is in alignment with the timing mark pointer. At this point, the valves for No. 1 cylinder should be closed.

NOTE: *Make sure both valves are closed with the valve springs up as high as they will go. An easy way to find the compression stroke is to remove the distributor cap and observe which spark plug lead the rotor is pointing to. If the rotor points to No. 1 spark plug lead, No. 1 cylinder is on its compression stroke. When the rotor points to the No. 2 spark plug lead, No. 2 cylinder is on its compression stroke.*

5. Set the No. 1 piston at TDC of the compression stroke, then check and/or adjust the valve clearance on Stanza (1982 model only) Nos. 1, 4, 6 and 7; on the Stanza (1983–86 and 1986–88 Stanza wagon), Nos. 1, 2, 4 and 6.

6. To adjust the clearance, loosen the locknut with a wrench and turn the adjuster with a screwdriver while holding the locknut. The correct size feeler gauge (0.012 in.) 0.30mm should pass with a slight drag between the rocker arm and the valve stem.

7. Turn the crankshaft one full revolution to position the No. 4 piston at TDC of the compression stroke. Check and/or adjust the valves (counting from the front to the rear) on the Stanza (1982 model only), Nos. 2, 3, 5 and 8; on the Stanza (1983–86 and 1986–88 Stanza wagon), Nos. 3, 5, 7 and 8.

8. Replace the valve cover and torque the bolts on the valve cover down evenly. Check oil level.

1989–92 240SX
KA24E and KA24DE Engines

NOTE: *On the 240SX KA24E engine no routine valve adjustment is necessary or possible. These models are equipped with hydraulic lash adjusters, which continually take up excess clearance in the valve train.*

Datsun/Nissan recommends that valve adjustment on the KA24DE engine should only be done if valve noise increases.

KA24DE ENGINE

1. Run the engine until it reaches normal operating temperature and shut it off.

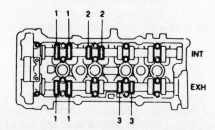

Valve adjustment step No. 1—KA24DE engine

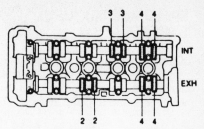

Valve adjustment step No. 2—KA24DE engine

2. Remove the rocker cover and all spark plugs.

3. Set No. 1 cylinder at TDC on compression stroke. Align pointer with TDC mark on crankshaft pulley. Check that the valve lifters on No. 1 cylinder are loose and valve lifters on No. 4 are tight. If not turn crankshaft one revolution 360° and align as above.

4. Check both No. 1 intake and both No. 1 exhaust valves, both No. 2 intake valves and both No. 3 exhaust valves. Using a feeler gauge, measure the clearance between valve lifter and camshaft. Record any valve clearance measurements which are out of specification. Intake Valve clearance (hot) is 0.012–0.015 in. (0.30–0.38mm) and exhaust valve clearance (hot) is 0.013–0.016 in. (0.33–0.40mm).

5. Turn crankshaft one revolution 360° and align mark on crankshaft pulley with pointer. Check both No. 2 exhaust valves, both No. 3 intake valves, both No. 4 intake valves and both No. 4 exhaust valves. Using a feeler gauge, measure the clearance between valve lifter and camshaft. Record any valve clearance measurements which are out of specification. Intake valve clearance (hot) is 0.012–0.015 in. (0.30–0.38mm) and exhaust valve clearance (hot) is 0.013–0.016 in. (0.33–0.40mm).

6. If all valve clearances are within specification, install all related parts as necessary.

7. If adjustement is necessary, adjust valve clearance while engine is cold by removing adjusting shim. Determine replacement adjusting shim size using formula. Using a micrometer determine thickness of removed shim. Calculate thickness of new adjusting shim so valve clearance comes within specified valves. R = thickness of removed shim, N = thickness of new shim, M = measured valve clearance.

- INTAKE: N = R + (M − 0.0138 in. [0.35mm])
- EXHAUST: N = R + (M − 0.0146 in. [0.37mm])

8. Shims are available in 37 sizes (thickness is stamped on shim − this side always installled down), select new shims with thickness as close as possible to calculated value.

IDLE SPEED AND MIXTURE ADJUSTMENTS

This Chapter contains only tune-up adjustment procedures for carburetors. Descriptions, adjustments, and overhaul procedures for fuel systems can be found in Chapter 5.

Caurbureted Engines

When the engine is running, the air/fuel mixture from the carburetor is being drawn into the engine by a partial vacuum which is created by the movement of the pistons downward on the intake stroke. The amount of air/fuel mixture that enters into the engine is controlled by the throttle plate(s) in the bottom of the carburetor. When the engine is not running the throttle plate is closed, completely blocking off the bottom of the carburetor from the inside of the engine. The throttle plates are connected by the throttle linkage to the accelerator pedal in the passenger compartment of the vehicle. When you depress the pedal, you open the throttle plates in the carburetor to admit more air/fuel mixture to the engine.

When the engine is not running, the throttle plates are closed. When the engine is idling, it is necessary to have the throttle plates open slightly. To prevent having to hold your foot on the pedal when the engine is idling, an idle speed adjusting screw was added to the carburetor linkage.

The idle adjusting screw contacts a lever (throttle lever) on the outside of the carburetor. When the screw is turned, it either opens or closes the throttle plates of the carburetor, raising or lowering the idle speed of the engine. This screw is called the curb idle adjusting screw.

ADJUSTMENT

1982–83 Stanza Models 49 States
1984–85 Stanza Models Canada

NOTE: *Always refer to the underhood specifications sticker for any additional applicable procedures.*

1. Connect a tachometer to the engine according the manufacturer's instructions.
2. Start the engine and run it until it reaches normal operating temperatures.
3. Operate it at 2,000 rpm for 2 minutes under no load, then idle for 1 minute.

NOTE: *If the cooling fan is operating, wait until it stops.*

4. If equipped with a manual transaxle, place the shift selector in **NEUTRAL**; if equipped with an automatic transaxle, place the shift selector in **DRIVE**.

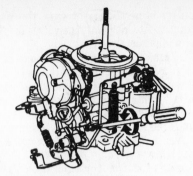
Adjusting idle speed—Stanza

5. If the idle speed is not correct, adjust the throttle adjusting screw at the carburetor.
6. When the idle speed is correct, stop the engine and disconnect the tachometer.

Electronic Fuel Injection (E.F.I.)

These cars use a rather complex electronic fuel injection system which is controlled by a series of temperature, altitude (for California) and air flow sensors which feed information into a central control unit. The control unit then relays an electronic signal to the injector nozzle at each cylinder, which allows a predetermined amount of fuel into the combustion chamber.

ADJUSTMENT PROCEDURE

1982–83 200SX (Z Series Engine)

NOTE: *Always refer to the underhood specifications sticker for any additional applicable procedures.*

1. Start the engine and run it until the water temperature indicator points to the middle of the temperature gauge. It might be quicker to take a short spin down the road and back.
2. Open the engine hood. Run the engine at about 2,000 rpm for a few minutes with the transmission in Neutral and all accessories off. If you have not already done so, check the ignition timing and make sure it is correct. Hook up a tachometer as per the manufacturer's instructions. For automatic transmission, set the parking brake, block the wheels and set the shift selector in the Drive position.
3. Run the engine at idle speed and disconnect the hose from the air induction pipe, then plug the pipe. Allow the engine to run for about a minute at idle speed.
4. Check the idle against the specifications given earlier in this Chapter. Adjust the idle speed by turning the idle speed adjusting screw, located near the air cleaner. Turn the screw clockwise for slower idle speed and counterclockwise for faster idle speed.

Idle speed adjusting screw—200SX (1982–83 Z series engine)

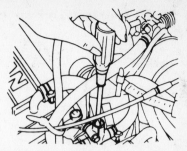

Adjusting the idle speed by turning the idle adjusting screw

5. Connect the hose and disconnect the tachometer. If idle speed increases, adjust it with the idle speed adjusting screw.

1984–86½ 200SX (CA20E and CA18ET Engines)
1984–86 Stanza CA20E Engine

NOTE: *Always refer to the underhood specifications sticker for any additional applicable procedures.*

1. Start the engine and warm the engine so it reaches normal operating temperature. The water temperature indicator should be in the middle of the gauge.

2. Then race the engine to 2,000–3,000 rpm a few times under no load and then allow it to return to the idle speed.

3. Connect a tachometer according to the instrument manufacturer's directions.

4. Check the idle speed on the manual transmission model in Neutral and on the automatic transmission model check in Drive.

NOTE: *For automatic transmission, set the parking brake, block the wheels and set the shift selector in the Drive position.*

5. Adjust the idle speed to the figure shown in the Tune-Up Specifications Chart by turning the idle speed adjusting screw shown in the appropriate illustration.

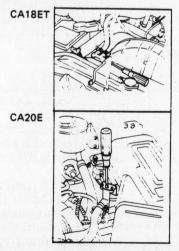

CA18ET

CA20E

Adjusting idle speed—200SX (1984–86½ model years)

6. Stop the engine. Remove the tachometer and road test for proper operation.

1986½–88 200SX CA20E Engine (Except VG30E Engine)
1987–89 Stanza CA20E Engine

NOTE: *Always refer to the underhood specifications sticker for any additional applicable procedures.*

1. Before adjusting the idle speed on the engine you must visually check the following items first: air cleaner for being clogged, hoses and ducts for leaks, EGR valve for proper operation, all electrical connectors, gaskets and the throttle valve and throttle valve switch.

2. Start the engine and warm the engine so it reaches normal operating temperature. The water temperature indicator should be in the middle of the gauge.

3. Then race the engine to 2,000–3,000 rpm a few times under no load and then allow it to return to the idle speed.

4. Connect a tachometer according to the instrument manufacturer's directions.

5. Check the idle speed on the manual transmission model in Neutral and on the automatic transmission model check in Drive.

NOTE: *For automatic transmission, set the parking brake, block the wheels and set the shift selector in the Drive position.*

6. If the idle speed has to be adjusted you must disconnect the A.A.C. valve harness connector (Auxiliary Air Control) and the throttle valve switch harness connector.

7. Adjust the idle speed to the figure shown

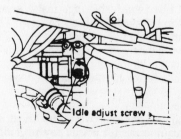

Adjusting idle speed 1986½–88 200SX models

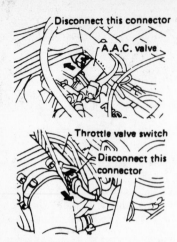

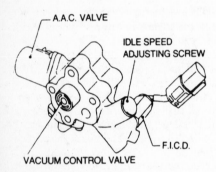

Disconnect A.A.C. valve connector and the throttle valve switch connector 1986½–88 model years

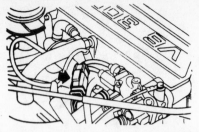

Idle up solenoid harness location—200SX VG30E engine

3. Run engine at about 2,000 rpm for about 2 minutes under no load.

4. Disconnect idle up solenoid harness connector and then race engine 2 or 3 times under no load, then run engine at idle speed.

5. Apply the parking brake securely and then put the transmission into Drive, if the car has an automatic. Adjust the idle speed to the figure shown in the Tune-Up Specifications Chart by turning the idle speed adjusting screw shown in the appropriate illustration.

6. Stop engine and connect idle-up solenoid harness connector.

7. Remove tachometer and road test for proper operation.

1989–92 240SX Models (KA24E and KA24DE Engines)
1990–92 Stanza

NOTE: *Always refer to the underhood specifications sticker for any additional applicable procedures.*

1. Before adjusting the idle speed on the engine you must visually check the following items first: air cleaner for being clogged, hoses and ducts for leaks, EGR valve for proper operation, all electrical connectors, gaskets and the throttle valve and throttle valve switch operation.

2. Start and warm the engine so it reaches normal operating temperature. The water temperature indicator should be in the middle of the gauge.

Idle air adjusting (I.A.A.) unit

in the Tune-Up Specifications Chart by turning the idle speed adjusting screw shown in the appropriate illustration.

8. Stop the engine. Connect the A.A.C. valve harness connector (Auxiliary Air Control) and the throttle valve switch harness connector.

9. Remove the tachometer and road test for proper operation.

1987–88 200SX (VG30E Engine)

NOTE: *Always refer to the underhood specifications sticker for any additional applicable procedures.*

1. Turn off the: headlights, heater blower, air conditioning, and rear window defogger. If the car has power steering, make sure the wheel is in the straight ahead position. The ignition timing must be correct to get an effective idle speed adjustment. Adjust the timing if do not know it to be correct. Connect a tachometer (a special adapter harness may be needed) according to the instrument manufacturer's directions.

2. Start engine and warm up until water temperature indicator points to the middle of the gauge.

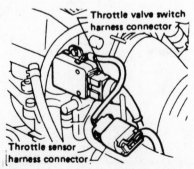

Throttle harness connector location on KA24E and KA24DE engines

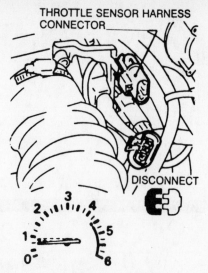

THROTTLE SENSOR HARNESS
CONNECTOR

DISCONNECT

**Throttle harness connector location on 1990–92
Stanza**

3. Then race the engine to 2,000–3,000 rpm a few times under no load and then allow it to return to the idle speed.

4. Connect a tachometer according to the instrument manufacturer's directions.

5. Check the idle speed in the Neutral position for both manual and automatic transmission models.

6. If the idle speed has to be adjusted you must disconnect the throttle sensor harness connector.

7. Adjust the idle speed to the figure shown in the Tune-Up Specifications Chart by turning the idle speed adjusting screw.

8. Stop the engine. Connect the the throttle sensor harness connector.

9. Remove the tachometer and road test for proper operation.

Engine and Engine Overhaul

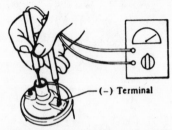

ENGINE ELECTRICAL

Ignition Coil

TESTING

200SX—Z Series Engine

1. Make a check of the power supply circuit. Turn the ignition OFF, Disconnect the connector from the top of the IC unit. Turn the ignition ON. Measure the voltage at each terminal of the connector in turn by touching the positive lead of the voltmeter to one of the terminals, and touching the negative lead of the voltmeter to a ground, such as the engine. In each case, battery voltage (12 volts) should be indicated. If not, check all wiring, the ignition switch, and all connectors for breaks, corrosion, discontinuity, etc., and repair as necessary.

2. Check the primary windings of the ignition coil. Turn the ignition OFF. Disconnect the harness connector from the negative coil terminal. Use an ohmmeter to measure the resistance between the positive and negative coil ter-

Checking the ignition coil secondary circuit

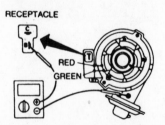

Testing the power supply circuit—1983 200SX

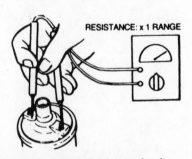

Checking the ignition coil primary circuit

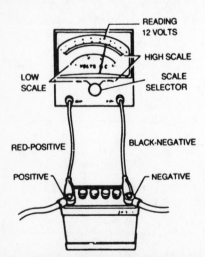

Testing battery voltage with voltmeter

minals. If resistance is 1.04–1.27Ω the coil is OK. Replace coil(s) if out of specification range.

3. Turn the ignition switch to the OFF position.

4. Disable the electronic fuel injection so engine will not start—disconnect the EFI injection fusible link.

5. Disconnect the high tension cable from

the distributor. Hold the cable with insulated pliers to avoid getting shocked. Position the wire about a ¼ in. (6mm) from the engine block and have an assistant turn over the engine using the starter. A good spark should jump from the cable to the engine block or ground.

NOTE: *The 1984-88 200SX, 1989-92 240SX and Stanza vehicles use a highly complex computerized ignition system.*

Stanza

PRIMARY RESISTANCE CHECK

Testing with a ohmmeter, the reading should be 0.84-1.02Ω for the Stanza models from 1982-86. On the Stanza models from 1987 and later a "Mold type" coil is used, first remove the coil wire then connect the leads of an ohmmeter to the positive (+) and negative (−) terminals at the the bottom of the coil assembly the reading should 0.8-1.0Ω for this type coil. If the reading is more than specified, replace the ignition coil assembly.

SECONDARY RESISTANCE CHECK

Turn the ignition key OFF, then remove the high tension and a primary coil wire from the coil using an ohmmeter, set it on the X1000 scale. Touch one lead to a primary terminal and the other lead to the center terminal. The resistance should be 8,200-12,400Ω; if not, replace the ignition coil.

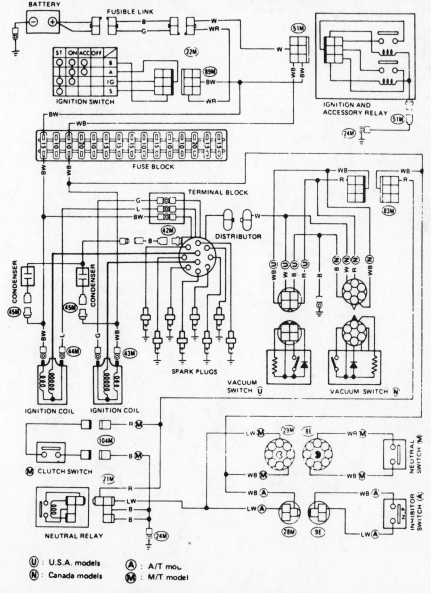

Ignition writing diagram 1982–83 200SX

Note: *On some later model vehicles, a power transistor is used with the ignition coil. The ignition signal from the E.C.U. is amplified by the power transistor, which turns the ignition coil primary circuit on and off, inducing the proper high voltage in the secondary circuit. On these models the the ignition coil is a small molded type.*

REMOVAL AND INSTALLATION

On all models, the coil assembly is either mounted to the wall of the engine compartment or the engine. To remove disconnect and mark all electrical connections--remove the coil assembly, then transfer coil mounting bracket if so equipped to the new coil. When installing the new coil make sure that the coil wire and all other electrical connections are properly installed.

Ignition Module

REMOVAL AND INSTALLATION

1. Remove the distributor cap and pull the rotor from the distributor shaft.

NOTE: *The rotor on most vehicles is held to the distributor shaft by a retaining screw, which must be removed.*

2. Remove the wiring harness and the vacuum controller from the housing.

3. Using 2 flat bladed tools, place one on each side of the reluctor and pry it from the distributor shaft.

NOTE: *When removing the reluctor, be careful not to damage or distort the teeth.*

4. Remove the roll pin from the reluctor.

5. Mark and remove the breaker plate assembly and separate the IC unit from it. Be careful not to loose the spacers when you remove the IC unit.

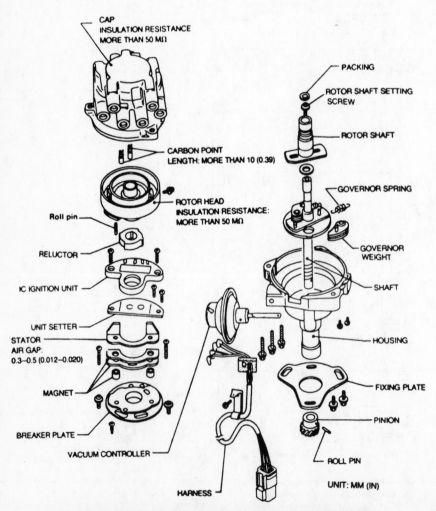

Distributor assembly—1984 and late 200SX, Stanza CA20E engines

6. To install, reverse the removal procedures. When you install the roll pin into the reluctor position the cutout direction of the roll pin in parallel with the notch in the reluctor. Make sure that the harness to the IC ignition unit is tightly secured, then adjust the air gap between the reluctor and the stator.

Distributor
REMOVAL

1. Unfasten the retaining clips and lift the distributor cap straight up. It will be easier to install the distributor. If the spark plug wires are not disconnected from the cap. If the wires

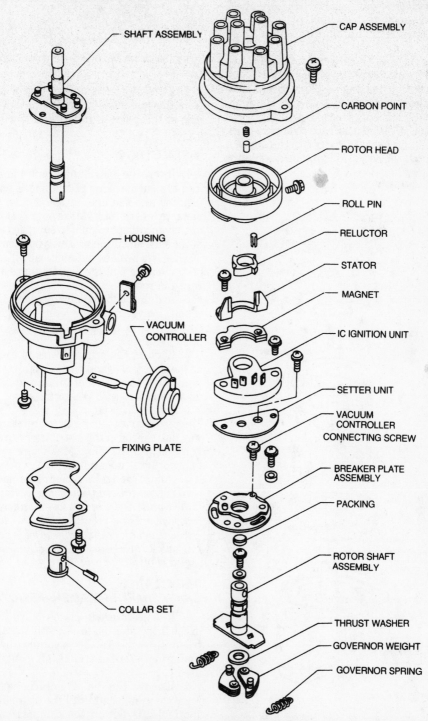

SHAFT ASSEMBLY

CAP ASSEMBLY

CARBON POINT

ROTOR HEAD

ROLL PIN

HOUSING

RELUCTOR

STATOR

MAGNET

VACUUM CONTROLLER

IC IGNITION UNIT

SETTER UNIT

VACUUM CONTROLLER CONNECTING SCREW

FIXING PLATE

BREAKER PLATE ASSEMBLY

PACKING

ROTOR SHAFT ASSEMBLY

COLLAR SET

THRUST WASHER

GOVERNOR WEIGHT

GOVERNOR SPRING

Distributor assembly—1982–83 200SX

must be removed from the cap remove the wires one at a time, mark or tag their positions to aid in installation.

2. Disconnect the distributor wiring harness and or the electrical connection if so equipped.

NOTE: *On late model Datsun/Nissan, a crankangle sensor is the basic component of the distributor. No vacuum lines are used, just one electrical connection.*

3. Disconnect the vacuum lines if so equipped.

4. Note the position of the rotor in relation to the base. Scribe a mark on the base of the distributor and on the engine block to facilitate reinstallation. Align the marks with the direction the metal tip of the rotor is pointing. (note the position of distributor base to engine block and distributor rotor to distributor assembly).

5. Remove the bolt(s) holding the distributor to the engine.

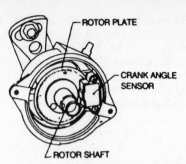

Distributor assembly with Crank Angle sensor

6. Carefully lift the distributor assembly from the engine--do not crank or move the engine at this point or initial timing will have to be set.

INSTALLATION

1. Insert the distributor shaft and assembly into the engine. Line up the mark on the distributor and the one on the engine with the metal tip of the rotor. Make sure that the vacuum advance diaphragm if so equipped is pointed in the same direction as it was pointed originally. This will be done automatically if the marks on the engine and the distributor are lined up with the rotor.

2. Install the distributor holddown bolt and clamp. Leave the screw loose enough so that you can move the distributor with moderate hand pressure.

3. Connect the primary wire to the coil and or the electrical connections. Install the distributor cap on the distributor housing. Secure the distributor cap with the spring clips.

4. Install the spark plug wires if removed. Make sure that the wires are pressed all the way into the top of the distributor cap and firmly onto the spark plug. Make sure the correct firing order is maintained.

5. Adjust the ignition timing as necessary.

NOTE: *If the crankshaft has been turned or the engine disturbed in any manner (i.e., disassembled and rebuilt) while the distributor was removed, or if the marks were not drawn, it will be necessary to initially time the engine. Follow the procedure given below.*

INSTALLATION
CRANKSHAFT OR CAMSHAFT ROTATED

1. It is necessary to place the No. 1 cylinder in the firing position to correctly install the distributor. To locate this position, the ignition timing marks on the crankshaft front pulley are used.

2. Remove the No. 1 cylinder spark plug. Turn the crankshaft until the piston in the No. 1 cylinder is UP on the compression stroke. This can be determined by placing your thumb

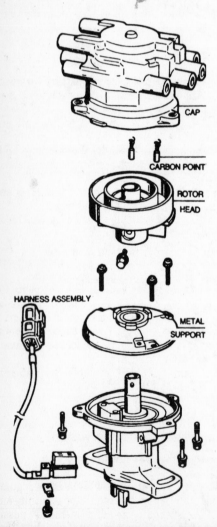

Distributor assembly—1987–88 Stanza (late model without ignition module)

over the spark plug hole and feeling the air being forced out of the cylinder. Stop turning the crankshaft when the timing marks that are used to time the engine are aligned on the front timing cover assembly.

3. Oil the distributor housing lightly where the distributor bears on the cylinder block.

4. Install the distributor so that the rotor, which is mounted on the shaft, points toward the No. 1 spark plug terminal tower position when the cap is installed. Of course you won't be able to see the direction in which the rotor is pointing if the cap is on the distributor. Lay the cap on the top of the distributor and make a mark on the side of the distributor housing just below the No. 1 spark plug terminal. Make sure that the rotor points toward that mark when you install the distributor.

5. When the distributor shaft has reached the bottom of the hole, move the rotor back and forth slightly until the driving lug on the end of the shaft enters the slots cut in the end of the oil pump shaft and the distributor assembly slides down into place.

6. When the distributor is correctly installed, the reluctor teeth should be aligned with the stator assembly. This can be accomplished by rotating the distributor body after it has been installed in the engine. Once again, line up the marks that you made before the distributor was removed.

7. Install the distributor holddown bolt.

8. Install the spark plug into the No. 1 spark plug hole and continue from Step 3 of the preceding distributor installation procedure.

If your engine has a distributor with a crankangle sensor, read the above procedure; you will be able to remove and install the distributor assembly.

You must remove the distributor cap, mark or tag all the spark plug wires and the electrical connections then remove them. Next, mark the postion of the base of the distributor with relation to the engine mounting location and the rotor position as opposed to the the base of the distributor cover assembly.

When installing the distributor, line up your marks and gently install the distributor and reconnect all spark wires and electrical connections. If you disturb the engine while the distributor is removed you will have to set inital timing.

Alternator

ALTERNATOR PRECAUTIONS

To prevent damage to the alternator and regulator, the following precautionary measures must be taken when working with the electrical system.

1. Never reverse battery connections.

2. Booster batteries for starting must be connected properly. Make sure that the positive cable of the booster battery is connected to the positive terminal of the battery that is getting the boost and negative cable to ground.

3. Disconnect the battery cables before using a fast charger; the charger has a tendency to force current through the diodes in the opposite direction for which they are designed. This burns out the diodes.

4. Never use a fast charger as a booster for starting the vehicle.

5. Never disconnect the voltage regulator while the engine is running.

6. Do not ground the alternator output terminal.

7. Do not operate the alternator on an open circuit with the field energized.

8. Do not attempt to polarize an alternator.

9. When steam cleaning the engine, be careful not to subject the alternator assembly to excessive heat or moisture.

REMOVAL AND INSTALLATION

1. Disconnect the negative battery terminal.

2. Disconnect the two lead wires and connector from the alternator.

3. Loosen the drive belt adjusting bolt and remove the belt.

4. Unscrew the alternator attaching bolts and remove the alternator from the vehicle.

To install:

5. Mount the alternator to the engine and partially tighten the attaching bolts.

6. Reconnect the lead wires and connector to the alternator.

7. Install the alternator drive belt.

8. Adjust the alternator belt correctly and completely tighten the mounting bolts.

The correct belt tension is about $\frac{1}{4}$-$\frac{1}{2}$ in. (6–13mm) play on the longest span of the drive belt. The alternator belt tension is quite critical. A belt that is too tight may cause alternator bearing failure; one that is too loose will cause a gradual battery discharge.

9. Connnect the battery cable. Start the engine and check for proper operation.

Regulator

REMOVAL AND INSTALLATION

All models are equipped with integral regulator assembly. Since the regulator is a internal part of the alternator no adjustments are possible or necessary. If the regulator fails, the alternator must be replaced.

Battery

REMOVAL AND INSTALLATION

1. Disconnect the negative (ground) cable from the terminal, and then the positive cable. Special pullers are available to remove the cable clamps.

NOTE: *To avoid sparks, always disconnect the ground cable first, and connect it last.*

2. Remove the battery holddown clamp.

3. Remove the battery, being careful not to spill the acid.

NOTE: *Spilled acid can be neutralized with a baking soda/water solution. If you somehow get acid into your eyes, flush it out with lots of water and get to a doctor.*

Clean the battery posts thoroughly before reinstalling, or when installing a new battery.

5. Clean the cable clamps, using a wire brush, both inside and out.

6. Install the battery and the holddown clamp or strap. Connect the positive, and then the negative cable. Do not hammer them in place. The terminals should be coated lightly (externally) with grease to prevent corrosion. There are also felt washers impregnated with an anti-corrosion substance which are slipped over the battery posts before installing the cables; these are available in auto parts stores.

NOTE: *Make absolutely sure that the battery is connected properly before you turn on the ignition switch. Reversed polarity can burn out your alternator and regulator within a matter of seconds.*

Starter

Datsun/Nissan began using a reduction gear starter in the Canadian versions 200SX model. They were also available as an option on later models. The differences between the gear reduction and conventional starters are: the gear reduction starter has a set of ratio reducing gears while the conventional starter does not; the brushes on the gear reduction starter are located on a plate behind the starter drive housing, while the conventional starter's brushes

ALTERNATOR AND REGULATOR SPECIFICATIONS

| Year | Engine ID/VIN | Engine Displacement Liters | Alternator | | Regulator | | |
			Output (amps)	Regulated Volts @ 75°F	Air Gap (in.)	Point Gap (in.)	Back Gap (in.)
1982	Z22E	2.2L	60	14.4–15.0	①	①	①
	CA20	2.0L	60	14.4–15.0	①	①	①
1983	Z22E	2.2L	60	14.4–15.0	①	①	①
	CA20	2.0L	60	14.4–15.0	①	①	①
1984	CA20E	2.0L	60	14.4–15.1	①	①	①
	CA18ET	1.8L	70	14.4–15.0	①	①	①
1985	CA20E	2.0L	60	14.4–15.0	①	①	①
	CA18ET	1.8L	70	14.4–15.0	①	①	①
1986	CA20E	2.0L	60	14.4–15.0	①	①	①
	CA18ET	1.8L	70	14.4–15.1	①	①	①
1987	CA20E	2.0L	60	14.1–14.7	①	①	①
	CA18ET	1.8L	67	14.1–14.7	①	①	①
	VG30E	3.0L	87	14.1–14.7	①	①	①
1988	CA20E	2.0L	67	14.1–14.7	①	①	①
	CA18ET	1.8L	70	14.4–15.1	①	①	①
	VG30E	3.0L	87	14.1–14.7	①	①	①
1989	KA24E	2.4L	77	14.1–14.7	①	①	①
	CA20E	2.0L	67	14.1–14.7	①	①	①
1990	KA24E	2.4L	77	14.1–14.7	①	①	①
1991	KA24DE	2.4L	77	14.1–14.7	①	①	①
	KA24E	2.4L	77	14.1–14.7	①	①	①
1992	KA24DE	2.4L	77	14.1–14.7	①	①	①
	KA24E	2.4L	77	14.1–14.7	①	①	①

Use all specifications as a guide for diagnosis of alternator and regulator
① Uses integral voltage regulator

are located in its rear cover. The extra gears on the gear reduction starter make the starter pinion gear turn at about half the speed of the starter, giving the starter twice the turning power of a conventional starter.

REMOVAL AND INSTALLATION

1. Disconnect the negative battery cable from the battery.
2. Disconnect the starter wiring at the starter, taking note of the positions for correct installation.
3. Remove the bolts attaching the starter to the engine and remove the starter from the vehicle.

To install:

4. Install the starter to the engine.
5. Tighten the attaching bolts evenly. Be careful not overtorque the mounting bolts as this will crack the nose of the starter case assembly.
6. Install the starter wiring in the correct location.
7. Connect the negative battery cable.
8. Start the engine a few times to make sure of proper operation.

SOLENOID REPLACEMENT

NOTE: *The starter solenoid is also known as the magnetic switch assembly.*

1. Remove the starter from the engine as outlined above.
2. Place the starter in a vise or equivalent to hold the starter in place while you are working on the solenoid. DO NOT tighten the vise too tight around the case of the starter. The case will crack if you tighten the vise too much.
3. Loosen the locknut and remove the connection from the starter motor going to the **M** terminal of the solenoid or bottom terminal of the solenoid.
4. Remove the securing screws and remove the solenoid.
5. Install the solenoid to the starter and tighten the securing screws.
6. Install the connection and locknut at bottom terminal of the starter.

Sending Units and Sensors

REMOVAL AND INSTALLATION

Coolant Temperature Sensor

1. Disconnect the negative battery cable.
2. Drain the cooling system until coolant level is below coolant sensor.
3. Disconnect electrical connector from the sensor.
4. Remove the sensor from the engine. On some applications, the coolant sensor threads into the thermostat housing.

5. Installation is the reverse of the removal procedure. Fill and bleed cooling system.

Oil Pressure Switch

1. Disconnect the negative battery cable.
2. Disconnect electrical connector from the oil pressure switch.
3. Remove the oil pressure switch from the engine.
4. Installation is the reverse of the removal procedure. Check oil level.

ENGINE MECHANICAL

Engine Overhaul Tips

Most engine overhaul procedures are fairly standard. In addition to specific parts replacement procedures and complete specifications for your individual engine, this Chapter also is a guide to accepted rebuilding procedures. Examples of standard rebuilding practice are shown and should be used along with specific details concerning your particular engine.

Competent and accurate machine shop services will ensure maximum performance, reliability and engine life.

In most instances it is more profitable for the do-it-yourself mechanic to remove, clean and inspect the component, buy the necessary parts and deliver these to a shop for actual machine work.

On the other hand, much of the rebuilding work (crankshaft, block, bearings, piston rods, and other components) is well within the scope of the do-it-yourself mechanic.

TOOLS

The tools required for an engine overhaul or parts replacement will depend on the depth of your involvement. With a few exceptions, they will be the tools found in a mechanic's tool kit, discussed in Chapter 1. More in-depth work will require any or all of the following:

- a dial indicator (reading in thousandths) mounted on a universal base
- micrometers and telescope gauges
- jaw and screw-type pullers
- scraper
- valve spring compressor
- ring groove cleaner
- piston ring expander and compressor
- ridge reamer
- cylinder hone or glaze breaker
- Plastigage®
- engine stand

The use of most of these tools is illustrated in this Chapter. Many can be rented for a one-time use from a local parts jobber or tool supply house specializing in automotive work.

Occasionally, the use of special tools is called for. See the information on Special Tools and Safety Notice in the front of this book before substituting another tool.

INSPECTION TECHNIQUES

Procedures and specifications are given in this Chapter for inspecting, cleaning and assessing the wear limits of most major components. Other procedures such as Magnaflux® and Zyglo® can be used to locate material flaws and stress cracks. Magnaflux® is a magnetic process applicable only to ferrous materials. The Zyglo® process coats the material with a fluorescent dye penetrant and can be used on any material. Check for suspected surface cracks can be more readily made using spot check dye. The dye is sprayed onto the suspected area, wiped off and the area sprayed with a developer. Cracks will show up brightly.

OVERHAUL TIPS

Aluminum has become extremely popular for use in engines, due to its low weight. Observe the following precautions when handling aluminum parts:

• Never hot tank aluminum parts (the caustic hot tank solution will eat the aluminum.

• Remove all aluminum parts (identification tag, etc.) from engine parts prior to the tanking.

• Always coat threads lightly with engine oil or anti-seize compounds before installation, to prevent seizure.

• Never overtorque bolts or spark plugs especially in aluminum threads.

Stripped threads in any component can be repaired using any of several commercial repair kits (Heli-Coil®, Microdot®, Keenserts®, etc.).

When assembling the engine, any parts that will be in frictional contact must be prelubed to provide lubrication at initial start-up. Any product specifically formulated for this purpose can be used, but engine oil is not recommended as a prelube.

When semi-permanent (locked, but removable) installation of bolts or nuts is desired, threads should be cleaned and coated with Loctite® or other similar, non-hardening sealant.

REPAIRING DAMAGED THREADS

Several methods of repairing damaged threads are available. Heli-Coil®, Keenserts® and Microdot® are among the most widely used. All involve basically the same principle—drilling out stripped threads, tapping the hole and installing a prewound insert—making welding, plugging and oversize fasteners unnecessary.

Two types of thread repair inserts are usually supplied: a standard type for most Inch Coarse,

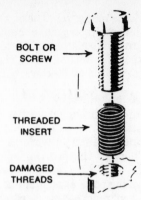

Damaged bolt holes can be repaired with thread repair inserts

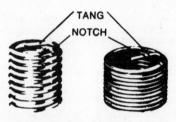

Standard thread repair insert (left) and spark plug insert thread insert (right)

Drill out the damaged threads with specific drill. Drill completely through the hole or the bottom of a blind hole

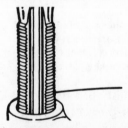

With the tap supplied, tap the hole to receive the thread insert. Keep the tap well oiled and back it out frequently to avoid clogging the threads

Inch Fine, Metric Coarse and Metric Fine thread sizes and a spark lug type to fit most spark plug port sizes. Consult the individual manufacturer's catalog to determine exact applications. Typical thread repair kits will con-

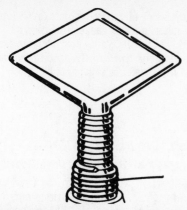

Screw the threaded insert onto the installation tool until the tang engages the slot. Screw the insert into the tapped hole until it is ¼–½ turn below the top surface. After installation break off the tang with a hammer and punch.

tain a selection of prewound threaded inserts, a tap (corresponding to the outside diameter threads of the insert) and an installation tool. Spark plug inserts usually differ because they require a tap equipped with pilot threads and a combined reamer/tap section. Most manufacturers also supply blister-packed thread repair inserts separately in addition to a master kit containing a variety of taps and inserts plus installation tools.

Before effecting a repair to a threaded hole, remove any snapped, broken or damaged bolts or studs. Penetrating oil can be used to free frozen threads. The offending item can be removed with locking pliers or with a screw or stud extractor. After the hole is clear, the thread can be repaired.

Checking Engine Compression

A noticeable lack of engine power, excessive oil consumption and/or poor fuel mileage measured over an extended period are all indicators of internal engine war. Worn piston rings, scored or worn cylinder bores, blown head gaskets, sticking or burnt valves and worn valve seats are all possible culprits here. A check of each cylinder's compression will help you locate the problems.

A screw-in type compression gauge is more accurate that the type you simply hold against the spark plug hole, although it takes slightly longer to use. It's worth it to obtain a more accurate reading. Follow the procedures below.

1. Warm up the engine to normal operating temperature, then switch it off.

2. Remove all the spark plugs. Use care; they will be hot.

3. Disconnect the high tension lead from the

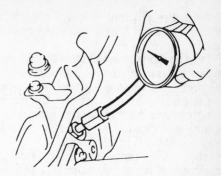

The screw-in type compression gauge is more accurate

CA18ET ENGINE

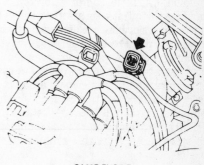

CA20E ENGINE

Distributor harness connector locations, 1984 and later 200SX engines

ignition coil or the distributor harness connection if so equipped.

4. On carbureted cars, fully open the throttle either by operating the carburetor throttle linkage by hand or by having an assistant floor the accelerator pedal. On fuel injected cars, disconnect all injector connections.

5. Screw the compression gauge into the No.1 spark plug hole until the fitting is snug.

NOTE: *Be careful not to crossthread the plug hole. On aluminum cylinder heads use extra care, as the threads in these heads are easily ruined.*

6. Ask an assistant to depress the accelerator pedal fully on both carbureted and fuel injected vehicles. Then, while you read the compression

gauge, ask the assistant to crank the engine four times in short bursts using the ignition switch.

7. Read the compression gauge at the end of each series of cranks, and record the highest of these readings. Repeat this procedure for each of the engine's cylinders. Compare the highest reading of each cylinder to the compression pressure specification note in the Tune-Up Specifications chart in Chapter 2.

A cylinder's compression pressure is usually acceptable if it is not less than 80% of maximum. The difference between any two cylinders should be no more than 12-14 pounds.

8. If a cylinder is unusually low, pour a tablespoon of clean engine oil into the cylinder through the spark plug hole and repeat the compression test. If the compression comes up after adding the oil, it appears that the cylinder's piston rings or bore are damaged or worn. If the pressure remains low, the valves may not be seating properly (a valve job is needed), or the head gasket may be blown near that cylinder. If compression in any two adjacent cylinders is low, and if the addition of oil doesn't help the compression, there is leakage past the head gasket. Oil and coolant water in the combustion chamber can result from this problem. There

may be evidence of water droplets on the engine dipstick when a head gasket has blown.

NOTE: *When analyzing compression test results, look for uniformity among cylinders, rather than specific pressures.*

Engine

REMOVAL AND INSTALLATION

200SX and 240SX – Rear Wheel Drive Models

The following procedure can be used on all years and models. Slight variations may occur due to extra connections, etc., but the basic procedure should cover all years and models.The engine and transmission are removed together as assembly and then separated when out of the car. Always observe the following cautions:

• Make sure the vehicle is on a flat and level surface and that wheels are tightly chocked. Use the chocks on both sides of the rear wheels on front wheel drive cars.

• Allow the exhaust system to cool completely before starting work to prevent burns and possible fire as fuel lines are disconnected.

• Release fuel pressure from the fuel system before attempting to disconnect any fuel lines.

GENERAL ENGINE SPECIFICATIONS

Year	Engine ID/VIN	Engine Displacement Liters	Fuel System Type	Net Horsepower @ rpm	Net Torque @ rpm (ft. lbs.)	Bore × Stroke (in.)	Compression Ratio	Oil Pressure @ rpm
1982–83	Z22E	2.2L	EFI	102 @ 5200	129 @ 2800	3.43 × 3.62	8.5:1	50–60
	CA20	2.0L	2 bbl.	88 @ 5200	112 @ 2800	3.33 × 3.46	8.5:1	50–60
1984	CA20E	2.0L	EFI	102 @ 5200	116 @ 3200	3.33 × 3.46	8.5:1	57 @ 4000
	CA18ET	1.8L	EFI	120 @ 5200	134 @ 3200	3.27 × 3.29	8.0:1	71 @ 4000
1985–86	CA20E	2.0L	EFI	102 @ 5200	116 @ 3200	3.33 × 3.46	8.5:1	57 @ 4000
	CA18ET	1.8L	EFI	120 @ 5200	134 @ 3200	3.27 × 3.29	8.0:1	71 @ 4000
1987	CA20E	2.0L	EFI	102 @ 5200	116 @ 3200	3.33 × 3.46	8.5:1	43 @ 2000
	CA18ET	1.8L	EFI	120 @ 5200	134 @ 3200	3.27 × 3.29	8.0:1	43 @ 2000
	VG30E	3.0L	EFI	160 @ 5200	174 @ 4000	3.43 × 3.27	9.0:1	43 @ 2000
1988	CA20E	2.0L	EFI	99 @ 5200	116 @ 2800	3.33 × 3.46	8.5:1	60.5 @ 3200
	VG30E	3.0L	EFI	165 @ 5200	168 @ 3600	3.43 × 3.27	9.0:1	59 @ 3200
	CA18ET	1.8L	EFI	120 @ 5200	134 @ 3200	3.27 × 3.29	8.0:1	43 @ 2000
1989	KA24E	2.4L	EFI	135 @ 5600	142 @ 4400	3.50 × 3.78	9.0:1	65 @ 3000
	CA20E	2.0L	EFI	94 @ 5400	114 @ 2800	3.33 × 3.47	8.5:1	61 @ 3200
1990	KA24E	2.4L	EFI	140 @ 5600	152 @ 4400	3.50 × 3.78	8.6:1	60–70 @ 3000
1991	KA24DE	2.4L	EFI	155 @ 5600	160 @ 4400	3.50 × 3.78	9.5:1	60–70 @ 3000
	KA24E	2.4L	EFI	138 @ 5600	148 @ 4400	3.50 × 3.78	8.6:1	60–70 @ 3000
1992	KA24DE	2.4L	EFI	155 @ 5600	160 @ 4400	3.50 × 3.78	9.5:1	60–70 @ 3000
	KA24E	2.4L	EFI	138 @ 5600	148 @ 4800	3.50 × 3.78	8.6:1	60–70 @ 3000

NOTE: Horsepower and torque are SAE net figures. They are measured at the rear of the transmission with all accessories installed and operating. Since the figures vary when a given engine is installed in different models, some are representative rather than exact.

VALVE SPECIFICATIONS

Year	Engine ID/VIN	Engine Displacement Liters	Seat Angle (deg.)	Face Angle (deg.)	Spring Test Pressure (lbs. @ in.)	Spring Installed Height (in.)	Stem-to-Guide Clearance (in.)		Stem Diameter (in.)	
							Intake	Exhaust	Intake	Exhaust
1982	Z22E	2.2L	45	45	115.3 @ 1.18①	1.575	0.0008–0.0021	0.0016–0.0029	0.3136–0.3142	0.3128–0.3434
	CA20	2.0L	44	—	47 @ 1.58②	1.736	0.0008–0.0021	0.0016–0.0029	0.2742–0.2748	0.2734–0.2740
1983	Z22E	2.2L	45	45	115.3 @ 1.18①	1.575	0.0008–0.0021	0.0016–0.0029	0.3136–0.3142	0.3128–0.3434
	CA20	2.0L	44	—	47 @ 1.58②	1.736	0.0008–0.0021	0.0016–0.0029	0.2742–0.2748	0.2734–0.2740
1984	CA20E	2.0L	45	45	118.2 @ 1.00	1.967③	0.0008–0.0021	0.0016–0.0029	0.2742–0.2748	0.2734–0.2740
	CA18ET	1.8L	45	45	118.2 @ 1.00	1.967③	0.0008–0.0021	0.0016–0.0029	0.2742–0.2748	0.2734–0.2740
1985	CA20E	2.0L	45	45	118.2 @ 1.00	1.967③	0.0008–0.0021	0.0016–0.0029	0.2742–0.2748	0.2734–0.2740
	CA18ET	1.8L	45	45	118.2 @ 1.00	1.967③	0.0008–0.0021	0.0016–0.0029	0.2742–0.2748	0.2734–0.2740
1986	CA20E	2.0L	45	45	118.2 @ 1.00	1.967③	0.0008–0.0021	0.0016–0.0029	0.2742–0.2748	0.2734–0.2740
	CA18ET	1.8L	45	45	118.2 @ 1.00	1.967③	0.0008–0.0021	0.0016–0.0029	0.2742–0.2748	0.2734–0.2740
1987	CA20E	2.0L	45	45	118.2 @ 1.00	1.967③	0.0008–0.0021	0.0016–0.0029	0.2742–0.2748	0.2734–0.2740
	CA18ET	1.8L	45	45	118.2 @ 1.00	1.967③	0.0008–0.0021	0.0016–0.0029	0.2742–0.2748	0.2734–0.2740
	VG30E	3.0L	45	45	117.7 @ 1.18	2.016③	0.0008–0.0021	0.0016–0.0029	0.2742–0.2748	0.3128–0.3134
1988	CA20E	2.0L	45	45	118.2 @ 1.00	1.967③	0.0008–0.0021	0.0016–0.0029	0.2742–0.2748	0.2734–0.2740
	CA18ET	1.8L	45	45	118.2 @ 1.00	1.967③	0.0008–0.0021	0.0016–0.0029	0.2742–0.2748	0.2734–0.2740
	VG30E	3.0L	45	45	117.7 @ 1.18	2.016③	0.0008–0.0021	0.0016–0.0029	0.2742–0.2748	0.3128–0.3134
1989	KA24E	2.4L	45	45	135.8 @ 1.480	2.261③	0.0008–0.0021	0.0016–0.0028	0.2742–0.2748	0.3129–0.3134
	CA20E	2.0L	45	45	129.9 @ 2.32	1.959③	0.0008–0.0021	0.0016–0.0029	0.2742–0.2748	0.2734–0.2740
1990	KA24E	2.4L	45	45	135.8 @ 1.480	2.261③	0.0008–0.0021	0.0016–0.0028	0.2742–0.2748	0.3129–0.3134
1991	KA24DE	2.4L	45	45	123 @ 1.024	1.756③	0.0008–0.0021	0.0016–0.0029	0.2742–0.2748	0.2734–0.2740
	KA24E	2.4L	45	45	135.8 @ 1.480	2.261③	0.0008–0.0021	0.0016–0.0028	0.2742–0.2748	0.3129–0.3134
1992	KA24DE	2.4L	45	45	123 @ 1.024	1.756③	0.0008–0.0021	0.0016–0.0029	0.2742–0.2748	0.2734–0.2740
	KA24E	2.4L	45	45	135.8 @ 1.480	2.261③	0.0008–0.0021	0.0016–0.0028	0.2742–0.2748	0.3129–0.3134

① Outer Spring-Inner Spring 57 lbs. @ 0.98 inches
② Outer Spring-Inner Spring 24 @ 1.38 inches
③ Figures are for free height (use spring test pressure as a guide on multi-valve engine applications).

• When lifting the engine out, guide it carefully to avoid hitting parts such as the master cylinder.

• Mount the engine securely and then release the tension of lifting chains to avoid injury as you work on the engine.

1. Mark the location of the hinges on the hood. Unbolt and remove the hood.

CAMSHAFT SPECIFICATIONS

All measurements given in inches.

Year	Engine ID/VIN	Engine Displacement Liters	Journal Diameter					Elevation		Bearing Clearance	Camshaft End Play
			1	2	3	4	5	In.	Ex.		
1982	Z22E	2.2L	1.2967–1.2974	1.2967–1.2974	1.2967–1.2974	1.2967–1.2974	1.2967–1.2974	NA	NA	0.0018–0.0035	0.008
	CA20	2.0L	1.8085–1.8092	1.8085–1.8092	1.8085–1.8092	1.8085–1.8092	1.8077–1.8085	0.354	0.354	0.0040	0.0028–0.0055
1983	Z22E	2.2L	1.2967–1.2974	1.2967–1.2974	1.2967–1.2974	1.2967–1.2974	1.2967–1.2974	NA	NA	0.0018–0.0035	0.008
	CA20	2.0L	1.8085–1.8092	1.8085–1.8092	1.8085–1.8092	1.8085–1.8092	1.8077–1.8085	0.354	0.354	0.0040	0.0028–0.0055
1984	CA20E	2.0L	1.8085–1.8092	1.8085–1.8092	1.8085–1.8092	1.8085–1.8092	1.8077–1.8055	0.335	0.374	0.0040	0.0028–0.0055
	CA18ET	1.8L	1.8085–1.8092	1.8085–1.8092	1.8085–1.8092	1.8085–1.8092	1.8077–1.8085	0.354	0.354	0.0040	0.0028–0.0055
1985	CA20E	2.0L	1.8085–1.8092	1.8085–1.8092	1.8085–1.8092	1.8085–1.8092	1.8077–1.8055	0.335	0.374	0.0040	0.0028–0.0055
	CA18ET	1.8L	1.8085–1.8092	1.8085–1.8092	1.8085–1.8092	1.8085–1.8092	1.8077–1.8085	0.354	0.354	0.0040	0.0028–0.0055
1986	CA20E	2.0L	1.8085–1.8092	1.8085–1.8092	1.8085–1.8092	1.8085–1.8092	1.8077–1.8055	0.335	0.374	0.0040	0.0028–0.0055
	CA18ET	1.8L	1.8085–1.8092	1.8085–1.8092	1.8085–1.8092	1.8085–1.8092	1.8077–1.8085	0.354	0.354	0.0040	0.0028–0.0055
1987	CA20E	2.0L	1.8085–1.8092	1.8085–1.8092	1.8085–1.8092	1.8085–1.8092	1.8077–1.8055	0.335	0.374	0.0040	0.0028–0.0055
	CA18ET	1.8L	1.8085–1.8092	1.8085–1.8092	1.8085–1.8092	1.8085–1.8092	1.8077–1.8085	0.354	0.354	0.0040	0.0028–0.0055
	VG30E	3.0L	1.8866–1.8874①	1.8472–1.8480	1.8472–1.8480	1.8472–1.8480	1.6701–1.6709	NA	NA	0.0018–0.0035	0.0012–0.0024
1988	CA20E	2.0L	1.8085–1.8092	1.8085–1.8092	1.8085–1.8092	1.8085–1.8092	1.8077–1.8055	0.335	0.374	0.0040	0.0028–0.0055
	CA18ET	1.8L	1.8085–1.8092	1.8085–1.8092	1.8085–1.8092	1.8085–1.8092	1.8077–1.8085	0.354	0.354	0.0040	0.0028–0.0055
	VG30E	3.0L	1.8866–1.8874①	1.8472–1.8480	1.8472–1.8480	1.8472–1.8480	1.6701–1.6709	NA	NA	0.0018–0.0035	0.0012–0.0024
1989	KA24E	2.4L	1.2967–1.2974	1.2967–1.2974	1.2967–1.2974	1.2967–1.2974	1.2967–1.2974	0.409	0.409	0.0018–0.0035	0.0028–0.0059
	CA20E	2.0L	1.8085–1.8092	1.8085–1.8092	1.8085–1.8092	1.8085–1.8092	1.8077–1.8055	0.335	0.374	0.0018–0.0035	0.0028–0.0059
1990	KA24E	2.4L	1.2967–1.2974	1.2967–1.2974	1.2967–1.2974	1.2967–1.2974	1.2967–1.2974	0.409	0.409	0.0018–0.0035	0.0028–0.0059
1991	KA24DE	2.4L	1.0998–1.1006	0.9423–0.9431	0.9423–0.9431	0.9423–0.9431	0.9423–0.9431	NA	NA	0.0018–0.0035	0.0028–0.0059
	KA24E	2.4L	1.2967–1.2974	1.2967–1.2974	1.2967–1.2974	1.2967–1.2974	1.2967–1.2974	0.409	0.409	0.0018–0.0035	0.0028–0.0059
1992	KA24DE	2.4L	1.0998–1.1006	0.9423–0.9431	–.0423–0.9431	0.9423–0.9431	0.9423–0.9431	NA	NA	0.0018–0.0035	0.0028–0.0059
	KA24E	2.4L	1.2967–1.2974	1.2967–1.2974	1.2967–1.2974	1.2967–1.2974	1.2967–1.2974	0.409	0.409	0.0018–0.0035	0.0028–0.0059

① Front of engine—left hand camshaft only

2. Disconnect the battery cables. Remove the battery.

3. Drain the coolant and automatic transmission fluid.

4. Remove the radiator and radiator shroud after disconnecting the automatic transmission coolant tubes.

5. Remove the air cleaner.

6. Remove the fan and pulley.

7. Disconnect:

CRANKSHAFT AND CONNECTING ROD SPECIFICATIONS
All measurements are given in inches.

Year	Engine ID/VIN	Engine Displacement Liters	Crankshaft				Connecting Rod		
			Main Brg. Journal Dia.	Main Brg. Oil Clearance	Shaft End-play	Thrust on No.	Journal Diameter	Oil Clearance	Side Clearance
1982	Z22E	2.2L	2.1631–2.1636	0.0008–0.0024	0.002–0.0071	3	1.967–1.9675	0.001–0.0022	0.008–0.012
	CA20	2.0L	2.0847–2.0852	0.0016–0.0024	0.002–0.007	3	1.7701–1.7706	0.0008–0.0024	0.008–0.012
1983	Z22E	2.2L	2.1631–2.1636	0.0008–0.0024	0.002–0.0071	3	1.967–1.9675	0.001–0.0022	0.008–0.012
	CA20	2.0L	2.0847–2.0852	0.0016–0.0024	0.002–0.007	3	1.7701–1.7706	0.0008–0.0024	0.008–0.012
1984	CA20E	2.0L	2.0847–2.0852	0.0016–0.0024	0.012	3	1.7701–1.7706	0.0008–0.0024	0.008–0.012
	CA18ET	1.8L	2.0847–2.0852	0.0016–0.0024	0.0020–0.0071	3	1.7701–1.7706	0.0008–0.0024	0.008–0.012
1985	CA20E	2.0L	2.0847–2.0852	0.0016–0.0024	0.012	3	1.7701–1.7706	0.0008–0.0024	0.008–0.012
	CA18ET	1.8L	2.0847–2.0852	0.0016–0.0024	0.0020–0.0071	3	1.7701–1.7706	0.0008–0.0024	0.008–0.012
1986	CA20E	2.0L	2.0847–2.0852	0.0008–0.0019	0.0020–0.0071	3	1.7701–1.7706	0.0004–0.0014	0.008–0.012
	CA18ET	1.8L	2.0847–2.0852	0.0016–0.0024	0.0020–0.0071	3	1.7701–1.7706	0.0008–0.0024	0.008–0.012
1987	CA20E	2.0L	2.0847–2.0852	0.0008–0.0019	0.0020–0.0071	3	1.7701–1.7706	0.0004–0.0014	0.008–0.012
	CA18ET	1.8L	2.0847–2.0852	0.0016–0.0024	0.0020–0.0071	3	1.7701–1.7706	0.0008–0.0024	0.008–0.012
	VG30E	3.0L	2.4790–2.4793	0.0011–0.0022	0.0020–0.0067	4	1.9667–1.9675	0.0006–0.0021	0.0079–0.0138
1988	CA20E	2.0L	2.0847–2.0852	0.0008–0.0019	0.0020–0.0071	3	1.7701–1.7706	0.0004–0.0014	0.008–0.012
	CA18ET	1.8L	2.0847–2.0852	0.0016–0.0024	0.0020–0.0071	3	1.7701–1.7706	0.0008–0.0024	0.008–0.012
	VG30E	3.0L	2.4790–2.4793	0.0011–0.0022	0.0020–0.0067	4	1.9667–1.9675	0.0006–0.0021	0.0079–0.0138
1989	KA24E	2.4L	2.3609–2.3612	0.0008–0.0019	0.0020–0.0071	3	1.7701–1.7706	0.0004–0.0014	0.008–0.012
	CA20E	2.0L	2.0847–2.0852	0.0008–0.0019	0.0020–0.0071	3	1.7701–1.7706	0.0004–0.0014	0.008–0.012
1990	KA24E	2.4L	2.3609–2.3612	0.0008–0.0019	0.0020–0.0071	3	1.7701–1.7706	0.0004–0.0014	0.008–0.012
1991	KA24DE	2.4L	2.3609–2.3612	2.3609–2.3612	2.3609–2.3612	3	1.9672–1.9675	0.0004–0.0014	0.008–0.016
	KA24E	2.4L	2.3609–2.3612	0.0008–0.0019	0.0020–0.0071	3	1.7701–1.7706	0.0004–0.0014	0.008–0.012
1992	KA24DE	2.4L	2.3609–2.3612	2.3609–2.3612	2.3609–2.3612	3	1.9672–1.9675	0.0004–0.0014	0.008–0.016
	KA24E	2.4L	2.3609–2.3612	0.0008–0.0019	0.0020–0.0071	3	1.7701–1.7706	0.0004–0.0014	0.008–0.012

PISTON AND RING SPECIFICATIONS

All measurements are given in inches.

Year	Engine ID/VIN	Engine Displacement Liters	Piston Clearance	Ring Gap			Ring Side Clearance		
				Top Compression	Bottom Compression	Oil Control	Top Compression	Bottom Compression	Oil Control
1982	Z22E	2.2L	0.001–0.0018	0.0098–0.0157	0.0059–0.0118	0.0118–0.0354	0.0016–0.0029	0.0012–0.0025	—
	CA20	2.0L	0.001–0.0018	0.0098–0.0157	0.0059–0.0118	0.0118–0.0354	0.0016–0.0029	0.0012–0.0025	0.0020–0.0057
1983	Z22E	2.2L	0.001–0.0018	0.0098–0.0157	0.0059–0.0118	0.0118–0.0354	0.0016–0.0029	0.0012–0.0025	
	CA20	2.0L	0.0010–0.0018	0.0098–0.0157	0.0059–0.0118	0.0118–0.0354	0.0016–0.0029	0.0012–0.0025	0.0020–0.0057
1984	CA20E	2.0L	0.0010–0.0018	0.0098–0.0138	0.0059–0.0098	0.0079–0.0236	0.0016–0.0029	0.0012–0.0025	—
	CA18ET	1.8L	0.0010–0.0018	①	0.0059–0.0098	0.0079–0.0236	0.0016–0.0029	0.0012–0.0025	—
1985	CA20E	2.0L	0.0010–0.0018	0.0098–0.0201	0.0059–0.0122	0.0079–0.0299	0.0016–0.0029	0.0012–0.0025	—
	CA18ET	1.8L	0.0010–0.0018	②	0.0059–0.0122	0.0079–0.0299	0.0016–0.0029	0.0012–0.0025	—
1986	CA20E	2.0L	0.0010–0.0018	0.0098–0.0201	0.0059–0.0122	0.0079–0.0299	0.0016–0.0029	0.0012–0.0025	—
	CA18ET	1.8L	0.0010–0.0018	②	0.0059–0.0122	0.0079–0.0299	0.0016–0.0029	0.0012–0.0025	—
1987	CA20E	2.0L	0.0010–0.0018	0.0098–0.0201	0.0059–0.0122	0.0079–0.0299	0.0016–0.0029	0.0012–0.0025	—
	CA18ET	1.8L	0.0010–0.0018	②	0.0059–0.0122	0.0079–0.0299	0.0016–0.0029	0.0012–0.0025	—
	VG30E	3.0L	0.0010–0.0018	0.0083–0.0173	0.0071–0.0173	0.0079–0.0299	0.0016–0.0029	0.0012–0.0025	0.0006–0.0075
1988	CA20E	2.0L	0.0010–0.0018	0.0098–0.0201	0.0059–0.0122	0.0079–0.0299	0.0016–0.0029	0.0012–0.0025	—
	CA18ET	1.8L	0.0010–0.0018	②	0.0059–0.0122	0.0079–0.0299	0.0016–0.0029	0.0012–0.0025	—
	VG30E	3.0L	0.0010–0.0018	0.0083–0.0173	0.0071–0.0173	0.0079–0.0299	0.0016–0.0029	0.0012–0.0025	0.0006–0.0075
1989	KA24E	2.4L	0.0008–0.0016	0.0110–0.0169	③	0.0079–0.0236	0.0016–0.0031	0.0012–0.0028	0.0026–0.0053
	CA20E	2.0L	0.0010–0.0018	0.0098–0.0201	0.0059–0.0129	0.0079–0.0299	0.0016–0.0029	0.0012–0.0028	0.0026–0.0053
1990	KA24E	2.4L	0.0008–0.0016	0.0110–0.0169	③	0.0079–0.0236	0.0016–0.0031	0.0012–0.0028	0.0026–0.0053
1991	KA24DE	2.4L	0.0008–0.0016	0.0110–0.0205	0.0177–0.0272	0.0079–0.0272	0.0016–0.0031	0.0012–0.0028	—
	KA24E	2.4L	0.0008–0.0016	0.0110–0.0205	③	0.0079–0.0272	0.0016–0.0031	0.0012–0.0028	0.0026–0.0053
1992	KA24DE	2.4L	0.0008–0.0016	0.0110–0.0205	0.0177–0.0272	0.0079–0.0272	0.0016–0.0031	0.0012–0.0028	—
	KA24E	2.0L	0.0008–0.0016	0.0110–0.0205	③	0.0079–0.0272	0.0016–0.0031	0.0012–0.0028	0.0026–0.0053

① Piston grades #1 and #2: 0.0098–0.0126 in.
Piston grades #3, 4 and 5: 0.0075–0.0102 in.
② Piston grades #1 and #2: 0.0098–0.0150
Piston grades #3, 4, and 5: 0.0110–0.0165
③ For rings punched with R or T—0.0177–0.0236
For rings punched with N—0.0217–0.0276

TORQUE SPECIFICATIONS

All readings in ft. lbs.

Year	Engine ID/VIN	Engine Displacement Liters	Cylinder Head Bolts	Main Bearing Bolts	Rod Bearing Bolts	Crankshaft Damper Bolts	Flywheel Bolts	Manifold	
								Intake	Exhaust
1982	Z22E	2.2L	51–58	33–40	33–40	87–116	101–116	12–15	12–15
	CA20	2.0L	51–58	33–40	22–27	90–98	72–80	13–16	13–17
1983	Z22E	2.2L	51–58	33–40	33–40	87–116	101–116	12–15	12–15
	CA20	2.0L	58–65	33–40	22–27	90–98	72–80	13–16	13–17
1984	CA20E	2.0L	①	33–40	24–27	90–98	72–80	14–19	14–22
	CA18ET	1.8L	①	33–40	24–27	90–98	72–80	14–19	14–22
1985	CA20E	2.0L	①	33–40	24–27	90–98	72–80	14–19	14–22
	CA18ET	1.8L	①	33–40	24–27	90–98	72–80	14–19	14–22
1986	CA20E	2.0L	①	33–40	24–27	90–98	72–80	14–19	14–22
	CA18ET	1.8L	①	33–40	24–27	90–98	72–80	14–19	14–22
1987	CA20E	2.0L	②	33–40	24–27	90–98	72–80	14–19	14–22
	CA18ET	1.8L	①	33–40	24–27	90–98	72–80	14–19	14–22
	VG30E	3.0L	③	67–74	33–40	90–98	72–80	12–14	13–16
1988	CA20E	2.0L	④	33–40	24–27	90–98	72–80	14–19	14–22
	CA18ET	1.8L	①	33–40	24–27	90–98	72–80	14–19	14–22
	VG30E	3.0L	③	67–74	⑤	90–98	72–80	12–14	13–16
1989	KA24E	2.4L	⑥	34–38	⑦	87–116	105–112	12–15	12–15
	CA20E	2.0L	④	33–40	24–27	90–98	72–80	14–19	14–22
1990	KA24E	2.4L	⑥	34–38	⑦	87–116	105–112	12–15	12–15
1991	KA24DE	2.4L	⑧	34–38	⑦	87–116	105–112	12–14	27–35
	KA24E	2.4L	⑥	34–38	⑦	87–116	105–112	12–15	12–15
1992	KA24DE	2.4L	⑧	34–38	⑦	87–116	105–112	12–14	27–35
	KA24E	2.4L	⑥	34–38	⑦	87–116	105–112	12–15	12–15

① A. Torque to 22 ft. lbs. (in sequence)
  B. Torque to 58 ft. lbs. (in sequence)
  C. Loosen all bolts
  D. Torque to 22 ft. lbs. (in sequence)
  E. Torque to 54–61 ft. lbs. (in sequence)
② Tighten in two steps: 1st—22 ft. lbs.; 2nd—
  58 ft. lbs. Then loosen all bolts completely.
  Final torque is in two steps: 1st—22 ft. lbs.;
  2nd—54–61 ft. lbs. If angle torquing, turn all
  bolts 90–95 degrees clockwise. (All steps
  in sequence.)
③ Torque all bolts in the proper sequence to 22 ft. lbs.
  Torque all bolts in the proper sequence to 43 ft. lbs.
  Loosen all bolts completely.
  Torque all bolts in the proper sequence to 22 ft. lbs.
  Torque all bolts in the proper sequence to 40–47 ft. lbs.
④ Tighten in two steps: 1st—22 ft. lbs.; 2nd—
  58 ft. lbs. Then loosen all bolts completely.
  Final torque is in 2 steps: 1st—22 ft. lbs.;
  2nd—54–61 ft. lbs. (If angle torquing, tighten
  bolt 8 to 83–88 degrees and all other bolts
  to 75–80 degrees clockwise.) NOTE: No. 8
  bolt is the longest bolt.
⑤ 1988 model
  Tighten in 2 steps:
  1st—10–12 ft. lbs.
  2nd—28–33 ft. lbs.
⑥ Tighten all bolts in numerical order to 22 ft. lbs. Then tighten all bolts to 58 ft. lbs. Loosen all bolts completely.
  Tighten all bolts to 22 ft. lbs. Then tighten to 54–61 ft. lbs. Always tighten and loosen bolts in numerical order—
  see text.
⑦ 2 steps:
  Tighten to 10–12 ft. lbs. Then tighten to 28–33 ft. lbs.
⑧ See text for procedure.

a. water temperature gauge wire
b. oil pressure sending unit wire
c. ignition distributor primary wire
d. starter motor connections
e. fuel hose

CAUTION: *On all fuel injected models, the fuel pressure must be released before the fuel lines can be disconnected. See the pressure releasing procedure under Gasoline Engine Fuel Filter in Chapter 1.*

f. alternator leads
g. heater hoses
h. throttle and choke connections
i. engine ground cable
j. thermal transmitter wire
k. wire to fuel cut-off solenoid
l. vacuum cut solenoid wire

NOTE: *A good rule of thumb when disconnecting the rather complex engine wiring of today's cars is to put a piece of masking tape on the wire and on the connection you removed the wire from, then mark both pieces of tape 1, 2, 3, etc. When replacing wiring, simply match the pieces of tape.*

CAUTION: *On models with air conditioning, it is necessary to remove the compressor and the condenser from their mounts. DO NOT attempt to unfasten any of the air conditioner hoses; simply move the compressor out of the way and support with a piece of stiff wire. Never allow the compressor to hang by the hoses. See Chapter 1 for additional warnings.*

8. Disconnect the power brake booster hose from the engine.

9. Remove the clutch operating cylinder and return spring.

10. Disconnect the speedometer cable from the transmission. Disconnect the backup light

Gearshift lever removal

switch and any other wiring or attachments to the transmission. On manual transmission models, remove the boot, withdraw the lock pin, and remove the lever from inside the car.

12. Detach the exhaust pipe from the exhaust manifold. Remove the front section of the exhaust system. Be careful not to break the retaining bolts to manifold. If the bolts or studs break in the manifold remove the manifold and drill and tap the hole.

13. Mark the relationship of the driveshaft flanges and remove the driveshaft.

14. Place a jack under the transmission. Remove the rear crossmember.

15. Attach a hoist to the lifting hooks on the engine (at either end of the cylinder head). Support the engine.

NOTE: *On 1984 and later 200SX models, do not loosen the front engine mounting insulator cover securing nuts. When the cover is removed, the damper oil will flow out and the mounting insulator will not function.*

16. Unbolt the front engine mounts. Tilt the engine by lowering the jack under the transmission and raising the hoist. Remove the engine/transmission assembly from the vehicle.

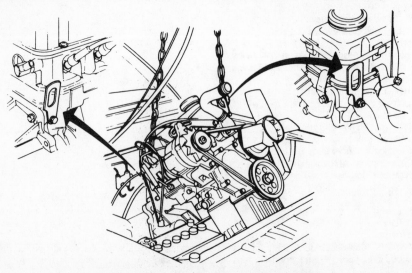

Removing the engine assembly from the vehicle

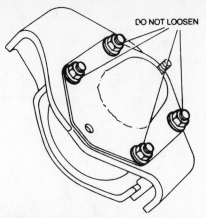

DO NOT LOOSEN

On the 1984 and later 200SX, do not loosen the front engine mounting insulation cover securing bolts

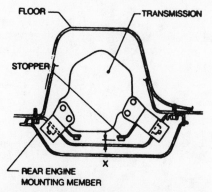

FLOOR — — TRANSMISSION

STOPPER

REAR ENGINE
MOUNTING MEMBER

X

When installing the 1984 and later 200SX engine, adjust the rear mounting stopper clearance (X) to 0.51 inch

To install:

17. With the engine/transmission assembly mounted safely on the engine hoist slowly lower the engine/transmission assembly into place.

NOTE: *When installing the CA20E and CA18ET engines into 1984 and later 200SXs, the rear engine mounting bracket must be adjusted. Using the accompanying illustration as a guide, adjust the rear mounting stopper clearance to 13mm.*

18. Support the transmission with a jack or equivalent until the crossmember is installed.

19. Tighten the front engine mounts. It may be necessary to lower or raise the engine hoist to correctly position the engine assembly to line up with the mount holes. Remove the engine hoist.

20. Install the crossmember then remove the jack or equivalent supporting the transmission.

21. Install the driveshaft in the correct marked position.

22. Reconnect the front exhaust system to the exhaust manifold. Be careful not to tighten retaining bolts to manifold to tight. If the bolts or studs break in the manifold remove the manifold and drill and tap the hole.

23. Reconnect all wiring at the transmission and the speedometer cable.

24. On manual transmission models, install the lever, lock pin and shift boot.

25. Install the clutch cylinder and return spring. Reconnect the power brake hose to the engine if so equipped.

26. Install all wiring, brackets, vacuum hoses and water hoses to the engine. Make sure all connections are tight and in the correct location. It is always a good idea to replace all the old water hoses, drive belts, clamps, spark plugs oil and oil filter when installing the engine.

27. Install the fan and fan pulley.

28. Install the radiator shroud than the radiator reconnect the transmission lines if so equipped.

29. Refill the radiator and all other fluid levels.

30. Install the air cleaner, battery and reconnect the battery cables.

31. Install the hood, aligning the match marks made earlier.

32. Check all fluids, start engine, let it warm up and check for leaks.

33. Road test vehicle after you are sure there are no leaks. Check vehicle for proper operation. Recheck all fluid levels.

Stanza and Stanza Wagon—Front Wheel Drive Models

The following procedure can be used on all years and models. Slight variations may occur due to extra connections, etc., but the basic procedure should cover all years and models.

CAUTION: *On EFI equipped models, release the fuel pressure in the system before disconnecting the fuel lines. Situate the vehicle on as flat and solid a surface as possible. Place chocks or equivalent at front and rear of rear wheels to stop vehicle from rolling.*

NOTE: *The engine and transaxle must be removed as a single unit. The engine and transaxle is removed from the top of the vehicle. If equipped with 4WD remove the engine, transaxle and transfer case as an assembly.*

1. Mark the location of the hinges on the hood. Remove the hood by holding at both sides and unscrewing bolts. This requires 2 people.

2. Disconnect the battery cables and remove the battery.

3. Drain the coolant from the radiator, then remove the radiator and the heater hoses.

4. Remove the air cleaner-to-rocker cover hose and the air cleaner cover, then place a clean rag in the carburetor or throttle body opening to keep out the dirt or any foreign object.

NOTE: *Disconnect and label all the necessary vacuum hoses and electrical connectors, for reinstallation purposes. A good rule of thumb when disconnecting the rather complex engine wiring of today's cars is to put a piece of masking tape on the wire and on the connection you removed the wire from, then mark both pieces of tape 1, 2, 3, etc. When replacing wiring, simply match the pieces of tape.*

5. If equipped, disconnect the air pump cleaner and remove the carbon canister.

6. Remove the auxiliary fan, the washer tank and the radiator grille if necessary. Remove the radiator together with the fan motor assembly as a unit.

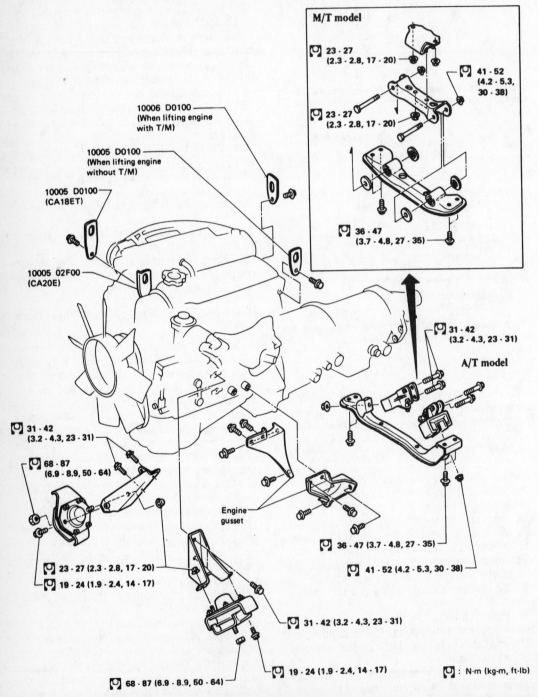

Engine removal—200SX

7. Remove the clutch control wire or cable from the transaxle. Remove the right and the left buffer rods but do not alter the length of these rods. Disconnect the speedometer cable from the transaxle and plug the hole with a clean rag.

NOTE: *Remove the EGR vacuum control valve with the bracket from the body.*

8. If equipped with air conditioning, loosen the idler pulley nut and the adjusting bolt, then remove the compressor belt. Remove the compressor to one side and suspend on a wire. Remove the condenser and the receiver drier and place them on the right fender.

NOTE: *If equipped with AC, DO NOT attempt to unfasten any of the refrigerant hoses.*

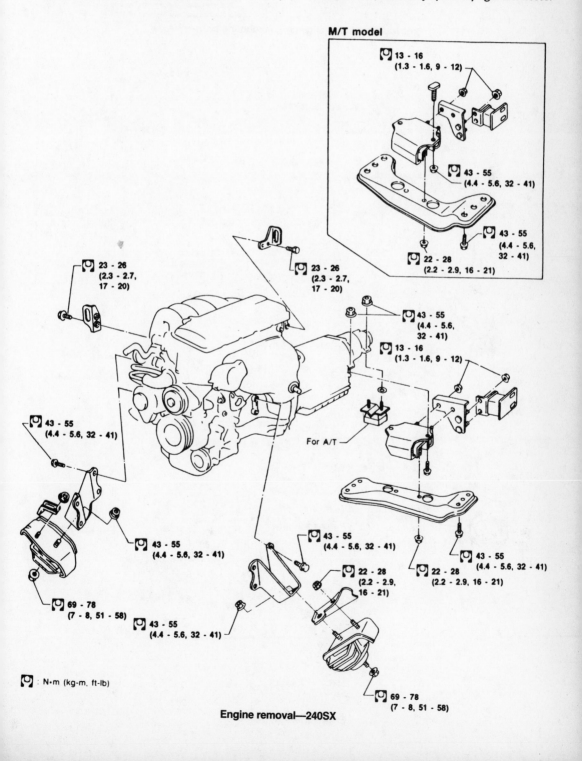

Engine removal—240SX

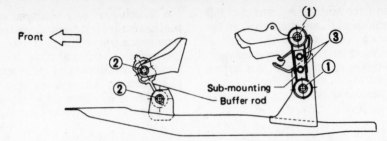

Procedure for tightening engine mounting bolts—Stanza

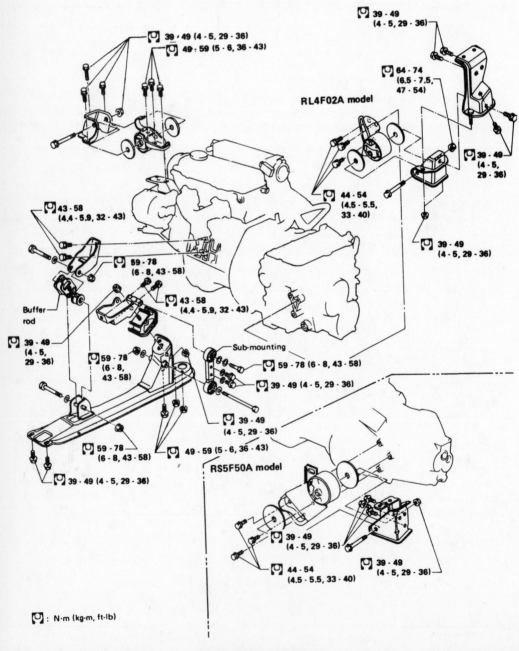

Engine removal—Stanza

See Chapter 1 for additional warnings and service procedures. If equipped with power steering, loosen the idler pulley nut and adjusting bolt, then remove the drive belt and the power steering pulley.

9. If equipped with a manual transaxle, disconnect the transaxle shifting rods by removing the securing bolts. If equipped with an automatic transaxle, disconnect the mounting bracket and the control wire from the transaxle.

On 4WD drive applications matchmark and remove the driveshaft from the transfer assembly.

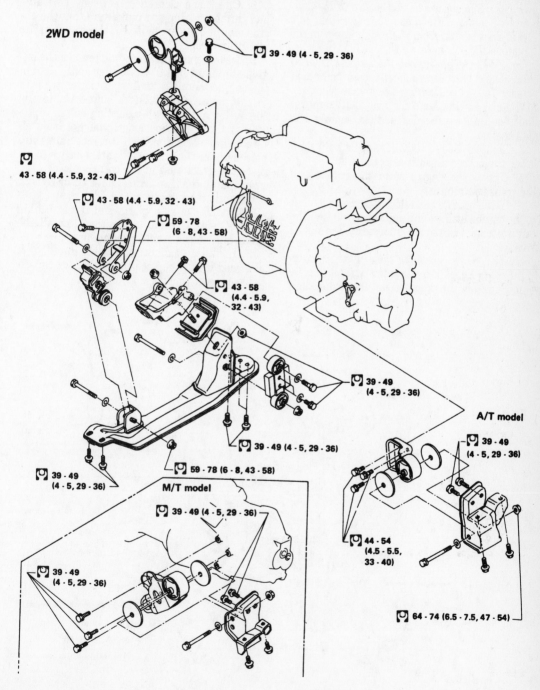

Engine removal—Stanza Wagon 2WD

10. Attach the engine sling at each end of the engine block. Connect a chain or cable to the engine slingers.

11. Unbolt the exhaust pipe from the exhaust manifold. There are 3 bolts which attach the pipe to the manifold and bolts which attach the pipe support to the engine.

NOTE: *Remove the tie rod ends and the lower ball joints. Disconnect the right and left side drive shafts from their side flanges and remove the bolt holding the radius link support. When drawing out the halfshafts, it is necessary to loosen the strut head bolts also becareful not to damage the grease seals.*

12. Refer to Chapter 7 for axle shaft removal and installation procedures, then remove the axle shafts.

13. Remove the radius link support bolt, then lower the transaxle shift selector rods.

14. Unbolt the engine from the engine and the transaxle mounts.

15. Using an overhead lifting device, attach it to the engine lifting sling and slowly remove the engine and transaxle assembly from the vehicle.

NOTE: *When removing the engine, be careful not to knock it against the adjacent parts.*

16. Separate the engine from the transaxle if necessary. Install all the necessary parts on the engine before lowering it into the vehicle, such as, spark plugs, water pump etc.

To install:

17. Lower the engine and transaxle as an assembly into the car and onto the frame, make sure to keep it as level as possible.

18. Check the clearance between the frame and clutch housing and make sure that the engine mount bolts are seated in the groove of the mounting bracket.

19. Install the motor mounts, remove the engine sling and install the buffer rods, tighten the engine mount bolts first, then apply a load to the mounting insulators before tightening the buffer rod and sub-mounting bolts.

20. If the buffer rod length has not been altered, they should still be correct. Shims are placed under the engine mounts, be sure to replace the exact ones in the correct places.

21. Install the transaxle shift selector rods or cable and attaching parts.

22. Install the axle shafts and the attaching parts. On 4WD drive applications install the driveshaft to the transfer assembly.

23. Install the exhaust pipe to the manifold, it is a good idea to replace the gasket for the exhaust pipe at this time.

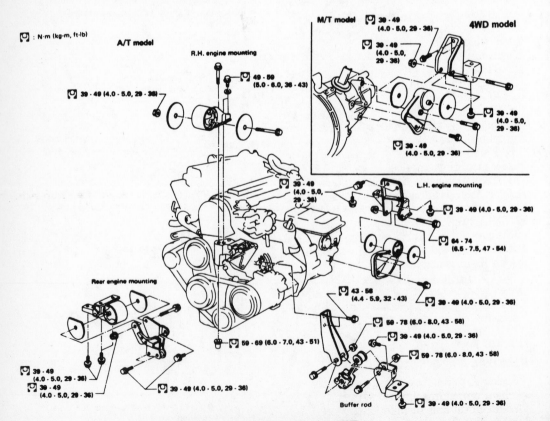

Engine removal—Stanza Wagon 4WD

24. Install clutch cable if so equipped and speedometer cable.

25. Install the condenser, receiver drier, air conditioning compressor, power steering pump and all drive belts.

26. Install the radiator with fan motor attached as assembly, radiator grille as necessary, washer tank and the auxiliary fan.

27. Install air pump cleaner, if so equipped and the carbon canister.

28. Install all other attaching parts such as brackets etc. and the air cleaner that were removed and connect all the vacuum hoses and the electrical connectors.

29. Connect the radiator and heater hoses and refill the system with the correct amount of antifreeze.

30. Install the battery and reconnect the battery cables.

31. Install the hood in the same location as you removed it from.

32. Fill and check all fluids, start engine, let it warm up and check for leaks.

33. Road test vehicle after you are sure there are no leaks. Check vehicle for proper operation. Recheck all fluid levels.

Rocker Arm Cover

REMOVAL AND INSTALLATION

1. Disconnect the negative battery cable. Remove or disconnect any electrical lines, hoses or tubes which may interfere with the removal procedures.

NOTE: *It may be necessary to remove the air cleaner (carburetor models) or the air duct (EFI and turbo models).*

2. Remove the rocker arm cover-to-cylinder head mounting screws , then lift the cover from the cylinder head.

3. Using a scraper or equivalent, clean the gasket mounting surfaces.

4. To install, use a NEW gasket and/or RTV sealant, then position the rocker arm cover in place. Torque the cover bolts-to-cylinder head EVENLY (working from the center to the end of the cover) to 5-8 ft. lbs. on Z series engine, 2-4 ft. lbs. on C and V series engines and 5-7 ft. lbs. on K series engines.

NOTE: *When using RTV sealant apply a even bead and make sure the surface that you are working on is very clean before applying sealer.*

Rocker Arm Shaft

REMOVAL AND INSTALLATION

Rocker Arm Shaft removal, installation and overhaul procedures are included in the Camshaft Removal and Installation service procedures in this Chapter.

Thermostat

REMOVAL AND INSTALLATION

NOTE: *On 200SX V6 engine it may be necessary to remove radiator shroud, coolant fan assembly and water suction pipe retaining bolts to gain access to the thermostat housing.*

1. Drain the engine coolant into a clean container so that the level is below the thermostat housing.

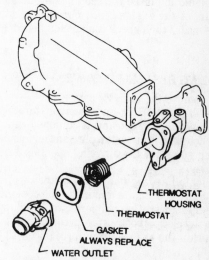

Thermostat location—CA series engines

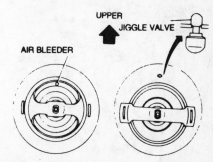

Always install the thermostat with the spring facing "down" and jiggle valve facing "up"

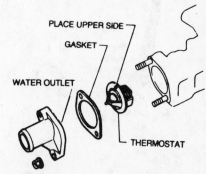

18–22 N·M (1.8–2.2 KG-M, 13–16 FT.LB.)

Thermostat location—Z series engine

2. Disconnect the upper radiator hose at the water outlet.

3. Loosen the two securing nuts and remove the water outlet, gasket, and the thermostat from the thermostat housing.

To install:

4. Install the thermostat to the engine, using a new gasket with sealer and with the thermostat spring toward the inside of the engine.

5. Reconnect the upper radiator hose.

6. Refill and bleed the cooling system. Make sure to let the engine reach normal operating temperature then check coolant for the correct level.

COOLING SYSTEM BLEEDING

1. Remove the radiator cap.

2. Fill the radiator and reservoir tank with the proper type of coolant. If equipped with an air relief plug, remove the plug and add coolant until it spills out the air relief opening. Install the plug.

3. Install and tighten the radiator cap.

4. Start the engine and allow the coolant to come up to operating temperature. If equipped allow the electric cooling fan to come on at least once. Run the heater at full force and with the

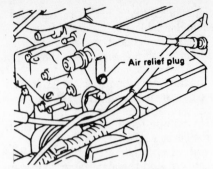

Air relief plug—Stanza KA24E engine

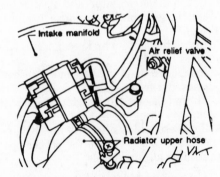

Air relief plug—240SX KA24DE engine

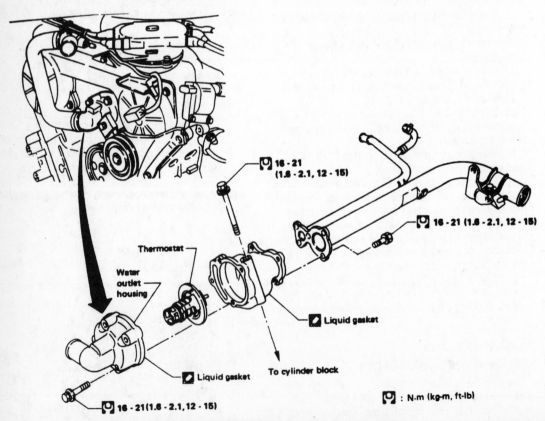

Thermostat and housing assembly—VG30E series engine

temperature lever in the HOT position. Be sure the heater control valve is functioning.

5. Shut the engine off and recheck the coolant level, refill as necessary.

Intake Manifold
REMOVAL AND INSTALLATION
1982-83 200SX–Z Series Engine

NOTE: *Always release the fuel pressure on fuel injected engines before removing any fuel system component.*

1. Drain the coolant and disconnect the battery cable.

2. Remove the air cleaner hoses.

3. Remove the radiator hoses from the manifold.

4. Remove the throttle cable and disconnect the fuel pipe and the return fuel line on fuel injection engines. Plug the fuel pipe to prevent spilling fuel.

NOTE: *When unplugging wires and hoses, mark each hose and its connection with a piece of masking tape, then match code the two pieces of tape with the numbers 1, 2, 3, etc. When assembling, simply match the pieces of tape.*

5. Remove all remaining wires, tubes and the E.G.R. and P.C.V. lines from the rear of the intake manifold. Remove the manifold supports.

6. Unbolt and remove the intake manifold. Remove the manifold with injectors, E.G.R. valve, fuel assembly, etc., still attached.

To install:

7. Clean the gasket mounting surfaces then install the intake manifold on the engine. Always use a new intake manifold gasket. Tighten the intake manifold bolts EVENLY in 2–3 stages (working from the center to the ends) to specifications.

8. Connect all electrical connections, tubes and the E.G.R. and P.C.V. lines to the rear of the intake manifold. Install the manifold supports.

9. Install the throttle cable and reconnect the fuel pipe and the return fuel lines.

10. Install the radiator hoses to the intake manifold.

11. Install the air cleaner hoses.

12. Refill the coolant level and connect the battery cable. Start the engine and check for leaks.

1984-88 200SX–CA Series Engine
Stanza–CA20E Engine

1. Disconnnect the negative battery cable and drain the cooling system.

2. Remove the air cleaner hoses.

3. Remove the radiator hoses from the manifold.

4. Relieve the fuel pressure. Remove the throttle cable and disconnect the fuel pipe and the fuel return line. Plug the fuel pipe to prevent spilling fuel.

5. Remove all remaining wires, tubes and the EGR and PCV tubes from the rear of the intake manifold. Remove the manifold supports.

6. Unbolt and remove the intake manifold. Remove the manifold with the fuel injectors/injection body, EGR valve, fuel pipes and associated running gear still attached.

7. Remove the intake manifold gasket and clean the gasket surfaces.

To install:

8. Install the intake manifold manifold with a new gasket. Tighten the intake manifold bolts EVENLY in 2–3 stages (working from the center to the ends) to specifications (14-19 ft. lbs.)

9. Install the intake manifold supports. Connect the the fuel pipe, fuel return line and the throttle cable. Reconnect all necessary lines, hoses and or electrical connections.

10. Connect the radiator hoses to the intake manifold. Connect the air cleaner hoses.

11. Fill the cooling system and connect the negative battery cable. Roadtest the vehicle for proper operation.

200SX–VG30E Engine

NOTE: *When removing and installing the collector assembly and intake manifold follow the sequence patterns.*

1. Relieve the fuel system pressure, disconnect the negative battery cable and drain the cooling system.

2. Disconnect the valve cover-to-throttle chamber hose at the valve cover.

3. Disconnect the heater housing-to-water inlet tube at the water inlet.

4. Remove the bolt holding the water and fuel tubes to the head.

5. Remove the heater housing-to-thermostat housing tube.

6. Remove the intake collector cover and then remove the collector itself.

7. Disconnect the fuel line and remove the

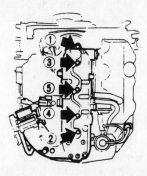

Removing collector—loosen bolts in this order

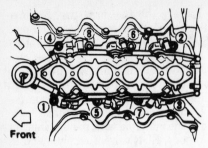

Removing intake manifold—loosen bolts in this order

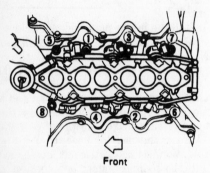

Installing intake manifold—tighten bolts in this order

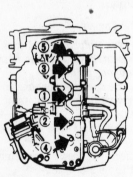

Installing collector to intake manifold—tighten bolts in this order

intake manifold bolts. Remove the intake manifold assembly, with the fuel tube assembly still attached, from the vehicle.

To install:

8. Install the intake manifold manifold with a new gasket. Tighten the intake manifold bolts in 2–3 stages in the proper sequence to specifications.

9. Connect the fuel line.

10. Install the intake manifold collector with a new gasket. Install the collector cover assembly.

11. Connect the heater-to-thermostat housing tube.

12. Attach the water and fuel tubes to the cylinder head with the mounting bolt.

13. Connect the valve cover-to-throttle chamber hose.

14. Fill the cooling system to the proper level and connect the negative battery cable.

15. Road test the vehicle for proper operation. Make all the necessary engine adjustments.

240SX—KA24E and KA24DE Engines
Stanza—KA24E Engine

1. Relieve the fuel system pressure, disconnect the negative battery cable and drain the cooling system.

2. Remove the air duct between the air flow meter and the throttle body.

3. Disconnect the throttle cable.

4. Disconnect the fuel supply and return lines from the fuel injector assembly. Plug the lines to prevent leakage.

5. Disconnect and tag the electrical connectors and the vacuum hoses to the throttle body and intake manifold/collector assembly.

6. Remove the spark plug wires.

7. Disconnect the EGR valve tube from the exhaust manifold.

8. Remove the intake manifold mounting brackets.

9. Unbolt the intake manifold collector/throttle body from the intake manifold or just remove the mounting bolts and separate the intake manifold from the cylinder head with the collector attached.

10. Using a putty knife or equivalent, clean the gasket mounting surfaces. Check the intake manifold for cracks and warpage.

To install:

11. Install the intake manifold and gasket on the engine. Tighten the mounting bolts 12–15 ft. lbs. from the center working to the end, in 2–3 stages. If the collector was separated from the intake manifold, torque the collector bolts to 12–15 ft. lbs. from the center working to the end.

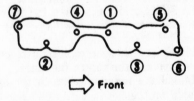

Intake manifold bolt torque sequence—KA24E engine

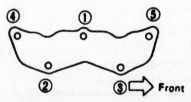

Intake manifold collector bolt torque sequence—KA24E engine

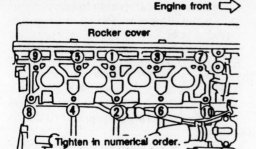

Intake manifold bolt torque sequence—KA24DE engine

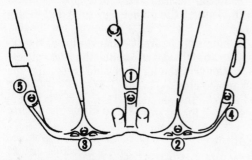

Tighten in numerical order.

Intake manifold collector bolt torque sequence—KA24DE engine

12. Install intake manifold mounting brackets.

13. Connect the EGR valve tube to the exhaust manifold.

14. Install the spark plug wires.

15. Connect the electrical connectors and the vacuum hoses to the throttle body and intake manifold/collector assembly.

16. Connect the fuel line(s) to the fuel injector assembly.

17. Connect the throttle cable.

18. Connect the air duct between the air flow meter and the throttle body.

19. Fill the cooling system to the proper level and connect the negative battery cable.

20. Make all the necessary engine adjustments. Road test the vehicle for proper operation.

Stanza—CA20 Engine

1. Remove the air cleaner assembly together with all of the hoses.

NOTE: *When unplugging wires and hoses, mark each hose and its connection with a piece of masking tape, then match code the 2 pieces of tape with the numbers 1, 2, 3, etc. When assembling, simply match up the pieces of tape.*

2. Disconnect and label the throttle linkage,

the fuel and the vacuum lines from the carburetor and the intake manifold components.

NOTE: *The carburetor can be removed from the manifold at this point or can be removed as an assembly with the intake manifold.*

3. Remove the intake manifold bolts or nuts and the manifold from the engine.

To install:

4. Using a putty knife or equivalent, clean the gasket mounting surfaces.

5. Install the intake manifold and gasket on the engine. Always use a new gasket. Tighten the mounting bolts from the, center working to the end, in two or three stages. Torque the intake manifold bolts to 14-19 ft. lbs.

6. Install throttle linkage, fuel and vacuum lines and the air cleaner assembly.

7. Start engine and check for leaks.

Exhaust Manifold

REMOVAL AND INSTALLATION

All Models Except 200SX with VG30 Engine

1. Remove the air cleaner assembly, if necessary for access. Remove the heat shield.

2. Disconnect and tag the high tension wires from the spark plugs on the exhaust side of the engine.

3. Disconnect the exhaust pipe from the exhaust manifold. On turbocharged engines remove the exhaust pipe from the turbocharger assembly.

NOTE: *Soak the exhaust pipe retaining bolts with penetrating oil if necessary to loosen them.*

4. On the carbureted models, remove the air induction and/or the EGR tubes from the exhaust manifold. On the fuel injected models, disconnect the exhaust gas sensor electrical connector.

5. Remove the exhaust manifold mounting nuts and the manifold from the cylinder head.

To install:

6. Using a putty knife or equivalent, clean the gasket mounting surfaces.

7. Install the manifold onto the engine, use new gaskets and from the, center working to the end. Torque the exhaust manifold nuts/bolts EVENLY to 14-22 ft. lbs.

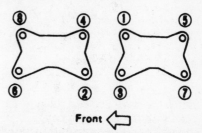

Exhaust manifold torque sequence—KA24E engine

8. Install the air induction and/or the EGR tubes to the exhaust manifold or the exhaust gas sensor electrical connector.

9. Reconnect exhaust pipe. On turbocharged engines reconnect the exhaust pipe to the turbocharger assembly.

10. Connect spark plug wires and air cleaner and any related hoses.

11. Start engine and check for exhaust leaks.

200SX – VG30E Engine

1. Remove the exhaust manifold sub-cover and manifold cover. Remove the E.G.R. tube from the right side exhaust manifold. Remove the exhaust manifold stay.

2. Disconnect the left side exhaust manifold at the exhaust pipe by removing retaining nuts and disconnect the right side manifold from the connecting pipe.

NOTE: *Soak the exhaust pipe retaining bolts with penetrating oil if necessary to loosen them.*

3. Remove bolts for each manifold in the order shown.

To install:

4. Clean all gasket surfaces. Install new gaskets.

5. Install the manifold to the engine, torquing manifold bolts alternately in two stages in the exact reverse order of removal to 13-16 ft. lbs.

6. Reconnect the exhaust pipe and the connecting pipe. Be careful not break these bolts.

7. Install the exhaust manifold stay and the E.G.R. tube to the right side manifold.

8. Install the exhaust manifold covers. Start the engine and check for exhaust leaks.

Turbocharger

REMOVAL AND INSTALLATION

200SX – CA18ET Engine

1. Drain the engine coolant.

2. Remove the air duct and hoses, and the air intake pipe.

3. Disconnect the front exhaust pipe at the exhaust manifold end (exhaust outlet in the illustration).

4. Remove the heat shield plates.

5. Tag and disconnect the oil delivery tube and return hose.

6. Disconnect the water inlet tube.

7. Unbolt and remove the turbocharger from the exhaust manifold.

NOTE: *The turbocharger unit should only be serviced internally by an engine specialist trained in turbocharger repair.*

To install:

8. Install the turbocharger to the exhaust manifold torque these bolts evenly and to 22-25 ft. lbs. Torque the turbocharger outlet to housing 16-22 ft. lbs. if the outlet was removed.

9. Reconnect the water inlet tube.

10. Connect the oil delivery tube and return hose.

11. Connect the front exhaust pipe at the exhaust manifold end and install the heat shields.

12. Connect the air duct and hoses, and the air intake pipe.

13. Refill the cooling system, start the engine and check for leaks.

Radiator

REMOVAL AND INSTALLATION

NOTE: *The cooling system can be drained from opening the drain cock at the bottom of the radiator or by removing the bottom hose at the radiator. Be careful not to damage the fins or core tubes when removing and installing the radiator to the vehicle. NEVER open the radiator cap when hot.*

1. Disconnect the negative battery cable.

2. Drain the cooling system.

3. Remove the undercover, if equipped.

4. Disconnect the reservoir tank hose.

5. Disconnect all temperature switch connectors.

6. Disconnect and plug the transmission or transaxle cooling lines from the bottom of the radiator, if equipped.

7. Remove the fan shroud and position the shroud over the fan and clear of the radiator if so equipped. Remove the condenser and radiator fan assembly from the radiator if so equipped.

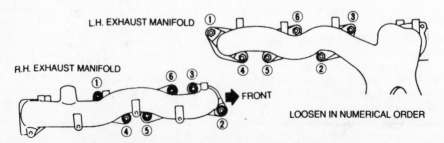

Exhaust manifold torque sequence—VG30E engine

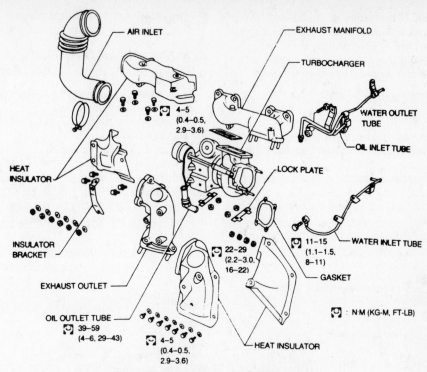

AIR INLET

EXHAUST MANIFOLD

TURBOCHARGER

WATER OUTLET TUBE

OIL INLET TUBE

4–5
(0.4–0.5, 2.9–3.6)

HEAT INSULATOR

LOCK PLATE

INSULATOR BRACKET

11–15
(1.1–1.5, 8–11)

WATER INLET TUBE

22–29
(2.2–3.0, 16–22)

EXHAUST OUTLET

GASKET

OIL OUTLET TUBE
39–59
(4–6, 29–43)

4–5
(0.4–0.5, 2.9–3.6)

HEAT INSULATOR

: N·M (KG-M, FT-LB)

Turbocharger assembly—CA18ET engine

8. Disconnect the upper and lower hoses from the radiator.

9. Remove the radiator retaining bolts or the upper supports.

10. Lift the radiator off the mounts and out of the vehicle.

To install:

11. Lower the radiator onto the mounts and bolt in place.

12. Install the lower shroud, if removed.

13. Connect the upper and lower radiator hoses--use NEW water hose clamps.

14. Install the fan shroud assembly as necessary. Install the condenser and radiator fan assembly as necessary.

15. Connect the transaxle or transmission cooling lines, if removed.

16. Reconnect all electrical connectors.

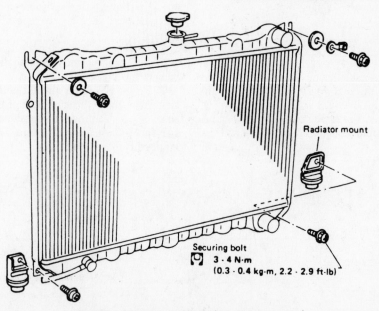

Radiator mount

Securing bolt
3 · 4 N·m
(0.3 · 0.4 kg·m, 2.2 · 2.9 ft·lb)

Radiator mounting—200SX CA series engines

17. Connect the reservoir tank hose.
18. Fill the cooling system to the proper level. Bleed the cooling system.
19. Connect the negative battery cable.
20. Start the engine and check for leaks.

Engine Oil Cooler

REMOVAL AND INSTALLATION

1. Disconnect the negative battery cable.
2. Remove engine oil cooler assembly inlet and outlet lines.
3. Remove the engine oil cooler assembly retaining bolts.
4. Installation is the reverse of the procedures.

Engine Fan

REMOVAL AND INSTALLATION

Belt Driven

1. Disconnect the negative battery cable.
2. Remove the fan shroud.
3. Remove the drive belt, fan assembly/pulley retaining bolts.
4. Remove the fan assembly.
5. Installation is the reverse of the removal procedure. Check fan coupling for rough operation before installation. Adjust the drive belt.

If necessary remove the radiator for additional clearance to remove the fan assembly.

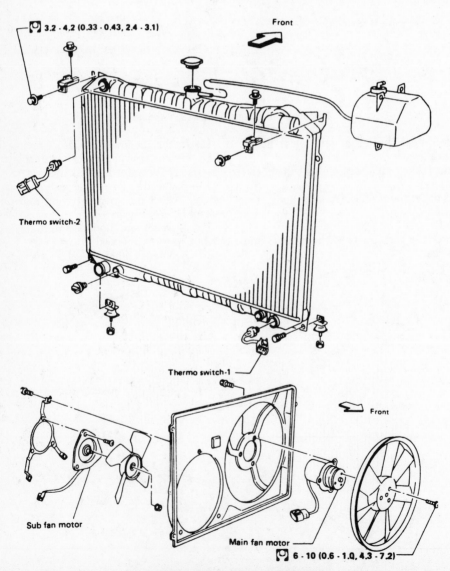

3.2 - 4.2 (0.33 - 0.43, 2.4 - 3.1)

Front

Thermo switch-2

Thermo switch-1

Sub fan motor

Main fan motor

Front

6 - 10 (0.6 - 1.0, 4.3 - 7.2)

Radiator mounting—Stanza CA20E engine

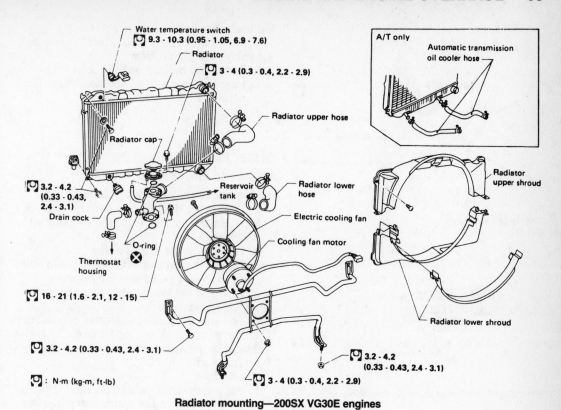

Water temperature switch
9.3 - 10.3 (0.95 - 1.05, 6.9 - 7.6)

Radiator

3 - 4 (0.3 - 0.4, 2.2 - 2.9)

Radiator upper hose

Radiator cap

A/T only

Automatic transmission
oil cooler hose

Radiator
upper shroud

3.2 - 4.2
(0.33 - 0.43,
2.4 - 3.1)

Drain cock

Reservoir
tank

Radiator lower
hose

Electric cooling fan

Cooling fan motor

O-ring

Thermostat
housing

Radiator lower shroud

16 - 21 (1.6 - 2.1, 12 - 15)

3.2 - 4.2 (0.33 - 0.43, 2.4 - 3.1)

3.2 - 4.2
(0.33 - 0.43, 2.4 - 3.1)

: N·m (kg-m, ft-lb)

3 - 4 (0.3 - 0.4, 2.2 - 2.9)

Radiator mounting—200SX VG30E engines

Radiator cap

Reservoir tank

A/T models only

Automatic
transmission
oil cooler hose

Upper radiator
hose

Radiator fan

Radiator drain plug

Cooling fan

Lower radiator
hose

Radiator shroud

Radiator mounting—240SX

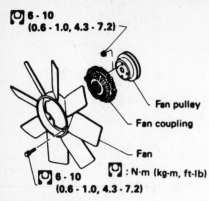

⬡ 6 - 10
(0.6 - 1.0, 4.3 - 7.2)

Fan pulley

Fan coupling

Fan

⬡ 6 - 10 **⬡ : N·m (kg-m, ft-lb)**
(0.6 - 1.0, 4.3 - 7.2)

Engine fan assembly

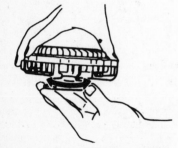

Checking clutch fan or coupling operation

Electric

1. Disconnect the negative battery cable.
2. Unplug the condenser and radiator fan motor wiring harness connectors.
3. Remove the radiator shroud bolts.
4. Separate the shroud and cooling fan assembly from the radiator and remove.

To install:

5. Mount the radiator shroud and cooling fan assembly onto the radiator.
6. Install the radiator shroud bolts.
7. Plug in the radiator and condenser fan motor harness connectors.
8. Connect the negative battery cable.

Water Pump

REMOVAL AND INSTALLATION

All Engines Except 200SX with VG30E

1. Disconnect the negative battery cable.
2. Drain the coolant from the radiator and cylinder block.
3. Remove all the drive belts.
4. Unbolt the fan assembly/water pump pulley and the water pump attaching bolts.
5. Separate the water pump with the gasket from the cylinder block.
6. Remove all gasket material or sealant from the water pump mating surfaces. All sealant must be removed from the groove in the water pump surface also.

To install:

7. Apply a continuous bead of high temperature liquid gasket to the water pump housing mating surface. The housing must be attached to the cylinder block within 5 minutes after the sealant is applied. After the pump housing is bolted to the block, wait at least 30 minutes for the sealant to cure before starting the engine.
8. Position the water pump (and gasket) onto the block and install the attaching bolts. Torque the small retaining bolts to about 5 ft.

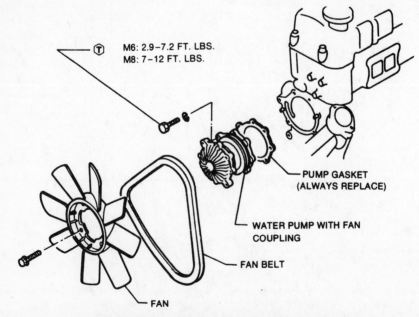

Ⓣ M6: 2.9–7.2 FT. LBS.
M8: 7–12 FT. LBS.

PUMP GASKET
(ALWAYS REPLACE)

WATER PUMP WITH FAN
COUPLING

FAN BELT

FAN

Removing water pump assembly—Z series engine

lbs. and large retaining bolts 12–14 ft. lbs. EVENLY in steps.

9. Install the water pump pulley/fan assembly.

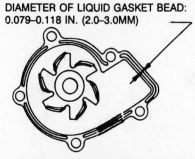

DIAMETER OF LIQUID GASKET BEAD: 0.079–0.118 IN. (2.0–3.0MM)

Apply a continuous bead of high temperature sealant to the water pump housing mating surface

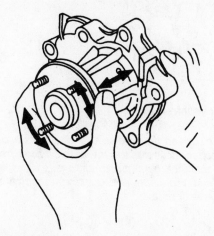

Checking water pump for excessive end play and rough operation

10. Install the drive belts and adjust the tension.

11. Fill the cooling system to the proper level. Bleed the cooling system.

12. Connect the negative battery cable.

200SX with VG30E Engine

1. Disconnect the negative battery cable and drain the coolant from the radiator and the left side drain cocks on the cylinder block.

2. Remove the radiator shroud.

3. Remove the power steering, compressor and alternator drive belts.

4. Remove the cooling fan and coupling.

5. Disconnect the water pump hoses.

6. Remove the water pump pulley, then the upper and lower timing covers.

NOTE: *Be careful not to get coolant on the timing belt and to avoid deforming the timing cover. Make sure there is enough clearance between the timing cover and the hose clamp.*

7. Remove the water pump retaining bolts, note different lengths, and remove the pump.

8. Make sure the gasket sealing surfaces are clean and free of all the old gasket material.

To install:

9. Mount the water pump and gasket onto the cylinder block. Torque the retaining bolts EVENLY in steps to 12–15 ft. lbs.

10. Install the upper and lower timing belt covers.

11. Connect the water pump hoses.

12. Install the cooling fan and coupling assembly.

13. Install and tension the drive belts.

14. Install the radiator shroud.

15. Fill and bleed the cooling system and connect the negative battery cable.

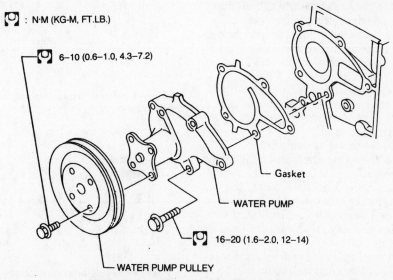

: N·M (KG-M, FT.LB.)

6–10 (0.6–1.0, 4.3–7.2)

Gasket

WATER PUMP

16–20 (1.6–2.0, 12–14)

WATER PUMP PULLEY

Water pump assembly—CA series engines

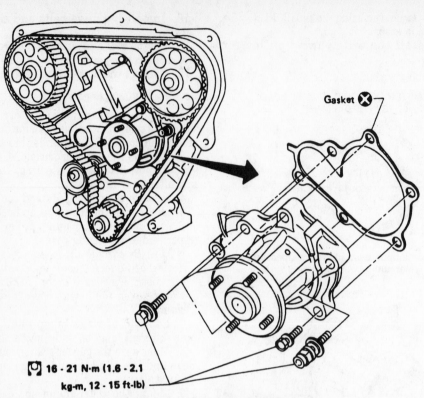

Gasket ⊗

⌷ 16 - 21 N·m (1.6 - 2.1
kg-m, 12 - 15 ft-lb)

Water pump assembly—200SX VG30E engine

Cylinder Head

REMOVAL AND INSTALLATION

NOTE: *To prevent distortion or warping of the cylinder head, allow the engine to cool completely before removing the head bolts.*

200SX–Z Series Engine

1. Crank the engine until the No. 1 piston is at TDC of the compression stroke, disconnect the battery, and drain the cooling system.

2. Remove the radiator hoses and the heater hoses. Unbolt the alternator mounting bracket and move the alternator to one side, if necessary.

3. If the car is equipped with air conditioning, unbolt the compressor and place it to one side. Do not disconnect the compressor lines. Severe injury could result.

4. Remove the power steering pump.

5. Mark and remove the spark plug wires and spark plugs.

6. Disconnect the throttle linkage, the air cleaner or its intake hose assembly. Release the fuel pressure. Disconnect the fuel line, the return fuel line and any other vacuum lines or electrical leads.

NOTE: *A good rule of thumb when disconnecting the rather complex engine wiring of today's automobiles is to put a piece of mask-*

ing tape on the wire or hose and one the connection you removed the wire or hose from, then mark both pieces of tape 1, 2, 3, etc. When replacing wiring, simply match the pieces of tape.

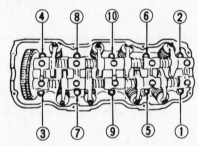

Cylinder head bolt loosening sequence—200SX Z series engine

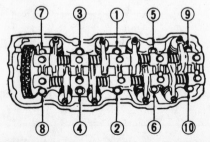

Cylinder head bolt torque sequence—200SX Z series engine

7. Remove the E.G.R. tube from around the rear of the engine.

8. Remove the exhaust air induction tubes from the exhaust manifold.

9. Unbolt the exhaust manifold from the exhaust pipe.

10. Remove the intake manifold supports from under the manifold if so equipped. Remove the P.C.V. valve from around the rear of the engine if necessary.

11. Remove the valve cover.

12. Mark the relationship of the camshaft sprocket to the timing chain with paint or chalk. If this is done, it will not be necessary to locate the factory timing marks. Before removing the camshaft sprocket, it will be necessary to wedge the chain in place so that it will not fall down into the front cover. The factory procedure is to wedge the timing chain in place with

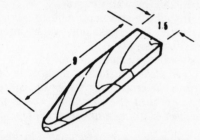

Wood wedge dimensions—9 in. (229mm) × 1.5 in. (38mm)—used to hold chain in place

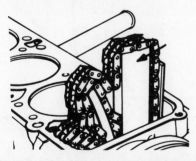

Wedge the chain with a wooden block (arrow). If you don't you will be fishing for the chain in the engine

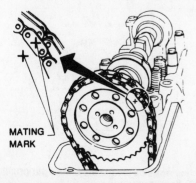

MATING MARK

Matchmark the timing chain to camshaft sprocket

the wooden wedge. The problem with this procedure is that it may allow the chain tensioner to move out far enough to cock itself against the chain. If this happens, you'll find that the chain won't go back over the sprocket after you've put the sprocket back on. In this case, you'll have to remove the front cover and push the tensioner back. After you've wedged the chain, unbolt the camshaft sprocket and remove it.

13. Working from both ends in, loosen the cylinder head bolts and remove them. Remove the bolts securing the cylinder head to the front cover assembly.

14. Lift the cylinder head off the engine block. It may be necessary to tap the head lightly with a rubber mallet to loosen it.

To install:

15. Thoroughly clean the cylinder block and head surfaces and check both for warpage.

16. Fit the new head gasket. Don't use sealant. Make sure that no open valves are in the way of raised pistons, and do not rotate the crankshaft or camshaft separately because of possible damage which might occur to the valves.

17. Temporarily tighten the two center right and left cylinder head bolts to 14 ft. lbs.

18. Install the camshaft sprocket together with the timing chain to the camshaft. Make sure the marks you made earlier line up with each other. If you get into trouble, see Timing Chain Removal and Installation for timing procedures.

19. Install the cylinder head bolts and torque them to 20 ft. lbs., then 40 ft. lbs., then 58 ft. lbs. in the order (sequence) shown in the illustration.

20. Clean and regap the spark plugs then install them in the cylinder head. DO NOT over torque the spark plugs.

21. Install the valve cover with a new gasket.

22. Install the intake manifold supports to the manifold if so equipped. Install the P.C.V. valve if it was removed.

23. Connect the exhaust pipe to exhaust manifold (use NEW exhaust gasket).

24. Install the exhaust air induction tubes to the exhaust manifold.

25. Install the E.G.R. tube from around the rear of the engine.

26. Connect the throttle linkage, the air cleaner or its intake hose assembly (fuel injection). Reconnect the fuel line, the return fuel line and any other vacuum lines or electrical leads.

27. Install the power steering pump if so equipped and correctly adjust the drive belt.

28. Install the air conditioning compressor and correctly adjust the drive belt.

29. Install the alternator mounting bracket,

alternator, electrical connections to the alternator and adjust the drive belt.

30. Reconnect the heater and radiator hoses.

NOTE: *It is always wise to drain the crankcase oil after the cylinder head has been installed to avoid contamination.*

31. Refill the cooling system. Adjust the valves.

32. Start engine, run engine to normal operating temperature, check for the correct coolant level.

33. Check for leaks and roadtest vehicle for proper operation.

200SX–CA20E and CA18ET Engines
Stanza and Stanza Wagon–CA20E

1. Relieve the fuel system pressure, disconnect the negative battery cable and drain the cooling system.

2. Remove the air intake pipe.

3. Remove the cooling fan and radiator shroud.

4. Remove the alternator drive belt, power steering pump drive belt and the air conditioner compressor drive belt, if equipped.

5. Position the No. 1 cylinder at TDC of the compression stroke and remove the upper and lower timing belt covers.

6. Loosen the timing belt tensioner and return spring, then remove the timing belt.

NOTE: *When the timing belt has been removed, do not rotate the crankshaft and the camshaft separately, because the valves will hit the tops of the pistons.*

7. Remove the exhaust manifold.

8. Remove the camshaft pulley.

9. Remove the water pump pulley.

10. Remove the crankshaft pulley.

11. Remove the alternator adjusting bracket.

12. Remove the water pump.

13. Remove the oil pump.

14. Loosen the cylinder head bolts in sequence and in several steps.

15. Remove the cylinder head and manifold as an assembly.

To install:

16. Clean the cylider head gasket surfaces.

17. Lay the cylinder head gasket onto the block and lower the head onto the gasket.

18. Install the cylinder head bolts. When installing the bolts, tighten the two center bolts temporarily to 15 ft. lbs. and install the head bolts loosely. They will be torqued after the timing belt and front cover are installed.

19. Install the oil pump.

20. Install the water pump.

21. Install the alternator adjusting bracket.

22. Install the crankshaft, water pump and camshaft pulleys.

23. Install the exhaust manifold.

NOTE: *Before installing the timing belt, be certain the crankshaft pulley key is near the top and that the camshaft knock pin or sprocket aligning mark is at the top.*

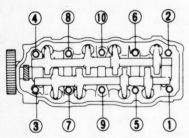

Cylinder head bolt loosening sequence—200SX CA series engine

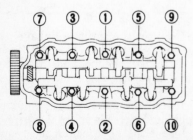

Cylinder head bolt torque sequence—200SX CA series engine. Bolt No. 8 is the longest

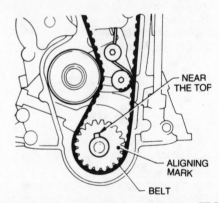

Set the CA series engines No. 1 cylinder at TDC on the compression stroke. The keyway on the crankshaft sprocket will be almost at 12:00 position

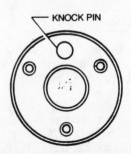

CA series engines camshaft knock pin position for cylinder head assembly

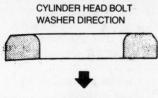

CYLINDER HEAD BOLT
WASHER DIRECTION

CYLINDER HEAD SIDE

Cupped washer installation—cylinder head installation

24. Install the timing belt and timing belt covers. After the timing belt and covers have been installed, torque all the head bolts in the torque sequence provided. Tighten all bolts to 22 ft. lbs. (29 Nm). Re-tighten all bolts to 58 ft. lbs. (78 Nm). Loosen all bolts completely and then re-tighten them once again to 22 ft. lbs. (29 Nm). Tighten all bolts to a final torque of 54–61 ft. lbs. (74–83 Nm) or if using an angle torque wrench, give all bolts a final turn to 75–80 degrees except bolt No. 8 which is 83–88 degrees. The No. 8 bolt is longer.

NOTE: *Newer models use cupped washers on the cylinder head bolts, always make sure that the flat side of the washer is facing downward before tightening the cylinder head bolts.*

25. Install the drive belts.
26. Install the cooling fan and radiator shroud.
27. Fill the cooling system to the proper level and connect the negative battery cable.
28. Make all the necessary engine adjustments. Road test the vehicle for proper operation.

200SX–VG30E Engine

NOTE: *To remove or install the cylinder head, you'll need a special hex-head wrench ST10120000 (J24239-01) or equivalent. The collector assembly and intake manifold have special bolt sequence for removal and installation. The distributor assembly is located in the cylinder head; mark and remove it if necessary.*

See note at 200SX VG30E "Camshaft Removal And Installation" before starting this procedure.

1. Release the fuel pressure. See the procedure in this Chapter for timing belt removal. Set the engine to Top Dead Center and then remove the timing belt.

NOTE: *Do not rotate either the crankshaft or camshaft from this point onward, or the valves could be bent by hitting the pistons.*

2. Drain the coolant from the engine. Then, disconnect all the vacuum hoses and water hoses connected to the intake collector.

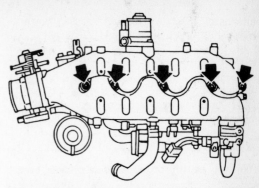

To remove the collector (VG30E engine), loosen the arrowed bolts

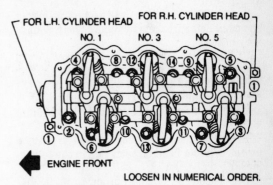

FOR L.H. CYLINDER HEAD   FOR R.H. CYLINDER HEAD
NO. 1   NO. 3   NO. 5

ENGINE FRONT

LOOSEN IN NUMERICAL ORDER.

To remove the cylinder head (VG30E engine), loosen the bolts in numerical order

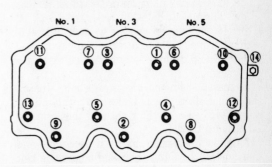

No. 1   No. 3   No. 5

Torquing pattern for the right side cylinder head—VG30E engine

3. Remove the collector cover and the collector.
4. Remove the intake manifold and fuel tube assembly.
5. Remove the exhaust collector bracket. Remove the exhaust manifold covers. Disconnect the exhaust manifold when it connects to the exhaust pipe (three bolts).
6. Remove the camshaft pulleys and the rear timing cover securing bolts.
7. Loosen cylinder head bolts a little at a time, in numerical order.
8. Remove the cylinder head with the exhaust manifold attached.

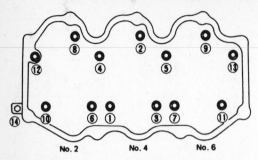

No. 2   No. 4   No. 6

Torquing pattern for the left side cylinder head—VG30E engine

To install:

9. Check the positions of the timing marks and camshaft sprockets to make sure they have not shifted.

10. Install the head with a new gasket. Apply clean engine oil to the threads and seats of the bolts and install the bolts with washers in the correct position. Note that bolts 4, 5, 12, and 13 are 127mm long. The other bolts are 106mm long.

11. Torque the bolts according to the pattern for the cylinder head on each side in the following stages:

 a. Torque all bolts, in order, to 22 ft. lbs.

 b. Torque all bolts, in order, to 43 ft. lbs.

 c. Loosen all bolts completely.

 d. Torque all bolts, in order, to 22 ft. lbs.

 e. Torque all bolts, in order, to 40-47 ft. lbs. If you have a special wrench available that torques bolts to a certain angle, torque them 60-65° tighter rather than going to 40-47 ft. lbs.

12. Install the rear timing cover bolts. Install the camshaft pulleys. Make sure the pulley marked R3 goes on the right and that marked L3 goes on the left.

13. Align the timing marks if necessary and then install the timing belt and adjust the belt tension.

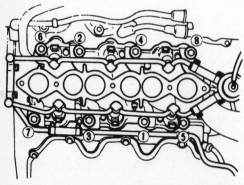

Torquing pattern for the intake manifold—VG30E engine

14. Install the front upper and lower belt covers.

15. Make sure that the rocker cover bolts, trays and washers are free of oil. Install the rocker covers.

16. Install the intake manifold and fuel tube. Torque NUTS as follows:

 a. Torque in numbered order to 26-43 in. lbs.

 b. Torque in numbered order to 17-20 ft. lbs.

17. Torque the BOLTS on the intake manifold as follows:

 a. Torque in numbered order to 26-43 inch lbs.

 b. Torque in numbered order to 12-14 ft. lbs.

18. Install the exhaust manifold if removed from the cylinder head.

19. Connect the exhaust manifold to the exhaust pipe connection (replace the exhaust pipe gasket). Install the exhaust collector bracket.

20. Install the collector and collector cover. Refer to Intake Manifold Removal And Installation for the correct torque pattern.

21. Connect all the vacuum hoses and water hoses to the intake collector.

22. Refill the cooling system. Start the engine and check the engine timing. After the engine reaches the normal operating temperture check for the correct coolant level.

23. Roadtest the vehicle for proper operation.

240SX–KA24E Engine
1990-92 Stanza–KA24E Engine

NOTE: *After finishing this procedure allow the rocker cover-to-cylinder head rubber plugs to dry for 30 minutes before starting the engine. This will allow the liquid gasket sealer used to seal these plugs to dry completely.*

1. Drain coolant from the radiator and remove drain plug from the cylinder block. Release the fuel pressure.

2. Remove the power steering drive belt, power steering pump, idler pulley and power steering brackets.

3. Mark and disconnect all the vacuum hoses, spark plug wires and electrical connections to gain access to cylinder head. Remove the air induction hose from the collector assembly.

4. Disconnect the accelerator bracket. If necessary mark the position and remove the accelerator cable wire end from the throttle drum.

5. Remove the bolts that hold intake manifold collector to the intake manifold. Remove and position the collector assembly to the side.

6. Remove the bolts that hold intake manifold to the cylinder. Remove the intake manifold. Unplug the exhaust gas sensor and remove the exhaust cover and exhaust pipe at exhaust

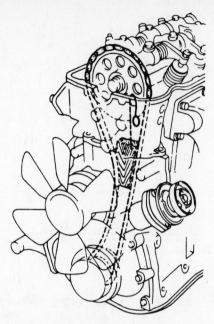

Support the timing chain with a block of wood

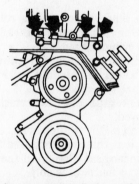

Remove the front cover to cylinder retaining bolts

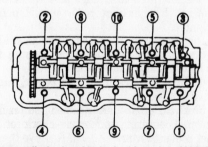

Loosen cylinder head bolts in this order—KA24E and KA24DE series engines

manifold connection. Remove the exhaust manifold from the cylinder head.

7. Remove the rocker cover. If cover sticks to the cylinder head, tap it with a rubber hammer.

NOTE: *After removing the rocker cover matchmark the timing chain with the camshaft sprocket with paint or equivalent. This*

step is very important for the correct installation of the timing chain to sprocket.

8. Set No.1 cylinder piston at T.D.C. on its compression stroke. Remove the No.1 spark plug and make sure that the piston is UP.

9. Loosen the camshaft sprocket bolt. Do not turn engine when removing the bolt.

10. Support the timing chain with a block of wood as illustrated.

11. Remove the camshaft sprocket.

12. Remove the front cover to cylinder head retaining bolts.

NOTE:

The cylinder head bolts should be loosened in two or three steps in the correct order to prevent head warpage or cracking.

13. Remove the cylinder head bolts in the correct order.

To install:

14. Confirm that the No. 1 is at T.D.C. on its compression stroke as follows:

   a. Align timing mark with 0^0 mark on the crankshaft pulley.

   b. Make sure the distributor rotor head is set at No. 1 on the distributor cap.

   c. Confirm that the knock pin on the camshaft is set at the top position.

15. Install the cylinder head with a new gasket and torque the head bolts in numerical order in 5 steps (a, b, c, d, e). Do not rotate crankshaft and camshaft separately, or valves will hit the piston heads.

Align timing mark with 0 on the timing scale

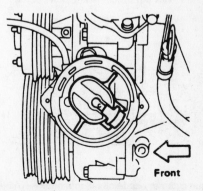

View of rotor at No. 1 cylinder firing location

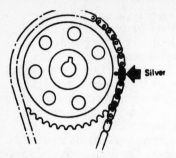

Matchmark timing chain with camshaft sprocket

a. Torque all bolts to 22 ft. lbs.
b. Torque all bolts to 58 ft. lbs.
c. Loosen all bolts completely.
d. Torque all bolts to 22 ft. lbs.
e. Torque all bolts to 54-61 ft. lbs., or if you are using an angle wrench, turn all bolts 80-85° clockwise.

16. Remove the block of wood holding timing chain in the correct location. Position the timing chain on the camshaft sprocket by aligning each matchmark. Install the camshaft sprocket to the camshaft.

17. Tighten the camshaft sprocket bolt and the front cover to cylinder head retaining bolts.

18. Install the intake manifold and collector assembly with new gaskets.

19. Install the exhaust manifold with new gaskets.

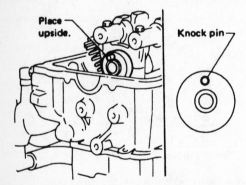

Confirm knock pin on camshaft is set at the top position

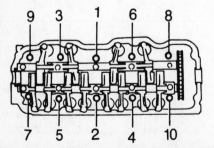

Torque cylinder head bolts in this order—KA24E and KA24DE series engines

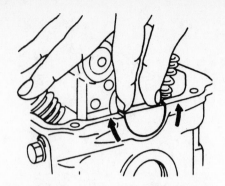

Installing rubber plugs in the correct manner

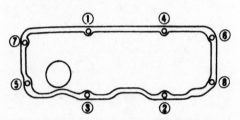

Correct rocker cover bolt torque sequence

20. Apply liquid gasket to the rubber plugs and install the rubber plugs in the correct location in the cylinder head.

21. Install the rocker cover with new gasket in place. Tighten the retaining bolts in the correct order.

22. Reconnect the accelerator bracket and cable if removed.

23. Connect all the vacuum hoses, and electrical connections that were removed to gain access to cylinder head. Reconnect the air induction hose to collector assembly.

24. Clean and regap the spark plugs if necessary. Install the spark plugs and spark plug wires in the correct location. Do not overtighten.

25. Install the power steering brackets, idler pulley, and power steering pump. Install the drive belt and adjust the belt.

26. Install the drain plug in the cylinder block. Refill the cooling system.

27. Start the engine, after the engine reaches the normal operating temperture check for the correct coolant level.

28. Roadtest the vehicle for proper operation.

240SX—KA24DE Engine

1. Release the fuel system pressure.

2. Disconnect the negative battery cable and drain the cooling system. Drain the engine oil.

3. Remove all vacuum hoses, fuel lines, wires, electrical connections as necessary.

4. Remove the front exhaust pipe and A.I.V. pipe.

5. Remove the air duct, cooling fan with coupling and radiator shroud.

6. Remove the the fuel injector tube assembly with injectors.

7. Disconnect and mark spark plug wires. Remove the spark plugs.

8. Set No. 1 piston at TDC on compression stroke. Remove the rocker cover assembly.

9. Mark and remove the distributor assembly.

10. Remove the cam sprocket, brackets and camshafts. These parts should be reassembled in their original position. Bolts should be loosened in 2–3 steps.

11. Loosen cylinder head bolts in two or three steps in sequence.

12. Remove the cam sprocket cover. Remove the upper chain tensioner and upper chain guides.

13. Remove the upper timing chain and idler sprocket bolt. Lower timing chain will not disengaged from the crankshaft sprocket.

14. Remove the cylinder head with the intake manifold, collector and exhaust manifold assembly.

To install:

15. Check all components for wear. Replace as necessary. Clean all mating surfaces and replace the cylinder head gasket.

16. Install cylinder head. Tighten cylinder head in the following sequence:

   a. Tighten all bolts in sequence to 22 ft. lbs.

   b. Tighten all bolts in sequence to 59 ft. lbs.

   c. Loosen all bolts in sequence completely.

   d. Tighten all bolts in sequence to 18–25 ft. lbs.

   e. Tighten all bolts to 86 to 91 degrees clockwise, or if an angle wrench is not available, tighten all bolts to in sequence to 55–62 ft. lbs.

17. Install upper timing chain assemble in the correct position. Align all timing marks.

18. Install all other components in the reverse order of the removal procedure. Refill and check all fluid levels. Road test the vehicle for proper operation.

Stanza—CA20 Engine

1. Disconnect the negative battery cable and drain the cooling system.

2. Support vehicle safely, remove the right front wheel.

3. Remove all spark plugs. Tag and disconnect all lines, hoses and wires which may interfere with cylinder removal.

4. Position the No. 1 cylinder at TDC of the compression stroke and remove the dust cover and the under cover.

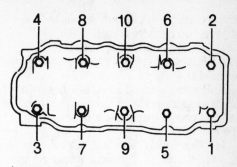

Loosen in numerical order.

• Tightening order

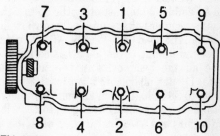

This bolt is the longest.

Removal and installation bolt torque sequence—Stanza CA20 series

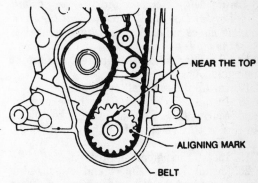

NEAR THE TOP

ALIGNING MARK

BELT

Make sure the crankshaft pulley key is near the top position—CA series engines

5. Remove the alternator drive belt, power steering pump drive belt and air conditioning compressor drive belt if so equipped.

6. Remove the crankshaft pulley.

7. Support engine and remove right side engine insulator and mounting bracket.

8. Remove front upper and lower timing belt covers.

9. Loosen timing belt tensioner and return spring, then remove the timing belt.

NOTE: *When the timing belt has been removed, do not rotate the crankshaft and the camshaft separately, because the valves will hit the piston heads.*

10. Remove rocker shafts with rocker arms

and securing bolts. The bolts should be loosened in two or three stages.

11. Remove camshaft sprocket.

12. Disconnect exhaust pipe from the exhaust manifold.

13. Remove cylinder head together with manifolds as an assembly. The bolts should be loosened in two or three stages in sequence.

To install:

14. Thoroughly clean both the cylinder block and head mating surfaces. Avoid scratching either.

15. Install a new head gasket on the block and the cylinder head with manifolds attached as an assembly. When installing the bolts tighten the two center bolts temporarily to 15 ft. lbs. and install the head bolts loosely. After the timing belt and front cover have been installed, torque all the head bolts in the torque sequence. Tighten all bolts to 22 ft. lbs. Retighten all bolts to 58 ft. lb. Loosen all bolts completely and then retighten them once again to 22 ft. lbs. Tighten all bolts to a final torque of 54-61 ft. lbs.

NOTE: *Newer models utilize cupped washers, always make sure that the flat side of the washer is facing downward before tightening the cylinder head bolts. Before installing the timing belt, be certain that the crankshaft pulley key is near the top and that the camshaft knock pin or sprocket aligning mark is at the top.*

16. Reconnect exhaust pipe to exhaust manifold.

17. Install the camshaft sprocket.

18. Install the rocker shafts with rocker arms and securing bolts. The bolts should be tighten in two or three stages from the center to the ends.

19. Install timing belt and tensioner.

20. Install the front upper and lower timing belt covers and the right side engine insulator and mounting bracket.

21. Install the crankshaft pulley. Install and adjust, the alternator drive belt, power steering pump drive belt and air conditioning compressor drive belt if so equipped.

22. Install the dust and under covers.

23. Install all spark plugs. Reconnect all lines, hoses and wires that were removed.

24. Install the right front wheel.

25. Connect the negative battery cable and refill the cooling system.

26. Start engine, check engine timing and for oil or water leaks.

27. Road test for proper operation.

CLEANING AND INSPECTION

All Cylinder Heads

1. With the valves installed to protect the valve seats, remove deposits from the combus-

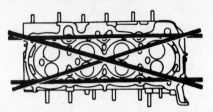

MEASURING POINTS

Use a straightedge to measure cylinder head flatness at these points

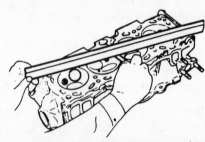

Check the cylinder head flatness and warpage with a straightedge and feeler gauge. Warpage should not exceed 0.004 inch

tion chambers and valve heads with a scraper and a wire brush. Be careful not to damage the cylinder head gasket surface. After the valves are removed, clean the valve guide bores with a valve guide cleaning tool. Using cleaning solvent to remove dirt, grease and other deposits, clean all bolt holes; be sure the oil passages are clean.

2. Remove all deposits from the valves with a fine wire brush or buffing wheel.

3. Inspect the cylinder head for cracks or excessively burned areas in the exhaust outlet ports.

4. Check the cylinder head for cracks and inspect the gasket surface for burrs and nicks. Replace the head if it is cracked.

5. On cylinder heads that incorporate valve seat inserts, check the inserts for excessive wear, cracks or looseness.

RESURFACING

Cylinder Head Flatness

When a cylinder head is removed, check the flatness of the cylinder head gasket surface.

1. Place a straight edge across the gasket surface of the cylinder head. Using feeler gauges, determine the clearance at the center of the straightedge.

2. If warpage exceeds 0.10mm over the total length, the cylinder head must be resurfaced. Cylinder head height after resurfacing must not exceed specifications.

3. If necessary to refinish the cylinder head gasket surface, do not plane or grind off more than 0.2mm from the original gasket surface.

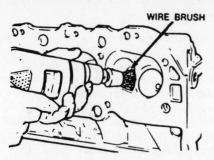

Clean the combustion chambers with a wire brush. Make sure you remove the deposits and do not scratch the head

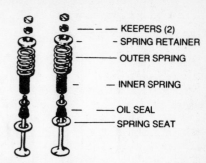

Typical valve components—not all engines have double valve springs

NOTE: *Cylinder head resurfacing should be done only by a competent machine shop or engine rebuilding facility.*

Valves and Valve Stem Seals (Cylinder Head Removed)

REMOVAL AND INSTALLATION

All Engines

The cylinder head must be removed on all engines before the valves can be removed.

A valve spring compressor is needed to remove the valves and springs; these are available at most auto parts and auto tool shops. A small magnet is very helpful for removing the keepers and spring seats.

Set the head on its side on the bench. Install the spring compressor so that the fixed side of the tool is flat against the valve head in the combustion chamber, and the screw side is against the retainer. Slowly turn the screw in towards the head, compressing the spring. As the spring compresses, the keepers will be revealed; pick them off of the valve stem with the magnet as they are easily fumbled and lost. When the keepers are removed, slowly back the screw out and remove the retainers and springs. Remove the compressor and pull the valves out of the head from the other side. Remove the valve seals by hand and remove the spring seats with the magnet.

Since it is very important that each valve and

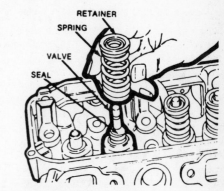

Always install new stem seals

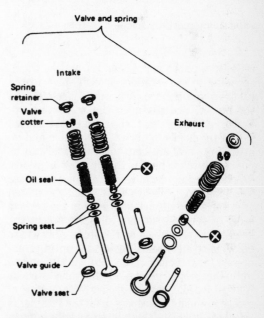

Exploded view of valves—KA24E engine (always replace oil seals after each diassembly)

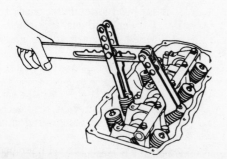

Compressing the valve springs using a valve spring compressor tool

its spring, retainer, spring seat and keepers is reassembled in its original location, you must keep these parts in order. The best way to do this is to cut either eight (four cylinder) or twelve (six cylinder) holes in a piece of heavy cardboard or wood. Label each hole with the

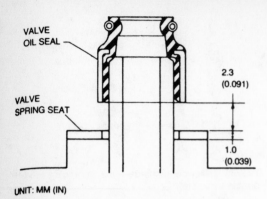

UNIT: MM (IN)

Proper valve stem seal installation—CA series engines

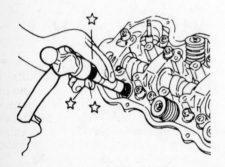

Valve spring seat installation—CA series engines

cylinder number and either IN or EX, corresponding to the location of each valve in the head. As you remove each valve, insert it into the holder, and assemble the seats, springs, keepers and retainers to the stem on the labeled side of the holder. This way each valve and its attending parts are kept together, and can be put back into the head in their proper locations.

After lapping each valve into its seat (see Valve Lapping), oil each valve stem, and install each valve into the cylinder head in the reverse order of removal, so that all parts except the keepers are assembled on the stem. Always use NEW valve stem seals. Install the spring compressor, and compress the retainer and spring until the keeper groove on the valve stem is fully revealed. Coat the groove with a wipe of grease (to hold the keepers until the retainer is released) and install both keepers, wide end up. Slowly back the screw of the compressor out until the spring retainer covers the keepers. Remove the tool. Lightly tap the end of each valve stem with a rubber hammer to ensure proper fit of the retainers and keepers. Adjust the valves.

NOTE: *On some engines there are 2 intake valves and 1 exhaust valve for each cylinder.*

INSPECTION

Before the valves can be properly inspected, the stem, lower end of the stem and the entire valve face and head must be cleaned. An old valve works well for clipping carbon from the valve head, and a wire brush, gasket scraper or putty knife can be used for cleaning the valve face and the area between the face and lower stem. Do not scratch the valve face during cleaning. Clean the entire stem with a rag soaked in thinners to remove all varnish and gum.

Thorough inspection of the valves requires the use of a micrometer, and a dial indicator is needed to measure the inside diameter of the valve guides. If these instruments are not available to you, the valves and head can be taken to a reputable machine shop for inspection. Refer to the Valve Specifications chart for valve stem and stem-to-guide specifications.

If the above instruments are at your disposal, measure the diameter of each valve stem at the locations illustrated. Jot these measurements down. Using the dial indicator, measure the inside diameter of the valve guides at their bottom, top and midpoint 90° apart. Jot these measurements down also. Subtract the valve stem measurement from the valve guide inside measurement; if the clearance exceeds that listed in the specifications chart under Stem-to-Guide Clearance, replace the valve(s). Stem-to-guide

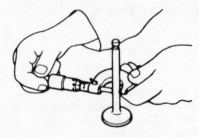

Measuring valve stem diameter on the center of the valve stem

Use an inside indicator to measure valve guide inner diameter (I.D.)

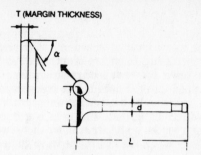

Critical valve dimensions. When the valve head has been worn down to 0.020 inch in margin thickness (T), replace the valve. Grinding allowance for the valve stem tip is 0.008 inch or less

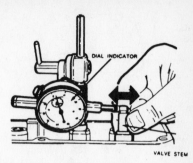

Measuring stem-to-guide clearance

clearance can also be checked at a machine shop, where a dial indicator would be used.

Check the top of each valve stem for pitting and unusual wear due to improper rocker adjustment, etc. The stem tip can be ground flat if it is worn, but no more than 0.5mm can be removed; if this limit must be exceeded to make the tip flat and square, then the valve must be replaced. If the valve stem tips are ground, make sure you fix the valve securely into a jig designed for this purpose, so the tip contacts the grinding wheel squarely at exactly 90°. Most machine shops that handle automotive work are equipped for this job.

STEM-TO-GUIDE CLEARANCE

Valve stem-to-guide clearance should be checked upon assembling the cylinder head, and is especially necessary if the valve guides have been reamed or knurled, or if oversize valves have been installed. Excessive oil consumption often is a result of too much clearance between the valve guide and valve stem.

1. Clean the valve stem with lacquer thinner or a similar solvent to remove all gum and varnish. Clean the valve guides using solvent and an expanding wire-type valve guide cleaner (a rifle cleaning brush works well here).

2. Mount a dial indicator so that the stem is at 90° to the valve stem and as close to the valve guide as possible.

3. Move the valve off its seat, and measure

the valve guide-to-stem clearance by rocking the stem back and forth to actuate the dial indicator. Measure the valve stems using a micrometer and compare to specifications, to determine whether stem or guide wear is responsible for excessive clearance.

Valve Guide
INSPECTION

Valve guides should be cleaned as outlined earlier, and checked when valve stem diameter and stem-to-guide clearance is checked. Generally, if the engine is using oil through the guides (assuming the valve seals are OK) and the valve stem diameter is within specification, it is the guides that are worn and need replacing.

REMOVAL AND INSTALLATION

The valve guides in all engines covered in this guide may be replaced. To remove the guide(s), heat the cylinder head to 302-320°F (150-160°C). Drive out the guides using a 2 ton press (many machine shops have this equipment) or a hammer and brass drift which has been modified with washers as in the accompanying illustration.

NOTE: *Some valve guides are retained by snaprings, which must be removed prior to guide removal.*

With the guide(s) removed, the cylinder head valve guide holes should be reamed to accept the new guides. The head should then be heated again and the new guides pressed or driven into place. On engines which utilize valve guide

A—VALVE GUIDE I.D.
B—LARGER THAN THE VALVE GUIDE O.D.

WASHERS

A—VALVE GUIDE I.D.   B—LARGER THAN THE VALVE GUIDE O.D.

A brass drift can be modified for valve guide removal

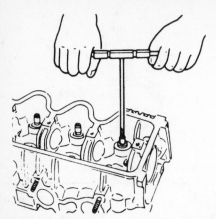

Always use 2 hands on the reamer handle when reaming valve guides

snaprings, install the snapring to the guide first, then install the guide into the head. Ream the new valve guide bores to 8.00-8.01mm (all engines except CA20E/CA18ET; or 7.00-7.01mm (CA20E/CA18ET). On the KA24E engine reamed valve guide finished sizes are 7.00-7.01mm intake valve and 8.00-8.01mm exhaust valve.

KNURLING

Valve guides which are not excessively worn or distorted may, in some cases, be knurled rather than reamed. Knurling is a process in which metal inside the valve guide bore is displaced and raised (forming a very fine cross-hatch pattern), thereby reducing clearance. Knurling also provides for excellent oil control. The possibility of knurling rather than reaming the guides should be discussed with a machinist.

REFACING

Valve refacing should only be handled by a reputable machine shop. During the course of a normal valve job, refacing is necessary when simply lapping the valves into their seats will not correct the seat and face wear. When the valves are reground (resurfaced), the valve seats must also be recut, again requiring special equipment and experience.

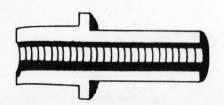

Cross-section of a knurled valve guide

VALVE LAPPING

The valves must be lapped into their seats after resurfacing, to ensure proper sealing. Even if the valves have not been refaced, they should be lapped into the head before reassembly.

Set the cylinder head on the workbench, combustion chamber side up. Rest the head on wooden blocks on either end, so there are 50-75mm between the tops of the valve guides and the bench.

1. Lightly lube the valve stem with clean engine oil. Coat the valve seat completely with valve grinding compound. Use just enough compound that the full width and circumference of the seat are covered.

2. Install the valve in its proper location in the head. Attach the suction cup end of the valve lapping tool to the valve head. It usually helps to put a small amount of saliva into the suction cup to aid it sticking to the valve.

3. Rotate the tool between the palms, changing position and lifting the tool often to prevent grooving. Lap the valve in until a smooth, evenly polished seat and valve face are evident.

Valve refacing

Lapping the valves

4. Remove the valve from the head. Wipe away all traces of grinding compound from the valve face and seat. Wipe out the port with a solvent soaked rag, and swab out the valve guide with a piece of solvent soaked rag to make sure there are no traces of compound grit inside the guide. This cleaning is very important, as the engine will ingest any grit remaining when started.

5. Proceed through the remaining valves, one at a time. Make sure the valve faces, seats, cylinder ports and valve guides are clean before reassembling the valve train.

Valve Seats

REPLACEMENT

Check the valve seat inserts for any evidence of pitting or excessive wear at the valve contact surface. The valve seats in all engines covered here can be replaced. Because the cylinder head must be machined to accept the new seat inserts, consult an engine specialist or machinist about this work.

NOTE: *When repairing a valve seat, first check the valve and guide; if wear is evident here, replace the valve and/or guide, then correct the valve seat.*

Valve Springs and Valve Stem Seals (Cylinder Head Installed)

REMOVAL AND INSTALLATION

The valve springs and valve stem seals can be removed without removing the camshaft, while the cylinder head is in place. Follow the valve and valve stem seals removal and installation procedure if the cylinder head has already been removed.

1. Remove the rocker cover. Set the cylinder on which you will be working to TDC on the compression stroke.

2. Remove the rocker shaft assembly.

3. Remove the spark plug from the cylinder on which you are working.

4. Install an air hose adaptor into the spark plug hole and apply about 71 psi of pressure into the cylinder. This will hold the valves in place, preventing them from droppng into the cylinder when the springs are removed.

5. Install a valve spring compressing tool; remove the valve spring and valve steam seal. Use care not to lose the keepers.

NOTE: *Always install new oil seals during reassembly.*

6. Reassemble the valve and components. Making sure the air pressure in the cylinder is at 71 psi while the springs are being installed.

7. Remove air adapator and install the spark plug.

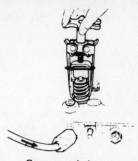

Compressed air

Using shop air pressure to keep the valve from dropping into the cylinder. Note the valve spring compressor

8. Install the rocker shaft and rocker cover with a new gasket.

HEIGHT AND PRESSURE CHECK

1. Place the valve spring on a flat, clean surface next to a square.

2. Measure the height of the spring, and rotate it against the edge of the square to measure distortion (out-of-roundness). If spring height varies between springs by more than 1.5mm or if the distortion exceeds 1.5mm, replace the spring(s) in question. Outer valve spring squareness should not exceed 2.2mm; inner spring squareness should not exceed 1.9mm.

A valve spring tester is needed to test spring test pressure, so the valve springs usually must

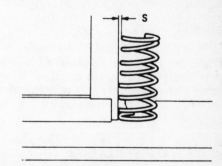

Measuring spring height and squareness—make sure closed coils face downward

Valve spring pressure test

be taken to a machinist or engine specialist for this test.

Valve Lifters

REMOVAL AND INSTALLATION

1. Disconnect the negative battery cable.
2. Remove the cylinder head, if required.
3. Remove the rocker arms and shafts.
4. Withdraw the lifters from the head or from the bore in the rocker. Tag each lifter to the corresponding cylinder head opening or rocker. If the lifter is installed in the rocker, remove the snapring first. Be careful not to bend the snapring during removal.

NOTE: *Do not place the lifters on their sides because air will be allowed to enter the lifter. When storing lifters, set them straight up.*

To install:

5. Install the lifters in their original locations. Use new lifter snaprings as needed. New lifters should be soaked in a bath of clean engine oil prior to installation to remove the air.
6. Install the rocker arms and shafts.
7. Install the cylinder head and leave the valve cover off.
8. Check the lifters for proper operation by pushing hard on each lifter with fingertip pressure. If the valve lifter moves more than 0.04 in. (1mm), air may be inside it. Make sure the rocker arm is not on the cam lobe when making this check. If there was air in the lifters, bleed the air by running the engine at 1000 rpm for 10 minutes.

OVERHAUL

The lifters used on Datsun/Nissan engine applications are not overhauled. If a problem (noise or wear) exists, replace the lifter. When replacing a lifter assembly it is recommended the entire set of lifters be replaced.

Oil Pan

REMOVAL AND INSTALLATION

200SX – CA and Z Series Engines

1. Disconnect the negative battery cable.
2. Raise the front of the vehicle and support safely.
3. Drain the oil pan.
4. Remove the power steering bracket from the suspension crossmember.
5. Separate the stabilizer bar from the transverse link.
6. Separate the tension rod from the transverse link.
7. Remove the front engine mounting insulator nuts.
8. Lift the engine.
9. Loosen the oil pan bolts in the proper sequence. On Z series engine application follow the CA series pattern.
10. Remove the suspension crossmember bolts and remove the screws that secure the power steering oil tubes to the crossmember.
11. Lower the suspension crossmember until there is sufficient clearance to remove the oil pan.
12. Insert a seal cutter between the oil pan and the cylinder block.
13. Tapping the seal cutter with a hammer, slide the cutting tool around the entire edge of the oil pan. Do not drive the seal cutter into the oil pump or rear seal retainer portion or the aluminum mating surface will be deformed.
14. Lower the oil pan from the cylinder block and remove it from the front side of the engine.

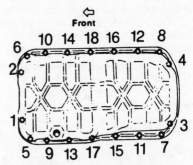

Oil pan bolt tightening sequence 200SX—loosen in the reverse order

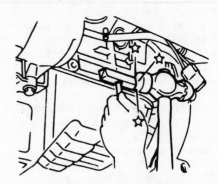

Using a seal cutter on the oil pan gasket

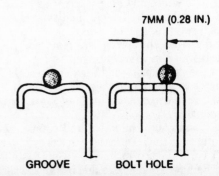

Apply sealer on the inside of the bolt holes

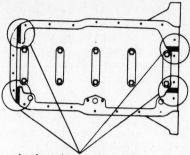

Apply sealant at these points

Oil pan sealant points—200SX Z series engine

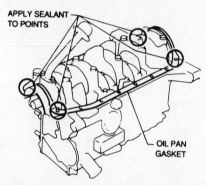

Apply sealant to the engine oil pan mating surfaces here; also to the corresponding points on the oil pan—CA series engines

To install:

15. Carefully scrape the old gasket material away from the pan and cylinder block mounting surfaces.

16. First apply sealant to the oil pump gasket and rear oil seal retainer gasket surfaces. Then, apply a continuous bead (3.5–4.5mm) of liquid gasket around the oil pan to the 4 corners of the cylinder block mounting surface. Wait 5 minutes and then install the pan. Tighten the oil pan bolts in sequence to 5–6 ft. lbs. On Z series engine application follow the CA series pattern.

17. Raise the crossmember from the lowered position. Attach the power steering tubes and install the crossmember bolts.

18. Install the front engine mounting insulator nuts.

19. Connect the tension rod and stabilizer bar to the transverse link.

20. Attach the power steering bracket to the crossmember.

21. Lower the vehicle.

22. Fill the crankcase to the proper level.

23. Connect the negative battery cable. Start the engine and check for leaks.

200SX—VG30E Engine

1. Remove the front hood if necessary, connect a lifting sling to the engine, and apply upward pressure. Drain the oil pan.

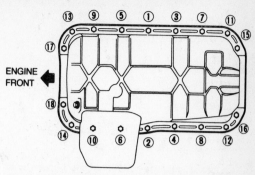

Oil pan torque sequence—200SX VG30E engine

2. Remove the covers from under the engine. Then, remove the engine mount insulator nuts and bolts.

3. Remove the five engine mounting bolts and remove the center crossmember assembly.

4. Remove the exhaust pipe connecting nuts. Unbolt and remove the oil pan.

To install:

5. Clean all the sealing surfaces. Apply sealant to the four joints on the lower surface of the block. Apply sealant to the corresponding areas of the oil pan gasket on both upper and lower surfaces.

6. Install the pan and gasket. Torque the pan bolts EVENLY in the order shown in the illustration to 5-6 ft. lbs and then lower engine assembly.

7. Install the exhaust pipe connection.

8. Install the center crossmember assembly and engine mount bolts.

9. Install the under covers to the engine and refill the oil pan with the specified quantity of clean oil. Operate the engine and check for leaks.

240SX

1. Disconnect the negative battery cable.

2. Raise the front of the vehicle and support safely.

3. Drain the oil pan.

4. Separate the front stabilizer bar from the side member.

5. Position a block of wood between a floor jack and the engine and then raise the engine slightly in its mounts.

6. Remove the oil pan retaining bolts in the proper sequence.

7. Insert a seal cutter between the oil pan and the cylinder block.

8. Tapping the cutter with a hammer, slide it around the entire edge of the oil pan. Do not drive the seal cutter into the oil pump or rear seal retainer portion or the aluminum mating surface will be deformed.

9. Lower the oil pan from the cylinder block and remove it from the front side of the engine.

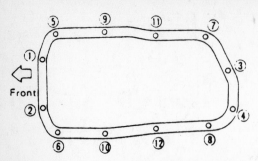

Oil pan torque sequence—240SX engine. Loosen bolts in reverse order

To install:

10. To install, carefully scrape the old gasket material away from the pan and cylinder block mounting surfaces and then apply a continuous bead (3.5–4.5mm) of liquid gasket around the oil pan to the 4 corners of the cylinder block mounting surface. Wait 5 minutes and then install the pan.

11. Install the oil pan and tighten the mounting bolts from the inside, out, to 3.6–5.1 ft. lbs. Wait 30 minutes before refilling the crankcase to allow for the sealant to cure properly.

12. Connect the front stabilizer to the side bar.

13. Lower the vehicle.

14. Fill the crankcase to the proper level.

15. Connect the negative battery cable. Start the engine and check for leaks.

Stanza—CA Series Engine

1. Disconect the negative battery cable.
2. Drain the oil pan.
3. Raise and support the front of the vehicle safely.
4. Remove the front exhaust pipe section and the center crossmember.
5. Remove the oil pan bolts.
6. Insert a seal cutter between the oil pan and the cylinder block.
7. Tapping the cutter with a hammer, slide it around the entire edge of the oil pan. Do not drive the seal cutter into the oil pump or rear seal retainer portion or the aluminum mating surface will be deformed.
8. Lower the oil pan from the cylinder block and remove it.

To install:

9. Carefully scrape the old gasket material away from the pan and cylinder block mounting surfaces and then apply a thin continuous bead of liquid gasket around the oil pan and to the 4 corners of the cylinder block mounting surface. Do the same to the oil pan gasket; both upper and lower surfaces. Wait 5 minutes and then install the pan. Wait 30 minutes before refilling

the crankcase to allow the sealant to cure properly.

10. Install the oil pan and tighten the mounting bolts from the center of the oil pan--to the end of the oil pan to 4–5 ft. lbs. (5–7 Nm).

11. Install the center crossmember and front exhaust pipe section.

12. Lower the vehicle.

13. Fill the crankcase to the proper level.

14. Connect the negative battery cable. Start the engine and check for leaks.

Stanza—KA24E Engine

1. Disconnect the negative battery cable.
2. Raise the vehicle and support safely.
3. Drain the oil pan.
4. Remove the right side splash cover.
5. Remove the right side undercover.
6. Remove the center member.
7. Remove the forward section of the exhaust pipe.
8. Remove the front buffer rod and its bracket if necessary.
9. Remove the engine gussets if necessary.
10. Remove the oil pan bolts.
11. Insert a seal cutter between the oil pan and the cylinder block.
12. Tapping the cutter with a hammer, slide it around the entire edge of the oil pan. Do not drive the seal cutter into the oil pump or rear seal retainer portion or the aluminum mating surface will be deformed.
13. Lower the oil pan from the cylinder block and remove it.

To install:

14. Carefully scrape the old gasket material away from the pan and cylinder block mounting surfaces and then apply a thin continuous bead of liquid gasket around the oil pan and to the 4 corners of the cylinder block mounting surface. Do the same to the oil pan gasket; both upper and lower surfaces. Wait 5 minutes and then install the pan. Wait 30 minutes before refilling the crankcase to allow the sealant to cure properly.

15. Install the oil pan and tighten the mounting bolts from the center of the oil pan to the end of the oil pan to 5–6 ft. lbs.

16. Install the engine gussets as necessary.

17. Install the front buffer rod and its bracket as necessary.

18. Install the forward section of the exhaust pipe using new gaskets.

19. Install the center member.

20. Install the right side undercover.

21. Install the right side splash cover.

22. Lower the vehicle.

23. Fill the crankcase to the proper level.

24. Connect the negative battery cable. Start the engine and check for leaks.

Oil Pump

REMOVAL AND INSTALLATION

200SX–Z Series Engine

Before attempting to remove the oil pump, you must perform the following procedures: Drain the oil from the oil pan. Turn the crankshaft so that No. 1 piston is at TDC on its compression stroke. Remove the distributor cap and mark the position of the distributor rotor in relation to the distributor base with a piece of chalk.

1. Remove the front stabilizer bar, if so equipped.
2. Remove the splash shield.
3. Remove the oil pump body with the drive spindle assembly.

To install:

4. Fill the pump housing with engine oil, align the punch mark on the spindle with the hole in the pump. No. 1 piston should be at TDC on its compression stroke.
5. With a new gasket placed over the drive spindle, install the oil pump and drive spindle assembly. Make sure the tip of the drive spindle

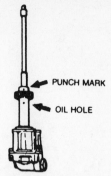

Oil pump alignment—Z series engine

fits into the distributor shaft notch securely. The distributor rotor should be pointing to the matchmark you made earlier.

NOTE: *Great care must be taken not to disturb the distributor rotor while installing the oil pump, or the ignition timing will be wrong.*

6. Install the splash shield and front stabilizer bar if it was removed.
7. Install the distributor cap.
8. Refill the engine oil. Start the engine, check ignition timing and check for oil leaks.

All Models–CA Series Engines

1. Disconnect the negative battery cable.
2. Drain the oil pan.
3. Remove all accessory drive belts.
4. Remove the alternator.
5. Remove the timing belt covers.
6. Remove the timing belt.
7. On 200SX and the Stanza Wagon, unbolt the engine from its mounts and lift or jack the engine up from the body. On the Stanza (except Wagon) remove the center member from the body.
8. Remove the oil pan.
9. Remove the oil pump assembly along with the oil strainer. Remove the O-ring from the oil pump body and replace it.
10. Replace the front seal.

To install:

11. If installing a new or rebuilt oil pump, first pack the pump full of petroleum jelly to prevent the pump from cavitating when the engine is started. Apply RTV sealer to the front oil seal end of the pan prior to installation.
12. Install the pump and torque the oil pump mounting bolts to 8–12 ft. lbs. Make sure the oil pump body O-ring is properly seated.
13. Install the oil pan.
14. On the Stanza (except Wagon), install the center member. On 200SX and the Stanza Wagon, lower and re-mount the engine.
15. Install the timing belt.
16. Install the timing belt covers.

Removing oil pump assembly—Z series engine

1. Oil pump body
2. Inner rotor and shaft
3. Outer rotor
4. Oil pump cover
5. Regulator valve
6. Regulator spring
7. Washer
8. Regulator cap
9. Cover gasket

Exploded view of the oil pump—Z series engine

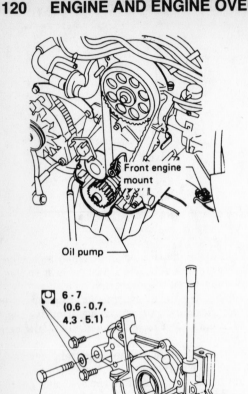

Oil pump

6 - 7
(0.6 - 0.7,
4.3 - 5.1)

12 - 16
(1.2 - 1.6,
9 - 12)

: N·m (kg-m, ft-lb)

Oil pump location—CA series engines

17. Install the alternator.
18. Install and tension the drive belts.
19. Fill the crankcase to the proper level.
20. Connect the negative battery cable. Start the engine and check for leaks.

1990-92 Stanza—KA24E Engine

The oil pump assembly consists of an inner and outer gear located in the front cover. Removal of the front cover is necessary to gain access to the oil pump.

1. Disconnect the negative battery cable.
2. Remove the front cover with the strainer tube.
3. Loosen the oil pump cover retaining screw and mounting bolts and separate the oil pump cover from the front cover.
4. Remove the oil pump inner and outer gears.

To install:

5. Thoroughly clean the oil pump cover mating surfaces and the gear cavity.
6. Install the outer gear into the cavity.
7. Install the inner gear so the grooved side is facing up (towards the oil pump cover). Make sure the gears mesh properly and pack the pump cavity with petroleum jelly.
8. Install the oil pump cover. On KA24E engine, torque the cover screws to 2.2–3.6 ft. lbs. and the bolts to 12–15 ft. lbs.
9. Install the front cover with a new seal.
10. Connect the negative battery cable. Start the engine and check for leaks.

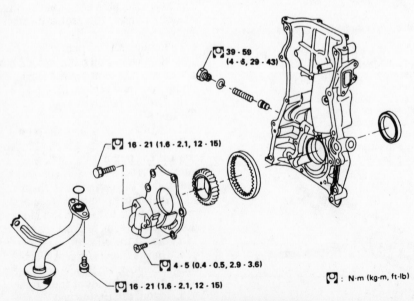

39 - 59
(4 - 6, 29 - 43)

16 - 21 (1.6 - 2.1, 12 - 15)

16 - 21 (1.6 - 2.1, 12 - 15)

4 - 5 (0.4 - 0.5, 2.9 - 3.6)

: N·m (kg-m, ft-lb)

Oil pump assembly—Stanza KA24E engine

240SX—KA24DE Engine

1. Remove the drive belts.
2. Remove the cylinder head and oil pans.
3. Remove the oil strainer and baffle plate.
4. Remove the front cover assembly (oil pump assembly is mounted in the front cover). Remove the oil pump.

To install:

5. Clean the mating surfaces of liquid gasket and apply a fresh bead of ⅛ in. (3mm) thickness.
6. Coat the oil pump gears with oil. Using a new oil seal and O-ring, install the front cover assembly.
7. Install the oil strainer, baffle plate, oil pans, cylinder head and drive belts.

240SX—KA24E Engine

1. Disconnect the negative battery cable.
2. Drain the oil pan.
3. Turn the crankshaft so No. 1 piston is at TDC on its compression stroke.
4. Remove the distributor cap and mark the position of the distributor rotor in relation to the distributor base with a piece of chalk.
5. Remove the splash shield.
6. Remove the oil pump body with the drive spindle assembly.

To install:

7. To install, fill the pump housing with engine oil, align the punch mark on the spindle

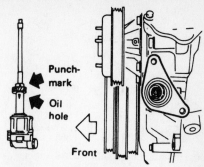

Oil pump drive spindle alignment

with the hole in the pump. No. 1 piston should be at TDC on its compression stroke.

8. With a new gasket and seal placed over the drive spindle, install the oil pump and drive spindle assembly. Make sure the tip of the drive spindle fits into the distributor shaft notch securely. The distributor rotor should be pointing to the matchmark made earlier.
9. Install the splash shield.
10. Install the distributor cap.
11. Fill the crankcase to the proper level.
12. Connect the negative battery cable. Start the engine and check for leaks. Check the ignition timing.

200SX—VG30 Engine

1. Disconnect the negative battery cable.
2. Remove the oil pan.

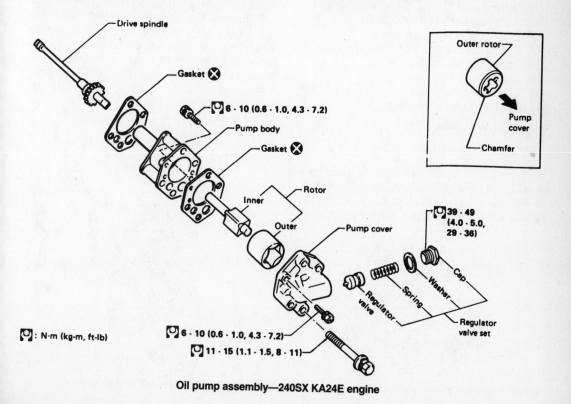

Oil pump assembly—240SX KA24E engine

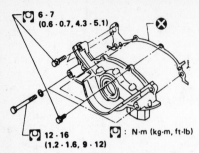

Oil pump installation—200SX VG30E engine

3. Remove the timing belt.

4. Remove the crankshaft timing sprocket using a suitable puller.

5. Remove the timing belt plate.

6. Remove the oil pump strainer and pick-up tube from the oil pump.

7. Remove the mounting bolts and remove the oil pump and gasket.

8. Replace the oil pump seal.

To install:

9. Before installing the oil pump, remove the front cover and pack the pump's cavity with petroleum jelly, then make sure the O-ring is fitted properly. Torque the front cover screws to 3–4 ft. lbs.

10. Mount the oil pump with a new gasket. Torque the 8mm retaining bolts to 16–22 ft. lbs. and the 6mm bolts to 5–6 ft. lbs.

11. Install the oil pump strainer and pick-up tube with a new O-ring. Torque the pick-up tube mounting bolts to 12–15 ft. lbs.

12. Install the timing belt plate.

13. Install the crankshaft timing sprocket.

14. Install the timing belt.

15. Install the oil pan.

16. Connect the negative battery cable. Start the engine and check for leaks.

Crankshaft Damper

REMOVAL AND INSTALLATION

To remove the crankshaft damper matchmark the crankshaft pulley to the damper. Remove the crankshaft pulley (outside) retaining bolts if so equipped. Remove the (cen-ter) crankshaft pulley to damper bolt, then use a puller tool to remove the pulley/damper from the crankshaft. When installing the damper and crankshaft pulley torque the center bolt to the correct specification.

Timing Chain Cover

REMOVAL AND INSTALLATION

200SX—Z Series Engine

NOTE: *It may be necessary to remove additional components to perform this operation if you cannot cut the gasket cleanly as described in Step 10. The CA20E, CA18ET and VG30E are belt driven engines.*

1. Disconnect the negative battery cable from the battery, drain the cooling system, and remove the radiator together with the upper and lower radiator hoses.

2. Loosen the alternator drive belt adjusting screw and remove the drive belt. Remove the bolts, which attach the alternator bracket to the engine and set the alternator aside out of the way.

3. Mark and remove the distributor.

4. Remove the oil pump attaching screws, and take out the pump and its drive spindle.

5. Remove the cooling fan and the fan pulley together with the drive belt.

6. Remove the water pump.

7. Remove the crankshaft pulley bolt and remove the crankshaft pulley.

8. Remove the bolts holding the front cover to the front of the cylinder block, the four bolts which retain the front of the oil pan to the bottom of the front cover, and the two bolts which are screwed down through the front of the cylinder head and into the top of the front cover.

9. Carefully pry the front cover off the front of the engine.

To install:

10. Cut the exposed front section of the oil

Removing crankshaft pulley with puller

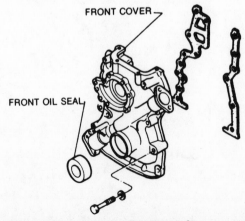

FRONT COVER

FRONT OIL SEAL

Timing chain front cover—Z series engine

pan gasket away from the oil pan. Do the same to the gasket at the top of the front cover. Remove the two side gaskets and clean all of the mating surfaces.

11. Cut the portions needed from a new oil pan gasket and top front cover gasket.

12. Apply sealer to all of the gaskets and position them on the engine in their proper places.

13. Apply a light coating of grease to the crankshaft oil seal and carefully mount the front cover to the front of the engine and install all of the mounting bolts. Tighten the 8mm bolts to 7-12 ft. lbs. and the 6mm bolts to 36-72 inch lbs. Tighten the oil pan attaching bolts to 48-84 inch lbs.

14. Before installing the oil pump, place the gasket over the shaft and make sure that the mark on the drive spindle faces (aligned) with the oil pump hole.

15. Install the oil pump after priming it with oil.

16. Install the crankshaft pulley and bolt.

17. Install the water pump with a new gasket. Install the fan pulley and cooling fan. Install the drive belt and adjust the belt to the correct tension.

18. Install the distributor in the correct position. Reconnect the alternator bracket and alternator if it was removed. Install the drive belt and adjust the belt to the correct tension.

19. Reconnect the upper and lower radiator hoses and refill the cooling system.

20. Reconnect the negative battery cable. Start the engine, check ignition timing and check for leaks.

240SX—KA24DE Engine

1. Remove the negative battery cable.
2. Drain the engine oil and coolant.
3. Remove the cylinder head assembly.
4. Raise and support the vehicle safely. Remove the oil pan, oil strainer and baffle plate.

5. Remove the crankshaft pulley using a suitable puller. Removal of the radiator may be necessary to gain clearance.

6. Support the engine and remove the front engine mount.

7. Loosen the front cover bolts in two or three steps and remove the front cover.

To install:

8. Clean all mating surfaces of liquid gasket material.

9. Apply a continious bead of liquid gasket to the mating surface of the timing cover. Install the oil pump drive spacer and front cover. Tighten front cover bolts (in even steps) to 5-6 ft. lbs. (6–8 Nm). Wipe excess liquid gasket material.

10. Install front engine mount.

11. Install crankshaft pulley and tighten bolt to specifications. Set No. 1 piston at TDC on the compression stroke.

12. Install the oil strainer and baffle. Install the oil pan.

13. Install the cylinder head assembly.

14. Lower the vehicle, connect the negative battery cable, refill fluid levels, start the engine and check for leaks. Road test the vehicle for proper operation.

240SX—KA24E Engine

1. Disconnect the negative battery cable.
2. Drain the cooling system and oil pan. To drain the cooling system, open the radiator drain cock and remove the engine block drain plug. The block plug is located on the left side of the block near the engine freeze plugs.
3. Remove the radiator shroud and the cooling fan.
4. Loosen the alternator drive belt adjusting screw and remove the drive belt.
5. Remove the power steering and air conditioning drive belts.
6. Remove the spark plugs and the distribu-

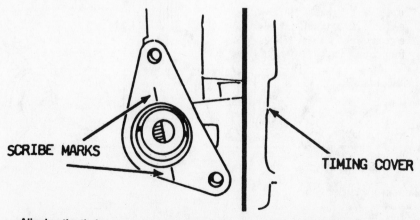

Aligning the timing cover and distributor/oil pump drive—240SX KA24E engine

tor cap. Set the No. 1 piston to TDC of the compression stroke. Carefully remove the the distributor. Before removal, scribe alignment marks in the timing cover and flat portion of the oil pump/distributor drive spindle. This alignment is critical and if not done properly, it could cause difficulty is aligning the distributor and setting the timing.

7. Remove the power steering pump, idler pulley and the power steering brackets.

8. Remove the air conditioning compressor idler pulley.

9. Remove the crankshaft pulley bolt and remove the crankshaft pulley with a 2- jawed puller.

10. Remove the oil pump attaching screws, and withdraw the pump and its drive spindle.

11. Remove the rocker arm cover.

12. Remove the oil pan.

13. Remove the bolts holding the front cover to the front of the cylinder block, the 4 bolts which retain the front of the oil pan to the bottom of the front cover, and the 4 bolts which are screwed down through the front of the cylinder head and into the top of the front cover. Carefully pry the front cover off the front of the engine. Clean all the old sealant from the surface of the front cover and the cylinder block.

14. Replace the crankshaft oil seal and the 2 timing chain cover oil seals in the block. These

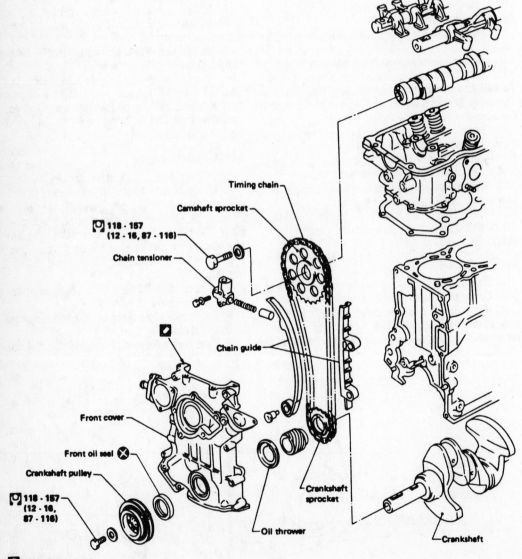

Timing chain cover—240SX KA24E engine

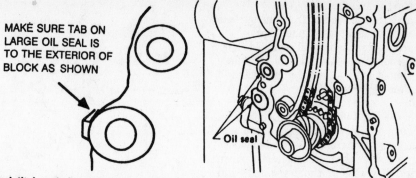

MAKE SURE TAB ON LARGE OIL SEAL IS TO THE EXTERIOR OF BLOCK AS SHOWN

Oil seal

Cylinder block timing chain cover seals—make sure tab on larger seal is positioned as shown—240SX KA24E engine

two seals should be installed in the block and not in the timing cover.

To install:

15. Verify the No. 1 piston is at TDC of the compression stroke. Apply a very thin bead of high temperature liquid gasket to both sides of the front cover and to where the cover mates with the cylinder head. Apply a light coating of grease to the crankshaft and timing cover oil seals and carefully bolt the front cover to the front of the engine.

NOTE: *When installing the front cover, be careful not to damage the cylinder head gasket or to disturb the position of the oil seals in the block. Make sure the tab on the larger block oil seal is pointing to the exterior of the block.*

16. Install new rubber plugs in the cylinder head.

17. Install the oil pan.

18. Install the rocker arm cover.

19. Before installing the oil pump, place the gasket over the shaft and make sure the mark on the drive spindle faces (aligned) with the oil pump hole. Install the oil pump and distributor driving spindle into the front cover with a new gasket.

20. Install the crankshaft pulley and bolt. Torque the pulley bolt to 87–116 ft. lbs. (118–157 Nm).

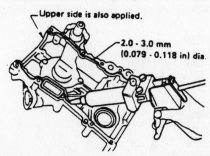

Upper side is also applied.

2.0 - 3.0 mm (0.079 - 0.118 in) dia.

Applying sealant to front cover—240SX KA24E engine

21. Install the distributor and the spark plugs.

22. Install the compressor idler pulley. Install power steering pump brackets, idler pulley and power steering pump. Install the drive belts and adjust the tension.

23. Install the radiator shroud and the cooling fan.

24. Refill the cooling system and crankcase to the proper levels.

25. Connect the negative battery cable.

26. Start the engine, check/set the ignition timing and check for engine leaks. Road test the vehicle for proper operation.

Stanza—KA24E Engine

1. Disconnect the negative battery cable.

2. Raise the front of the vehicle and support safely.

3. Remove the right front wheel.

4. Remove the dust cover and undercover.

5. Drain the oil pan.

6. Set the No. 1 piston at TDC of the compression stroke.

7. Remove the alternator and air conditioning compressor drive belts.

8. Remove the alternator and adjusting bar.

9. Remove the oil separator.

10. Remove the power steering pump pulley, pump stay and mounting bracket.

11. Discharge the air conditioning system and remove the compressor and mounting bracket.

12. Remove the crankshaft pulley and oil pump drive boss.

13. Remove the oil pan.

14. Remove the oil strainer mounting bolt.

15. Remove the bolts that attach the front cover to the head and the block.

16. Remove the rocker cover.

17. Support the engine with a suitable lifting device.

18. Unbolt the right side engine mount bracket from the block and lower the engine.

19. Remove the front cover.

20. Clean all the old sealant from the surface of the front cover and the cylinder block.

21. Replace the crankshaft oil seal and the 2 timing chain cover oil seals in the block. These two seals should be installed in the block and not in the timing cover.

To install:

22. Verify the No. 1 piston is at TDC. Apply a very thin bead of high temperature liquid gasket to both sides of the front cover and to where the cover mates with the cylinder head. Apply a light coating of grease to the crankshaft and timing cover oil seals and carefully mount the front cover to the front of the engine.

NOTE: *When installing the front cover, be careful not to damage the cylinder head gasket or to disturb the position of the oil seals in the block. Make sure the tab on the larger block oil seal is pointing to the exterior of the block.*

23. Install new rubber plugs in the cylinder head.

24. Raise the engine and install the right engine mount bracket bolts. Torque the bolts to 58–65 ft. lbs. (78–88 Nm).

25. Install the rocker arm cover.

26. Install the front cover bolts.

27. Install the oil strainer mounting bolt.

28. Install the oil pan.

29. Install the oil pump drive boss and the crankshaft pulley. Torque the pulley bolt to 87–116 ft. lbs. (118–157 Nm).

30. Install the air conditioning compressor bracket and mount the compressor.

31. Install the power steering bracket, pump stay and power steering pump.

32. Install the oil separator.

33. Install the dust cover and undercover.

34. Mount the right front wheel and lower the vehicle.

35. Fill the crankcase to the proper level and charge the air conditioning system.

36. Make all the necessary engine adjustments.

Front Cover Oil Seal

REPLACEMENT

1. Disconnect the negative battery cable.

2. Remove the crankshaft pulley.

3. Using a suitable tool, pry the oil seal from the front cover.

NOTE: *When removing the oil seal, be careful not the gouge or scratch the seal bore or crankshaft surfaces.*

4. Wipe the seal bore with a clean rag.

5. Lubricate the lip of the new seal with clean engine oil.

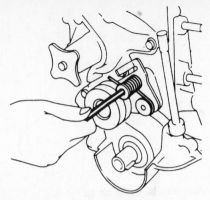

Timing chain front cover oil seal installation

6. Install the seal into the front cover with a suitable seal installer.

7. Install the crankshaft pulley.

8. Connect the negative battery cable.

Timing Chain, Gears and Tensioner

REMOVAL AND INSTALLATION

200SX—Z Series

1. Before beginning any disassembly procedures, position the No. 1 piston at TDC on the compression stroke.

2. Remove the front cover as previously outlined. Remove the camshaft cover and remove the fuel pump if it runs off a cam lobe in front of the camshaft sprocket.

3. With the No. 1 piston at TDC, the timing marks in the camshaft sprocket and the timing chain should be visible. Mark both of them with paint. Also mark the relationship of the camshaft sprocket to the camshaft. At this point you will notice that there are three sets of timing marks and locating holes in the sprocket. They are for making adjustments to compensate for timing chain stretch.

4. With the timing marks on the cam sprocket clearly marked, locate and mark the timing marks on the crankshaft sprocket. Also mark the chain timing mark. Of course, if the chain is not to be re-used, marking it is useless.

5. Unbolt the camshaft sprocket and remove the sprocket along with the chain. As you re-

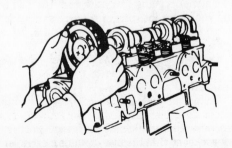

Removing the camshaft sprocket

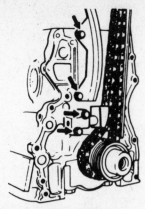

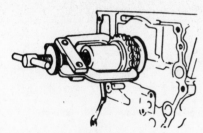

Tensioner and chain guide removal

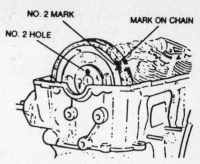

Use the No. 2 mark and hole to align camshaft—Z series engine

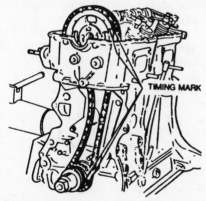

Crankshaft sprocket removal

Timing chain and sprocket alignment—Z series engine

move the chain, hold it where the chain tensioner contacts it. When the chain is removed, the tensioner is going to come apart. Hold on to it and you won't lose any of the parts. There is no need to remove the chain guide unless it is being replaced.

6. Using a two-armed gear puller, remove the crankshaft sprocket assembly.

To install:

7. Install the timing chain and the camshaft sprocket together after first positioning the chain over the crankshaft sprocket. Position the sprocket so that the marks made earlier line up. This is assuming that the engine has not

been disturbed. The camshaft and crankshaft keys should both be pointed upward. If a new chain and/or gear is being installed, position the sprocket so that the timing marks on the chain align with the marks on the crankshaft sprocket and the camshaft sprocket (with both keys pointing up). The marks are on the right hand side of the sprockets as you face the engine. The L18 has 42 pins between the mating marks of the chain and sprockets when the chain is installed correctly. The L20B has 44 pins. The 1977-78 L24 engine used in the 810 has 42 pins between timing marks. The L24 (1979-84), Z20E and Z20S engines do not use the pin counting method for finding correct valve timing. Instead, position the key in the crankshaft sprocket so that it is pointing upward and install the camshaft sprocket on the camshaft with its dowel pin at the top using the No. 2 (No. 1 on the L24) mounting hole and timing mark. The painted links of the chain should be on the right hand side of the sprockets as you face the engine.

NOTE: *Count the pins. There are two pins per link. This is an important step. If you do not get the exact number of pins between the timing marks, valve timing will be incorrect and the engine will either not run at all, in which case you stand the chance of bending the valves, or the engine will run very poorly.*

8. Install the chain tensioner and the front cover assembly.

If timing chain assembly uses chain guides, the guides do not have to be removed to replace the timing chain. Check the timing chain for cracks and excessive wear.

TIMING CHAIN ADJUSTMENT

When the timing chain stretches excessively, the valve timing will be adversely affected. There are three sets of holes and timing marks on the camshaft sprocket.

If the stretch of the chain roller links is excessive, adjust the camshaft sprocket location by transferring the set position of the camshaft sprocket from the factory position of No. 1 or No. 2 to one of the other positions as follows:

1. Turn the crankshaft until the No. 1 piston is at TDC on the compression stroke. Examine whether the camshaft sprocket location notch is to the left of the oblong groove on the camshaft retaining plate. If the notch in the sprocket is to the left of the groove in the retaining plate, then the chain is stretched and needs adjusting.

2. Remove the camshaft sprocket together with the chain and reinstall the sprocket and chain with the locating dowel on the camshaft inserted into either the No. 2 or 3 hole of the sprocket. The timing mark on the timing chain must be aligned with the mark on the sprocket. The amount of modification is 4° of crankshaft rotation for each mark.

3. Recheck the valve timing as outlined in Step 1. The notch in the sprocket should be to the right of the groove in the camshaft retaining plate.

4. If and when the notch cannot be brought to the right of the groove, the timing chain is worn beyond repair and must be replaced.

240SX and 1990-92 Stanza—KA24E Engine

1. Disconnect the negative battery cable.
2. Set the No. 1 piston at TDC of the compression stroke.
3. Remove the front cover.
4. If necessary, define the timing marks with chalk or paint to ensure proper alignment.
5. Hold the camshaft sprocket stationary with an open-end wrench or similar tool and remove the camshaft sprocket bolt.
6. Remove chain tensioner.
7. Remove the chain guides.
8. Remove the timing chain.

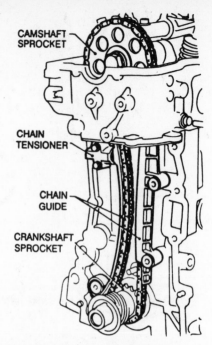

Timing chain assembly—KA24E engine

9. Remove the sprocket oil slinger, oil pump drive gear and crankshaft gear.

To install:

10. Install the crankshaft sprocket, oil pump drive gear and oil slinger onto the end of the crankshaft. Make sure the crankshaft sprocket timing marks face toward the front.

11. Install the camshaft sprocket, bolt and washer. The alignment mark must face towards the front. Tighten the bolt just enough to hold the sprocket in place.

12. Verify that the No. 1 piston is at TDC of

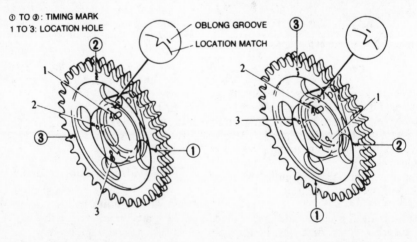

Timing chain adjustment

the compression stroke. The crankshaft keyways should be at the 12 o'clock position.

13. Install the timing chain by aligning the marks on the chain with the marks on the crankshaft and camshaft sprockets. Torque the camshaft sprocket bolt to 87–116 ft. lbs. (118–157 Nm) once the timing chain is in place and aligned.

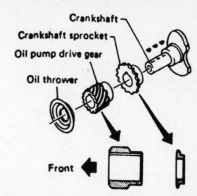

Correct installation of crankshaft sprocket, oil pump, drive gear, oil thrower—KA24E engine

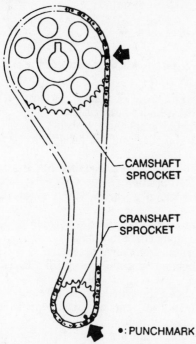

CAMSHAFT SPROCKET

CRANSHAFT SPROCKET

●: PUNCHMARK

Timing chain and sprocket alignment—KA24E engine

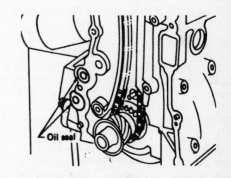

Oil seals in left side of engine block—KA24E engine

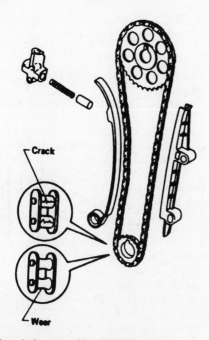

Crack

Wear

Timing chain assembly—KA24E engine

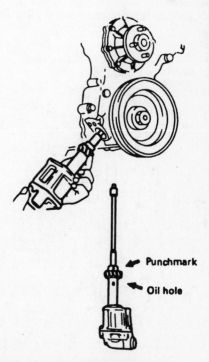

Punchmark

Oil hole

Installing oil pump—240SX KA24E engine

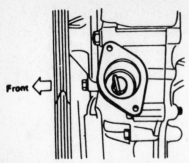

Drive spindle for oil pump in correct location—240SX KA24E engine

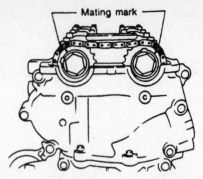

Timing chain installation—240SX KA24DE engine

14. Install the chain tensioner and chain guide.
15. Install the front cover.
16. Connect the negative battery cable.

240SX—KA24DE Engine

1. Release the fuel system pressure.
2. Disconnect the negative battery cable and drain the cooling system. Drain engine oil.
3. Remove the cylinder head assembly.
4. Remove the oil pan.
5. Remove the oil strainer, crankshaft pulley.
6. Remove the front cover assembly.
7. Remove the lower timing chain tensioner, tension arm, lower timing chain guide.
8. Remove the lower timing chain and idler sprocket.
To install:
9. Check all components for wear. Replace as

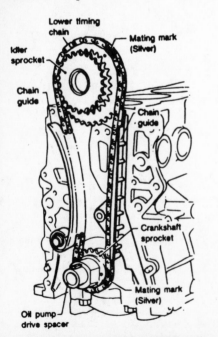

Timing chain installation—240SX KA24DE engine

necessary. Clean all mating surfaces and replace the cylinder head gasket.
10. Install crankshaft sprocket. Make sure that mating marks of crankshaft sprocket face front of the engine.
11. Rotate crankshaft so that No. 1 piston is set a TDC position.
12. Install idler sprocket and lower timing chain.
13. Install chain tension arm, chain guide and lower timing chain tensioner.
14. Install front cover assembly.
15. Install crankshaft pulley, oil strainer and oil pan.
16. Install the cylinder head assembly.
17. Install all remaining components in reverse order of removal.
18. Connect the negative battery cable. Refill all fluid levels. Road test the vehicle for proper operation.

Timing Belt/Cover
REMOVAL AND INSTALLATION
200SX—CA Series Engines

1. Remove the battery ground cable. Release the fuel pressure.
2. On the CA20E engine, remove the air intake ducts.
3. Remove the cooling fan.
4. Remove the power steering, alternator, and air conditioner compressor belts if so equipped.
5. Set the No. 1 cylinder at TDC on the compression stroke.
6. Remove the front upper and lower timing belt covers.
7. Loosen the timing belt tensioner and return spring, then remove the timing belt.
To install:
8. Carefully inspect the condition of the timing belt. There should be no breaks or cracks anywhere on the belt. Especially check around the bottoms of the teeth, where they intersect the belt; cracks often show up here. Evidence of

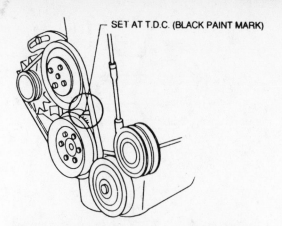

SET AT T.D.C. (BLACK PAINT MARK)

Timing marks for finding TDC—CA series engines

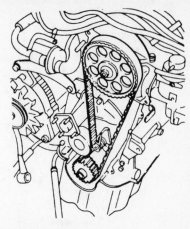

Timing belt with covers removed

any wear or damage on the belt means the belt should be replaced.

9. To install the belt, first make sure that No. 1 cylinder is set at TDC on compression. Install the belt tensioner and return spring.

NOTE: *If the coarse stud has been removed, apply Loctite® or another locking thread sealer to the stud threads before installing.*

10. Make sure the tensioner bolts are not se-

curely tightened before the drive belt is installed. Make sure the tensioner pulley can be rotated smoothly.

11. Make sure the timing belt is in good condition and clean. Do not bend it. Place the belt in position, aligning the white lines on the timing belt with the punch mark on the camshaft pulleys and the crankshaft pulley. Make sure the

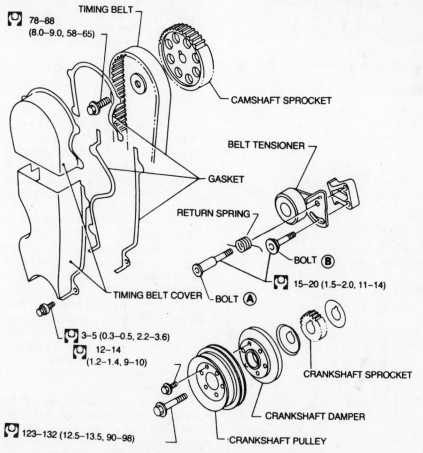

78–88
(8.0–9.0, 58–65)

TIMING BELT

CAMSHAFT SPROCKET

BELT TENSIONER

GASKET

RETURN SPRING

BOLT **B**

15–20 (1.5–2.0, 11–14)

TIMING BELT COVER   BOLT **A**

3–5 (0.3–0.5, 2.2–3.6)

12–14
(1.2–1.4, 9–10)

CRANKSHAFT SPROCKET

CRANKSHAFT DAMPER

123–132 (12.5–13.5, 90–98)

CRANKSHAFT PULLEY

Timing belt assembly—CA series engines

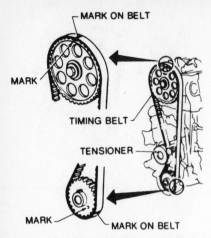

Timing belt installation—CA series engines

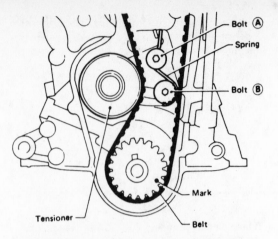

Set the tensioner spring by first hooking one end to the side of bolt "B" then the other of the tensioner pawl bracket

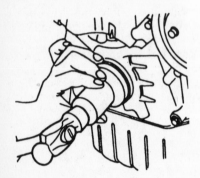

Installing the belt tensioner and return spring

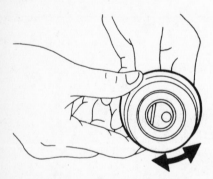

Spin the tensioner pulley to make sure it works smoothly

arrow on the belt is pointing toward the front belt covers.

12. Tighten the belt tensioner and assemble the spring. To set the spring, first hook one end on bolt B side, then hook the other end on the tensioner bracket pawl. Rotate the crankshaft two turns clockwise, then tighten bolt B then bolt A. At this point, belt tension will automatically be at the specified value.

13. Install the upper and lower timing belt covers.

14. Install and adjust all the drive belts.

15. Install the cooling fan and reconnect the air intake ducts on the CA20E engine.

16. Connect the battery cable, start engine and check the ignition timing.

200SX—VG30E Engine-1987

NOTE: *After removing timing belt, do not rotate the crankshaft or camshaft separately, because valves will hit piston heads. Review the complete procedure before starting this repair.*

Timing belt replacement interval is 60,000 miles--this interval is recommended by Nissan for reliable vehicle operation.

1. Raise vehicle and safely support.

2. Remove the engine under covers and drain engine coolant from the radiator. Be careful not to allow coolant to contact drive belts.

3. Remove the front right side wheel and tire assembly. Remove the engine side cover.

4. Remove the engine coolant reservoir tank and radiator hoses.

5. Remove the A.S.C.D. (speed control device) actuator.

6. Remove all the drive belts from the engine. When removing the power steering drive belt, loosen the idler pulley from the right side wheel housing.

7. Remove the idler bracket of the compressor drive belt and crankshaft pulley.

8. Remove the timing belt covers. Rotate the engine with a socket wrench on the crankshaft pulley bolt to align the two sets of timing marks. The marks are on the camshaft pulleys and rear belt covers.

9. Remove the rocker covers. Loosen the rocker shaft securing bolts so that rockers will no longer bear on the cam lobes. Remove all spark plugs.

10. Use a hexagon wrench to turn the belt

tensioner clockwise and tighten the tensioner locknut just enough to hold the tensioner in position. This is done to remove tension. Then remove the old belt.

NOTE: *Be careful not to bend the new belt in-*

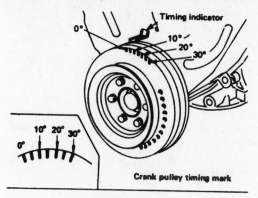

Crank pulley timing mark

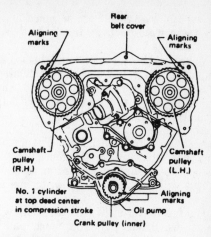

Timing marks—200SX VG30E engine

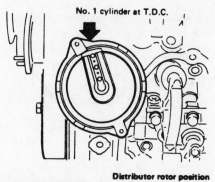

Distributor rotor position

Set No. 1 cylinder at TDC on compression stroke—200SX VG30E engine

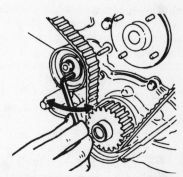

Set tensioner after timing belt installation—1987 200SX VG30E engine

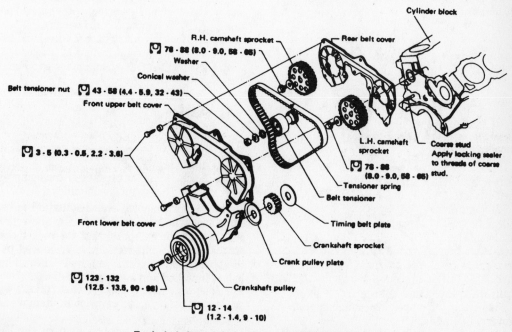

Exploded view of timing belt—200SX VG30E engine

stalling it. Timing belts are designed to flex only the way they turn around the pulleys.

To install:

11. Make sure that all pulleys and the belt are free of oil and water. Install the new belt, aligning the arrow on the timing belt forward. Align the white lines on the timing belt with the punchmarks on all three pulleys.

12. Loosen the tensioner locknut to allow spring tension to tension the belt. Then, using the hexagon wrench, turn the tensioner first clockwise, then counterclockwise in three cycles. This will seat the belt. Now, torque the tensioner locknut to 32-43 ft. lbs.

13. Tighten rocker shaft bolts alternately in three stages. Before tightening each pair of bolts, turn the engine over so the affected rocker will not touch its cam lobe. Final torque is 13-16 ft. lbs. Install the rocker covers with new gaskets.

14. Install lower and upper timing belt covers.

15. Install crankshaft pulley and idler bracket of the compressor drive belt. Tighten the crankshaft pulley bolt to 90-98 ft. lbs.

16. Install the drive belts. Clean and regap the spark plugs if necessary then install in the cylinder head.

17. Install the coolant reservoir tank, radiator hoses, A.S.C.D. actutator.

18. Install the right front wheel. Install engine under cover and side covers.

19. Refill the cooling system. Check ignition timing and roadtest for proper operation.

200SX–VG30E Engine-1988

Timing belt replacement is recommended at 60,000 miles.

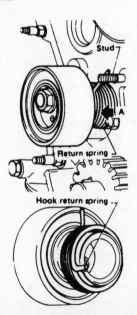

Tensioner assembly—200SX VG30E engine

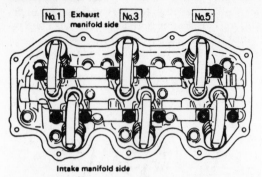

R.H. rocker shafts

Bolt location right side rocker shaft—200SX VG30E engine

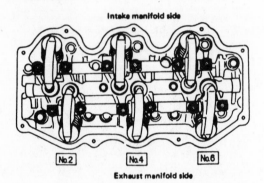

L.H. rocker shafts

Bolt location left side rocker shaft—200SX VG30E engine

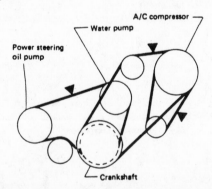

Installing drive belts in correct position—200SX VG30E engine

Timing belt removal and installation is the same as on the 1987 model. Use the above procedure with the exception that the rocker covers and rocker shafts bolts are not removed, but the spark plugs are still removed. The timing belt is installed and adjusted as follows:

1. Confirm No. 1 cylinder is at T.D.C. on its compression stroke. Install tensioner and tensioner spring. If stud is removed apply locking sealant to threads before installing.

2. Swing tensioner fully clockwise with hexagon wrench and temporarily tighten locknut.

3. Set timing belt, align the arrow on the timing belt forward. Align the white lines on the timing belt with the punchmarks on all three pulleys.

NOTE: *There are 133 total timing belt teeth. If timing belt is installed correctly there will be 40 teeth between lefthand and righthand camshaft sprocket timing marks. There will be 43 teeth between the lefthand camshaft*

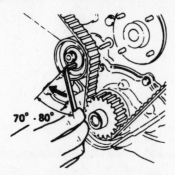

Set tensioner after timing belt installation—1988 200SX VG30E engine

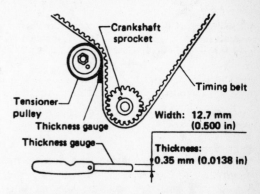

Set thickness gauge first at this location

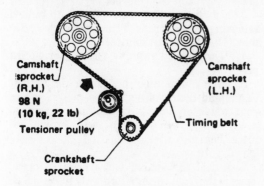

Apply force at marked position then loosen tensioner

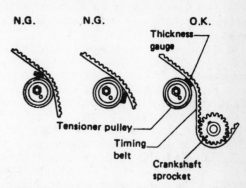

Thickness gauge in correct position for proper adjustment

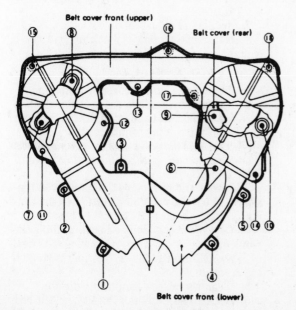

Timing belt cover bolt locations—200SX VG30E engine

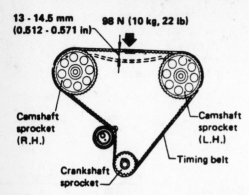

Check timing belt deflection—1988 200SX VG30E engine

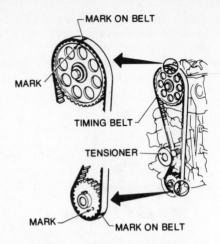

Timing mark alignment—Stanza CA20 engine

sprocket and the crankshaft sprocket timing marks.

4. Loosen tensioner locknut, keeping tensioner steady with a hexagon wrench.

5. Swing tensioner 70-80° clockwise with hexagon wrench and temporarily tighten locknut.

6. Install all the spark plugs. Turn crankshaft clockwise 2 or 3 times, then slowly set No. 1 cylinder at T.D.C. on its compression stroke.

7. Push middle of timing belt between righthand camshaft sprocket and tensioner pulley with a force of 22 ft. lbs.

8. Loosen tensioner locknut, keeping tensioner steady with a hexagon wrench.

9. Using a feeler gauge or equivalent as shown in the illustration which is 0.35mm thick and 13mm wide, set gauge at the bottom of tensioner pulley and timing belt. Turn crankshaft clockwise and position gauge completely between tensioner pulley and timing belt. The timing belt will move about 2.5 teeth.

10. Tighten tensioner locknut, keeping tensioner steady with a hexagon wrench.

11. Turn crankshaft clockwise or counterclockwise and remove the gauge.

12. Rotate the engine 3 times, then set No. 1 at T.D.C. on its compression stroke.

13. Check timing belt deflection on 1988 model year only. Timing belt deflection is 13.0-14.5mm at 22 lbs. of pressure. If it is out of specified range, readjust the timing belt.

Stanza—CA Series Engine

NOTE: *For additional information, refer to 200SX (C Series Engine) service procedures and illustrations.*

FRONT COVER

1. Disconnect the battery cables. Remove the upper and lower alternator securing bolts until the alternator can be moved enough to remove the drive belt from the pulley.

2. Loosen the idler pulley locknut and turn the adjusting bolt until the air conditioner compressor belt can be removed.

3. Unbolt and remove the crankshaft pulley, removing the alternator belt along with it. Remove the crankshaft damper.

4. Unbolt and remove the water pump pulley.

5. Remove the upper and lower timing belt covers and their gaskets. If the gaskets are in good condition after removal, they can be reused; if they are in way damaged or broken, replace them.

To install:

6. Install the timing belt covers in place. Torque the front cover bolts evenly to 2.2-3.6 ft. lbs.; torque the crank pulley damper bolt to 90-98 ft. lbs.; torque the crank pulley bolt to 9-10 ft. lbs.; torque the water pump pulley bolts to 4.3-7 ft. lbs.

7. Install and adjust all drive belts.

8. Connect the battery cables and start engine.

TIMING BELT/CRANKSHAFT OIL SEAL

1. Remove the timing cover assembly.

2. If necessary, remove the spark plug, then turn the crankshaft to position the No. 1 piston at TDC of the compression stroke.

NOTE: *Note the position of the timing marks on the camshaft sprocket, the timing belt and the crankshaft sprocket.*

3. Loosen and/or remove the timing belt tensioner. Mark the rotation direction of the timing belt, then remove it from the sprockets.

4. To remove the front oil seal, pull off the crankshaft sprocket, then pry out the oil seal with a small pry bar (be careful not to scratch the crankshaft).

5. Clean the oil seal mounting surface.

6. Install a new oil seal, the timing belt and tensioner. Torque the tensioner pulley bolts to

13-16 ft. lbs., the timing cover bolts to 2.5-4 ft. lbs., the crankshaft pulley bolt to 90-98 ft. lbs.

7. Install the timing belt covers.

8. Start engine and check timing. Road test the vehicle.

Camshaft Sprocket
REMOVAL AND INSTALLATION

1. Remove the timing chain/belt.

2. Remove the sprocket retaining bolt and remove the sprocket from the camshaft. On engines with a timing chain the chain and sprocket are removed at the same time.

3. To install reverse the removal procedures. On V6 engines the right hand and left hand camshaft sprockets are different parts. Install them in the correct location. The right hand sprocket has an R3 identification and the left hand pulley has L3 identification.

NOTE: *On the belt driven engines make sure to install the crank pulley plate in the correct position. On chain driven engines make sure oil thrower, oil pump drive gear are installed in the correct position.*

Camshaft and Bearings

NOTE: *Since these engines do not use replaceable camshaft bearings, overhaul is performed by replacement of the camshaft or the cylinder head. Check the camshaft bearing surfaces (in the cylinder head) with an internal micrometer and the bearing surfaces (of the camshaft) with a micrometer.*

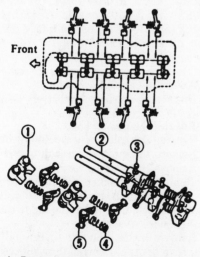

1. Rocker bracket
2. Rocker shaft
3. Bolt
4. Spring
5. Rocker arm

Rocker shaft assembly—Z series engine

REMOVAL AND INSTALLATION
200SX—Z Series Engine

NOTE: *Removal of the cylinder head from the engine is optional. Mark and keep all parts in order for correct installation.*

1. Remove the camshaft sprocket from the camshaft together with the timing chain, after setting the No. 1 piston at TDC on its compression stroke.

2. Loosen the bolts holding the rocker shaft assembly in place and remove the six center bolts. Do not pull the four end bolts out of the rocker assembly because they hold the unit together.

NOTE: *When loosening the bolts, work from the ends in and loosen all of the bolts a little at a time so that you do not strain the camshaft or the rocker assembly.*

3. After removing the rocker assembly, remove the camshaft. Slide the camshaft carefully out of the front of the vehicle.

NOTE: *Mark and keep the disassembled parts in order.*

If you disassembled the rocker unit, assemble as follows.

4. Install the mounting brackets, valve rockers and springs observing the following considerations:

a. The two rocker shafts are different. Both have punch marks in the ends that face the front of the engine. The rocker shaft that

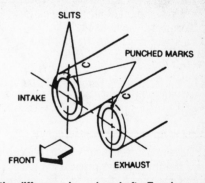

Note the difference in rocker shaft—Z series engine

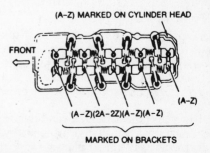

Rocker shaft mounting brackets are assembled in this order—Z series engine

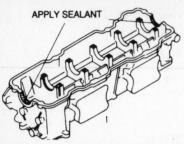

APPLY SEALANT

Apply sealant to these points on the cylinder head just before installing the camshaft—Z series engine

goes on the side of the intake manifold has two slits in its end just below the punch mark. The exhaust side rocker shaft does not have slits.

b. The rocker arms for the intake and exhaust valves are interchangeable between cylinders one and three and are identified by the mark 1. Similarly, the rockers for cylinders two and four are interchangeable and are identified by the mark 2.

c. The rocker shaft mounting brackets are also coded for correct placement with either an A or a Z plus a number code.

5. Check camshaft runout, endplay wear and journal clearance.

To install:

6. Apply sealant to the end camshaft saddles. Place the camshaft on the head with its dowel pin pointing up.

7. Fit the rocker assembly on the head, making sure you mount it on its knock pin.

8. Torque the bolts to 11-18 ft. lbs., in several stages working from the middle bolts and moving outwards on both sides.

NOTE: *Make sure the engine is on TDC of the compression stroke for No. 1 piston or you may damage some valves.*

9. Adjust the valves.

200SX and Stanza—CA Series Engine

1. Disconnect the negative battery cable and relieve the fuel system pressure if necessary.

2. Set the No. 1 piston to TDC of the compression stroke.

3. Remove the timing belt.

4. Remove the valve rocker cover.

5. Fully loosen all rocker arm adjusting screws (the valve adjusting screws). Loosen the rocker shaft mounting bolts in 2-3 stages and then remove the rocker shafts as an assembly. Keep all components in the correct order for reassembly.

6. Hold the camshaft pulley and remove the pulley mounting bolt. Remove the pulley. Remove the camshaft thrust plate.

7. Carefully pry the camshaft oil seal out of the front of the cylinder head.

8. Slide the camshaft out the front of the cylinder head, taking extreme care not to score any of the journals.

To install:

9. Coat the camshaft with clean engine oil.

10. Carefully slide the camshaft into the cylinder head, coat the end with oil and install a new oil seal. Install the camshaft thrust plate and wedge the camshaft with a small wooden block inserted between one of the cams and the cylinder head. Torque the thrust plate bolt to 58-65 ft. lbs. (78-88 Nm). Remove the wooden block.

11. Lubricate the rocker shafts lightly with clean engine oil and install them, with the rocker arms, into the head. Both shafts have punch marks on their leading edges, while the intake shaft is also marked with 2 slits on its leading edge.

NOTE: *To prevent the rocker shaft springs from slipping out of the shaft, insert the bracket bolts into the shaft prior to installation.*

12. Tighten the rocker shaft bolts gradually, in 2-3 stages (from the center of the shaft to the end of the shaft assembly) to 13-16 ft. lbs. (18-22 Nm).

13. Install the camshaft pulley and then install the timing belt.

14. Adjust the valves as required and install the cylinder head cover.

15. Connect the negative battery cable.

200SX—VG30E Engine

NOTE: *On the 1987 200SX with VG30E engine, Nissan recommends that the engine assembly be removed from the vehicle, then the cylinder heads disassembled. On the 1988 200SX with VG30E engine, Nissan recommends that the the cylinder heads be removed from the engine, with the engine mounted in the vehicle, and then remove the camshafts. This procedure is for removing the camshafts with the engine in the vehicle.*

1. Disconnect the negative battery cable.

2. Drain the cooling system.

3. Remove the timing belt.

4. Remove the collector assembly.

5. Remove the intake manifold.

6. Remove the cylinder head.

7. Remove the rocker shafts with rocker arms. Bolts should be loosened in several steps in the proper sequence (from the end to the center of the shaft assembly).

8. Remove hydraulic valve lifters and lifter guide. Hold hydraulic valve lifters with wire so they will not drop from lifter guide.

9. Using a dial gauge, measure the camshaft endplay. If the camshaft endplay exceeds the limit — 0.0012-0.0024 in. (0.030-0.060mm),

select the thickness of a cam locate plate so the endplay is within specification. For example, if camshaft end play measures 0.0031 in. (0.08mm) with shim 2 used, then change shim 2 to shim 3 so the camshaft end play is 0.0020 in. (0.05mm).

10. Remove the camshaft front oil seal and slide camshaft out the front of the cylinder head assembly.

To install:

11. Install camshaft, locater plates, cylinder head rear cover and front oil seal. Set camshaft knock pin at 12 o'clock position. Install cylinder head with new gasket to engine.

12. Install valve lifter guide assembly. Assemble valve lifters in their original position. After installing them in the correct location remove the wire holding them in lifter guide.

13. Install rocker shafts in correct position (see illustration) with rocker arms. Tighten bolts in 2–3 stages (from the center to the end of the shaft assembly) to 13–16 ft. lbs. (18–22 Nm). Before tightening, be sure to set camshaft lobe at the position where lobe is not lifted or the valve closed. Set each cylinder 1 at a time or follow the procedure below. The cylinder head, intake manifold, collector and timing belt must be installed:

a. Set No. 1 piston at TDC of the compression stroke and tighten rocker shaft bolts for No. 2, No. 4 and No. 6 cylinders.

b. Set No. 4 piston at TDC of the compression stroke and tighten rocker shaft bolts for No. 1, No. 3 and No. 5 cylinders.

c. Torque specification for the rocker shaft retaining bolts is 13–16 ft. lbs. (18–22 Nm).

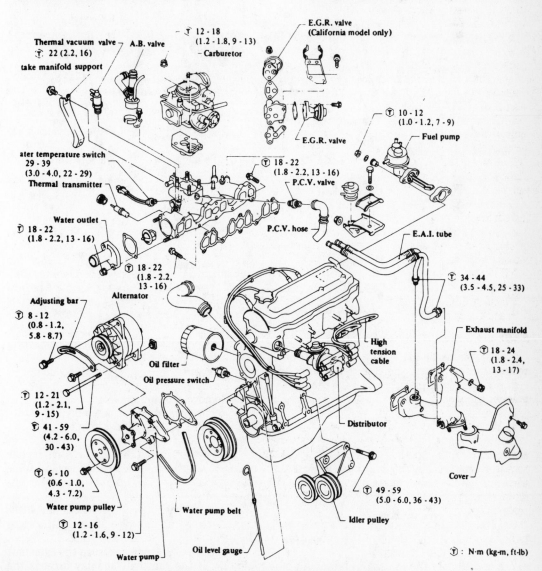

Engine outer components—Stanza CA20 engine

14. Fill the cooling system to the proper level.
15. Connect the negative battery cable.

240SX and 1990-92 Stanza—KA24E Engine

1. Disconnect the negative battery cable.
2. Remove the timing chain.
3. Remove the cylinder head. Do not remove the camshaft sprocket at this time.

4. Loosen the rocker shaft bolt evenly in proper sequence. Start from the outside and work toward the center.

5. Mount a dial indicator to the cylinder head and set the stylus of the indicator on the head of the camshaft sprocket bolt. Zero the indicator and measure the camshaft endplay by moving the camshaft back and forth. Endplay should be

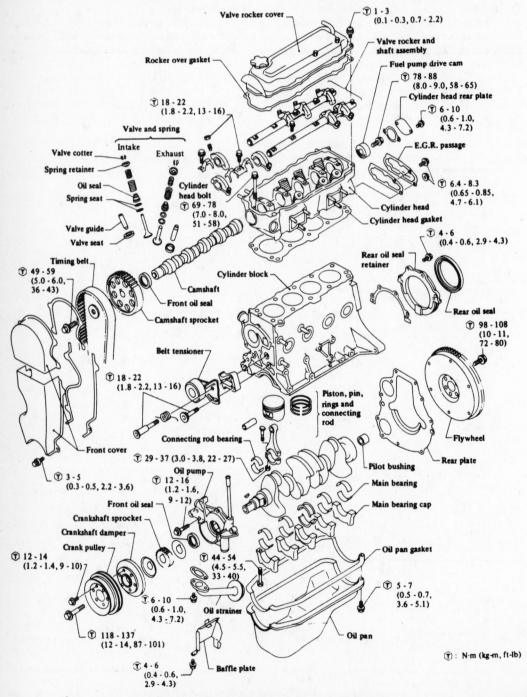

Engine internal components—Stanza CA20 engine

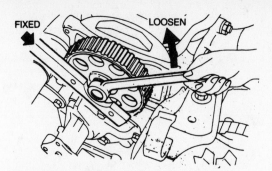

FIXED

LOOSEN

Use a sprocket holding tool when loosening the cam sprocket—CA series engine

within 0.0028–0.0059 in. (0.07–0.15mm).

6. Remove the camshaft brackets and lift the camshaft with sprocket from the cylinder head.

To install:

7. Clean all cylinder head, intake and exhaust manifold gasket surfaces. Lubricate the camshaft and rocker arm/shaft assemblies with a liberal coating of clean engine oil. Lay the camshaft and sprocket into the cylinder head so the knock pin is at the front of the head at the 12 o'clock postion. Install the camshaft brackets. The camshaft bracket directional arrows must face the toward the front of the engine.

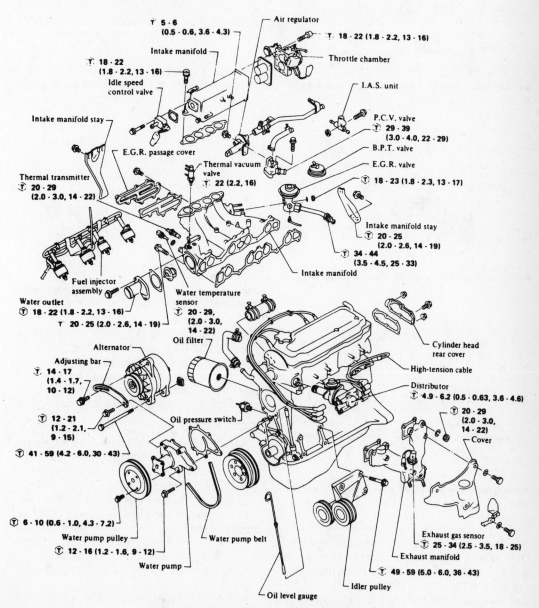

Engine outer components—Stanza CA20E engine

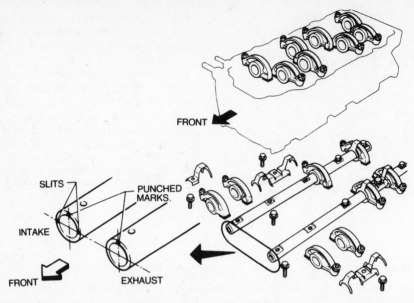

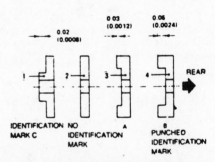

Note location marks on the end of the shafts, slits on the intake shaft—rocker shaft assembly CA series engine

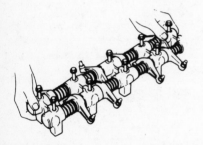

Rocker shaft assembly removed—CA series engine

Select shim thickness so that camshaft thickness is within specifications—200SX VG30E engine

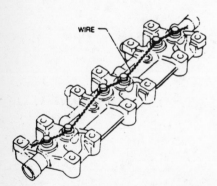

Holding the valve lifters in place—200SX VG30E engine

8. Install the rocker shaft and rocker arms. Both intake and exhaust rocker shafts are stamped with an **F** mark. This mark must face the front of the engine during installation. Install the rocker arm bolts and spring clips so the cut outs are facing as shown. Torque the rocker arm bolts (in several stages) in the proper sequence to 27–30 ft. lbs. (37–41 Nm).

9. Install the timing chain.

10. Install the cylinder head. Use new rubber plugs when installing the cylinder head.

11. Connect the negative battery cable.

240SX—KA24DE Engine

NOTE: *Modify service steps as necessary. This is a complete disassembly repair procedure. Review the complete procedure before starting this repair.*

1. Release the fuel system pressure.

2. Disconnect the negative battery cable and drain the cooling system. Drain the engine oil.

3. Remove all vacuum hoses, fuel lines, wires, electrical connections as necessary.

4. Remove the front exhaust pipe and A.I.V. pipe.

5. Remove the air duct, cooling fan with coupling and radiator shroud.

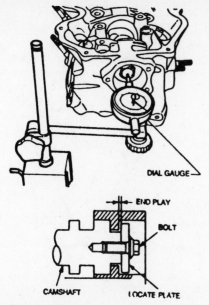

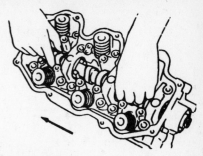

Remove the camshaft in the direction of the arrow—200SX VG30E engine

Using a dial indicator to measure camshaft end-play—200SX VG30E engine

6. Remove the the fuel injector tube assembly with injectors.

7. Disconnect and mark spark plug wires. Remove the spark plugs.

8. Set No. 1 piston at TDC on compression stroke. Remove the rocker cover assembly.

9. Mark and remove the distributor assembly.

10. Remove the cam sprocket, brackets and camshafts. These parts should be reassembled in their original position. Bolts should be loosened in 2 or 3 steps (loosen all bolts in the reverse of the tightening order).

To install:

11. Install camshafts and camshafts brackets. Torque camshaft brackets in two or three steps in sequence. After completing assembly check valve clearance.

12. Install camshaft sprockets.

13. Install chain guide between both camshaft sprockets and distributor assembly.

14. Install all remaining components in reverse order of removal.

15. Connect the negative battery cable. Refill all fluid levels. Road test the vehicle for proper operation.

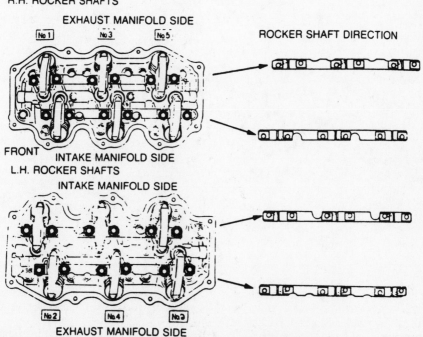

Rocker shaft/arm installation—200SX VG30E engine

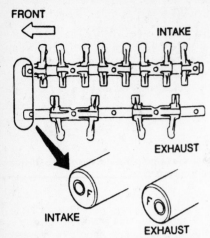

Rocker arm shaft positioning—KA24E engine

CHECKING CAMSHAFT RUNOUT

Camshaft runout should be checked when the camshaft has been removed from the cylinder head. An accurate dial indicator is needed for this procedure; engine specialists and most

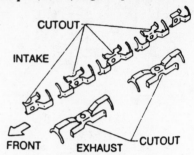

Spring clip installation—KA24E engine

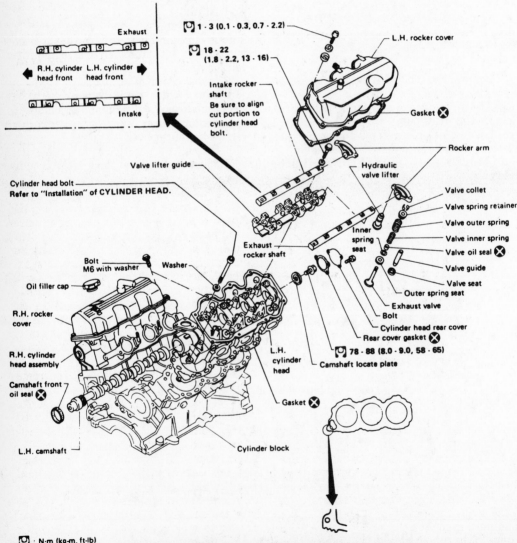

: N·m (kg-m, ft-lb)

Exploded view cylinder head assembly—200SX VG30E engine

Rocker shaft bolt LOOSENING sequence—KA24E engine. TIGHTEN IN REVERSE OF THE LOOSENING SEQUENCE

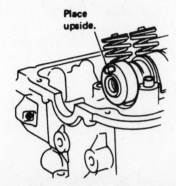

Knock pin

Place upside.

Install camshaft in correct position—KA24E engine

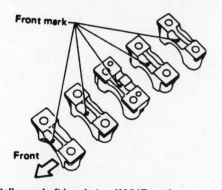

Front mark

Front

Install camshaft brackets—KA24E engine

machine shops have this equipment. If you have access to a dial indicator, or can take your cam to someone who does, measure cam bearing journal runout. The maximum (limit) runout on the CA20E, CA18ET and KA24E camshafts is 0.02mm. The runout limit on the Z20 and Z22 series camshafts is 0.20mm. The maximum (limit) runout on the VG30E camshaft is 0.01mm. If the runout exceeds the limit replace the camshaft.

CHECKING CAMSHAFT LOBE HEIGHT

Use a micrometer to check cam (lobe) height, making sure the anvil and the spindle of the micrometer are positioned directly on the heel and tip of the cam lobe. Use the specifications in the chart to determine the lobe wear.

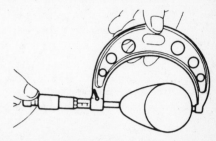

Use a micrometer to check camshaft cam lobe height

Engine Series	Lobe	Lobe Height (in.)	Wear Limit (in.)
Z20, Z22	Int. and Exh.	1.5148 to 1.5168	0.0098
CA18ET	Intake	1.5055 to 1.5075	0.008
	Exhaust	1.5289 to 1.5309	
CA20E	Int. and Exh.	1.5289 to 1.5309	0.008
KA24E	Int. and Exh.	1.7653–1.7728	0.008
VG30E	Int. and Exh.	1.5566–1.5641	0.0059

CHECKING CAMSHAFT JOURNALS AND CAMSHAFT BEARING SADDLES

While the camshaft is still removed from the cylinder head, the camshaft bearing journals should be measured with a micrometer. Compare the measurements with those listed in the Camshaft Specifications chart in this Chapter. If the measurements are less than the limits listed in the chart, the camshaft will have to be replaced, since the camshafts in all of the engines covered in this guide run directly on the cylinder head surface; no actual bearings or bushings are used, so no oversize bearings or bushings are available.

Using an inside dial gauge or inside micrometer, measure the inside diameter of the camshaft saddles (the camshaft mounts that are either integrally cast as part of the cylinder head, or are a bolted on, one piece unit. The Z-series engines use a saddle-and-cap arrangement. The inside diameter of the saddles on all engines except the CA20E/CA18ET is 48.00-48.01mm. The CA20E/CA18ET measurement is 46.00-46.01mm. The inside diameter on the KA24E with the camshaft bracket and rocker shaft torqued to specifications is 31.5-33.00mm. On the VG30E engine contact a Nissan dealer or local machine shop for that specification. The

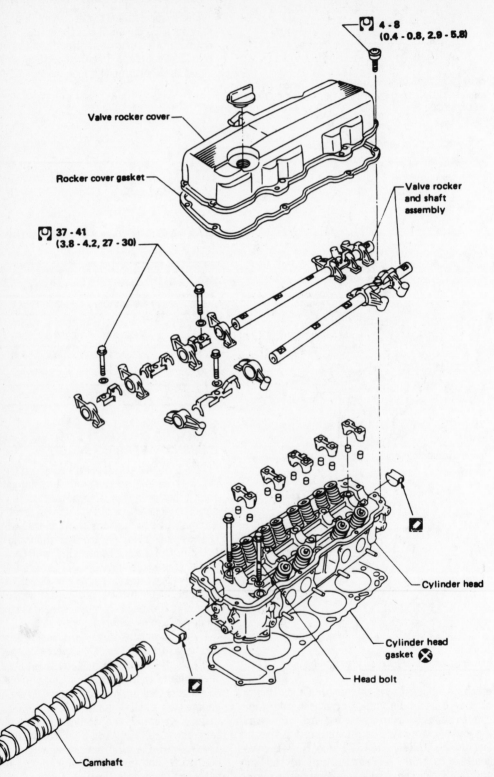

4 - 8
(0.4 - 0.8, 2.9 - 5.8)

Valve rocker cover

Rocker cover gasket

Valve rocker
and shaft
assembly

37 - 41
(3.8 - 4.2, 27 - 30)

Cylinder head

Cylinder head
gasket

Head bolt

Camshaft

Exploded view cylinder head assembly—240SX KA24E engine

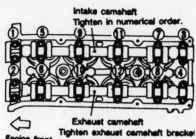

Intake camshaft
Tighten in numerical order.

Exhaust camshaft
Tighten exhaust camshaft bracket in the same procedure.

Engine front

Camshaft bracket torque sequence—240SX KA24DE engine

① Oil filler cap
② Rocker cover
③ Camshaft bracket
④ Intake camshaft
⑤ Exhaust camshaft
⑥ Shim
⑦ Valve lifter
⑧ Valve cotter
⑨ Spring retainer
⑩ Valve spring
⑪ Spring seat
⑫ Intake valve
⑬ Exhaust valve
⑭ Rubber plug
⑮ Cylinder head
⑯ Cylinder head bolt

camshaft journal oil clearances are listed in the Camshaft Specifications chart in this Chapter. If the saddle inside diameters exceed those listed above, the cylinder head must be replaced.

CHECKING CAMSHAFT ENDPLAY

After the camshaft has been installed, endplay should be checked. The camshaft sprocket should not be installed on the cam.

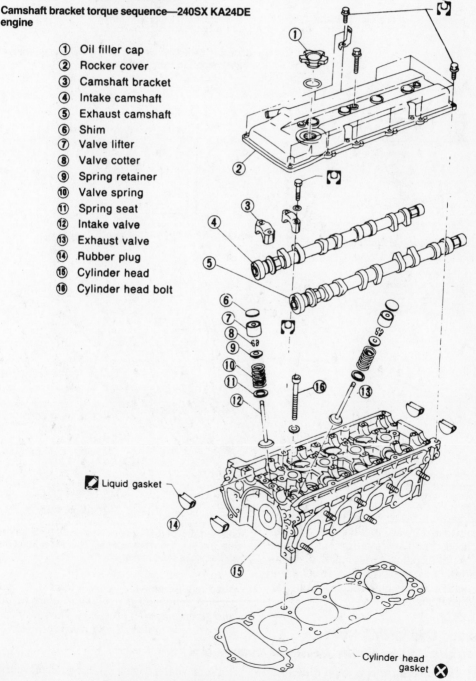

Liquid gasket

Cylinder head gasket

Exploded view cylinder head assembly—240SX KA24DE engine

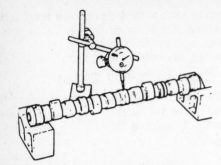

Check camshaft run-out with a dial indicator

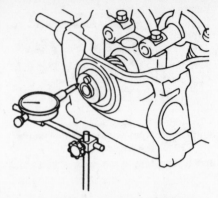

Checking camshaft endplay with a dial gauge—move the camshaft forward and backward

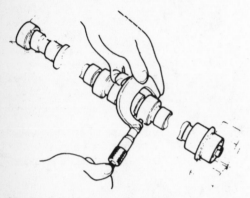

Measuring camshaft journal diameter

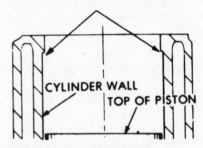

CYLINDER WALL

TOP OF PISTON

Ridge caused by cylinder wear

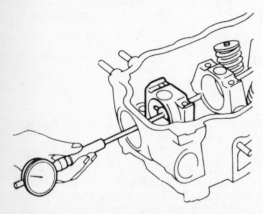

Use an inside micrometer or dial indicator gauge to measure camshaft bearing saddle diameters

Use a dial gauge to check the endplay, by moving the camshaft forward and backward in the cylinder head. Endplay specifications for the CA20E, CA18ET, Z20/22 series and KA24E engines should not exceed 0.20mm. On the VG30E engine the camshaft endplay should be between 0.03-0.06mm.

Pistons and Connecting Rods

REMOVAL AND INSTALLATION

NOTE: *This procedure is a rebuilding process. It generally requires removing the complete engine assembly from the vehicle, but may be done with the engine in place (head and pan removed) if necessary. The out-of-car procedure is preferred and recommended.*

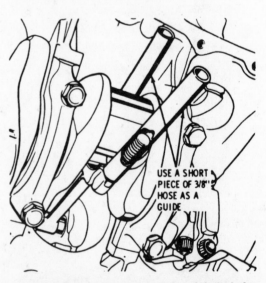

USE A SHORT PIECE OF 3/8" HOSE AS A GUIDE

Install lengths of rubber hose on the rod bolts before removing the piston assemblies. This will protect the cylinder walls from damage.

All Engines

1. Remove the engine assembly. Remove the cylinder head.

2. Remove the oil pan.

3. Remove any carbon buildup from the cylinder wall at the top end of the piston travel with a ridge reamer tool.

4. Position the piston to be removed at the bottom of its stroke so that the connecting rod bearing cap can be reached easily from under the engine.

5. Unscrew the connecting rod bearing cap nuts and remove the cap and lower half of the bearing. Cover the rod bolts with lengths of rubber tubing or hose to protect the cylinder walls when the rod and piston assembly is driven out.

6. Push the piston and connecting rod up and out of the cylinder block with a length of wood. Use care not to scratch the cylinder wall with the connecting rod or the wooden tool.

To install:

7. Keep all of the components from each cylinder together and install them in the cylinder from which they were removed.

8. Coat the bearing face of the connecting rod and the outer face of the pistons with engine oil.

9. Install the piston rings. Insure the correct placement of the piston rings for your model and engine size.

10. Turn the crankshaft until the rod journal of the particular cylinder you are working on is brought to the TDC position.

11. With the piston and rings clamped in a ring compressor, the notched mark on the head of the piston toward the front of the engine, and the oil hole side of the connecting rod toward the correct side of the engine, push the piston and connecting rod assembly into the cylinder bore until the big bearing end of the connecting rod contacts and is seated on the rod journal of the crankshaft. Use care not to scratch the cylinder wall with the connecting rod.

12. Push down farther on the piston and turn the crankshaft while the connecting rod rides around on the crankshaft rod journal. Turn the crankshaft until the crankshaft rod journal is at BDC (bottom dead center).

13. Align the mark on the connecting rod bearing cap with that on the connecting rod and tighten the bearing cap bolts to the specified torque.

14. Install all of the piston/connecting rod assemblies in the manner outlined above.

15. Install the oil strainer, pickup tube and oil pan.

16. Install the cylinder head.

17. Install engine assembly in vehicle if necessary.

18. Check all fluid levels and road test.

IDENTIFICATION AND POSITIONING

The pistons are marked with a number or **F** in the piston head. When installed in the engine the number or **F** markings are to be facing toward the front of the engine.

The connecting rods are installed in the engine with the oil hole facing toward the fuel pump side (right) of the engine.

NOTE: *It is advisable to number the pistons, connecting rods, and bearing caps in some manner so that they can be reinstalled in the same cylinder, facing in the same direction from which they are removed. The CA-series rod and cap assemblies are factory-numbered.*

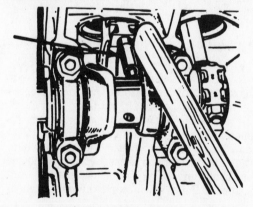

Tap out the piston assemblies with a wooden hammer handle—note hose covering rod bolts (arrow)

RING COMPRESSOR

Tap the piston assemblies down into the bores with a wooden hammer handle. Make sure the pistons and bores are well-lubed

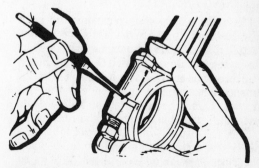

Matchmark each rod cap to its connecting rod

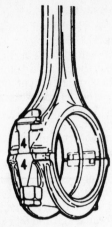

Number each rod and cap with its cylinder number for correct assembly

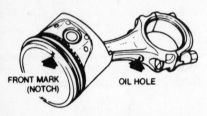

Piston and rod positioning—Z series and CA series engines

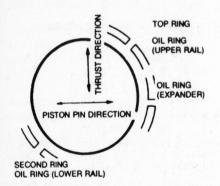

Piston ring placement—Z series and CA series engines

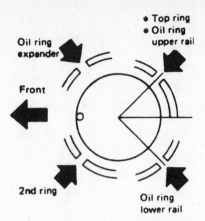

Piston ring placement—KA series and VG series engines

the clearance between the ring and its groove. If clearance is greater than the maximum listed under Ring Side Clearance in the Piston and Ring chart, replace the ring(s) and if necessary, the piston.

To check ring endgap, insert a compression ring into the cylinder. Lightly oil the cylinder bore and push the ring down into the cylinder with a piston, to the bottom of its travel. Measure the ring endgap with a feeler gauge. If the gap is not within specification, replace the ring; DO NOT file the ring ends.

CYLINDER BORE INSPECTION

Place a rag over the crankshaft journals. Wipe out each cylinder with a clean, solvent soaked rag. Visually inspect the cylinder bores for roughness, scoring or scuffing; also check the bores by feel. Measure the cylinder bore diameter with an inside micrometer, or a telescope gauge and micrometer. Measure the bore at points parallel and perpendicular to the engine centerline at the top (below the ridge) and bottom of the bore. Subtract the bottom mea-

Moving the bore gauge as shown, take the minimum diameter.

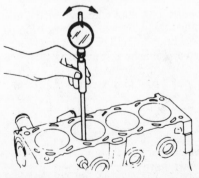

Checking cylinder bore diameter with a telescope gauge

CLEANING AND INSPECTION

Clean the piston after removing the rings (See Piston Ring and Wrist Pin Removal and Installation), by first scraping any carbon from the piston top. Do not scratch the piston in any way during cleaning. Use a broken piston ring or ring cleaning tool to clean out the ring grooves. Clean the entire piston with solvent and a stiff bristle brush (NOT a wire brush).

Once the piston is thoroughly cleaned, insert the side of a good piston ring (both No. 1 and No. 2 compression on each piston) into its respective groove. Using a feeler gauge, measure

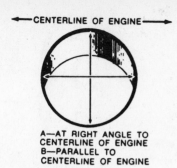

A—AT RIGHT ANGLE TO CENTERLINE OF ENGINE
B—PARALLEL TO CENTERLINE OF ENGINE

Cylinder bore measuring points

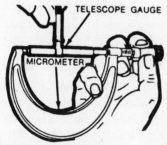

Measure the telescope gauge with a micrometer to determine cylinder bore diameter

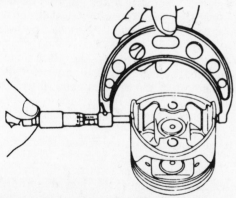

Measuring piston diameter—check diameter on the wrist pin axis, and 90° from the axis

surements from the top to determine cylinder taper.

Measure the piston diameter with a micrometer; since this micrometer may not be part of your tool kit, you may have to have the pistons checked at a machine shop. Take the measurements at right angles to the wrist pin center line, about 1 in. (25mm) down the piston skirt from the top.

Compare this measurement to the bore diameter of each cylinder. The difference is the piston clearance. If the clearance is greater than that specified in the Piston and Ring Specifications chart, have the cylinders honed or rebored and replace the pistons with an oversize set. Piston clearance can also be checked by invert-

ing a piston into an oiled cylinder, and sliding in a feeler gauge between the two.

NOTE: *When any one cylinder needs boring, all cylinders must be bored.*

Piston Ring and Wrist Pin
REMOVAL

A piston ring expander is necessary for removing piston rings without damaging them; any other method (screwdriver blades, pliers, etc.) usually results in the rings being bent, scratched or distorted, or the piston itself being damaged. When the rings are removed, clean the ring grooves using an appropriate ring groove cleaning tool, using care not to cut too deeply. Thoroughly clean all carbon and varnish from the piston with solvent.

All the Datsun/Nissan pistons covered in this guide have pressed in wrist pins, requiring a special press for removal. Take the piston and connecting rod assemblies to an engine specialist or machinist for wrist pin removal. The pins must also be pressed in during assembly.

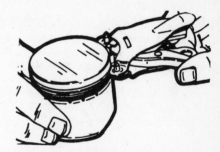

Removing the piston rings with a ring expander tool

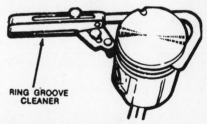

RING GROOVE CLEANER

Use a ring groove cleaner to properly clean the ring groove

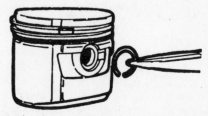

Wrist pin clips are removed with a needle-nose or snapring pliers

Wrist pins must be pressed in and out with a special press

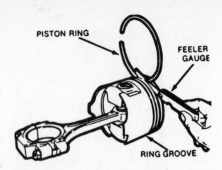

Measuring piston ring side clearance

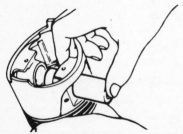

Wrist pin-to-piston fit should be such that the pin can be slid in smoothly by hand at room temperature

PISTON RING END GAP

Piston ring end gap should be checked while the rings are removed from the pistons. Incorrect end gap indicates that the wrong size rings are being used; ring breakage could occur.

Compress the piston rings to be used in a cylinder, one at a time, into that cylinder. Squirt clean oil into the cylinder, so that the rings and the top 50mm of cylinder wall are coated. Using

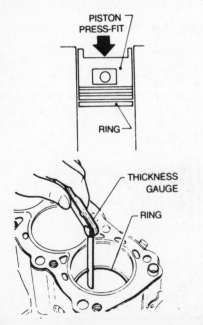

Checking ring end gap and piston-to-bore clearance

an inverted piston, press the rings approximately 25mm below the deck of the block. Measure the ring end gap with a feeler gauge, and compare to the Ring Gap chart in this Chapter. Replace the ring if necessary.

PISTON RING SIDE CLEARANCE CHECK AND INSTALLATION

Check the pistons to see that the ring grooves and oil return holes have been properly cleaned. Slide a piston ring into its groove, and check the side clearance with a feeler gauge. Make sure you insert the gauge between the ring and its lower land (lower edge of the groove), because any wear that occurs forms a step at the inner portion of the lower land. If the piston grooves have worn to the extent that relatively high steps exist on the lower land, the piston should be replaced, because these will interfere with the operation of the new rings and ring clearances will be excessive. Piston rings are not furnished in oversize widths to compensate for ring groove wear.

Install the rings on the piston, lowest ring first, using a piston ring expander. There is a high risk of breaking or distorting the rings, or scratching the piston, if the rings are installed by hand or other means.

Position the rings on the piston; spacing of the various piston ring gaps is crucial to proper oil retention and even cylinder wear.

Connecting Rod

INSPECTION AND BEARING REPLACEMENT

Connecting rod side clearance and big end bearing inspection and replacement should be performed while the rods are still installed in the engine. Determine the clearance between the connecting rod sides and the crankshaft using a feeler gauge. If clearance is below the minimum tolerance, check with a machinist about machining the rod to provide adequate clearance. If clearance is excessive, substitute an unworn rod and recheck; if clearance is still

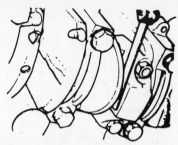

Checking connecting rod side clearance—make sure the feeler gauge is between the shoulder of the crank journal and the side of the rod

outside specifications, the crankshaft must be welded and reground, or replaced.

1. To check connecting rod big end bearing clearances, remove the rod bearing caps one at a time. Using a clean, dry shop rag, thoroughly clean all oil from the crank journal and bearing insert in the cap.

NOTE: *The Plastigage® gauging material you will be using to check clearances with is soluble in oil; therefore any oil on the journal or bearing could result in an incorrect reading.*

2. Lay a strip of Plastigage® along the full length of the bearing insert (along the crank journal if the engine is out of the car and inverted). Reinstall the cap and torque to specifications listed in the Torque Specifications chart.

3. Remove the rod cap and determine bearing clearance by comparing the width of the now flattened Plastigage® to the scale on the Plastigage® envelope. Journal taper is determined by comparing the width of the Plastigage® strip near its ends. Rotate the crankshaft 90° and retest, to determine journal eccentricity.

NOTE: *Do not rotate the crankshaft with the Plastigage® installed.*

4. If the bearing insert and crank journal appear intact and are within tolerances, no further service is required and the bearing caps can be reinstalled (remove Plastigage® before installation). If clearances are not within toler-

ances, the bearing inserts in both the connecting rod and rod cap must be replaced with undersize inserts, and/or the crankshaft must be reground. To install the bearing insert halves, press them into the bearing caps and connecting rods. Make sure the tab in each insert fits into the notch in each rod and cap. Lube the face of each insert with engine oil prior to installing each rod into the engine.

5. The connecting rods can be further inspected when they are removed from the engine and separated from their pistons. Rod alignment (straightness and squareness) must be checked by a machinist, as the rod must be set in a special fixture. Many machine shops also perform a Magnafluxing service, which is a process that shows up any tiny cracks that you may be unable to see.

Engine Core Plugs (Freeze Plugs)
REMOVAL

Drain the cooling system. Using a blunt tool such as a drift, strike the bottom edge of the cup plug. With the cup plug rotated, grasp firmly with pliers or other suitable tool and remove the plug.

NOTE: *Do not drive cup plug into the block casting as restricted cooling may result.*

INSTALLATION

Thoroughly clean inside of cup plug hole in cylinder block or head. Be sure to remove old sealer. Lightly coat inside of cup plug hole with sealer. Make certain the new plug is cleaned of all oil and grease. Using proper drive tool, drive plug into hole. Refill the cooling system.

Rear Main Bearing Oil Seal
REMOVAL AND INSTALLATION

1. Remove the transmission or transaxle.
2. Remove the flywheel or drive plate.
3. Remove the rear oil seal retainer from the block. On the early models, the seal retainer is part of the block--using a small pry bar, pry the

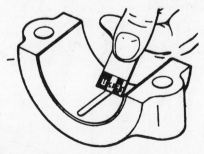

Check connecting rod bearing clearance with Plastigage®

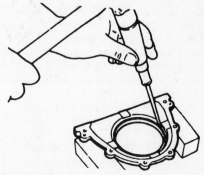

Rear seal removal

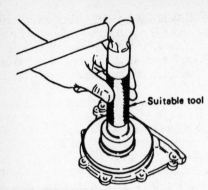

Suitable tool

Rear seal installation

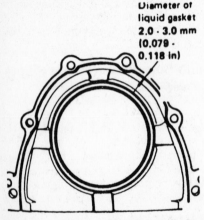

Diameter of liquid gasket 2.0 - 3.0 mm (0.079 - 0.118 in)

On most engines, apply a 0.08–0.12 inch (2–3mm) of liquid gasket to the rear oil seal retainer

rear main oil seal from around the crankshaft.

4. Using a suitable prying tool, remove the oil seal from the retainer.

To install:

5. Thoroughly scrape the surface of the retainer to remove any traces of the existing sealant or gasket material.

6. Wipe the seal bore with a clean rag.

7. Apply clean engine oil to the new oil seal and carefully install it into the retainer using the proper seal installation tool.

8. Install the rear oil seal retainer into the engine, along with a new gasket. Apply a 0.08–0.12 in. (2–3mm) of liquid gasket to the rear oil seal retainer prior to installation as necessary. Torque the bolts to 3–6 ft. lbs. (4–8 Nm).

On early models apply lithium grease around the sealing lip of the oil seal and install the seal by driving it into the cylinder block using an oil installation tool.

9. Install the flywheel or driveplate.

10. Install the transmission or transaxle.

Crankshaft and Main Bearings

REMOVAL AND INSTALLATION

NOTE: *Before removing the crankshaft, check main bearing clearances as described* under *"Main Bearing Clearance Check" below.*

1. Remove the piston and connecting rod assemblies.

2. Check crankshaft thrust clearance (end play) before removing the crank from the block. Using a pry bar, pry the crankshaft the extent of its travel forward, and measure thrust clearance at the center main bearing (No. 4 bearing on 6-cylinder engines, No. 3 on 4-cylinder engines) with a feeler gauge. Pry the crankshaft the extent of its rearward travel, and measure the other side of the bearing. If clearance is greater than specified, the thrust washers must be replaced (see Main Bearing Replacement, below).

3. Using a punch, mark the corresponding man bearing caps and saddles according to position. One punch on the front main cap and saddle, two on the second, three on the third, etc. This ensures correct reassembly.

4. Remove the main bearing caps after they have been marked.

5. Remove the crankshaft from the block.

6. Follow the crankshaft inspection, main bearing clearance checking and replacement procedures below before reinstalling the crankshaft.

INSPECTION

Crankshaft inspection and servicing should be handled exclusively by a reputable machinist, as most of the necessary procedures require a dial indicator and fixing jig, a large micrometer, and machine tools such as a crankshaft grinder. While at the machine shop, the crankshaft should be thoroughly cleaned (especially the oil passages), magnafluxed (to check for minute cracks) and the following checks made: Main journal diameter, crank pin (connecting rod journal) diameter, taper and out-of-round, and runout. Wear, beyond specification limits, in any of these areas means the crankshaft must be reground or replaced.

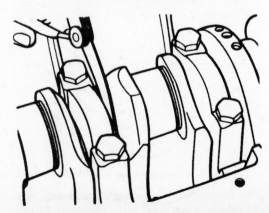

Check crankshaft endplay with a feeler gauge

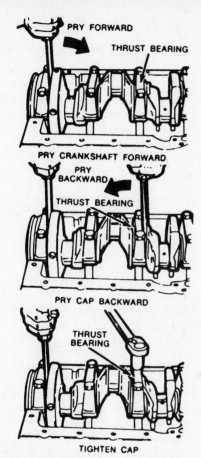

Checking crankshaft thrust

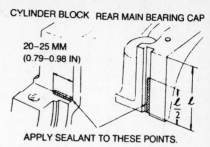

CYLINDER BLOCK   REAR MAIN BEARING CAP

20–25 MM
(0.79–0.98 IN)

APPLY SEALANT TO THESE POINTS.

Apply sealant on engine main bearing caps

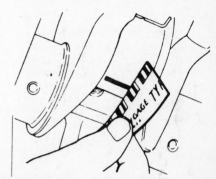

Check main bearing clearance on the crankshaft journal as well as on the bearing cap—use Plastigage®

MAIN BEARING CLEARANCE CHECK

Checking main bearing clearances is done in the same manner as checking connecting rod big end clearances.

1. With the crankshaft installed, remove the main bearing cap. Clean all oil from the bearing insert in the cap and from the crankshaft journal, as the Plastigage® material is oil soluble.

2. Lay a strip of Plastigage® along the full width of the bearing cap (or along the width of the crank journal if the engine is out of the car and inverted).

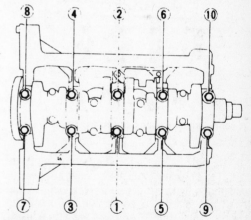

CA series engines main bearing cap bolt torque sequence

3. Install the bearing cap and torque to specification. Tighten bearing caps gradually in two or three stages.

NOTE: *Do not rotate the crankshaft with the Plastigage® installed.*

4. Remove the bearing cap and determine bearing clearance by comparing the width of the now flattened Plastigage® with the scale on the Plastigage® envelope. Journal taper is determined by comparing the width of the Plastigage® strip near its ends. Rotate the crankshaft 90° and retest, to determine journal eccentricity.

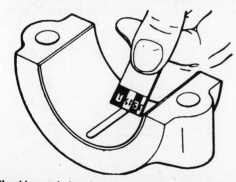

Checking main bearing clearance with Plastigage®

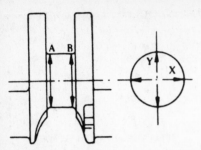

Check crankshaft journal eccentricity and taper with a micrometer at these points

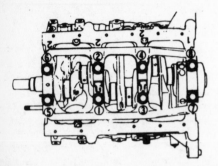

VG30 engine main bearing cap bolt torque sequence

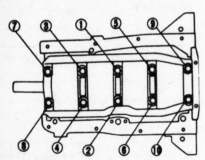

KA series engines main bearing cap bolt torque sequence

5. Repeat the above for the remaining bearings. If the bearing journal and insert appear in good shape (with no unusual wear visible) and are within tolerances, no further main bearing service is required. If unusual wear is evident and/or the clearances are outside specifications, the bearings must be replaced and the cause of their wear found.

MAIN BEARING REPLACEMENT

Main bearings can be replaced with the crankshaft both in the engine (with the engine still in the car) and out of the engine (with the engine on a workstand or bench). Both procedures are covered here. The main bearings must be replaced if the crankshaft has been reground; the replacement bearings being available in various undersize increments from most auto parts jobbers or your local Datsun/Nissan dealer.

Engine Out of Car

1. Remove the crankshaft from the engine block.
2. Remove the main bearing inserts from the bearing caps and from the main bearing saddles. Remove the thrust washers from the No. 3 (4-cylinder) or No. 4 (6-cylinder) crank journal.
3. Thoroughly clean the saddles, bearing caps, and crankshaft.
4. Make sure the crankshaft has been fully checked and is ready for reassembly. Place the upper main bearings in the block saddles so that the oil grooves and/or oil holes are correctly aligned with their corresponding grooves or holes in the saddles.
5. Install the thrust washers on the center main bearing, with the oil grooves facing out.
6. Lubricate the faces of all bearings with clean engine oil, and place the crankshaft in the block.
7. Install the main bearing caps in numbered order with the arrows or any other orientation marks facing forward. Torque all bolts except the center cap bolts in sequence in two or three passes to the specified torque. Rotate the crankshaft after each pass to ensure even tightness.
8. Align the thrust bearing by prying the crankshaft the extent of its axial travel several times with a pry bar. On last movement hold the crankshaft toward the front of the engine and torque the thrust bearing cap to specifications. Measure the crankshaft thrust clearance (end play) as previously described in this Chapter. If clearance is outside specifications (too sloppy), install a new set of oversize thrust washers and check clearance again.

Engine and Crankshaft Installed

1. Remove the main bearing caps and keep them in order.
2. Make a bearing rollout pin from a cotter pin as shown.
3. Carefully roll out the old inserts from the upper side of the crankshaft journal, noting the positions of the oil grooves and/or oil holes so the new inserts can be correctly installed.
4. Roll each new insert into its saddle after lightly oiling the crankshaft side face of each.

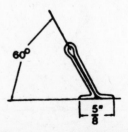

Make a bearing roll-out tool from a cotter pin

Make sure the notches and/or oil holes are correctly positioned.

5. Replace the bearing inserts in the caps with new inserts. Oil the face of each, and install the caps in numbered order with the arrows or other orientation marks facing forward. Torque the bolts to the specified torque in two or three passes in the sequence shown.

Cylinder Block

Most inspection and service work on the cylinder block should be handled by a machinist or professional engine rebuilding shop. Included in this work are bearing alignment checks, line boring, deck resurfacing, hot-tanking and cylinder honing or boring. A block that has been checked and properly serviced will last much longer than one which has not had the proper attention when the opportunity was there for it.

Cylinder deglazing (honing) can, however, be performed by the owner/mechanic who is careful and takes his or her time. The cylinder bores become glazed during normal operation as the rings continually ride up and down against them. This shiny glaze must be removed in order for a new set of piston rings to be able to properly seat themselves.

Cylinder hones are available at most auto tool stores and parts jobbers. With the piston and rod assemblies removed from the block, cover the crankshaft completely with a rag or cover to keep grit from the hone and cylinder material off of it. Chuck a hone into a variable speed power drill and insert it into the cylinder.

NOTE: *Make sure the drill and hone are kept square to the cylinder bore throughout the entire honing operation.*

Start the hone and move it up and down in the cylinder at a rate which will produce approximately a 60° crosshatch pattern. DO NOT extend the hone below the cylinder bore! After developing the pattern, remove the hone and recheck piston fit. Wash the cylinders with a detergent and water solution to remove the hone and cylinder grit. Wipe the bores out several times with a clean rag soaked in clean engine oil. Remove the cover from the crankshaft, and check closely to see that no grit has found its way onto the crankshaft.

Flywheel and Ring Gear
REMOVAL AND INSTALLATION

NOTE: *The clutch cover and the pressure plate are balanced as an assembly; if replacement of either part becomes necessary, replace both parts as an assembly.*

1. On manual transmission/transaxle applications, refer to the "Clutch Removal and Installation" procedures in Chapter 7 and remove the clutch assembly. On automatic transmission/transaxle applications, remove the automatic transmission/transaxle assembly from the vehicle—refer to the necessary service procedures in Chapter 7.

2. Remove the flywheel/drive plate-to-crankshaft bolts and the flywheel/driveplate.

NOTE: *If necessary the clutch disc should be inspected and/or replaced at this time; the clutch lining wear limit is 0.30mm above the rivet heads.*

3. To install, reverse the removal procedures. Torque the flywheel-to crankshaft bolts to specifications, the clutch cover-to-flywheel bolts and the bearing housing-to-clutch housing bolts to specifications on manual transmission/transaxle applications. On automatic transmission/transaxle applications, torque the driveplate-to crankshaft bolts to specifications, install torque converter then the transmission assembly. Refer to the Torque Specification Chart and Chapter 7 service procedures.

EXHAUST SYSTEM

Safety Precautions

For a number of reasons, exhaust system work can be dangerous. Always observe the following precautions:

1. Support the vehicle securely by using jackstands or equivalent under the frame of the vehicle.

2. Wear safety goggles to protect your eyes from metal chips that may fly free while working on the exhaust system.

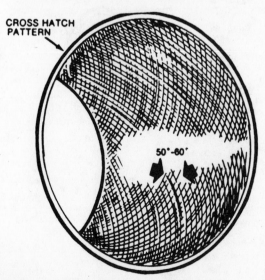

CROSS HATCH PATTERN

50°-60°

Proper cylinder bore cross-hatching after honing

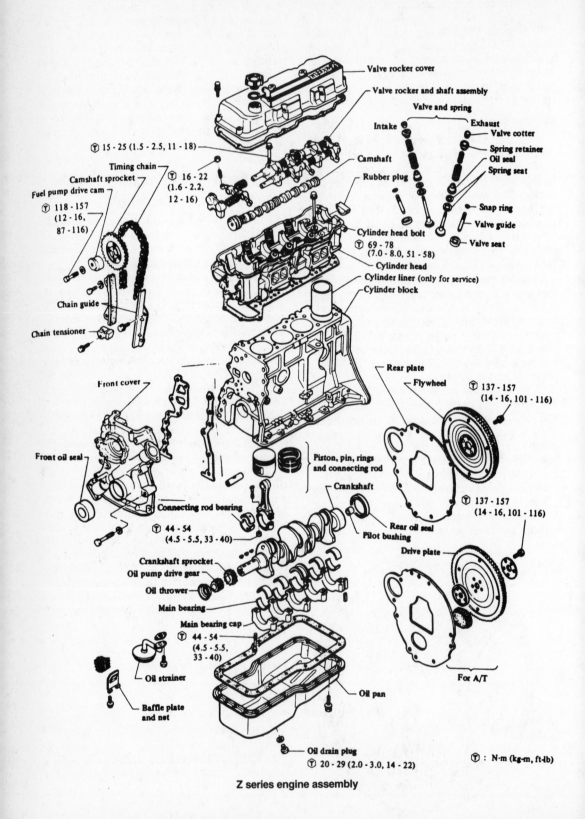

Valve rocker cover

Valve rocker and shaft assembly

Valve and spring

Intake

Exhaust

Valve cotter

Spring retainer

Oil seal

Spring seat

Camshaft

Rubber plug

Snap ring

Valve guide

Valve seat

Ⓣ 15 - 25 (1.5 - 2.5, 11 - 18)

Timing chain

Camshaft sprocket

Fuel pump drive cam

Ⓣ 118 - 157 (12 - 16, 87 - 116)

Ⓣ 16 - 22 (1.6 - 2.2, 12 - 16)

Cylinder head bolt

Ⓣ 69 - 78 (7.0 - 8.0, 51 - 58)

Cylinder head

Cylinder liner (only for service)

Cylinder block

Chain guide

Chain tensioner

Front cover

Rear plate

Flywheel

Ⓣ 137 - 157 (14 - 16, 101 - 116)

Front oil seal

Piston, pin, rings and connecting rod

Crankshaft

Connecting rod bearing

Ⓣ 44 - 54 (4.5 - 5.5, 33 - 40)

Rear oil seal

Pilot bushing

Ⓣ 137 - 157 (14 - 16, 101 - 116)

Drive plate

Crankshaft sprocket

Oil pump drive gear

Oil thrower

Main bearing

Main bearing cap

Ⓣ 44 - 54 (4.5 - 5.5, 33 - 40)

Oil strainer

For A/T

Baffle plate and net

Oil pan

Oil drain plug

Ⓣ 20 - 29 (2.0 - 3.0, 14 - 22)

Ⓣ : N·m (kg-m, ft-lb)

Z series engine assembly

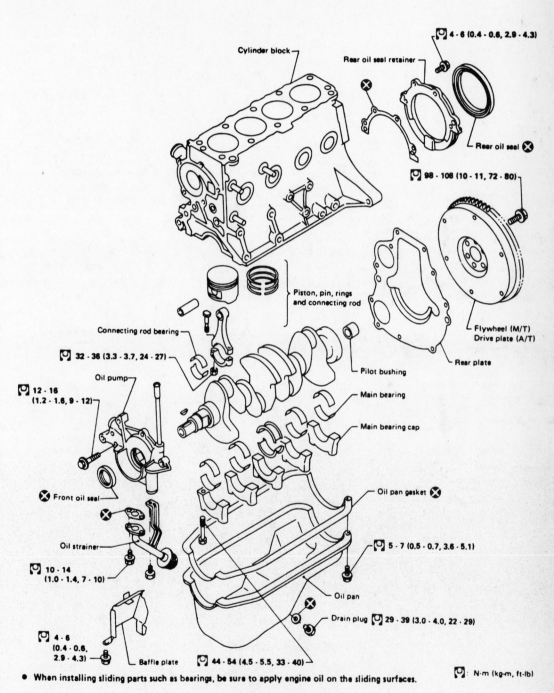

Cylinder block

Rear oil seal retainer

4 - 6 (0.4 - 0.6, 2.9 - 4.3)

Rear oil seal

98 - 108 (10 - 11, 72 - 80)

Piston, pin, rings and connecting rod

Connecting rod bearing

32 - 36 (3.3 - 3.7, 24 - 27)

Flywheel (M/T) Drive plate (A/T)

Pilot bushing

Rear plate

Oil pump

Main bearing

12 - 16 (1.2 - 1.6, 9 - 12)

Main bearing cap

Front oil seal

Oil pan gasket

Oil strainer

5 - 7 (0.5 - 0.7, 3.6 - 5.1)

10 - 14 (1.0 - 1.4, 7 - 10)

Oil pan

Drain plug 29 - 39 (3.0 - 4.0, 22 - 29)

4 - 6 (0.4 - 0.6, 2.9 - 4.3)

Baffle plate   44 - 54 (4.5 - 5.5, 33 - 40)

: N·m (kg-m, ft-lb)

● When installing sliding parts such as bearings, be sure to apply engine oil on the sliding surfaces.

CA series engine assembly

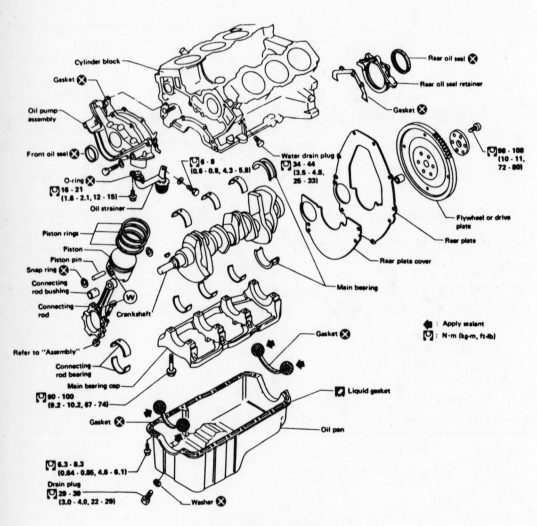

Cylinder block

Gasket ⊗

Oil pump assembly

Front oil seal ⊗

O-ring ⊗
🔧 16 · 21
(1.6 · 2.1, 12 · 15)

Oil strainer

Piston rings

Piston

Piston pin

Snap ring ⊗

Connecting rod bushing

Connecting rod

Crankshaft

Refer to "Assembly"

Connecting rod bearing

Main bearing cap

🔧 90 · 100
(9.2 · 10.2, 67 · 74)

Gasket ⊗

🔧 6.3 · 8.3
(0.64 · 0.85, 4.6 · 6.1)

Drain plug
🔧 29 · 39
(3.0 · 4.0, 22 · 29)

Washer ⊗

🔧 6 · 8
(0.6 · 0.8, 4.3 · 5.8)

Water drain plug
🔧 34 · 44
(3.5 · 4.5, 25 · 33)

Main bearing

Rear oil seal ⊗

Rear oil seal retainer

Gasket ⊗

🔧 98 · 108
(10 · 11, 72 · 80)

Flywheel or drive plate

Rear plate

Rear plate cover

Gasket ⊗

Liquid gasket

Oil pan

◀ : Apply sealant

🔧 : N·m (kg-m, ft-lb)

VG30E engine assembly

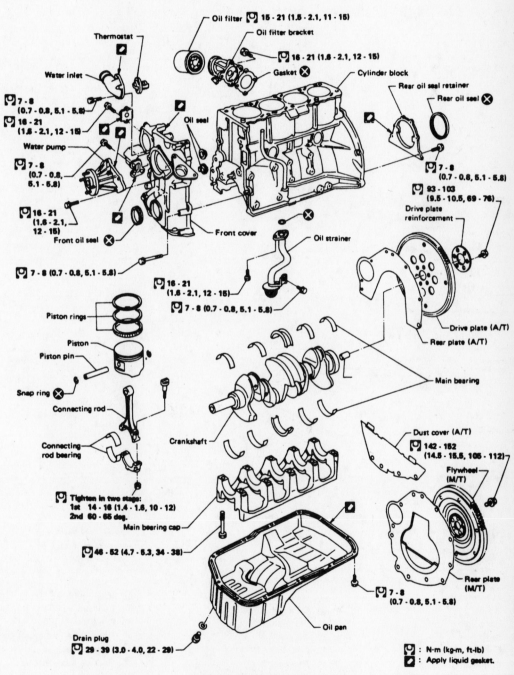

Oil filter 15 - 21 (1.5 - 2.1, 11 - 15)

Oil filter bracket

Thermostat

16 - 21 (1.6 - 2.1, 12 - 15)

Water inlet

Gasket

Cylinder block

Rear oil seal retainer

Rear oil seal

7 - 8
(0.7 - 0.8, 5.1 - 5.8)

16 - 21
(1.6 - 2.1, 12 - 15)

Oil seal

Water pump

7 - 8
(0.7 - 0.8,
5.1 - 5.8)

7 - 8 (0.7 - 0.8, 5.1 - 5.8)

93 - 103
(9.5 - 10.5, 69 - 76)

Drive plate
reinforcement

16 - 21
(1.6 - 2.1,
12 - 15)

Front oil seal

Front cover

Oil strainer

Drive plate (A/T)

Rear plate (A/T)

7 - 8 (0.7 - 0.8, 5.1 - 5.8)

16 - 21
(1.6 - 2.1, 12 - 15)

7 - 8 (0.7 - 0.8, 5.1 - 5.8)

Piston rings

Piston

Piston pin

Main bearing

Snap ring

Connecting rod

Dust cover (A/T)

Connecting
rod bearing

Crankshaft

142 - 152
(14.5 - 15.5, 105 - 112)

Flywheel
(M/T)

Tighten in two stage:
1st 14 - 16 (1.4 - 1.6, 10 - 12)
2nd 60 - 65 deg.

Main bearing cap

46 - 52 (4.7 - 5.3, 34 - 38)

Rear plate
(M/T)

7 - 8
(0.7 - 0.8, 5.1 - 5.8)

Drain plug
29 - 39 (3.0 - 4.0, 22 - 29)

Oil pan

: N·m (kg-m, ft-lb)
: Apply liquid gasket.

KA24E engine assembly

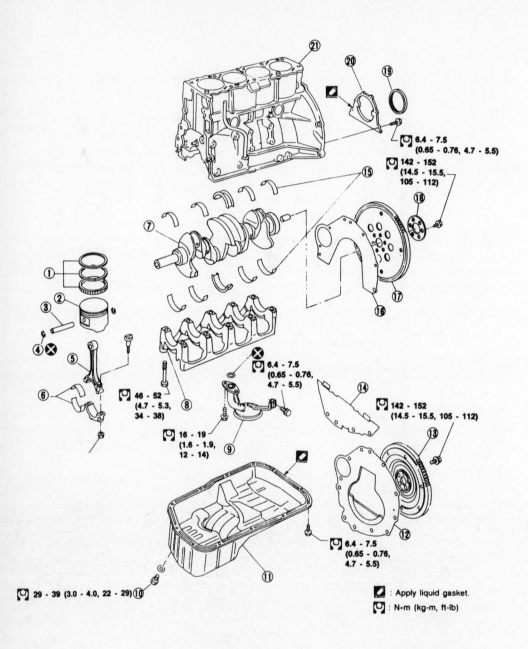

6.4 - 7.5
(0.65 - 0.76, 4.7 - 5.5)

142 - 152
(14.5 - 15.5, 105 - 112)

6.4 - 7.5
(0.65 - 0.76, 4.7 - 5.5)

46 - 52
(4.7 - 5.3, 34 - 38)

16 - 19
(1.6 - 1.9, 12 - 14)

142 - 152
(14.5 - 15.5, 105 - 112)

6.4 - 7.5
(0.65 - 0.76, 4.7 - 5.5)

29 - 39 (3.0 - 4.0, 22 - 29)

: Apply liquid gasket.

: N•m (kg-m, ft-lb)

① Piston rings	⑧ Main bearing cap	⑮ Main bearing
② Piston	⑨ Oil strainer	⑯ Rear plate (A/T)
③ Piston pin	⑩ Drain plug	⑰ Drive plate (A/T)
④ Snap ring	⑪ Oil pan	⑱ Drive plate reinforcement
⑤ Connecting rod	⑫ Rear plate (M/T)	⑲ Rear oil seal
⑥ Connecting rod bearing	⑬ Flywheel (M/T)	⑳ Rear oil seal retainer
⑦ Crankshaft	⑭ Dust cover (A/T)	㉑ Cylinder block

KA24DE engine assembly

3. If you are using a torch, be careful not to come close to any fuel lines.

4. Always use the proper tool for the job.

Special Tools

A number of special exhaust tools can be rented or bought from a local auto parts store. It may also be quite helpful to use solvents designed to loosen rusted nuts or bolts. Remember that these products are often flammable, apply only to parts after they are cool.

Front Pipe

REMOVAL AND INSTALLATION

NOTE: *Always replace the exhaust gaskets (exhaust pipe gasket to manifold) with new ones when reassembling. Clean the exhaust pipe flange completely before installing new exhaust gasket.*

1. Support the vehicle securely by using jackstands or equivalent under the frame of the vehicle.

2. Remove the exhaust pipe clamps and any front exhaust pipe shield.

3. Soak the exhaust manifold front pipe mounting studs with penetrating oil. Remove attaching nuts and gasket from the manifold.

NOTE: *If these studs snap off while removing the front pipe, the manifold will have to be removed, the stud drilled out and the hole tapped.*

4. Remove any exhaust pipe mounting hanger or bracket.

5. Remove front pipe from the catalytic connverter.

To install:

6. Install the front pipe on the manifold with seal if so equipped.

7. Install the pipe on the catalytic connverter. Assemble all parts loosely and position pipe to insure proper clearance from body of vehicle.

8. Tighten mounting studs, bracket bolts on exhaust clamps.

9. Install exhaust pipe shield.

10. Start engine and check for exhaust leaks.

Catalytic Converter

REMOVAL AND INSTALLATION

CAUTION: *The catalytic converter becomes extremely hot during operation. Allow the system to cool completely before beginning any work. Check the temperature of the con-*

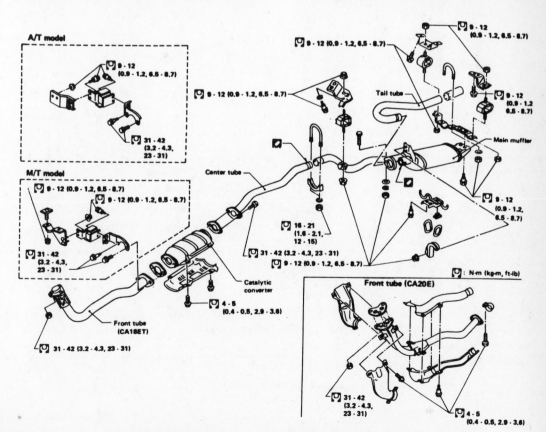

Exploded view exhaust system—200SX (CA series engines)

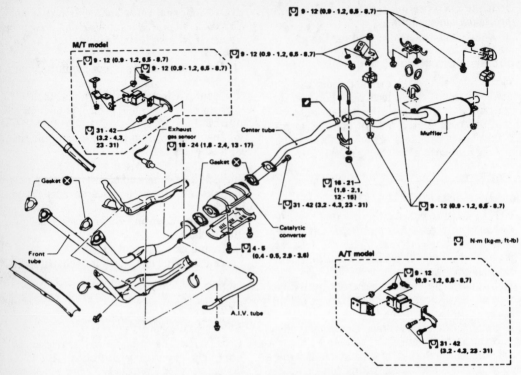

Exploded view exhaust system—200SX (VG30E series engine)

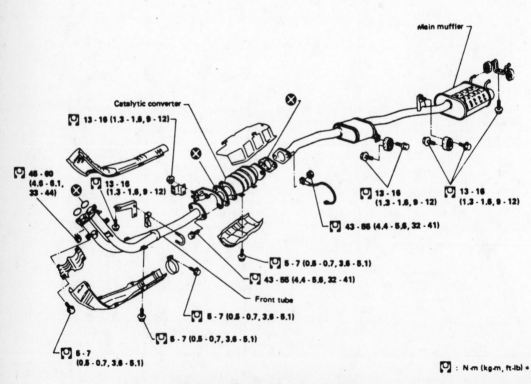

Exploded view exhaust system—240SX

verter before working; wear gloves and eye protection when working.

1. Remove the converter lower shield.
2. Disconnect converter from front pipe.
3. Disconnect converter from center pipe.

NOTE: *Assemble all parts loosely and position converter before tightening the exhaust clamps.*

4. Remove catalytic converter.
5. To install reverse the removal procedures. Always use new clamps and exhaust seals, start engine and check for leaks.

Tailpipe And Muffler

REMOVAL AND INSTALLATION

1. Remove tailpipe connection at center pipe.
2. Remove all brackets and exhaust clamps.
3. Remove tailpipe from muffler. On some models the tailpipe and muffler are one piece.
4. To install reverse the removal procedures. Always use new clamps and exhaust seals, start engine and check for leaks.

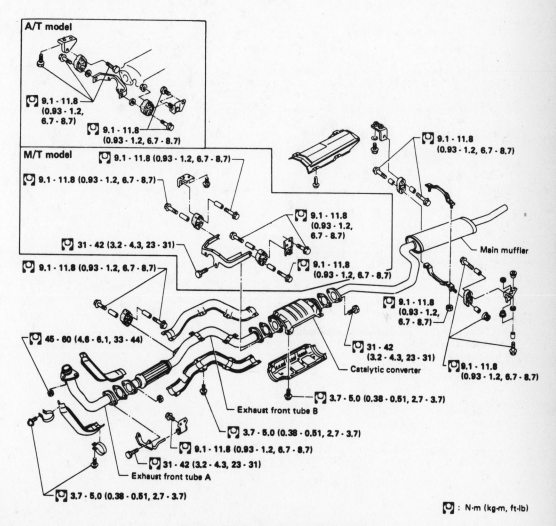

Exploded view exhaust system—Stanza

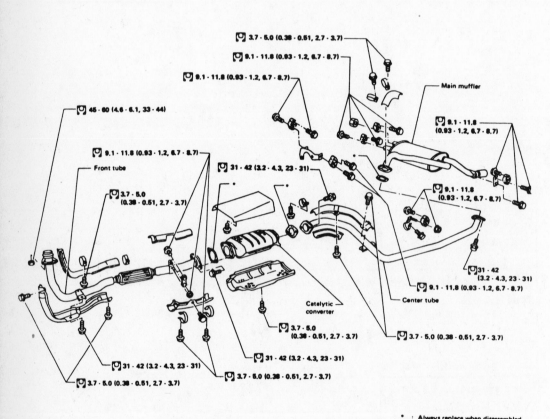

3.7 - 5.0 (0.38 - 0.51, 2.7 - 3.7)

9.1 - 11.8 (0.93 - 1.2, 6.7 - 8.7)

9.1 - 11.8 (0.93 - 1.2, 6.7 - 8.7)

Main muffler

45 - 60 (4.6 - 6.1, 33 - 44)

9.1 - 11.8 (0.93 - 1.2, 6.7 - 8.7)

9.1 - 11.8 (0.93 - 1.2, 6.7 - 8.7)

Front tube

31 - 42 (3.2 - 4.3, 23 - 31)

3.7 - 5.0 (0.38 - 0.51, 2.7 - 3.7)

9.1 - 11.8 (0.93 - 1.2, 6.7 - 8.7)

31 - 42 (3.2 - 4.3, 23 - 31)

9.1 - 11.8 (0.93 - 1.2, 6.7 - 8.7)

Center tube

Catalytic converter

3.7 - 5.0 (0.38 - 0.51, 2.7 - 3.7)

3.7 - 5.0 (0.38 - 0.51, 2.7 - 3.7)

31 - 42 (3.2 - 4.3, 23 - 31)

31 - 42 (3.2 - 4.3, 23 - 31)

3.7 - 5.0 (0.38 - 0.51, 2.7 - 3.7)

3.7 - 5.0 (0.38 - 0.51, 2.7 - 3.7)

* : Always replace when disassembled.

: N·m (kg-m, ft-lb)

Exploded view exhaust system—Stanza 4WD

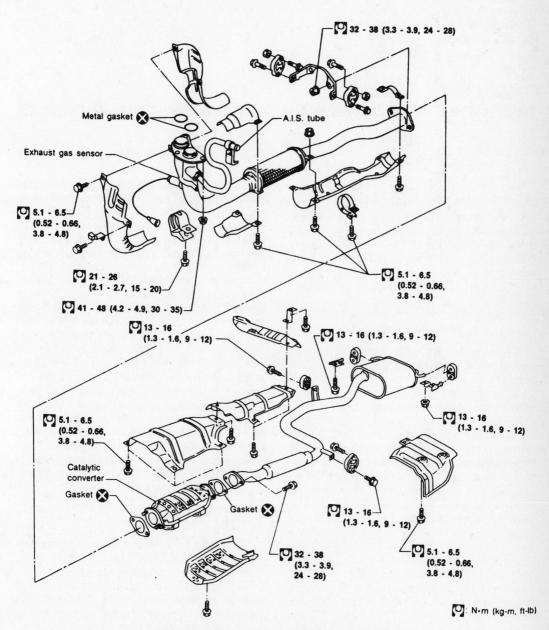

Exploded view exhaust system—Stanza (1990–92)

Emission Controls

EMISSION CONTROLS

There are three sources of automotive pollutants: Crankcase fumes, exhaust gases and gasoline evaporation. The pollutants formed from these substances fall into three categories: unburnt hydrocarbons (HC), carbon monoxide (CO) and oxides of nitrogen (NOx). The equipment that is used to limit these pollutants is commonly called emission control equipment.

Crankcase Emission Controls

The crankcase emission control equipment consists of a positive crankcase ventilation valve (PCV), a closed or open oil filler cap and hoses to connect this equipment.

When the engine is running, a small portion of the gases which are formed in the combustion chamber during combustion leak by the piston rings and enter the crankcase. Since these gases are under pressure they tend to escape from the crankcase and enter into the atmosphere. If these gases were allowed to remain in the crankcase for any length of time, they would contaminate the engine oil and cause sludge to build up. If the gases are allowed to escape into the atmosphere, they would pollute the air, as they contain unburned hydrocarbons. The crankcase emission control equipment recycles these gases back into the engine combustion chamber where they are burned.

Crankcase gases are recycled in the following manner: while the engine is running, clean filtered air is drawn into the crankcase through the air filter and then through a hose leading to the rocker cover. As the air passes through the crankcase it picks up the combustion gases and carries them out of the crankcase, up through the PCV valve and into the intake manifold. After they enter the intake manifold they are drawn into the combustion chamber and burned.

The most critical component in the system is the PCV valve. This vacuum controlled valve regulates the amount of gases which are recycled into the combustion changer. At low engine speeds the valve is partially closed, limiting the flow of gases into the intake manifold. As engine speed increases, the valve opens to admit greater quantities of the gases into the intake manifold. If the valve should become blocked or plugged, the gases will be prevented from escaping from the crankcase by the normal route. Since these gases are under pressure, they will find their own way out of the crankcase. This alternate route is usually a weak oil seal or gasket in the engine. As the gas escapes by the gasket it also creates an oil leak. Besides causing oil leaks, a clogged PCV valve also allows these gases to remain in the crankcase for an extended period of time, promoting the formation of sludge in the engine.

The above explanation and the troubleshooting procedure which follows applies to all engines with PCV systems.

TESTING

Check the PCV system hoses and connections, to see that there are no vacuum leaks. Then replace or tighten, as necessary.

With the engine running at idle, remove the ventilation hose from the PCV valve. If the valve is working properly, a hissing noise will be heard as air passes through it and a strong vacuum should be felt when a finger is placed over the valve inlet. Refer to the illustrations.

To check the valve, remove it and blow through both of its ends. When blowing from the side which goes toward the intake manifold, very little air should pass through it. When blowing from the crankcase (valve cover) side, air should pass through freely. Replace the

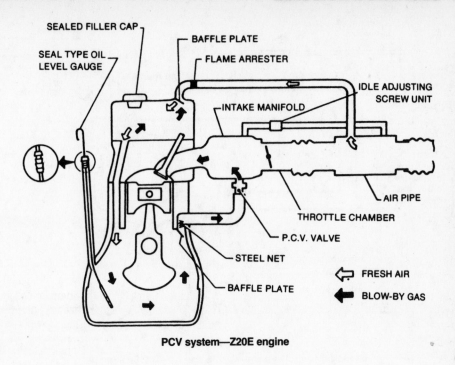

SEALED FILLER CAP

SEAL TYPE OIL
LEVEL GAUGE

BAFFLE PLATE

FLAME ARRESTER

INTAKE MANIFOLD

IDLE ADJUSTING
SCREW UNIT

AIR PIPE

THROTTLE CHAMBER

P.C.V. VALVE

STEEL NET

BAFFLE PLATE

FRESH AIR

BLOW-BY GAS

PCV system—Z20E engine

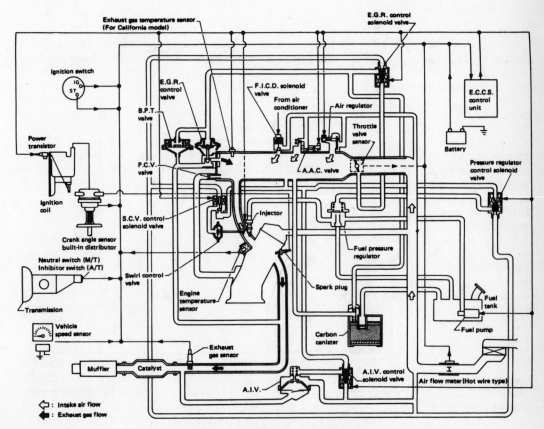

Exhaust gas temperature sensor
(For California model)

E.G.R. control
solenoid valve

Ignition switch

E.G.R.
control
valve

F.I.C.D. solenoid
valve

From air
conditioner

Air regulator

E.C.C.S.
control
unit

B.P.T.
valve

Throttle
valve
sensor

Battery

Power
transistor

P.C.V.
valve

A.A.C. valve

Pressure regulator
control solenoid
valve

Ignition
coil

S.C.V. control
solenoid valve

Injector

Fuel pressure
regulator

Crank angle sensor
built-in distributor

Neutral switch (M/T)
Inhibitor switch (A/T)

Swirl control
valve

Spark plug

Fuel
tank

Engine temperature
sensor

Fuel pump

Transmission

Vehicle
speed sensor

Carbon
canister

Muffler

Catalyst

Exhaust
gas sensor

A.I.V.

A.I.V. control
solenoid valve

Air flow meter (Hot wire type)

: Intake air flow

: Exhaust gas flow

Emission control system—KA24E engine

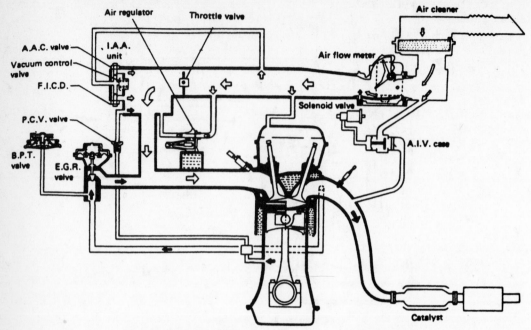

Emission control system—CA20E engine—CA18ET similar

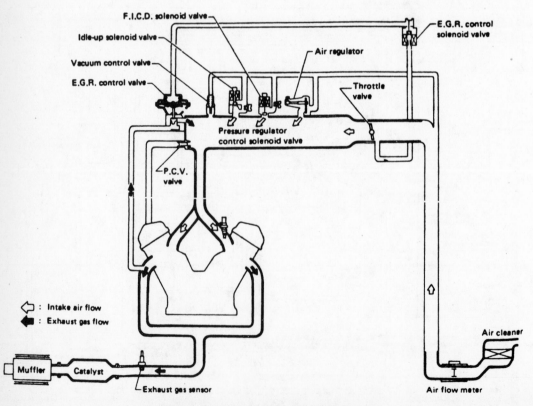

Emission control system—VG30E engine

valve with a new one, if the valve fails to function as outlined.

REMOVAL AND INSTALLATION

To remove the PCV valve, simply loosen the hose clamp and remove the valve from the manifold-to-crankcase hose and intake manifold. Install the PCV valve in the reverse order of removal procedure.

Disconnect all hoses and clean with compressed air. If any hose cannot be freed of obstructions--replace the hose.

Evaporative Emission Control System

When raw fuel evaporates, the vapors contain hydrocarbons. To prevent these fumes from escaping into the atmosphere, the fuel evaporative emission control system was developed.

The system consists of a sealed fuel tank, a vapor/liquid separator (certain models only), a vapor vent line, a carbon canister, a vacuum signal line and a canister purge line.

In operation, fuel vapors and/or liquid are routed to the liquid/vapor separator or check valve where liquid fuel is directed back into the fuel tank as fuel vapors flow into the charcoal filled canister. The charcoal absorbs and stores the fuel vapors when the engine is not running or is at idle. When the throttle valves in the carburetor (or air intakes for fuel injection) are opened, vacuum from above the throttle valves is routed through a vacuum signal line to the purge control valve on the canister. The control valve opens and allows the fuel vapors to be drawn from the canister through a purge line and into the intake manifold and the combustion chambers.

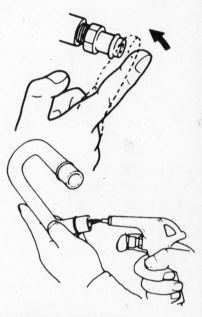

PCV valve and hose inspection

P.C.V. valve operation

Engine not running or backfiring	Cruising
Idling or decelerating	Acceleration or high load

⇦ : Fresh air
⬅ : Blow-by gas

Breather separator

P.C.V. valve

Crankcase emission control system—KA24DE engine

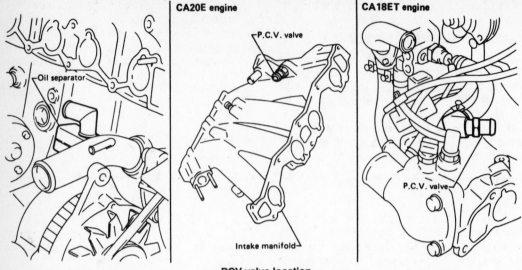

PCV valve location

INSPECTION AND SERVICE

Check the hoses for proper connections and damage. Replace as necessary. Check the vapor separator tank for fuel leaks, distortion and dents, and replace as necessary.

Carbon Canister and Purge Control Valve

To check the operation of the carbon canister purge control valve, disconnect the rubber hose between the canister control valve and the T-fitting, at the T-fitting. Apply vacuum to the hose leading to the control valve. The vacuum condition should be maintained indefinitely. If the control valve leaks, remove the top cover of the valve and check for a dislocated or cracked diaphragm. If the diaphragm is damaged, a repair kit containing a new diaphragm, retainer, and spring is available and should be installed or replace the carbon cannister assembly.

REMOVAL AND INSTALLATION

Removal and installation of the various evaporative emission control system components consists of disconnecting the hoses, loosening retaining screws, and remove the part which is to be replaced or checked. Install in the reverse order. When replacing hose, make sure that it is fuel and vapor resistant type hose.

Dual Spark Plug Ignition System

The 1982–83 Z-series and CA-series engines have two spark plugs per cylinder. This arrangement allows the engine to burn large amounts of recirculated exhaust gases without affecting performance. In fact, the system works so well it improves gas mileage under most circumstances.

Both spark plugs fire simultaneously, which

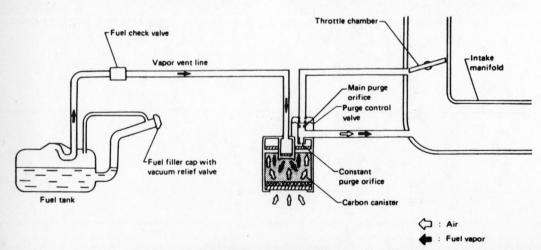

Evaporative emission control

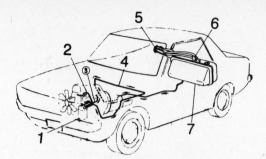

1. Carbon canister
2. Vacuum signal line
3. Canister vent line
4. Vapor vent line
5. Fuel filler cap with vacuum relief valve
6. Fuel check valve
7. Fuel tank

Evaporative emission control system schematic

When checking the purge control valve apply vacuum (inhale) to the hose

substantially shortens the time required to burn the air/fuel mixture when exhaust gases (EGR) are not being recirculated. When gases are being recirculated, the dual spark plug system brings the ignition level up to that of a single plug system which is not recirculating exhaust gases.

ADJUSTMENT

The only adjustments necessary are the normal tune-up and maintenance procedures outlined in Chapters 1 and 2.

Spark Timing Control System

The spark timing control system has been used in different forms on Nissan/ Datsuns since 1972. The first system, Transnmission Controlled Spark System (TCS) was used on most Nissan/Datsuns through 1979. This system consists of a thermal vacuum valve, a vacuum switching valve, a high gear detecting switch, and a number of vacuum hoses. Basically, the system is designed to retard full spark advance except when the car is in high gear and the engine is at normal operating temperature. At all other times, the spark advance is retarded to one degree or another.

The 1980 and later Spark Timing Control System replaces the TCS system. The major difference is that it works solely from engine water temperature changes rather than a transmission mounted switch. The system includes a thermal vacuum valve, a vacuum delay valve, and attendant hoses. It performs the same function as the earlier TCS system. To retard full spark advance at times when high levels of pollutants would otherwise be given off.

INSPECTION AND ADJUSTMENTS

Normally the Spark Timing Control systems should be trouble-free. However, if you suspect a problem in the system, first check to make

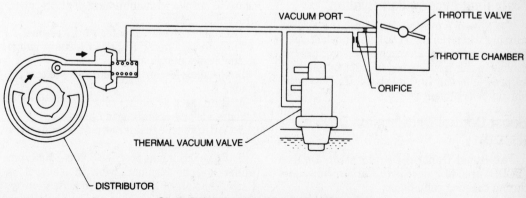

Spark timing control system—CA20E engine

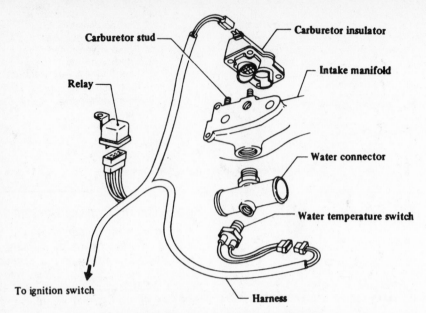

Carburetor stud

Relay

Carburetor insulator

Intake manifold

Water connector

Water temperature switch

To ignition switch

Harness

Coolant water heated fuel heater—CA20 engine

sure all wiring and hoses are connected and free from dirt. Also check to make sure the distributor vacuum advance is working properly. If everything appears all right, connect a timing light to the engine and make sure the initial timing is correct.

To test the Spark Timing Control System, connect a timing light and check the ignition timing while the temperature gauge is in the cold position. Write down the reading. Allow the engine to run with the timing light attached until the temperature needle reaches the center of the gauge. As the engine is warming up, check with the timing light to make sure the ignition timing retards. When the temperature needle is in the middle of the gauge, the ignition timing should advance from its previous position. If the ignition timing does not change, replace the thermal vacuum valve.

Early Fuel Evaporation System

The system's purpose is to heat the air/fuel mixture when the engine is below normal operating temperature. The carbureted engines use coolant water heat instead of exhaust gas heat to prewarm the fuel mixture. This system should be trouble-free.

Boost Control Deceleration Device (BCDD)

The Boost Control Deceleration Device (BCDD) used to reduce hydrocarbon emissions during coasting conditions.

High manifold vacuum during coasting pre-

vents the complete combustion of the air/fuel mixture because of the reduced amount of air. This condition will result in a large amount of HC emission. Enriching the air/fuel mixture for a short time (during the high vacuum condition) will reduce the emission of the HC.

However, enriching the air/fuel mixture with only the mixture adjusting screw will cause poor engine idle or invite an increase in the carbon monoxide (CO) content of the exhaust gases. The BCDD consists of an independent system that kicks in when the engine is coasting and enriches the air/fuel mixture, which reduces the hydrocarbon content of the exhaust gases. This is accomplished without adversely affecting engine idle and the carbon monoxide content of the exhaust gases.

ADJUSTMENT

Normally, the BCDD does not need adjustment. However, if the need should arise because of suspected malfunction of the system, proceed as follows:

1. Connect the tachometer to the engine.
2. Connect a quick response vacuum gauge to the intake manifold.
3. Disconnect the solenoid valve electrical leads.
4. Start and warm up the engine until it reaches normal operating temperature.
5. Adjust the idle speed to the proper specification.
6. Raise the engine speed to 3,000–3,500 rpm under no-load (transmission in Neutral or Park), then allow the throttle to close quickly. Take notice as to whether or not the engine

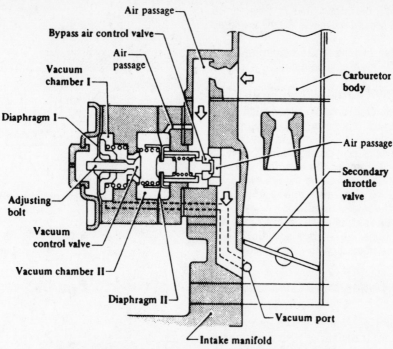

Boost controlled deceleration device system—CA20 engine

rpm returns to idle speed and if it does, how long the fall in rpm is interrupted before it reaches idle speed.

At the moment the throttle is snapped closed at high engine rpm, the vacuum in the intake manifold reaches between −23 in.Hg and −27.7 in.Hg and then gradually falls to about −16.5 in. Hg at idle speed. The process of the fall of the intake manifold vacuum and the engine rpm will take one of the following three forms:

a. When the operating pressure of the BCDD is too high, the system remains inoperative, and the vacuum in the intake manifold decreases without interruption just like that of an engine without a BCDD.

b. When the operating pressure is lower than that of the case given above, but still

higher than the proper set pressure, the fall of vacuum in the intake manifold is interrupted and kept constant at a certain level (operating pressure) for about one second and then gradually falls down to the normal vacuum at idle speed.

c. When the set of operating pressure of the BCDD is lower than the intake manifold vacuum when the throttle is suddenly released, the engine speed will not lower to idle speed.

To adjust the set operating pressure of the BCDD, remove the adjusting screw cover from the BCDD mechanism mounted on the side of the carburetor.

The adjusting screw is a left-hand threaded screw; it turns in the opposite of the usual direction to loosen or tighten. Late models may have an adjusting nut instead of a screw. Turning the screw ⅛ of a turn in either direction will change the operation pressure about 0.8 in. Hg. Turning the screw counterclockwise will increase the amount of vacuum needed to operate the mechanism. Turning the screw clockwise will decrease the amount of vacuum needed to operate the mechanism.

The operating pressure for the BCDD on most models should be between −19.9 to −22.05 in. Hg. The decrease in intake manifold

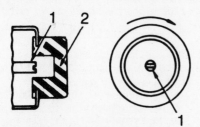

BCDD adjusting screw cover assembly

vacuum should be interrupted at these levels for about one second when the BCDD is operating correctly.

Don't forget to install the adjusting screw cover after the system is adjusted.

Intake Manifold Vacuum Control

The vacuum control valve is provided to reduce the engine lubricating oil consumption when the intake manifold vacuum increases to a vey high level during deceleration. The vacuum control valve senses the manifold vacuum. As the manifold vacuum increases beyond the specified valve, the valve opens and air is sucked into the intake manifold.

Aside from a routine check of the hoses and their connections, no service or adjustments should ever be necessary on this system.

Automatic Temperature Controlled Air Cleaner

The rate at which fuel is drawn into the airstream in a carburetor varies with the temperature of the air that the fuel is being mixed with. The air/fuel ratio cannot be held constant for efficient fuel combustion with a wide range of air temperatures. Cold air being drawn into the engine causes a richer air/fuel mixture, and thus, more hydrocarbons in the exhaust gas. Hot air being drawn into the engine causes a leaner air/fuel mixture and more efficient combustion for less hydrocarbons in the exhaust gases.

The automatic temperature controlled air cleaner is designed so that the temperature of the ambient air being drawn into the engine is automatically controlled, to hold the tempera-

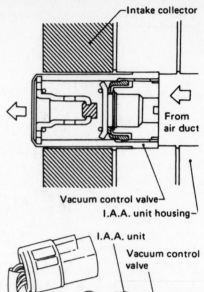

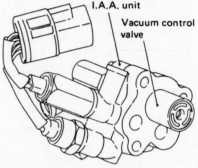

Intake manifold vacuum control

ture of the air and, consequently, the fuel/air ratio at a constant rate for efficient fuel combustion.

A temperature sensing vacuum switch controls vacuum applied to a vacuum motor operating a valve in the intake snorkle of the air cleaner. When the engine is cold or the air being drawn into the engine is cold, the vacuum mo-

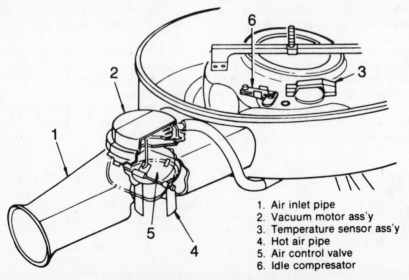

1. Air inlet pipe
2. Vacuum motor ass'y
3. Temperature sensor ass'y
4. Hot air pipe
5. Air control valve
6. Idle compresator

Automatic temperature controlled air cleaner

tor opens the valve, allowing air heated by the exhaust manifold to be drawn into the engine. As the engine warms up, the temperature sensing unit shuts off the vacuum applied to the vacuum motor which allows the valve to close, shutting off the heated air and allowing cooler, outside (under hood) air to be drawn into the engine.

TESTING

When the air around the temperature sensor of the unit mounted inside the air cleaner housing reaches 100°F (38°C), the sensor should block the flow of vacuum to the air control valve vacuum motor. When the temperature around the temperature sensor is below 100°F (38°C), the sensor should allow vacuum to pass onto the air valve vacuum motor thus blocking off the air cleaner snorkle to under hood (unheated) air.

When the temperature around the sensor is above 118°F (48°C), the air control valve should be completely open to under hood air.

If the air cleaner fails to operate correctly, check for loose or broken vacuum hoses. If the hoses are not the cause, replace the vacuum motor in the air cleaner.

Exhaust Gas Recirculation (EGR)

Exhaust gas recirculation is used to reduce combustion temperatures in the engine, thereby reducing the oxides of nitrogen emissions.

An EGR valve is mounted on the center of the intake manifold. The recycled exhaust gas is drawn into the bottom of the intake manifold riser portion through the exhaust manifold heat stove and EGR valve. A vacuum diaphragm is connected to a timed signal port at the carburetor flange.

As the throttle valve is opened, vacuum is applied to the EGR valve vacuum diaphragm. When the vacuum reaches about 2 in. Hg, the diaphragm moves against string pressure and is in a fully up position at 8 in. Hg of vacuum. As the diaphragm moves up, it opens the exhaust gas metering valve which allows exhaust gas to be pulled into the engine intake manifold. The system does not operate when the engine is idling because the exhaust gas recirculation would cause a rough idle.

On some later models, a thermal vacuum valve inserted in the engine thermostat housing controls the application of the vacuum to the EGR valve. When the engine coolant reaches a predetermined temperature, the thermal vacuum valve opens and allows vacuum to be routed to the EGR valve. Below the predetermined temperature, the thermal vacuum valve closes and blocks vacuum to the EGR valve.

Most vehicles have a B.P.T. valve installed between the EGR valve and the thermal vacuum valve. The B.P.T. valve has a diaphragm which is raised or lowered by exhaust back pressure. The diaphragm opens or closes an air bleed, which is connected into the EGR vacuum line. High pressure results in higher levels of EGR, because the diaphragm is raised, closing off the air bleed, which allows more vacuum to reach and open the EGR valve. Thus the amount of recirculated exhaust gas varies with exhaust pressure.

Some early models use a V.V.T. (venturi vacuum transducer) valve instead of the B.P.T. valve. The V.V.T. valve monitors exhaust pressure and carburetor vacuum in order to activate the diaphragm which controls the throttle vacuum applied to the EGR control valve. This system expands the operating range of the EGR flow rate as compared to the B.P.T. unit.

TESTING

NOTE: *A quick service check for the EGR valve operation is with the engine running at idle, push up on the EGR control valve diaphragm with your finger. When this is done, the engine idle should become rough and uneven.*

1. Remove the EGR valve and apply enough vacuum to the diaphragm to open the valve.

2. The valve should remain open for over 30 seconds after the vacuum is removed.

3. Check the valve for damage, such as warpage, cracks, and excessive wear around the valve and seat.

4. Clean the seat with a brush and com-

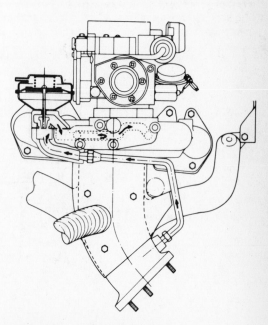

EGR system—carbureted models

CA20E ENGINE

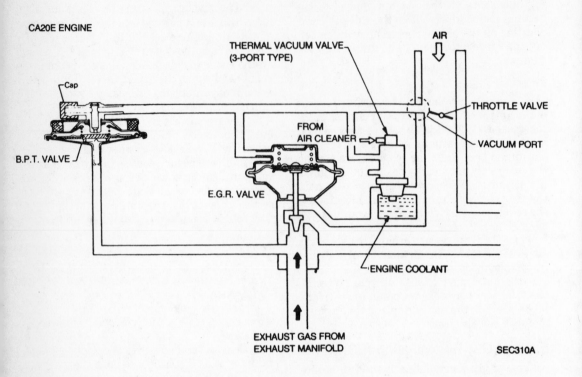

THERMAL VACUUM VALVE
(3-PORT TYPE)

AIR

Cap

THROTTLE VALVE

FROM
AIR CLEANER

VACUUM PORT

B.P.T. VALVE

E.G.R. VALVE

ENGINE COOLANT

EXHAUST GAS FROM
EXHAUST MANIFOLD

SEC310A

CA18ET ENGINE

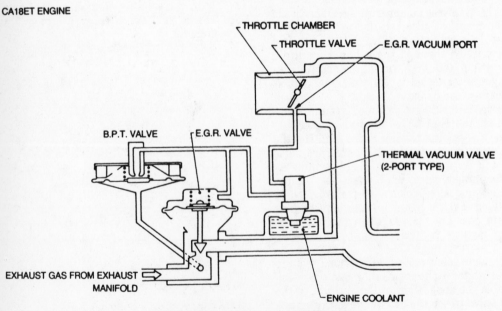

THROTTLE CHAMBER

THROTTLE VALVE

E.G.R. VACUUM PORT

B.P.T. VALVE

E.G.R. VALVE

THERMAL VACUUM VALVE
(2-PORT TYPE)

EXHAUST GAS FROM EXHAUST
MANIFOLD

ENGINE COOLANT

EGR system—CA20E and CA18ET engines

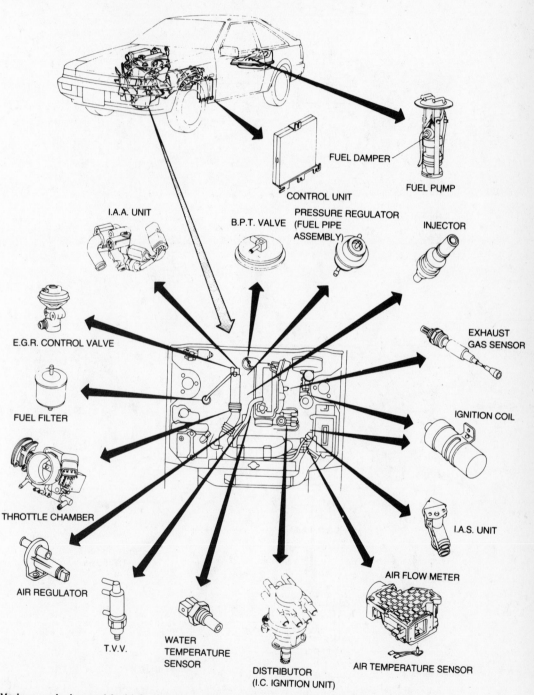

FUEL DAMPER

CONTROL UNIT

FUEL PUMP

I.A.A. UNIT

B.P.T. VALVE

PRESSURE REGULATOR (FUEL PIPE ASSEMBLY)

INJECTOR

E.G.R. CONTROL VALVE

EXHAUST GAS SENSOR

FUEL FILTER

IGNITION COIL

THROTTLE CHAMBER

I.A.S. UNIT

AIR REGULATOR

T.V.V.

WATER TEMPERATURE SENSOR

DISTRIBUTOR (I.C. IGNITION UNIT)

AIR FLOW METER

AIR TEMPERATURE SENSOR

Various emission and fuel injection component locations—200SX and 200SX Turbo CA20E and CA18ET engines

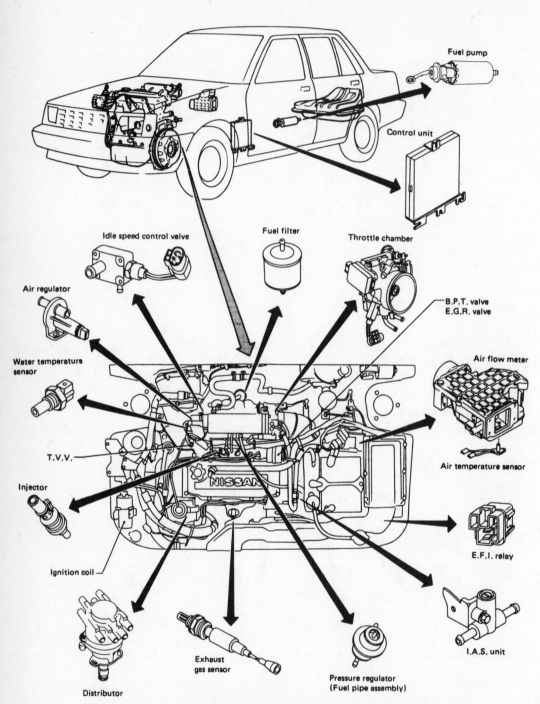

Fuel pump

Control unit

Idle speed control valve

Fuel filter

Throttle chamber

B.P.T. valve
E.G.R. valve

Air regulator

Air flow meter

Water temperature sensor

Air temperature sensor

T.V.V.

Injector

E.F.I. relay

Ignition coil

I.A.S. unit

Distributor

Exhaust gas sensor

Pressure regulator
(Fuel pipe assembly)

Various emission and fuel injection component locations—Stanza CA20E engine

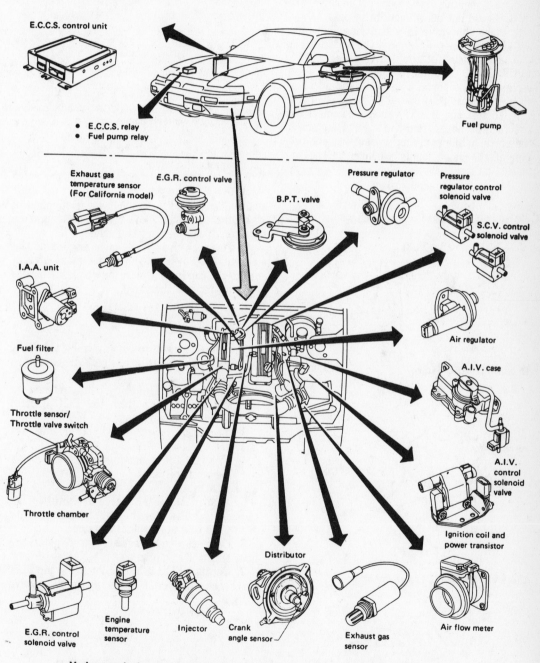

E.C.C.S. control unit

- E.C.C.S. relay
- Fuel pump relay

Fuel pump

Exhaust gas temperature sensor (For California model)

E.G.R. control valve

B.P.T. valve

Pressure regulator

Pressure regulator control solenoid valve

S.C.V. control solenoid valve

I.A.A. unit

Air regulator

Fuel filter

A.I.V. case

Throttle sensor/ Throttle valve switch

A.I.V. control solenoid valve

Throttle chamber

Ignition coil and power transistor

Distributor

E.G.R. control solenoid valve

Engine temperature sensor

Injector

Crank angle sensor

Exhaust gas sensor

Air flow meter

Various emission and fuel injection component locations—240SX KA24E engine

pressed air and remove any deposits from around the valve and port (seat).

5. To check the operation of the thermal vacuum valve, remove the valve from the engine and apply vacuum to the ports of the valve. The valve should not allow vacuum to pass.

6. Place the valve in a container of water with a thermometer and heat the water. When the temperature of the water reaches 134–145°F (57–63°C), remove the valve and apply vacuum to the ports. The valve should allow vacuum to pass through it.

7. To test the B.P.T. valve, disconnect the two vacuum hoses from the valve. Plug one of the ports. While applying pressure to the bottom of the valve, apply vacuum to the un-

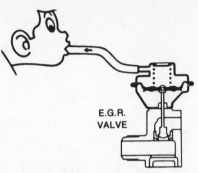

You can apply vacuum to the EGR valve by sucking on the air tube which is connected to it

plugged port and check for leakage. If any exists, replace the valve.

8. To test the check valve, remove the valve and blow into the side which connects the EGR valve. Air should flow. When air is supplied to the other side, air flow resistance should be greater. If not, replace the valve.

9. To check the V.V.T. valve disconnect the top and bottom center hoses and apply a vacuum to the top hose. Check for leaks. If a leak is present, replace the valve.

REMOVAL AND INSTALLATION

EGR Control Valve

1. Remove the nuts which attach the EGR tube and/or the BP tube to the EGR valve (if so equipped).

2. Unscrew the mounting bolts and remove the heat shield plate from the EGR control valve (if so equipped).

3. Tag and disconnect the EGR vacuum hose(s).

4. Unscrew the mounting bolts and remove the EGR control valve.

To install:

5. Install the EGR valve assembly with mounting bolts (torque the retaining bolts evenly) to intake manifold location.

6. Connect all vacuum hoses and install the heat shield if so equipped.

7. Connect EGR tube or BP tube to the EGR valve if so equipped. If replacing the EGR valve

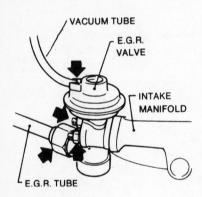

Removing the EGR valve

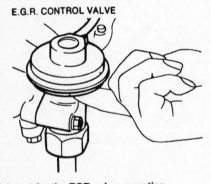

Quick test for the EGR valve operation

Clean seat of the EGR valve with a stiff brush

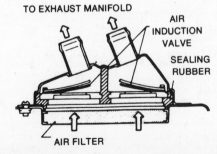

Cross section view of the air induction valve

assembly always be sure that the new valve is identical to the old one.

Air Induction System

The air induction system is used to send fresh, secondary air to the exhaust manifold by utilizing vacuum created by the exhaust pulsation in the manifold.

The exhaust pressure usually pulsates in response to the opening and closing of the exhaust valve and it periodically decreases below atmospheric pressure. If a secondary air intake pipe is opened to the atmosphere under a vacuum condition, secondary air can then be drawn into the exhaust manifold in proportion of the vacuum. Because of this, the air induction system is able to reduce the CO and HC content in the exhaust gases. The system consists of two air induction valves, a filter, hoses and E.A.I. tubes.

The only periodic maintenance required is replacement of the air induction filter as detailed in Chapter 1.

Fuel Shut-Off System

This system is designed to reduce HC emissions and also to improve fuel economy during deceleration.

The fuel shut-off system is operated when the engine runs at higher than 2200 rpm and the throttle valve is closed. These conditions are detected by the engine revolution switch and the the throttle valve switch. As the engine speed goes down to the recovery zone which is lower than 1,600 rpm, the fuel shut-off system does not operate even if the throttle valve is kept closed.

INSPECTION

Entire System

1. Disconnect harness connector on carburetor. Then connect jumper wires between each connector as illustrated.
2. Start the engine and make sure that the engine stops when engine speed increases to about 2,000 to 2,500 rpm. If not, check the harness connections for engine revolution switch and repair them as necessary. If the harness connections are OK--replace the engine revolution switch.

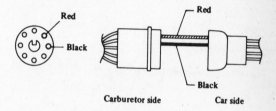

Fuel shut-off system testing procedure

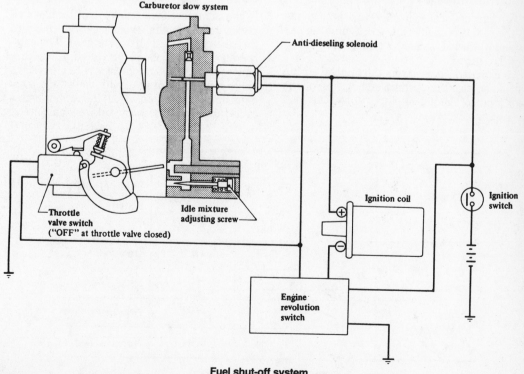

Fuel shut-off system

Throttle Valve Switch

1. Disconnect harness connector on the carburetor.
2. Check the continuity between the terminal of the connector and carburetor body when accelerator pedal is depressed or released--refer to the necessary illustrations.

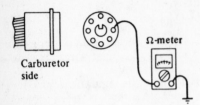

Carburetor side

Ω-meter

Fuel shut-off system testing procedure

The operation of throttle valve switch is as follows:

	Operation
Depressed	ON
Released	OFF

Fuel shut-off system testing chart

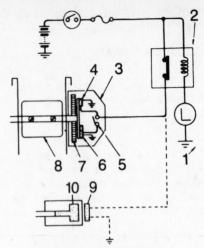

1 Alternator "L" terminal
2 Automatic-choke relay
3 Automatic-choke cover
4 P.T.C. heater (A)
5 Bimetal switch
6 P.T.C. heater (B)
7 Bimetal
8 Choke valve
9 Fast idle breaker P.T.C. heater
10 Wax

Electric choke system—1982 Stanza

Electric Choke

The purpose of the electric choke is to shorten the time the choke is in operation after the engine is started, thus shortening the time of high HC output.

An electric heater warms the bimetal spring which controls the opening and closing of the choke valve. The heater starts to heat as soon as the engine starts.

Catalytic Converter

The catalytic converter is a muffler like container built into the exhaust system to aid in the reduction of exhaust emissions. The catalyst element consists of individual pellets or a honeycomb monolithic substrate coated with a noble metal such as platinum, palladium, rhodium or a combination. When the exhaust gases come into contact with the catalyst, a chemical

Engine speed	Switch operation			Fuel shut-off system
	Engine revolution switch	Throttel valve switch	Anti-dieseling solenoid	
Higher than 2,200 rpm	OFF	OFF	OFF	Operated
		ON	ON	Not operated
Lower than 1,600 rpm	ON	OFF	ON	Not operated
		ON	ON	Not operated

Fuel shut-off system testing chart

reaction occurs which will reduce the pollutants into harmless substances like water and carbon dioxide.

There are essentially two types of catalytic converters: an oxidizing type is used on all models before 1980 year. It requires the addition of oxygen to spur the catalyst into reducing the engine's HC and CO emissions into H_2O and CO_2. Because of this need for oxygen, the Air Injection (air pump) system is used with all these models.

The oxidizing catalytic converter, while effectively reducing HC and CO emissions, does little, if anything in the way of reducing NOx emissions. Thus, the three way catalytic converter.

The three way converter, unlike the oxidizing type, is capable of reducing HC, CO and NOx emissions; all at the same time. In theory, it seems impossible to reduce all three pollutants in one system since the reduction of HC and CO requires the addition of oxygen, while the reduction of NOx calls for the removal of oxygen. In actuality, the three way system really can reduce all three pollutants, but only if the amount of oxygen in the exhaust system is precisely controlled. Due to this precise oxygen control requirement, the three way converter system is used only in cars equipped with an oxygen sensor system.

All models with the three way converter have an oxygen sensor warning light on the dashboard, which illuminates at the first 30,000 mile interval, signaling the need for oxygen sensor replacement. The oxygen sensor is part of the Mixture Ratio Feedback System. The Feedback System uses the three way converter as one of its major components.

No regular maintenance is required for the catalytic converter system, except for periodic replacement of the Air Induction System filter (if so equipped). Filter replacement procedures are in Chapter 1. The Air Induction System is used to supply the catalytic converter with fresh air. Oxygen present in the air is used in the oxidation process.

PRECAUTIONS

1. Use only unleaded fuel.
2. Avoid prolonged idling. The engine should run on longer than 20 min. at curb idle and no longer than 10 min. at fast idle.
3. Do not disconnect any of the spark plug leads while the engine is running.
4. Make engine compression checks as quickly as possible.

TESTING

At the present time there is no known way to reliably test catalytic converter operation in the field.

An infrared HC/CO tester is not sensitive enough to measure the higher tailpipe emissions from a failing converter. Thus, a bad converter may allow enough emissions to escape so that the car is no longer in compliance with

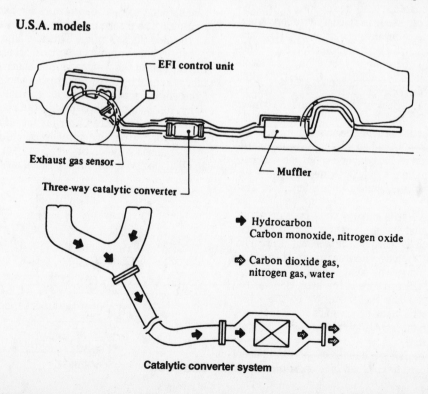

U.S.A. models

EFI control unit

Exhaust gas sensor

Three-way catalytic converter

Muffler

➡ Hydrocarbon
Carbon monoxide, nitrogen oxide

⇨ Carbon dioxide gas,
nitrogen gas, water

Catalytic converter system

Federal or state levels, but will still not cause the needle on a tester to move off zero.

The chemical reactions which occur inside a catalytic converter generate a great deal of heat. Most converter problems can be traced to fuel or ignition system problems which cause unusually high emissions. As a result of the increased intensity of the chemical reactions, the converter literally burns itself up.

A completely failed converter might cause a tester to show a slight reading; as a result, it is occasionally possible to detect one of these.

As long as you avoid severe overheating and the use of leaded fuels it is reasonably safe to assume that the converter is working properly.

NOTE: *If the catalytic converter becomes blocked the engine will not run. The converter assembly may be covered bu a manufacturer's emission warranty; contact your local Datsun/Nissan dealer for more information.*

Mixture Ratio Feedback System

The need for better fuel economy coupled to increasingly strict emission control regulations dictates a more exact control of the engine air/fuel mixture. Datsun/Nissan has developed a Mixture Ratio Feedback System in response to these needs. The system is installed on all 200SX, 1984 and later Stanza models and 240SX models.

The principle of the system is to control the air/fuel mixture exactly, so that more complete combustion can occur in the engine, and more thorough oxidation and reduction of the exhaust gases can occur in the catalytic converter. The object is to maintain a stoichiometric air/fuel mixture, which is chemically correct for theoretically complete combustion. The stoichiometric ratio is 14.7:1 (air to fuel). At that point, the converter's efficiency is greatest in oxidizing and reducing HC, CO, and NOx into CO_2, H_2O, O_2, and N_2.

Components used in the system include an oxygen sensor, installed in the exhaust manifold upstream of the converter, a three way oxidation reduction catalytic converter, an electronic control unit, and the fuel injection system itself.

The oxygen sensor reads the oxygen content of the exhaust gases. It generates an electric signal which is sent to the control unit. The control unit then decides how to adjust the mixture to keep it at the correct air/fuel ratio. For example, if the mixture is too lean, the control unit increases the fuel metering to the injectors. The monitoring process is a continual one, so that fine mixture adjustments are going on at all times.

The system has two modes of operation: open loop and closed loop. Open loop operation takes place when the engine is still cold. In this mode, the control unit ignores signals from the oxygen sensor and provides a fixed signal to the fuel injection unit. Closed loop operation takes place when the engine and catalytic converter have warmed to normal operating temperature. In closed loop operation, the control unit uses the oxygen sensor signals to adjust the mixture. The burned mixture's oxygen content is read by the oxygen sensor, which continues to signal the control unit, and so on. Thus, the closed loop mode is an interdependent system of information feedback.

Mixture is, of course, not readily adjustable in this system. All system adjustments require the use of a CO meter. Thus, they should be entrusted to a qualified technician (ASE certified) with access to the equipment and special training in the system's repair. The only regularly scheduled maintenance is replacement of the oxygen sensor at 30,000 mile intervals.

It should be noted that proper operation of the system is entirely dependent on the oxygen sensor. Thus, if the sensor is not replaced at the correct interval, or if the sensor fails during normal operation, the engine fuel mixture will be incorrect, resulting in poor fuel economy, starting problems, or stumbling and stalling of the engine when warm.

Oxygen Sensor

Inspection and Replacement

An exhaust gas sensor warning light will illuminate on the instrument panel when the car has reached 30,000 miles. This is a signal that the oxygen sensor must be replaced. It is important to replace the oxygen sensor every 30,000 miles, to ensure proper monitoring and control of the engine air/fuel mixture.

The following service procedure is recommend by Nissan Motor Company for all models to 1987 year, after this point complete Engine Self-Diagnosis is necessary. The oxygen sensor can be inspected using the following procedure:

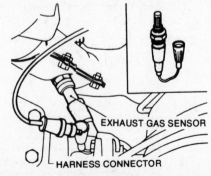

EXHAUST GAS SENSOR

HARNESS CONNECTOR

Oxygen sensor location—200SX

1. Start the engine and allow it to reach normal operating temperature.

2. Run the engine at approximately 2,000 rpm under no load. Block the front wheels and set the parking brake.

3. An inspection lamp has been provided on the bottom of the control unit, which is located in the passenger compartment. If the oxygen sensor is operating correctly, the inspection lamp will go on and off more than 9 times in 10 seconds. The inspection lamp can be more easily seen with the aid of a mirror.

4. If the lamp does not go on and off as specified, the system is not operating correctly. Check the battery, ignition system, engine oil and coolant levels, all fuses, the fuel injection wiring harness connectors, all vacuum hoses, the oil filler cap and dipstick for proper seating, and the valve clearance and engine compression. If all of these parts are in good order, and the inspection lamp still does not go on and off at least 9 times in 10 seconds the oxygen sensor is probably faulty. However, the possibility exists that the malfunction could be in the fuel injection control unit. The system should be tested by a qualified technician (ASE certified) with specific training in the "Mixture Ratio Feedback System".

To replace the oxygen sensor:

1. Disconnect the negative battery cable and the sensor electrical lead. Unscrew the sensor from the exhaust manifold.

2. Coat the threads of the replacement sensor with a nickel-based anti-seize compound. Do not use other types of compounds, since they may electrically insulate the sensor. Do not get compound on sensor housing. Install the sensor into the manifold. Installation torque for the sensor is about 18–25 ft. lbs. on 1988 and later models torque is 30–37 ft. lbs. (Note the 1987 200SX model oxygen sensor torque is 30–37 ft. lbs.) Connect the electrical lead. Be careful handling the electrical lead. It is easily damaged.

3. Reconnect the battery cable.

The oxygen sensor is installed in the exhaust manifold and is removed in the same manner as a spark plug. Exercise care when handling the sensor do not drop or handle the sensor roughly. Care should be used not to get compound on the sensor itself.

Maintenance Reminder Lights
RESETTING

On models with a sensor relay, reset the relay by pushing or inserting a small screwdriver into the reset hole. Reset relay at 30,000 mile intervals.

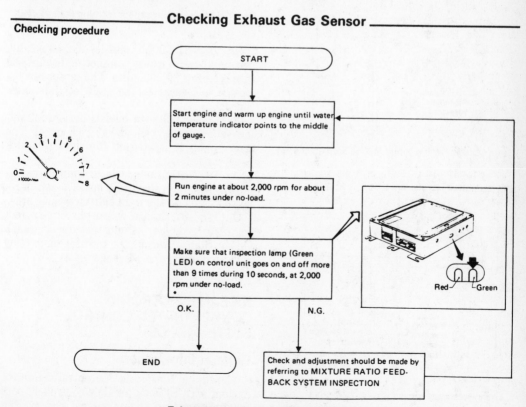

Checking Exhaust Gas Sensor

Checking procedure

START

Start engine and warm up engine until water temperature indicator points to the middle of gauge.

Run engine at about 2,000 rpm for about 2 minutes under no-load.

Make sure that inspection lamp (Green LED) on control unit goes on and off more than 9 times during 10 seconds, at 2,000 rpm under no-load.

O.K.

N.G.

Red — Green

END

Check and adjustment should be made by referring to MIXTURE RATIO FEEDBACK SYSTEM INSPECTION

Exhaust gas sensor testing procedure

WARNING LIGHT CONNECTOR LOCATIONS

After 30,000 miles on Datsun/Nissan (1982–1983) 200SX Model disconnect a green/green and white stripe wire under the right side of the instrument panel. On (1984) 200SX models disconnect white connector under the right side of the instrument panel.

Oxygen sensor warning lamp harness connector 1982–83 200SX

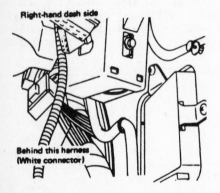

Oxygen sensor warning lamp harness connector 1984 200SX

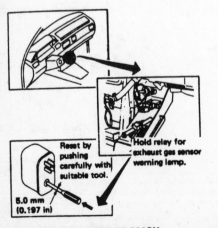

Sensor relay location 1985–87 200SX

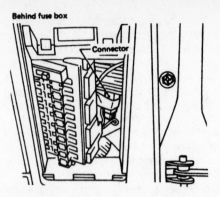

Oxygen sensor warning lamp harness connector 1985–87 200SX

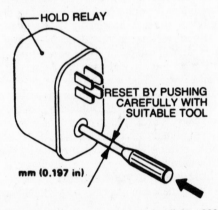

Resetting the oxygen sensor warning light—200SX

On 1985–87 200SX vehicles disconnect the warning lamp harness connnector behind the fuse box after 90,000 miles. The sensor relay is located is located to the right of the center console.

On 1984–86 Stanza models disconnect yellow-yellow/green, behind left kick panel. The sensor relay is located on the right side kick panel area.

On 1987 Stanza models disconnect green-brown (with tag), above fuse box. The sensor relay is located on the right side kick panel area.

On 1986–87 Stanza wagon disconnect red-yellow or red/blue, behind instrument panel. On the Stanza wagons the warning lamp relay is located under the passenger seat.

NISSAN ELECTRONIC CONCENTRATED CONTROL SYSTEM (ECCS)

General Information

The Nissan Electronic Concentrated Control System (ECCS) is an air flow controlled, port fuel injection and engine control system. The

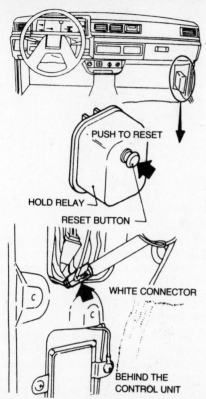

Disconnecting and resetting the oxygen sensor warning lamp 1984–87 Stanza (except station wagon)

ECCS electronic control unit consists of a microcomputer, inspection lamps, a diagnostic mode selector and connectors for signal input and output and for power supply. The electronic control unit, or ECU, controls the following functions:

- Amount of injected fuel
- Ignition timing
- Mixture ratio feedback
- Pressure regulator control
- Exhaust Gas Recirculation (EGR) operation
- Idle speed control
- Fuel pump operation
- Air regulator control
- Air Injection Valve (AIV) operation
- Self-diagnostics
- Air flow meter self-cleaning control
- Fail safe system

SYSTEM COMPONENTS

Crank Angle Sensor

The crank angle sensor is a basic component of the ECCS system. It monitors engine speed and piston position, as well as sending signals which the ECU uses to control fuel injection, ignition timing and other functions. The crank angle sensor has a rotor plate and a wave form-

ing circuit. On all models, the rotor plate has 360 slits for 1° signals (crank angle). On models equipped with VG30E engine, the rotor plate also consists of 6 slits for 120° signal (engine speed). On models equipped with CA20E, CA18ET, CA18DE and KA24E engines, the rotor plate also consists of 4 slits for 180° signal (engine speed).

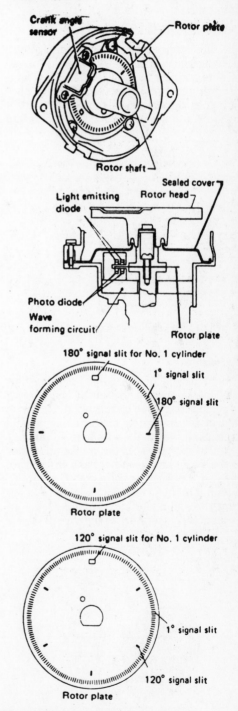

ECCS distributor with crank angle sensor

The light emitting diodes (LED's) and photo diodes are built into the wave forming circuit. When the rotor plate passes the space between the LED and the photo diode, the slits of the rotor plate continually cut the light which is sent to the photo diode from the LED. This generates rough shaped pulses which are converted into ON/OFF pulses by the wave forming circuit and then sent to the ECU.

Cylinder Head Temperature Sensor

The cylinder head temperature sensor monitors changes in cylinder head temperature and transmits a signal to the ECU. The temperature sensing unit employs a thermistor which is sensitive to the change in temperature, with electrical resistance decreasing as temperature rises.

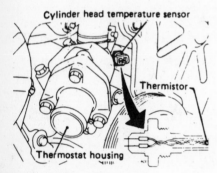

Cylinder head temperature sensor

Air Flow Meter

The air flow meter measures the mass flow rate of intake air. The volume of air entering the engine is measured by the use of a hot wire placed in the intake air stream. The control unit sends current to the wire to maintain it at a preset temperature. As the intake air moves past the wire, it removes heat and the control unit must increase the voltage to the wire to maintain it at the preset temperature. By measuring the amount of current necessary to maintain the temperature of the wire in the air

Air flow meter—except CA18ET engine

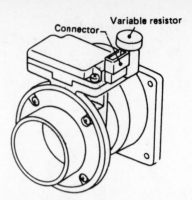

Air flow meter—CA18ET engine

stream, the ECU knows exactly how much air is entering the engine. A self-cleaning system briefly heats the hot air wire to approximately 1832°F (1000°C) after engine shutdown to burn off any dust or contaminants on the wire.

Exhaust Gas Sensor

The exhaust gas sensor, which is placed in the exhaust pipe, monitors the amount of oxygen in the exhaust gas. The sensor is made of ceramic titania which changes electrical resistance at the ideal air/fuel ratio (14.7:1). The control unit supplies the sensor with approximately 1 volt and takes the output voltage of the sensor depending on its resistance. The oxygen sensor is equipped with a heater to bring it to operating temperature quickly.

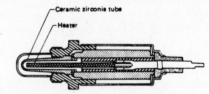

Exhaust gas sensor—zirconia tube type

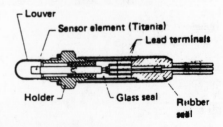

Exhaust gas sensor—titania type

Throttle Valve Switch

A throttle valve switch is attached to the throttle chamber and operates in response to accelerator pedal movement. The switch has an idle contact and a full throttle contact. The idle contact closes when the throttle valve is posi-

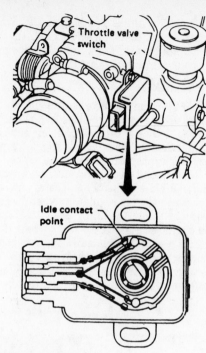

Throttle valve switch

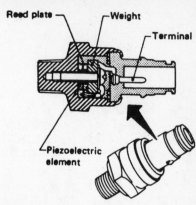

Detonation sensor (turbo sensor)

tioned at idle and opens when it is in any other position.

Fuel Injector

The fuel injector is a small, precision solenoid valve. As the ECU sends an injection signal to each injector, the coil built into the injector pulls the needle valve back and fuel is injected through the nozzle and into the intake manifold. The amount of fuel injected is dependent on how long the signal is (pulse duration); the longer the signal, the more fuel delivered.

Fuel Temperature Sensor

A fuel temperature sensor is built into the fuel pressure regulator. When the fuel temperature is higher than the preprogrammed level, the ECU will enrich the fuel injected to compensate for temperature expansion. The temperature sensor and pressure regulator should be replaced as an assembly if either malfunctions. The electric fuel pump with an integral damper is installed in the fuel tank. It is a vane roller type with the electric motor cooled by the fuel itself. The fuel filter is of metal construction in order to withstand the high fuel system pressure. The fuel pump develops 61–71 psi, but the pressure regulator keeps system pressure at 36 psi in operation.

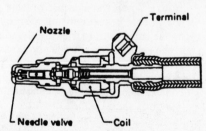

Fuel injector

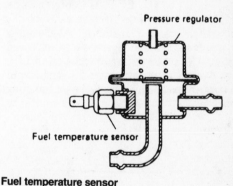

Fuel temperature sensor

Detonation Sensor (Turbo Model)

The detonation sensor is attached to the cylinder block and senses engine knocking conditions. A knocking vibration from the cylinder block is applied as pressure to the piezoelectric element. This vibrational pressure is then converted into a voltage signal which is delivered as output.

Power Transistor

The ignition signal from the ECU is amplified by the power transistor, which turns the ignition coil primary circuit on and off, inducing the necessary high voltage in the secondary circuit to fire the spark plugs. Ignition timing is controlled according to engine operating conditions, with the optimum timing advance for each driving condition preprogrammed into the ECU memory.

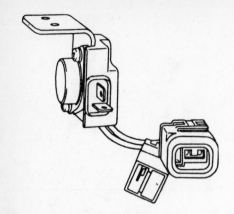

Power transitor—CA18ET engine

Power transistor and ignition coil

Vehicle Speed Sensor

The vehicle speed sensor provides a vehicle speed signal to the ECU. On conventional speedometers, the speed sensor consists of a reed switch which transforms vehicle speed into a pulse signal. On digital electronic speedometers, the speed sensor consists of an LED, photo diode, shutter and wave forming circuit. It operates on the same principle as the crank angle sensor.

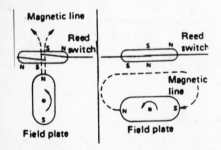

Vehicle speed sensor

Swirl Control Valve (SCV) Control Solenoid Valve

The SCV control solenoid valve cuts the intake manifold vacuum signal for the swirl control valve. It responds to ON/OFF signal from the ECU. When the solenoid is off, the vacuum

signal from the intake manifold is cut. When the control unit sends an ON signal, the coil pulls the plunger and feeds the vacuum signal to the swirl control valve actuator.

Idle-Up Solenoid Valve

An idle-up solenoid valve is attached to the intake collector to stabilize idle speed when the engine load is heavy because of electrical load, power steering load, etc. An air regulator provides an air bypass when the engine is cold in order to increase idle speed during warmup (fast idle). A bimetal, heater and rotary shutter are built into the air regulator. When bimetal temperature is low, the air bypass port is open. As the engine starts and electric current flows through a heater, the bimetal begins to rotate the shutter to close off the air bypass port. The air passage remains closed until the engine is stopped and the bimetal temperature drops.

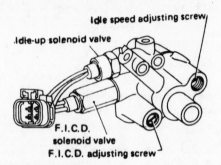

Idle-up solenoid valve

Air Injection Valve (AIV)

The Air Injection Valve (AIV) sends secondary air to the exhaust manifold, utilizing a vacuum caused by exhaust pulsation in the exhaust manifold. When the exhaust pressure is below atmospheric pressure (negative pressure), secondary air is sent to the exhaust manifold. When the exhaust pressure is above atmospheric pressure, the reed valves prevent secondary air from being sent to the air cleaner. The AIV control solenoid valve cuts the intake manifold vacuum signal for AIV control. The solenoid valve actuates in response to the ON/OFF signal from the ECU. When the solenoid is off, the vacuum signal from the intake manifold

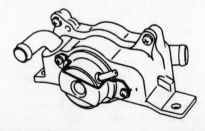

Air injection valve

is cut. As the control unit outputs an on signal, the coil pulls the plunger downward and feeds the vacuum signal to the AIV control valve.

Exhaust Gas Recirculation (EGR) Vacuum Cut Solenoid Valve

The EGR vacuum cut solenoid valve is the same type as that of the AIV. The EGR system is controlled by the ECU; at both low and high engine speed (rpm), the solenoid valve turns on and the EGR valve cuts the exhaust gas recirculation into the intake manifold. The pressure regulator control solenoid valve also actuates in response to the ON/OFF signal from the ECU. When it is off, a vacuum signal from the intake manifold is fed into the pressure regulator. As the control unit outputs an on signal, the coil pulls the plunger downward and cuts the vacuum signal.

Electronic Control Unit (ECU)

The ECU consists of a microcomputer, inspection lamps, a diagnostic mode selector, and connectors for signal input and output, and for power supply. The unit has control of the engine.

Air Regulator

The air regulator provides an air bypass when the engine is cold for the purpose of a fast idle during warm-up. A bimetal, heater and rotary shutter are built into the air regulator. When the bimetal temperature is low, the air bypass port is open. As the engine starts and

electric current flows through a heater, the bimetal begins to rotate the shutter to close off the bypass port. The air passage remains closed until the engine is stopped and the bimetal temperature drops.

Idle Air Adjusting (IAA) Unit

The IAA consists of the AAC valve, FICD solenoid valve and an idle adjust screw. It receives signals from the ECU and controls the idle speed to the pre-set valve.

The FICD solenoid valve compensates for change in the idle speed caused by the operation of the air compressor. A vacuum control valve is installed in this unit to prevent an abnormal rise in the intake manifold vacuum pressure during deceleration

Auxiliary Air Control (AAC) Valve

The AAC valve is attached to the intake collector. The ECU actuates the AAC valve by an ON/OFF pulse of approximately 160 Hz. The longer that ON duty is left on, the larger the amount of air that will flow through the AAC valve.

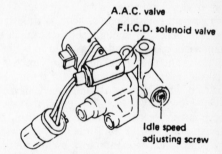

Auxiliary air control (AAC) valve

SYSTEM OPERATION

In operation, the on-board computer (control unit) calculates the basic injection pulse width by processing signals from the crank angle sensor and air flow meter. Receiving signals from each sensor which detects various engine operating conditions, the computer adds various en-

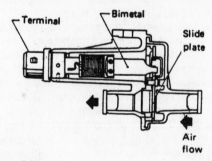

Air regulator

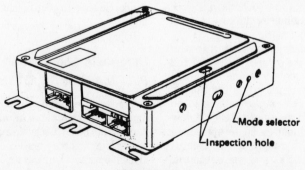

Control unit

richments (which are preprogrammed) to the basic injection amount. In this manner, the optimum amount of fuel is delivered through the injectors. The fuel is enriched when starting, during warm-up, when accelerating, when cylinder head temperature is high and when operating under a heavy load. The fuel is leaned during deceleration according to the closing rate of the throttle valve. Fuel shut-off is accomplished during deceleration, when vehicle speed exceeds 137 mph, or when engine speed exceeds 6400 rpm for about 500 revolutions.

The mixture ratio feedback system (closed loop control) is designed to control the air/fuel mixture precisely to the stoichiometric or optimum point so that the 3-way catalytic converter can minimize CO, HC and NOx emissions simultaneously. The optimum air/fuel fuel mixture is 14.7:1. This system uses an exhaust gas (oxygen) sensor located in the exhaust manifold to give an indication of whether the fuel mixture is richer or leaner than the stoichiometric point. The control unit adjusts the injection pulse width according to the sensor voltage so the mixture ratio will be within the narrow window around the stoichiometric fuel ratio. The system goes into closed loop as soon as the oxygen sensor heats up enough to register. The system will operate under open loop when starting the engine, when the engine temperature is cold, when exhaust gas sensor temperature is cold, when driving at high speeds or under heavy load, at idle (after mixture ratio learning is completed), during deceleration, if the exhaust gas sensor malfunctions, or when the exhaust gas sensor monitors a rich condition for more than 10 seconds and during deceleration.

Ignition timing is controlled in response to engine operating conditions. The optimum ignition timing in each driving condition is preprogrammed in the computer. The signal from the control unit is transmitted to the power transistor and controls ignition timing. The idle speed is also controlled according to engine operating conditions, temperature and gear position. On manual transmission models, if battery voltage is less than 12 volts for a few seconds, a higher idle speed will be maintained by the control unit to improve charging function.

There is a fail-safe system built into the ECCS control unit. If the output voltage of the air flow meter is extremely low, the ECU will substitute a preprogrammed value for the air flow meter signal and allow the vehicle to be driven as long as the engine speed is kept below 2000 rpm. If the cylinder head temperature sensor circuit is open, the control unit clamps the warmup enrichment at a certain amount. This amount is almost the same as that when

the cylinder head temperature is between 68–176°F (20–80°C). If the fuel pump circuit malfunctions, the fuel pump relay comes on until the engine stops. This allows the fuel pump to receive power from the relay.

SERVICE PRECAUTIONS

- Do not operate the fuel pump when the fuel lines are empty.
- Do not reuse fuel hose clamps.
- Do not disconnect the ECCS harness connectors before the battery ground cable has been disconnected.
- Make sure all ECCS connectors are fastened securely. A poor connection can cause an extremely high surge voltage in the coil and condenser and result in damage to integrated circuits.
- Keep the ECCS harness at least 4 in. away from adjacent harnesses to prevent an ECCS system malfunction due to external electronic "noise."
- Keep all parts and harnesses dry during service.
- Before attempting to remove any parts, turn **OFF** the ignition switch and disconnect the battery ground cable.
- Always use a 12 volt battery as a power source.
- Do not disconnect the battery cables with the engine running.
- Do not depress the accelerator pedal when starting.
- Do not rev up the engine immediately after starting or just prior to shutdown.
- Do not attempt to disassemble the ECCS control unit under any circumstances.
- If a battery cable is disconnected, the memory will return to the ROM (programmed) values. Engine operation may vary slightly, but this is not an indication of a problem. Do not replace parts because of a slight variation.
- If installing a 2-way or CB radio, keep the antenna as far as possible away from the electronic control unit. Keep the antenna feeder line at least 8 in. away from the ECCS harness and do not let the 2 run parallel for a long distance. Be sure to ground the radio to the vehicle body.

Diagnosis and Testing
SELF-DIAGNOSTIC SYSTEM

The self-diagnostic function is useful for diagnosing malfunctions in major sensors and actuators of the ECCS system. There are 5 modes in self-diagnostics on all models except Stanza. On Stanza, there are 2 modes in self-diagnostics

Mode 1

EXCEPT STANZA

During closed loop operation, the green inspection lamp turns ON when a lean condition is detected and OFF when a rich condition is detected. During open loop operation, the red inspection lamp stays OFF.

STANZA

During this mode, the red LED in the ECU and the CHECK ENGINE LIGHT on the instrument panel stay ON. If either remain OFF, check the bulb in the CHECK ENGINE light or the red LED.

Mode 2

EXCEPT STANZA

The green inspection lamp function is the same as in Mode 1. During closed loop operation, the red inspection lamp turns ON and OFF simultaneously with the green inspection lamp when the mixture ratio is controlled within the specified value. During open loop operation, the red inspection lamp stays OFF.

STANZA

This models uses Mode 2 for self-diagnostic results and exhaust gas sensor monitor.

When in Mode 2 (self-diagnostic results), a malfunction code is indicated by the number of flashes from the red LED or the CHECK ENGINE LIGHT.

When in Mode 2 (exhaust gas sensor monitor), the CHECK ENGINE LIGHT and red LED display the condition of the fuel mixture (rich/lean) which is monitored by the exhaust gas senor. If 2 exhaust sensors are used (right side and left side), the left exhaust gas sensor monitor operates first, when selecting this mode.

Mode 3

This mode is the same as the former self-diagnosis mode.

Mode 4

During this mode, the inspection lamps monitor the ON/OFF condition of the idle switch, starter switch and vehicle speed sensor.

In ON/OFF diagnosis system, the operation of the following switches can be detected continuously:
- Idle switch
- Starter switch
- Vehicle speed sensor

1. Idle switch and starter switch — the switches ON/OFF status at the point when Mode IV is selected is stored in ECU memory. When either switch is turned from **ON** to **OFF**

or **OFF** to **ON**, the red LED on ECU alternately comes on and goes off each time switching is detected.

2. Vehicle speed sensor — The switches ON/OFF status at the point when Mode IV is selected is stored in ECU memory. When vehicle speed is 12 mph (20 km/h) or slower, the green LED on ECU is off. When vehicle speed exceeds 12 mph (20 km/h), the green LED on ECU comes ON.

Mode 5

The moment a malfunction is detected, the display will be presented immediately by flashing the inspection lamps during the driving test.

In real time diagnosis, if any of the following items are judged to be faulty, a malfunction is indicated immediately:
- Crank angle sensor
- Ignition signal
- Air flow meter output signal
- Fuel pump (some models)

Consequently, this diagnosis is a very effective measure to diagnose whether the above systems cause the malfunction or not, during driving test. Compared with self-diagnosis, real time diagnosis is very sensitive, and can detect malfunctioning conditions in a moment. Further, items regarded to be malfunctions in this diagnosis are not stored in ECU memory.

To switch the modes, turn the ignition switch **ON**, then turn the diagnostic mode selector on the control unit fully clockwise and wait for the inspection lamps to flash. Count the number of flashes until the inspection lamps have flashed the number of the desired mode, then immediately turn the diagnostic mode selector fully counterclockwise.

NOTE: *When the ignition switch is turned OFF during diagnosis in each mode, and then turned back on again after the power to the control unit has dropped off completely, the diagnosis will automatically return to Mode 1.*

The stored memory will be lost if the battery terminal is disconnected, or Mode 4 is selected after selecting Mode 3. However, if the diagnostic mode selector is kept turned fully clockwise, it will continue to change in the order of Mode 1, 2, 3, etc., and in this case, the stored memory will not be erased.

In Mode 3, the control unit constantly monitors the function of sensors and actuators regardless of ignition key position. If a malfunction occurs, the information is stored in the control unit and can be retrieved from the memory by turning **ON** the diagnostic mode selector on the side of the control unit. When activated, the malfunction is indicated by flashing a red and green LED (also located on the control unit). Since all the self-diagnostic results are stored in the control unit memory, even intermittent malfunctions can be diagnosed. A malfunctioning part's group is indicated by the number of both red and green LED's flashing. First, the red LED flashes and the green flashes follow. The red LED refers to the number of tens, while the green refers to the number of units. If the red LED flashes twice and the green LED flashes once, a Code 21 is being displayed. All malfunctions are classified by their trouble code number.

The diagnostic result is retained in the control unit memory until the starter is operated 50 times after a diagnostic item is judged to be malfunctioning. The diagnostic result will then be canceled automatically. If a diagnostic item which has been judged malfunctioning and stored in memory is again judged to be malfunctioning before the starter is operated 50 times, the second result will replace the previous one and stored in the memory until the starter is operated 50 more times.

In Mode 5 (real time diagnosis), if the crank angle sensor, ignition signal or air flow meter output signal are judged to be malfunctioning, the malfunction will be indicated immediately. This diagnosis is very effective for determining whether these systems are causing a malfunction during the driving test. Compared with self-diagnosis, real time diagnosis is very sensitive and can detect malfunctioning conditions immediately. However, malfunctioning items in this diagnosis mode are not stored in memory.

TESTING PRECAUTIONS

• Before connecting or disconnecting control unit ECU harness connectors, make sure the ignition switch is **OFF** and the negative battery cable is disconnected to avoid the possibility of damage to the control unit.

• When performing ECU input/output signal diagnosis, remove the pin terminal retainer from the 20 and 16-pin connectors to make it easier to insert tester probes into the connector.

• When connecting or disconnecting pin connectors from the ECU, take care not to bend or break any pin terminals. Check that there are no bends or breaks on ECU pin terminals before attempting any connections.

• Before replacing any ECU, perform the ECU input/output signal diagnosis to make sure the ECU is functioning properly or not.

• After performing the Electronic Control System Inspection, perform the ECCS self-diagnosis and driving test.

• When measuring supply voltage of ECU controlled components with a circuit tester, separate one tester probe from another. If the 2 tester probes accidentally make contact with each other during measurement, a short circuit will result and damage the power transistor in the ECU.

Fuel System

5

CARBURETED FUEL SYSTEMS

Mechanical Fuel Pump

The fuel pump is a mechanically operated, diaphragm type driven by the fuel pump eccentric on the camshaft. The pump is located on the right rear side of the cylinder head (CA20 engine).

REMOVAL AND INSTALLATION

CAUTION: *Never smoke when working around gasoline! Avoid all sources of sparks or ignition. Gasoline vapors are EXTREMELY volatile!*

1. Disconnect the fuel lines from the fuel pump. Be sure to keep the line leading from the fuel tank up high to prevent the excess loss of fuel.

2. Remove the two fuel pump mounting nuts and the fuel pump assembly from the right side of the engine.

3. To install, use a new gasket, sealant and reverse the removal procedures. Torque the fuel pump bolts to 7–9 ft. lbs. Replace the fuel line hose clamps as necessary.

TESTING

Static Pressure

CAUTION: *Never smoke when working around gasoline! Avoid all sources of sparks or ignition. Gasoline vapors are EXTREMELY volatile!*

1. Disconnect the fuel line at the carburetor. Using a T-connector, connect two rubber hoses to the connector, then install it between the fuel line and the carburetor fitting.

NOTE: *When disconnecting the fuel line, be sure to place a container under the line to catch the excess fuel.*

2. Connect a fuel pump pressure gauge to the T-connector and secure it with a clamp.

3. Start the engine and check the pressure at various speeds. The pressure should be 2.8–3.8 psi (19.3–26.2 kpa). There is usually enough gas in the float bowl to perform this test.

4. If the pressure is OK, perform a capacity test. Remove the gauge and the T-connector as-

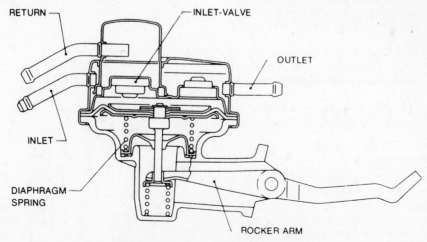

Engine fuel pump—CA20 engine series

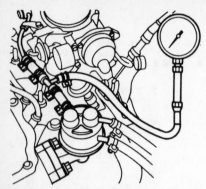

Testing mechanical fuel pump

sembly, then reinstall the fuel line to the carburetor.

Capacity Test

1. Disconnect the fuel line from the carburetor and place the line in a graduated container.
2. Fill the carburetor float bowl with gas.
3. Start the engine and run it for one minute at about 1,000 rpm. The pump should deliver 1.5 liters of fuel per minute.

Carburetor

The carburetor is a 2-barrel down-draft type with a low speed (primary) side and a high speed (secondary) side.

All models have an electrically operated antidieseling solenoid. As the ignition switch is turned off, the valve is energized and shuts off the supply of fuel to the idle circuit of the carburetor.

ADJUSTMENTS

Throttle Linkage Adjustment

1. Disconnect the negative battery cable.
2. Remove the air cleaner.
3. Open the automatic choke valve by hand, while turning the throttle valve by pulling the throttle lever, then set the choke valve in the open position.

NOTE: *If equipped with a vacuum controlled throttle positioner, use a vacuum hand pump to retract the the throttle positioner rod.*

4. Adjust the throttle cable at the carburetor bracket, so that a 1.0–2.0mm of free pedal play exists.

Dashpot Adjustment

A dashpot is used on carburetors with automatic transaxles and some manual transaxles. The dashpot slowly closes the throttle on automatic transmissions to prevent stalling and serves as an emission control device on all late model vehicles.

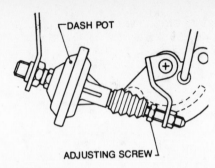

Dashpot adjustment

The dashpot should be adjusted to contact the throttle lever on deceleration at approximately 1,400–1,600 rpm of engine operation.

NOTE: *Before attempting to adjust the dashpot, make sure the idle speed, timing and mixture adjustments are correct.*

1. Loosen the locknut (turn the dashpot, if necessary) and make sure the engine speed drops smoothly from 2,000 rpm to 1,000 rpm in 3 seconds.
2. If the dashpot has been removed from the carburetor, it must be adjusted when installed. Adjust the gap between the primary throttle valve and the inner carburetor wall, when the dashpot stem comes in contact with the throttle arm. The dashpot gap is 0.66–0.86mm (manual transaxle) or 0.49–0.69mm (automatic transaxle).

Secondary Throttle Linkage Adjustment

All carburetors discussed in this book are two stage type carburetors. On this type of carburetor, the engine runs on the primary barrel most of the time, with the secondary barrel being used for acceleration. When the throttle valve on the primary side opens to an angle of approximately 50° (from its fully closed position), the

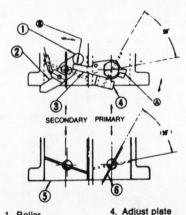

1. Roller
2. Connecting lever
3. Return plate
4. Adjust plate
5. Throttle chamber
6. Throttle valve

Secondary throttle linkage adjustment

secondary throttle valve is pulled open by the connecting linkage. The 50° angle of throttle valve opening works out to a clearance measurement of 7.4–8.4mm (Stanza) between the throttle valve and the carburetor body. The easiest way to measure this is to use a drill bit. Drill bits from sizes H to P (standard letter size drill bits) should fit. If an adjustment is necessary, bend the connecting link between the two linkage assemblies.

Float Level Adjustment

The fuel level is normal if it is within the lines on the window glass of the float chamber (or the sight glass) when the vehicle is resting on level ground and the engine is off.

If the fuel level is outside the lines, remove the float housing cover. Have an absorbent cloth under the cover to catch the fuel from the fuel bowl. Adjust the float level by bending the needle seat on the float.

The needle valve should have an effective stroke of about 1.5mm. When necessary, the needle valve stroke can be adjusted by bending the float stopper.

NOTE: *Be careful not to bend the needle valve rod when installing the float and baffle plate, if removed.*

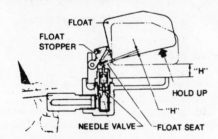

Float level adjustment

Fast Idle Adjustment

NOTE: *On the Stanza models, the fast idle cam lever is located next to the fast idle cam screw, so the choke cover does not have to be removed. On the 1985 Stanza, disconnect the Fast Idle Breaker harness at the carburetor.*
1. Remove the carburetor from the vehicle.
CAUTION: *Never smoke when working around gasoline! Avoid all sources of sparks or ignition. Gasoline vapors are EXTREMELY volatile!*
2. Remove the choke cover, then place the fast idle arm on the 2nd step of the fast idle cam. Using the correct wire gauge, measure the clearance A between the throttle valve and the wall of the throttle valve chamber (at the center of the throttle valve). It should be 0.66–0.80mm (MT) or 0.81–0.95mm (AT).

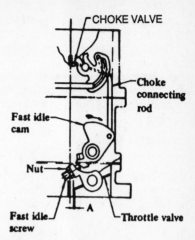

Adjusting the fast idle cam—Stanza

3. Install the carburetor on the engine.
4. Start the engine, warm it to operating temperatures and check the fast idle rpm. The cam should be at the 2nd step. Engine speed should be 2,400–2,700 rpm (MT) or 2,800–3,100 rpm (AT).
5. To adjust the fast idle speed, turn the fast idle adjusting screw counterclockwise to increase the fast idle speed and clockwise to decrease the fast idle speed.

Fast Idle Breaker Adjustment

1985-86 STANZA

1. Start the engine and warm it to operating temperatures without racing it.
2. Check the engine speed and the breaker operation; it should be high rpm at the start, then idle speed when warm.
3. Disconnect the fast idle breaker harness connector at the carburetor. Using an ohmmeter, check the fast idle breaker for continuity; place one lead on the breaker's ground wire and the other lead on the No. 8 pin of the harness connector.
NOTE: *Checking is performed when the*

Checking the continuity of the fast idle breaker— Stanza 1985 and later models

breaker is cold (less than 68°F) and the choke plate closed.

4. If there is no continuity, replace the breaker.

5. If an ohmmeter is not available, check the breaker with the engine running (harness connector installed), if the breaker does not warm up, replace it.

Cam Follow Lever Adjustment

STANZA

Hold the choke plate closed, turn the adjusting screw until there is no clearance between the cam follow lever and the fast idle cam.

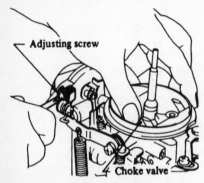

Adjusting the cam follow lever—Stanza

Automatic Choke Adjustment

1. With the engine cold, make sure the choke is fully closed (press the accelerator pedal all the way to the floor and release).

2. Check the choke linkage for binding. The choke plate should be easily opened and closed with your finger. If the choke sticks or binds, it can usually be freed with a liberal application of a carburetor cleaner made for the purpose. A couple of quick squirts normally does the trick; if not, the carburetor will have to be disassembled for repairs.

3. The choke is correctly adjusted when the index mark on the choke housing (notch) aligns with the center mark on the carburetor body. If the setting is incorrect, loosen the three screws clamping the choke body in place and rotate the choke cover left or right until the marks align. Tighten the screws carefully to avoid cracking the housing.

Choke Unloader Adjustment

NOTE: *The choke assembly must be cold for this adjustment.*

1. Close the choke valve completely.

2. Hold the choke valve closed by stretching a rubber band between the choke piston lever and a stationary part of the carburetor.

3. Open the throttle lever fully.

NOTE: *On the Stanza, the unloader adjusting lever is connected to the primary throttle plate shaft, an intermediate cam is connected to the choke lever by a choke rod.*

4. Adjustment is made by bending the unloader tongue. Gauge the gap between the choke plate and the carburetor body to 2.05–2.85mm.

Vacuum Break Adjustment

1. With the engine cold, close the choke completely.

2. Pull the vacuum break stem straight up as far as it will go.

3. Check the clearance between the choke plate and the carburetor wall. Clearance should be 3.12–3.72mm above 68°F; 1.65–2.25mm below 41°F.

4. On the Stanza models, adjustment is made by bending the tang at the choke plate lever assembly.

NOTE: *Remove the choke cover, then connect a rubber band to the choke lever to hold it shut.*

Accelerator Pump Adjustment

If a smooth constant stream of fuel is not injected into the carburetor bore when the throttle is opened, the accelerator pump is not functioning properly.

The Stanza accelerator pump is not adjustable; if it is not operating correctly, replace it.

Anti-Dieseling Solenoid

Check this valve if the engine continues to run after the key has been turned off.

1. Run the engine at idle speed and disconnect the lead wire at the anti-dieseling solenoid. The engine should stop.

2. If the engine does not stop, check the harness for current at the solenoid. If current is present, replace the solenoid. Installation torque for the solenoid is 13–25 ft. lbs. for CA20 engines.

CARBURETOR REMOVAL AND INSTALLATION

1. Remove the air cleaner.

2. Disconnect and mark the electrical connector(s), the fuel and the vacuum hoses from the carburetor.

3. Remove the throttle lever.

4. Remove the four nuts and washers retaining the carburetor to the manifold.

5. Lift the carburetor from the manifold. Do not tilt the carburetor over when removed from the manifold.

To install:

6. Remove and discard the gasket used between the carburetor and the manifold. Clean

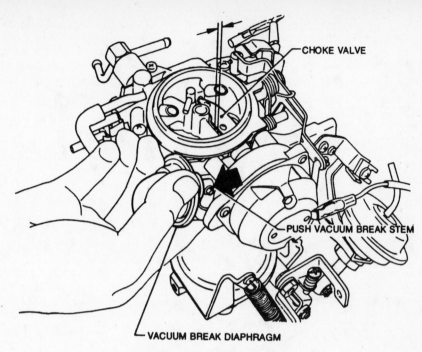

Vacuum break adjustment

all vacuum passages on intake manifold if necessary.

7. Install carburetor on the manifold, use a new base gasket and torque the carburetor mounting nuts EVENLY to 9–13 ft. lbs.

8. Install the throttle lever.

9. Connect the electrical connector(s), the fuel and the vacuum hoses to the carburetor. Replace the fuel line gas clamps as necessary.

10. Install the air cleaner.

11. Start engine, warm engine and adjust as necessary.

OVERHAUL

CAUTION: *Never smoke when working around gasoline! Avoid all sources of sparks or ignition. Gasoline vapors are EXTREMELY volatile!*

Efficient carburetion depends greatly on careful cleaning and inspection during overhaul, since dirt, gum, water and/or varnish in or on the carburetor parts are often responsible for poor performance.

Overhaul your carburetor in a clean, dust free area. Carefully disassemble the carburetor. Keep all similar and look-alike parts segregated during disassembly and cleaning to avoid accidental interchange during assembly. Make a note of all jet sizes.

When the carburetor is disassembled, wash all the parts (except diaphragms, electric choke units, pump plunger and any other plastic, leather, fiber or rubber parts) in clean carbure-

tor solvent. Do not leave parts in the solvent any longer than is necessary to sufficiently loosen the deposits. Excessive cleaning may remove the special finish from the float bowl and choke valve bodies, leaving these parts unfit for service. Rinse all parts in clean solvent and blow them dry with compressed air to allow them to air dry. Wipe clean all cork, plastic, leather and fiber parts with a clean, lint-free cloth.

Blow out all passages and jets with compressed air, be sure that there are no restrictions or blockages. Never use wire or similar tools for cleaning purposes; clean the jets and valves separately, to avoid accidental interchange.

Check all the parts for wear or damage. If wear or damage is found, replace the defective parts. Especially check the following:

1. Check the float needle and seat for wear. If wear is found, replace the complete assembly.

2. Check the float hinge pin for wear and the float(s) for dents or distortion. Replace the float if fuel has leaked into it.

3. Check the throttle and choke shaft bores for wear or an out-of-round condition. Damage or wear to the throttle arm, shaft or shaft bore will often require replacement of the throttle body. These parts require a close tolerance of fit; wear may allow air leakage, which could affect starting and idling.

NOTE: *Throttle shafts and bushings are not included in overhaul kits. They can be purchased separately.*

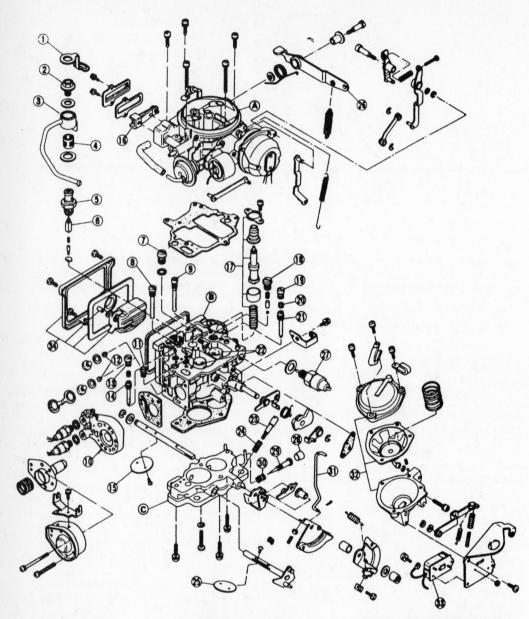

A. Choke chamber
B. Carburetor body
C. Throttle chamber
1. Lock lever
2. Filter set screw
3. Fuel nipple
4. Fuel filter
5. Needle valve body
6. Needle valve
7. Power valve
8. Secondary main air bleed
9. Primary main air bleed
10. B.C.D.D.
11. Secondary slow air bleed

12. Secondary main jet
13. Plug
14. Secondary slow jet
15. Primary throttle valve
16. Idle compensator
17. Accelerating pump parts
18. Plug for accelerating
    mechanism
19. Plug
20. Spring
21. Primary slow jet
22. Primary and secondary small
    venturi
23. Throttle adjusting screw

24. Throttle adjusting screw
    spring
25. Secondary throttle valve
26. Accelerating pump lever
27. Anti-dieseling solenoid valve
28. Blind plug
29. Idle adjusting screw
30. Idle adjusting screw spring
31. Choke connecting rod
32. Diaphragm chamber parts
33. Throttle valve switch
34. Float

Exploded view carburetor assembly—CA20 engine

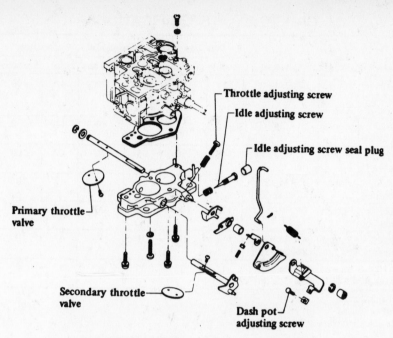

Throttle adjusting screw

Idle adjusting screw

Idle adjusting screw seal plug

Primary throttle valve

Secondary throttle valve

Dash pot adjusting screw

Exploded view carburetor assembly—CA20 engine

4. Inspect the idle mixture adjusting needles for burrs or grooves. Any such condition requires replacement of the needle, since you will not be able to obtain a satisfactory idle.

5. Test the accelerator pump check valves. They should pass air one way but not the other. Test for proper seating by blowing and sucking on the valve. Replace the valve if necessary. If the valve is satisfactory, wash the valve again to remove breath moisture.

6. Check the bowl cover for warped surfaces with a straightedge.

7. Closely inspect the valves and seats for wear and/or damage, replacing as necessary.

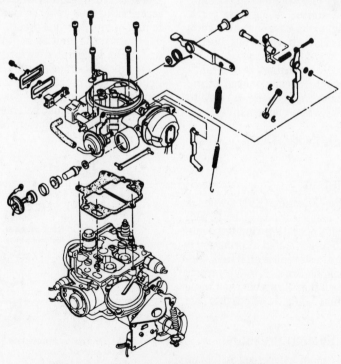

Exploded view carburetor assembly—CA20 engine

CARBURETOR SPECIFICATIONS

Year	Engine	Vehicle Model	Carb Model	Main Jet #		Main Air Bleed #		Slow Jet #		Float Level (in.)	Power Jet #
				Primary	Secondary	Primary	Secondary	Primary	Secondary		
1982	CA20 (Fed. & Canada)	Stanza	DCR342-33	111	160	90	60	47	100	0.91	45
	CA20 (California)	Stanza	DCR342-31	113	160	90	60	47	100	0.91	45
1983	CA20① (Federal)	Stanza	DCR342-25	111	160	95	60	47	100	0.91	45
	CA20 (California)	Stanza	DCR342-37① DCR342-38②	113	160	95	60	47	100	0.91	45
	CA20② (Canada)	Stanza	DCR342-36	113	160	95	60	47	100	0.91	40
1984	CA20S (Canada)	Stanza	DCR342-35① DCR342-36②	111	155	95	60	47	100	0.91	45① 40②
1985–86	CA20S (Canada)	Stanza	DCR342-35① DCR342-36②	111	155	95	60	47	100	③	45① 40②

① Manual Transmission
② Automatic Transmission
③ Use the sight adjusting glass on the side of the float bowl

8. After the carburetor is assembled, check the choke valve for freedom of operation.

Carburetor overhaul kits are recommended for each overhaul. These kits contain all gaskets and new parts to replace those that deteriorate most rapidly. Failure to replace all parts supplied with the kit (especially gaskets) can result in poor performance later.

After cleaning and checking all components, reassemble the carburetor, using new parts. When reassembling, make sure that all screws and jets are tight in their seats but do not overtighten as the tips will be distorted. Tighten all screws gradually in rotation. Do not tighten needle valves into their seats; uneven jetting will result. Always use new gaskets. Be sure to adjust the float level when reassembling.

GASOLINE FUEL INJECTION SYSTEM

General Description

The electronic fuel injection (EFI) system is an electronic type using various types of sensors to convert engine operating conditions into electronic signals. The generated information is fed to a control unit, where it is analyzed. Calculated electrical signals are sent to the various equipment to control the idle speed, the timing and amount of fuel being injected into the engine.

Relieving Fuel System Pressure

The fuel pressure must be released on fuel injected models before removing the any fuel related component. To relieve the fuel pressure, remove the gas cap. Remove/disconnect the fuel pump fuse, fuel pump relay or electrical fuel pump connection to disable the electrical fuel pump.

Start the engine and allow it to run. After the engine stalls from lack of fuel, crank the engine two or three times to relieve any remaining pressure. Turn ignition switch OFF and install/connect the fuse, relay or electrical connection to fuel pump. The fuel pressure will remain reduced until the ignition is switched ON or the fuel pump is operated by other means.

On some late models the CHECK ENGINE light will stay on after installation of the fuel component is completed. The memory code in the control unit must be erased. To erase the code, disconnect the battery cable for 1 minute then reconnect.

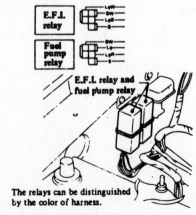

The relays can be distinguished by the color of harness.

Fuel pump relay—1982 200SX

Access plate and fuel pump electrical connection location—1984–88 200SX

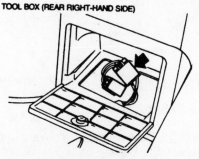

TOOL BOX (REAR RIGHT-HAND SIDE)

Unplug the electrical connection to release the fuel pressure 1984 and later 200SX

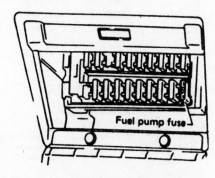

Fuel pump fuse

Removing the fuel pump fuse 1987 Stanza

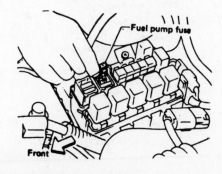

Fuel pump fuse

Front

Fuel pump fuse location—240SX

Electric Fuel Pump

REMOVAL AND INSTALLATION

200SX Model (External Mount Electric Pump)

1. Safely relieve the fuel pressure before disconnecting the fuel lines or any of the fuel system components. Reducing the fuel pressure to zero is a very important step for correct removal of the electric fuel pump.

2. Disconnect the negative batery cable. Disconnect the electrical harness connector at the pump. The 200SX pump is located near the center of the car, except on 1984 200SX, on which the pump is located near the fuel tank assembly.

3. Clamp or plug the hose between the fuel tank and the pump to prevent gas from spewing out from the tank.

4. Remove the inlet and outlet hoses at the pump. Unclamp the inlet hose and allow the fuel lines to drain into a suitable container.

5. Unbolt and remove the pump. The 200SX pump and fuel damper can be removed at the same time.

To install:

6. Install the fuel pump in the correct position. Reconnect all hoses. Use new clamps and be sure all hoses are properly seated on the fuel pump body.

7. Reconnect the electrical harness connector at the pump. Start engine and check for fuel leaks.

200SX and 240SX (In-Tank Electric Pump)

1. Safely relieve the fuel pressure before disconnecting the fuel lines or any of the fuel system components. Reducing the fuel pressure to zero is a very important step for correct removal of the electric fuel pump.

2. Disconnect the negative battery cable. Open the trunk lid, disconnect the fuel gauge electrical connector and remove the fuel tank inspection cover.

NOTE: *If vehicle has no fuel tank inspection cover the fuel tank must be lowered or removed to gain access to the in-tank fuel pump. When installing fuel check valve, be careful of its designated direction.*

3. Disconnect the fuel outlet and the return hoses. Remove the fuel tank if necessary.

4. Remove the ring retaining bolts and the O-ring, then lift the fuel pump assembly from the fuel tank. Plug the opening with a clean rag to prevent dirt from entering the system.

NOTE: *When removing or installing the fuel pump assembly, be careful not to damage or deform it. Install a new O-ring.*

To install:

5. Install fuel pump assembly in tank with a

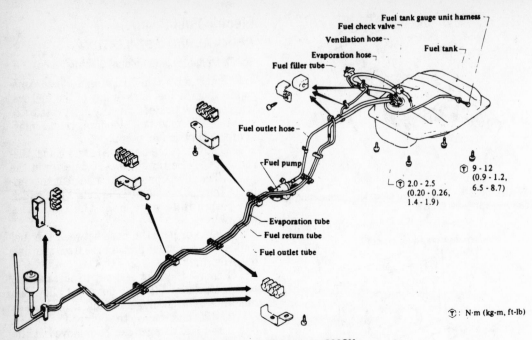

Fuel tank gauge unit harness

Fuel check valve

Ventilation hose

Fuel tank

Evaporation hose

Fuel filler tube

Fuel outlet hose

Fuel pump

9 - 12
(0.9 - 1.2,
6.5 - 8.7)

2.0 - 2.5
(0.20 - 0.26,
1.4 - 1.9)

Evaporation tube

Fuel return tube

Fuel outlet tube

⊤: N·m (kg-m, ft-lb)

External mounted fuel pump—200SX

new O-ring. Install the ring retaining bolts. Install the fuel tank if removed.

6. Reconnect the fuel lines and the electrical connection.

7. Install the fuel tank inspection cover.

8. Connect battery cable, start engine and check for fuel leaks. On some late models the CHECK ENGINE light will stay on after installation is completed. The memory code in the control unit must be erased. To erase the code disconnect the battery cable for 10 seconds, then reconnect it.

Stanza Model (External Mount Electric Pump)

The Stanza (1984–86) fuel pump is located under the vehicle in front of the fuel tank, the (1987 and later) Stanza vehicles use in-tank fuel pump.

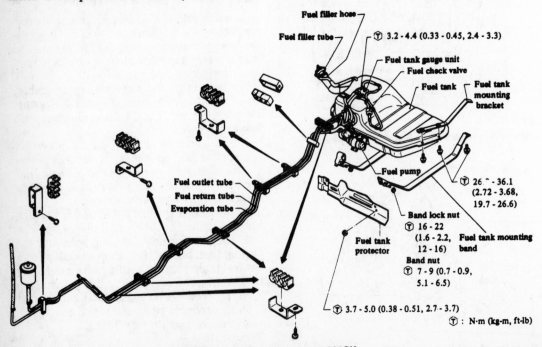

Fuel filler hose

Fuel filler tube

3.2 - 4.4 (0.33 - 0.45, 2.4 - 3.3)

Fuel tank gauge unit

Fuel check valve

Fuel tank

Fuel tank mounting bracket

Fuel outlet tube

Fuel return tube

Evaporation tube

Fuel pump

26.~ - 36.1
(2.72 - 3.68,
19.7 - 26.6)

Band lock nut
16 - 22
(1.6 - 2.2,
12 - 16)

Fuel tank mounting band

Band nut
7 - 9 (0.7 - 0.9,
5.1 - 6.5)

Fuel tank protector

3.7 - 5.0 (0.38 - 0.51, 2.7 - 3.7)

⊤: N·m (kg-m, ft-lb)

External mounted fuel pump—200SX

NOTE: *Before disconnecting the fuel lines or any of the fuel system components, release the fuel pressure.*

1. Disconnect the negative battery cable.

2. Raise and support the rear of the vehicle on jackstands.

3. Disconnect the electrical connector from the fuel pump.

4. Place fuel container under the fuel lines, then disconnect the fuel lines and drain the excess fuel into the container.

5. Remove the mounting braces and the fuel pump from the vehicle.

To install:

6. Install the vehicle fuel lines to the pump.

7. Install the mounting braces and mount pump to vehicle.

8. Connect fuel pump electrical connector.

9. Reconnect battery cable, start engine and check for leaks.

Stanza Model (In-Tank Electric Pump)

1. Disconnect the negative battery cable.

2. Open the trunk lid, disconnect the fuel gauge electrical connector and remove the fuel tank inspection cover.

NOTE: *If vehicle has no fuel tank inspection cover the fuel tank must be removed. When installing fuel check valve, be careful of its designated direction.*

3. Disconnect the fuel outlet and the return hoses.

4. Using a large brass drift pin and a hammer, drive the fuel tank locking ring in the counterclockwise direction.

5. Remove the locking ring and the O-ring, then lift the fuel pump assembly from the fuel tank. Plug the opening with a clean rag to prevent dirt from entering the system. When removing the fuel tank gauge unit, be careful not to damage or deform it. Install a new O-ring.

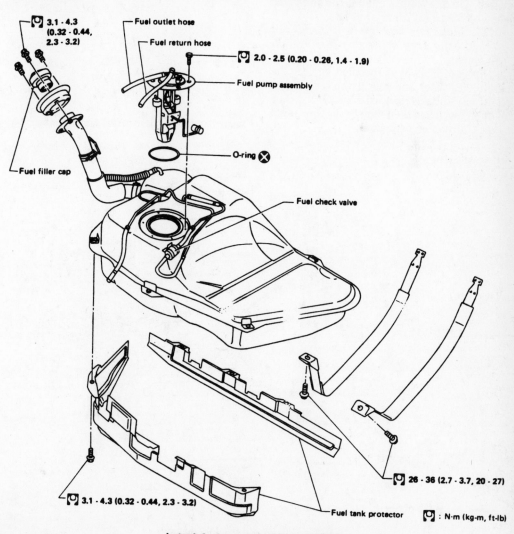

In-tank fuel pump assembly—200SX

To install:

6. Install fuel pump assembly in tank. With a new O-ring install the fuel tank locking ring in place.

7. Reconnect the fuel lines and the electrical connection.

8. Install the fuel tank inspection cover.

9. Connect battery cable, start engine and check for leaks.

TESTING

1. Release the fuel pressure. Connect a fuel pressure gauge (special tool J–25400–34 or equivalent) between the fuel filter outlet and fuel feed pipe.

2. Start the engine and read the pressure. All models except the 240SX, it should be 30 psi (207 kPa) at idle, and 37 psi (255 kPa) at the moment the accelerator pedal is fully depressed. On the 240SX model the pressure should be 33 psi (227.5 kPa) at idle.

NOTE: *Make sure that the fuel filter is not blocked before replacing any fuel system components.*

3. If pressure is not as specified, replace the pressure regulator and repeat the test. If the pressure is still incorrect, check for clogged or deformed fuel lines, then replace the fuel pump or check valve if so equipped.

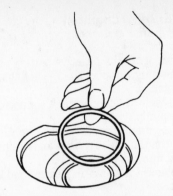

Installing new O-ring in the fuel tank assembly

Removing the lock ring on the fuel tank assembly

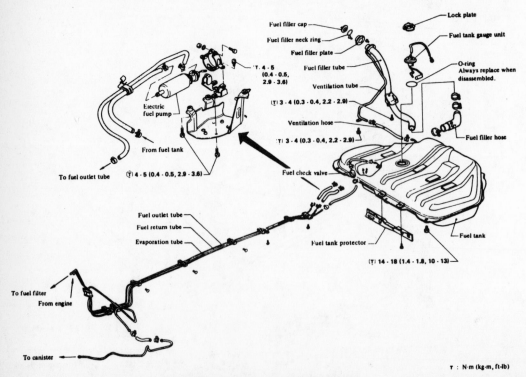

External fuel pump—1984–86 Stanza

Throttle Body/Chamber

REMOVAL AND INSTALLATION

All Models

1. Disconnect the negative battery cable and remove the intake duct from the throttle chamber.

2. Disconnect and mark the vacuum hoses and the electrical harness connector from the throttle chamber. Disconnect the accelerator cable from the throttle chamber.

3. Remove the mounting bolts and the throttle chamber from the intake manifold (early years) or intake manifold collector assembly.

4. To install, use a new gasket and reverse the removal procedures. Torque the throttle chamber bolts to 13–16 ft. lbs. in two steps EVENLY. Adjust the throttle cable if necessary.

Check the throttle for smooth operation and make sure the by-pass port is free from obstacles and is clean. Check to make sure the idle speed adjusting screw moves smoothly. Do not touch the EGR vacuum port screw or, on some later models, the throttle valve stopper screw, as they are factory adjusted.

Because of the sensitivity of the air flow meter, there cannot be any air leaks in the system. Even the smallest leak could unbalance the system and affect the performance of the automobile.

During every check pay attention to vacuum hose connections, dipstick and oil filler cap for evidence of air leaks. Should you encounter any, take steps to correct the problem.

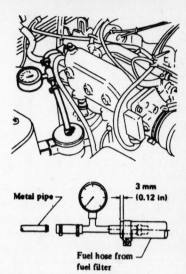

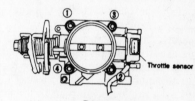

Installation of fuel pressure test gauge

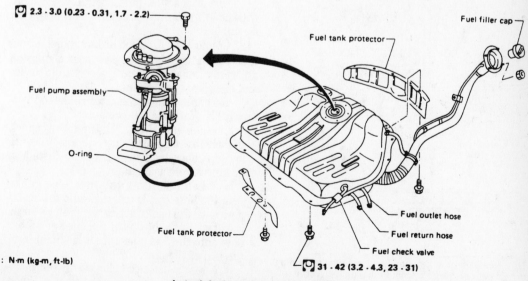

Throttle sensor

Tighten in numerical order.

Throttle chamber bolts
Tightening procedure
1) Tighten all bolts to 9 to 11 N·m
   (0.9 to 1.1 kg-m, 6.5 to 8.0 ft-lb).
2) Tighten all bolts to 18 to 22 N·m
   (1.8 to 2.2 kg-m, 13 to 16 ft-lb).

Throttle chamber tightening procedure

2.3 - 3.0 (0.23 - 0.31, 1.7 - 2.2)

Fuel tank protector

Fuel filler cap

Fuel pump assembly

O-ring

Fuel tank protector

Fuel outlet hose

Fuel return hose

Fuel check valve

: N·m (kg-m, ft-lb)

31 - 42 (3.2 - 4.3, 23 - 31)

In-tank fuel pump assembly—Stanza

Fuel Injectors/Rail Assembly
REMOVAL AND INSTALLATION
200SX—Z-Series Engine

NOTE: *Review the entire procedure before starting this repair.*

1. Release fuel pressure by following the correct procedure.

2. Disconnect the negative battery cable and the accelerator cable.

3. Disconnect the injector harness connector.

4. Tag and disconnect the vacuum hose at the fuel pipe connection end. Disconnect the air regulator and its harness connector, and tag and disconnect any other hoses that may hinder removal of the injection assembly.

5. Disconnect the fuel feed hose and fuel return hose from the fuel pipe.

NOTE: *Place a rag under the fuel pipe to prevent splashing of the fuel.*

6. Remove the vacuum hose connecting the pressure regulator to the intake manifold.

7. Remove the bolts securing the fuel pipe and pressure regulator.

8. Remove the screws securing the fuel injectors. Remove the fuel pipe assembly, by pulling out the fuel pipe, injectors and pressure regulator as an assembly.

9. Unfasten the hose clamp on the injectors and remove the injectors from the fuel pipe.

To install:

10. Install the fuel injectors in the fuel pipe with new hose clamps.

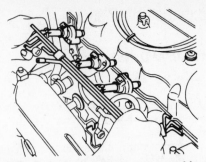

Removing the fuel pipe and injector assembly—Z series engine

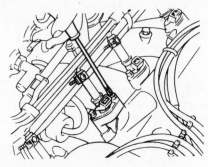

Removing the injector securing screws

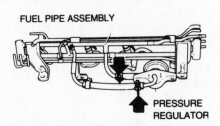

FUEL PIPE ASSEMBLY

PRESSURE REGULATOR

Fuel pressure regulator location and connections

11. Install the fuel pipe assembly, injectors with new O-rings and pressure regulator as an assembly.

12. Connect the fuel feed hose and fuel return hose to the fuel pipe. Use new hose clamps on all connections. Reconnect all vacuum hoses and electrical connections.

13. Reconnect the accelerator cable and battery cable. Note the following:

a. When installing the injectors, check that there are no scratches or abrasion at the lower rubber insulator. Securely install it, making sure it is air-tight.

b. When installing the fuel hose, make sure the hose end is inserted onto the metal pipe until the end contacts the unit, as far as it will go. Push the end of the injector rubber hose onto the fuel pipe until it is 25mm from the end of the pipe.

c. Never reuse hose clamps on the injection system. Always renew the clamps. When

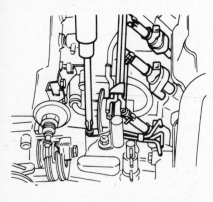

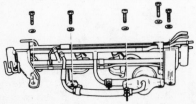

Top: Removing the Z-series fuel pressure regulator to fuel pipe screws. Bottom: Fuel pipe assembly retaining screws

tightening clamps, make sure the screw does not come in contact with adjacent parts.

14. Start the engine and check for fuel leaks.

200SX — CA Series Engine

NOTE: *On the CA20E engine on late model 200SX vehicles the collector assembly may not have to be removed — modify Step 2 of the service procedure below.*

1. Release fuel pressure by following the correct service procedure. Refer to Fuel Pressure Release Procedure. Disconnect the negative battery cable.

2. On the CA20E engine, drain the engine coolant. Disconnect the fuel injection wiring harness, the ignition wires, and remove the collector with the throttle chamber. Tag and disconnect all related hoses.

3. On the CA18ET engine, disconnect the air intake pipe, the fuel injection wiring harness, the ignition wires and accelerator cable. Remove the throttle chamber.

4. On all engines, disconnect the fuel hoses and pressure regulator vacuum hoses.

5. Remove the fuel injectors with the fuel rail assembly.

6. Remove the fuel injector hose-to-fuel rail clamp(s), then pull the injector from the fuel rail.

To install:

7. To remove the fuel hose from the injector, use a hot soldering iron to cut (melt) a line in the fuel hose (to the braided reinforcement), starting at the injector socket to ¾ in. (19mm)

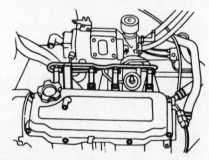

Injector assembly—CA20E/CA18ET engines

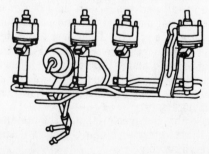

Injector assembly and fuel pressure regulator— CA20E/CA18 ET engines

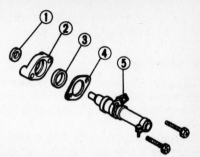

Fuel injector and related hardware. When replacing injector always replace the lower rubber (1) and upper rubber insulator (3)

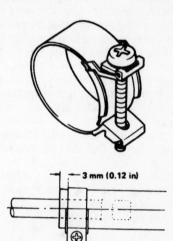

Always replace the hose clamps. Note proper installation

long. Remove the hose from the injector, by hand.

NOTE: *Do NOT allow the soldering iron to cut all the way through the hose, nor touch the injector seat or damage the plastic socket connector.*

8. To install a new fuel hose, clean the injector tail section, wet the inside of the new hose with fuel, push the hose into the fuel injector hose socket as far as it will go;retain it with a new hose clamp if necessary. Assemble the injector(s) onto the fuel rail.

9. Install the injectors with new O-rings and fuel rail as an assembly.

10. Connect the fuel hoses and pressure regulator vacuum hoses.

11. On the CA18ET engine, connect the air intake pipe, the fuel injection wiring harness, the ignition wires and accelerator cable. Install the throttle chamber.

12. On the CA20E engine, reconnect the fuel injection wiring harness, the ignition wires, and install the collector with the throttle chamber if necessary. Reconnect all related hoses and refill the cooling system if necessary.

13. Reconnect the battery cable. Start the engine and check for fuel leaks.

200SX—VG30 Engine

1. Release fuel pressure by following the correct procedure. Refer to Fuel Pressure Release Procedure. Disconnect the negative battery cable.

2. Disconnect these items at the intake collector: the air inatke duct; accelerator linkage; PCV hose; air regulator pressure hose; B.C.D.D. hose; fuel hoses; E.G.R tube; wiring harness clamps; wiring harness connectors; intake collector cover. Then, drain some coolant out of the cooling system and disconnect the coolant hoses connecting into the collector.

3. Remove the intake collector assembly.

4. Remove the bolts securing the fuel tube.

5. Remove the bolts securing the injectors and remove the injectors, fuel tubes, and pressure regulator as an assembly.

To install:

6. To remove the fuel hoses, heat a sharp knife until it is hot. Cut into the braided rein-

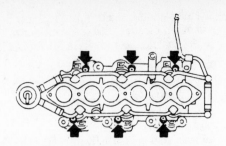

Removing the fuel injector/pressure regulator assembly—200 SX (VG30E engine)

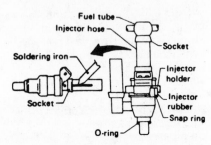

Removing the fuel injector hose.

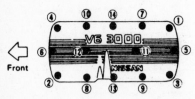

Removing the intake collector cover—200SX (VG30E engine)

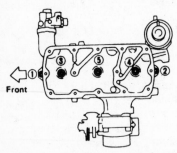

Removing the intake collector—200SX (VG30E engine)

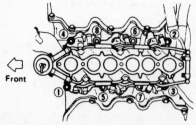

Removing the fuel tube securing bolts—200SX (VG30E engine)

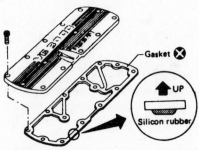

Removing the intake collector cover gasket—200SX (VG30E engine)

forcement from the mark on the hose to the end of the fuel tube connection.

NOTE: *Make sure the knife does not cut all the way through the hose and nick the injector tail piece or connector fitting.*

7. Pull the hose off of the injectors. DO NOT install the injectors in a vise to hold them as you pull off the hoses.

8. To install new hose, clean the exterior of the injector tail piece and the end of the fuel tube with a safe solvent. Then, wet the inside diameter of the new hose with fuel. Push the ends of the hoses and fittings onto the injector tail piece and the end of the fuel tube as far as they will go by hand, retain it with a new hose clamp if necessary

9. Assemble the injector(s) onto the fuel rail. Install the injectors with new O-rings and fuel rail as an assembly.

10. Install the intake collector assembly.

11. Connect the air intake duct; accelerator

linkage; PCV hose; air regulator pressure hose; B.C.D.D. hose; fuel hoses; E.G.R tube; wiring harness clamps; wiring harness connectors and intake collector cover to the collector assembly.

12. Connect the coolant hoses to the collector and refill the cooling system to the proper level.

13. Reconnect the battery cable. Start the engine and check for fuel leaks.

240SX

NOTE: *For the KA24DE engine on late model 240SX vehicles the BPT valve may NOT have to be removed — modify Step 3 of the service procedure below.*

1. Relieve the fuel system pressure.
2. Disconnect the negative battery cable.
3. Remove the BPT valve.
4. Remove the fuel tube retaining bolts.
5. Remove the fuel tube and injector assembly from the intake manifold.
6. Withdraw the injectors from the fuel tube.

To install:

7. Clean the injector tail piece and insert the injectors into the fuel tube with new O-rings.
8. Position the injector and fuel tube assembly onto the intake manifold and install the injector tube retaining bolts.
9. Pressurize the fuel system and check for leaks at all fuel connections.
10. Install the BPT valve if necessary.
11. Connect the negative battery cable.

Fuel injector and rail assembly

Stanza—CA Series Engine

NOTE: *On the CA20E engine on late model Stanza vehicles, the collector assembly may NOT have to be removed — modify Step 4 of the service procedure below.*

1. Refer to the Fuel Pressure Release Procedure in this Chapter and reduce the fuel pressure to zero. Disconnect the negative battery cable.
2. Remove the fuel inlet and outlet hoses from the fuel rail.
3. Disconnect the EFI electrical harness from the fuel injectors and the vacuum hose from the fuel pressure regulator, located at the center of the fuel rail.
4. Remove the fuel rail securing bolts, the collector/throttle chamber (if necessary) and the injector securing bolts.
5. Remove the fuel injectors with the fuel rail assembly.

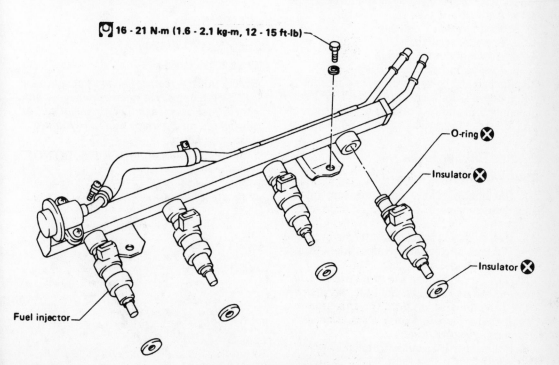

16 - 21 N·m (1.6 - 2.1 kg-m, 12 - 15 ft-lb)

O-ring ✖

Insulator ✖

Insulator ✖

Fuel injector

Fuel injector and rail assembly

6. Remove the fuel injector hose-to-fuel rail clamp(s), then pull the injector from the fuel rail.

To install:

7. To remove the fuel hose from the injector, use a hot soldering iron. Cut (melt) a line in the fuel hose (to the braided reinforcement), starting at the injector socket to ¾ in. (19mm) long. Remove the hose from the injector, by hand.

NOTE: *Do NOT allow the soldering iron to cut all the way through the hose, nor touch the injector seat or damage the plastic socket connector.*

8. To install a new fuel hose, clean the injector tail section, wet the inside of the new hose with fuel, push the hose into the fuel injector hose socket (as far as it will go). Assemble the injector(s) onto the fuel rail.

9. Install the injectors with new O-rings and securing bolts.

10. Install the collector and the throttle chamber if necessary and the fuel rail securing bolts.

11. Connect the EFI electrical harness to the fuel injectors and the vacuum hose to the fuel pressure regulator.

12. Connect all the fuel lines.

13. Start engine and check for fuel leaks.

Stanza—KA24E Engine

1. Relieve fuel pressure from system. Disconnect the negative battery cable.

2. Remove or disconnect the following:
   a. Air duct
   b. Fuel hoses
   c. Pressure regulator
   d. Accelerator wire bracket
   e. Injector harness connectors

3. Remove the bolts securing the fuel tube.

4. Remove bolts securing injectors and remove injectors and fuel tube as an assembly.

5. Reverse the service procedure to install.

Injector Rubber Hose

REMOVAL AND INSTALLATION

1. On injector rubber hose, measure off a point approximately 0.79 in. (20mm) from socket end.

2. Heat soldering iron (150 watt) for 15 minutes. Cut hose into braided reinforcement from mark to socket end.

NOTE: *Do NOT allow the soldering iron to cut all the way through the hose, nor touch the injector seat or damage the plastic socket. Never place injector in a vise when disconnecting rubber hose.*

3. Pull rubber hose out with hand.

To install:

4. Clean exterior of injector tail piece.

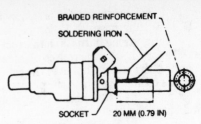

Removing the fuel injector hose.

5. Wet inside of new rubber hose with fuel.

6. Push end of rubber hose with hose socket onto injector tail piece by hand as far as it will go. Clamp is not necessary at this connection.

NOTE: *After properly connecting fuel hose to injector, check connection for fuel leakage.*

Fuel Pressure Regulator

REMOVAL AND INSTALLATION

1. Relieve fuel pressure from system. Disconnect the negative battery cable.

2. Disengage vacuum tube connecting regulator to intake manifold from pressure regulator.

3. Remove screws securing pressure regulator.

4. Unfasten hose clamps, and disconnect pressure regulator from fuel hose.

NOTE: *Place a rag under fuel pipe to absorb any remaining fuel.*

5. To install, reverse the removal procedure.

FUEL TANK

REMOVAL AND INSTALLATION

1982–83 200SX Models

NOTE: *Always replace O-rings and gas hose retaining clamps. Do not kink or twist any hose or fuel lines when they are installed. Do not tighten hose clamps excessively to avoid damaging hoses.*

Release the fuel pressure using the proper procedure.

When installing fuel check valve, be careful of its designated direction.

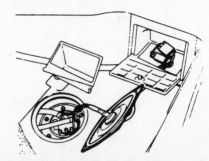

Access plate location—1984–88 200SX

1. Remove the battery ground cable.
2. Drain the fuel from the fuel tank.
3. Remove the protector from the luggage compartment, and then remove the following parts:

    a. Harness connector for the fuel tank gauge unit.
    b. Ventilation hose.
    c. Evaporation hoses
    d. Fuel filler hose (Hatchback)

4. Remove the following parts from beneath the floor.

    a. Fuel outlet hose
    b. Fuel return hose
    c. Evaporation hose
    d. Fuel filler hose (Hardtop)

5. Remove the bolts which secure the fuel tank and remove the tank.

Reservoir Tank – Hatchback

1. Remove the battery cable.
2. Remove the protector from the luggage compartment. Also remove the right hand speaker and side lower finisher.
3. Remove the evaporation hoses and then remove the reservoir tank.

To install:

4. Install the reservior tank in place and fuel tank assembly in the correct position. While supporting the tank in place torque the gas tank strap retaining bolts EVENLY.

5. Reconnect all lines, hoses and the electrical connection.
6. Install the protector in the luggage compartment. Connect the battery ground cable.

1984–88 200SX and 240SX Models

NOTE: *Always replace O-rings and gas hose retaining clamps. Do not kink or twist any hose or fuel lines when they are installed. Do not tighten hose clamps excessively to avoid damaging hoses.*

Release the fuel pressure using the correct procedure. When installing fuel check valve, be careful of its designated direction.

The following procedure can be used on all years and models. Slight variations may occur due to extra connections, etc. but the basic procedure should cover all years and models.

1. Remove the battery ground cable.
2. Drain the fuel from the fuel tank.
3. Remove the access plate if so equipped from the trunk area. Disconnect the hoses, evaporative (vent) tube line if so equipped and fuel pump electrical connection.
4. Raise the rear of vehicle and safely support it with the proper jackstands.
5. Remove the fuel tank protector assembly.
6. Disconnect the fuel filler hose at the gas tank.
7. Remove the gas tank strap retaining bolts

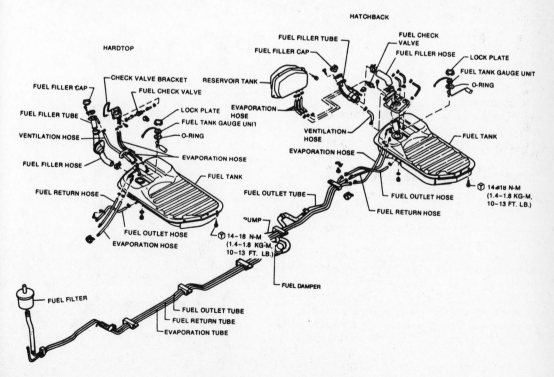

Fuel tank and lines 1982–83 200SX

and slowly lower the tank assembly down from the vehicle.

To install:

8. Install the tank in the correct position.

9. While supporting the tank in place torque the gas tank strap retaining bolts EVENLY to 20–27 ft. lbs.

10. Reconnect the fuel filler hose at the gas tank using a new clamp.

11. Install the fuel tank protector assembly and connect the evaporative (vent) tube line if so equipped.

12. Lower the vehicle, connect all hoses with new clamps and the electrical connection. Install the access plate if so equipped.

13. Refill the gas tank. Reconnect the battery ground cable.

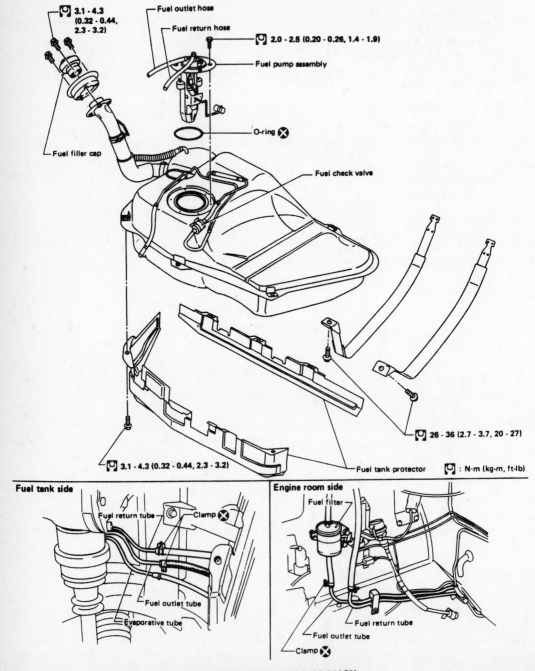

Fuel tank assembly—1984–88 200SX

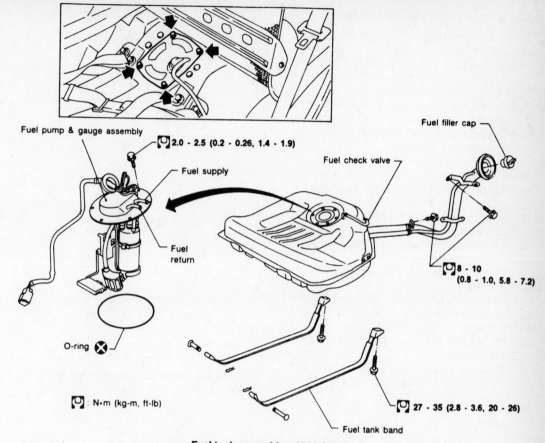

Fuel pump & gauge assembly

[○] 2.0 - 2.5 (0.2 - 0.26, 1.4 - 1.9)

Fuel supply

Fuel filler cap

Fuel check valve

Fuel return

[○] 8 - 10 (0.8 - 1.0, 5.8 - 7.2)

O-ring ⊗

[○] : N·m (kg-m, ft-lb)

[○] 27 - 35 (2.8 - 3.6, 20 - 26)

Fuel tank band

Fuel tank assembly—1992 Stanza

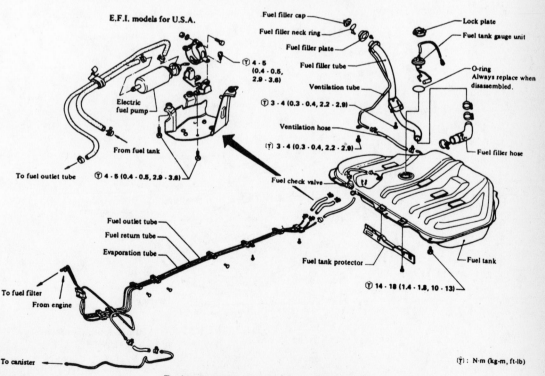

E.F.I. models for U.S.A.

Fuel filler cap

Fuel filler neck ring

Fuel filler plate

Fuel filler tube

Lock plate

Fuel tank gauge unit

(T) 4 - 5 (0.4 - 0.5, 2.9 - 3.6)

Electric fuel pump

Ventilation tube

O-ring
Always replace when disassembled.

(T) 3 - 4 (0.3 - 0.4, 2.2 - 2.9)

From fuel tank

Ventilation hose

Fuel filler hose

To fuel outlet tube

(T) 4 - 5 (0.4 - 0.5, 2.9 - 3.6)

(T) 3 - 4 (0.3 - 0.4, 2.2 - 2.9)

Fuel check valve

Fuel outlet tube

Fuel return tube

Evaporation tube

Fuel tank protector

Fuel tank

To fuel filter

From engine

(T) 14 - 18 (1.4 - 1.8, 10 - 13)

To canister

(T) : N·m (kg-m, ft-lb)

Fuel tank assembly and lines—1985 Stanza

Stanza and Stanza 2WD and 4WD Wagons

NOTE: *Always replace O-rings and gas hose retaining clamps. Do not kink or twist any hose or fuel lines when they are installed. Do not tighten hose clamps excessively to avoid damaging hoses.*

Release the fuel pressure using the correct procedure

When installing fuel check valve, be careful of its designated direction.

The following procedure can be used on all years and models. Slight variations may occur due to extra connections, etc. but the basic procedure covers all years and models.

1. Drain the fuel tank. Disconnect the negative battery cable.
2. Remove the rear seat cushion.
3. Remove the inspection cover.
4. Disconnect the fuel gauge electrical harness connector.
5. Disconnect the fuel filler (if so equipped) and the ventilation hoses. Disconnect the fuel outlet, return and evaporation hoses, at the front of the tank. Plug open fuel lines. Remove the tank protector.
6. Remove the fuel tank mounting bolts and the tank from the vehicle.

Access plate location—Stanza

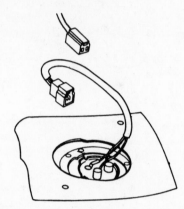

Removing the electrical connection fuel gauge assembly

2WD model

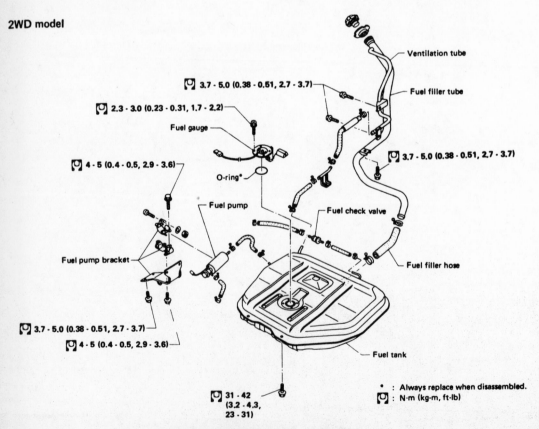

Fuel tank assembly—Stanza 2WD wagon

To install:

7. Install the fuel tank to vehicle and torque the mounting bolts EVENLY to 20–27 ft. lbs.

8. Reconnect all fuel lines, ventilation hoses and the electrical connection.

9. Install the inspection cover and rear seat cushion.

10. Start engine and check for fuel leaks.

SENDING UNIT REPLACEMENT

NOTE: *Always replace O-rings and gas hose retaining clamps. Do not kink or twist any hose or fuel lines when they are installed. Do not tighten hose clamps excessively to avoid damaging hoses.*

Release the fuel pressure using the correct procedure. When installing fuel check valve, be careful of its designated direction.

The following procedure can be used on all years and models. Slight variations may occur due to extra connections, etc. but the basic procedure covers all years and models.

1. Release the fuel pressure. Disconnect the negative battery cable.

2. On Stanza models, remove the rear seat cushion — remove the inspection cover. On later model 200SX vehicles the inspection cover or

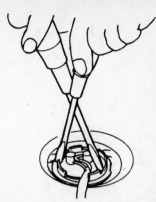

Removing the lockring in the fuel tank assembly

access plate in the trunk areas must be removed..

3. If vehicle has no inspection cover or access plate (1982–83 200SX and 240SX models) to fuel sending unit assembly the fuel tank must be removed from the vehicle. Refer to the necessary service procedures in this Chapter.

4. Disconnect fuel tank gauge harness connector and all fuel/vapor line connections.

5. Remove the lock plate and remove the fuel tank gauge unit — Refer to "Electric Fuel

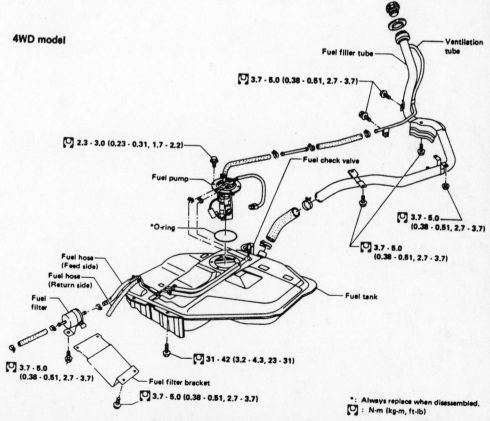

Fuel tank assembly—Stanza 4WD wagon

Replacing the O-ring in the fuel tank assembly

Pump In-Tank" service procedures in this Chapter.

6. Installation is the reverse of the removal procedure. When taking out fuel gauge/fuel pump assembly, be careful not to damage the assembly. Install a new O-ring in the fuel tank before installing the lock ring. Always use new gas hose clamps on all connections.

CHILTON'S
FUEL ECONOMY & TUNE-UP TIPS

Tune-up • Spark Plug Diagnosis • Emission Controls

Fuel System • Cooling System • Tires and Wheels

General Maintenance

CHILTON'S FUEL ECONOMY & TUNE-UP TIPS

Fuel economy is important to everyone, no matter what kind of vehicle you drive. The maintenance-minded motorist can save both money and fuel using these tips and the periodic maintenance and tune-up procedures in this Repair and Tune-Up Guide.

There are more than 130,000,000 cars and trucks registered for private use in the United States. Each travels an average of 10-12,000 miles per year, and, and in total they consume close to 70 billion gallons of fuel each year. This represents nearly ⅔ of the oil imported by the United States each year. The Federal government's goal is to reduce consumption 10% by 1985. A variety of methods are either already in use or under serious consideration, and they all affect you driving and the cars you will drive. In addition to "down-sizing", the auto industry is using or investigating the use of electronic fuel delivery, electronic engine controls and alternative engines for use in smaller and lighter vehicles, among other alternatives to meet the federally mandated Corporate Average Fuel Economy (CAFE) of 27.5 mpg by 1985. The government, for its part, is considering rationing, mandatory driving curtailments and tax increases on motor vehicle fuel in an effort to reduce consumption. The government's goal of a 10% reduction could be realized — and further government regulation avoided — if every private vehicle could use just 1 less gallon of fuel per week.

How Much Can You Save?

Tests have proven that almost anyone can make at least a 10% reduction in fuel consumption through regular maintenance and tune-ups. When a major manufacturer of spark plugs sur-

TUNE-UP

1. Check the cylinder compression to be sure the engine will really benefit from a tune-up and that it is capable of producing good fuel economy. A tune-up will be wasted on an engine in poor mechanical condition.

2. Replace spark plugs regularly. New spark plugs alone can increase fuel economy 3%.

3. Be sure the spark plugs are the correct type (heat range) for your vehicle. See the Tune-Up Specifications.

Heat range refers to the spark plug's ability to conduct heat away from the firing end. It must conduct the heat away in an even pattern to avoid becoming a source of pre-ignition, yet it must also operate hot enough to burn off conductive deposits that could cause misfiring.

The heat range is usually indicated by a number on the spark plug, part of the manufacturer's designation for each individual spark plug. The numbers in bold-face indicate the heat range in each manufacturer's identification system.

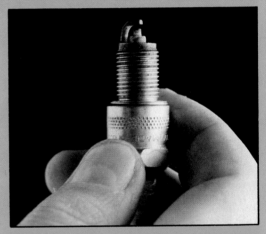

Periodically, check the spark plugs to be sure they are firing efficiently. They are excellent indicators of the internal condition of your engine.

On AC, Bosch (new), Champion, Fram/Autolite, Mopar, Motorcraft and Prestolite, a higher number indicates a hotter plug. On Bosch (old), NGK and Nippondenso, a higher number indicates a colder plug.

4. Make sure the spark plugs are properly gapped. See the Tune-Up Specifications in this book.

5. Be sure the spark plugs are firing efficiently. The illustrations on the next 2 pages show you how to "read" the firing end of the spark plug.

6. Check the ignition timing and set it to specifications. Tests show that almost all cars have incorrect ignition timing by more than 2°.

Manufacturer	Typical Designation
AC	R **45** TS
Bosch (old)	WA **145** T30
Bosch (new)	HR **8** Y
Champion	RBL **15** Y
Fram/Autolite	**415**
Mopar	P-**62** PR
Motorcraft	BRF-**42**
NGK	BP **5** ES-15
Nippondenso	W **16** EP
Prestolite	14GR **5** 2A

veyed over 6,000 cars nationwide, they found that a tune-up, on cars that needed one, increased fuel economy over 11%. Replacing worn plugs alone, accounted for a 3% increase. The same test also revealed that 8 out of every 10 vehicles will have some maintenance deficiency that will directly affect fuel economy, emissions or performance. Most of this mileage-robbing neglect could be prevented with regular maintenance.

Modern engines require that all of the functioning systems operate properly for maximum efficiency. A malfunction anywhere wastes fuel. You can keep your vehicle running as efficiently and economically as possible, by being aware of your vehicle's operating and performance characteristics. If your vehicle suddenly develops performance or fuel economy problems it could be due to one or more of the following:

PROBLEM	POSSIBLE CAUSE
Engine Idles Rough	Ignition timing, idle mixture, vacuum leak or something amiss in the emission control system.
Hesitates on Acceleration	Dirty carburetor or fuel filter, improper accelerator pump setting, ignition timing or fouled spark plugs.
Starts Hard or Fails to Start	Worn spark plugs, improperly set automatic choke, ice (or water) in fuel system.
Stalls Frequently	Automatic choke improperly adjusted and possible dirty air filter or fuel filter.
Performs Sluggishly	Worn spark plugs, dirty fuel or air filter, ignition timing or automatic choke out of adjustment.

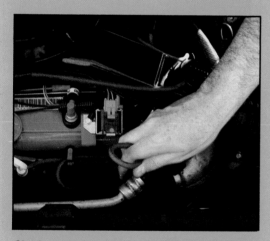

Check spark plug wires on conventional point type ignition for cracks by bending them in a loop around your finger.

Be sure that spark plug wires leading to adjacent cylinders do not run too close together. (Photo courtesy Champion Spark Plug Co.)

7. If your vehicle does not have electronic ignition, check the points, rotor and cap as specified.

8. Check the spark plug wires (used with conventional point-type ignitions) for cracks and burned or broken insulation by bending them in a loop around your finger. Cracked wires decrease fuel efficiency by failing to deliver full voltage to the spark plugs. One misfiring spark plug can cost you as much as 2 mpg.

9. Check the routing of the plug wires. Misfiring can be the result of spark plug leads to adjacent cylinders running parallel to each other and too close together. One wire tends to pick up voltage from the other causing it to fire "out of time".

10. Check all electrical and ignition circuits for voltage drop and resistance.

11. Check the distributor mechanical and/or vacuum advance mechanisms for proper functioning. The vacuum advance can be checked by twisting the distributor plate in the opposite direction of rotation. It should spring back when released.

12. Check and adjust the valve clearance on engines with mechanical lifters. The clearance should be slightly loose rather than too tight.

SPARK PLUG DIAGNOSIS

Normal

APPEARANCE: This plug is typical of one operating normally. The insulator nose varies from a light tan to grayish color with slight electrode wear. The presence of slight deposits is normal on used plugs and will have no adverse effect on engine performance. The spark plug heat range is correct for the engine and the engine is running normally.

CAUSE: Properly running engine.

RECOMMENDATION: Before reinstalling this plug, the electrodes should be cleaned and filed square. Set the gap to specifications. If the plug has been in service for more than 10-12,000 miles, the entire set should probably be replaced with a fresh set of the same heat range.

Oil Deposits

APPEARANCE: The firing end of the plug is covered with a wet, oily coating.

CAUSE: The problem is poor oil control. On high mileage engines, oil is leaking past the rings or valve guides into the combustion chamber. A common cause is also a plugged PCV valve, and a ruptured fuel pump diaphragm can also cause this condition. Oil fouled plugs such as these are often found in new or recently overhauled engines, before normal oil control is achieved, and can be cleaned and reinstalled.

RECOMMENDATION: A hotter spark plug may temporarily relieve the problem, but the engine is probably in need of work.

Incorrect Heat Range

APPEARANCE: The effects of high temperature on a spark plug are indicated by clean white, often blistered insulator. This can also be accompanied by excessive wear of the electrode, and the absence of deposits.

CAUSE: Check for the correct spark plug heat range. A plug which is too hot for the engine can result in overheating. A car operated mostly at high speeds can require a colder plug. Also check ignition timing, cooling system level, fuel mixture and leaking intake manifold.

RECOMMENDATION: If all ignition and engine adjustments are known to be correct, and no other malfunction exists, install spark plugs one heat range colder.

Photos Courtesy Fram Corporation

Carbon Deposits

APPEARANCE: Carbon fouling is easily identified by the presence of dry, soft, black, sooty deposits.

CAUSE: Changing the heat range can often lead to carbon fouling, as can prolonged slow, stop-and-start driving. If the heat range is correct, carbon fouling can be attributed to a rich fuel mixture, sticking choke, clogged air cleaner, worn breaker points, retarded timing or low compression. If only one or two plugs are carbon fouled, check for corroded or cracked wires on the affected plugs. Also look for cracks in the distributor cap between the towers of affected cylinders.

RECOMMENDATION: After the problem is corrected, these plugs can be cleaned and reinstalled if not worn severely.

MMT Fouled

APPEARANCE: Spark plugs fouled by MMT (Methycyclopentadienyl Maganese Tricarbonyl) have reddish, rusty appearance on the insulator and side electrode.

CAUSE: MMT is an anti-knock additive in gasoline used to replace lead. During the combustion process, the MMT leaves a reddish deposit on the insulator and side electrode.

RECOMMENDATION: No engine malfunction is indicated and the deposits will not affect plug performance any more than lead deposits (see Ash Deposits). MMT fouled plugs can be cleaned, regapped and reinstalled.

High Speed Glazing

APPEARANCE: Glazing appears as shiny coating on the plug, either yellow or tan in color.

CAUSE: During hard, fast acceleration, plug temperatures rise suddenly. Deposits from normal combustion have no chance to fluff-off; instead, they melt on the insulator forming an electrically conductive coating which causes misfiring.

RECOMMENDATION: Glazed plugs are not easily cleaned. They should be replaced with a fresh set of plugs of the correct heat range. If the condition recurs, using plugs with a heat range one step colder may cure the problem.

Ash (Lead) Deposits

APPEARANCE: Ash deposits are characterized by light brown or white colored deposits crusted on the side or center electrodes. In some cases it may give the plug a rusty appearance.

CAUSE: Ash deposits are normally derived from oil or fuel additives burned during normal combustion. Normally they are harmless, though excessive amounts can cause misfiring. If deposits are excessive in short mileage, the valve guides may be worn.

RECOMMENDATION: Ash-fouled plugs can be cleaned, gapped and reinstalled.

Detonation

APPEARANCE: Detonation is usually characterized by a broken plug insulator.

CAUSE: A portion of the fuel charge will begin to burn spontaneously, from the increased heat following ignition. The explosion that results applies extreme pressure to engine components, frequently damaging spark plugs and pistons.

Detonation can result by over-advanced ignition timing, inferior gasoline (low octane) lean air/fuel mixture, poor carburetion, engine lugging or an increase in compression ratio due to combustion chamber deposits or engine modification.

RECOMMENDATION: Replace the plugs after correcting the problem.

Photos Courtesy Champion Spark Plug Co.

EMISSION CONTROLS

13. Be aware of the general condition of the emission control system. It contributes to reduced pollution and should be serviced regularly to maintain efficient engine operation.

14. Check all vacuum lines for dried, cracked or brittle conditions. Something as simple as a leaking vacuum hose can cause poor performance and loss of economy.

15. Avoid tampering with the emission control system. Attempting to improve fuel econ-

FUEL SYSTEM

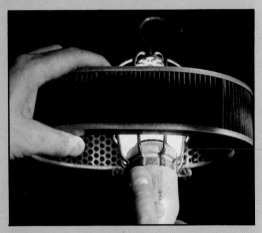

Check the air filter with a light behind it. If you can see light through the filter it can be reused.

Extremely clogged filters should be discarded and replaced with a new one.

18. Replace the air filter regularly. A dirty air filter richens the air/fuel mixture and can increase fuel consumption as much as 10%. Tests show that ⅓ of all vehicles have air filters in need of replacement.

19. Replace the fuel filter at least as often as recommended.

20. Set the idle speed and carburetor mixture to specifications.

21. Check the automatic choke. A sticking or malfunctioning choke wastes gas.

22. During the summer months, adjust the automatic choke for a leaner mixture which will produce faster engine warm-ups.

COOLING SYSTEM

29. Be sure all accessory drive belts are in good condition. Check for cracks or wear.

30. Adjust all accessory drive belts to proper tension.

31. Check all hoses for swollen areas, worn spots, or loose clamps.

32. Check coolant level in the radiator or ex-pansion tank.

33. Be sure the thermostat is operating properly. A stuck thermostat delays engine warm-up and a cold engine uses nearly twice as much fuel as a warm engine.

34. Drain and replace the engine coolant at least as often as recommended. Rust and scale

TIRES & WHEELS

38. Check the tire pressure often with a pencil type gauge. Tests by a major tire manufacturer show that 90% of all vehicles have at least 1 tire improperly inflated. Better mileage can be achieved by over-inflating tires, but never exceed the maximum inflation pressure on the side of the tire.

39. If possible, install radial tires. Radial tires deliver as much as ½ mpg more than bias belted tires.

40. Avoid installing super-wide tires. They only create extra rolling resistance and decrease fuel mileage. Stick to the manufacturer's recommendations.

41. Have the wheels properly balanced.

omy by tampering with emission controls is more likely to worsen fuel economy than improve it. Emission control changes on modern engines are not readily reversible.

16. Clean (or replace) the EGR valve and lines as recommended.

17. Be sure that all vacuum lines and hoses are reconnected properly after working under the hood. An unconnected or misrouted vacuum line can wreak havoc with engine performance.

23. Check for fuel leaks at the carburetor, fuel pump, fuel lines and fuel tank. Be sure all lines and connections are tight.

24. Periodically check the tightness of the carburetor and intake manifold attaching nuts and bolts. These are a common place for vacuum leaks to occur.

25. Clean the carburetor periodically and lubricate the linkage.

26. The condition of the tailpipe can be an excellent indicator of proper engine combustion. After a long drive at highway speeds, the inside of the tailpipe should be a light grey in color. Black or soot on the insides indicates an overly rich mixture.

27. Check the fuel pump pressure. The fuel pump may be supplying more fuel than the engine needs.

28. Use the proper grade of gasoline for your engine. Don't try to compensate for knocking or "pinging" by advancing the ignition timing. This practice will only increase plug temperature and the chances of detonation or pre-ignition with relatively little performance gain.

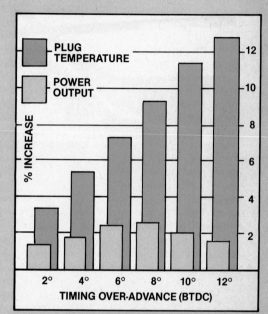

Increasing ignition timing past the specified setting results in a drastic increase in spark plug temperature with increased chance of detonation or preignition. Performance increase is considerably less. (Photo courtesy Champion Spark Plug Co.)

that form in the engine should be flushed out to allow the engine to operate at peak efficiency.

35. Clean the radiator of debris that can decrease cooling efficiency.

36. Install a flex-type or electric cooling fan, if you don't have a clutch type fan. Flex fans use curved plastic blades to push more air at low speeds when more cooling is needed; at high speeds the blades flatten out for less resistance. Electric fans only run when the engine temperature reaches a predetermined level.

37. Check the radiator cap for a worn or cracked gasket. If the cap does not seal properly, the cooling system will not function properly.

42. Be sure the front end is correctly aligned. A misaligned front end actually has wheels going in differed directions. The increased drag can reduce fuel economy by .3 mpg.

43. Correctly adjust the wheel bearings. Wheel bearings that are adjusted too tight increase rolling resistance.

Check tire pressures regularly with a reliable pocket type gauge. Be sure to check the pressure on a cold tire.

GENERAL MAINTENANCE

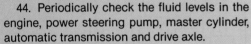

Check the fluid levels (particularly engine oil) on a regular basis. Be sure to check the oil for grit, water or other contamination.

A vacuum gauge is another excellent indicator of internal engine condition and can also be installed in the dash as a mileage indicator.

44. Periodically check the fluid levels in the engine, power steering pump, master cylinder, automatic transmission and drive axle.

45. Change the oil at the recommended interval and change the filter at every oil change. Dirty oil is thick and causes extra friction between moving parts, cutting efficiency and increasing wear. A worn engine requires more frequent tune-ups and gets progressively worse fuel economy. In general, use the lightest viscosity oil for the driving conditions you will encounter.

46. Use the recommended viscosity fluids in the transmission and axle.

47. Be sure the battery is fully charged for fast starts. A slow starting engine wastes fuel.

48. Be sure battery terminals are clean and tight.

49. Check the battery electrolyte level and add distilled water if necessary.

50. Check the exhaust system for crushed pipes, blockages and leaks.

51. Adjust the brakes. Dragging brakes or brakes that are not releasing create increased drag on the engine.

52. Install a vacuum gauge or miles-per-gallon gauge. These gauges visually indicate engine vacuum in the intake manifold. High vacuum = good mileage and low vacuum = poorer mileage. The gauge can also be an excellent indicator of internal engine conditions.

53. Be sure the clutch is properly adjusted. A slipping clutch wastes fuel.

54. Check and periodically lubricate the heat control valve in the exhaust manifold. A sticking or inoperative valve prevents engine warm-up and wastes gas.

55. Keep accurate records to check fuel economy over a period of time. A sudden drop in fuel economy may signal a need for tune-up or other maintenance.

Chassis Electrical

6

HEATING AND AIR CONDITIONING

CAUTION: *At no time should you attempt to discharge or recharge the air conditioning system. In many cases it is illegal for an uncertified operator to do so. If an air conditioning repair is anticipated, take the vehicle to a certified repair facility so that the system may be discharged and the refrigerant properly recovered or recycled. After the your repair is completed, return the vehicle for evacuation of the system and recharging.*

Heater Unit Assembly

REMOVAL & INSTALLATION
1982 and Later 200SX
240SX

NOTE: *On the 1984-88 200SX and 240SX models no factory removal and installation procedures are available; use this procedure as a guide. Refer to the exploded view of each heater system--modify service steps as necessary.*

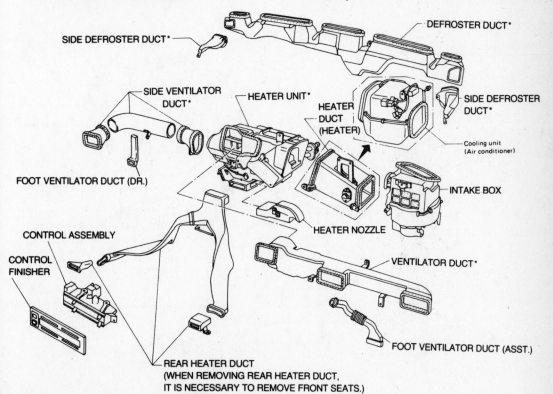

SIDE DEFROSTER DUCT*

DEFROSTER DUCT*

SIDE VENTILATOR DUCT*

HEATER UNIT*

HEATER DUCT (HEATER)

SIDE DEFROSTER DUCT*

Cooling unit (Air conditioner)

FOOT VENTILATOR DUCT (DR.)

INTAKE BOX

CONTROL ASSEMBLY

HEATER NOZZLE

CONTROL FINISHER

VENTILATOR DUCT*

FOOT VENTILATOR DUCT (ASST.)

REAR HEATER DUCT
(WHEN REMOVING REAR HEATER DUCT, IT IS NECESSARY TO REMOVE FRONT SEATS.)

*For removal, it is necessary to remove instrument assembly.

Heater assembly 1982–83 200SX

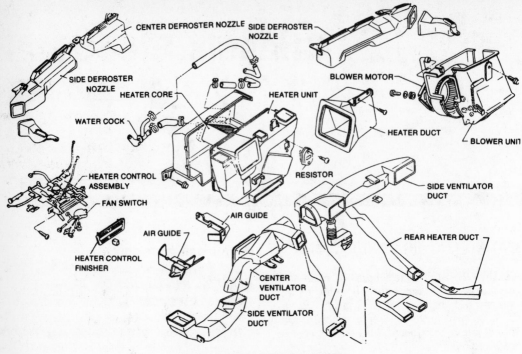

Heater assembly 1984–86½ 200SX

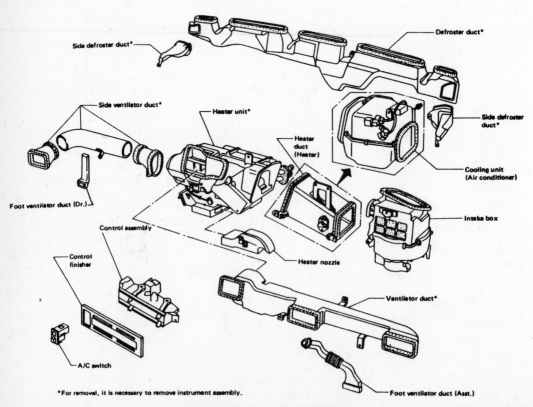

*For removal, it is necessary to remove instrument assembly.

Heater assembly 1986½–88 200SX

1. Set the TEMP lever to the HOT position and drain the coolant.

2. Disconnect the heater hoses from the driver's side of the heater unit.

3. Remove the front seats. To do this, remove the plastic covers over the ends of the seat runners, both front and back, to expose the seat mounting bolts. Remove the bolts and remove the seats.

4. Remove the console box and the floor carpets.

5. Remove the instrument panel lower covers from both the driver's and passenger's sides of the car. Remove the lower cluster lids.

6. Remove the left hand side ventilator duct.

7. Remove the radio, sound balancer and stereo cassette deck if so equipped.

8. Remove the instrument panel-to-transmission tunnel stay.

9. Remove the rear heater duct from the floor of the vehicle.

10. Remove the center ventilator duct.

11. Remove the left and right hand side air guides from the lower heater outlets.

12. Disconnect the wire harness connections.

13. Remove the two screws at the bottom sides of the heater unit and the one screw and the top of the unit and remove the unit together with the heater control assembly.

NOTE: *On late models, the heater control cables and control assembly may have to be removed before the heater unit is removed. Always mark control cables before removing them to ensure correct adjustment and proper operation.*

To install:

14. Install the heater assembly with retaining bolts in the vehicle. Reconnect all electrical and heater control cable connections if removed.

15. Install the left and right hand side air guides to the lower heater outlets.

16. Install the center ventilator duct.

17. Install the rear heater duct to the floor of the vehicle and all components that were removed to gain access to the rear heater duct retaining bolts.

18. Install the instrument panel lower covers, floor carpets, console box and seats if removed.

19. Reconnect the two heater hoses with new hose clamps. Connect the battery ground cable and refill the cooling system.

20. Run the engine for a few minutes with

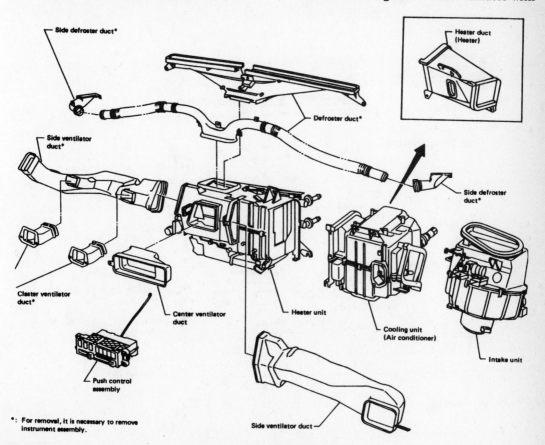

— Side defroster duct*

Heater duct
(Heater)

Defroster duct*

Side ventilator duct*

Side defroster duct*

Cluster ventilator duct*

Center ventilator duct

Heater unit

Cooling unit
(Air conditioner)

Intake unit

Push control assembly

*: For removal, it is necessary to remove instrument assembly.

Side ventilator duct

Heater assembly 1989–92 240SX

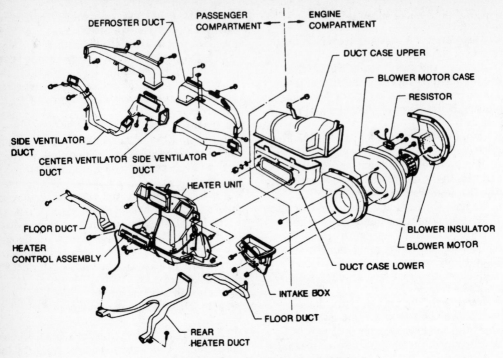

Heater assembly—Stanza (early models)

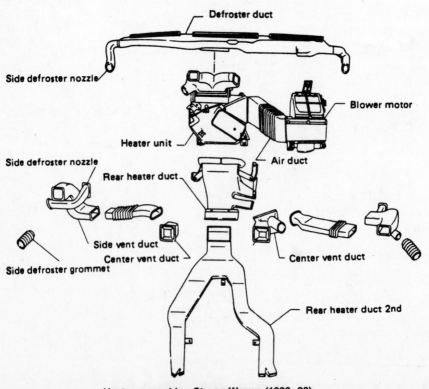

Heater assembly—Stanza Wagon (1986–88)

the heater on to make sure the coolant level is correct. Check for any coolant leaks and the heater system for proper operation.

Stanza

The air conditioning evaporator core is mounted in the engine compartment on some models. No air conditioning interference is experienced when removing the heater core on these vehicles. When refilling the cooling system be sure to bleed the air from it, refer to Section 1.

1. Disconnect the negative battery cable. Remove the instrument panel.

2. Disconnect the heater hoses and vacuum lines in the engine compartment.

3. Disconnect the control lever and electrical connectors. Remove the heater control assembly.

4. Unbolt and remove the heater unit assembly.

To install:

5. Install the heater unit in the vehicle.

6. Install the heater control assembly, control lever and electrical connections.

7. Connect the heater hoses and vacuum tube.

8. Install the instrument panel and refill the cooling system.

9. Start engine and check system for proper operation.

Heater Blower

REMOVAL & INSTALLATION

1982 and Later 200SX
240SX

NOTE: *On all 1984-88 200SX models the blower motor is located behind the glove box, facing the floor in the intake unit of the heater housing.*

1. Disconnect the battery ground cable. Remove the instrument panel lower cover and cluster lid on the right hand side.

2. Disconnect the control cable and harness connector from the blower unit.

3. Remove the three bolts and remove the blower unit.

4. Remove the three screws holding the blower motor in the case, unplug the hose running from the rear of the motor into the case and pull the motor together with the fan cage out of the case.

5. Installation is the reverse of removal. With the blower motor assembly removed, check the case for any debris or signs of fan contact. Inspect the fan for wear spots, cracked blades or hub, loose retaining nut or poor alignment. Make sure the electrical connection is installed in the correct position. Check system for proper operation.

Stanza

NOTE: *On all 1987 and later Stanza models, the blower motor is located behind the glove box, facing the floor in the intake unit of the heater housing.*

EARLY MODELS

1. Disconnect the negative battery cable. Working in the engine compartment, disconnect the blower motor insulator upper fasteners.

2. Remove the blower motor retaining bolts.

3. Push the blower motor insulator down by hand and remove the motor.

4. Installation is the reverse of the removal procedures. With the blower motor assembly removed, check the case for any debris or signs of fan contact. Inspect the fan for wear spots, cracked blades or hub, loose retaining nut or

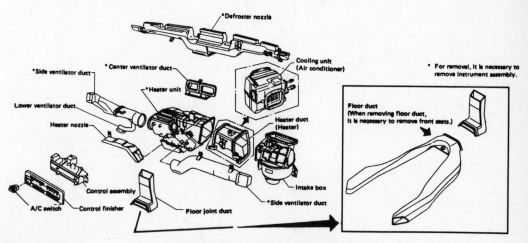

Heater assembly—Stanza (1987 and later)

poor alignment. Check system for proper operation.

LATER MODELS

1. Disconnect the negative battery cable. Disconnect the electrical harness from the blower motor.

2. Remove the retaining bolts from the bottom of the blower unit and lower the blower motor from the case.

3. To install, reverse the removal procedures. With the blower motor assembly removed, check the case for any debris or signs of fan contact. Inspect the fan for wear spots, cracked blades or hub, loose retaining nut or

poor alignment. Check system for proper operation.

Heater Core

REMOVAL & INSTALLATION

1982 and Later 200SX
240SX

1. Disconnect the negative battery cable.

2. Remove the heater unit assembly (refer to the necessary service procedures and illustrations) and the heater core hoses.

3. Remove the heater core from the heater unit box.

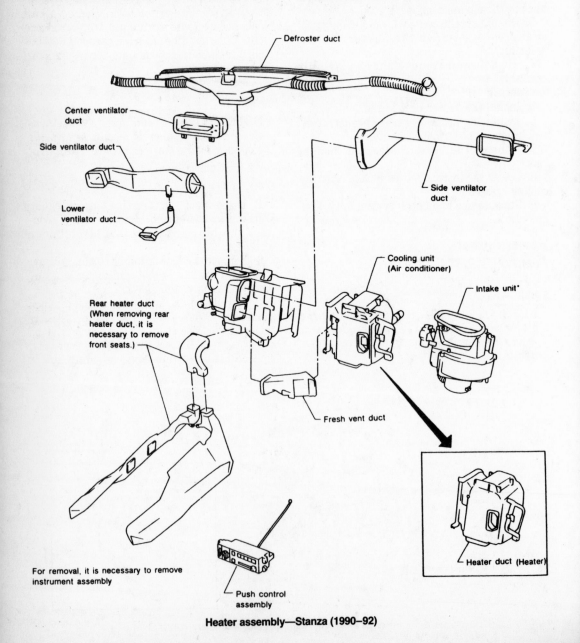

Heater assembly—Stanza (1990–92)

4. Installation is the reverse of removal. Clean heater case of all debris before installation. Check system for proper operation.

Stanza

NOTE: *When refilling the cooling system, be sure to bleed the air from it. Refer to Section 1.*

1. Remove pedal bracket mounting bolts, the steering column mounting bolts, the brake and the clutch pedal cotter pins.

2. Move the pedal bracket and the steering column to the left.

3. Disconnect the air mix door control cable and the heater valve control lever, then remove the control lever.

4. Remove the core cover and disconnect the hoses at the core. Remove the heater core.

5. Installation is the reverse of the removal procedures. On later models it may be necessary to remove the complete heater assembly and then remove the heater core from the assembly (remove the heater assembly case bolts/clips and separate the cases, then pull the heater core from the case). Clean heater case of all debris before installation. Check system for proper operation.

Heater Water Control Valve
REMOVAL & INSTALLATION
All Models

1. Disconnect the negative battery cable.

2. Drain the cooling system. Remove all the necessary components in order to gain access to the valve retaining assembly.

3. Disconnect the electrical, vacuum or mechanical connections from the valve.

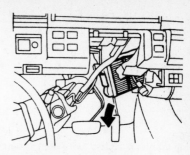

Removing the heater core—Stanza

4. Disconnect the heater hose from the valve. Remove the control valve from the vehicle.

5. Installation is the reverse of the removal procedure. Refill the cooling system and bleed the system. Check system for proper operation.

Control Head And Fan Switch Assembly
REMOVAL & INSTALLATION
200SX and 240SX

1. Disconnect the negative battery cable. Remove the heater control trim panel. Remove the instrument lower trim panels.

2. Disconnect control cables from the heater unit assembly.

3. Disconnect harness (electrical) connectors and ground wire.

4. Disconnect heater control assembly mounting bolts.

5. Installation is the reverse of the removal procedures. Make sure the ground wire makes good connection. Adjust the heater control cables by clamping the cables while pushing cable outer case and lever in the correct (forward) di-

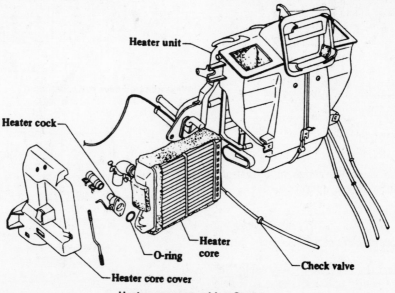

Heater unit

Heater cock

O-ring

Heater core

Heater core cover

Check valve

Heater core assembly—Stanza

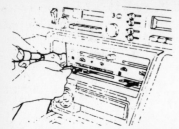

Removing control head and fan switch assembly

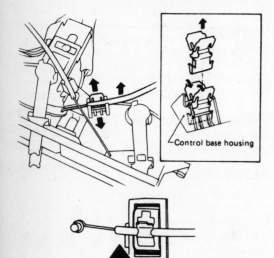

Removing control cables at heater unit assembly door levers

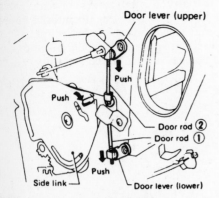

Ventilator door control rod adjustment

rection to the complete range of operation. Check system for proper operation.

Stanza

NOTE: *On some vehicles, the fan switch cannot be removed from the control head assembly.*

1. Disconnect the negative battery cable. Remove cluster cover and instrument lower covers.

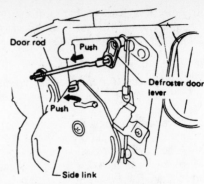

Defroster door control rod adjustment

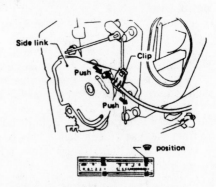

Air control cable adjustment

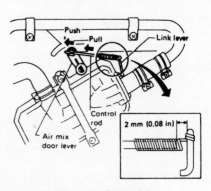

Water control valve rod adjustment

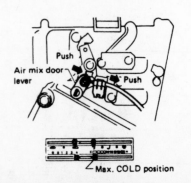

Temperature control cable adjustment

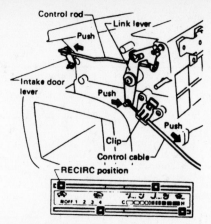

Intake door control cable adjustment

2. Remove control cables by unfastening clamps at door levers.

3. Disconnect electrical connector and remove heater control head assembly mounting bolts. Remove ground wire from intake box.

4. Remove heater control head assembly.

5. To install reverse the removal procedures. Make sure the ground wire makes good connection. Adjust the heater control cables by clamping the cables while pushing cable outer case and lever in the correct (forward) direction to the complete range of operation. Check system for proper operation.

AIR CONDITIONING

CAUTION: *At no time should you attempt to discharge or recharge the air conditioning*

system. *In many cases it is illegal for an uncertified operator to do so. If an air conditioning repair is anticipated, take the vehicle to a certified repair facility so that the system may be discharged and the refrigerant properly recovered or recycled. After the your repair is completed, return the vehicle for evacuation of the system and recharging.*

Special Precautions

1. All refrigerant service work must be done with the proper recycling equipment used by a certified operator. Do not allow the freon to discharge to the air.

2. Any amount of water will make the system less effective. When any part of the system has been removed, plug or cap the lines to prevent moisture from the air entering the system. When installing a new component, do not uncap the fittings until ready to attach the lines.

3. When assembling a fitting, always use a new O-ring and lightly lubricate the fitting with compressor oil.

4. When a compressor is removed, do not leave it on its side or upside down for more than 10 minutes. The oil may leak into the low pressure chamber.

5. The proper amount of oil must be maintained in the system (add to low pressure side only) to prevent compressor damage and to maintain system efficiency. Be sure to measure and adjust the amount of oil removed or added to the system, especially when replacing the compressor.

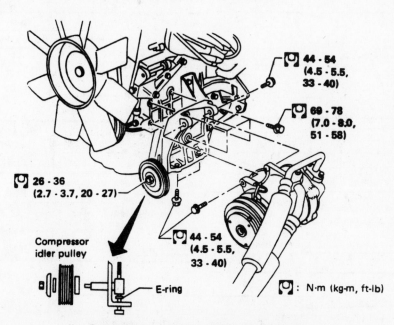

Compressor mounting—200SX CA20E engine

General Specifications

COMPRESSOR

Model	ATSUGI make NVR 140S
Type	Vane rotary
Displacement cm³ (cu in)/Rev.	140 (8.54)
Direction of rotation	Clockwise (Viewed from drive end)
Drive belt	Poly V

LUBRICATION OIL

Model	ATSUGI make NVR 140S
Type	SUNISO 5GS
Capacity mℓ (US fl oz, Imp fl oz) Total in system	200 (6.8, 7.0)
Amount of oil which can be drained	Approx. 100 (3.4, 3.5)
Compressor (Service parts) charging amount	200 (6.8, 7.0)

REFRIGERANT

Type	R-12
Capacity kg (lb)	0.9 - 1.0 (2.0 - 2.2)

A/C General Specifications—240SX 1989

General Specifications

COMPRESSOR

Model	CALSONIC make V-5
Type	V-5 variable displacement
Displacement cm³ (cu in)/rev.	
Max.	146 (8.91)
Min.	3 (0.18)
Cylinder bore x stroke mm (in)	36.1 (1.421) x [0.6 - 28.6 (0.024 - 1.126)]
Direction of rotation	Clockwise (viewed from drive end)
Drive belt	Poly V

LUBRICATION OIL

Model	CALSONIC make V-5
Type	SUNISO 5GS or equivalent
Capacity mℓ (US fl oz, Imp fl oz) Total in system	236 (8.0, 8.3)
Compressor (Service part) charging amount	236 (8.0, 8.3)

REFRIGERANT

Type	R-12
Capacity kg (lb)	0.8 - 0.9 (1.8 - 2.0)

A/C General Specifications—240SX 1990-2

General Specifications

COMPRESSOR

Model	HITACHI make MJS170
Type	Swash plate
Displacement cm³ (cu in)/Rev.	170 (10.37)
Cylinder bore x stroke mm (in)	40.0 x 22.6 (1.575 x 0.890)
Direction of rotation	Clockwise (Viewed from drive end)
Drive belt	Poly V

LUBRICATION OIL

Model	HITACHI make MJS170
Type	SUNISO 5GS
Capacity mℓ (US fl oz, Imp fl oz) Total in system	150 (5.1, 5.3)
Remaining oil in system after oil return operation and draining it	30 (1.0, 1.1)
Compressor (Service parts) charging amount	150 (5.1, 5.3)

REFRIGERANT

Type	R-12
Capacity kg (lb)	0.9 - 1.1 (2.0 - 2.4)

A/C General Specifications—200 SX 1984–88

General Specifications

COMPRESSOR

Model	ATSUGI make NVR 140S
Type	Vane rotary
Displacement cm³ (cu in)/Rev.	140 (8.54)
Direction of rotation	Clockwise (Viewed from drive end)
Drive belt	Poly V

LUBRICATION OIL

Model	ATSUGI make NVR 140S
Type	SUNISO 5GS or equivalent
Capacity mℓ (US fl oz, Imp fl oz)	
Total in system	200 (6.8, 7.0)
Amount of oil which can be drained	Approx. 100 (3.4, 3.5)
Compressor (Service parts) charging amount	200 (6.8, 7.0)

REFRIGERANT

Type	R-12
Capacity kg (lb)	0.75 - 0.85 (1.65 - 1.87)

A/C General Specifications—Stanza 1990–92

Compressor
REMOVAL & INSTALLATION
All Models

1. Have the system fully discharged using refrigerant recovery equipment.
2. Disconnect the negative battery cables.
3. Remove all the necessary components in order to gain access to the compressor mounting bolts. Remove compressor revolution sensor if so equipped.
4. Remove the compressor drive belt.

GENERAL SPECIFICATIONS
COMPRESSOR

Model	MJS170
Type	Swash plate
Displacement cm³ (cu in)/rev.	170 (10.37)
Cylinder bore x stroke mm (in)	40.0 x 22.6 (1.575 x 0.890)
Direction of rotation	Clockwise (viewed from drive end)
Type of driving belt	B type

LUBRICATING OIL

Model	MJS170
Type	SUNISO 5GS
Capacity mℓ (US fl oz, Imp fl oz)	150 (5.1, 5.3)

REFRIGERANT

Type	R-12
Capacity kg (lb)	0.8 - 1.0 (1.8 - 2.2)

A/C General Specifications—Stanza 1982–89

NOTE: *To facilitate removal of the compressor belt, remove the idler pulley and bracket as an assembly beforehand from the underside of the car.*

5. Disconnect and plug the refrigerant lines with a clean shop towel.

NOTE: *Be sure to use 2 wrenches (one to loosen fitting—one to hold fitting in place) when disconnecting the refrigerant lines.*

6. Disconnect and tag all electrical connections.
7. Remove the compressor mounting bolts. Remove the compressor from the vehicle.

To install:

8. Install the compressor on the engine and evenly torque all the mounting bolts.
9. Connect all the electrical connections and unplug and reconnect all refrigerant lines (replace O-rings).
10. Install the equipment removed to gain access to the compressor mounting bolts. Install compressor revolution sensor if so equipped.
11. Install and adjust the drive belt.
12. Connect the negative battery cable.
13. Have the system evacuated and recharged.

Condenser
REMOVAL & INSTALLATION
All Models

1. Have the system fully discharged using refrigerant recovery equipment.
2. Disconnect the negative battery cables.
3. Remove the necessary components in order to gain access to the condenser retaining

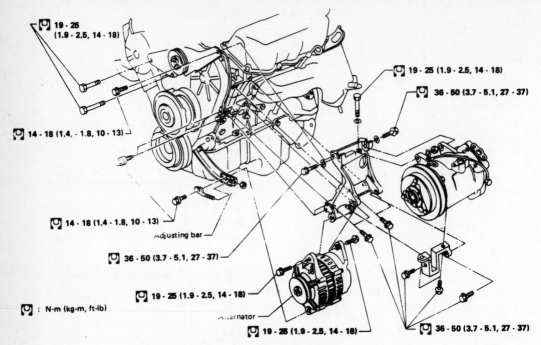

19 - 25
(1.9 - 2.5, 14 - 18)

19 - 25 (1.9 - 2.5, 14 - 18)

36 - 50 (3.7 - 5.1, 27 - 37)

14 - 18 (1.4 - 1.8, 10 - 13)

14 - 18 (1.4 - 1.8, 10 - 13)

Adjusting bar

36 - 50 (3.7 - 5.1, 27 - 37)

19 - 25 (1.9 - 2.5, 14 - 18)

: N·m (kg-m, ft-lb)

Alternator

19 - 25 (1.9 - 2.5, 14 - 18)

36 - 50 (3.7 - 5.1, 27 - 37)

Compressor mounting—200SX VG30E engine

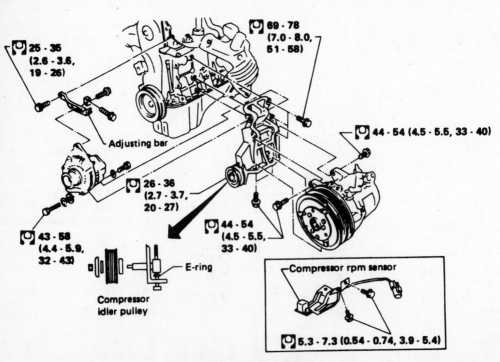

69 - 78
(7.0 - 8.0,
51 - 58)

25 - 35
(2.6 - 3.6,
19 - 26)

Adjusting bar

44 - 54 (4.5 - 5.5, 33 - 40)

26 - 36
(2.7 - 3.7,
20 - 27)

43 - 58
(4.4 - 5.9,
32 - 43)

44 - 54
(4.5 - 5.5,
33 - 40)

E-ring

Compressor
idler pulley

Compressor rpm sensor

5.3 - 7.3 (0.54 - 0.74, 3.9 - 5.4)

Compressor mounting—Stanza

bolts (radiator grille, hood lock stay etc.). Remove the condenser fan motor if so equipped.

4. Remove the condenser refrigerant lines and plug them with a clean shop towel.

NOTE: *On the 200SX models the receiver drier assembly should be removed before removing the condenser.*

5. Remove the condenser retaining bolts. Remove the condenser from the vehicle.

To install:

6. Install the condenser in the vehicle and evenly torque all the mounting bolts.

NOTE: *Always use new O-rings in all refrigerant lines.*

7. Reconnect all the refrigerant lines.

8. Install the equipment removed to gain access to the condenser mounting bolts. If removed, install the condenser fan motor.

9. Connect the negative battery cable.

10. Have the system evacuated and recharged.

Evaporator Core/Cooling Unit

REMOVAL & INSTALLATION

1982-83 200SX

1. Have the system fully discharged using refrigerant recovery equipment.

2. Disconnect battery ground cable.

3. Remove the instrument lower cover and cluster lid cover.

4. Disconnect refrigerant lines and electrical harness from the cooling unit.

NOTE: *Be sure to use two wrenches when removing or connecting pipe joints. Always plug pipe openings immediately after pipe disconnection.*

5. Remove the cooling unit with drain tube.

6. Remove the clips fixing the upper case to lower case.

7. Remove the evaporator core from the cooling unit.

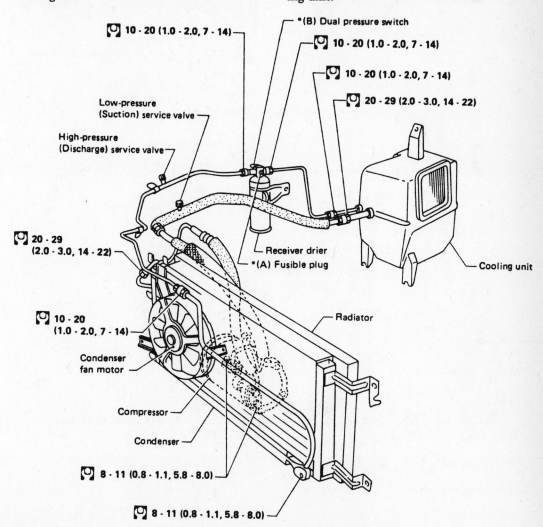

A/C condenser with condenser fan motor

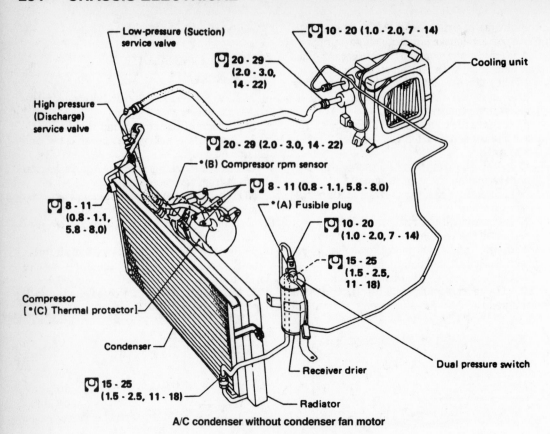

Low-pressure (Suction) service valve

10 - 20 (1.0 - 2.0, 7 - 14)

20 - 29 (2.0 - 3.0, 14 - 22)

Cooling unit

High pressure (Discharge) service valve

20 - 29 (2.0 - 3.0, 14 - 22)

*(B) Compressor rpm sensor

8 - 11 (0.8 - 1.1, 5.8 - 8.0)

*(A) Fusible plug

8 - 11 (0.8 - 1.1, 5.8 - 8.0)

10 - 20 (1.0 - 2.0, 7 - 14)

15 - 25 (1.5 - 2.5, 11 - 18)

Compressor [*(C) Thermal protector]

Condenser

Receiver drier

Dual pressure switch

15 - 25 (1.5 - 2.5, 11 - 18)

Radiator

A/C condenser without condenser fan motor

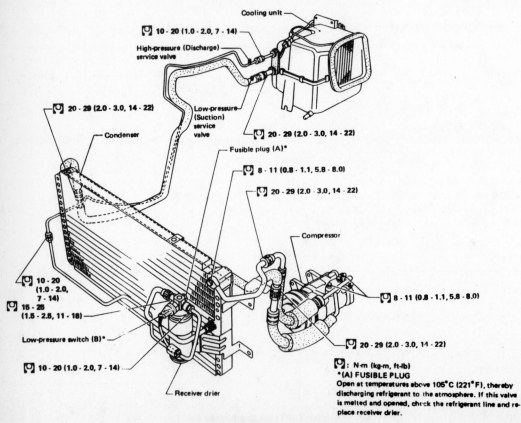

Cooling unit

10 - 20 (1.0 - 2.0, 7 - 14)

High-pressure (Discharge) service valve

Low-pressure (Suction) service valve

20 - 29 (2.0 - 3.0, 14 - 22)

20 - 29 (2.0 - 3.0, 14 - 22)

Condenser

Fusible plug (A)*

8 - 11 (0.8 - 1.1, 5.8 - 8.0)

20 - 29 (2.0 - 3.0, 14 - 22)

Compressor

10 - 20 (1.0 - 2.0, 7 - 14)

15 - 25 (1.5 - 2.5, 11 - 18)

Low-pressure switch (B)*

8 - 11 (0.8 - 1.1, 5.8 - 8.0)

20 - 29 (2.0 - 3.0, 14 - 22)

10 - 20 (1.0 - 2.0, 7 - 14)

: N·m (kg-m, ft-lb)
*(A) FUSIBLE PLUG
Open at temperatures above 105°C (221°F), thereby discharging refrigerant to the atmosphere. If this valve is melted and opened, check the refrigerant line and replace receiver drier.

Receiver drier

Condenser assembly—1988 200SX

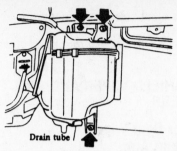

Removing cooling unit retaining bolts—1983 200SX

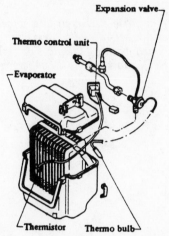

Evaporator housing/cooling unit assembly—1983 200SX

To install:

8. Install the evaporator core in the cooling unit. Connect lower and upper case with retaining clips.

9. Install the cooling unit with retaining bolts in the vehicle.

10. Connect all electrical connections. Reconnect the pressure pipes with new O-rings. Install the instrument lower cover and cluster lid cover.

11. Connect battery cable.

12. Have the system evacuated and recharged. Make sure the oil level is correct for the system. Check system for proper operation.

1984-88 200SX
1989-92 240SX

On these vehicles there is no removal and installation procedure for evaporator core or cooling unit given by Datsun/Nissan. Use the early model procedures as a guide.

1982-86 Stanza

NOTE: *On Stanza models from 1987 and on Stanza wagons from 1986, the cooling unit which contains the evaporator is under the dash connected to the heater unit.*

1. Have the system discharged using refrigerant recovery equipment.

2. Disconnect battery ground cable.

3. Remove air cleaner and disconnect vacuum check valve fixing bolt.

4. Disconnect evaporator upper case fixing bolts.

5. Remove evaporator upper case while scraping off sealer.

6. Disconnect inlet and outlet pipes at evaporator.

NOTE: *Be sure to use two wrenches when removing or connecting pipe joints. Always plug pipe openings immediately after pipe disconnection.*

7. Remove evaporator from evaporator lower case.

To install:

8. Install the evaporator in the evaporator lower case.

9. Connect inlet and outlet pipes at evaporator with new O-rings.

10. Install the upper evaporator case (with suitable type sealer--to seal assembly) with fixing bolts.

11. Install the air cleaner and vacuum check valve fixing bolt.

12. Connect battery cable.

13. Have the system evacuated and recharged. Make sure the oil level is correct for the system. Check system for proper operation.

1987-92 Stanza
1986-88 Stanza Wagons

On these vehicles there is no removal and installation procedure for evaporator core or cooling unit given by Datsun/Nissan. Use the early model procedures as a guide and refer to the exploded view of the heater assembly if necessary.

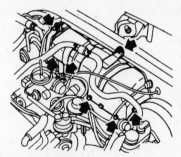

Evaporator upper case—Stanza

Removing evaporator assembly—Stanza

ENTERTAINMENT SYSTEMS

Radio/Cassette Deck
REMOVAL & INSTALLATION

1982-83 200SX

1. Disconnect the battery. Before removing the radio (audio assembly), you must remove the center instrument cluster which holds the heater controls, etc. Remove the two side screws in the cluster. Remove the heater control and the control panel. Remove the two bolts behind the heater control panel and the two bolts at the case of the cluster. Pull the cluster out of the way after disconnecting the lighter wiring and any other control cables.

2. Remove the radio knobs and fronting panel.

3. Remove the five screws holding the radio assembly in place.

4. Remove the radio after unplugging all connections.

5. Installation is the reverse of removal. Check radio for proper operation.

1984-88 200SX
240SX
Stanza

NOTE: *On some applications, an auxiliary fuse is located in the rear of the radio. If all other power sources check OK, remove the radio and check the fuse.*

1. Disconnect the neagative battery cable.

2. Remove all necessary trim panel(s) or ashtray assembly.

3. Remove the radio mounting bolts and the radio.

4. Disconnect the electrical harness connector and the antenna plug from the radio.

To install:

5. Connect the electrical harness connector and the antenna plug to the radio.

6. Install the radio and tighten the bolts.

7. Install all necessary trim panel(s) or ashtray assembly.

8. Check radio system for proper operation.

WINDSHIELD WIPER AND WASHERS

Front or Rear Wiper Blade and Arm
REMOVAL & INSTALLATION

All Models

NOTE: *On some new models a wiper arm lock is used to keep the wiper arm off the glass surface when washing the glass or replacing the blade. On most models the wiper arms are*

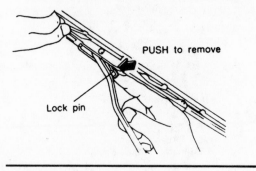

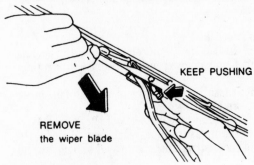

Wiper blade/arm replacement

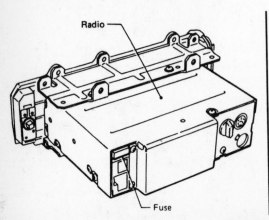

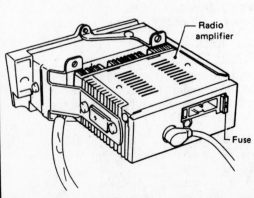

Radio fuse check

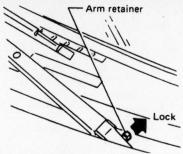

Wiper blade removal lock

a different length. They have an identifying mark and care must be taken to install them properly.

1. Pull the wiper arm up.
2. Push the lock pin, then remove the wiper blade.
3. Insert the new wiper blade to the wiper arm until a click sounds.
4. Make sure the wiper blade contacts the glass. Otherwise, the arm may be damaged.
5. To remove the arm assembly, lift the end of the wiper arm at the base and remove the attaching nut. If a lock type application is used-- push the lock up. On early models, remove the attaching nut at the base of the wiper arm.

Before reinstalling wiper arm, clean up the pivot area with a brush. This will reduce the possibility of the wiper arm coming loose.

Front Wiper Motor and Linkage

REMOVAL & INSTALLATION
200SX and Stanza (1982-89)

1. Disconnect the negative battery cable.
2. Open the hood and disconnect the motor wiring connection.
3. Unbolt the motor from the body.
4. Disconnect the wiper linkage from the motor and remove the motor.
5. Installation is the reverse of removal. Check wiper arm/blade assembly to cowl clearance and complete system for proper operation.

240SX
1990-92 Stanza

1. Remove the wiper arm.
2. Remove the cowl cover. Remove the wiper motor so that the wiper motor link comes out of hole in the front cowl top panel.
3. Disconnect the ball joint which connects motor link and wiper link. Remove the wiper motor from the vehicle.
4. Remove wiper link pivot blocks on driver and passenger sides. Remove the wiper link and pivot blocks as an assembly from the oblong hole on the left side of cowl top.
5. To install reverse the removal procedures. Apply a small amount of grease to ball joints before installation.

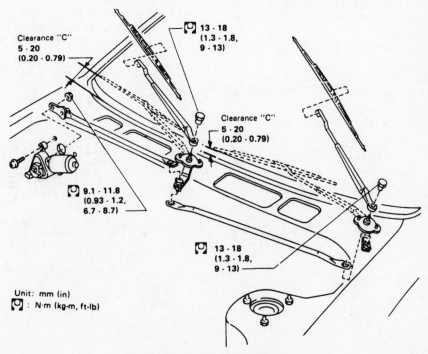

Clearance "C"
5 - 20
(0.20 - 0.79)

13 - 18
(1.3 - 1.8,
9 - 13)

Clearance "C"
5 - 20
(0.20 - 0.79)

9.1 - 11.8
(0.93 - 1.2,
6.7 - 8.7)

13 - 18
(1.3 - 1.8,
9 - 13)

Unit: mm (in)
: N·m (kg-m, ft-lb)

Wiper motor linkage 1984—88 200SX

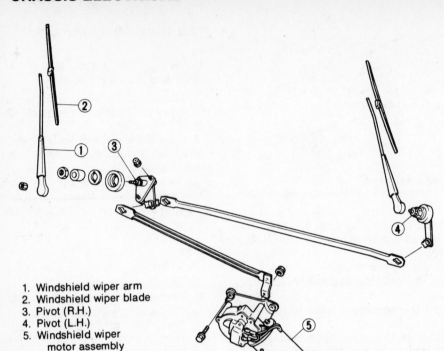

1. Windshield wiper arm
2. Windshield wiper blade
3. Pivot (R.H.)
4. Pivot (L.H.)
5. Windshield wiper
   motor assembly

Wiper system—Stanza

Rear Wiper Motor

REMOVAL & INSTALLATION

1. Disconnect the negative battery cable. Position the wiper arm to raise the wiper blade off the rear window glass. Remove the attaching nut and washers and work the wiper arm off the motor shaft.

2. Remove the attaching screws and remove the hatchback/liftback area inner finish panel. Carefully peel the plastic water shield off the sealer if so equipped.

3. Disconnect the electrical connector at the motor. Remove the motor mounting bolts and remove the motor.

4. Install the motor in reverse of the removal procedure. Torque the rear window wiper arm-to-motor nut to 9–13 ft. lbs. (13–18 Nm).

3.8 - 5.1
(0.39 - 0.52, 2.8 - 3.8)

3.8 - 5.1
(0.39 - 0.52, 2.8 - 3.8)

: N·m (kg-m, ft-lb)

Wiper system 1990–92 Stanza

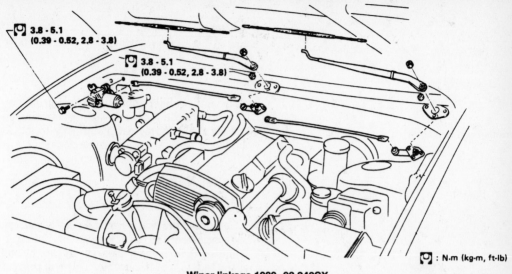

3.8 - 5.1
(0.39 - 0.52, 2.8 - 3.8)

3.8 - 5.1
(0.39 - 0.52, 2.8 - 3.8)

⬚ : N·m (kg-m, ft-lb)

Wiper linkage 1989–92 240SX

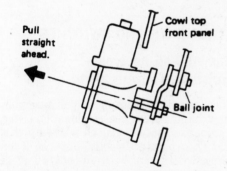

Pull
straight
ahead.

Cowl top
front panel

Ball joint

Remove wiper motor to gain access to ball joint

Rear window wiper motor—1983 200SX

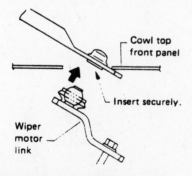

Cowl top
front panel

Insert securely.

Wiper
motor
link

Install ball joint to wiper linkage securely

5. Before installing the water shield, run a fresh ring of sealer around the outer edge if necessary.

Windshield Washer Fluid Reservoir
REMOVAL & INSTALLATION
Front and Rear

1. Disconnect the negative battery cable and reservoir electrical connector.

2. Disconnect the fluid tube from the washer motor. If the tube is too tight to remove, do not force. Heat the tube with a heat gun if the tube has no extra slack or cut the tube at the motor end.

3. Remove the reservoir retaining bolts and slide out of the bracket.

4. Installation is the reverse of removal. Apply petroleum jelly to the motor nipple before installing the washer tube.

NOTE: *A check valve is installed in the washer fluid line. Be careful not to connect check valve to washer tube in the wrong direction.*

Windshield Washer Motor
REMOVAL & INSTALLATION
Front and Rear

Remove the washer reservoir/motor assembly from the vehicle and drain into a suitable container. Remove all connections. Pull the mo-

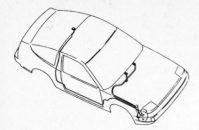

Washer hose routing

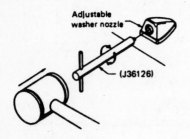

Clean pivot area before installing wiper arm/blade

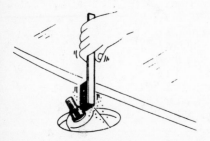

Washer nozzle adjustment

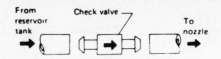

Washer system check valve

tor from the rubber grommet. If having difficulty, lubricate the grommet with penetrating oil and try again. Apply petroleum jelly to install the motor. Reconnect all connections.

Washer Nozzle
ADJUSTMENT

To adjust the washer nozzle spray pattern use special tool J36126 or equivalent. Before attempting to turn the nozzle, gently tap the end of the tool to free the nozzle. This will prevent rounding out the center of the nozzle.

INSTRUMENTS AND SWITCHES

Instument Pad Assembly
REMOVAL AND INSTALLATION

When removing instrument pad assembly, remove the defroster grille, combination meter, A/C or heater control, and all necessary trim panels. These parts are mostly plastic, so do not use excessive force and be careful not to damage them.

On 240SX models, when removing the Head-

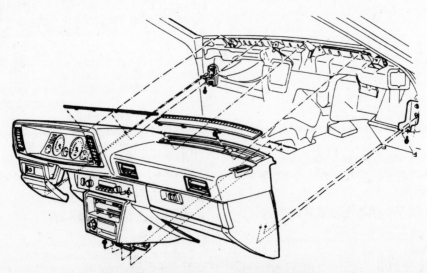

Instrument panel/pad assembly 1983 200SX

Up Display (HUD) finisher, be careful not to scratch the HUD's reflective surface. To prevent this, cover the finisher and reflective surface with a protective covering.

Instrument Cluster/Combination Meter

REMOVAL & INSTALLATION

200SX and 240SX

1. Disconnect the negative battery cable.
2. Remove the steering wheel and steering wheel covers, as required.
3. Remove the screws holding the cluster lid in place and remove the lid.
4. On 200SX, remove the 2 screws and 7 pawls to release the cluster. On 240SX, the cluster is held with 3 screws.
5. Carefully withdraw the cluster assembly from the instrument panel and disconnect the speedometer cable (analog) and electrical wiring from the rear of the cluster. Make sure the wiring is labeled clearly to avoid confusion during installation.
6. Remove the cluster. Be careful not to damage the printed circuit.
7. Installation is the reverse of the removal procedure.

Stanza

1. Disconnect the negative battery cable.
2. Remove the steering wheel and the steering column covers.
3. Remove the instrument cluster lid by removing its screws.
4. Remove the instrument cluster screws.
5. Gently withdraw the cluster from the instrument pad and disconnect all wiring and speedometer cable. Make sure the wires are marked clearly to avoid confusion during installation. Be careful not to damage the printed circuit.
6. Remove the cluster.
7. Installation is the reverse of removal.

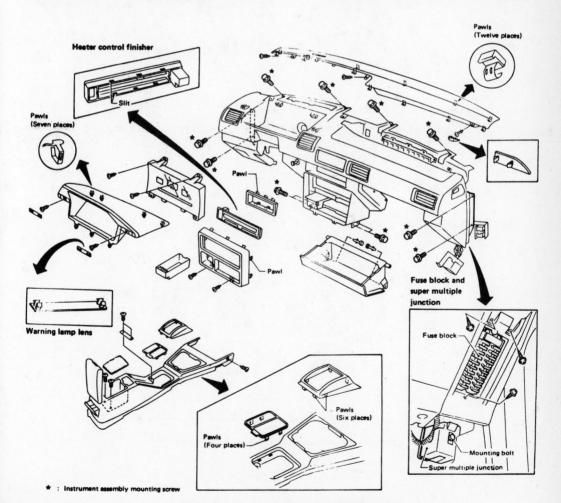

Instrument panel/pad assembly 1984–88 200SX

HEAD-UP DISPLAY (H.U.D.)

- When removing H.U.D. finisher, be extremely careful not to scratch H.U.D.'s reflective surface. To avoid scratching, cover H.U.D.'s reflective surface or finisher with a cloth or vinyl sheet. **L**

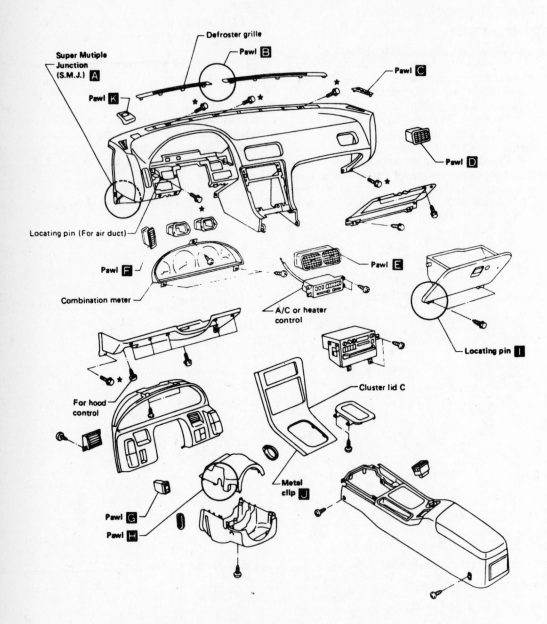

★ : Instrument panel assembly mounting bolts

Instrument panel assembly 1990–92 240SX (part 1)

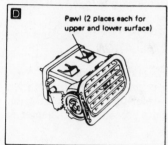

A — Mounting bolt — Super Multiple Junction (S.M.J.) — Instrument harness — Fuse block

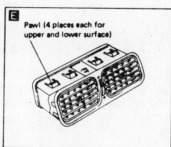

B — Pawl

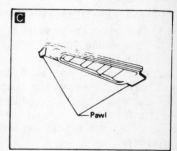

C — Pawl

D — Pawl (2 places each for upper and lower surface)

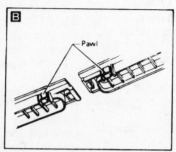

E — Pawl (4 places each for upper and lower surface)

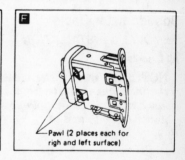

F — Pawl (2 places each for righ and left surface)

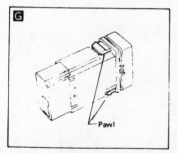

G — Pawl

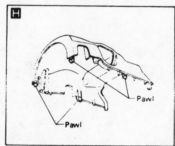

H — Pawl — Pawl

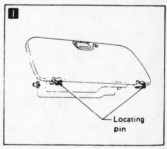

I — Locating pin

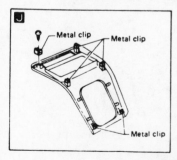

J — Metal clip — Metal clip — Metal clip

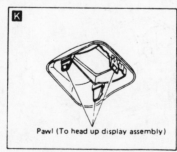

K — Pawl (To head up display assembly)

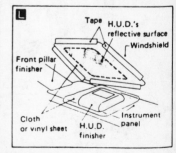

L — Tape — H.U.D.'s reflective surface — Windshield — Front pillar finisher — Cloth or vinyl sheet — H.U.D. finisher — Instrument panel

Instrument panel assembly 1990–92 240SX (part 2)

Speedometer

NOTE: *If equipped with a digital speedometer, the entire cluster assembly must be replaced if the speedometer is faulty.*

REMOVAL & INSTALLATION

Analog (Needle Type) Speedometers

1. Disconnect the negative battery cable.
2. Remove the cluster.
3. Disconnect the speedometer cable and remove the speedometer fasteners.
4. Carefully remove the speedometer from the cluster. Be careful not to damage the printed circuit board.
5. Installation is the reverse of the removal procedure.

Speedometer Cable

REMOVAL & INSTALLATION

All Models

NOTE: *The speedometer cable connector to the instrument cluster/combination meter has a snap release--simply press on the connector tab to release it.*

1. Loosen the lock nut at the rear extension housing on transmission/transaxle assembly.
2. Disconnect the negative battery cable. Remove the instrument cluster/ combination meter.
3. Slide the speedometer cable up to free it.
4. Detach the speedometer cable from all retaining (4) points.
5. Remove the grommet from the upper dash panel by hand.
6. Pull out the speedometer cable from the vehicle.
7. Installation is the reverse of the removal procedure. Make sure that the speedometer cable assembly is properly lubricated. Install the cable end and hollow portion in the transmission/transaxle rear extension in the correct manner. Torque the lock nut to 7-11 ft. lbs.

Windshield Wiper Switch

REMOVAL & INSTALLATION

On 200SX, 240SX and Stanza model vehicles, the wiper switch is part of the Combination Switch Assembly--refer to Turn Signal/Combination Switch service procedures in Chapter 8.

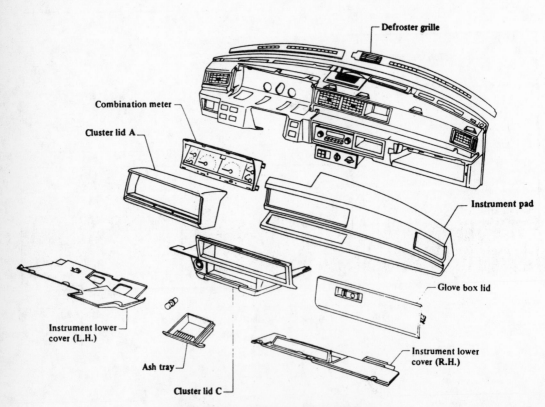

Instrument panel/pad assembly 1983 Stanza

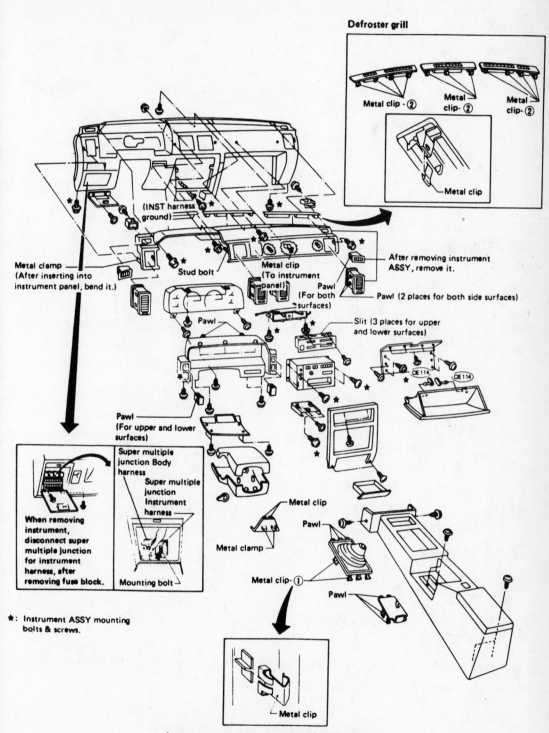

Defroster grill

Metal clip - ②   Metal clip- ②   Metal clip- ②

Metal clip

(INST harness ground)

Metal clamp
(After inserting into
instrument panel, bend it.)

Stud bolt

Metal clip
(To instrument
panel)

Pawl
(For both
surfaces)

After removing instrument
ASSY, remove it.

Pawl (2 places for both side surfaces)

Slit (3 places for upper
and lower surfaces)

Pawl

DE 114   DE 114

Pawl
(For upper and lower
surfaces)

Super multiple
junction Body
harness

Super multiple
junction
Instrument
harness

When removing
instrument,
disconnect super
multiple junction
for instrument
harness, after
removing fuse block.

Mounting bolt

Metal clip

Metal clamp

Pawl

Metal clip- ①

Pawl

★: Instrument ASSY mounting
bolts & screws.

Metal clip

Instrument panel/pad assembly 1987 Stanza

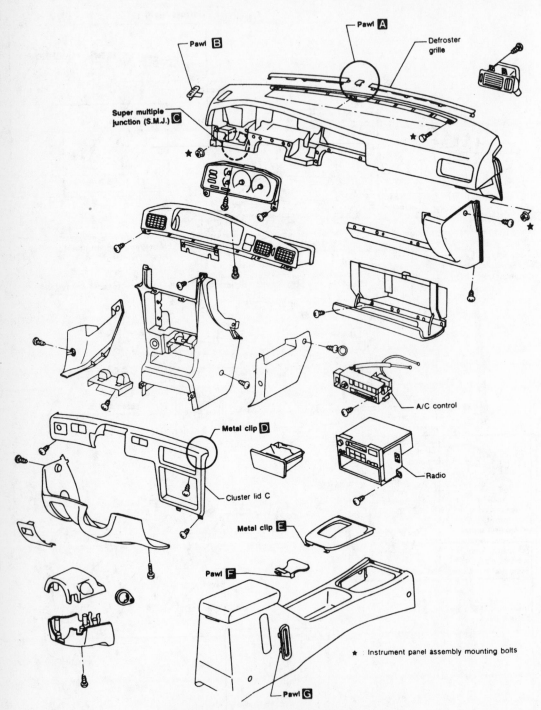

Pawl **A**

Pawl **B**

Defroster grille

Super multiple junction (S.M.J.) **C**

A/C control

Metal clip **D**

Radio

Cluster lid C

Metal clip **E**

Pawl **F**

★ Instrument panel assembly mounting bolts

Pawl **G**

Instrument panel assembly 1990–92 Stanza (part 1)

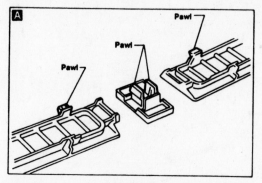

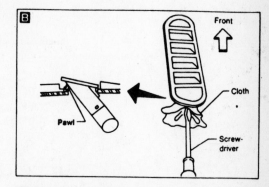

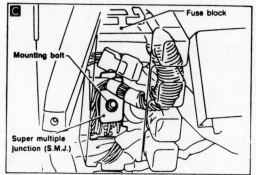

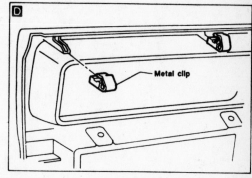

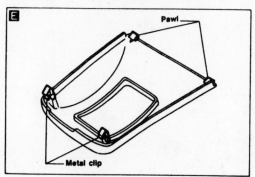

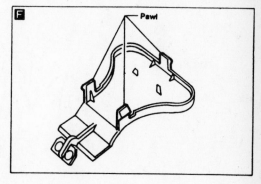

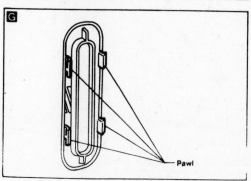

Instrument panel assembly 1990–92 Stanza (part 2)

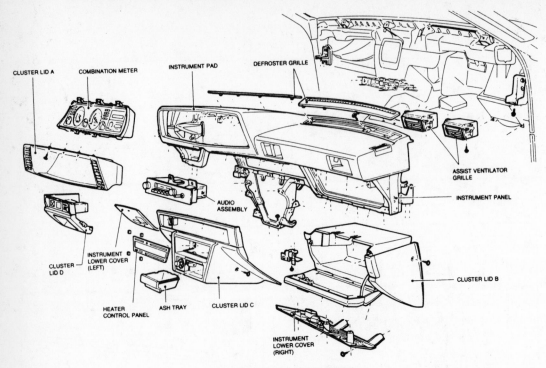

CLUSTER LID A

COMBINATION METER

INSTRUMENT PAD

DEFROSTER GRILLE

ASSIST VENTILATOR GRILLE

INSTRUMENT PANEL

AUDIO ASSEMBLY

CLUSTER LID D

INSTRUMENT LOWER COVER (LEFT)

HEATER CONTROL PANEL

ASH TRAY

CLUSTER LID C

CLUSTER LID B

INSTRUMENT LOWER COVER (RIGHT)

Instrument panel—1982 200SX

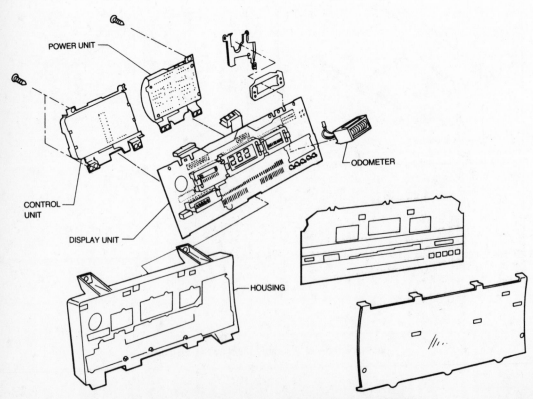

POWER UNIT

ODOMETER

CONTROL UNIT

DISPLAY UNIT

HOUSING

Electronic digital instrument cluster assembly—1984 200SX

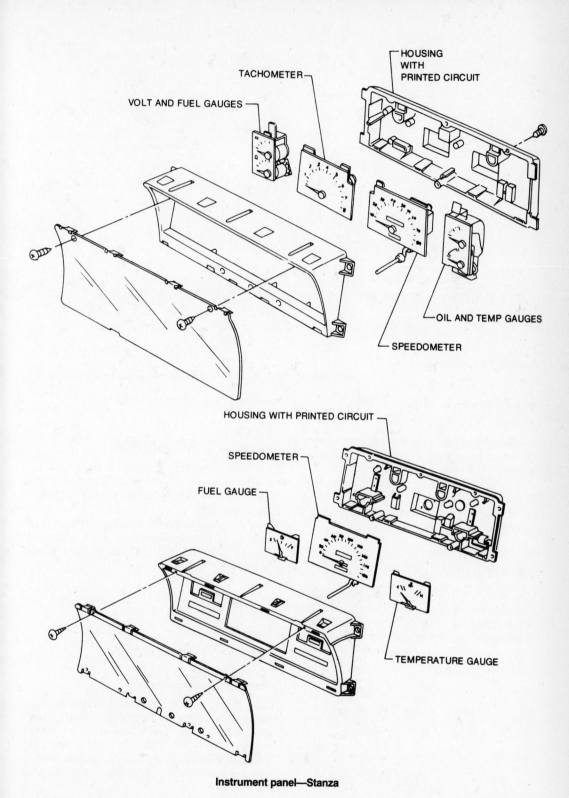

TACHOMETER

VOLT AND FUEL GAUGES

HOUSING
WITH
PRINTED CIRCUIT

OIL AND TEMP GAUGES

SPEEDOMETER

HOUSING WITH PRINTED CIRCUIT

SPEEDOMETER

FUEL GAUGE

TEMPERATURE GAUGE

Instrument panel—Stanza

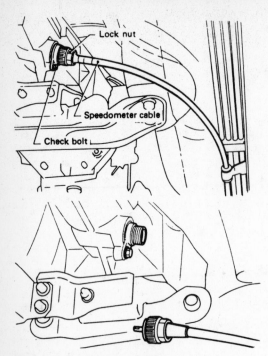

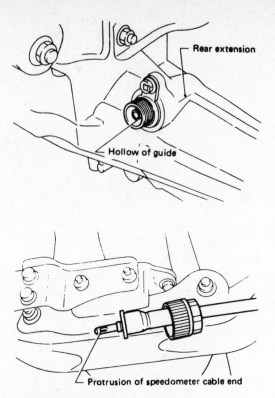

Removing the speedometer cable

Installing the speedometer cable

Rear Windshield Wiper Switch
REMOVAL & INSTALLATION

1. Disconnect the negative battery cable.
2. Remove the rear wiper switch mounting screws or push in retaining clips to dash.
3. Disconnect the electrical connectors from the rear of the switch, then remove it.
4. Installation is the reverse of the removal procedure.

Headlight Switch
REMOVAL & INSTALLATION

On 200SX, 240SX and Stanza vehicles, the headlight switch is part of the Combination Switch Assembly--refer to Turn Signal/Combination Switch service procedures in Chapter 8.

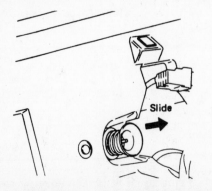

Slide the speedometer cable out from the vehicle

Clock
REMOVAL & INSTALLATION

1. Disconnect the negative battery cable.
2. Remove all necessary trim panels--remove the clock assembly mounting screws or push in retaining clips
3. Disconnect the electrical connectors from the rear of the clock assembly, then remove it.
4. Installation is the reverse of the removal procedure.

LIGHTING

Headlights
REMOVAL & INSTALLATION
1982-83 200SX
Stanza (Sealed Beam Type)

1. Remove the headlight retaining ring screws. These are the three or four short screws in the assembly. There are also two longer screws at the top and side of the headlight which are used to aim the headlight. Do not tamper with these or the headlight will have to be re-aimed.
2. Remove the ring on round headlights by turning it clockwise.
3. Pull the headlight bulb from its socket and disconnect the electrical plug.

To install:

4. Connect the plug to the new bulb.

5. Position the headlight in the shell. Make sure that the word TOP is, indeed, at the top and that the knobs in the headlight lens engage the slots in the mounting shell.

6. Place the retaining ring over the bulb and install the screws.

7. Check headlight system for proper operation; if you didn't turn the aiming screws during removal, the new lamp will be in identical aim to the old one.

1984-88 200SX
240SX

NOTE: *If headlamps do not open on these models, first check the fusible link for the headlight motor. Also check the retract*

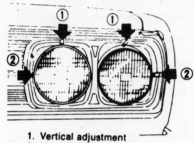

1. Vertical adjustment
2. Horizontal adjustment

Headlight adjusting screws—early models

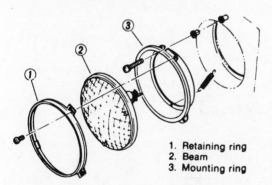

1. Retaining ring
2. Beam
3. Mounting ring

Exploded view of the standard headlight assembly

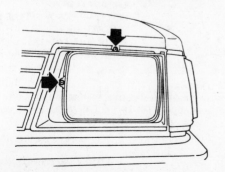

Headlight adjustment—Stanza

switch. If headlamps do not retract, check the retract control relay.

1. Open the headlamp. Disconnect the neagative battery cable.

2. Unbolt and remove the finisher.

3. Remove the headlamp lid.

4. Remove the bulb retaining ring. Unplug and remove the headlamp bulb.

5. Reverse the removal procedure to install. Install headlamp rubber cap with electrical connector firmly so that the lip makes contact with the headlamp body. Adjust the headlamp lid so it is flush with the hood and fender, and so the lid joint is as shown in the accompanying illustration. This is done by adjusting the lid mounting screws while open and close the headlamp by operating the manual knob on the headlamp motor. Make sure the lid is not interfering with the protector. Adjust the headlights if necessary.

Stanza (Halogen Headlamp)

The headlight is a semi-sealed beam type which uses a replaceable halogen bulb. A bulb can be replaced from the inside the engine compartment without removing the headlight assembly. Use care and caution when working with this type bulb--high pressure halogen gas is sealed inside the halogen bulb.

1. Disconnect the negative battery cable. On some late model vehicles, remove the Anti-lock brake system electrical connectors and bracket assembly to gain access to the bulb. Turn the bulb retaining ring counterclockwise until it is free of the headlight reflector, and remove it.

2. Disconnect the electrical connector at the rear of the bulb. Then, remove the bulb carefully without rotating or shaking it.

3. Install in reverse order. Check headlight operation--adjust headlamp aim if necessary.

NOTE: *Do not remove a healdight bulb and leave the reflector empty. If you do this, the reflector will become contaminated by dust and moisture. Do not remove one bulb until another is available for immediate replacement. Do not touch the glass portion of the bulb. Handle it only by the plastic base!*

MANUAL OPERATION OF HEADLIGHTS DOORS

1. Turn OFF both headlight switch and retractable headlight switch.

2. Disconnect the battery negative terminal.

3. Remove the motor shaft cap.

4. Turn the motor shaft counterclockwise by hand until the headlights are opened or closed.

5. Reinstall the motor shaft cap and connect the battery cable.

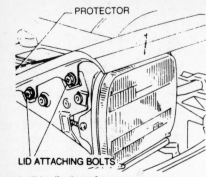

Headlight lid adjustment

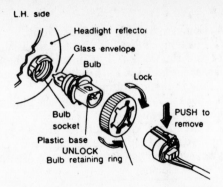

Headlight (halogen bulb) removal and installation

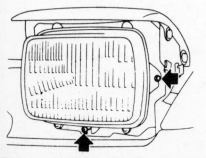

Headlight adjustment—1984 and later 200SX and 240SX

Signal And Marker Lights
REMOVAL & INSTALLATION
Front Turn Signal And Parking Lights

1. Remove turn signal/parking light lens with retaining screws.

2. Slightly depress the bulb and turn it counterclockwise to release it.

3. To install the bulb carefully push down and turn bulb clockwise at the same time.

4. Install the turn signal/parking light lens with retaining screws.

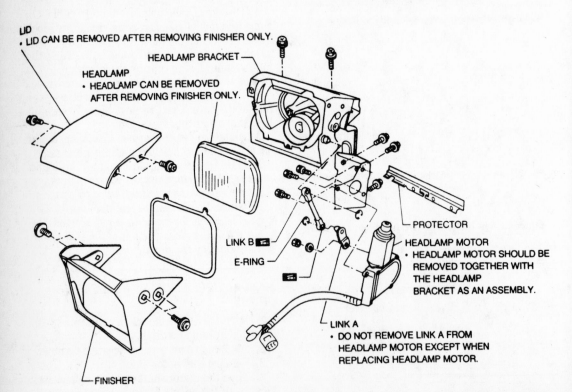

Headlamp assembly—1984 and later 200SX and 240SX

R.H. side with anti-lock braking system

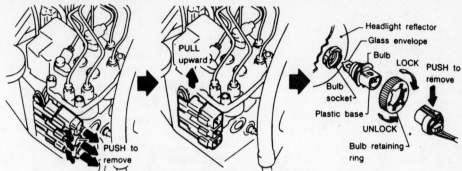

Headlight (halogen bulb) removal and installation—1992 Stanza

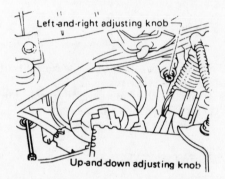

Headlight (halogen bulb) adjustment—Stanza

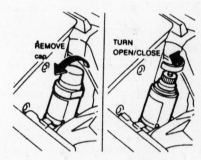

Manual operation of power headlight doors

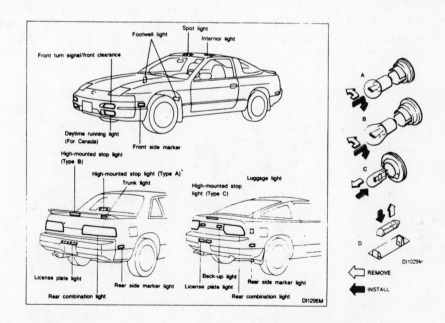

Replacement procedures

All other lights are either type A, B, C or D.
When replacing a bulb, first remove the lens
and/or cover.

Light bulb removal and installation—240SX

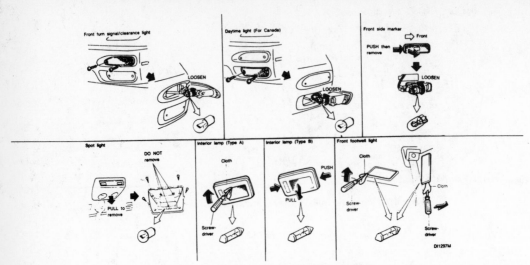

Light bulb removal and installation—240SX

Side Marker Lights

1. Remove side marker light lens with retaining screws.
2. Turn the bulb socket counterclockwise to release it from lens.
3. Pull bulb straight out.
4. To install bulb carefully push straight in.
5. Turn the bulb socket clockwise to install it in lens.
6. Install side marker light lens with retaining screws.

Rear Turn Signal, Brake And Parking Lights

1. Remove rear trim panel in rear of vehicle if necessary to gain access to the bulb socket.

2. Slightly depress the bulb and turn it counterclockwise to release it.
3. To install the bulb carefully push down and turn bulb clockwise at the same time.
4. Install trim panel if necessary.

HEADLIGHT ALIGNMENT

Preparation

Headlamps should be adjusted with a special alignment tool. State regulations may vary this procedure — check your local regulations. Use this procedure for temporary adjustments.

Verify the headlamp dimmer and high beam indicator operation. Inspect and correct all

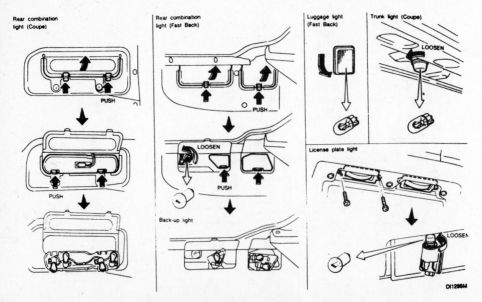

Light bulb removal and installation—240SX

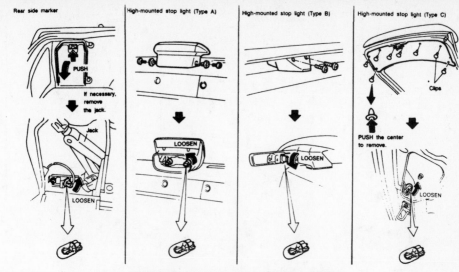

Light bulb removal and installation—240SX

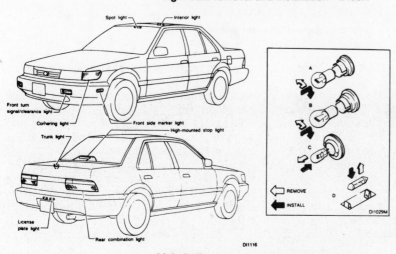

Replacement procedures

All other lights are either type A, B, C or D. When replacing a bulb, first remove the lens and/or cover.

Light bulb removal and installation—Stanza

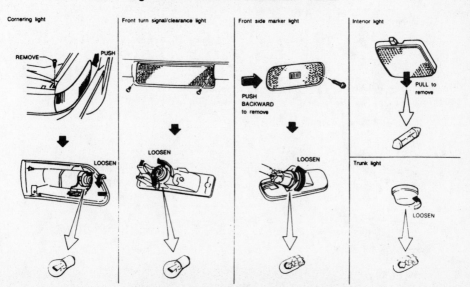

Light bulb removal and installation—Stanza

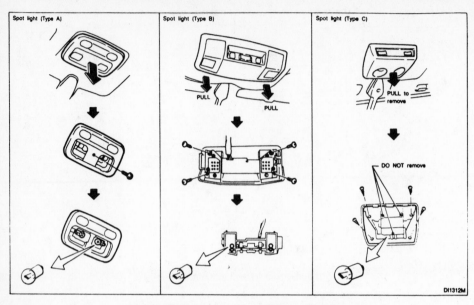

Light bulb removal and installation—Stanza

components that could interfere with the proper headlamp alignment.

Verify proper tire inflation on all wheels. Clean headlamp lenses and make sure that there are no heavy loads in the trunk or hatch luggage area. The fuel tank should be FULL. Add 6.5 lbs. of weight over the fuel tank for each estimated gallon of missing fuel.

Alignment Screen Preparation

1. Position the vehicle on a LEVEL surface perpendicular to a flat wall 25 feet away.
2. From the floor UP, tape a line on the wall

at the centerline of the vehicle. Sight along the centerline of the vehicle (from the rear of the vehicle forward) to verify accuracy of the the line placement.

3. Rock the vehicle side to side and up and down (on front bumper assembly) a few times to allow the suspension to stabilize.

4. Measure the distance from the center of the headlamp lens to the floor. Transfer measurements to the alignment screen with tape. Use this mark for UP/DOWN adjustment reference.

5. Measure distance from the centerline of

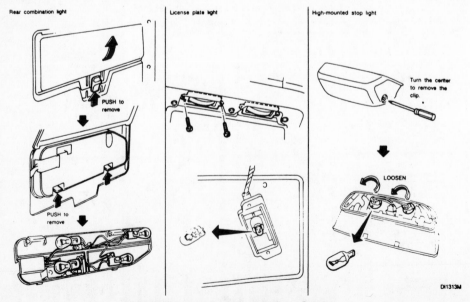

Light bulb removal and installation—Stanza

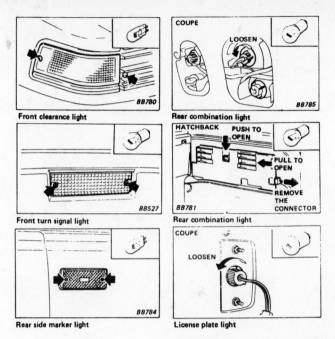

Front clearance light — BB780

Rear combination light — COUPE, LOOSEN — BB785

Front turn signal light — BB527

Rear combination light — HATCHBACK, PUSH TO OPEN, PULL TO OPEN, REMOVE THE CONNECTOR — BB781

Rear side marker light — BB784

License plate light — COUPE, LOOSEN

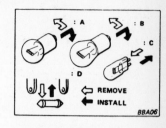

: A   : B   : C   : D   REMOVE   INSTALL — BBA06

OTHER LIGHTS

All other lights are either type A, B, C or D. When replacing a bulb, first remove the lens and/or cover.

Light bulb removal and installation—200SX

the vehicle to the center of each headlamp being aligned. Transfer measurements to screen with tape to each side of the vehicle centerline. Use this mark for LEFT/RIGHT adjustment reference.

Adjustment

A properly aimed low beam headlamp will project the top edge of high intensity pattern on the the alignment screen from 2 in. (50mm) above to 2 in. (50mm) below the headlamp centerline. The side-to-side outboard edge of high intensity pattern should be from 2 in. (50mm) left to 2 in. (50mm) right of the headlamp centerline.

The preferred headlamp alignment is 0 for the up/down adjustment and 0 for the left/right adjustment.

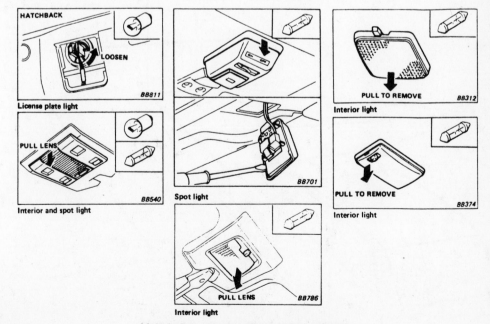

License plate light — HATCHBACK, LOOSEN — BB811

Interior and spot light — PULL LENS — BB540

Spot light — BB701

Interior light — PULL TO REMOVE — BB312

Interior light — PULL TO REMOVE — BB374

Interior light — PULL LENS — BB786

Light bulb removal and installation—200SX

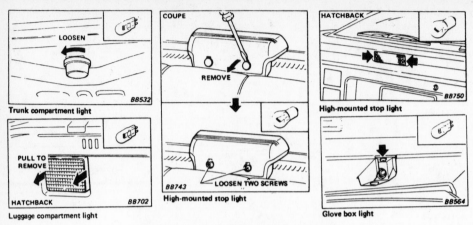

Light bulb removal and installation—200SX

On halogen applications, the high beam pattern should be correct when the low beams are aligned properly. The high beam pattern on vehicles with multiple sealed beam headlamps should be aligned with the low beam lamp covered (do not cover illuminated headlamp for more than 15 seconds) or disconnected.

To adjust headlamps, adjust the alignment screws to achieve the specified high intensity pattern.

FOG LAMP ALIGNMENT

A properly aligned fog lamp will project a pattern on the alignment screen 4 in. (102mm) below the fog lamp centerline and straight ahead.

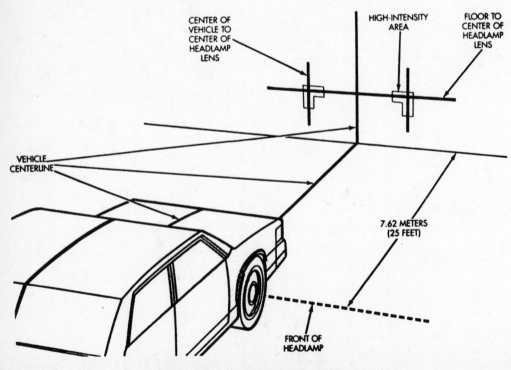

Headlight alignment screen low beam pattern

Item	Wattage (W)	Bulb No.
Front turn signal/clearance light	27/8	1157
Front side marker light	3.8	194
Rear combination light		
Turn signal	27	1156
Stop/Tail	27/8	1157
Back-up	27	1156
Rear side marker light	3.8	194
License plate light	7.5	89
High-mounted stop light	18	921
Interior light	10	
Spot light	8	
Foot well light	3	
Trunk light (Coupe)	3.4	
Luggage compartment light (Fast Back)	5	
Daytime light (For Canada)	27	1156

Light Bulb Chart

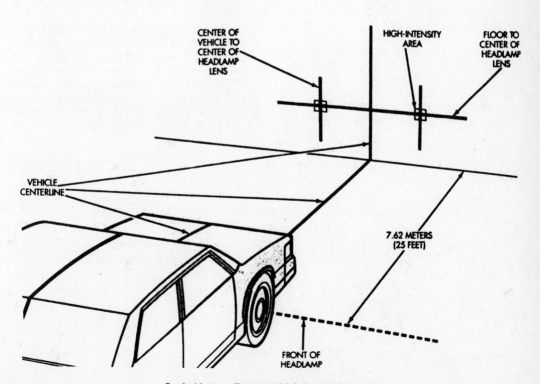

Sealed beam alignment high beam pattern

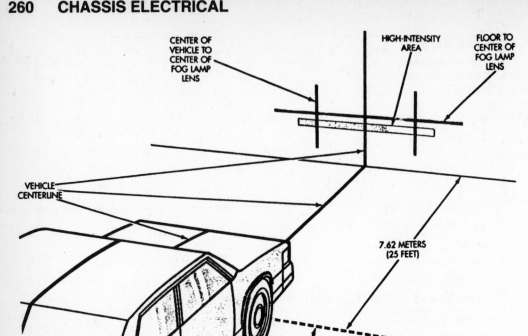

Fog lamp alignment

CIRCUIT PROTECTION

Fuses

REMOVAL & INSTALLATION

The fuses can be easily inspected to see if they are blown. Simply pull the fuse from the block, inspect it and replace it with a new one, if necessary. A vehicle can be equipped with 2 or more fuse block/panels-the engine compartment and passenger compartment are the locations.

NOTE: *When replacing a blown fuse, be certain to replace it with one of the correct amperage.*

Fusible Links

A fusible link is a protective device used in an electrical circuit. When current increases beyond a certain amperage, the fusible metal wire of the link melts, thus breaking the electrical circuit and preventing further damage to the other components and wiring. Whenever a fusible link is melted because of a short circuit, correct the cause before installing a new link. All fusible links are the plug in kind. To replace them, simply unplug the bad link and insert the new one.

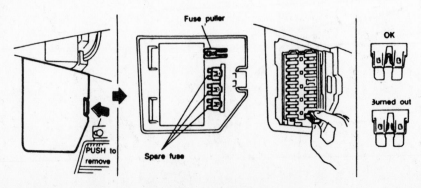

Typical late model fuse box

Circuit Breakers

Circuit breakers are also located in the fuse block. A circuit breaker is an electrical switch which breaks the circuit during an electrical overload. The circuit breaker will remain open until the short or overload condition in the circuit is corrected.

Flashers

To replace the turn signal or hazard warning flasher, carefully pull it from the electrical connector. If necessary remove any component/trim panel that restricts removal. On some applications, a combination flasher is used for turn signals and hazard warning lights.

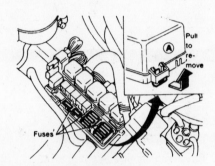

Engine compartment fuse block

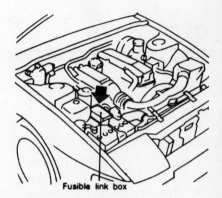

Fusible link locations 1989 240SX

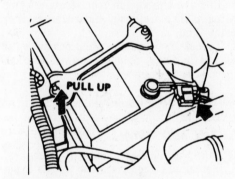

Fusible link locations 1988 200SX

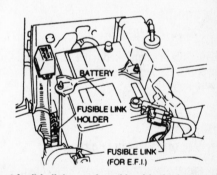

Most fusible links are found beside the battery

Drive Train

7

MANUAL TRANSMISSION

Identification

On all models covered in this book, the manual transmission serial number is stamped on the front upper face of the transmission case.

Adjustments
LINKAGE AND SHIFTER

All models are equipped with an integral linkage system. No adjustments are either possible or necessary.

Shifter Lever
REMOVAL AND INSTALLATION

The shifter lever is removed by removing the shifter lever trim panel, positioning the rubber boot (remove boot retainers) on the shifter assembly in an up position and then removing the snap-ring that retains the shifter lever in the transmission unit.

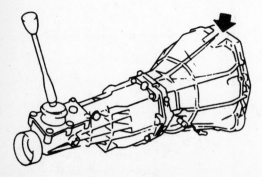

Manual transmission serial number

Back-Up Light Switch
REMOVAL AND INSTALLATION

1. Raise vehicle and support safely.
2. Disconnect the electrical connections from the switch.
3. Remove the switch from transmission housing; place a drain pan under transmission to catch fluid.
4. To install reverse removal procedures and check the fluid level. Replace the switch mounting gasket is so equipped.

Extension Housing Seal (In Vehicle)
REMOVAL AND INSTALLATION

1. Raise the vehicle and support safely.
2. Matchmark the driveshaft (if the drive-

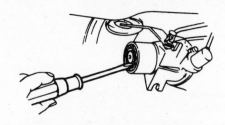

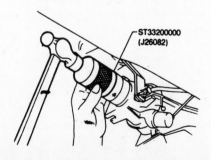

ST33200000
(J26082)

Removing the extension housing oil seal

shaft is not installed in the correct position it may cause a vibration) and differential companion flanges. Remove the center bearing and mounting brackets from the crossmember as required.

3. Loosen the companion flange bolts and lower the driveshaft from the differential.

4. Carefully withdraw the driveshaft from the transmission. Plug the extension opening to prevent leakage.

5. Using the proper tool, remove the oil seal from the extension.

To install:

6. Wipe all seal contact surfaces clean. Coat the lip of the new seal with clean transmission fluid.

7. Using the proper drift tool, drive the new seal into the extension housing.

8. Insert the driveshaft into the extension housing making sure the splines are properly engaged.

9. Raise the driveshaft and align the companion flange marks. Install and tighten the flange bolts to 29–33 ft. lbs. Install the center bearing, if removed.

10. Lower the vehicle. Check the fluid level and add as necesary.

Transmission

REMOVAL AND INSTALLATION

200SX And 240SX

1. Raise and support the vehicle safely. Disconnect the negative battery cable.

2. Disconnect the back-up light switch on all units and neutral switch, if equipped.

3. Disconnect the accelerator linkage.

4. Matchmark then unbolt the driveshaft at the rear and remove. If equipped with a center bearing, unbolt it from the crossmember. Plug the end of the transmission extension to prevent leakage.

5. Disconnect the speedometer drive cable from the transmission.

6. Place the shift lever in the N position. Remove the E-ring and pull the shifter lever out of the transmission.

7. Remove the clutch operating (slave) cylinder from the clutch housing.

8. Support the engine with a large wood block and a jack under the oil pan. Do not place the jack under the oil pan drain plug.

9. Unbolt the transmission from the crossmember. Support the transmission with a jack and remove the crossmember.

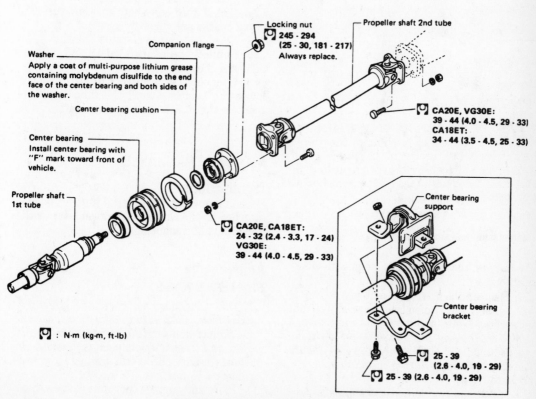

Washer

Apply a coat of multi-purpose lithium grease containing molybdenum disulfide to the end face of the center bearing and both sides of the washer.

Center bearing cushion

Center bearing
Install center bearing with "F" mark toward front of vehicle.

Propeller shaft 1st tube

Companion flange

Locking nut
245 - 294
(25 - 30, 181 - 217)
Always replace.

Propeller shaft 2nd tube

CA20E, VG30E:
39 - 44 (4.0 - 4.5, 29 - 33)
CA18ET:
34 - 44 (3.5 - 4.5, 25 - 33)

CA20E, CA18ET:
24 - 32 (2.4 - 3.3, 17 - 24)
VG30E:
39 - 44 (4.0 - 4.5, 29 - 33)

Center bearing support

Center bearing bracket

25 - 39
(2.6 - 4.0, 19 - 29)

25 - 39 (2.6 - 4.0, 19 - 29)

: N·m (kg-m, ft-lb)

Driveshaft assembly 200SX (all engines)

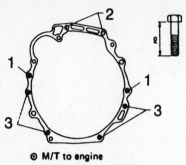

- ⊙ M/T to engine
- ⊛ Engine gusset to M/T

Transmission bolt locations—200SX (CA series engines)

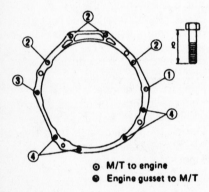

- ⊙ M/T to engine
- ⊛ Engine gusset to M/T

Transmission bolt locations—200SX (VG series engine)

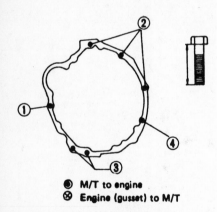

- ⊛ M/T to engine
- ⊗ Engine (gusset) to M/T

Transmission bolt locations—240SX

10. Lower the rear of the engine to allow clearance.

11. Remove the starter assembly.

12. Unbolt the transmission assembly from the engine. Lower and move it to the rear.

NOTE: *Tagging the transmission-to-engine bolts upon removal is necessary to insure proper tightening during installation.*

To install:

13. Clean the engine and transmission mating surfaces. Lightly lubricate the clutch disc and main drive gear splines and control lever sliding surfaces with grease.

14. Lubricate the rear extension oil seal lip and bushing with clean transmission fluid.

15. Properly support the transmission and raise onto the engine.

16. Use the following torque specifications to bolt the transmission to the engine:

a. On 200SX with 4 cylinder engine, tighten the 4 longer bolts to 29–36 ft. lbs. and the 4 shorter bolts to 22–29 ft. lbs.

b. On the 200SX with V6 engine, tighten the long mounting bolts (65mm and 60mm) to 29–36 ft. lbs. (39–49 Nm). Tighten the short bolts (55mm and 25mm) to 22–29 ft. lbs. (29–39 Nm).

c. On 240SX, torque the 70mm, 60mm, 25mm bolts (1, 2, 4) and engine-to-gusset bolts to 29–36 ft. lbs. (39–49 Nm). Torque the 30mm bolts (3) to 22–29 ft. lbs. (29–39 ft. lbs.)

17. Install the starter assembly.

18. Raise the rear of the engine to its original position.

19. Bolt the crossmember in place. Remove the jack.

20. Bolt the clutch operating cylinder to the clutch housing.

21. Install the shift lever and secure with snapring.

22. Connect the speedometer cable.

23. Install the driveshaft making sure the flange marks are aligned properly.

24. Reconnect the accelerator linkage.

25. Connect the neutral safety and back-up light switches.

26. Connect the negative battery cable and lower the vehicle. Check the fluid level and roadtest the vehicle for proper operation.

MANUAL TRANSAXLE

Identification

The manual transaxle serial number label is attached on the clutch withdrawal lever or the upper part of the housing.

Adjustments

SHIFTER LINKAGE

NOTE: *On Stanza models (RS5F31A transaxle) from 1982-86 adjustment is possible. On Stanza models (RS5F50A transaxle) from 1987 and later no adjustment is possible. On Stanza wagon (RS5F50A transaxle) no adjustment is possible.*

1. Raise and support the front of the vehicle on jackstands.

Transaxle serial number—Stanza

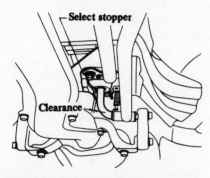

Adjusting the select plate clearance—Stanza

2. Under the vehicle, at the shift control area, loosen the select stopper securing bolts.

3. Shift the gear selector into 1st gear.

4. Adjust the clearance between the control lever and select stopper by sliding the select stopper so that the clearance is 1.00mm.

5. Torque the stopper securing bolts to 5.8-8.0 ft. lbs. Check that the control lever can be shifted without binding or dragging.

Back-Up Light Switch
REMOVAL AND INSTALLATION

1. Raise vehicle and support safely.
2. Disconnect the electrical connections.
3. Remove swith from transaxle housing, when removing place drain pan under transaxle to catch fluid.
4. To install reverse removal procedures.

Transaxle
REMOVAL AND INSTALLATION
1982-86 Stanza
RS5F31A Transaxle

1. Disconnect the battery. Removing the battery may allow greater ease of access.
2. Raise and safely support the vehicle and drain the gear oil.
3. Remove the wheel bearing locknut while depressing the brake pedal.
4. Remove the brake caliper assembly. The brake hose does not need to be disconnected from the caliper. Support the caliper.
5. Remove the tie rod and and lower ball joint securing nuts.
6. Loosen but do not remove the upper strut mounting nuts.
7. Separate the halfshafts from the knuckle by lightly tapping.
8. Separate the ball joint from steering

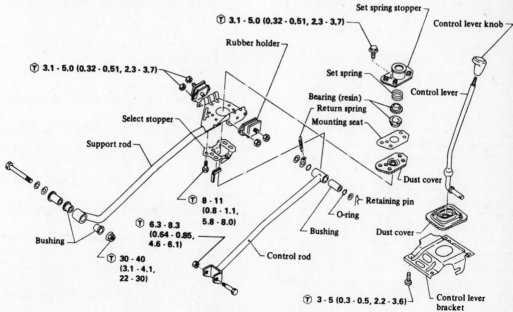

Ⓣ : N·m (kg-m, ft-lb)

Transmission gear control—Stanza (RS5F31A type transaxle)

knuckle and move assembly aside to allow room to remove halfshafts.

9. Remove halfshafts by prying against the reinforcement locations on halfshaft. Do not pull halfshafts; this will damage the sliding boots and oil seals.

10. After removing halfshafts, insert a suitable bar to prevent the side gears from rotating and falling into the differential case.

11. Remove the wheel protector and undercover.

12. Separate the control rod and support rod from the transaxle.

13. Remove the exhaust tube securing nut and bolt.

14. Remove the engine gusset bolt and engine mounting.

15. Remove the clutch control cable from the withdrawal lever.

16. Disconnect the speedometer cable.

17. Disconnect the wire connectors from the backup light and neutral safety switches.

18. Support the engine.

19. Support the transaxle with an suitable transmission jack.

20. Remove the starter.

21. Remove the engine mounting bolts.

22. Remove the transaxle to engine bolts.

23. Carefully lower transaxle down and away from engine. Take care not to damage halfshafts or other components in the area.

To install:

24. Clean all mating surfaces.

25. Apply a light coat of lithium based grease to the input shaft splines.

26. Carefully raise the transaxle to the engine.

27. Tighten transaxle to engine bolts to proper torque 22-30 ft. lbs.

28. Install the starter.

29. Connect cables and electrical connectors.

30. Install the exhaust tube securing bolts.

31. Check wheel bearing by installing halfshaft to hub and torqueing nut to 145–203 ft. lbs. (196–275 Nm). Spin wheel in both directions several times and measure the bearing preload. If preload is not 3.1–10.8 lb. (13.9–48.1 N) pull, as measured by pulling on a lug stud, the wheel bearing should be replaced.

32. If bearing preload was checked, remove halfshaft for hub.

33. Set the seal protector KV38105500 on the transaxle and install the halfshafts. Make certain to properly align serrations and then withdraw tool.

34. Push the halfshaft, then press-fit the circular clip on the halfshaft into the clip groove of the side gear.

35. Pull back on the halfshaft to make certain it is fully locked in place.

36. Tighten wheel bearing locknut to 145–203 ft. lbs. (196–275 Nm).

37. Install ball joint bolt and tie rod.

38. Install brake caliper assembly.

39. Tighten strut bolts and install wheels.

40. Fill transaxle axle to proper level (5.9 pints API gear oil) with gear lubricant.

41. Install the undercover and wheel house protector.

42. Lower the vehicle.

43. Install and connect the battery.

1987 and later Stanza
1986-88 Stanza Wagon 2WD/4WD
RS5F50A Transaxle

1. Disconnect the battery. Remove the battery and its bracket.

2. Raise and safely support vehicle. Drain gear oil.

3. Remove the wheel bearing locknut while depressing the brake pedal.

4. Remove the brake caliper assembly. The brake hose does not need to be disconnected from the caliper. Support the caliper.

5. Remove the tie rod and and lower ball joint securing nuts.

6. Loosen but do not remove the upper strut mounting nuts.

7. Separate the halfshafts from the knuckle by lightly tapping.

8. Separate the ball joint from steering knuckle and move assembly aside to allow room to remove halfshafts.

9. Remove halfshafts by prying against the reinforment locations on halfshaft.

10. Remove bolts securing exhaust to front tube.

11. If equipped with 4WD, disconnect (matchmark for correct installation) driveshaft and remove transfer case.

12. Lower vehicle and remove the air cleaner and airflow meter assembly.

13. Disconnect cables and electrical connections from transaxle.

14. Remove transaxle to engine bolts and mount bolts.

15. Carefully lower transaxle from engine.

To install:

16. Carefully raise the transaxle to the engine.

17. Tighten transaxle to engine bolts to proper torque 29-40 ft. lbs.

18. If equipped with 4WD, install the transfer case and driveshaft.

19. Connect cables and electrical connectors.

20. Install the exhaust pipe.

21. Install the air cleaner and airflow meter assemblies.

22. Check wheel bearing by installing halfshaft to hub and torqueing nut to 174–231

ft. lbs. (235–314 Nm). Spin wheel in both directions several times and measure the bearing preload. If preload is not 1.1–10.1 lb. (4.9–45.1N) pull, as measured by pulling on a lug stud, the wheel bearing should be replaced.

23. After bearing preload has been checked, remove halfshaft from hub.

24. Set the installation KV381060700 and KV381060800 tools on the transaxle and install the halfshafts. Make certain to properly align serrations and then withdraw tool.

25. Push the halfshaft, then press-fit the circular clip on the halfshaft into the clip groove of the side gear.

26. Pull back on the halfshaft to make certain it is fully locked in place.

27. Tighten wheel bearing locknut to 174–231 ft. lbs. (235–314 Nm).

28. Install ball joint bolt and tierod.

29. Install brake caliper assembly.

30. Tighten strut bolts and install wheels.

31. Lower vehicle and fill transaxle axle to proper level (10 pints API GL-4 gear oil) with gear lubricant.

32. Install and connect the battery.

CHECKING FLUID LEVEL

With the vehicle on a level surface, place a drain pan under the vehicle and remove the oil filler plug. The transaxle is correctly filled if the oil just begins to run out of the hole or is level with the bottom of the fill hole.

On vehicles without a filler plug, remove the speedometer cable from the transaxle case. Check that the fluid level is within 0.35 in. of the inside case lip. On the 4WD Stanza, remove filler plug, and, using a straight wire, check that the level is 3.82–4.13 in. (97–105mm) from the top of the housing.

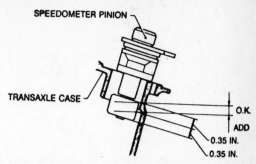

Check transaxle fluid level—Stanza 2WD

Halfshaft

REMOVAL AND INSTALLATION

NOTE: *Installation of the halfshafts will require a special tool for the spline alignment of the halfshaft end and the transaxle case. This procedure should not be performed without access to this tool. The Kent Moore tool numbers are J-34296 and J-34297.*

1. Raise the front of the vehicle and support it with jackstands.

2. Remove the wheel. Remove the brake caliper assembly. The brake hose does not need to be disconnected from the caliper. Be careful not to depress the brake pedal, or the piston will pop out. Do not twist the brake hose.

3. Pull out the cotter pin from the castellated nut on the wheel hub and then remove the wheel bearing lock nut.

NOTE: *Cover the boots with a shop towel or waste cloth so not to damage them when removing the halfshaft.*

Removing the wheel bearing locknut

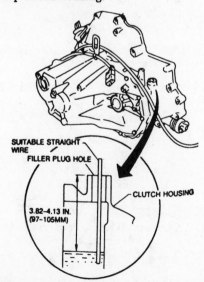

Check transaxle fluid level—Stanza 4WD

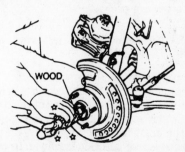

Separating the halfshaft from the steering knuckle

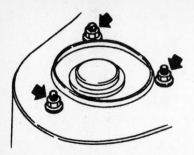

Loosen (DO NOT REMOVE) strut mounting nuts

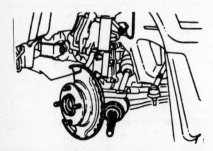

Removing the halfshaft from the steering knuckle

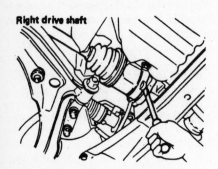

Removing right halfshaft from transaxle

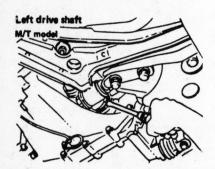

Removing left halfshaft from transaxle—manual transaxle

4. Separate the halfshaft from the steering knuckle by tapping it with a block of wood and a mallet. It may be necessary to loosen (do not remove) the strut mounting bolts to gain clearance for steering knuckle removal from the halfshaft.

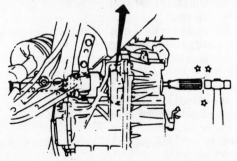

Left drive shaft
A/T model

Removing left halfshaft from transaxle—automatic transaxle

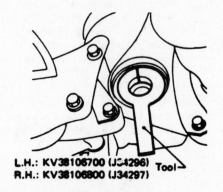

L.H.: KV38106700 (J34296) **Tool**
R.H.: KV38106800 (J34297)

Set special tool along the inner circumference of oil seal transaxle side

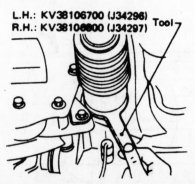

L.H.: KV38106700 (J34296) **Tool**
R.H.: KV38106800 (J34297)

Insert halfshaft into transaxle with special tool aligned properly

5. Remove the tie rod ball joint.

NOTE: *Always use a new nut and cotter pin when installing the tie rod ball joint.*

6. On models with a manual transaxle, using a suitable tool, reach through the engine cross-member and carefully tap the right side inner CV-joint out of the transaxle case.

7. If no support bracket is used disregard this step. Using a block of wood on an hydraulic floor jack, support the engine under the oil pan if necessary. Remove the support bearing bracket from the engine and then withdraw the right halfshaft if so equipped.

8. On models with manual transaxle, carefully insert a small prybar between the left CV-joint inner flange and the transaxle case mounting surface and pry the halfshaft out of the case. Withdraw the shaft from the steering knuckle and remove it.

9. On models with automatic transaxle, insert a dowel through the right side halfshaft hole (remove the right side halfshaft the same way as on manual transaxle models) and use a small mallet to tap the left halfshaft out of the transaxle case. Withdraw the shaft from the steering knuckle and remove it

NOTE: *Be careful not to damage the pinion mating shaft and the side gear while tapping the left halfshaft out of the transaxle case.*

10. When installing the shafts into the transaxle, use a new oil seal and then install an alignment tool along the inner circumference of the oil seal.

11. Insert the halfshaft into the transaxle, align the serrations and then remove the alignment tool.

12. Push the halfshaft, then press-fit the circular clip on the shaft into the clip groove on the side gear.

NOTE: *After insertion, attempt to pull the flange out of the side joint to make sure that the circular clip is properly seated in the side gear and will not come out.*

13. Install support bearing bracket retaining bolts and insert the halfshaft in the steering knuckle if so equipped. Tighten the strut mounting bolts if loosen.

14. Connect the tie rod end in the correct position use new nut and cotter pin.

15. Install the caliper assembly and the wheel bearing locknut. Tighten the nut to 174-231 ft. lbs.

16. Install a new cotter pin on the wheel hub and install the wheel.

17. Bleed the brake system if necessary. Road test the vehicle for proper operation.

CLUTCH

CAUTION: *The clutch driven disc contains asbestos, which has been determined to be a cancer causing agent. Never clean clutch surface with compressed air! Avoid inhaling any dust from any clutch surface! When cleaning clutch surfaces, use a commercially available brake cleaning fluid.*

Adjustments

PEDAL HEIGHT AND FREE PLAY

On all vehicles and clutch type operating systems, refer to the Clutch Specifications Chart for clutch pedal height above floor and pedal free play.

On all models with a hydraulically operated clutch system, pedal height is usually adjusted with a stopper which limits the upward travel of the pedal. Pedal free-play is adjusted at the master cylinder pushrod. If the pushrod is non-

CLUTCH SPECIFICATIONS

Year	Model	Pedal Height Above Floor (in.)	Pedal Free-Play (in.)
1982	Stanza	6.00	0.43–0.63
1983–84	Stanza	6.05	0.43–0.63
1985–86	Stanza	6.02	0.47–0.67
1987–89	Stanza	6.73–7.13	0.04–0.12
1990–92	Stanza	6.50–6.89	0.04–0.12
	Stanza Wagon	9.29–9.69	0.04–0.12
1982–83	200SX	6.70	0.04–0.20
1984–85	200SX	7.60–7.99	0.04–0.06
1986–88	200SX	7.44–7.83 ①	0.039–0.118
1989–92	240SX	7.32–7.72	0.039–0.118

① 7.72–8.11 on VG30E engine

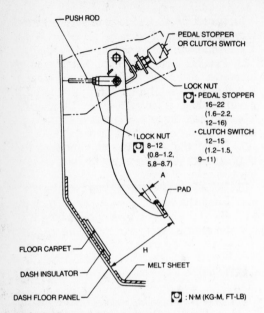

Clutch adjusting points—200SX

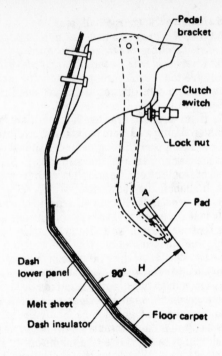

Adjusting clutch pedal—1987 Stanza

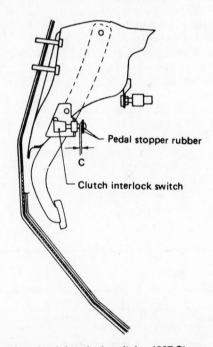

Adjusting clutch interlock switch—1987 Stanza

adjustable, free-play is adjusted by placing shims between the master cylinder and the firewall.

On all models with a mechanical clutch system follow the service procedure below:

1. Loosen the locknut and adjust the pedal height by means of the pedal stopper. Tighten the locknut.

2. Push the withdrawal lever in by hand until resistance is felt. Adjust withdrawal lever play at the lever tip end with the locknuts. Withdrawal lever play should be 0.08-0.12 inch (2-3mm).

3. Depress and release the clutch pedal several times and then recheck the withdrawal lever play again. Readjust if necessary.

4. Measure the pedal free travel at the center of the pedal pad.

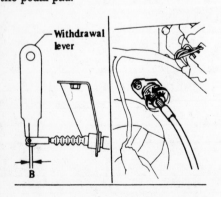

Withdrawal lever play "B":
2 - 3 mm (0.08 - 0.12 in)

Clutch pedal free height and free play—1984 Stanza

Driven Disc And Pressure Plate
REMOVAL AND INSTALLATION

NOTE: *The clutch cover and pressure plate are balanced as an assembly. If replacement of either part becomes necessary--replace both parts (and the release bearing) as an assembly.*

The flywheel should be inspected for wear or scoring and resurfaced/replaced as necessary.

1. Remove the transmission/transaxle from the engine.

2. Insert a clutch aligning bar or similar tool all the way into the clutch disc hub. This must be done so as to support the weight of the clutch disc during removal. Mark the clutch assembly-to-flywheel relationship with paint or a center punch so that the clutch assembly can be assembled in the same position from which it is removed.

3. Loosen the bolts in sequence, a turn at a time. Remove the bolts.

4. Remove the pressure plate and clutch disc.

5. Remove the release mechanism from the transmission housing. Apply lithium based molybdenum disulfide grease to the bearing sleeve inside groove, the contact point of the withdrawal lever and bearing sleeve, the contact surface of the lever ball pin and lever.

To install:

6. Inspect the release bearing and replace if necessary. Apply a small amount of grease to the transmission splines. Install the disc on the splines and slide back and forth a few times. Remove the disc and remove excess grease on hub. Be sure no grease contacts the disc or pressure plate.

7. Install the disc to flywheel, aligning it with a splined dummy shaft.

8. Install the pressure plate. Tighten the bolts evenly and in a criss-cross pattern to 16-22 ft. lbs.

9. Remove the dummy shaft.

10. Replace the transmission/transaxle. Check system for proper operation.

Clutch Master Cylinder

REMOVAL AND INSTALLATION

1. Disconnect the clutch pedal arm from the pushrod.

2. Disconnect the clutch hydraulic line from the master cylinder.

NOTE: *Take precautions to keep brake fluid from coming in contact with any painted surfaces.*

3. Remove the nuts attaching the master cylinder and remove the master cylinder and pushrod toward the engine compartment side.

4. Install the master cylinder in the reverse order of removal and bleed the clutch hydraulic system.

OVERHAUL

1. Remove the master cylinder from the vehicle.

2. Drain the clutch fluid from the master cylinder reservoir.

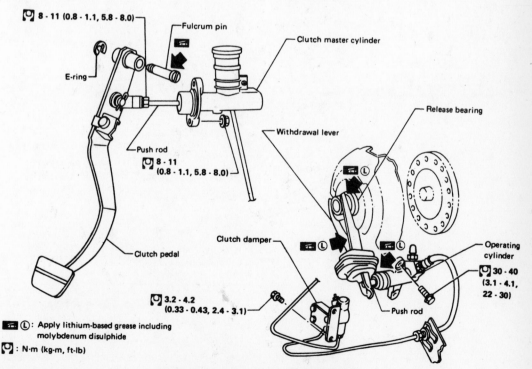

Hydraulic clutch control assembly—200SX

3. Remove the boot and circlip and remove the pushrod.

4. Remove the stopper, piston, cup and return spring.

5. Clean all of the parts in clean brake fluid.

6. Check the master cylinder and piston for wear, corrosion and scores and replace the parts as necessary. Light scoring and glaze can be removed with crocus cloth soaked in brake fluid.

7. Generally, the cup seal should be replaced each time the master cylinder is disassembled. Check the cup and replace it if it is worn, fatigued, or damaged.

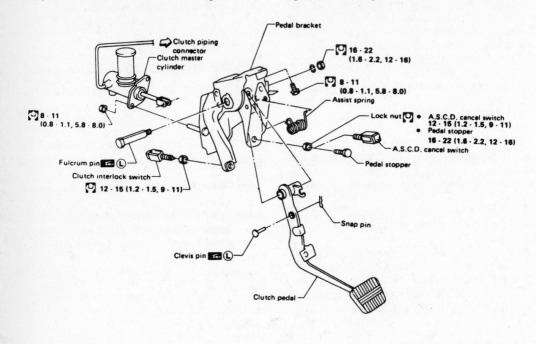

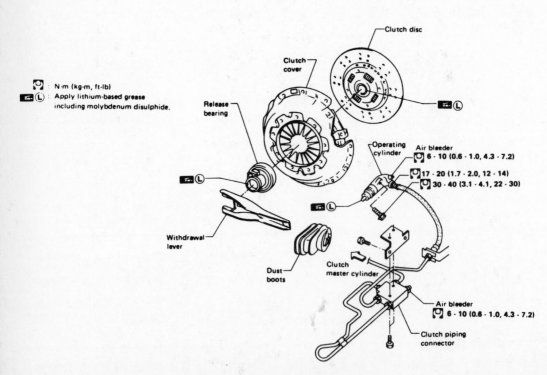

Hydraulic clutch control assembly—240SX

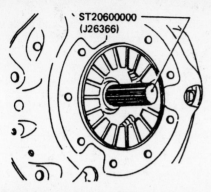

Insert special tool (dummy shaft or equivalent) into clutch disc hub when installing clutch cover (pressure plate) and disc

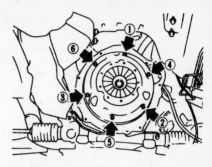

Tighten clutch cover (pressure plate) retaining bolts in sequence and in equal 2 stages—remove the assembly by reverse of the installation sequence

8. Check the clutch fluid reservoir, filler cap, dust cover and the pipe for distortion and damage and replace the parts as necessary.

9. Lubricate all new parts with clean brake fluid.

10. Reassemble the master cylinder parts in the reverse order of disassembly, taking note of the following:

a. Reinstall the cup seal carefully to prevent damaging the lipped portions.

b. Adjust the height of the clutch pedal after installing the master cylinder in position on the vehicle.

c. Fill the master cylinder and clutch fluid reservoir and then bleed the clutch hydraulic system.

Clutch Slave Cylinder
REMOVAL AND INSTALLATION

1. Remove the slave cylinder attaching bolts and the pushrod from the shift fork.

2. Disconnect the flexible fluid hose from the slave cylinder and remove the unit from the vehicle.

3. Install the slave cylinder in the reverse order of removal and bleed the clutch hydraulic system.

OVERHAUL

1. Remove the slave cylinder from the vehicle.

2. Remove the pushrod and boot.

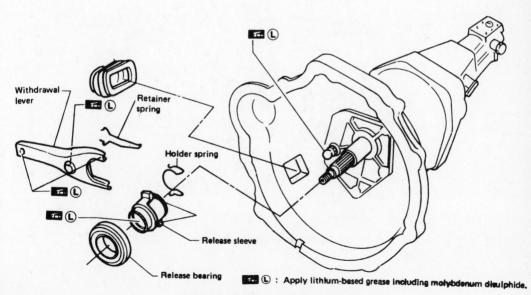

Withdrawal lever — Retainer spring — Holder spring — Release sleeve — Release bearing

: Apply lithium-based grease including molybdenum disulphide.

Clutch release mechanism—240SX

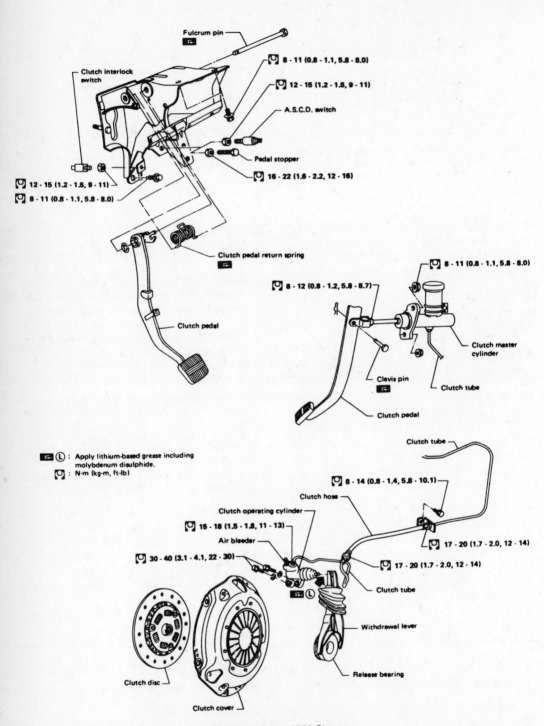

Fulcrum pin

8 - 11 (0.8 - 1.1, 5.8 - 8.0)

12 - 15 (1.2 - 1.5, 9 - 11)

Clutch interlock switch

A.S.C.D. switch

Pedal stopper

12 - 15 (1.2 - 1.5, 9 - 11)

8 - 11 (0.8 - 1.1, 5.8 - 8.0)

16 - 22 (1.6 - 2.2, 12 - 16)

Clutch pedal return spring

8 - 11 (0.8 - 1.1, 5.8 - 8.0)

8 - 12 (0.8 - 1.2, 5.8 - 8.7)

Clutch pedal

Clutch master cylinder

Clevis pin

Clutch tube

Clutch pedal

Clutch tube

: Apply lithium-based grease including molybdenum disulphide.
: N·m (kg-m, ft-lb)

8 - 14 (0.8 - 1.4, 5.8 - 10.1)

Clutch hose

Clutch operating cylinder

15 - 18 (1.5 - 1.8, 11 - 13)

Air bleeder

30 - 40 (3.1 - 4.1, 22 - 30)

17 - 20 (1.7 - 2.0, 12 - 14)

17 - 20 (1.7 - 2.0, 12 - 14)

Clutch tube

Withdrawal lever

Clutch disc

Release bearing

Clutch cover

Clutch system—1989 Stanza

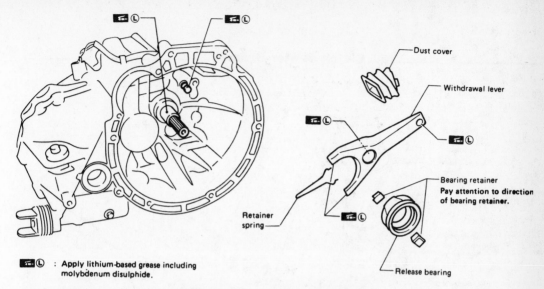

: Apply lithium-based grease including molybdenum disulphide.

Clutch release mechanism—1989 Stanza

3. Force out the piston by blowing compressed air into the slave cylinder at the hose connection.

CAUTION: *Be careful not to apply excess air pressure to avoid possible injury.*

4. Clean all of the parts in clean brake fluid.

5. Check and replace the slave cylinder bore and piston if wear or severe scoring exists. Light scoring and glaze can be removed with crocus cloth soaked in brake fluid.

6. Normally the piston cup should be replaced when the slave cylinder is disassembled. Check the piston cup and replace it if it is found to be worn, fatigued or scored.

7. Replace the rubber boot if it is cracked or broken.

8. Lubricate all of the new parts in clean brake fluid and reassemble in the reverse order of disassembly, taking note of the following:

a. Use care when reassembling the piston cup to prevent damaging the lipped portion of the piston cup.

b. Fill the master cylinder with brake fluid and bleed the clutch hydraulic system.

BLEEDING THE CLUTCH HYDRAULIC SYSTEM

1. Check and fill the clutch fluid reservoir to the specified level as necessary. During the bleeding process, continue to check and replenish the reservoir to prevent the fluid level from getting lower than ½ the specified level.

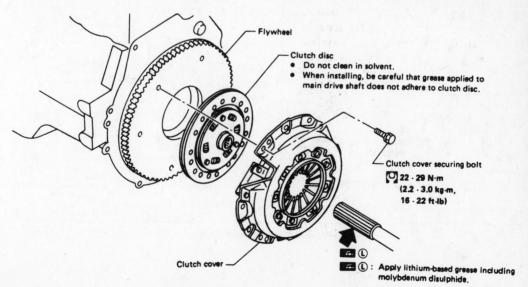

Clutch disc and clutch cover (pressure plate)

Clutch Master Cylinder

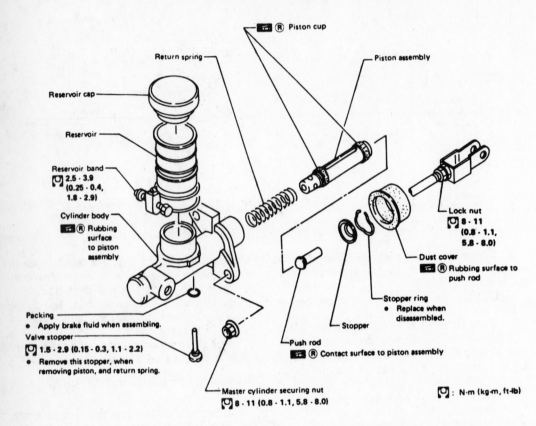

- ® Piston cup
- Piston assembly
- Return spring
- Reservoir cap
- Reservoir
- Reservoir band
  - 2.5 - 3.9 (0.25 - 0.4, 1.8 - 2.9)
- Cylinder body
  - ® Rubbing surface to piston assembly
- Lock nut
  - 8 - 11 (0.8 - 1.1, 5.8 - 8.0)
- Dust cover
  - ® Rubbing surface to push rod
- Stopper ring
  - • Replace when disassembled.
- Stopper
- Packing
  - • Apply brake fluid when assembling.
- Valve stopper
  - 1.5 - 2.9 (0.15 - 0.3, 1.1 - 2.2)
  - • Remove this stopper, when removing piston, and return spring.
- Push rod
  - ® Contact surface to piston assembly
- Master cylinder securing nut
  - 8 - 11 (0.8 - 1.1, 5.8 - 8.0)
- : N·m (kg·m, ft-lb)

Operating Cylinder

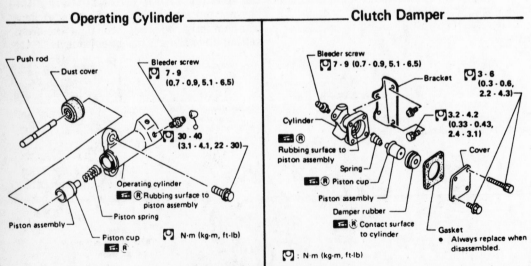

- Push rod
- Dust cover
- Bleeder screw
  - 7 - 9 (0.7 - 0.9, 5.1 - 6.5)
- 30 - 40 (3.1 - 4.1, 22 - 30)
- Operating cylinder
  - ® Rubbing surface to piston assembly
- Piston assembly
- Piston spring
- Piston cup
  - ®
- : N·m (kg·m, ft-lb)

Clutch Damper

- Bleeder screw
  - 7 - 9 (0.7 - 0.9, 5.1 - 6.5)
- Bracket
- 3 - 6 (0.3 - 0.6, 2.2 - 4.3)
- 3.2 - 4.2 (0.33 - 0.43, 2.4 - 3.1)
- Cylinder
  - ®
  - Rubbing surface to piston assembly
- Spring
- ® Piston cup
- Piston assembly
- Damper rubber
  - ® Contact surface to cylinder
- Cover
- Gasket
  - • Always replace when disassembled.
- : N·m (kg·m, ft-lb)

Hydraulic clutch control—all models

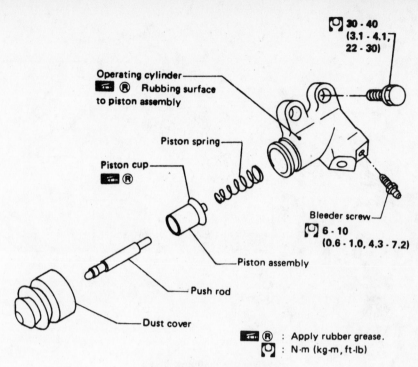

Slave cylinder—1989 Stanza

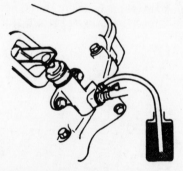

Run a hose from the bleeder screw into a clear container filled with brake fluid

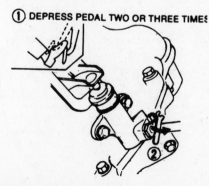

Pump the clutch pedal several times and then open the bleeder screw

2. Remove the dust cap from the bleeder screw on the clutch slave cylinder (and clutch piping connector if so equipped) and connect a tube to the bleeder screw and insert the other end of the tube into a clean glass or metal container.

NOTE: *Take precautionary measures to prevent the brake fluid from getting on any painted surfaces.*

3. Pump the clutch pedal SLOWLY several times, hold it down and loosen the bleeder screw.

4. Tighten the bleeder screw and release the clutch pedal gradually. Repeat this operation until air bubbles disappear from the brake fluid being expelled out through the bleeder screw.

5. Repeat until all evidence of air bubbles completely disappears from the brake fluid being pumped out through the tube.

6. When the air is completely removed, securely tighten the bleeder screw and replace the dust cap.

7. Check and refill the master cylinder reservoir as necessary.

8. Depress the clutch pedal several times to check the operation of the clutch and check for leaks.

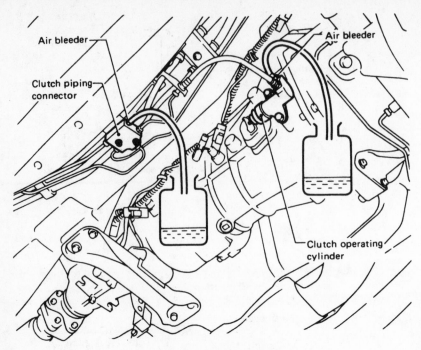

Bleeding procedure—240SX

AUTOMATIC TRANSMISSION

Identification

The automatic transmission serial number label is attached to the side of the transmission housing on all models and to the rear tailshaft section on the 240SX model.

Fluid Pan and Filter

REMOVAL AND INSTALLATION

1. Jack up the front of the car and support it safely on stands.

2. Slide a drain pan under the transmission. Loosen the rear oil pan bolts first, to allow most of the fluid to drain off without making a mess on your garage floor.

3. Remove the remaining bolts and drop the pan. Remove the 11 transmission filter retaining bolts and remove the filter from the transmission. Install a new filter in the correct position and torque the transmission filter retaining bolts to 2-3 ft. lbs.

4. Discard the old gasket, clean the pan, and reinstall the pan with a new gasket.

5. Tighten the retaining bolts in a crisscross pattern starting at the center.

NOTE: *The transmission case is aluminum, so don't exert too much force on the bolts. Torque the bolts to 3.6-5.1 ft. lbs.*

6. Refill the transmission through the dipstick tube and check the fluid level.

Adjustments

SHIFT LINKAGE

If the detents cannot be felt or the pointer indicator is improperly aligned while shifting

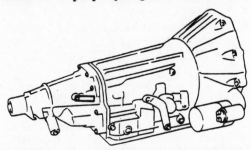

Automatic transmission serial number location—240SX

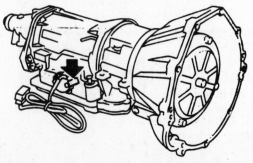

Automatic transmission serial number location—200SX

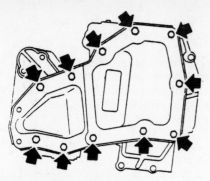

Transmission filter retaining bolts

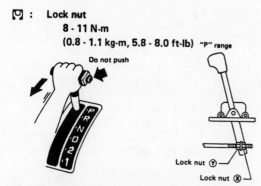

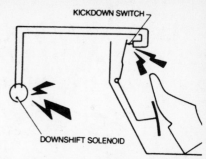

Kickdown switch and downshift solenoid

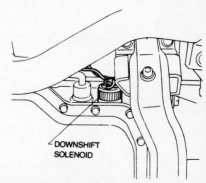

The downshift solenoid is located on the side of the transmission just above the oil pan

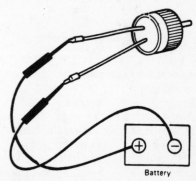

Check downshift solenoid operation by applying battery voltage

from the **P** range to range **1**, the linkage should be adjusted.

1. Place the shifter in the **P** position.
2. Loosen the locknuts.
3. Tighten the outer locknut **X** until it touches the trunnion, pulling the selector lever toward the **R** range side without pushing the button.
4. Back off the outer locknut **X** ¼–½ turns and then tighten the inner locknut **Y** to 5–11 ft. lbs. (8–15 Nm).
5. Move the selector lever from **P** to **1**. Make sure it moves smoothly.

NOTE: *Some late model vehicles have an automatic transmission interlock system. This interlock system prevents the transmission selector from being shifted from the P position unless the brake pedal is depressed.*

CHECKING KICK-DOWN SWITCH AND SOLENOID

1. Turn the key to the normal ON position, and depress the accelerator all the way. The solenoid in the transmission should make an audible click.
2. If the solenoid does not work, inspect the wiring, and test it electrically to determine whether the problem is in the wiring, the kickdown switch, or the solenoid.
3. If the solenoid requires replacement,

drain a little over 2 pts (1 liter) of fluid from the transmission before removing it.

Neutral Safety Switch/Inhibitor Switch

REMOVAL, INSTALLATION AND ADJUSTMENT

The switch unit is bolted to the the transmission case, behind the transmission shift lever. The switch prevents the engine from being started in any transmission position except Park or Neutral. It also controls the backup lights.

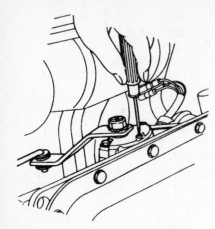

Removing screw from the inhibitor switch

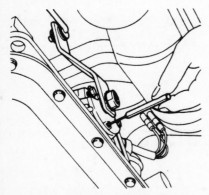

Inhibitor switch adjustment with aligning pin

1. Place the transmission selector lever in the Neutral range.
2. Remove the screw from the switch.
3. Loosen the attaching bolts. With a aligning pin (2.0mm diameter) move the switch until the pin falls into the hole in the rotor.
4. Tighten the attaching bolts equally.
5. Make sure while holding the brakes on, that the engine will start only in Park or Neutral. Check that the backup lights go on only in reverse.

Back-Up light Switch

REMOVAL AND INSTALLATION

Refer to the "Neutral Safety Switch/Inhibitor Switch" service procedures; this switch also controls the back-up lights.

Transmission

REMOVAL AND INSTALLATION

200SX And 240SX

1. Disconnect the battery cable.
2. Remove the accelerator linkage.
3. Detach the shift linkage.

4. Disconnect the neutral safety switch and downshift solenoid wiring.
5. Raise and safely support the vehicle. Remove the drain plug and drain the torque converter. If there is no converter drain plug, drain the transmission. If there is no transmission drain plug, remove the pan to drain. Replace the pan to keep out dirt.
6. Remove the front exhaust pipe.
7. Remove the vacuum tube and speedometer cable.
8. Disconnect the fluid cooler tubes. Plug the tube ends to prevent leakage.
9. Remove the driveshaft and remove the starter.
10. Support the transmission with a jack under the oil pan. Support the engine also.
11. Remove the rear crossmember.
12. Mark the relationship between the torque converter and the driveplate. Remove the bolts holding the torque converter to the driveplate (rotate engine if necessary). Unbolt the transmission from the engine and remove it.

NOTE: *The transmission bolts are different lengths. Tag each bolt according to location*

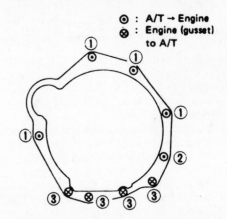

Transmisison mounting bolt locations on 240SX; bolt (1) is 40mm, bolt (2) is 50mm, bolt (3) is 25mm and gusset bolts are 20mm

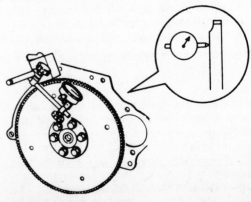

Checking drive plate runout

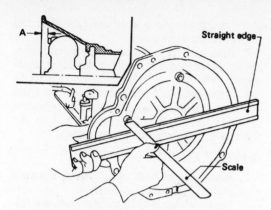

Installation of torque converter—refer to text

to insure proper installation. This is particularly important on the 240SX.

13. Check the driveplate runout with a dial indictator. Runout must be no more than 0.020 in.

To install:

14. If the torque converter was removed from the engine for any reason, after it is installed, the distance from the face of the converter to the edge of the converter housing must be checked prior to installing the transmission. This is done to ensure proper installation of the torque converter. On 200SX, the dimension should be 1.38 in. (35mm) or more. On 240SX, the dimension should be 1.02 in. (26mm) or more.

15. Install the transmission and bolt the driveplate to the converter and transmission to the engine. Torque the driveplate-to-torque converter and converter housing-to-engine bolts to 29–36 ft. lbs. (39–49 Nm) on all except 240SX. For 240SX, torque the transmission mounting bolts as follows: tighten bolts (1) and (2) to 29–36 ft. lbs. (39–49 Nm); tighten bolt (3) to 22–29 ft. lbs. (29–39 Nm); tighten the gusset-to-engine bolts to 22–29 ft. lbs. (29–39 Nm).

NOTE: *After the converter is installed, rotate the crankshaft several times to make sure the transmission rotates freely and does not bind.*

16. Install the rear crossmember.

17. Remove the engine and transmission supports.

18. Install the starter and connect the driveshaft. Torque the flange bolts to 29–33 ft. lbs. (34–44 Nm).

19. Unplug, connect and tighten the fluid cooler tubes.

20. Connect the speedometer cable and the vacuum tube.

21. Connect the front exhaust pipe using new gaskets.

22. Connect the switch wiring to the transmission.

23. Connect the shift linkage.

24. Connect the negative battery cable, fill the transmission to the proper level and make any necessary adjustment.

25. Perform a road test and check the fluid level.

AUTOMATIC TRANSAXLE

Identification

The automatic transaxle serial number label is attached to upper portion of the oil pan on all Stanza models.

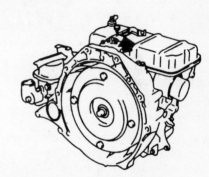

Transaxle serial number—Stanza wagon

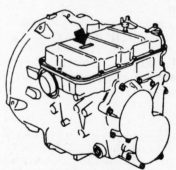

AUTOMATIC TRANSAXLE

Transaxle serial number—Stanza

Fluid Pan

REMOVAL AND INSTALLATION

1. Raise and support the vehicle on jackstands.

2. Place a container under the transaxle to catch the oil when the pan is removed.

3. Remove the transaxle pan bolts.

NOTE: *If the pan sticks, bump it with a soft hammer to break it loose.*

4. Using a putty knife, clean the gasket mounting surfaces.

5. To install, use a new gasket, sealant and reverse the removal procedures. Torque the oil

pan bolts EVENLY to 3.6-5.1 ft. lbs. Refill the transaxle.

FILTER SERVICE (OIL STRAINER)

NOTE: *The oil strainer should not have to be replaced under normal operation--changing the transaxle fluid is all that is required for maintenance purposes.*

1. Remove the transmission oil pan.
2. Remove the oil strainer plate bolts from the control valve body assembly and remove the oil strainer. On some later models, the transaxle assembly must be disassembled to remove oil strainer.
3. Installation is the reverse of the removal procedure. Tighten oil strainer retaining screws evenly--replace any gasket for strainer mounting.

Adjustments

THROTTLE WIRE CA20 ENGINE

The throttle wire is adjusted by means of double nuts on the carburetor side.

1. Loosen the adjusting nuts at the carburetor throttle wire bracket.
2. With the throttle fully opened, turn the threaded shaft inward as far as it will go and tighten the 1st nut against the bracket.
3. Back off the 1st nut 1-1½ turns and tighten the 2nd nut against the bracket.
4. The throttle wire stroke between the threaded shaft and the cam should be 27.5-31.5mm.

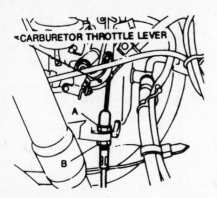

Throttle wire adjustment

THROTTLE CABLE FUEL INJECTED ENGINE

NOTE: *The throttle cable is operated via a cam on the throttle shaft of the injection unit. The adjustment is located on the side of the air intake plenum.*

1. Loosen the 2 locknuts that position the ca-ble. Open the throttle lever and hold it at the fully open position.
2. Back off both locknuts. Slide the outer cable as far as it will go away from the throttle cam.
3. Turn the nut on the side away from the throttle until it just starts to hold. Then, back it off ¾-1¼ revolutions. Tighten the nut on the throttle side to lock this position securely.

CONTROL CABLE

1. Place selector lever in **P** range. Make sure that control lever locks at **P** range.
2. Loosen lock nuts. Screw front lock nut until it touches select rod end while holding select rod horizontal.
3. Tighten back lock nut. Make sure that selector lever moves smoothly in each range.

Neutral Safety Switch/Inhibitor Switch

The inhibitor switch allows the back-up lights to work when the transaxle is placed in reverse and acts as a neutral switch, by allowing the current to pass to the starter when the transaxle is placed in Neutral or Park.

REMOVAL AND INSTALLATION

1. Raise and support the vehicle on jackstands.
2. Remove the transaxle control cable connection.
3. Disconnect electrical harness, remove switch retaining screws. Remove the switch from the vehicle.
4. Installation is the reverse of the removal procedure. Adjust the inhibitor switch.

ADJUSTMENT

1. Raise and support the vehicle on jackstands.
2. Loosen the inhibitor switch adjusting screws. Place the select lever in the Neutral position.
3. Using a 2.5mm diameter pin (RL3F01A transaxle--early model Stanza) or a 4mm diameter pin (RL4F02A type transaxle--late model

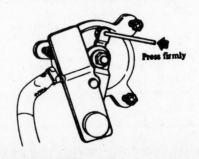

Adjusting the inhibitor switch

Stanza) place the pin into the adjustment holes on both the inhibitor switch and the switch lever (the switch lever should be as near vertical position as possible).

4. Tighten the adjusting screws EVENLY to 1.4-1.9 ft. lbs. Check the switch for continuity by making sure the vehicle starts only in P or N.

Back-Up Light Switch
REMOVAL AND INSTALLATION

Refer to the Neutral Safety Switch/Inhibitor Switch service procedures.

Transaxle
REMOVAL AND INSTALLATION

1. Disconnect the negative battery terminal.
2. Raise and safely support the vehicle.

NOTE: *On Stanza wagon, remove air cleaner, airflow meter and disconnect the front exhaust pipe. On 4WD vehicles remove driveshaft (matchmark for correct installation),*

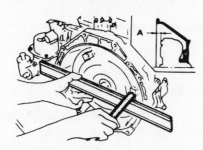

Removing the automatic transaxle—Stanza

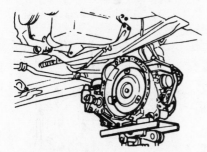

Checking flexplate runout

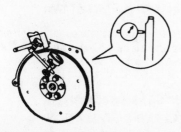

Installing the torque converter assembly—automatic transaxle

support rod, transfer control actuator, all electrical connections and transfer gussets as necessary.

3. Remove the left front wheel assembly and the left front fender protector. Drain the transaxle fluid.

4. Remove the cailper assembly. Remove the cotter pin and hub nut.

5. Remove the tie rod ball joint. Separate the axle shaft from the knuckle by slightly tapping it with a suitable tool.

6. Disconnect the speedometer cable, the throttle wire from the throttle lever.

7. Remove the control cable from the rear of the transaxle, then the oil level gauge tube.

8. Place a floor jack under the transaxle. Properly support under the engine.

9. Disconnect and plug the oil cooler hoses from the lines. Remove the torque converter to drive plate bolts.

NOTE: *When removing the torque converter to drive plate bolts, turn the crankshaft for access to the bolts and place alignment marks on the converter to drive plate for alignment purposes.*

10. Remove the engine mount securing bolts and the starter motor.

11. Remove the transaxle bolts; note and record the location of the bolts as some are different sizes. Pull the transaxle away from the engine and lower it from the vehicle.

To install:

12. Before installing the transaxle check the drive plate for runout. The maximum allowable runout is 0.020 in. (0.5mm). Measure the distance between the torque converter and the transaxle housing, on RL3F01A type transaxle (early models) it should be more than 0.831 in. or (22mm). On the RL4F02A type transaxle (later models) it should be 0.75 in. or (19mm). This measurement is for correct torque converter installation.

13. Install the transaxle assembly in vehicle.

14. On RL3F01A transaxle, torque the converter to drive plate bolts to 36-51 ft. lbs. and converter housing to engine 12-16 ft. lbs. On the RL4F02A type transaxle, torque the converter to drive plate bolts to 29-36 ft. lbs. and converter housing to engine bolts to 29-36 ft. lbs. except 25mm bolts torque to 22-30 ft. lbs.

15. Install the starter motor and all electrical connections.

16. Install the control cable to the rear of the transaxle, then the oil level gauge tube.

17. Install the axle shaft with new circlip. Install the tie rod ball joint wtih new cotter pin.

18. Install the hub nut and torque to (145-203 ft. lbs. RL3F01A transaxle) (174-231 ft. lbs. RL4F02A transaxle). Install the brake caliper assembly , bleed brakes if necessary.

19. Reconnect the speedometer cable and throttle wire to the throttle lever.

20. Install all securing bolts and brackets. On Stanza wagon, install air cleaner and airflow meter and connect the front exhaust pipe also.

21. On 4WD vehicles install driveshaft, support rod, transfer control actuator, all electrical connections and transfer gussets as necessary.

22. Install the left front wheel assembly and the left front fender protector. Refill the transaxle fluid.

23. Lower the vehicle. Reconnect the negative battery cable and road test for proper operation.

Halfshafts

REMOVAL AND INSTALLATION

Refer to the Manual Transaxle procedures with this exception: insert a dowel or equivalent through the right side halfshaft hole and use a small mallet to tap the left halfshaft out of the transaxle case. Withdraw the shaft from the steering knuckle and remove it. Be careful not to damage the pinion mating shaft and the side gear while tapping the left halfshaft out of the transaxle case.

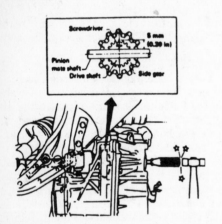

Removing the left halfshaft on models with an automatic transaxle

TRANSFER SYSTEM STANZA 4WD

Transfer Case

CHECKING TRANSFER OIL

Remove the plug and place a tool inside the case--fluid level should be to the top of the plug.

Adapter Oil Seal

REMOVAL AND INSTALLATION

Refer to the illustrations as guide for oil seal removal and installation.

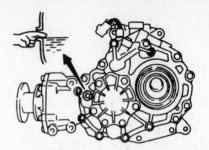

Checking transfer case oil—Stanza Wagon 4WD

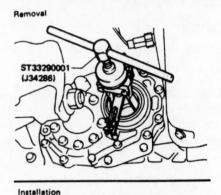

Removal

ST33290001 (J34286)

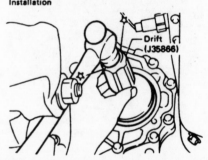

Installation

Drift (J35866)

Replacing adapter oil seal—Stanza Wagon 4WD

Driveshaft Oil Seal

REMOVAL AND INSTALLATION

Refer to the illustrations as guide for oil seal removal and installation.

Transfer Control Actuator

REMOVAL AND INSTALLATION

Refer to the illustrations as guide for electrical component removal and installation procedures.

Transfer Case Assembly

REMOVAL AND INSTALLATION

1. Drain the gear oil from the transaxle and the transfer case.

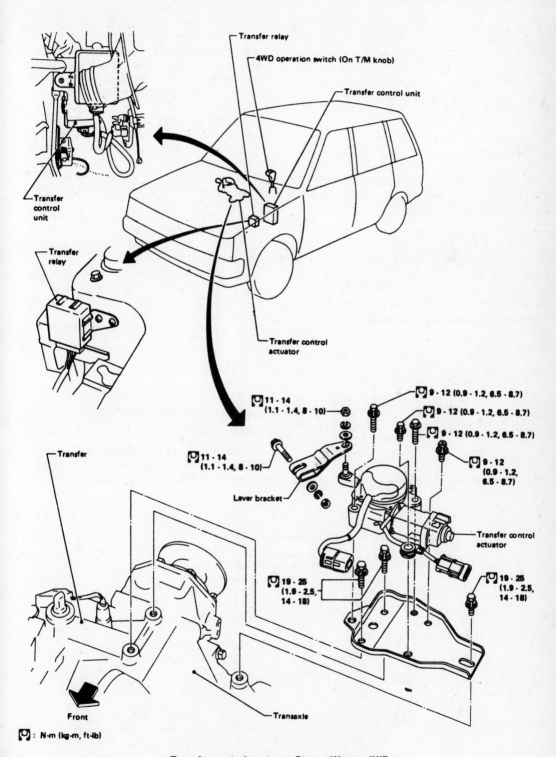

Transfer control system—Stanza Wagon 4WD

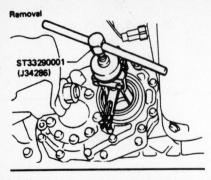

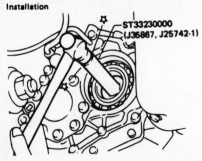

Replacing driveshaft oil seal—Stanza Wagon 4WD

2. Disconnect and remove the forward exhaust pipe.

3. Using chalk or paint, matchmark the flanges on the driveshaft and then unbolt and remove the driveshaft from the transfer case.

4. Unbolt and remove the transfer control actuator from the side of the transfer case.

5. Disconnect and remove the right side halfshaft.

6. Unscrew and withdraw the speedometer

pinion gear from the transfer case. Position it out of the way and secure it with wire.

7. Unbolt and remove the front, rear and side transfer case gussets (support members).

8. Use an hydraulic floor jack and a block of wood to support the transfer case, remove the transfer case-to-transaxle mounting bolts and then remove the case itself. Be careful when moving it while supported on the jack.

To install:

9. Install the transfer case in the vehicle. Tighten the transfer case-to-transaxle mounting bolts and the transfer case gusset mounting bolts to 22-30 ft. lbs. (30-40 Nm).

10. Be sure to use a multi-purpose grease to lubricate all oil seal surfaces prior to reinstallation.

11. Install the speedometer pinion gear.

12. Install the halfshaft.

13. Connect the transfer control actuator to the side of the transfer case.

14. Install the driveshaft to the transfer case.

15. Install the forward exhaust pipe.

16. Refill all fluid levels, the transfer case and the transaxle use different types and weights of lubricant then road test for proper operation.

DRIVELINE

Driveshaft and Universal Joints

REMOVAL AND INSTALLATION

200SX and 240SX

These models use a driveshaft with three U-joints and a center support bearing. The driveshaft is balanced as an assembly.

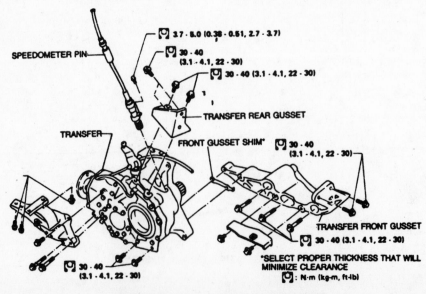

Transfer case removal—Stanza Wagon 4WD

1. Raise and safely support the vehicle.

2. Matchmark the flanges on the driveshaft and differential so the driveshaft can be reinstalled in its original orientation; this will help maintain drive line balance.

3. Unbolt the rear flange and the center bearing bracket.

4. Withdraw the driveshaft from the transmission and pull the driveshaft down and back to remove.

5. Plug the transmission extension housing to prevent oil leakage.

To install:

6. Lubricate the sleeve yoke splines with clean engine oil prior to installation. Insert the driveshaft into the transmission and align the flange matchmarks.

7. Install the flange and the center bearing bolts.

8. On 200SX and 240SX, torque the center bearing support bracket bolts to 19–29 ft. lbs.

9. On 200SX with CA20E and VG30E en-

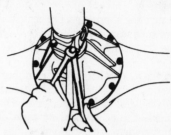

Disconnecting the rear driveshaft flange

Matchmark the driveshaft flange to the axle flange before removing

Remove the center bearing bracket

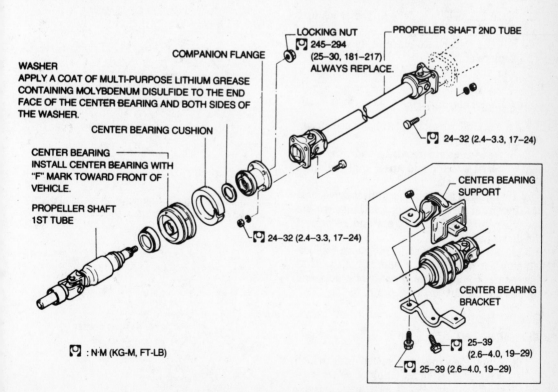

Exploded view of 2 piece driveshaft assembly

gines, torque the flange bolts to 29–33 ft. lbs. (39–44 Nm) and on the 240SX torque to 29–33 ft. lbs. (39–44 Nm).

U-JOINT REPLACEMENT

Disassembly

1. Mark the relationship of all components for reassembly.
2. Remove the snaprings. On early units, the snaprings are seated in the yokes. On later units, the snaprings seat in the needle bearing races.
3. Tap the yoke with brass or rubber mallet to release one bearing cap. Be careful not to lose the needle rollers.
4. Remove the other bearing caps. Remove the U-joint spiders from the yokes.

Inspection

1. Spline backlash should not exceed 0.5mm.
2. Driveshaft runout should not exceed 0.6mm.
3. On later model with snaprings seated in the needle bearing races, different thicknesses of snaprings are available for U-joint adjustment. Play should not exceed 0.02mm.
4. U-joint spiders must be replaced if their bearing journals are worn more than 0.15mm from their original diameter.

Assembly

1. Place the needle rollers in the races and hold them in place with grease.
2. Put the spider into place in its yokes.
3. Replace all seals.
4. Tap the races into position and secure them with snaprings.

DRIVESHAFT VIBRATION

To check and correct an unbalanced driveshaft, proceed as follows:
1. Remove the undercoating and other foreign material which could upset shaft balance. Roadtest the vehicle.
2. If vibration is noted, disconnect driveshaft at differential carrier companion flange, rotate companion flange 180° degress and reconnect the driveshaft.
3. Roadtest the vehicle, if vibration still exists replace driveshaft assembly. Note that driveshaft should be free of dents or cracks and runout should not exceed 0.6mm.

Center Bearing

REPLACEMENT

The center bearing is a sealed unit which must be replaced as an assembly if defective.
1. Remove the driveshaft assembly.
2. Paint a matchmark across where the flanges behind the center yoke are joined. This is for assembly purposes. If you don't paint or somehow mark the relationship between the two shafts, they may be out of balance when you put them back together.
3. Remove the bolts and separate the shafts. Make a matchmark on the front driveshaft half which lines up with the mark you made on the flange half.
4. You must devise a way to hold the driveshaft while unbolting the companion flange from the front driveshaft. Do not place the front driveshaft tube in a vise, because the chances are it will get crushed. The best way is to grip the flange somehow while loosening the nut. It is going to require some strength to remove.
5. Press the companion flange off the front driveshaft and press the center bearing from its mount.
6. The new bearing is already lubricated. Install it into the mount, making sure that the seals and so on are facing the same way as when removed. Also make sure the F mark is facing the front of the car.
7. Slide the companion flange on to the front driveshaft, aligning the marks made during removal. Install the washer and lock nut. If the washer and locknut are separate pieces, tighten them to 145-175 ft. lbs. If they were a unit. tighten it to 180-217 ft. lbs. Check that the

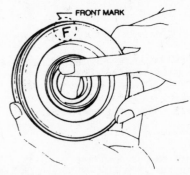

Before installing the center bearing, position the "F" mark so it is facing the front of the car

Always use a new nut, and stake it after tightening

bearing rotates freely around the driveshaft. Stake the nut (always use a new nut).

8. Connect the companion flange to the other half of the driveshaft, aligning the marks made during removal. Tighten the bolts securely.

9. Install the driveshaft.

REAR AXLE

Identification

There are different types of rear axles used on the cars covered in this manual. A solid rear axle is used on 1982-84 200SX (except the 1984 Turbo model). Independent rear suspension (I.R.S.) is used on 1984-88 200SX and the 240SX model. In this I.R.S. design, separate axle driveshafts are used to transmit power from the differential to the wheels.

Determining Axle Ratio

The drive axle is said to have a certain axle ratio. This number (usually a whole number and a decimal fraction) is actually a comparison of the number of gear teeth on the ring gear and the pinion gear. For example, a 4.11 rear means that theoretically, there are 4.11 teeth on the ring gear and one tooth on the pinion gear or, put another way, the driveshaft must turn 4.11 times to turn the wheels once. Actually, on a 4.11 rear, there might be 37 teeth on the ring gear and 9 teeth on the pinion gear. By dividing the number of teeth on the pinion gear into the number of teeth on the ring gear, the numerical axle ratio (4.11) is obtained. This also provides a good method of ascertaining exactly what axle ratio one is dealing with.

Another method of determining gear ratio is to jack up and support the car so that both rear wheels are off the ground. Make a chalk mark on the rear wheel and the driveshaft. Put the transmission in neutral. Turn the rear wheel one complete turn and count the number of turns that the driveshaft makes. The number of turns that the driveshaft makes in one complete revolution of the rear wheel is an approximation of the rear axle ratio.

Axle Shaft
(Solid Rear Axle)

REMOVAL AND INSTALLATION

NOTE: *Bearings must be pressed on and off the shaft with an arbor press. Unless you have access to one, it is not advisable to attempt any repair work on the axle shaft and bearing assemblies.*

1. Remove the hub cap or wheel cover. Loosen the lug nuts.

2. Raise the rear of the car and support it safely on stands.

3. Remove the rear wheel. Remove the four brake backing plate retaining nuts. Detach the parking brake linkage from the brake backing plate.

4. Attach a slide hammer to the axle shaft and remove it. Use a slide hammer and a two pronged puller to remove the oil seal from the housing.

NOTE: *If a slide hammer is not available, the axle can sometimes be pried out using pry bars on opposing sides of the hub.*

If endplay is found to be excessive, the bearing should be replaced. Shimming the bearing is not recommended as this ignores end play of the bearing itself and could result in improper seating of the bearing.

5. Using a chisel, carefully nick the bearing retainer in three or four places. The retainer

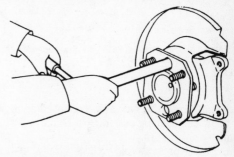

Removing the brake backing plate nuts

Use a slide hammer tool to remove the axle shaft—solid rear axle models

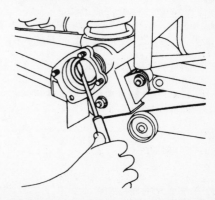

Carefully remove the oil seal—replace the seal before axle shaft installation

Use a chisel to cut the axle bearing retainer

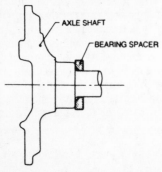

AXLE SHAFT

BEARING SPACER

Install the bearing spacer with the chamber side facing the axle shaft flange

does not have to be cut, only collapsed enough to allow the bearing retainer to be slid off the shaft.

6. Pull or press the old bearing off and install the new one by pressing it into position.

7. Install the outer bearing retainer with its raised surface facing the wheel hub, and then install the bearing and the inner bearing retainer in that order on the axle shaft.

8. With the smaller chamfered side of the in-

ner bearing retainer facing the bearing, press on the retainer. The edge of the retainer should fully touch the bearing.

9. Clean the oil seal seat in the rear axle housing. Apply a thin coat of chassis grease.

10. Using a seal installation tool, drive the oil seal into the rear axle housing. Wipe a thin coat of bearing grease on the lips of the seal.

11. Determine the number of retainer gaskets which will give the correct bearing-to-outer retainer clearance of 0.25mm.

12. Insert the axle shaft assembly into the axle housing, being careful not to damage the seal. Insure that the shaft splines engage those of the differential pinion. Align the vent holes of the gasket and the outer bearing retainer. Install the retaining bolts.

13. Install the nuts on the bolts and tighten them evenly, and in a criss-cross pattern, to 20 ft. lbs.

Halfshaft (Independent Rear Suspension)
REMOVAL AND INSTALLATION
200SX

NOTE: *When removing the halfshaft be careful not to damage the oil seal in the differential carrier. Do not damage the CV-boot.*

1. Raise and support the rear of the car.

2. Remove the spring stay.

3. Disconnect the halfshaft on the wheel side by removing the four flange bolts.

4. Grasp the halfshaft at the center and extract it from the differential carrier by prying it with a suitable pry bar.

5. Installation is in the reverse order of removal. Install the differential end first and then

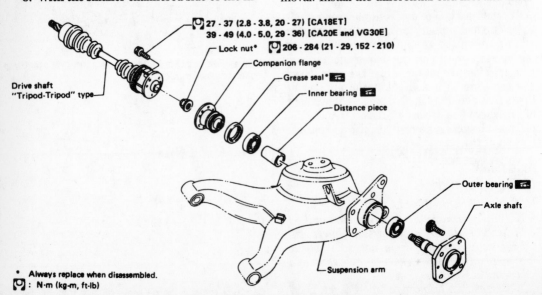

27 - 37 (2.8 - 3.8, 20 - 27) [CA18ET]
39 - 49 (4.0 - 5.0, 29 - 36) [CA20E and VG30E]
Lock nut*   206 - 284 (21 - 29, 152 - 210)
Companion flange
Grease seal*
Inner bearing
Distance piece
Drive shaft "Tripod-Tripod" type
Outer bearing
Axle shaft
Suspension arm

* Always replace when disassembled.
: N·m (kg-m, ft-lb)

Rear axle shaft assembly (IRS type)

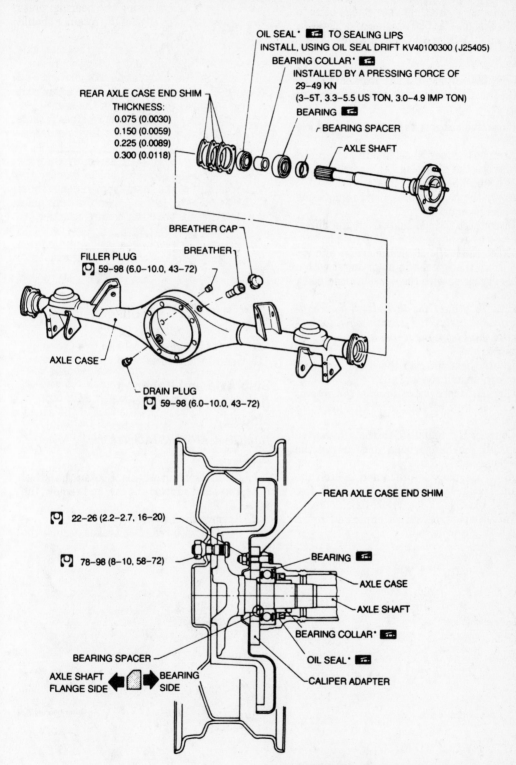

OIL SEAL* [img] TO SEALING LIPS
INSTALL, USING OIL SEAL DRIFT KV40100300 (J25405)
BEARING COLLAR* [img]
INSTALLED BY A PRESSING FORCE OF
29–49 KN
(3–5T, 3.3–5.5 US TON, 3.0–4.9 IMP TON)
BEARING [img]

REAR AXLE CASE END SHIM
THICKNESS:
0.075 (0.0030)
0.150 (0.0059)
0.225 (0.0089)
0.300 (0.0118)

BEARING SPACER
AXLE SHAFT

BREATHER CAP
BREATHER
FILLER PLUG
[img] 59–98 (6.0–10.0, 43–72)

AXLE CASE

DRAIN PLUG
[img] 59–98 (6.0–10.0, 43–72)

REAR AXLE CASE END SHIM

[img] 22–26 (2.2–2.7, 16–20)

[img] 78–98 (8–10, 58–72)

BEARING [img]
AXLE CASE
AXLE SHAFT
BEARING COLLAR* [img]
OIL SEAL* [img]
BEARING SPACER
AXLE SHAFT
FLANGE SIDE   BEARING
SIDE
CALIPER ADAPTER

*: ALWAYS REPLACE ONCE THEY HAVE BEEN REMOVED.
[img] : N·M (KG-M, FT-LB)
UNIT: MM(IN)

Solid rear axle assembly

the wheel end. Tighten the four flange bolts to 20-27 ft. lbs. on CA18ET engine and 29-36 ft. lbs. on the CA20E and VG30E engines.

240SX

NOTE: *When removing the rear halfshafts, cover the CV-boots with cloth to prevent damage.*

1. Raise and support the rear of the vehicle safely.

2. Remove the rear wheel and tire assembly.

3. Remove the adjusting cap and cotter pin from the wheel bearing locknut.

4. Apply the parking brake and remove the rear wheel locknut.

5. Disconnect the halfshaft from the differential side by removing the side flange bolts.

6. Grasp the halfshaft at the center and extract if from the wheel hub by prying it with a suitable prybar or with the use of a wood block and mallet.

NOTE: *To protect the threads of the shaft, temporarily install the locknut when loosening the shaft from the wheel hub.*

To install:

7. Insert the shaft into the wheel hub and temporarily install the locknut.

NOTE: *Take care not to damage the oil seal or either end of the halfshaft during installation.*

8. Connect the halfshaft to the differential and install the flange bolts and torque the flange bolts to 25-33 ft. lbs.

9. Apply the parking brake and tighten the locknut. Torque the locknut to 174-231 ft. lbs. (1989-90) 152–203 ft. lbs. (1991-92).

10. Install a new locknut cotter pin and install the adjusting cap.

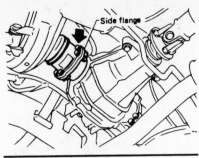

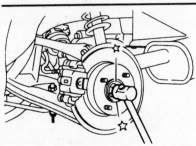

Removing the halfshaft assembly—240SX

11. Mount the rear wheel and tire assembly.

12. Lower the vehicle.

Stub Axle and Bearings (Independent Rear Suspension Models)

REMOVAL AND INSTALLATION

200SX

1. Block the front wheels. Loosen the wheel nuts, raise and support the car, and remove the wheel.

2. Remove the halfshaft.

3. On cars with rear disc brakes, unbolt the

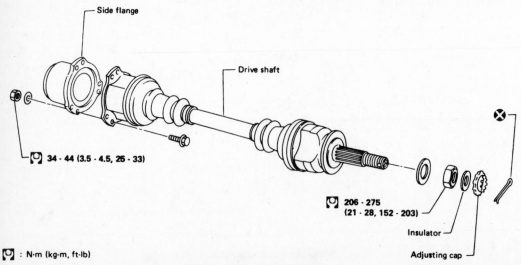

Side flange

Drive shaft

34 - 44 (3.5 - 4.5, 25 - 33)

206 - 275
(21 - 28, 152 - 203)

Insulator

Adjusting cap

[🔧] : N·m (kg-m, ft-lb)

Halfshaft assembly—240SX

caliper and move it aside. Do not allow the caliper to hang by the hose. Support the caliper with a length of wire or rest it on a suspension member.

4. Remove the brake disc on models with rear disc brakes. Remove the brake drum on cars with drum brakes.

5. Remove the stub axle nut. You will have to hold the stub axle at the outside while removing the nut from the axle shaft side. The nut will require a good deal of force to remove, so be sure to hold the stub axle firmly.

6. Remove the stub axle with a slide hammer and an adapter. The outer wheel bearing will come off with the stub axle.

7. Remove the companion flange from the lower arm.

8. Remove and discard the grease seal and inner bearing from the lower arm using a drift made for the purpose or a length of pipe of the proper diameter. The outer bearing can be removed from the stub axle with a puller. If the grease seal or the bearings are removed, new parts must be used on assembly.

To install:

9. Clean all the parts to be reused in solvent.

10. Sealed type bearings are used. When the new bearings are installed, the sealed side must face out. Install the sealed side of the outer bearing facing the wheel, and the sealed side of the inner bearing facing the differential.

11. Press the outer bearing onto the stub axle.
NOTE: *When a spacer is reused, make sure that both ends are not collapsed or deformed. When installing, make sure that the larger side faces the axle shaft flange.*

12. The bearing housing is stamped with a

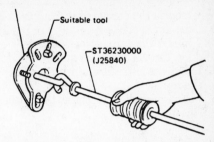

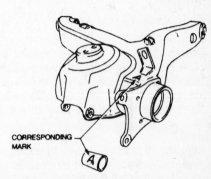

Using special tool to remove the stub or axle shaft.

Make sure you install a spacer which is marked the same as the mark on the bearing housing

letter. Select a spacer with the same marking. Install the spacer on the stub axle.

13. Install the stub axle into the lower arm.

14. Install the new inner bearing into the lower arm with the stub axle in place. Install a new grease seal.

15. Install the companion flange onto the stub axle.

16. Install the stub axle nut. On 1984-87

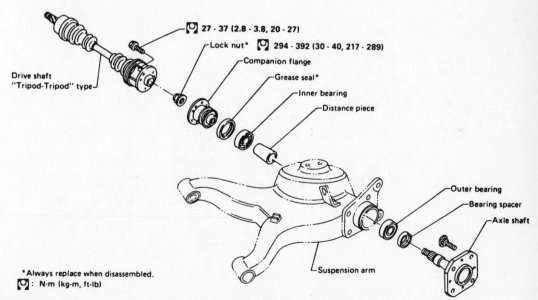

* Always replace when disassembled.

[symbol]: N·m (kg-m, ft-lb)

Exploded view rear axle shaft assembly (IRS type)

200SX models the torque specification is 217-289 ft. lbs. for the axle stub nut. On the 1988 200SX model the torque specification is 152-210 ft. lbs. for the axle stub nut.

17. Install the brake disc or drum, and the caliper if removed.

18. Install the halfshaft. Install the wheel and lower the car.

Front Oil Seal (Pinion Seal)

REMOVAL AND INSTALLATION

1. Remove the driveshaft.
2. Loosen drive pinion nut; a special tool, J34311, is required to hold companion flange.
3. Remove companion flange (matchmark for correct installation) using suitable puller.
4. Remove the front oil seal from differential carrier.

To install:

5. Apply multi-purpose grease to sealing lips of oil seal. Press front oil seal into carrier.
6. Install companion flange and drive pinion nut. Torque drive pinion nut to specification.

7. Install the driveshaft. Check fluid level. Refer to the specifications below:

• The drive pinion nut torque specification for model H190-ML (200SX solid rear axle type) is total preload 10-19 in. lbs. is obtained (94-217 ft. lbs.)

• The drive pinion nut torque specification for (1984-85 200SX) model R200 (IRS type) is 137-159 ft. lbs.

• The drive pinion nut torque specification for (1986-88 200SX and 240SX) model R200 (IRS type) is 137-217 ft. lbs.

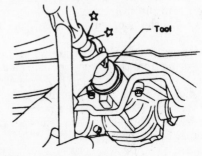

Installing the front oil seal

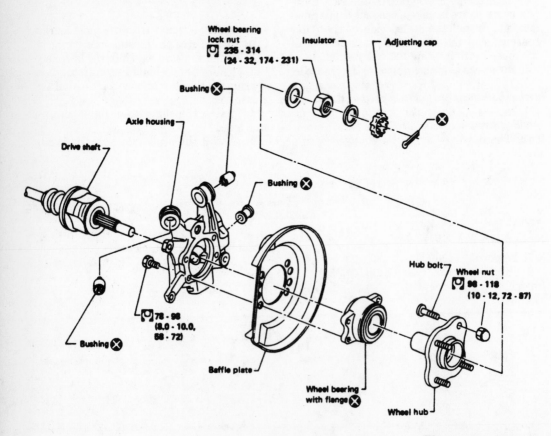

: N·m (kg-m, ft-lb)

Rear axle hub assembly—240SX

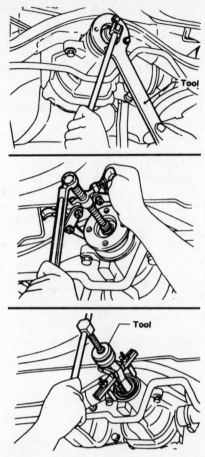

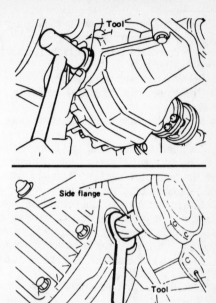

Installing side oil seal

Removing the companion flange and front oil seal

• The drive pinion nut torque specification for (1985-88 200SX) model R180 (IRS type) is 123-145 ft. lbs.

• The drive pinion nut torque specification for (1986-88 Stanza Wagon) model R180 is 123-145 ft. lbs.

Side Oil Seal

REMOVAL AND INSTALLATION

1. Remove the halfshaft.
2. Remove side flange if so eqipped (matchmark for correct installation) using suitable puller.

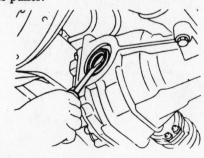

Removing side oil seal

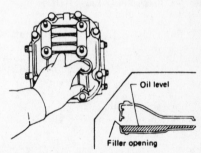

Checking the final drive unit fluid level

3. Remove the oil seal.

To install:

4. Apply multi-purpose grease to sealing lips of oil seal. Press oil seal into carrier.

5. Install side flange if so equipped with special tool J39352 or equivalent.

6. Install the halfshaft. Check fluid level.

Differential Carrier/Rear Axle Assembly

REMOVAL AND INSTALLATION

NOTE: *This is a complete rear axle housing and rear suspension service procedure--modify the steps as necessary. Use the illustrations to help you.*

1. Raise the rear of the vehicle and support safely. Drain the oil from the differential. Position a floor jack underneath the differential unit.

2. Disconnect the brake hydraulic lines and the parking brake cable. Remove the brake cali-

per leaving the brake line connected. Plug the brake lines to prevent lakage.

3. Disconnect the sway bar from the control arms on either side.

4. Remove the rear exhaust pipe.

5. Disconnect the driveshaft and the rear axle shafts.

6. Remove the rear shock absorbers from the control arms.

7. Unbolt the differential unit from the chassis at the differential mounting insulator. Remove the mounting member from the front of the final drive unit if so equipped.

8. Lower the rear assembly out of the vehicle using the floor jack. It is best to have at least one other person helping to balance the assembly. After the final drive is removed, support the center suspension member to prevent damage to the insulators.

9. Installation is the reverse of the removal procedure.

Differential Carrier (Stanza 4WD)

REMOVAL AND INSTALLATION

1. Jack up the rear of the vehicle and drain the oil from the differential. Support with jackstands. Position the floor jack underneath the differential unit.

2. Disconnect the brake hydraulic lines and the parking brake cable.

3. Disconnect the sway bar from the control arms on either sides.

4. Remove the rear exhaust tube.

5. Disconnect the driveshaft and the rear axle shafts.

6. Remove the rear shock absorbers from the control arms.

7. Unbolt the differential unit from the chassis, at the differential mounting insulator.

8. Lower the rear assembly out of the car using the floor jack. It is best to have at least one other person helping to balance the assembly.

To install:

9. Install the differential unit to the chassis. Torque the rear cover-to-insulator nuts to 72-87 ft. lbs.; the mounting insulator-to-chassis bolts to 22-29 ft. lbs.; the driveshaft-to-flange bolts to 43-51 ft. lbs. Torque the strut nuts to 51-65 ft. lbs.; and the sway bar-to-control arm nuts to 12-15 ft. lbs.

10. Reconnect the rear exhaust tube.

11. Connect the brake hydraulic lines and the parking brake cable.

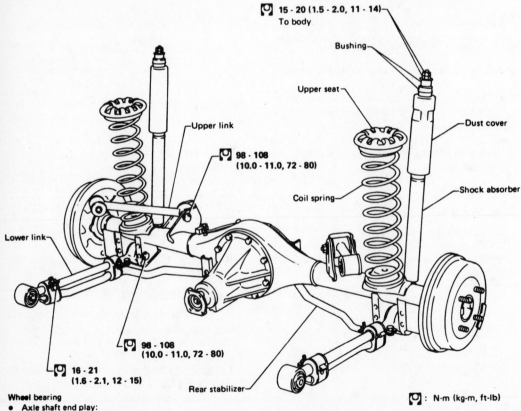

15 - 20 (1.5 - 2.0, 11 - 14)
To body

Bushing

Upper seat

Upper link

98 - 108
(10.0 - 11.0, 72 - 80)

Dust cover

Coil spring

Shock absorber

Lower link

98 - 108
(10.0 - 11.0, 72 - 80)

16 - 21
(1.6 - 2.1, 12 - 15)

Rear stabilizer

Wheel bearing
● Axle shaft end play:
0.2 - 0.5 mm (0.008 - 0.020 in)

: N·m (kg-m, ft-lb)

Rear axle and rear suspension—200SX (4-link type)

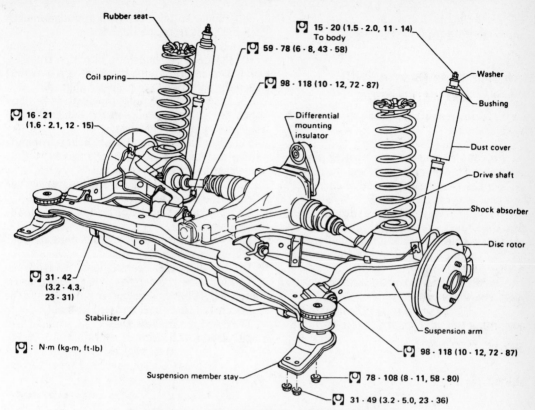

Rubber seat

Coil spring

15 - 20 (1.5 - 2.0, 11 - 14)
To body

59 - 78 (6 - 8, 43 - 58)

98 - 118 (10 - 12, 72 - 87)

Differential
mounting
insulator

Washer

Bushing

Dust cover

Drive shaft

Shock absorber

Disc rotor

16 - 21
(1.6 - 2.1, 12 - 15)

31 - 42
(3.2 - 4.3,
23 - 31)

Stabilizer

Suspension arm

98 - 118 (10 - 12, 72 - 87)

: N·m (kg-m, ft-lb)

Suspension member stay

78 - 108 (8 - 11, 58 - 80)

31 - 49 (3.2 - 5.0, 23 - 36)

Rear axle and rear suspension—200SX (IRS type)

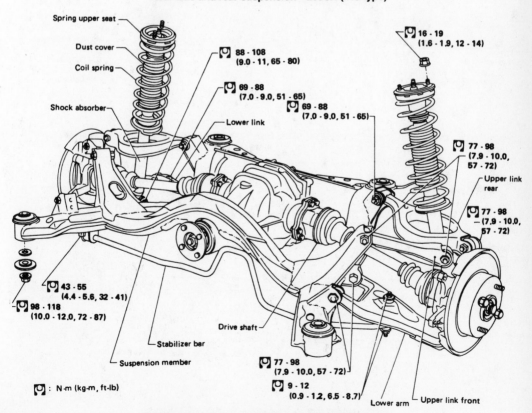

Spring upper seat

Dust cover

Coil spring

Shock absorber

Lower link

88 - 108
(9.0 - 11, 65 - 80)

69 - 88
(7.0 - 9.0, 51 - 65)

69 - 88
(7.0 - 9.0, 51 - 65)

16 - 19
(1.6 - 1.9, 12 - 14)

77 - 98
(7.9 - 10.0,
57 - 72)

Upper link
rear

77 - 98
(7.9 - 10.0,
57 - 72)

43 - 55
(4.4 - 5.6, 32 - 41)

98 - 118
(10.0 - 12.0, 72 - 87)

Stabilizer bar

Suspension member

Drive shaft

77 - 98
(7.9 - 10.0, 57 - 72)

9 - 12
(0.9 - 1.2, 6.5 - 8.7)

Lower arm

Upper link front

: N·m (kg-m, ft-lb)

Rear axle and rear suspension—240SX (IRS type)

12. Bleed the brake system.

13. Road test for proper operation.

Rear Halfshafts (Stanza 4WD)

REMOVAL AND INSTALLATION

1. Raise the rear of the vehicle and support it with jackstands.

2. Remove the wheel and tire.

3. Pull out the wheel bearing cotter pin and then remove the adjusting cap and insulator.

4. Set the parking brake and then remove the wheel bearing lock nut.

5. Disconnect and plug the hydraulic brake lines. Disconnect the parking brake cable.

6. Using a block of wood and a small mallet, carefully tap the halfshaft out of the knuckle/backing plate assembly.

7. Unbolt the radius rod and the transverse link at the wheel end.

NOTE: *Before removing the transverse link mounting bolt, matchmark the toe-in adjusting plate to the link.*

8. Using a suitable pry bar, carefully remove the halfshaft from the final drive.

To install:

9. Position the halfshaft into the knuckle and then insert it into the final drive; make sure the serrations are properly aligned.

10. Push the shaft into the final drive and then press-fit the circlip on the halfshaft into the groove on the side gear.

11. After insertion, pull the halfshaft by hand to be certain that it is properly seated in the side gear and will not come out.

12. Connect the radius rod and the transverse link at the wheel end.

13. Install the knuckle/backing plate assembly.

14. Connect the hydraulic brake lines and the parking brake cable.

15. Install wheel bearing lock nut (torque 174-231 ft. lbs. refer to the illustrations), insulator, adjusting cap and cotter pin.

16. Install the wheel and tire assembly.

17. Bleed the brake system.

18. Road test for proper operation.

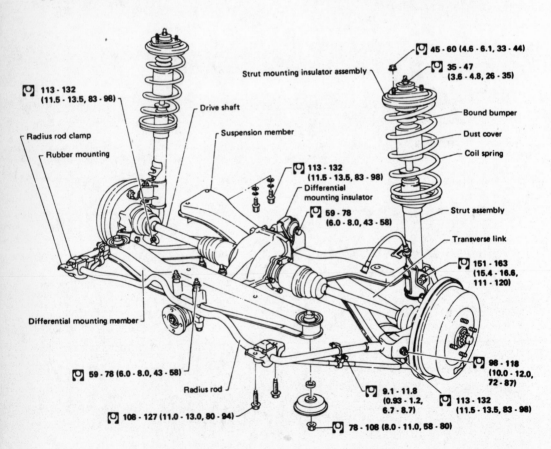

Rear axle and rear suspension—Stanza 4WD Wagon

FRONT SUSPENSION

MacPherson Strut

REMOVAL AND INSTALLATION

200SX

1. Jack up the car and support it safely. Remove the wheel/tire assembly.

2. Remove the brake caliper. Remove the disc and hub assembly. .

3. Remove the tension rod arm and knuckle arm to lower strut assembly retaining bolts.

4. Pry the lower assembly down to detach it from the strut.

5. Support strut assembly with a suitable stand or jack.

When installing a bushing, do not allow it to project beyond the surface area of the washer.

Do not allow the bushings and washers to come in contact with grease, oil, soapy water, etc.

*: Always replace whenever disassembled.

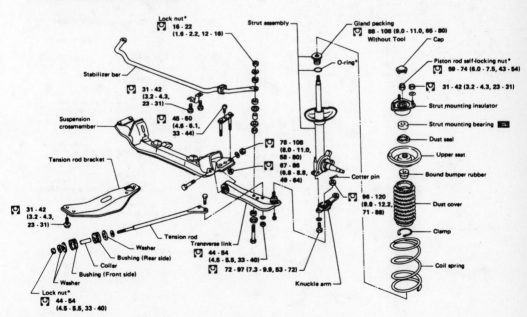

- Final tightening should be carried out under unladen condition**
  with tires on ground when installing each bushing.
  **Fuel, radiator coolant and engine oil are filled up.
  Spare tire, jack, hand tools and mats are in designed position.

Front suspension—200SX 1984–88

6. Open the hood, and remove the nuts holding the top of the strut to the tower.

7. Lower the jack/stand slowly and cautiously until the strut assembly can be removed.

To install:

8. Install the strut assembly on the vehicle and torque the strut-to-knuckle arm to 53–72 ft. lbs. Torque the tension rod to transverse link to 33–40 ft. lbs. and the strut to tower (hood ledge) bolts to 23–31 ft. lbs.

NOTE: *The self-locking nuts holding the top of the strut must always be replaced when removed.*

9. Bleed the brakes.

10. Install the wheel.

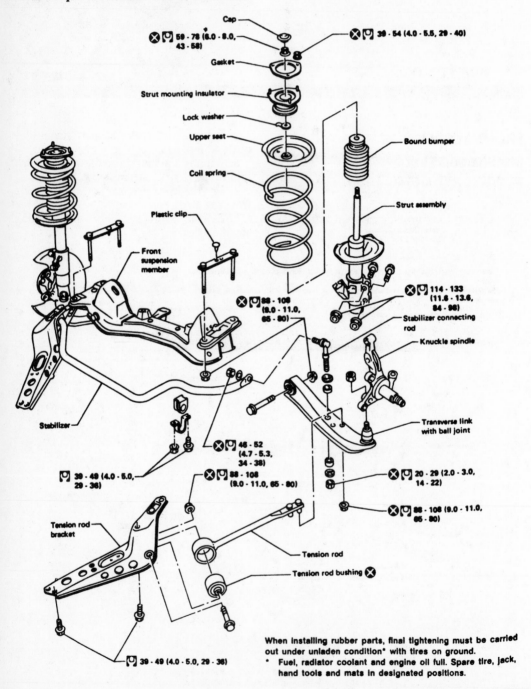

Front suspension—240SX 1989–92

240SX
Stanza
Stanza Wagon 2WD and 4WD

1. Raise and safely support the vehicle.
2. Remove the wheel. Mark the position of the strut-to-steering knuckle location.
3. Detach the brake tube from the strut.

4. Support the control arm.
5. Remove the strut-to-steering knuckle bolts.
6. Support the strut assembly and remove the 3 upper strut to hood ledge nuts. Remove the strut assembly from the vehicle.

To install:

CAUTION:
When disassembling and assembling, be careful not to damage piston rod.

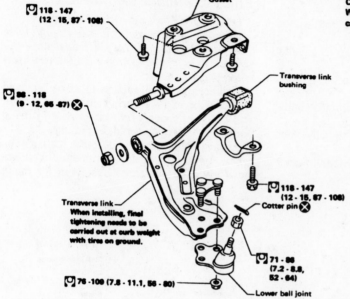

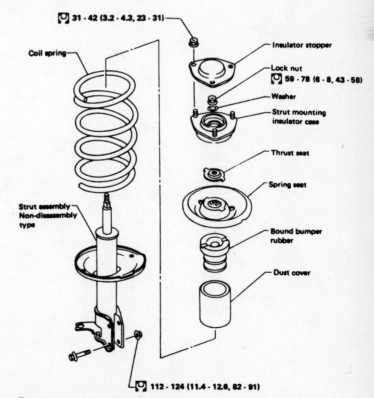

Front suspension—Stanza 1982–89

7. Install the strut assembly onto the vehicle and torque the following:
- 240SX model – Strut-to-body (hood ledge) nuts: 29–40 ft. lbs.
- 240SX model – Strut-to-knuckle bolts: 114–133 ft. lbs.
- 1982–86 Stanza – Strut-to-body (hood ledge) nuts: 23–31 ft. lbs.
- 1982–86 Stanza – Strut-to-knuckle bolts: 56–80 ft. lbs.
- 1987–89 Stanza – Strut-to-body (hood ledge) nuts: 23–31 ft. lbs.
- 1987–89 Stanza – Strut-to-knuckle bolts: 82–91 ft. lbs.
- 1990–92 Stanza – Strut-to-body (hood ledge) nuts: 29–40 ft. lbs.
- 1990–92 Stanza – Strut-to-knuckle bolts: 116–123 ft. lbs.
- Stanza Wagon 2WD – Strut-to-body (hood ledge) nuts: 23–31 ft. lbs.
- Stanza Wagon 2WD – Strut-to-knuckle bolts: 72–87 ft. lbs.
- Stanza Wagon 4WD – Strut-to-body (hood ledge) nuts: 11–17 ft. lbs.
- Stanza Wagon 4WD – Strut-to-knuckle bolts: 72–87 ft. lbs.

8. If brake hose was disconnected from the brake caliper, bleed brakes and install the wheel.

STRUT CARTRIDGE REPLACEMENT

CAUTION: *The coil springs are under considerable tension, and can exert enough force to cause serious injury. Disassemble the struts only using the proper tools, and use extreme caution.*

Coil springs on all models must be removed with the aid of a coil spring compressor. If you don't have one, don't try to improvise by using something else: you could risk injury.

Always follow manufacturer's instructions when operating a spring compressor. You can now buy cartridge shock absorbers for many

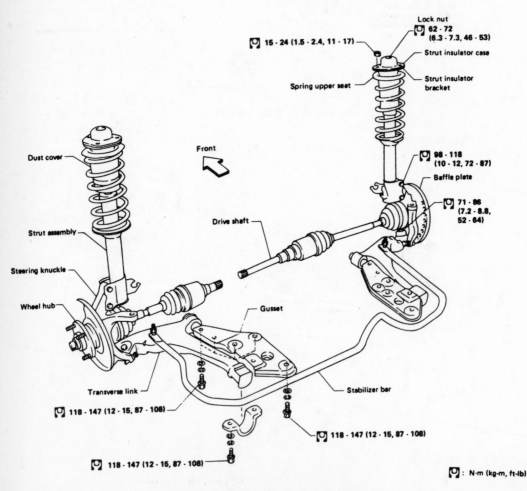

Lock nut
62 - 72
(6.3 - 7.3, 46 - 53)

15 - 24 (1.5 - 2.4, 11 - 17)

Strut insulator case

Spring upper seat

Strut insulator bracket

Dust cover

Front

98 - 118
(10 - 12, 72 - 87)

Baffle plate

71 - 86
(7.2 - 8.8, 52 - 64)

Strut assembly

Drive shaft

Steering knuckle

Wheel hub

Gusset

Transverse link

Stabilizer bar

118 - 147 (12 - 15, 87 - 108)

118 - 147 (12 - 15, 87 - 108)

118 - 147 (12 - 15, 87 - 108)

: N·m (kg-m, ft-lb)

Front suspension—Stanza Wagon 4WD

Datsun/Nissan: installation procedures are not the same as those given here. In this case, follow the instructions that come with the shock absorbers.

To remove the coil spring, you must first remove the strut assembly from the vehicle. See above procedures.

1. Secure the strut assembly in a vise.

2. Attach the spring compressor to the spring, leaving the top few coils free.

3. Remove the dust cap from the top of the strut to expose the center nut.

4. Compress the spring just far enough to permit the strut insulator to be turned by hand. Remove the self locking center nut.

5. Take out the strut insulator, strut bearing, oil seal, upper spring seat and bound bumper rubber from the top of the strut. Note their sequence of removal and be sure to assemble them in the same order.

6. Remove the spring with the spring compressor still attached.

7. Reassembly the strut assembly and observe the following:

a. Make sure you assemble the unit with the shock absorber piston rod fully extended.

b. When assembling, take care that the rubber spring seats, both top and bottom, and the spring are positioned in their grooves before releasing the spring.

8. To remove the shock absorber: Remove the dust cap, if so equipped, and push the piston rod down until it bottoms. With the piston in this position, loosen and remove the gland packing shock absorber retainer. This calls for Datsun/ Nissan Special Tool ST35490000 or equivalent tool J26083.

NOTE: *If the gland tube is dirty, clean it before removing to prevent dirt from contaminating the fluid inside the strut tube.*

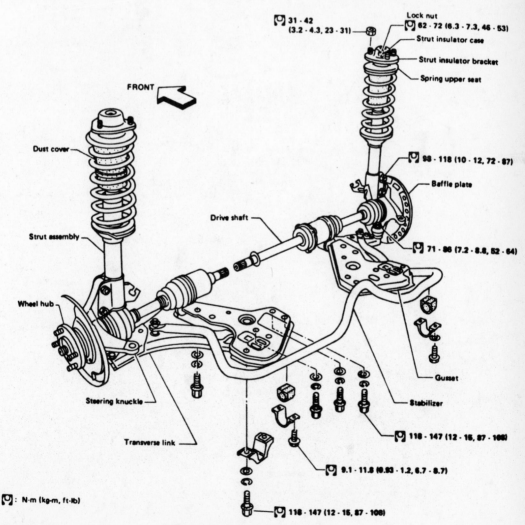

Front suspension—Stanza 1990–92

9. Remove the O-ring from the top of the piston rod guide and lift out the piston rod together with the cylinder. Drain all of the fluid from the strut and shock components into a suitable container. Clean all parts.

NOTE: *The piston rod, piston rod guide and cylinder are a matched set: single parts of this shock assembly should not be exchanged with parts of other assemblies.*

10. Assembly the shock absorber into the assembly with the following notes:

a. After installing the cylinder and piston rod assembly (the shock absorber kit) in the outer casing, remove the piston rod guide, if so equipped, from the cylinder and pour the correct amount of new fluid into the cylinder and strut outer casing. To find this amount consult the instructions with your shock ab-

When installing rubber parts, final tightening must be carried out under unladen condition* with tires on ground.
* Fuel, radiator coolant and engine oil full. Spare tire, jack, hand tools and mats in designated positions.

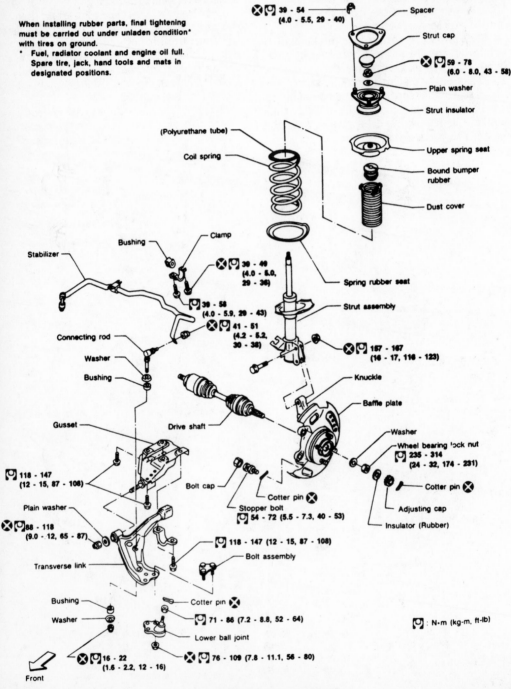

Front suspension—Stanza 1990–92

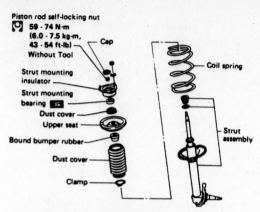

Piston rod self-locking nut
59 - 74 N·m
(6.0 - 7.5 kg-m,
43 - 54 ft-lb)
Without Tool
Cap
Strut mounting insulator
Strut mounting bearing
Dust cover
Upper seat
Bound bumper rubber
Dust cover
Clamp
Coil spring
Strut assembly

Spring and strut assembly—200SX

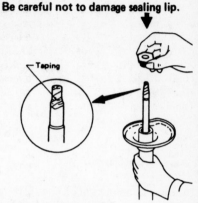

Be careful not to damage sealing lip.

Taping

Spring and strut disassembly

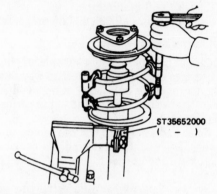

ST35652000
(–)

Spring and strut disassembly

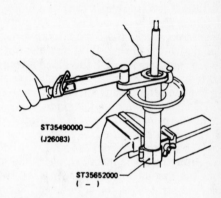

ST35490000
(J26083)

ST35652000
(–)

Spring and strut disassembly

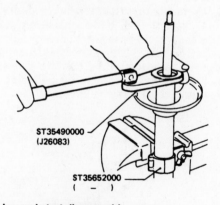

ST35490000
(J26083)

ST35652000
(–)

Spring and strut disassembly

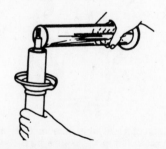

Spring and strut disassembly

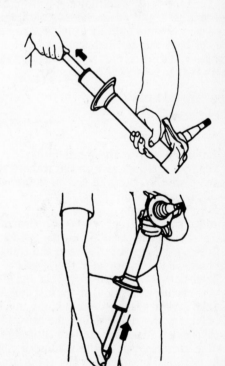

Spring and strut disassembly

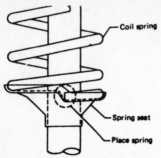

Spring and strut disassembly

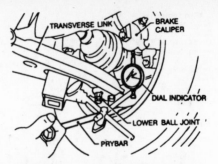

Measuring balljoint play with a dial indicator

sorber kit. The amount of oil should be listed. Use only Nissan Genuine Strut Oil or its equivalent.

NOTE: *It is important that the correct amount of fluid be poured into the strut to assure correct shock absorber damping force.*

b. Install the O-ring, fluid and any other cylinder components. Fit the gland packing and tighten it after greasing the gland packing-to-piston rod mating surfaces.

NOTE: *When tightening the gland packing, extend the piston rod about 3 to 5 in. (76–127mm) from the end of the outer casing to expel most of the air from the strut.*

c. After the kit is installed, bleed the air from the system in the following manner: hold the strut with its bottom end facing down. Pull the piston rod out as far as it will go. Turn the strut upside down and push the piston in as far as it will go. Repeat this procedure several times until an equal pressure is felt on both the pull out and the push in strokes of the piston rods. The remaining assembly is the reverse of disassembly.

Lower Ball Joints

INSPECTION

Dial Indicator Method

1. Raise and support the vehicle safely.
2. Clamp a dial indicator to the transverse link and place the tip of the dial on the lower edge of the brake caliper.
3. Zero the indicator.
4. Make sure the front wheels are straight ahead and the brake pedal is fully depressed.
5. Insert a long prybar between the transverse link and the inner rim of the wheel.
6. Push down and release the prybar and observe the reading (deflection) on the dial indicator. Take several readings and use the maximum dial indicator deflection as the ball joint vertical endplay. Make sure to zero the indicator after each reading. If the reading is not within specifications, replace the transverse link or the ball joint. Ball joint vertical endplay specifications are as follows:

- 200SX and 240SX – 0 in. (0mm)
- Stanza:
  1982–89 – 0.004–0.039 in. (0.1–1.0mm)
  1990–92 – 0 in. (0mm)
- Stanza Wagon – 0.098 in. (2.5mm) or less

Visual Approximation Method

The lower ball joint should be replaced when play becomes excessive. An effective way to visually approximate ball joint verticle endplay without the use of a dial indicator is to perform the following:

1. Raise and safely support the vehicle until the wheel is clear of the ground. Do not place the jack under the ball joint; it must be unloaded.
2. Place a long prybar under the tire and move the wheel up and down. Keep one hand on top of the tire while doing this.
3. If ¼ in. (6mm) or more of play exists at the top of the tire, the ball joint should be replaced. Be sure the wheel bearings are properly adjusted before making this measurement. A double check can be made; while the tire is being moved up and down, observe the ball joint. If play is seen, replace the ball joint.

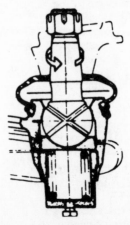

Cross section of a ball joint; note the plug at the bottom for a grease fitting. Make sure the rubber boot is in good condition

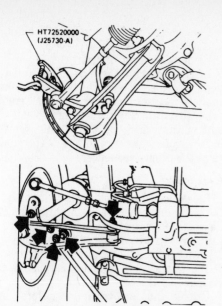

Removal of lower ball joint assembly—200SX

Separate ball joint from the knuckle arm with press—200SX

REMOVAL AND INSTALLATION

Rear Wheel Drive

If there is a plugged hole in the bottom of the joint for installation of a grease fitting, install a fitting. The ball joint should be greased every 15,000 miles or 1 year.

NOTE: *The transverse link (lower control arm) must be removed and then the ball joint must be pressed out.*

1. Raise and support the vehicle safely.
2. Remove the front wheels.
3. Separate the knuckle arm from the tie rod using the proper tool.
4. Separate the knuckle arm from the strut.
5. Remove the stabilizer bar and tension rod.
6. Remove the transverse link and knuckle arm.
7. Separate the knuckle arm from the ball joint with a suitable press.
8. Replace the transverse link/ball joint assembly.

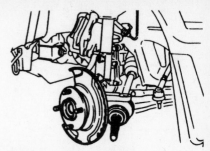

Lower ball joint removal—Stanza

9. Installation is the reverse of the removal procedure. Final tightening needs to be carried out under Unladen conditions with tires on ground. All fluid levels and fuel full and all components installed in the correct position.

Front Wheel Drive

1. Raise and support the vehicle safely.
2. Remove the front wheel.
3. Remove the wheel bearing locknut.
4. Separate the tie rod end ball joint from the steering knuckle with a ball joint remover, being careful not to damage the ball joint dust cover if the ball joint is to be used again.
5. Loosen, but do not remove the strut retaining upper nuts.
6. Remove the nut that attaches the ball joint to the transverse link.
7. Separate the halfshaft from the knuckle by lightly taping the end of the shaft.
8. Separate the ball joint from the knuckle using the proper tool.
9. Installation is the reverse of the removal procedure. Always replace the ball joint retaining bolts and cotter pins after each diassembly.

Lower Control Arm (Transverse Link)
REMOVAL AND INSTALLATION
200SX and 240SX

1. Raise and support the vehicle safely.
2. Remove the front wheel.
3. Remove the cotter pin and castle nut from the side rod (steering arm) ball joint and separate the ball joint from the side rod using the proper tool.

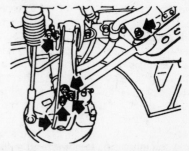

Removal of transverse link assembly—200SX

Separate the ball joint from the knuckle arm with press transverse link removal—200SX

4. Separate the steering knuckle arm from the MacPherson strut.

5. Remove the tension rod and stabilizer bar from the lower arm.

6. Remove the nuts or bolts connecting the lower control arm (transverse link) to the suspension crossmember.

7. Remove the lower control arm (transverse link) with the suspension ball joint and knuckle arm still attached.

8. When installing the control arm, temporarily tighten the nuts and/or bolts securing the control arm to the suspension crossmember. Tighten them fully only after the vehicle is sitting on its wheels. Lubricate the ball joints after assembly. Check wheel alignment.

1982–89 Stanza
Stanza 2WD and 4WD Wagon

NOTE: *Always use new nuts when installing the ball joint assembly to the control arm.*

1. Raise the vehicle and support it safely.

2. Remove the front wheels.

3. Remove the lower ball joint bolts from the control arm.

NOTE: *If equipped with a stabilizer bar, disconnect it at the control arm.*

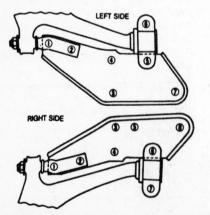

Transverse link gusset bolt torque sequence—Stanza Wagon 4WD

4. Remove the control arm-to-body bolts.

5. Remove the gusset.

6. Remove the control arm.

7. Installation is the reverse of the removal procedure. Always replace the ball joint retaining bolts and cotter pins after each diassembly. Final tightening should be made with the weight of the vehicle on the wheels. On the Stanza Wagon, make sure to torque the gusset bolts in the proper sequence.

1990–92 Stanza

1. Raise the vehicle and support it safely.

2. Unbolt and remove the stabilizer bar. The bar is removed by unfastening the clamp bolts and the bolts that hold the bar to the transverse link gusset plate. When removing the clamps, note the relationship between the clamp and paint mark on the bar.

3. Unbolt and remove the transverse link and gusset.

4. Inspect the transverse link, gusset and bushings for cracks, damage and deformation.

5. To install, bolt the transverse link and gusset into place. Lower the vehicle and torque the the bolts and nuts in the proper sequence as illustrated. Torque the nuts to 30–35 ft. lbs. and the bolts to 87–108 ft. lbs. The vehicle must at curb weight and the tires must be on the ground. After installation is complete, check the front end alignment.

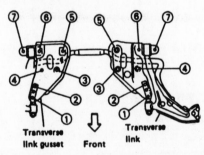

Transverse link gusset bolt torque sequence—Stanza 1990–92

Tension Rod and Stabilizer Bar
REMOVAL AND INSTALLATION
200SX and 240SX

1. Raise and support the vehicle safely.

2. Remove the tension rod-to-frame lock nuts.

3. Remove the 2 mounting bolts at the transverse link, lower control arm, and then slide out the tension rod.

4. On 240SX, to remove the tension rod, remove the bolt and nut that holds the rod to the tension rod bracket (through the bushing),

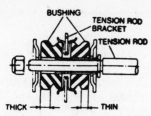

Tension rod bushings positioning—RWD models

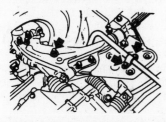

Tension rod and bar attaching points—240SX

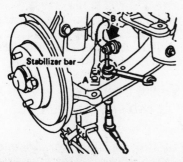

Hold the stabilizer connecting rod with a wrench when removing and installing the mounting nuts

then swing the rod upward and remove the tranverse link bolts, nuts, bushings and washers. If the bushings are worn replace them.

5. Unbolt the stabilizer bar at each transverse link or connecting rod. On 240SX, engage the flats of stabilizer bar connecting rod with a wrench to keep the rod from moving when removing the nuts.

6. Remove the 4 stabilizer bar bracket bolts, and remove the stabilizer bar.

7. During installation observe the following:

   a. Tighten the stabilizer bar-to-transverse link bolts to 12–16 ft. lbs. and 34–38 ft. lbs. on 240SX.

   b. Tighten the stabilizer bar bracket bolts to 22–29 ft. lbs. and 29–36 ft. lbs. on 240SX.

   c. Tighten the tension rod-to-transverse link nuts to 31–43 ft. lbs. On 240SX, torque the plain nuts to 65–80 ft. lbs. and the nuts with bushings and washers to 14–22 ft. lbs. Make sure to hold the connecting rod stationary.

   d. Tighten the tension rod-to-frame nut (bushing end) to 33–40 ft. lbs. Always use a new locknut when reconnecting the tension rod to the frame.

   e. Be certain the tension rod bushings are installed properly. Make sure the stabilizer bar ball joint socket is properly positioned.
   NOTE: *Never tighten any bolts or nuts to their final torque unless the vehicle is resting, unsupported, on the wheels.*

Stanza
Stanza Wagon 2WD and 4WD

NOTE: *On this service procedure, modify the steps to the correct application; perform only the necessary service steps.*

1. Raise and support the vehicle safely. Disconnect the parking brake cable at the equalizer on the Stanza Wagon (2WD).

2. On the Stanza Wagon (4WD), remove the mounting nuts for the transaxle support rod and the transaxle control rod.

3. Disconnect the front exhaust pipe at the manifold and position it aside (not required on Stanza car).

4. On the Stanza Wagon (4WD), matchmark the flanges and then separate the driveshaft from the transfer case.

5. Remove the stabilizer bar-to-transverse

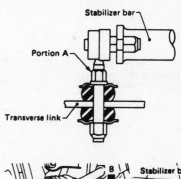

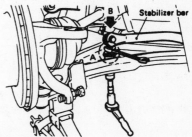

Stabilizer bar removal and installation—Stanza

View from B

O.K.   N.G.

Install stabilizer bar and joint socket in the correct position

link (lower, control arm) mounting bolts. Engage the flats of stabilizer bar connecting rod with a wrench to keep the rod from moving when removing (and installing) the bolts.

6. Matchmark the stabilizer bar to the mounting clamps.

7. Remove the stabilizer bar mounting clamp bolts and then pull the bar out, around the link and exhaust pipe.

8. Installation is the reverse of the removal procedure. Never tighten the mounting bolts unless the vehicle is resting on the ground with normal weight upon the wheels. Be sure the stabilizer bar ball joint socket is properly positioned.

Front Axle, Knuckle and Bearing
REMOVAL AND INSTALLATION
Stanza

1. Raise and support the front of the vehicle safely and remove the wheels.

2. Remove wheel bearing lock nut.

3. Remove brake cliper assembly. Make sure not to twist the brake hose.

4. Remove tie rod ball joint.

NOTE: *Cover axle boots with cloth so as not to damage them when removing driveshaft. Make a matching mark on strut housing and ajusting pin before removing them.*

5. Separate halfshaft from the knuckle by slightly tapping it.

6. Mark and remove the strut mounting bolts.

7. Remove lower ball joint from knuckle.

8. Remove knuckle from lower control arm.

To install:

NOTE: *To replace the wheel bearings and races they must be pressed in and out of the knuckle assembly. To pack the wheel bearings they will have to be removed from the knuckle assembly. Refer to the illustrations.*

9. Install the knuckle to the lower control arm and connect the ball joint, use a NEW retaining nut and cotter pin on ball joint assembly.

10. Connect the knuckle to the strut and to the halfshaft.

11. Install the tie rod ball joint, use a NEW cotter pin.

12. Install the brake caliper assembly.

13. Install the wheel bearing lock nut torque hub nut to 145–203 ft. lbs. (1982–87 Stanza with plain rotor assembly — see illustrations) and all other appications to 174–231 ft. lbs.

14. Install the front wheels. Check front end alignment.

Front Wheel Bearings
REMOVAL AND INSTALLATION
Rear Wheel Drive

NOTE: *After the wheel bearings have been removed or replaced or the front axle reas-*

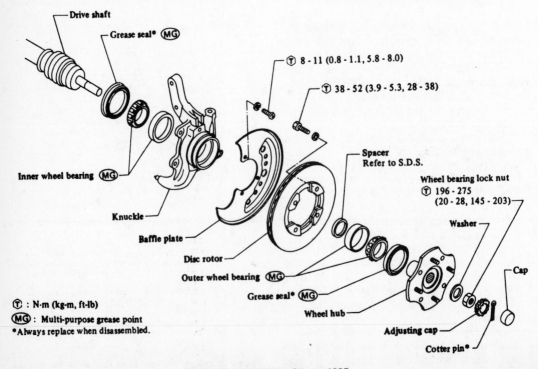

— Drive shaft
— Grease seal* (MG)
Ⓣ 8 - 11 (0.8 - 1.1, 5.8 - 8.0)
Ⓣ 38 - 52 (3.9 - 5.3, 28 - 38)
Inner wheel bearing (MG)
Knuckle
Baffle plate
Disc rotor
Outer wheel bearing (MG)
Grease seal* (MG)
Wheel hub
Spacer Refer to S.D.S.
Wheel bearing lock nut
Ⓣ 196 - 275
(20 - 28, 145 - 203)
Washer
Cap
Adjusting cap
Cotter pin*

Ⓣ : N·m (kg-m, ft-lb)
(MG) : Multi-purpose grease point
*Always replace when disassembled.

Front axle assembly—Stanza 1985

sembled, be sure to adjust wheel bearing preload. Refer to the adjustment procedure below. On the 1989–92 240SX there is just one wheel bearing, pressed into the hub and no adjusting cap. Review the complete service procedure.

1. Raise and support the vehicle safely.

2. Remove the front wheels and the brake caliper assemblies.

NOTE: *Brake hoses do not need to be disconnected from the brake caliper assemblies. Make sure the brake hoses are secure and do not let cailper assemblies hang unsupported from the vehicle.*

3. Work off center hub cap by using thin tool. If necessary tap around it with a soft hammer while removing.

4. Pry off cotter pin and take out adjusting cap and wheel bearing lock nut.

5. Remove wheel hub with disc brake rotor from spindle with bearings installed. Remove the outer bearing from the hub.

6. Remove inner bearing and grease seal

from hub using long brass drift pin or equivalent.

7. If it is necessary to replace the bearing outer races, drive them out of the hub with a brass drift pin and mallet.

8. Install the outer bearing race with a tool (tool number KV401021S0) until it seats in the hub flush.

NOTE: *Place a large glob of grease into the palm of one hand and push the bearing through it with a sliding motion. The grease must be forced through the side of the bearing and between each roller. Continue until the grease begins to ooze out the other side through the gaps between the rollers. The bearing must be completely packed with grease.*

9. Pack each wheel bearing with high temperature wheel bearing grease. Pack hub and hub cap with the recommended wheel bearing grease up to shaded portions.

10. Install the inner bearing and grease seal in the proper position in the hub.

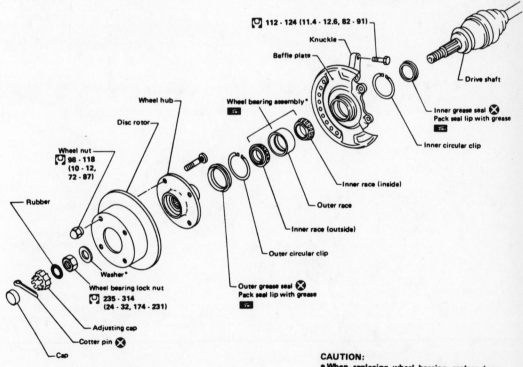

Front axle assembly—Stanza 1987

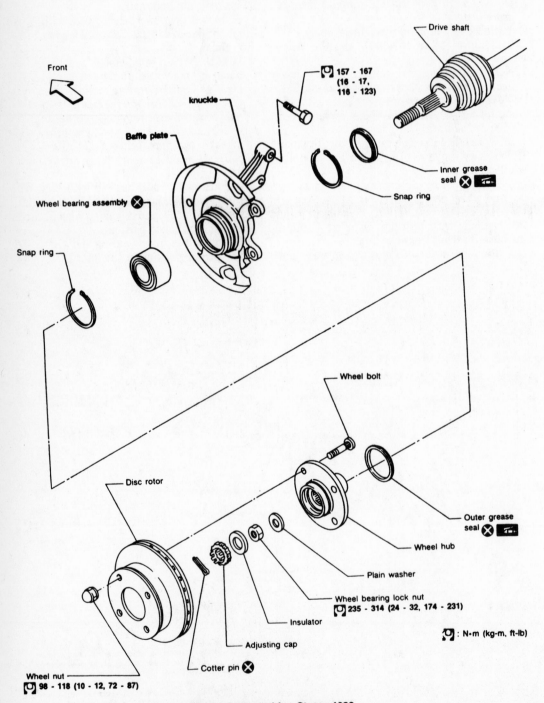

Front

Drive shaft

knuckle

157 - 167
(16 - 17,
116 - 123)

Baffle plate

Inner grease
seal

Snap ring

Wheel bearing assembly

Snap ring

Wheel bolt

Disc rotor

Outer grease
seal

Wheel hub

Plain washer

Wheel bearing lock nut
235 - 314 (24 - 32, 174 - 231)

Insulator

: N·m (kg-m, ft-lb)

Adjusting cap

Cotter pin

Wheel nut
98 - 118 (10 - 12, 72 - 87)

Front axle assembly—Stanza 1992

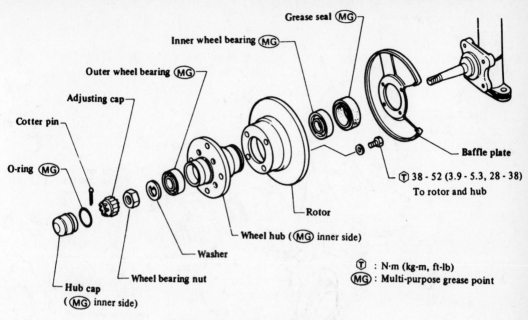

Grease seal (MG)

Inner wheel bearing (MG)

Outer wheel bearing (MG)

Adjusting cap

Cotter pin

O-ring (MG)

Hub cap
((MG) inner side)

Wheel bearing nut

Washer

Wheel hub ((MG) inner side)

Rotor

Baffle plate

(T) 38 - 52 (3.9 - 5.3, 28 - 38)
To rotor and hub

(T) : N·m (kg-m, ft-lb)
(MG) : Multi-purpose grease point

Front axle assembly—200SX 1982–83

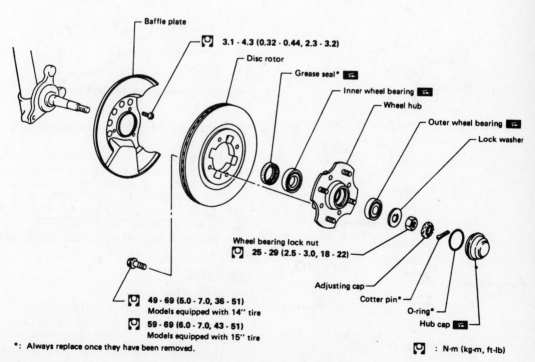

Baffle plate

3.1 - 4.3 (0.32 - 0.44, 2.3 - 3.2)

Disc rotor

Grease seal*

Inner wheel bearing

Wheel hub

Outer wheel bearing

Lock washer

Wheel bearing lock nut
25 - 29 (2.5 - 3.0, 18 - 22)

Adjusting cap

Cotter pin*

O-ring*

Hub cap

49 - 69 (5.0 - 7.0, 36 - 51)
Models equipped with 14" tire

59 - 69 (6.0 - 7.0, 43 - 51)
Models equipped with 15" tire

*: Always replace once they have been removed.

: N·m (kg-m, ft-lb)

Front axle assembly—200SX 1984–88

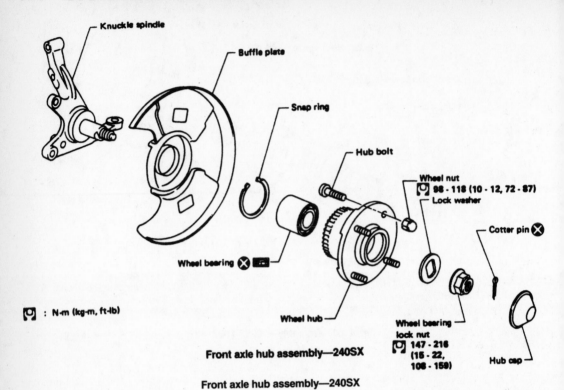

Front axle hub assembly—240SX

Front axle hub assembly—240SX

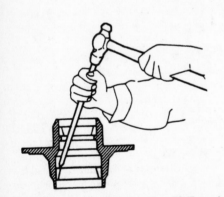

Removing inner front wheel bearing—RWD model

Packing front wheel bearings—RWD model

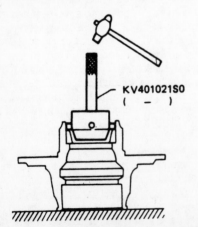

KV401021S0
(–)

Installing race in hub with special tool—RWD model

11. Install the wheel hub with disc brake rotor to the spindle.

12. Install the outer wheel bearing, lock washer, wheel bearing lock nut, adjusting cap, cotter pin (always use a new cotter pin and O-ring for installation after adjustment), spread cotter pin then install the O-ring and dust cap.

13. Install the brake caliper assemblies and bleed brakes if necessary. Install the front wheels.

ADJUSTMENT

Rear Wheel Drive

NOTE: *Before adjustment clean all parts. Apply wheel bearing grease sparingly to the threaded portion of spindle and contact surface between lock washer and outer wheel bearing.*

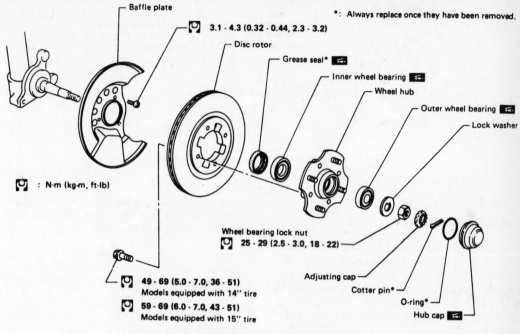

Baffle plate

🔧 3.1 - 4.3 (0.32 - 0.44, 2.3 - 3.2)

*: Always replace once they have been removed.

Disc rotor

Grease seal* 🔧

Inner wheel bearing 🔧

Wheel hub

Outer wheel bearing 🔧

Lock washer

🔧 : N·m (kg-m, ft-lb)

Wheel bearing lock nut
🔧 25 - 29 (2.5 - 3.0, 18 - 22)

Adjusting cap

Cotter pin*

O-ring*

Hub cap 🔧

🔧 49 - 69 (5.0 - 7.0, 36 - 51)
Models equipped with 14" tire

🔧 59 - 69 (6.0 - 7.0, 43 - 51)
Models equipped with 15" tire

Installing grease seal—RWD model

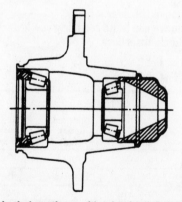

Pack shaded portions with wheel bearing grease—RWD model

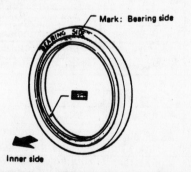

Mark: Bearing side

Inner side

Spread cotter pin after wheel bearing installation—RWD model

1. Raise and support the vehicle safely, remove the front wheels and the brake caliper assemblies.

2. Torque wheel bearing lock nut to 18–22 ft. lbs.

NOTE: *On the 1989–92 240SX model, the wheel bearing lock nut torque is 108–159 ft. lbs. On this model, make sure that the wheel bearing is properly seated and then just torque it to the specification. There is just one wheel bearing and no adjusting cap on this model, just use a new cotter pin after the torque spsecification is reached.*

3. Turn the wheel hub several times in both directions to seat wheel bearing correctly.

4. Again tighten wheel bearing nut to specification 18–22 ft. lbs.

5. Loosen lock nut approximately 60°. Install adjusting cap and align groove of nut with hole in spindle. If alignment cannot be obtained, change position of adjusting cap. Also, if alignment cannot be obtained, loosen lock nut slightly but not more than 15°.

NOTE: *Measure the wheel bearing preload and axial play. Repeat above procedures until correct starting torque is obtained.*

6. Spread the cotter pin and install hub cap with a new O-ring.

7. Install cailper assemblies and front wheels.

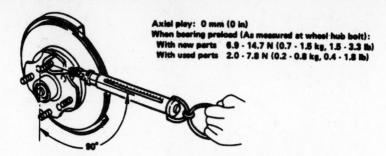

Axial play: 0 mm (0 in)
When bearing preload (As measured at wheel hub bolt):
With new parts   6.9 - 14.7 N (0.7 - 1.5 kg, 1.5 - 3.3 lb)
With used parts 2.0 - 7.8 N (0.2 - 0.8 kg, 0.4 - 1.8 lb)

Measure wheel bearing preload and axial play—RWD model

Front End Alignment
CASTER AND CAMBER

Caster is the forward or rearward tilt of the upper end of the kingpin, or the upper ball joint, which results in a slight tilt of the steering axis forward or backward. Rearward tilt is referred to as a positive caster, while forward tilt is referred to as negative caster.

Camber is the inward or outward tilt from the vertical, measured in degrees of the front wheels at the top. An outward tilt gives the wheel positive camber. Proper camber is critical to assure even tire wear.

TOE

Toe is the amount, measured in a fraction of an inch or millimeters, that the wheels are closer together at one end than the other. Toe-in means that the front wheels are closer together at the front than the rear. Toe-out means the rears are closer than the front.

REAR SUSPENSION

Coil Springs
REMOVAL AND INSTALLATION

200SX (4-Link Type Suspension)

1. Raise the car and support it with jackstands.
2. Support the center of the differential with a jack.
3. Remove the rear wheels.
4. Remove the bolts securing the lower ends of the shock absorbers.

WHEEL ALIGNMENT SPECIFICATIONS

Year	Model		Caster Range (deg.)	Caster Preferred Setting (deg.)	Camber Range (deg.)	Camber Preferred Setting (deg.)	Toe-In (in.)
1982–83	200SX		$1^3/_4$–$3^1/_4$	$2^1/_2$	$-^{11}/_{16}$–$^{13}/_{16}$	$^1/_{16}$	$^3/_{64}$
1982–84	Stanza	(Front)	$^{11}/_{16}$–$2^3/_{16}$	—	$-^3/_4$–$^3/_4$	—	0–$^5/_{64}$
		(Rear)	—	—	0–$1^1/_2$	—	$^{13}/_{64}$–$^5/_{16}$
1984	200SX		$2^3/_4$–$4^1/_4$	$3^1/_2$	$-^3/_8$–$1^1/_{16}$	$1^7/_8$	$^3/_{64}$
1985–86	200SX		$2^3/_4$–$4^1/_4$	$3^1/_2$	$-^1/_4$–$1^1/_{20}$	$^1/_3$	$^3/_8$
	Stanza	(Front)	$^{11}/_{16}$–$2^3/_{16}$	—	$-^7/_{16}$–$1^1/_{16}$	—	0–$^1/_{16}$
		(Rear)	—	—	0–$1^1/_2$	—	$^9/_{32}$–$^1/_4$
1987–88	200SX	(Front)	$2^3/_4$–$4^1/_4$	$3^1/_2$P	$^7/_{16}$N–$1^1/_{16}$P	$^1/_4$P	$^1/_{32}$N–$^1/_{32}$P
		(Rear)	—	—	$1^1/_4$N–$1^1/_4$P	$^1/_2$N	$^5/_{64}$N–0
	Stanza	(Front)	$1^1/_4$–$2^3/_4$	—	$-^7/_{16}$–$^1/_{16}$	—	$^1/_{32}$–$^1/_8$
		(Rear)	—	—	$-1^3/_{16}$–$^5/_{16}$	—	$^5/_{16}$–$^3/_{32}$
1989–92	240SX	(Front)	6P–7P	$6^1/_2$P	1N–0	$^1/_2$N	0
		(Rear)	—	—	1N–0	$^1/_2$N	0
	Stanza	(Front)	$^5/_8$–$2^1/_{16}$	—	$-^1/_2$–1	—	$^1/_{16}$–$^1/_8$
		(Rear)	—	—	$-1^5/_{16}$–$^3/_{16}$	—	0

NOTE: The minimum and maximum settings that are specified are a guide to use when checking alignment specifications.

5. Lower the jack under the differential slowly and carefully and remove the coil springs (note location of spring seat for correct installation) after they are fully extended.

6. Installation is in the reverse order of removal.

200SX (I.R.S. Type Suspension)

1. Set a suitable spring compressor on the coil spring.

2. Jack up the rear end of the car.

3. Compress the coil spring until it is of sufficient length to be removed. Remove the spring.

4. When installing the spring, be sure the upper and lower spring seat rubbers are not twisted and have not slipped off when installing the coil spring.

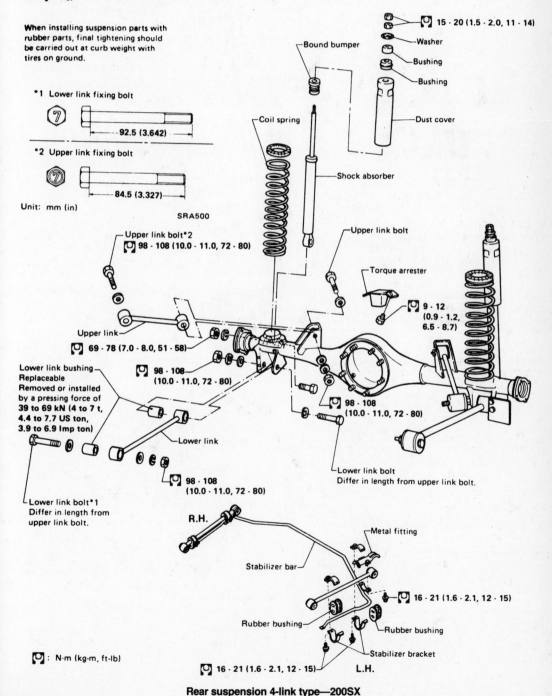

When installing suspension parts with rubber parts, final tightening should be carried out at curb weight with tires on ground.

*1 Lower link fixing bolt
92.5 (3.642)

*2 Upper link fixing bolt
84.5 (3.327)

Unit: mm (in)

SRA500

15 - 20 (1.5 - 2.0, 11 - 14)
Washer
Bushing
Bushing
Dust cover

Bound bumper

Coil spring

Shock absorber

Upper link bolt

Upper link bolt*2
98 - 108 (10.0 - 11.0, 72 - 80)

Torque arrester

9 - 12 (0.9 - 1.2, 6.5 - 8.7)

Upper link
69 - 78 (7.0 - 8.0, 51 - 58)

98 - 108 (10.0 - 11.0, 72 - 80)

Lower link bushing
Replaceable
Removed or installed by a pressing force of 39 to 69 kN (4 to 7 t, 4.4 to 7.7 US ton, 3.9 to 6.9 Imp ton)

Lower link

98 - 108 (10.0 - 11.0, 72 - 80)

98 - 108 (10.0 - 11.0, 72 - 80)

Lower link bolt
Differ in length from upper link bolt.

Lower link bolt*1
Differ in length from upper link bolt.

R.H.

Metal fitting

Stabilizer bar

16 - 21 (1.6 - 2.1, 12 - 15)

Rubber bushing

Rubber bushing

Stabilizer bracket

: N·m (kg-m, ft-lb)

16 - 21 (1.6 - 2.1, 12 - 15)   L.H.

Rear suspension 4-link type—200SX

When installing suspension parts with rubber parts,
final tightening needs to be carried out under
unladen condition* with tires on ground.
* Fuel, radiator coolant and engine oil full.
Spare tire, jack, hand tools and mats in
designed position.

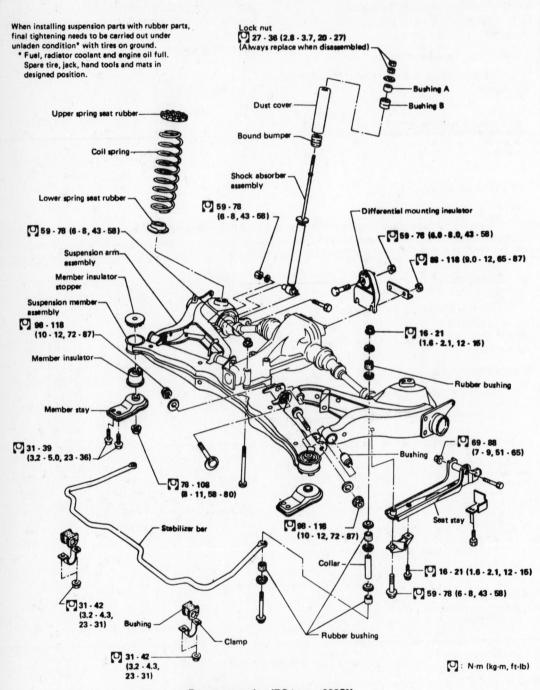

Lock nut
27 - 36 (2.8 - 3.7, 20 - 27)
(Always replace when disassembled)

Bushing A

Bushing B

Dust cover

Bound bumper

Upper spring seat rubber

Coil spring

Shock absorber
assembly

Lower spring seat rubber

59 - 78
(6 - 8, 43 - 58)

Differential mounting insulator

59 - 78 (6 - 8, 43 - 58)

59 - 78 (6.0 - 8.0, 43 - 58)

Suspension arm
assembly

88 - 118 (9.0 - 12, 65 - 87)

Member insulator
stopper

Suspension member
assembly

96 - 118
(10 - 12, 72 - 87)

16 - 21
(1.6 - 2.1, 12 - 15)

Member insulator

Rubber bushing

Member stay

Bushing

69 - 88
(7 - 9, 51 - 65)

31 - 39
(3.2 - 5.0, 23 - 36)

78 - 108
(8 - 11, 58 - 80)

Seat stay

Stabilizer bar

98 - 118
(10 - 12, 72 - 87)

Collar

16 - 21 (1.6 - 2.1, 12 - 15)

59 - 78 (6 - 8, 43 - 58)

31 - 42
(3.2 - 4.3,
23 - 31)

Bushing

Clamp

Rubber bushing

31 - 42
(3.2 - 4.3,
23 - 31)

: N·m (kg-m, ft-lb)

Rear suspension IRS type—200SX

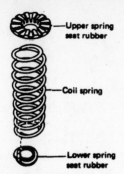

Rear coil spring assembly IRS suspension—200SX

Shock Absorber

REMOVAL AND INSTALLATION

200SX

1. Open the trunk and remove the cover panel if necessary to expose the shock mounts. Pry off the mount covers, if so equipped.
2. Remove the nut holding the top of the shock absorber. Unbolt the bottom of the shock absorber.
3. Remove the shock absorber.
4. Installation is the reverse of removal. Make sure rear shock retaining bushings and washer are installed in the correct position.

Stanza 2WD Wagon

1. Raise and support the rear of the vehicle on jackstands.

2. Remove the upper nut and the lower mounting bolt form the shock absorber.
3. Remove the shock absorber from the vehicle.
4. To install, reverse the removal procedures. Make sure rear shock retaining bushings and washer are installed in the correct position.

TESTING

Shock absorbers require replacement if the vehicle fails to recover quickly after a large bump, if there is a tendency for the vehicle to sway or if the suspension is overly susceptible to vibration.

A good way to test the shocks is to apply downward pressure to one corner of the vehicle until it is moving up and down for almost the full suspension travel, then release it and watch the recovery. If the vehicle bounces slightly about one more time and then comes to rest, the shocks are serviceable. If the vehicle goes on bouncing, the shocks require replacement.

Rear MacPherson Strut

REMOVAL AND INSTALLATION

240SX

1. Block the front wheels.
2. Raise and support the vehicle safely.
NOTE: *The vehicle should be far enough off the ground so the rear spring does not support any weight.*

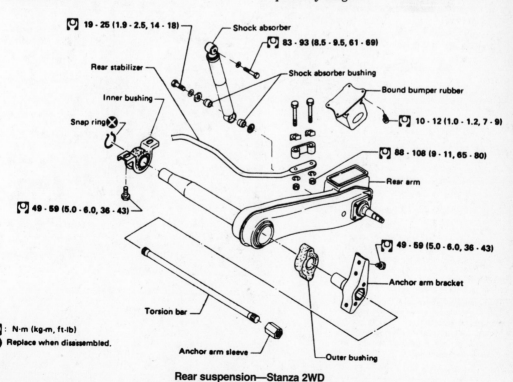

Rear suspension—Stanza 2WD

3. Working inside the luggage compartment, turn and remove the caps above the strut mounts. Remove the strut mounting nuts.

4. Remove the mounting bolt for the strut at the lower arm (transverse link) and then lift out the strut.

5. Installation is in the reverse order of removal. Install the upper end first and secure with the nuts snugged down but not fully tight-ened. Attach the lower end of the strut to the transverse link and the tighten the upper nuts to 12–14 ft. lbs. Tighten the lower mounting bolt to 65–80 ft. lbs.

1982–86 Stanza

1. Raise and support the rear of the vehicle on jackstands.

2. Remove the wheel.

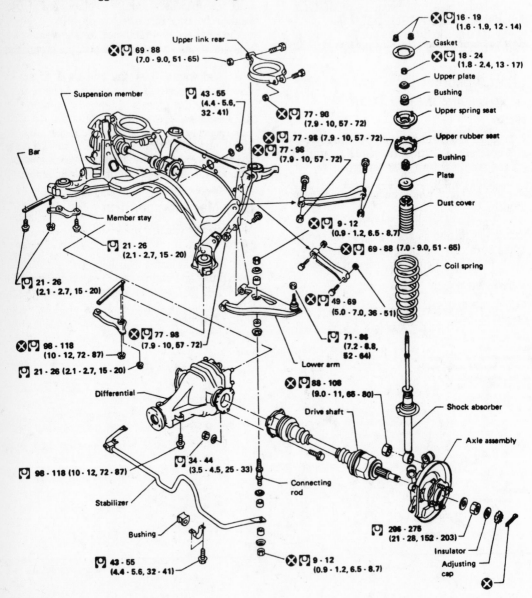

CAUTION:
Do not jack up at lower arm.

When installing rubber parts, final tightening must be carried out under unladen condition* with tires on ground.
* Fuel, radiator coolant and engine oil full. Spare tire, jack, hand tools and mats in designated positions.

⊡ : N·m (kg-m, ft-lb)

Rear suspension—240SX

3. Disconnect the brake tube and parking brake cable.

4. If necessary, remove the brake assembly and wheel bearing.

5. Disconnect the parallel links and radius rod assembly from the strut or knuckle.

6. Support the strut with a jackstand.

7. Remove the strut upper end nuts and then remove the strut from the vehicle.

8. Install the strut assembly to the vehicle and tighten the strut-to-parallel link nuts to 65–87 ft. lbs., the strut-to-radius rod nuts to 54–69 ft. lbs. and the strut-to-body nuts to 23–31 ft. lbs.

9. Reconnect the brake tube and parking brake cable.

10. Install the wheel.

1987 and Later Stanza

1. Remove wheel and unclip the rear brake line at the strut. Unbolt and remove the brake assembly, wheel bearings and backing plate. Position the brake caliper out of the way and suspend it so as not to stress the brake line.

2. Remove the radius rod mounting bolt, radius rod mounting bracket.

3. Remove the 2 parallel link mounting bolts.

4. Remove the rear seat and parcel shelf.

5. Position a floor jack under the strut and raise it just enought to support the strut.

6. Remove the 3 upper strut mounting nuts and then lift out the strut.

7. Install the strut assembly in the vehicle. Tighten all bolts sufficiently to safely support the vehicle and then lower the car to the ground so it rests on its own weight. Tighten the upper strut mounting nuts to 23–31 ft. lbs., the radius rod bracket bolts to 43–58 ft. lbs. and the parallel link mounting bolts to 65–87 ft. lbs.

8. Install the brake caliper.

9. Install the backing plate, brake assembly and wheel bearings.

10. Install the wheel.

Stanza 4WD Wagon

1. Block the front wheels.

2. Raise and support the rear of the vehicle with jackstands.

3. Position a floor jack under the transverse link on the side of the strut to be removed. Raise it just enough to support the strut.

4. Open the rear of the car and remove the 3 nuts that attach the top of the strut to the body.

5. Remove the wheel.

6. Remove the brake line from its bracket and position it out of the way.

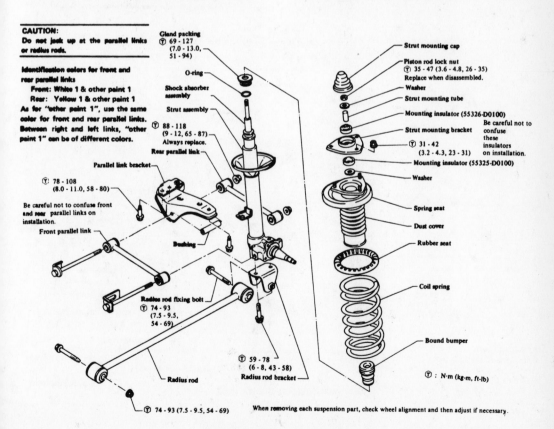

CAUTION:
Do not jack up at the parallel links or radius rods.

Identification colors for front and rear parallel links
Front: White 1 & other paint 1
Rear: Yellow 1 & other paint 1
As for "other paint 1", use the same color for front and rear parallel links. Between right and left links, "other paint 1" can be of different colors.

Gland packing
Ⓣ 69 - 127 (7.0 - 13.0, 51 - 94)

O-ring

Shock absorber assembly

Strut assembly
Ⓣ 88 - 118 (9 - 12, 65 - 87) Always replace.

Rear parallel link

Parallel link bracket

Ⓣ 78 - 108 (8.0 - 11.0, 58 - 80)

Be careful not to confuse front and rear parallel links on installation.

Front parallel link

Bushing

Radius rod fixing bolt
Ⓣ 74 - 93 (7.5 - 9.5, 54 - 69)

Ⓣ 59 - 78 (6 - 8, 43 - 58)

Radius rod

Radius rod bracket

Ⓣ 74 - 93 (7.5 - 9.5, 54 - 69)

Strut mounting cap

Piston rod lock nut
Ⓣ 35 - 47 (3.6 - 4.8, 26 - 35) Replace when disassembled.

Washer

Strut mounting tube

Mounting insulator (55326-D0100)

Strut mounting bracket

Ⓣ 31 - 42 (3.2 - 4.3, 23 - 31)

Be careful not to confuse these insulators on installation.

Mounting insulator (55325-D0100)

Washer

Spring seat

Dust cover

Rubber seat

Coil spring

Bound bumper

Ⓣ : N·m (kg-m, ft-lb)

When removing each suspension part, check wheel alignment and then adjust if necessary.

Rear suspension—Stanza 1985

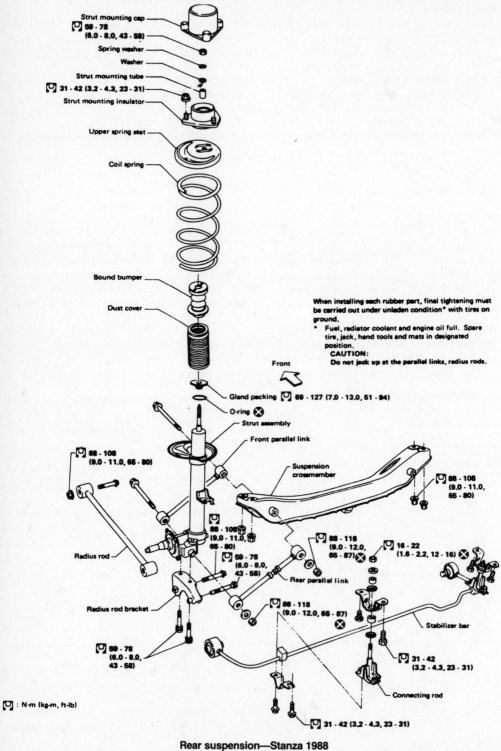

Strut mounting cap

59 - 78
(6.0 - 8.0, 43 - 58)

Spring washer

Washer

Strut mounting tube

31 - 42 (3.2 - 4.3, 23 - 31)

Strut mounting insulator

Upper spring seat

Coil spring

Bound bumper

Dust cover

When installing each rubber part, final tightening must
be carried out under unladen condition* with tires on
ground.
* Fuel, radiator coolant and engine oil full. Spare
tire, jack, hand tools and mats in designated
position.
CAUTION:
Do not jack up at the parallel links, radius rods.

Front

Gland packing   69 - 127 (7.0 - 13.0, 51 - 94)

O-ring ⊗

Strut assembly

Front parallel link

Suspension
crossmember

88 - 108
(9.0 - 11.0, 65 - 80)

88 - 108
(9.0 - 11.0,
65 - 80)

88 - 108
(9.0 - 11.0,
65 - 80)

59 - 78
(6.0 - 8.0,
43 - 58)

88 - 118
(9.0 - 12.0,
65 - 87) ⊗

16 - 22
(1.6 - 2.2, 12 - 16) ⊗

Radius rod

Rear parallel link

Radius rod bracket

88 - 118
(9.0 - 12.0, 65 - 87)
⊗

Stabilizer bar

59 - 78
(6.0 - 8.0,
43 - 58)

31 - 42
(3.2 - 4.3, 23 - 31)

Connecting rod

: N·m (kg-m, ft-lb)

31 - 42 (3.2 - 4.3, 23 - 31)

Rear suspension—Stanza 1988

7. Remove the 2 lower strut-to-knuckle mounting bolts.

8. Carefully lower the floor jack and remove the strut.

9. Install the strut assembly in the vehicle. Final tightening of the strut mounting bolts should take place with the wheels on the ground and the vehicle unladen. Tighten the upper strut-to-body nuts to 33–40 ft. lbs. Tighten the lower strut-to-knuckle bolts to 111–120 ft. lbs.

10. Connect the brake line.

11. Install the wheel.

OVERHAUL

NOTE: *It is necessary throughout strut work to keep all parts absolutely clean.*

1. Matchmark the strut mounting insulator for reassembly at the same angle.

2. Install a spring compressor and compress the spring until the spring insulator can be turned by hand.

3. Remove the rebound stop locknut so the threads on the piston rod will not be damaged. Use a tool such as ST35490000 (J26083) or equivalent to remove the packing. Then, force the piston rod downward until it bottoms.

When installing rubber parts, final tightening must be carried out under unladen condition* with tires on ground.
* Fuel, radiator coolant and engine oil full. Spare tire, jack, hand tools and mats in designated positions.
CAUTION:
Do not jack up at the parallel links or radius rods.

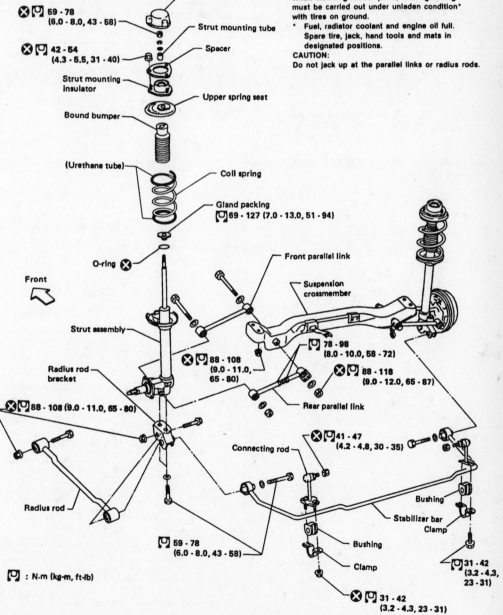

Rear suspension—Stanza 1992

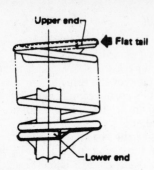

Correct position for spring-rear strut assembly—240SX

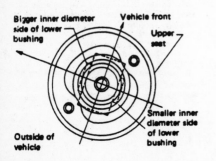

Correct position for upper spring seat-rear strut assembly—240SX

4. Withdraw the piston rod and guide from the strut cylinder.

5. Pour the correct amount of an approved strut fluid into the strut. Use 11.2 fl. oz. for non-adjustable struts and 11.0 fl. oz. for adjustable struts.

6. Lubricate the sealing lip of the gland packing. Tape over the strut rod threads and then install the gland packing. Tighten it with the special wrench. Torque to 65–80 ft. lbs.

7. Pump the strut rod up and down several times with it in its normal vertical position and upside down to remove air bubbles.

8. Install the upper spring seat and mounting insulator. Make sure the matchmark on the insulator corresponds with the location hole on the upper spring seat.

9. Position the spring so its end rests against the stop on the lower seat. Install the remaining spring retaining parts including the piston rod self locking nut (torque to 43–58 ft. lbs.) and the upper nut that retains the flexible washer (torque to 26–35 ft. lbs.).

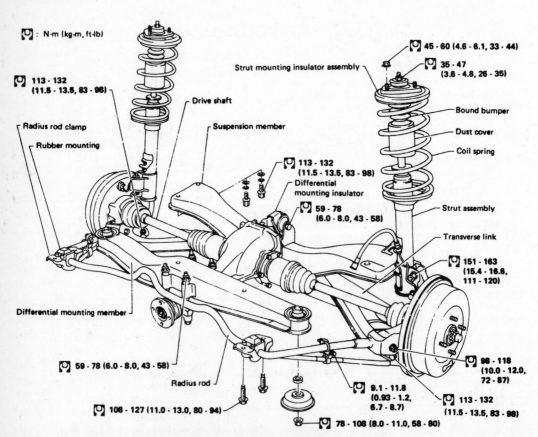

Rear axle and rear suspension—Stanza Wagon 4WD

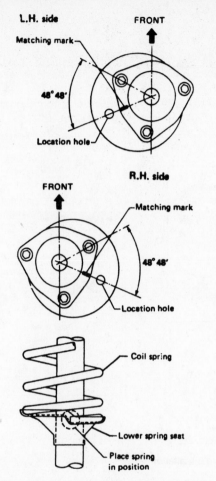

Correct position for upper spring seat and spring—
Stanza

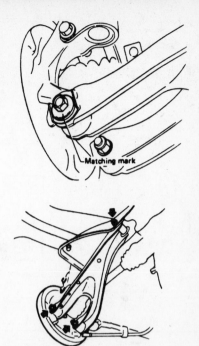

Transverse link removal—Stanza Wagon 4WD

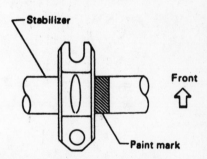

Stabilizer bar installation—Stanza 4WD

Transverse Link

REMOVAL AND INSTALLATION

Stanza Wagon 4WD

1. Raise and support the rear of the vehicle on jackstands.
2. Before removing transverse link retaining bolts, matchmark the toe-in adjustment.
3. Remove the link retaining bolts.
4. Installation is the reverse of the removal procedure. Final tightening of the transverse link mounting bolts should take place with the wheels on the ground and the vehicle unladen. Check rear alignment.

Stabilizer Bar

REMOVAL AND INSTALLATION

Stanza Wagon 4WD

1. Raise and support the rear of the vehicle on jackstands.
2. Before removing stabilizer retaining bolts, matchmark the brackets.

3. Remove the bracket retaining bolts. Remove the stabilizer bar.
4. Installation is the reverse of the removal procedure. Make sure the stabilizer retaining brackets are even spaced when installed.

Rear Wheel Bearings

REMOVAL AND INSTALLATION

1982–89 Stanza
Stanza Wagon 2WD

1. Raise and support the vehicle safely.
2. Remove the rear wheel. Release the parking brake.
3. Work off center hub cap by using thin tool. If necessary tap around it with a soft hammer while removing.
4. Pry off cotter pin and take out adjusting cap and wheel bearing lock nut.

NOTE: *During removal, be careful to avoid damaging O ring in dust cap if so equipped.*

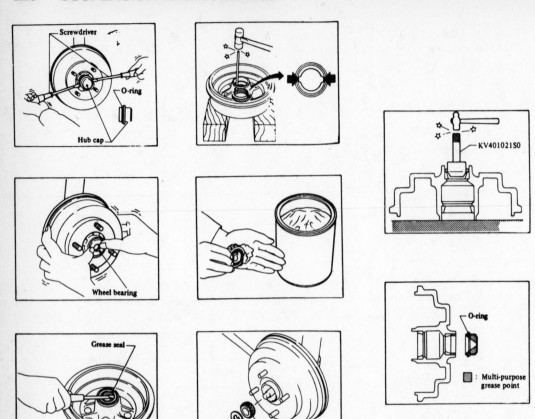

Rear wheel bearing and race: removal and installation—Stanza 1982–89

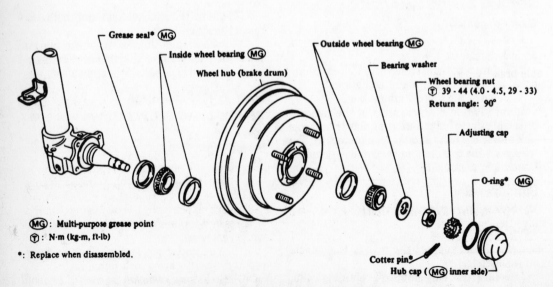

(MG) : Multi-purpose grease point

(T) : N·m (kg-m, ft-lb)

*: Replace when disassembled.

Rear axle assembly—Stanza 1982–86

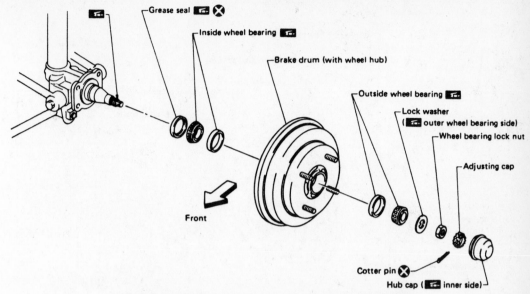

Grease seal

Inside wheel bearing

Brake drum (with wheel hub)

Outside wheel bearing

Lock washer
(outer wheel bearing side)

Wheel bearing lock nut

Adjusting cap

Front

Cotter pin

Hub cap (inner side)

Rear axle assembly—Stanza 1987–89 and Stanza Wagon 2WD

5. Remove rear drum with outer bearing and washer and inner bearing and seal inside the drum.

6. Remove inner bearing and seal from drum using long brass drift pin or equivalent.

To install:

7. Install the inner bearing (and seal in the correct position) assembly in the brake drum and install the drum on the vehicle.

NOTE: *The rear wheel bearings must be adjusted after installation. If a one-piece bearing is used, torque the wheel bearing lock nut.*

8. Install the outer bearing assembly, wheel bearing lock nut, adjusting cap and NEW cotter pin. Adjust the wheel bearings.

9. Install the center cap and the wheel assembly. To remove the wheel bearing races knock them out of the brake drum using a suitable brass punch.

1990–92 Stanza

NOTE: *On these vehicles a one-piece bearing hub assembly is used. This assembly does not require maintenance or adjustment after installation. If any problem is found (noise, excessive drag etc.), replace the wheel hub asembly.*

1. Raise and support the vehicle safely. Remove the rear wheel.

2. Remove the brake caliper (brake hose does not have to be disconnected from the caliper) and reposition.

3. Remove the wheel bearing locknut. Remove the bearing hub assembly.

4. Installation is the reverse of the removal procedure. Tighten wheel bearing locknut to 137–188 ft. lbs. Check that wheel bearing operates smoothly.

Stanza Wagon 4WD
240SX

NOTE: *This assembly does not require maintenance or adjustment after installation. If any problem is present, replace the component.*

1. Raise and support the vehicle safely.

2. Remove wheel bearing lock nut while depressing brake pedal.

3. Disconnect brake hydraulic line and parking brake cable.

4. Separate driveshaft from knuckle by slightly tapping it with suitable tool. Cover axle boots with waste cloth so as not to damage them when removing driveshaft.

5. Remove all knuckle retaining bolts and nuts. Make a match mark before removing adjusting pin if so equipped.

6. Remove knuckle and inner and outer circular clips. Remove wheel bearings.

To install:

NOTE: *To remove the wheel bearing races knock them out of the knuckle using a brass punch.*

7. Install the knuckle with wheel bearings to the driveshaft.

8. Connect brake hydraulic line and parking brake cable.

9. Install the wheel bearing lock nut.

10. Bleed brakes. Check rear alignment.

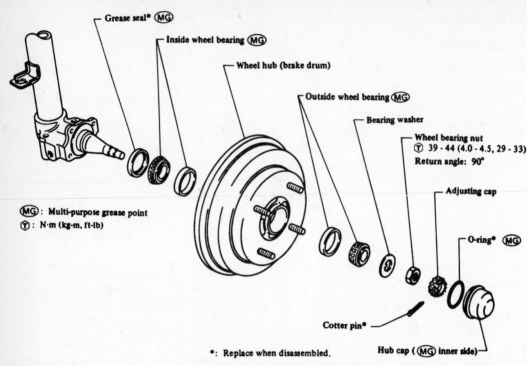

MG : Multi-purpose grease point
Ⓣ : N·m (kg-m, ft-lb)

*: Replace when disassembled.

Rear axle assembly—Stanza 1990–92

ADJUSTMENT

NOTE: *No adjustment is necessary on Stanza Wagon 4WD, 240SX and 1990–92 Stanza (one-piece bearing and hub assembly).*

Make sure all parts are cleaned. Apply multi-purpose grease sparingly to rubbing surface of the spindle, between surface of lock washer and outer wheel bearing, grease seal and dust cap.

1. Raise the rear of the vehicle and support it on jackstands.
2. Remove the wheel.
3. Remove the bearing dust cap with a pair of channel locks pliers or equivalent.
4. Remove the cotter pin and retaining nut cap, dispose of the cotter pin.
5. On 1982–86 Stanza models – tighten the wheel bearing locknut 29–33 ft. lbs.
On 1987–89 Stanza and Stanza Wagon 2WD – tighten the wheel bearing locknut 18–25 ft. lbs.
6. Rotate the drum back and forth a few revolutions to seat wheel bearing.
On 1987–89 Stanza and Stanza Wagon 2WD – loosen wheel bearing locknut so that the preload becomes 0 then torque to 6.5–8.7 ft. lbs. turn wheel hub several times in both directions and retorque to 6.5–8.7 ft. lbs.
7. On 1982–86 Stanza only, after turning the wheel, recheck the torque (29–33 ft. lbs. is

specification for these vehicles) of the nut, then loosen it 90° from its position.
8. Install the retaining nut cap. Align the cotter pin holes in the nut cap with hole in the spindle by tighten the nut no more than 15° to align the holes.
9. Install the NEW cotter pin, bend up its ends and install the dust cap.

Rear End Alignment
1984–88 200SX

The rear camber is preset at the factory and cannot be adjusted. The vehicle requires only rear toe adjustment.

1989–92 240SX

The rear camber and rear toe can be adjust on this model.

Stanza

The camber is preset at the factory and cannot be adjusted; if the camber alignment is not within specifications, check the associated parts, then repair or replace them. The only adjustment that can be performed is setting the toe.

STEERING

Steering Wheel

REMOVAL AND INSTALLATION

1. Position the wheels in the straight ahead direction. The steering wheel should be right side up and level.

2. Disconnect the battery ground cable.

3. Look at the back of your steering wheel. If there are countersunk screws in the back of the spokes, remove the screws and pull of the horn pad. Some models have a horn wire running from the pad to the steering wheel. Disconnect it. There are other types of horn buttons or rings. The first simply pulls off. The second, which is usually a large, semitriangular pad, must be pushed up, then pulled off. The third must be pushed in and turned clockwise.

On newer models, if it is hard to pull out horn pad, temporarily loosen fixing screw (behind back of steering wheel) of horn pad retaining spring.

4. Remove the rest of the horn switching mechanism, noting the relative location of the parts. Remove the mechanism only if it hinders subsequent wheel removal procedures.

5. Matchmark the top of the steering column shaft and the steering wheel flange.

6. Remove the attaching nut and remove the steering wheel with a puller.

NOTE: *Do not strike the shaft with a hammer, which may cause the column to collapse.*

7. Install the steering wheel in the reverse order of removal, aligning the punch marks. Coat the entire surface of the turn signal canceling pin and the horn contact slip ring with multipurpose grease. Do not drive or hammer the wheel into place, or you may cause the collapsible steering column to compress, in which case you'll have to buy a whole new steering column unit.

8. Torque the steering wheel nut to specifications. Reinstall the horn button, pad, or ring. Check system for proper operation.

Steering wheel retaining nut torque specification:

- 1982–83 200SX – 28–36 ft. lbs.
- 1982–86 Stanza – 27–38 ft. lbs.
- 1984–88 200SX and 1987–92 Stanza – 22–29 ft. lbs.
- 1989–92 240SX – 22–29 ft. lbs.

Turn Signal/Combination Switch

REMOVAL AND INSTALLATION

1. Disconnect the battery ground cable.

2. Remove the steering wheel as previously outlined. Observe the caution on the collapsible steering column.

3. Remove the steering column cover(s).

4. Disconnect the electrical connections from the combination switch assembly.

NOTE: *On most model vehicles, the control (lighting, wiper and washer, hazard and cruise control set) switches can be replaced without removing the combination base.*

5. To remove the combination switch base, remove the base attaching screw and turn after pushing on it.

6. Install the switch/combination base in the proper position. The switch base has a tab which must fit into a hole in the steering shaft in order for the system to return the switch to the neutral position after the turn has been made. Be sure to align the tab and the hole when installing.

7. Install the steering wheel and steering column cover(s) – observe steering wheel retaining nut torque upon installation.

8. Reconnect the battery cable. Turn key to the ON position and check system for proper operation. Make sure that the turn signals will cancel after the vehicle has made a turn.

Ignition Lock/Switch

REMOVAL AND INSTALLATION

The steering lock/ignition switch/warning buzzer switch assembly is attached to the steering column by special screws or bolts whose heads shear off during installation. The screws must be drilled out to remove the assembly or removed with an appropriate tool.

The ignition switch or warning switch can be replaced without removing the assembly. The

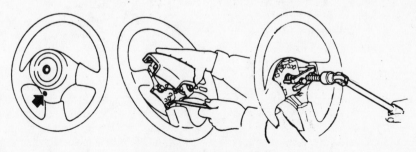

Removing the steering wheel

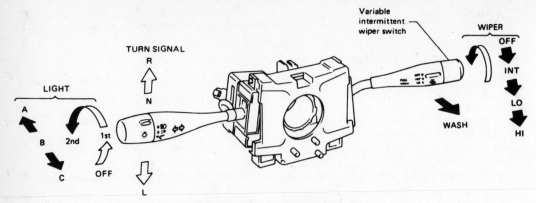

Combination switch operation

ignition switch is on the back of the assembly, and the warning switch on the side.

1. Disconnect the negative battery cable.
2. Remove the steering wheel, steering column cover(s) and combination switch.
3. Disconnect the switch wiring.
4. Lower the steering column, as required.
5. Break the self-shear screws with a drill or other appropriate tool.
6. Remove the steering lock from the column.

Ignition lock removal

To install:

7. Install the steering lock onto the column with new self-shear bolts or screws. Tighten the bolts or screws until the heads shear off.
8. Raise and secure the steering column.
9. Install the combination switch, steering column cover(s) and steering wheel.
10. Connect the negative battery cable.

Steering Column
REMOVAL AND INSTALLATION

1. Disconnect the negative battery cable.
2. Remove the steering wheel.
3. Remove the steering column covers.
4. Disconnect the combination switch and steering lock switch wiring.
5. Remove most of the steering column support bracket and clamp nuts and bolts. Leave a few of the fasteners loosely installed to support the column while disconnecting it from the steering gear.
6. Remove the bolt from the column lower joint.

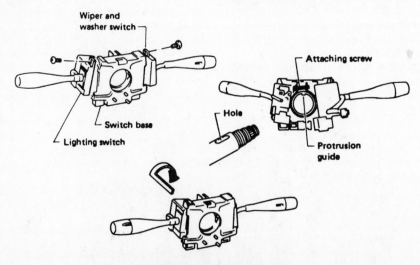

Combination switch replacement

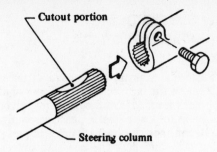

Steering column assembly installation

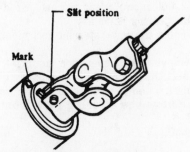

Steering column assembly installation

7. Remove the temporarily installed column support bracket bolts and withdraw the column from the (matchmark steering column-lower joint for correct installation) lower joint.

8. Withdraw the column spline shaft from the lower joint and remove the steering column. Be careful not to tear the column tube jacket insulator during removal.

To install:

9. Insert the column spline shaft into the lower joint and install all column fasteners finger-tight.

10. Install the lower joint bolt. The cutout portion of the spline shaft must perfectly aligned with the bolt. Torque the bolt to 23–31 ft. lbs. (17–22 ft. lbs. on later models) Tighten the steering bracket and clamp fasteners gradually. While tightening, make sure no stress is placed on the column.

11. Connect the combination switch and steering lock switch wiring.

12. Install the steering column covers.

13. Install the steering wheel.

14. Connect the negative battery cable.

15. After the installation is complete, turn the steering wheel from stop to stop and make sure it turns smoothly. The number of turns to the left and right stops must be equal.

Tie Rod Ends (Steering Side Rods)

REMOVAL AND INSTALLATION

1. Raise the front of the vehicle and support it on jackstands. Remove the wheel.

2. Locate the faulty tie rod end. It will have a

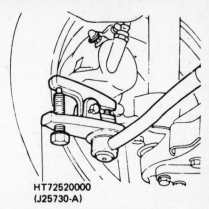

HT72520000
(J25730-A)

Removing the tie rod end (steering side rods) from the steering knuckle using special tool

lot of play in it and the dust cover will probably be ripped.

3. Remove the cotter pin and the tie rod ball joint stud nut. Note the position of the steering linkage.

4. Loosen the tie rod-to-steering gear locknut.

5. Using the Ball Joint Remover tool HT72520000 or equivalent, remove the tie rod ball joint from the steering knuckle.

6. Loosen the locknut and remove the tie rod end from the tie rod, counting the number of complete turns it takes to completely free it.

To install:

7. Install the new tie rod end, turning it in exactly as far as you screwed out the old one. Make sure it is correctly positioned in relationship to the steering linkage.

8. Fit the ball joint and nut, tighten them and install a NEW cotter pin. Torque the ball joint stud nut to specifications. Check front end alignment.

• The outer tie rod end-to-steering knuckle torque specification is 40–72 ft. lbs. on the 200SX model.

• The outer tie rod end-to-steering knuckle torque specification is 22–36 ft. lbs. on the 240SX model.

• The outer tie rod end-to-steering knuckle torque specification is 22–29 ft. lbs. on all Stanza models.

• Use these specifications as guide always replace the cotter pins and if necessary replace the retaining nut.

Manual Steering Gear

REMOVAL AND INSTALLATION

1. Raise and support the car on jackstands.

2. Using the Ball Joint Remover tool HT72520000 or equivalent, remove tie rod end from the steering knuckle.

3. Loosen, but do not remove, the steering gear mounting bolts.

4. Matchmark and remove the steering column lower joint.

5. Unbolt and remove the steering gear assembly.

To install:

6. Position and install the steering gear assembly to the vehicle. Torque the tie rod-to-steering knuckle nut to specifications. The outer tie rod end-to-steering knuckle torque specification is 40–72 ft. lbs. on the 200SX model and 22–29 ft. lbs. on all Stanza models. Torque the steering gear-to-frame clamp bolts EVENLY in steps, to 43–58 ft. lbs. on Stanza and 33–44 ft. lbs. on 200SX. Torque the lower joint-to-steering gear bolt to 23–31 ft. lbs. on all models.

NOTE: *When installing the lower steering joint to the steering gear, make sure that the wheels are aligned straight and the steering joint slot is aligned with the steering gear cap or spacer mark. Check front end alignment if necessary.*

Power Steering Gear

REMOVAL AND ADJUSTMENT

200SX

1. Raise and support the vehicle as necessary. Remove the bolt securing the lower shaft (matchmark shaft to joint assembly for correct installation) to power steering gear assembly.

2. Disconnect the hoses from the power steering gear and plug the hoses to prevent leakage.

3. Using the Ball Joint Remover tool HT72520000 or equivalent, remove tie rod ends from the steering knuckle.

4. Remove the power steering gear mounting bolts.

5. Remove the exhaust pipe mounting nut. Disconnect the control cable or linkage for the transmission and position it out of the way.

6. Remove the steering gear from the vehicle.

To install:

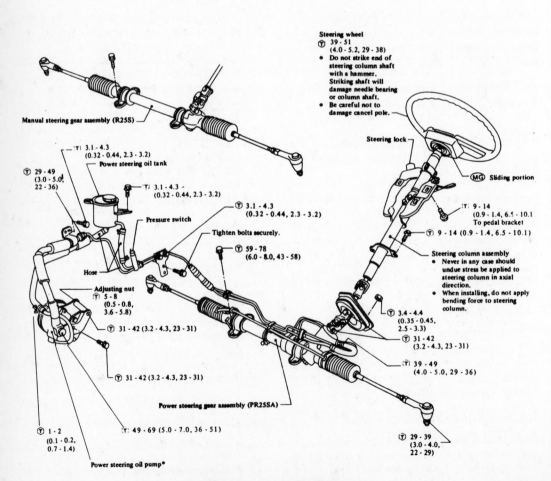

Steering wheel
39 - 51
(4.0 - 5.2, 29 - 38)
• Do not strike end of steering column shaft with a hammer. Striking shaft will damage needle bearing or column shaft.
• Be careful not to damage cancel pole.

Steering lock

Manual steering gear assembly (R25S)

3.1 - 4.3
(0.32 - 0.44, 2.3 - 3.2)
Power steering oil tank

29 - 49
(3.0 - 5.0, 22 - 36)

3.1 - 4.3
(0.32 - 0.44, 2.3 - 3.2)

Pressure switch

3.1 - 4.3
(0.32 - 0.44, 2.3 - 3.2)

MG Sliding portion

9 - 14
(0.9 - 1.4, 6.5 - 10.1
To pedal bracket

9 - 14 (0.9 - 1.4, 6.5 - 10.1)

Tighten bolts securely.

59 - 78
(6.0 - 8.0, 43 - 58)

Hose

Steering column assembly
• Never in any case should undue stress be applied to steering column in axial direction.
• When installing, do not apply bending force to steering column.

Adjusting nut
5 - 8
(0.5 - 0.8, 3.6 - 5.8)

3.4 - 4.4
(0.35 - 0.45, 2.5 - 3.3)

31 - 42 (3.2 - 4.3, 23 - 31)

31 - 42
(3.2 - 4.3, 23 - 31)

31 - 42 (3.2 - 4.3, 23 - 31)

39 - 49
(4.0 - 5.0, 29 - 36)

Power steering gear assembly (PR25SA)

49 - 69 (5.0 - 7.0, 36 - 51)

1 - 2
(0.1 - 0.2, 0.7 - 1.4)

29 - 39
(3.0 - 4.0, 22 - 29)

Power steering oil pump*

Steering system—1985 Stanza

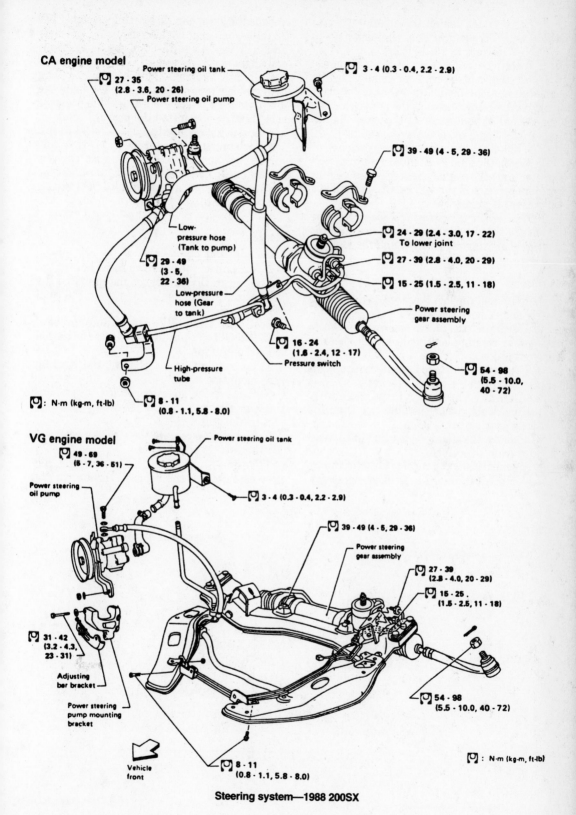

CA engine model

Power steering oil tank

27 - 35
(2.8 - 3.6, 20 - 26)
Power steering oil pump

3 - 4 (0.3 - 0.4, 2.2 - 2.9)

39 - 49 (4 - 5, 29 - 36)

Low-pressure hose (Tank to pump)

24 - 29 (2.4 - 3.0, 17 - 22)
To lower joint

29 - 49
(3 - 5,
22 - 36)

27 - 39 (2.8 - 4.0, 20 - 29)

15 - 25 (1.5 - 2.5, 11 - 18)

Low-pressure hose (Gear to tank)

Power steering gear assembly

16 - 24
(1.6 - 2.4, 12 - 17)
Pressure switch

High-pressure tube

54 - 98
(5.5 - 10.0, 40 - 72)

: N·m (kg-m, ft-lb)   8 - 11
(0.8 - 1.1, 5.8 - 8.0)

VG engine model

Power steering oil tank

49 - 69
(5 - 7, 36 - 51)

Power steering oil pump

3 - 4 (0.3 - 0.4, 2.2 - 2.9)

39 - 49 (4 - 5, 29 - 36)

Power steering gear assembly

27 - 39
(2.8 - 4.0, 20 - 29)

15 - 25
(1.5 - 2.5, 11 - 18)

31 - 42
(3.2 - 4.3,
23 - 31)

Adjusting bar bracket

Power steering pump mounting bracket

54 - 98
(5.5 - 10.0, 40 - 72)

: N·m (kg-m, ft-lb)

Vehicle front

8 - 11
(0.8 - 1.1, 5.8 - 8.0)

Steering system—1988 200SX

7. Position and install the steering gear to the vehicle. Torque the clamp retaining bolts to EVENLY in steps to 29–36 ft.lbs.

8. Install tie rod end to steering knuckle. Connect the control cable or linkage to the transmission and install the exhaust system.

9. Reconnect the hoses to the power steering gear. Install the bolt securing the lower shaft to power steering gear assembly torque to 17–22 ft. lbs. (26–31 ft. lbs. on older applications).

10. Check the fluid level. Bleed system as necessary. Start the engine check for leaks and for proper operation of the system. Check front end alignment if necessary.

NOTE: *When installing the lower steering joint to the steering gear, make sure that the wheels are aligned straight and the steering joint slot is aligned.*

240SX

1. Raise and support the front of the vehicle safely and remove the wheels.

2. Disconnect the power steering hose from the power steering gear and plug all hoses to prevent leakage.

3. Disconnect the tie rod ends from the steering knuckle using a suitable tools.

4. Remove the lower joint assembly (matchmark for correct installation) from the steering gear pinion.

5. Remove the steering gear and linkage assembly from the vehicle.

6. Installation is the reverse order of the removal procedure. Bleed system as necessary.

Torque the lower joint to steering assembly 17–22 ft. lbs. and gear housing mounting brackets EVENLY in steps to 65–80 ft. lbs. Check front end alignment if necessary.

• Observe tightening torque when installing high and low preesure pipes. The O-ring in the low pressure is larger than in the high pressure side. Take care to install the proper O-ring.

• Low pressure pipe torque – 20–29 ft. lbs.
• High pressure pipe torque – 11–18 ft. lbs.

NOTE: *When installing the lower steering joint to the steering gear, make sure that the wheels are aligned straight and the steering joint slot is aligned.*

Stanza

1. Raise and support the car on jackstands.

2. Disconnect the hose clamp and hose at the steering gear. Disconnect the flare nut and the tube at the steering gear, then drain the fluid from the gear.

3. Using the Ball Joint Remover tool HT72520000 or equivalent, remove the tie rod from the knuckle.

4. Loosen, but do not remove, the steering gear mounting bolts.

5. Remove the steering column lower joint (matchmark shaft to joint assembly – for correct installation).

6. Unbolt and remove the steering gear.

To install:

7. Position and install the power steering gear assembly to the vehicle. Torque the tie

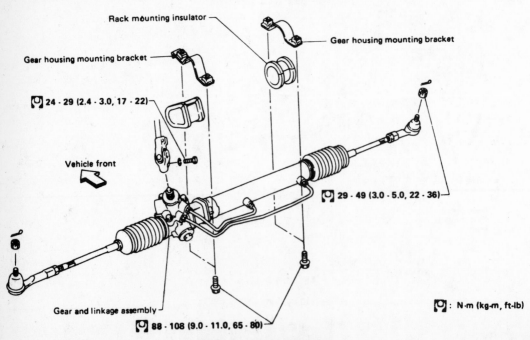

Rack mounting insulator

Gear housing mounting bracket

Gear housing mounting bracket

⟦◯⟧ 24 - 29 (2.4 - 3.0, 17 - 22)

Vehicle front

⟦◯⟧ 29 - 49 (3.0 - 5.0, 22 - 36)

Gear and linkage assembly

⟦◯⟧ 88 - 108 (9.0 - 11.0, 65 - 80)

⟦◯⟧ : N-m (kg-m, ft-lb)

Steering system—1992 240SX

rod-to-steering knuckle nut to 22–29 ft. lbs., the steering gear-to-frame clamp bolts to EVENLY in steps to 43–58 ft. lbs., the lower joint-to-steering column bolt to 23–31 ft. lbs.

• Torque the low pressure hose clip bolt to 9–17 inch lbs. and the high pressure hose-to-gear to 29–36 ft. lbs.

• On most later models, observe tightening torque when installing high and low preesure pipes. The O-ring in the low pressure is larger than in the high pressure side. Take care to install the proper O-ring.

• Low pressure pipe torque – 20–29 ft. lbs.
• High pressure pipe torque – 11–18 ft. lbs.

8. Bleed the power steering system and check the wheel alignment.

NOTE: *When installing the lower steering joint to the steering gear, make sure that the wheels are aligned straight and the steering joint slot is aligned with the steering gear cap or spacer mark.*

Power Steering Pump

REMOVAL AND INSTALLATION

1. Remove the hoses at the pump and plug the openings shut to prevent contamination. Position the disconnected lines in a raised attitude to prevent leakage.

2. Remove the pump belt.

3. Loosen the retaining bolts and any braces, and remove the pump.

4. Installation is the reverse of removal procedure. Use the following torque specifications as a guide pully locknut 23–31 ft. lbs. and pump bracket to engine 20–26 ft. lbs. Adjust the belt. Bleed the system.

BLEEDING THE POWER STEERING SYSTEM

1. Fill the pump reservoir and allow to remain undisturbed for a few minutes.

2. Raise the car until the front wheels are clear of the ground.

3. With the engine off, quickly turn the wheels right and left several times, lightly contacting the stops.

4. Add fluid if necessary.

5. Start the engine and let it idle.

6. Repeat Steps 3 and 4 with the engine idling.

7. Stop the engine, lower the car until the wheels just touch the ground. Start the engine, allow it to idle, and turn the wheels back and forth several times. Check the fluid level and refill if necessary.

Brakes

BRAKE SYSTEM

Adjustments

DRUM BRAKES

1. Raise and support the rear of the vehicle on jackstands.
2. Remove the rubber cover from the backing plate.
3. Insert a brake adjusting tool through the hole in the brake backing plate. Turn the toothed adjusting nut to spread the brake shoes, making contact with the brake drum.

NOTE: *When adjusting the brake shoes, turn the wheel until considerable drag is felt.*

4. When considerable drag is felt, back off the adjusting nut a few notches, so that the correct clearance is maintained between the brake drum and the brake shoes. Make sure that the wheel rotates freely.

BRAKE PEDAL

Pedal Freeplay

Before adjusting the pedal, make sure that the wheelbrakes are correctly adjusted. Adjust the pedal free play by means of the adjustable pushrod or by replacing shims between the master cylinder and the brake booster or firewall. Free play should be approximately 1–5mm on all models through 1984. On all models from 1985–1992 the pedal free play should be 1–3mm.

Pedal Height

Adjust the pedal height by means of the adjustable pedal arm stop pad in the driver's compartment on models through 1984. On later models, adjust the brake booster input rod by loosening the locknut and turning the rod.

The pedal height (floorboard-to-pedal pad) should be approximately 178mm for 1982–83 200SX model.

On the 1984–86½ 200SX, it should be 189–199mm on cars with a manual transmission and 191–201mm on cars with automatic transmission.

On the 1986½–88 200SX, it should be 185–195mm on cars with a manual transmission and 187–197mm on cars with automatic transmission.

The brake pedal free height for the 1989–92 240SX model is 177–187mm for manual transmission and 186–196mm for automatic transmission.

The brake pedal free height for the Stanza models is 159–169mm for manual transaxle

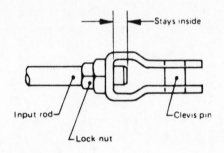

Pedal freeplay

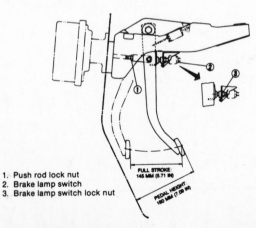

1. Push rod lock nut
2. Brake lamp switch
3. Brake lamp switch lock nut

Brake pedal height adjustment

and 169–179mm for automatic transaxle. The early Stanza models pedal height (floorboard to pedal pad) is 152mm.

Brake Light Switch

REMOVAL & INSTALLATION

1. Disconnect the negative battery cable.
2. Disconnect the wiring connector at the switch.
3. Remove the switch lock nut.
4. Remove the switch.
5. Install the switch and adjust it so the brake lights are not on unless the brake pedal is depressed.

ADJUSTMENT

Adjust the clearance between the brake pedal and the stop lamp switch or the ASCD switch, by loosening the locknut and adjusting the switch. The clearance should be approximately 0–1.0mm for Stanza (1982–84) or 0.30–1.00mm for Stanza and all other models. Use this service procedure as a guide if necessary.

NOTE: *The stop light switch is adjusted so that the switch is not activated when the brake pedal is relaxed.*

Brake Pedal

REMOVAL & INSTALLATION

Refer to the exploded view illustration as a guide for the removal and installation information.

Master Cylinder

REMOVAL & INSTALLATION

1. Disconnect the negative battery cable. Clean the outside of the master cylinder thoroughly, particularly around the cap and fluid lines. Disconnect the fluid lines and cap them to exclude dirt.
2. If equipped with a fluid level sensor, disconnect the wiring harness from the master cylinder.
3. Disconnect the brake fluid tubes, then plug the openings to prevent dirt from entering the system.
4. Remove the mounting bolts at the firewall or the brake booster (if equipped) and remove the master cylinder from the vehicle.

To install:

5. Bench bleed the master cylinder assembly

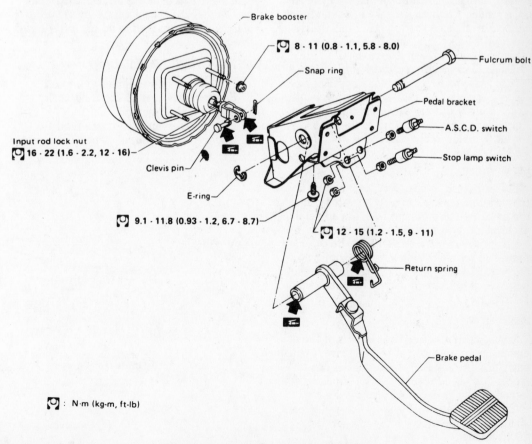

Brake pedal assembly—1986 Stanza wagon

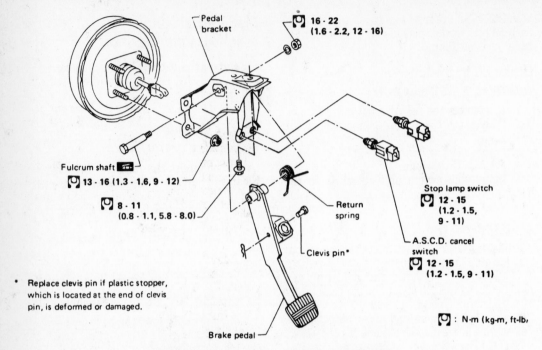

- Pedal bracket
- 16 - 22 (1.6 - 2.2, 12 - 16)

Fulcrum shaft
13 - 16 (1.3 - 1.6, 9 - 12)

8 - 11 (0.8 - 1.1, 5.8 - 8.0)

- Return spring
- Clevis pin*

Stop lamp switch
12 - 15 (1.2 - 1.5, 9 - 11)

A.S.C.D. cancel switch
12 - 15 (1.2 - 1.5, 9 - 11)

* Replace clevis pin if plastic stopper, which is located at the end of clevis pin, is deformed or damaged.

Brake pedal

: N·m (kg-m, ft-lb)

Brake pedal and bracket assembly—1992 240SX

before installation. Install the master cylinder to the vehicle. Connect all brake lines and fluid level sensor wiring is so equipped. Refill the reservoir with brake fluid and bleed the system. Adjust the brake system if necessary.

NOTE: *Ordinary brake fluid will boil and cause brake failure under the high temperatures developed in disc brake systems; use DOT 3 brake fluid in the brake systems. The adjustable pushrod is used to adjust brake pedal free-play. If the pushrod is not adjust-*

able, there will be shims between the cylinder and the mount. These shims, or the adjustable pushrod, are used to adjust brake pedal free play.

MASTER CYLINDER BLEEDING

1. Place the master cylinder in a vise.
2. Connect two lines to the fluid outlet orifices, and into the reservoir.
3. Fill the reservoir with brake fluid.
4. Using a wooden dowel, depress the push-

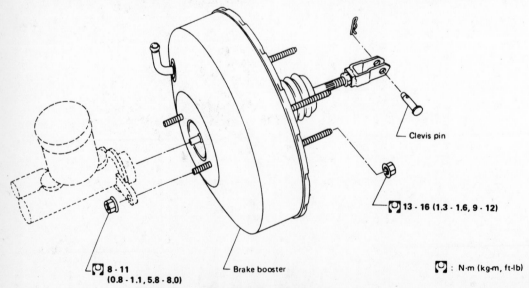

Clevis pin

13 - 16 (1.3 - 1.6, 9 - 12)

8 - 11 (0.8 - 1.1, 5.8 - 8.0)

Brake booster

: N·m (kg-m, ft-lb)

Brake booster—1992 240SX

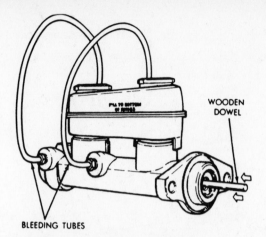

Bench bleeding the master cylinder

rod slowly, allowing the pistons to return. Do this several times until the air bubbles are all expelled.

5. Remove the bleeding tubes from the master cylinder, plug the outlets and install the caps.

OVERHAUL

NOTE: *Use this service procedure and exploded view illustrations as a guide for overhaul of the master cylinder assembly. If in doubt about overhaul condition or service procedure, REPLACE the complete assembly with a new master cylinder assembly.*

The master cylinder assembly can be disassembled using the illustrations as a guide. Clean all parts in clean brake fluid. Replace the cylinder or piston as necessary if clearance between the two exceed 0.15mm. Lubricate all parts with clean brake fluid on assembly. Master cylinder rebuilding kits, containing all the wearing parts are available to simplify overhaul.

Power Brake Booster
REMOVAL & INSTALLATION

NOTE: *Make sure all vacuum lines and connectors are in good condition. A small vacuum leak will cause a big problem in the power brake system.*

1. Disconnect the negative battery cable. Remove the master cylinder mounting nuts and pull the master cylinder assembly (brake lines connected) away from the power booster.

2. Detach the vacuum lines from the booster.

3. Detach the booster pushrod at the pedal clevis.

4. Unbolt the booster from under the dash and lift it out of the engine compartment.

To install:

5. Install the brake booster assembly to the vehicle. Install the master cylinder assembly to brake booster assembly.

6. Connect the booster pushrod to the pedal clevis. Connect the vacuum lines to brake booster.

7. Connect the battery. Start the engine and check brake operation.

Brake Proportioning Valve

All Datsun/Nissans covered in this manual are equipped with brake proportioning valves of several different types. The valves all do the same job, which is to separate the front and rear brake lines, allowing them to function independently, and preventing the rear brakes from locking before the front brakes. Damage, such as brake line leakage, in either the front or

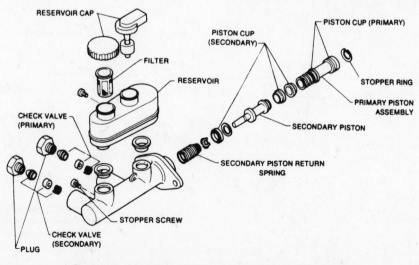

Exploded view master cylinder assembly 1981–84 200SX

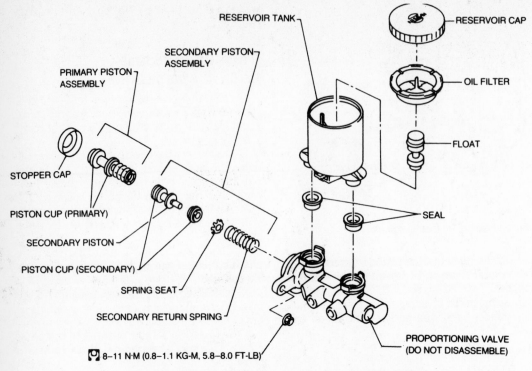

Exploded view master cylinder assembly 1984 and later 200SX

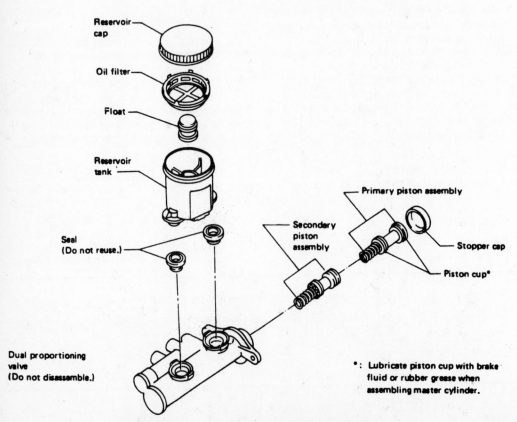

Exploded view master cylinder assembly 1989 240SX

Nabco

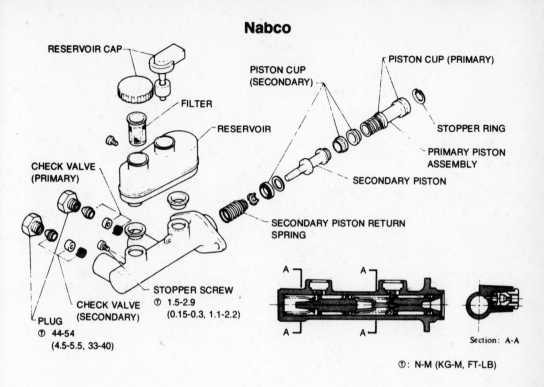

RESERVOIR CAP

FILTER

RESERVOIR

PISTON CUP (SECONDARY)

PISTON CUP (PRIMARY)

STOPPER RING

PRIMARY PISTON ASSEMBLY

CHECK VALVE (PRIMARY)

SECONDARY PISTON

SECONDARY PISTON RETURN SPRING

CHECK VALVE (SECONDARY)

STOPPER SCREW
Ⓣ 1.5-2.9
(0.15-0.3, 1.1-2.2)

PLUG
Ⓣ 44-54
(4.5-5.5, 33-40)

Section: A-A

Ⓣ: N-M (KG-M, FT-LB)

Tokico

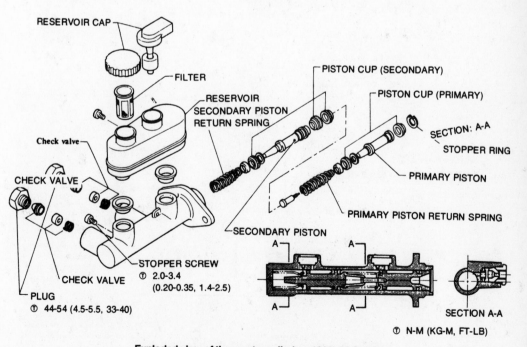

RESERVOIR CAP

FILTER

PISTON CUP (SECONDARY)

PISTON CUP (PRIMARY)

RESERVOIR
SECONDARY PISTON
RETURN SPRING

SECTION: A-A

STOPPER RING

Check valve

PRIMARY PISTON

CHECK VALVE

PRIMARY PISTON RETURN SPRING

SECONDARY PISTON

STOPPER SCREW
Ⓣ 2.0-3.4
(0.20-0.35, 1.4-2.5)

CHECK VALVE

PLUG
Ⓣ 44-54 (4.5-5.5, 33-40)

SECTION A-A

Ⓣ N-M (KG-M, FT-LB)

Exploded view of the master cylinders 1982–83 Stanza

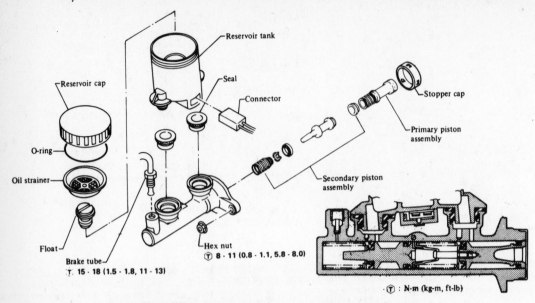

Exploded view of the master cylinder 1984 and later Stanza

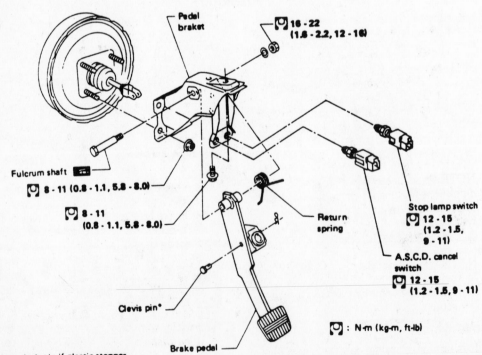

• Replace clevis pin if plastic stopper,
   which is located at the end of clevis
   pin, is deformed or damaged.

Brake booster and pedal assembly—1989 240SX

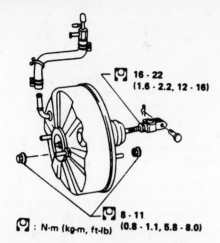

Brake booster assembly late model 200SX

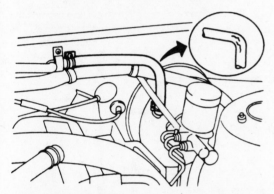

Check condition of the vacuum hose on power brake booster

rear brake system will not affect the normal operation of the unaffected system. If, in the event of a panic stop, the rear brakes lock up before the front brakes, it could mean the proportioning valve is defective. In that case, replace the entire proportioning valve.

REMOVAL & INSTALLATION

NOTE: *Models built in 1985 and later years do not use a separate proportioning valve.*

1. Disconnect and plug the brake lines at the valve.

2. Unscrew the mounting bolt(s) and remove the valve.

NOTE: *Do not disassemble the valve.*

3. Installation is in the reverse order of removal. Bleed the complete brake system.

Brake Hoses

It is important to use quality brake hose intended specifically for the application. Hose of less than the best quality, or hose not made to the specified length will tend to fatigue and may

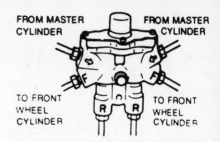

Proportioning valve—Stanza

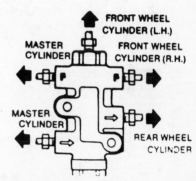

Cross section of proportioning valve—most models similar

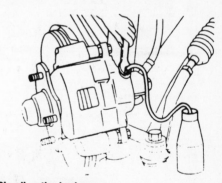

Bleeding the brakes

therefore create premature leakage and, consequently, a potential for brake failure. Note also that brake hose differs from one side of the car to the other and should therefore be ordered specifying the side on which it will be installed.

Make sure hose end mating surfaces are clean and free of nicks and burrs, which would prevent effective sealing. Use new copper seals on banjo fittings.

CAUTION: *When routing a brake hose to a vehicle, minimize hose twisting and bending upon installation.*

REMOVAL & INSTALLATION

NOTE: *The procedures below for Brake Hose Removal and Installation can be used as a* service guide for all years and models. Modify the service steps as necessary.

Refer to Brake Hydraulic Line illustrations for the torque specifications for the lines.

Front Brake Hose

1. Place a drain pan under the hose connections. First, disconnect the hose where it connects to the body bracket and steel tube.

2. Unbolt the hose bracket from the strut assembly.

3. Remove the bolt to disconnect the banjo connection at the caliper.

4. Position the new hose, noting that the body bracket and the body end of the hose are keyed to prevent installation of the hose in the wrong direction. First attach the hose to the banjo connector on the caliper (torque connection).

5. Bolt the hose bracket located in the center of the hose to the strut, allowing the bracket to position the hose so it will not be twisted.

6. Attach the hose to the body bracket and steel brake tube.

7. Torque all connections. Bleed the system thoroughly.

Rear Brake Hose

1. Place a drain pan under the hose connections. Disconnect the double nut (using a primary wrench and a backup wrench) at the tube

Without Anti-lock Braking System (ABS)

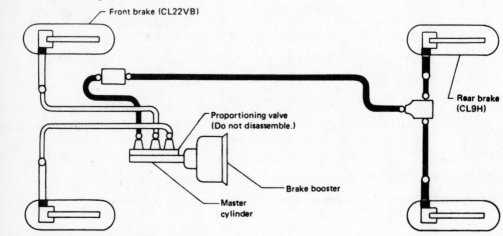

With Anti-lock Braking System (ABS)

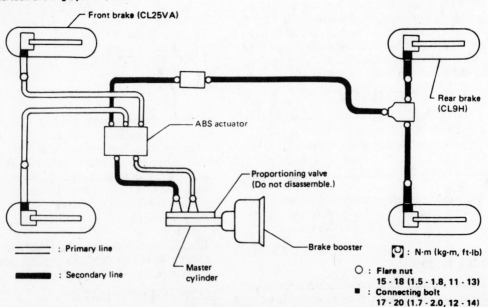

Brake hydraulic line—200SX and 240SX

mounted on the floor pan. Then, disconnect the hose at the retaining clip.

2. Disconnect the hose at the trailing arm tube. Install the new tube to the trailing arm connection first. Torque the connection. Then, making sure it is not twisted, connect it to the tube on the floor pan. Again, torque the connection. Bleed the system thoroughly.

Caliper Hose — Rear Disc Brakes

1. Place a drain pan under the hose connections. Disconnect the double nut (using a primary wrench and a backup wrench) at the tube mounted on the clip, located on the caliper-mounted bracket. Then, disconnect the banjo connector by removing the through bolt.

Without anti-lock braking system

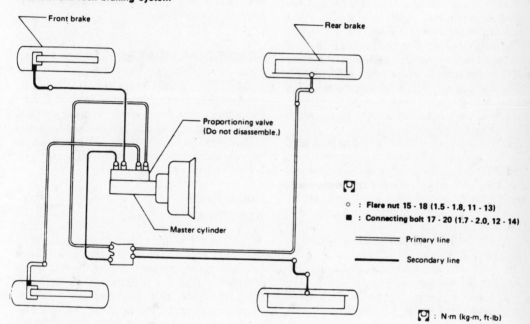

With anti-lock braking system

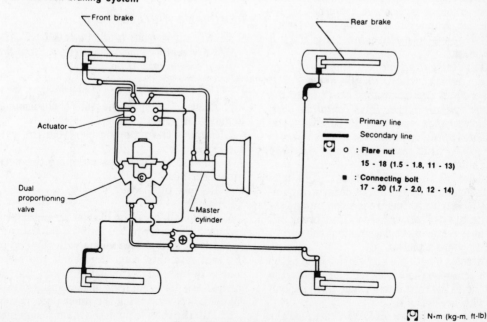

Brake hydraulic line—Stanza

2. Install the new hose by connecting the banjo connector first, using new copper seals and torquing the connection.

3. Making sure the hose is not twisted, make the connection to the tube, and torque the connection.

4. Secure the hose to the bracket with the retaining clip. Bleed the system thoroughly.

Brake System Bleeding

NOTE: *If vehicle is equipped with a Anti-Lock Brake System (ABS) refer to the service procedures later in this Chapter.*

The purpose of bleeding the brakes is to expel air trapped in the hydraulic system. The system must be bled whenever the pedal feels spongy, indicating that air, which is compressible, has entered the system. It must also be bled whenever the system has been opened or repaired. You will need a helper for this job.

Never reuse brake fluid which has been bled from the system. The service procedure is to bleed at the points farthest from the master cylinder assembly first. Follow this order when bleeding the brake system on your vehicle:

    a. 1982–88 200SX bleed in this order RR, LR, RF, LF wheels

    b. 1989–92 240SX bleed in this order LR, RR, LF, RF wheels

    c. 1982–85 Stanza bleed in this order RR, LF, LR, RF wheels

    d. 1986–92 Stanza, Stanza Wagon bleed in this order LR, RF, RR, LF wheels

BLEEDING PROCEDURE

1. Clean all dirt from around the master cylinder reservoir caps. Remove the caps and fill the master cylinder to the proper level with clean, fresh brake fluid meeting DOT 3 specifications.

NOTE: *Brake fluid picks up moisture from the air, which reduces its effectiveness and causes brake line corrosion. Don't leave the master cylinder or the fluid container open any longer than necessary. Be careful not to spill brake fluid on painted surfaces. Wipe up any spilled fluid immediately and rinse the area with clear water.*

2. Clean all the bleeder screws. You may want to give each one a shot of penetrating solvent to loosen it up. Seizure is a common problem with bleeder screws, which then break off, sometimes requiring replacement of the part to which they are attached.

3. Attach a length of clear vinyl tubing to the bleeder screw on the wheel cylinder. Insert the other end of the tube into a clear, clean jar half filled with brake fluid.

4. Have your helper SLOWLY depress the brake pedal. As this is done, open the bleeder (follow the correct bleeding order) screw 1/3–1/2 of a turn, and allow the fluid to run through the tube. Close the bleeder screw before the pedal reaches the end of its travel. Have your assistant slowly release the pedal. Repeat this process until no air bubbles appear in the expelled fluid.

5. Repeat the procedure on the other three brakes, checking the fluid level in the master cylinder reservoirs often. Do not allow the reservoirs to run dry, or the bleeding process will have to be repeated.

FRONT DISC BRAKES

CAUTION: *Brake shoes contain asbestos, which has been determined to be a cancer causing agent. Never clean the brake surfaces with compressed air! Avoid inhaling any dust from any brake surface! When cleaning brake surfaces, use a commercially available brake cleaning fluid.*

Brake Pads

INSPECTION

You should be able to check the pad lining thickness without removing the pads. Check the Brake Specifications chart at the end of this Chapter to find the manufacturer's pad wear limit. However, this measurement may disagree with your state inspection laws. When replacing pads, always check the surface of the rotors for scoring or wear. The rotors should be removed for resurfacing if badly scored.

REMOVAL & INSTALLATION

NOTE: *All 4 front brake pads MUST ALWAYS be replaced as a complete set. Bleed the brake system only if necessary.*

Type N22 Series — Disc Brake Assembly

1. Raise and support the front of the vehicle. Remove the wheels.

2. Remove the retaining clip from the outboard pad.

3. Remove the pad pins retaining the anti-squeal springs.

4. Remove the pads.

To install:

5. To install, open the bleeder screw slightly and push the outer piston into the cylinder until the dust seal groove aligns with the end of the seal retaining ring, then close the bleed screw. Be careful because the piston can be pushed too far, requiring disassembly of the caliper to repair. Install the inner pad.

6. Pull the yoke to push the inner piston into place. Install the outer pad.

7. Lightly coat the areas where the pins touch the pads, and where the pads touch the caliper (at the top) with grease. Do not allow grease to get on the pad friction surfaces.

8. Install the anti-squeal springs and pad pins. Install the clip.

9. Apply the brakes a few times to seat the pads. Check the master cylinder level. Add fluid if necessary. Bleed the brakes if necessary.

Type CL22V Series — Disc Brake Assembly

1. Raise the front of the car and support it with safety stands.

2. Unscrew and remove the lower pin bolt (sub pin).

3. Swing the cylinder body upward and then remove the pad retainer, the inner and outer

shims and the pads themselves. Do not depress the brake pedal when the cylinder body is in the raised position or the piston will pop out.

To install:

4. Clean the piston end of the cylinder body and the pin bolt holes. Be careful not to get oil on the rotor.

5. Pull the cylinder body to the outer side and install the inner pad.

6. Install the outer pad, the shim and the pad retainer.

7. Reposition the cylinder body and then tighten the pin bolt to 12–15 ft. lbs.

8. Apply the brakes a few times to seat the new pads. Check the fluid level and bleed the brakes if required.

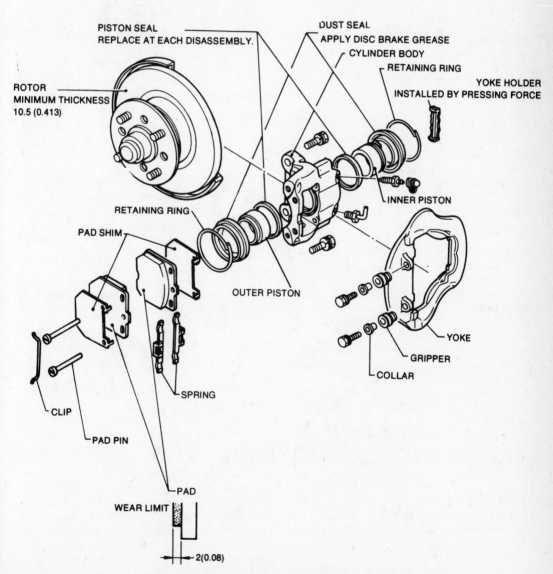

Exploded view of the N22 series disc brake assembly

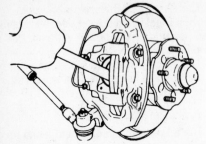

Pushing the inner piston in to install new brake pads

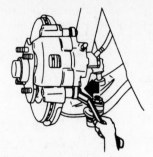

Remove the lower pin bolt

Do not push the piston in too far

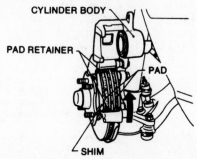

Raise the cylinder body to remove the brake pads

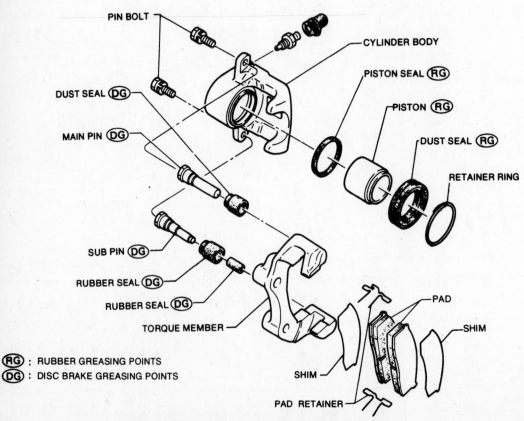

RG : RUBBER GREASING POINTS
DG : DISC BRAKE GREASING POINTS

Exploded view of the CL22V series disc brake assembly

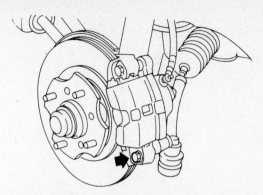

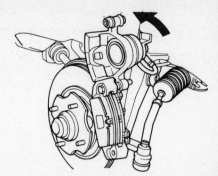

Remove the AD22V series disc brake assembly guide pin...

...and rotate the caliper up and away from the rotor. Do not apply the brakes with the caliper in this position!

Type AD22V Series – Disc Brake Assembly

1. Remove the road wheel.
2. Remove the lower caliper guide pin.
3. Rotate the brake caliper body upward.
4. Remove the brake pad retainer and the inner and outer pad shims.
5. Remove the brake pads. Do not depress the brake pedal when the caliper body is raised. The brake piston will be forced out of the caliper.

To install:

6. Clean the piston end of the caliper body and the pin bolt holes. Be careful not to get oil on the brake rotor.
7. Pull the caliper body to the outer side and install the inner brake pad. Make sure both new pads are kept clean!
8. Install the outer pad, shim and pad retainer.
9. Reposition the caliper body and then tighten the guide pin bolt to 23–30 ft. lbs.

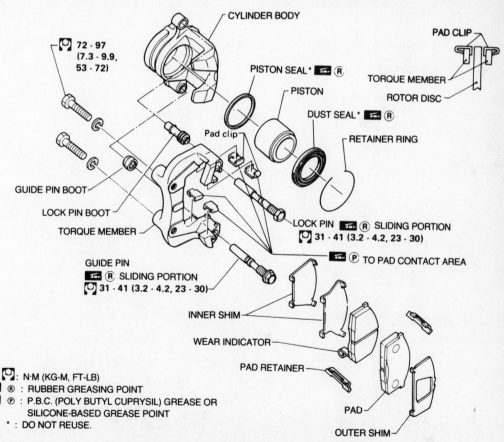

Exploded view of the AD22V series disc brake assembly

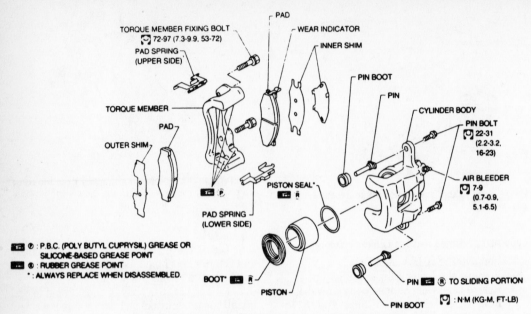

Exploded view of the CL28VB series disc brake assembly

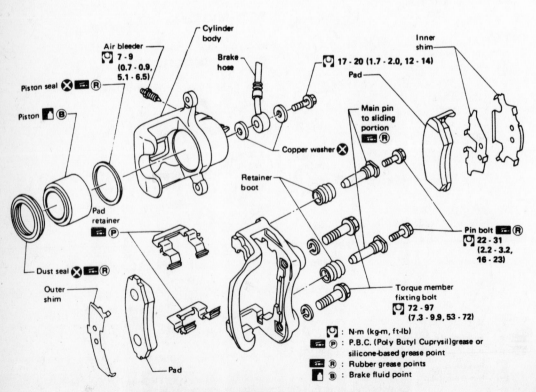

Exploded view of the CL22VB series disc brake assembly

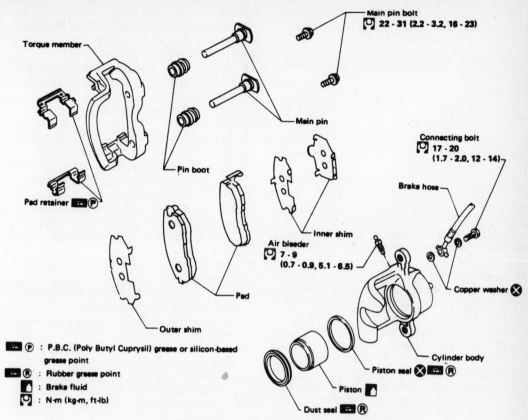

Exploded view of the CL25VB series disc brake assembly

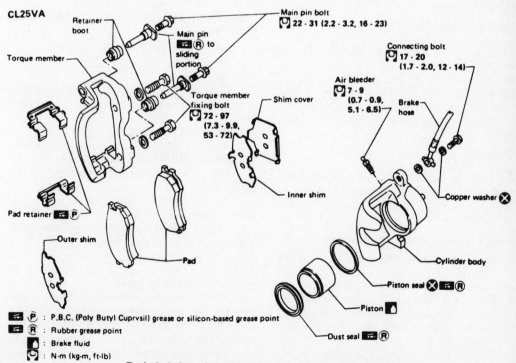

Exploded view of the CL25VA series disc brake assembly

10. Apply the brakes a few times to seat the pads. Bleed and adjust brakes if necessary before driving on the road.

Types CL28VB, CL22VB and CL25VB Series Disc Brake Assembly

NOTE: *Use this service procedure and illustrations as a guide for all other CL Series Disc Brake Systems.*

1. Raise the vehicle and support it securely. Remove the front wheel. Remove the pin (lower) bolt from the caliper.

2. Swing the caliper body upward on the upper bolt. Remove the pad retainers and inner and outer shims. Do not depress the brake pedal when the cylinder body is in the raised position or the piston will pop out. Avoid damaging the piston seal when removing/installing the pads and retainers.

To install:

3. Check the level of fluid in the master cylinder. If the fluid is near the maximum level, use a clean syringe to remove fluid until the level is down well below the lip of the reservoir. Then, use a large C-clamp to press the caliper piston back into the caliper, to allow room for the installation of the thicker new pads.

4. Install the new pads, utilizing new shims, in reverse order. Torque the lower retaining bolt to 16–23 ft. lbs. Bleed and adjust the brakes if necessary. Make sure you pump the brakes and get a hard pedal before driving the car.

Brake Calipers

REMOVAL & INSTALLATION

Refer to Brake Pads Removal and Installation procedure in this Chapter. Remove the brake pads. Remove both guide pins, torque member fixing bolts and brake hose connector. Remove the caliper assembly from the vehicle. The brake system must be bled after this repair.

OVERHAUL

NOTE: *Use the exploded view illustrations as guide for overhaul of the caliper assembly. If in doubt about caliper condition--replace the caliper assembly.*

Type N22 Series – Disc Brake Assembly

1. With the vehicle supported safely and the front wheels off, remove the brake fluid tube (brake line) from the caliper assembly.

2. Remove the caliper from the knuckle assembly by removing the mounting bolts, located at the rear of the caliper, and lifting the caliper from the rotor.

3. Remove the pads from the caliper.

4. Remove the gripper pin attaching nuts

and separate the yoke from the cylinder body.

5. Remove the yoke holder from the piston and remove the retaining rings and dust seals from the ends of both pistons.

6. Apply air pressure gradually into the fluid chamber of the caliper, to force the pistons from the cylinders.

7. Remove the piston seals.

To install:

8. Inspect the components for damage or excessive wear. Replace or repair as needed.

9. To assemble, install the piston seals in the cylinder bore. Lubricate seals and pistons.

10. Slide the A piston into the cylinder, followed by the B piston so that its yoke groove coincides with the yoke groove of the cylinder.

11. Install the dust seal and clamp tightly with the retaining ring.

12. Install the yoke holder on the A piston and install the gripper to yoke.

NOTE: *The use of soapy water will aid in the installation of the gripper pins.*

13. Support the end of B piston and press the yoke into the yoke holder.

14. Install the pads, anti squeal springs, pad pins and retain with the clip.

15. Tighten the gripper pin attaching nuts to 12–15 ft. lbs. and install the caliper on the spindle knuckle. Torque the caliper mounting bolts to 53–72 ft. lbs.

16. Bleed the system, check the fluid level, install the wheels and lower the vehicle.

Types CL22V and AD22V Series – Disc Brake Assembly

1. Disconnect and plug the brake line.

2. Unscrew the two mounting bolts and remove the caliper.

3. Remove the main pin and the sub pin and then separate the cylinder body from the torque member.

4. Remove the piston dust cover.

5. Apply compressed air gradually to the fluid chamber until the piston pops out.

6. Carefully pry out the piston seal.

To install:

7. Inspect the components for damage or excessive wear. Replace or repair as necessary.

8. Install the piston seal in the cylinder bore. Lubricate the seals and pistons.

9. Fit the dust seal onto the piston, insert the dust seal into the groove on the cylinder body and then install the piston.

10. Place the cylinder body and torque member together, grease the main and sub pins, install the pins and tighten them to 12–15 ft. lbs. on the CL22V, and 23–30 ft. lbs. on the AD22V.

11. Install the caliper and tighten the mounting bolts to 36–51 ft. lbs. on the CL22V, and 53–

72 ft. lbs. on the AD22V. Reconnect the brake line and install the wheels.

12. Bleed the system, check the fluid level and lower the vehicle.

Types CL28VB, CL22VB and CL25VB Series – Disc Brake Assembly

NOTE: *Use this service procedure and illustrations as a guide for all other CL type series calipers.*

1. Remove the brake pads as described above. Disconnect the brake hose and plug the open end of the hose. Remove the two caliper mounting bolts and remove the caliper.

2. Place a wooden block between the caliper piston and the pad retainer opposite it. Then, gently apply compressed air to the brake hose connection. This will remove the piston and dust seal. Note the direction in which the piston seal is installed.

To install:

3. Clean all parts in clean brake fluid. Inspect the inner cylinder bore for rust, scoring, or mechanical wear. Remove minor imperfections with emery paper. Replace the caliper body if these imperfections cannot be removed. Inspect the piston for such imperfections. If they exist, it must be replaced, as the surface is polished!

4. Inspect the lockpins, bolts, piston seal, bushings, and pin seals for damage and replace all parts as necessary.

5. Insert the piston seal into the groove on the caliper body. Install the inner edge of the rubber boot into the piston groove and then install the piston. Work the edge of the rubber boot into the groove in the caliper body.

6. Perform the remaining procedures in the reverse of removal. Torque the caliper mounting pins to 53–72 ft. lbs. Refill the system with clean brake fluid and bleed it thoroughly. Make sure you pump the brakes and get a hard pedal before operating the car.

Brake Disc (Rotor)
REMOVAL & INSTALLATION
200SX and 240SX Models
Rear Wheel Drive

1. Raise and support the front of the vehicle safely and remove the wheels.

2. Remove brake caliper assembly and wheel hub and bearing assembly if necessary. Make sure not to twist the brake hose.

3. Remove the brake disc/wheel hub from the vehicle.

4. Installation is the reverse of removal. Adjust the wheel bearings if necessary.

INSPECTION

Check the brake rotor for roughness, cracks or chips. The rotor can be machined on a brake lathe most auto parts stores have complete machine shop service. The rotors should be machined or replaced during every front disc brake pad replacement.

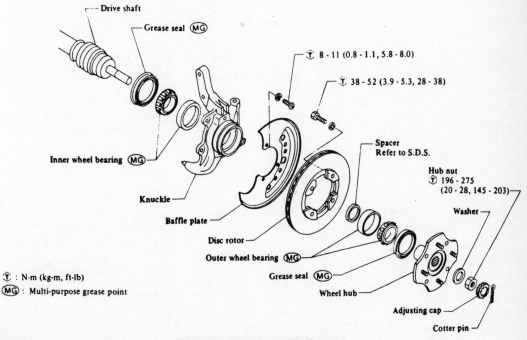

Front axle assembly—1983 Stanza

Stanza and Stanza Wagon Models
Front Wheel Drive

CAUTION: *Brake shoes contain asbestos, which has been determined to be a cancer causing agent. Never clean the brake surfaces with compressed air! Avoid inhaling any dust from any brake surface! When cleaning brake surfaces, use a commercially available brake cleaning fluid.*

EARLY TYPE ROTOR/DISC ASSEMBLY

1. Refer to the Caliper, Removal and Installation procedures, in this Chapter and remove the caliper and the cylinder body and the torque member from the steering knuckle. Do not disconnect the brake tube (if possible), support the assembly on a wire.

2. Remove the grease cap, the cotter pin, the adjusting cap, the wheel bearing locknut and the thrust washer from the drive shaft.

3. Using Wheel Hub Remover tools KV40101000 and ST36230000 press the wheel hub/disc assembly from the steering knuckle.

4. Remove the disc-to-wheel hub bolts and separate the disc from the wheel hub.

5. Install wheel hub/disc assembly to the vehicle. Refer to Chapter 8.

6. Install the caliper assembly and any other components to the vehicle.

7. Bleed brake system if necessary.

LATER TYPE ROTOR/DISC ASSEMBLY

1. Raise and safely support the vehicle.

2. Remove the caliper assembly as outlined.

3. Remove the rotor/disc assembly from the vehicle.

4. Installation is the reverse of removal procedure.

INSPECTION

Check the brake rotor for roughness, cracks or chips. The rotor can be machined on a brake lathe most auto parts stores have complete machine shop service. The rotors should be machined or replaced during every front disc brake pad replacement.

REAR DISC BRAKES

CAUTION: *Brake shoes contain asbestos, which has been determined to be a cancer causing agent. Never clean the brake surfaces with compressed air! Avoid inhaling any dust from any brake surface! When cleaning*

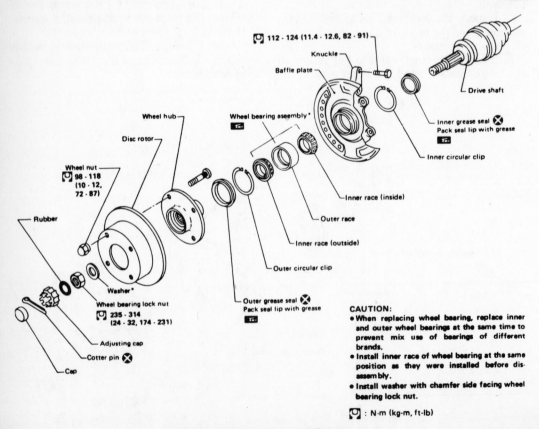

Front axle assembly—1987 Stanza

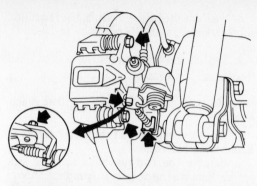

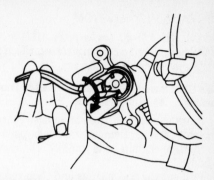

On the 200SX, remove the parking brake cable stay fixing bolt, pin bolts and lock spring before removing the pads and shims—1984 model shown

Use needle nose pliers to retract the piston

brake surfaces, use a commercially available brake cleaning fluid.

Brake Pads

INSPECTION

You should be able to check the pad lining thickness without removing the pads. Check the Brake Specifications chart at the end of this Chapter to find the manufacturer's pad wear limit. However, this measurement may disagree with your state inspection laws. When replacing pads, always check the surface of the rotors for scoring or wear. The rotors should be removed for resurfacing if badly scored.

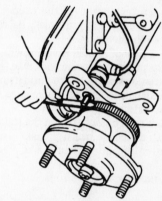

Remove the parking brake cable mounting brace bolt—CL11H caliper assembly

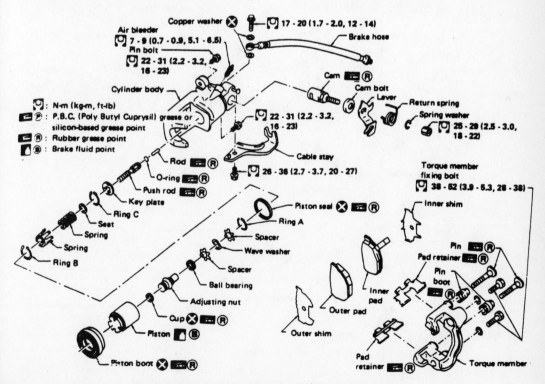

Exploded view of the CL11HB series disc brake assembly

REMOVAL & INSTALLATION

NOTE: *All 4 front brake pads MUST ALWAYS be replaced as a complete set. Bleed the brake system only if necessary.*

Types CL11H and CL9H Series – Disc Brake Assembly

1. Raise the rear of the car and support it with safety stands. Remove the brake pads.
2. Remove the pin bolts and lift off the caliper body.
3. Pull out the pad springs and then remove the pads and their shims.

To install:

4. Clean the piston end of the caliper body and the area around the pin holes. Be careful not to get oil on the rotor.
5. Using a pair of needle nosed pliers, carefully turn the piston clockwise back into the caliper body (remove some brake fluid from the master cylinder if necessary). Take care not to damage the piston boot.
6. Coat the pad contact area on the mounting support with a silicone based grease.
7. Install the pads, shims and the pad springs.

NOTE: *Always use new shims.*

8. Position the caliper body in the mounting support and tighten the pin bolts to 16–23 ft. lbs.
9. Replace the wheel, lower the car and bleed the system if necessary.

Types CL11HB and CL14B Series – Disc Brake Assembly

1. Raise the vehicle and support it securely. Remove the rear wheel.
2. Remove the two pin bolts and the lock spring. Remove the caliper, suspending it above the disc so as to avoid putting any strain on the hose.
3. Remove the pad retainers, pads, and shims.

NOTE: *Do not depress the brake pedal when the cylinder body is in the raised position or the piston will pop out. Avoid damaging the piston seal when removing/installing the pads and retainers.*

4. Check the level of fluid in the master cylinder. If the fluid is near the maximum level, use a clean syringe to remove fluid until the level is down well below the lip of the reservoir. Then, press the caliper piston back into the caliper by turning it clockwise (it has a helical

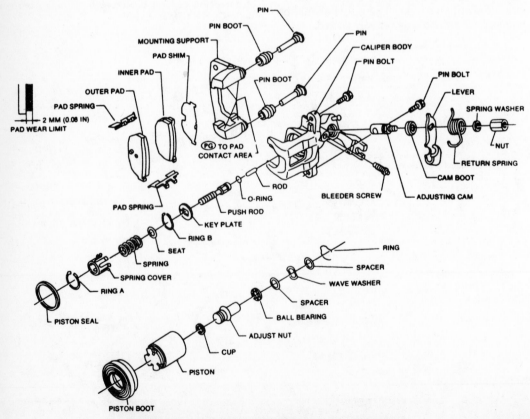

Exploded view of the CL11H series disc brake assembly

groove on the outer diameter). This will allow room for the installation of the thicker new pads.

5. Install the new pads using new shims in reverse order of the removal procedure. Torque the caliper pin bolts to 16–23 ft. lbs. Bleed the brakes if necessary. Make sure you pump the brakes and get a hard pedal before driving the car.

Brake Caliper

REMOVAL INSTALLATION AND OVERHAUL

Types CL11H, CL11HB, CL14B and CL9H Series – Disc Brake Assembly

1. See the appropriate procedure and remove the brake pads.
2. Disconnect the parking brake cable and brake hose. Unscrew the mounting bolts and remove the caliper assembly.
3. Remove the pin bolts and separate the caliper body from the mounting support.
4. Using needle nosed pliers, turn the piston counterclockwise and remove it.

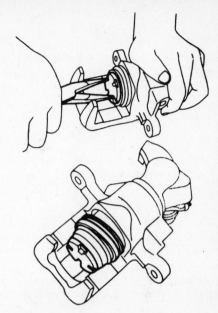

Turn the piston counterclockwise to remove it from the caliper body

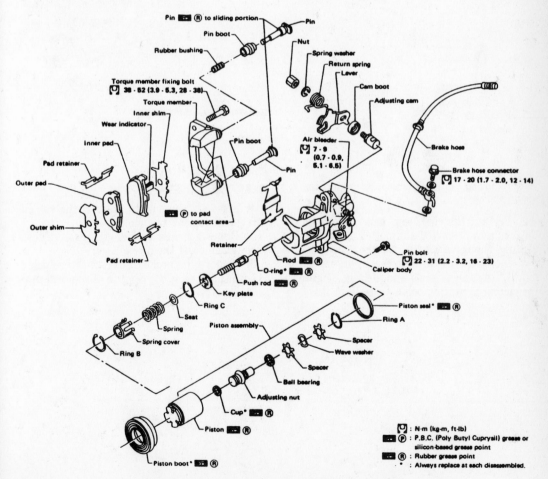

Exploded view of the CL9H series disc brake assembly

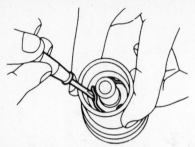

Prying off the ring from the inside of the piston—some rings may be the snap-ring type

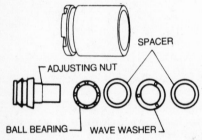

2 various CL11H caliper parts

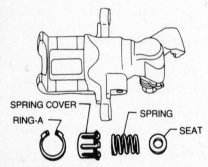

After removing the ring, remove the spring cover, spring and seat

5. Pry out the ring from inside the piston. You can now remove the adjusting nut, the ball bearing, the wave washer and the spacers.

6. Installation is in the reverse order of removal. Replace all seals and O-rings. Tighten the caliper mounting bolts to 28–38 ft. lbs.

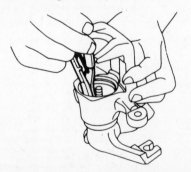

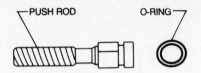

Remove the O-ring from the push rod—replace the O-ring during installation

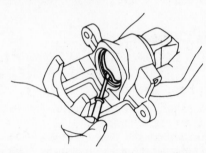

Carefully remove the oil seal—replace it during assembly

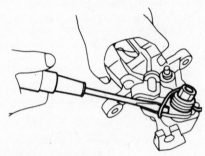

Removing the return spring

Brake Disc (Rotor)
REMOVAL & INSTALLATION

1. Raise and support the rear of the vehicle safely and remove the wheels.
2. Remove brake caliper assembly. Make sure not to twist the brake hose.
3. Remove the brake disc from the vehicle.
4. Installation is the reverse of removal procedure.

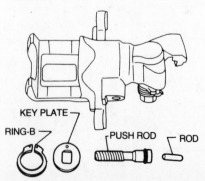

Remove the ring "B" with snap-ring pliers, then remove the key plate, push rod and rod

INSPECTION

Check the brake rotor for roughness, cracks or chips. The rotor can be machined on a brake lathe most auto parts stores have complete machine shop service. The rotors should be machined or replaced during every rear disc brake pad replacement.

REAR DRUM BRAKES

CAUTION: *Brake shoes contain asbestos, which has been determined to be a cancer causing agent. Never clean the brake surfaces with compressed air! Avoid inhaling any dust from any brake surface! When cleaning brake surfaces, use a commercially available brake cleaning fluid.*

Brake Drums

REMOVAL & INSTALLATION

200SX and 1990–92 Stanza Models

1. Raises the rear of the vehicle and support it on jack stands.
2. Remove the wheels.
3. Release the parking brake.
4. Pull off the brake drums. On some models there are two threaded service holes in each brake drum. If the drum will not come off, fit two correct size bolts in the service holes and screw them in: this will force the drum away from the axle.
5. If the drum cannot be easily removed, back off the brake adjustment.

NOTE: *Never depress the brake pedal while the brake drum is removed.*

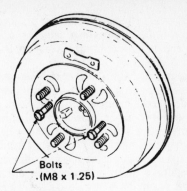

Brake drum removal

6. Installation is the reverse of removal procedure.

1982–89 Stanza and Stanza Wagon Models

NOTE: *For rear wheel bearing service procedures refer to Chapter 8.*

1. Raise the rear of the vehicle and support it on jackstands.
2. Remove the wheels.
3. Release the parking brake.
4. Remove the grease cap, the cotter pin and the adjusting cap and the wheel bearing nut.
5. Pull off the drum, taking care not to drop the tapered bearing assembly.
6. Install the drum assembly to the vehicle. Adjust the wheel bearings.
7. Install the wheels.

INSPECTION

After removing the brake drum, wipe out the accumulated dust with a damp cloth.

CAUTION: *Do not blow the brake dust out of*

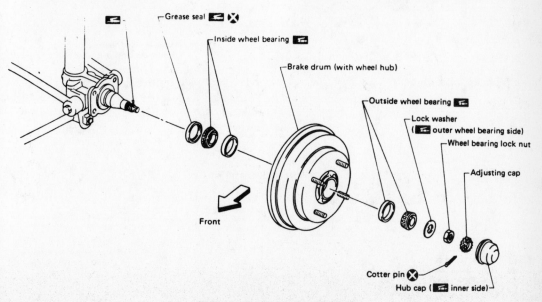

Brake drum and bearing removal

the drums with compressed air or lung power. Brake linings contain asbestos, a known cancer causing substance. Dispose of the cloth after use.

Inspect the drum for cracks, deep grooves, roughness, scoring, or out-of-roundness. Replace any brake drum which is cracked.

Smooth any slight scores by polishing the friction surface with the fine emery cloth or have the drum machined (trued) at a machine shop. Heavy or extensive scoring will cause excessive brake lining wear and should be removed from the brake drum through resurfacing.

Brake Shoes

INSPECTION

You should be able to check the brake shoe lining thickness after removing the brake drum. Check the Brake Specifications chart at the end of this Chapter to find the manufacturer's wear limits. However, this measurement may disagree with your state inspection laws. When replacing brake shoes, always check the surface of the brake drums for scoring or wear. The brake drums should resurfaced or machined if badly scored.

REMOVAL & INSTALLATION

NOTE: *If you are not thoroughly familiar with the procedures involved in brake replacement, disassemble and assemble one side at a time, leaving the other wheel intact, as a reference. This will reduce the risk of assembling brakes incorrectly. Special brake tools are available to make this repair easier. Refer to the illustrations — modify service steps for removal and installation.*

1. Raise the vehicle and remove the wheels.
2. Release the parking brake. Disconnect the cross rod from the lever of the brake cylinder if so equipped. Remove the brake drum. Place a heavy rubber band or clamp around the wheel cylinder to prevent the piston from coming out.
3. Remove the return springs, adjuster assembly, hold down springs and brake shoes.

To install:

4. Clean the backing plate and check the wheel cylinder for leaks.
5. The brake drums must be machined if scored or out of round.
6. Hook the return springs into the new shoes. The return spring ends should be between the shoes and the backing plate. The longer return spring must be adjacent to the wheel cylinder. A very thin film of grease may be applied to the pivot points at the ends of the brake shoes. Grease the shoe locating buttons on the backing plate, also. Be careful not to get grease on the linings or drums.
7. Install the adjuster assembly (rotate nut until adjuster rod is at its shortest point) between brake shoes. Place one shoe in the adjuster and piston slots, and pry the other shoe into position. Install hold down springs.

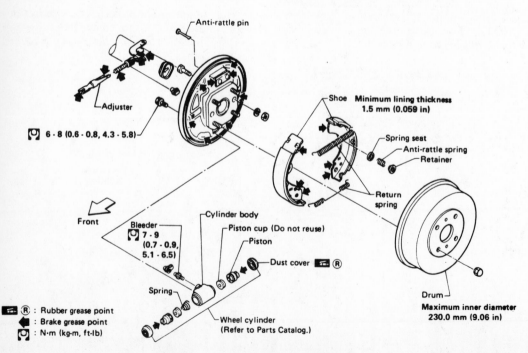

Rear drum brake assembly—(LT23 type)

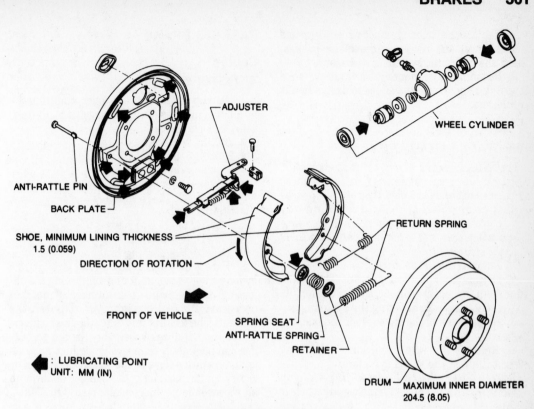

Rear drum brake assembly—Stanza

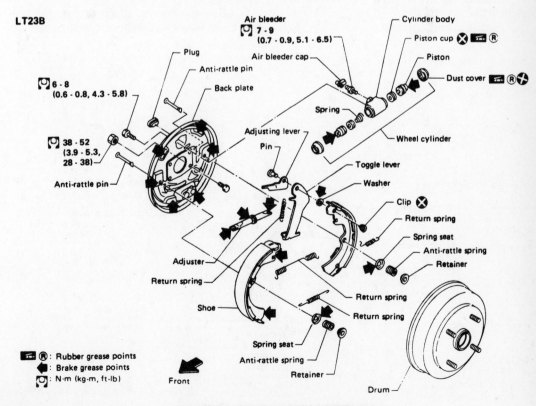

Rear drum brake assembly—(LT23B type)

8. Replace the drums (adjust wheel bearings if necessary) and wheels. Adjust the brakes. Bleed the hydraulic system if necessary.

9. Reconnect the handbrake, making sure that it does not cause the shoes to drag when it is released.

Wheel Cylinder

REMOVAL & INSTALLATION

CAUTION: *Brake shoes contain asbestos, which has been determined to be a cancer causing agent. Never clean the brake surfaces with compressed air! Avoid inhaling any dust from any brake surface! When cleaning brake surfaces, use a commercially available brake cleaning fluid.*

1. Remove the brake drum.

2. Disconnect the flare nut and the brake tube from the wheel cylinder, then plug the line to prevent dirt from entering the system.

3. Remove the brake shoes from the backing plate.

4. Remove the wheel cylinder-to-backing plate bolts and the wheel cylinders.

NOTE: *If the wheel cylinder is difficult to remove, bump it with a soft hammer to release it from the backing plate.*

5. Install the wheel cylinder assembly to the backing plate.

6. Connect all brake lines and install the brake drum.

7. Bleed the brake system.

PARKING BRAKE

Cables

ADJUSTMENT

1. Pull up the hand brake lever, counting the number of notches for full engagement. Full engagement should be:
- 200SX: 7–8 notches
- 240SX: 6–8 notches
- Stanza sedan
  1982–1988: 9–11 notches
  1989–92: 11–13 notches
- Stanza Wagon
  2WD: 11–17 notches
  4WD: 8–9 notches

2. Release the parking brake.

3. Except on 200SX, adjust the lever stroke by loosening the locknut and tightening the adjusting nut to reduce the number of notches necessary for full engagement. Tighten the locknut. The locknut and adjuster can be found inside the handbrake assembly, in the passenger compartment. Some vehicles just have an adjusting nut. Access to the locknut is gained by removing the parking brake console or through an access hole in the console itself. On 200SX, the lever stroke is adjusted by turning the equalizer under the vehicle.

4. Check the adjustment and repeat as necessary.

5. After adjustment, check to see that the rear brake levers, at the calipers, return to their

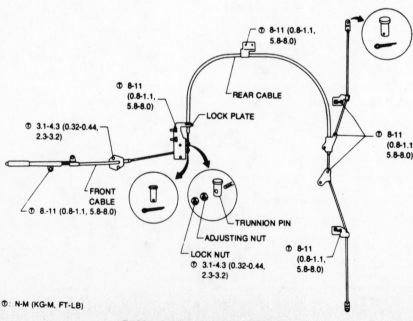

①: N·M (KG-M, FT-LB)

Parking brake assembly—Stanza

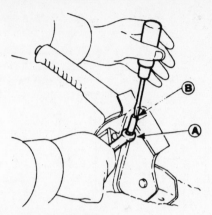

Parking brake adjustment

full off positions when the lever is released, and that the rear cables are not slack when the lever is released.

REMOVAL & INSTALLATION

Front Cable

1. Remove the parking brake console box.
2. Remove the heat insulator, if equipped.

3. Remove the front passenger seat, if required.
4. Disconnect the warning lamp switch plate connector.
5. Unbolt the lever from the floor.
6. Working from under the vehicle, remove the locknut, adjusting nut and equalizer.
7. Pull the front cable out through the compartment and remove it from the vehicle.

NOTE: *On some vehicles it may be necessary to separate the front cable from the lever by breaking the pin.*

8. Installation is the reverse of the removal procedure. Adjust the lever stroke.

Rear Cable

1. Back off on the adjusting nut or equalizer to loosen the cable tension.
2. Working from underneath the vehicle, disconnect the cable at the equalizer.
3. Remove the cable lock plate from the rear suspension member.
4. Disconnect the cable from the rear brakes.
5. Disconnect the cable from the suspension arm.

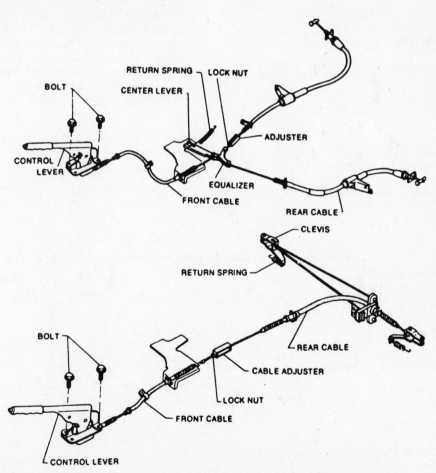

Two common types of parking brake cables—most vehicles are similar

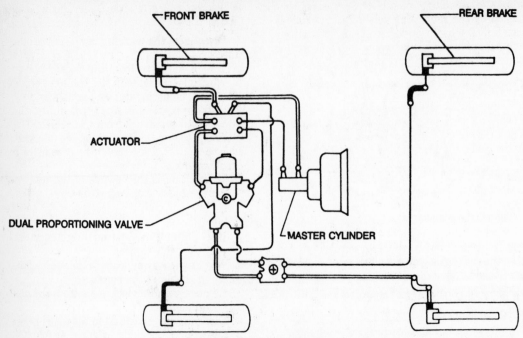

ABS brake system—Stanza

6. Remove the cable.

7. Installation is the reverse of the removal procedure. Adjust the lever stroke.

FOUR WHEEL ANTI-LOCK BRAKE SYSTEM

Description and Operation

STANZA

The ABS system employs a speed sensor at each wheel sending signals to the ECU. The control unit can trigger any or all of 4 solenoids within the hydraulic actuator. This system allows optimal control of the braking effort at each wheel. This model use a Dual Proportioning Valve (DPV) to further control distribution to the rear wheels. On this model the primary circuit is to the right front and left rear wheels.

240SX

The ABS system uses a 3 solenoid system within the actuator. Brake fluid line pressure is controlled separately to each of the wheels,

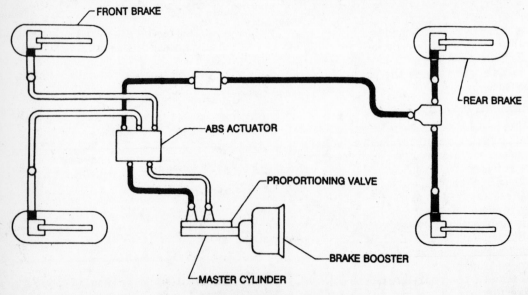

ABS brake system—240SX

while the signal line to both rear wheels is controlled by the remaining solenoid. This model uses only 3 sensors, one at each front wheel and one mounted in the side of the differential housing.

Troubleshooting

When the ECU detects a fault, the ANTI-LOCK warning lamp on the dash will be lite. The ECU will perform a self-diagnosis to identify the problem. When a vehicle has an a apparent ABS problem, it must be test driven above 19 mph (30 km/h) for at least 1 minute; this allows the ECU to test the system and store a diagnostic code if possible.

The stored code will be be displayed by the flashing of the LED on the electronic control unit. The display begins when the vehicle comes to a full stop after the self-diagnosis process. The engine must be running for the code to display. The stored code will repeat after a 5–10 second pause.

NOTE: *Both the ANTI-LOCK warning lamp and the LED will remain lit after repairs are made. The vehicle must be driven above 19 mph for at least 1 minute. If the ECU performs the self-diagnosis and finds no fault, the lamps will extinguish.*

Brake System Bleeding

PRECAUTIONS

• Carefully monitor the brake fluid level in the master cylinder at all times during the bleeding procedure. Keep the reservoir full at all times.

• Only use brake fluid that meets or exceeds DOT 3 specifications.

• Place a suitable container under the master cylinder to avoid spillage of brake fluid.

• Do not allow brake fluid to come in contact with any painted surface. Brake fluid makes excellent paint remover.

• Make sure to use the proper bleeding sequence.

BLEEDING PROCEDURE

The brake bleeding sequence varys from vehicle to vehicle and whether the vehicle is equipped with ABS or not. Bleeding sequences are as follows:

240SX (with ABS) — left rear caliper, right rear caliper, right front caliper, left front caliper, front side air bleeder on ABS actuator, rear side air bleeder on ABS actuator

Stanza — left wheel cylinder or caliper, right front caliper, right rear wheel cylinder or caliper, left front caliper

To bleed the brakes, use the following procedure:

1. If equipped with ABS, turn the ignition switch to the **OFF** position and disconnect the connectors from the ABS actuator. Wait a few minutes to allow for the system to bleed down, then disconnect the negative battery cable.

2. Connect a transparent vinyl tube to the bleeder valve. Submerge the tube in a container half filled with clean brake fluid.

3. Fully depress the brake pedal several times.

4. With the brake pedal depressed, open the air bleeder valve to release the air.

5. Close the air bleeder valve.

6. Release the brake pedal slowly.

7. Repeat Steps 3–6 until clear fluid flows from the air bleeder valve.

8. Check the fluid level in the master cylinder reservoir and add as necessary.

Anti-Lock Brake System Service

RELIEVING ANTI-LOCK BRAKE SYSTEM PRESSURE

To relieve the pressure from the ABS system, turn the ignition switch to the **OFF** position. Disconnect the connectors from the ABS actuator. Wait a few minutes to allow for the system to bleed down, then disconnect the negative battery cable.

ABS Actuator

REMOVAL & INSTALLATION

1. Relieve the pressure from the ABS system.

2. Disconnect the negative battery cable.

3. Disconnect the electrical harness connectors from the actuator.

4. Disconnect the fluid lines from the actuator. Plug the ends of the lines to prevent leakage.

5. On 240SX, remove the relay bracket.

6. Remove the actuator mounting bolts and nuts.

7. Remove the actuator from the mounting bracket.

To install:

8. Position the actuator onto the mounting bracket.

9. Install the actuator mounting fasteners.

10. On 240SX, install the relay bracket.

11. Connect the fluid lines and the harness connectors.

12. Connect the negative battery cable.

13. Bleed the brake system.

ABS Front Wheel Sensor

REMOVAL & INSTALLATION

1. Raise and support the vehicle safely.

2. Remove the front wheels.

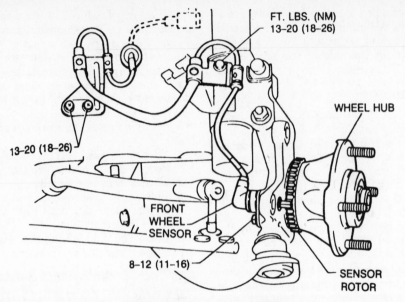

FT. LBS. (NM)
13–20 (18–26)

WHEEL HUB

13–20 (18–26)

FRONT
WHEEL
SENSOR

8–12 (11–16)

SENSOR
ROTOR

ABS front wheel sensor—240SX

3. Disconnect the sensor harness connector.

4. Detach the sensor mounting brackets.

5. Unbolt the sensor from the rear of the steering knuckle.

6. Withdraw the sensor from the sensor rotor. Remove the sensor mounting brackets from the sensor wiring.

NOTE: *During removal and installation, take care not to damage the sensor or the teeth of the rotor.*

To install:

7. Transfer the mounting brackets to the new sensor. Insert the sensor through the opening in the the rear of the knuckle and engage the sensor with the rotor teeth.

8. Install the sensor mounting bolts. Check and adjust the sensor-to-rotor clearance as described below. Once the clearance is set, tighten the sensor mounting bolt(s) to 8–12 ft. lbs. on 240SX and 13–17 ft. lbs. on Stanza.

9. Position and install the sensor mounting brackets. Make the sure the sensor wiring is routed properly.

10. Connect the sensor harness connector.

11. Mount the front wheels and lower the vehicle.

WHEEL SENSOR CLEARANCE ADJUSTMENT

1. Install the sensor.

2. Check the clearance between the edge of the sensor and rotor teeth using a feeler gauge. Clearances should be as follows:

a. On 240SX, front wheel sensor clearance should be 0.0108–0.0295 in. (0.275–0.75mm).

b. On Stanza, the clearance should be 0.008–0.039 in. (0.2–1.0mm).

3. To adjust the clearance, loosen the sensor mounting bolt(s) and move the sensor back and forth until the clearance is as specified.

4. Once the clearance is set, tighten the sensor mounting bolt(s) to 8–12 ft. lbs. on 240SX and 13–17 ft. lbs. on Stanza.

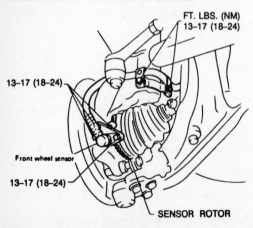

FT. LBS. (NM)
13–17 (18–24)

13–17 (18–24)

Front wheel sensor

13–17 (18–24)

SENSOR ROTOR

ABS front wheel sensor—Stanza

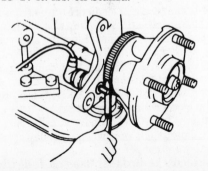

Checking front wheel sensor-to-rotor clearance

ABS Rear Wheel Sensor
REMOVAL & INSTALLATION

1. Raise and support the vehicle safely.
2. Remove the rear wheels.
3. Disconnect the sensor harness connector.
4. Detach the sensor mounting brackets.
5. Remove the sensor mounting bolts.
6. On Stanza, withdraw the sensor from the rear gusset. On 240SX, the sensor is located on the side of the differential carrier near the driveshaft companion flange.
7. Remove the sensor mounting brackets from the sensor wiring.

To install:

8. Transfer the mounting brackets to the new sensor.

9. Install the sensor. Check and adjust the sensor-to-rotor clearance as described below. Once the clearance is set, tighten the sensor mounting bolt(s) to to 13–20 ft. lbs.
10. Install the sensor mounting brackets. Make the sure the sensor wiring is routed properly.
11. Connect the sensor harness connector.
12. Mount the rear wheels and lower the vehicle.

WHEEL SENSOR CLEARANCE ADJUSTMENT

1. Install the rear wheel sensor.
2. Check the clearance between the edge of the sensor and rotor teeth using a feeler gauge. Clearances should be as follows:

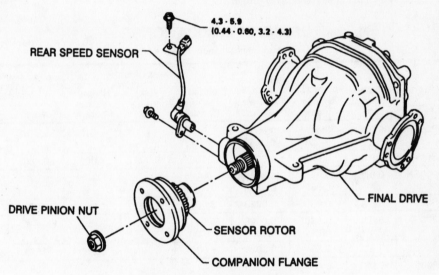

ABS rear wheel sensor—240SX

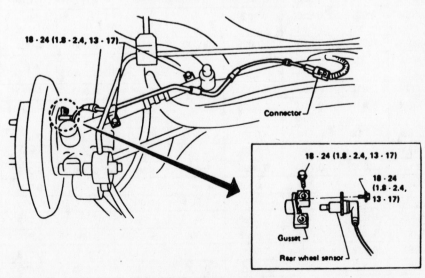

ABS rear wheel sensor—Stanza

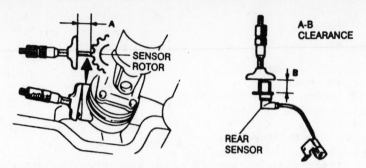

Checking rear wheel sensor-to-rotor clearance—240SX model

a. On 240SX, rear wheel sensor clearance should 0.0138–0.0246 in. (0.035–0.625mm).

b. On Stanza, the clearance should be 0.008–0.039 in. (0.2–1.0mm).

3. To adjust the clearance, loosen the sensor mounting bolt(s) and move the sensor back and forth until the clearance is as specified.

4. Once the clearance is set, tighten the sensor mounting bolt(s) to to 13–20 ft. lbs.

BRAKE SPECIFICATIONS
All measurements in inches unless noted

Year	Model	Master Cylinder Bore	Brake Disc		Brake Drum Diameter			Minimum Lining Thickness	
			Minimum Thickness	Maximum Runout	Original Inside Diameter	Max. Wear Limit	Maximum Machine Diameter	Front	Rear
1982	200SX	0.875	0.413/ 0.339	0.0047/ 0.0059	—	—	—	0.079	0.079
	Stanza	0.812	0.630	0.0059	8.000	8.090	8.060	0.080	0.059
1983	200SX	0.875	0.413/ 0.339	0.0047/ 0.0059	—	—	—	0.079	0.079
	Stanza	0.812	0.630	0.0028	8.000	8.090	8.060	0.079	0.059
1984	200SX	0.938	0.630/ 0.354	0.0028/ 0.0028	9.000	9.090	9.060	—	—
	Stanza	0.812	0.63	0.0028	8.000	8.090	8.060	0.079	0.059
1985	200SX	0.937	0.630/ 0.354	0.0028	—	—	—	0.08	0.08
	Stanza	0.812	0.630	0.0028	8.000	8.090	8.060	0.079	0.059
1986	200SX	0.937	0.630/ 0.354	0.0028	—	—	—	0.08	0.08
	Stanza	0.812	0.630	0.0028	8.000	8.090	8.060	0.079	0.059
1987	200SX	0.937	0.630/ 0.354	0.0028	—	—	—	0.08	0.08
	Stanza	0.812	0.630	0.0028	8.000	8.090	8.060	0.079	0.059
1988	200SX	0.937	0.630/ 0.354	0.0028	—	—	—	0.08	0.08
	Stanza	0.812	0.630	0.0028	8.000	8.090	8.060	0.079	0.059
1989	240SX	0.875	0.709	0.0028	—	—	—	0.079	0.079
	Stanza	1.000	0.787	0.0028	9.000	9.090	9.060	0.079	0.079
1990	240SX	0.937	0.709	0.0028	—	—	—	0.079	0.079
	Stanza	1.000	0.787	0.0028	9.000	9.090	9.060	0.079	0.079
1991	240SX	0.937	0.709	0.0028	—	—	—	0.079	0.079
	Stanza	1.000	0.787	0.0028	9.000	9.090	9.060	0.079	0.079
1992	240SX	0.937	0.709	0.0028	—	—	—	0.079	0.079
	Stanza	1.000	0.787	0.0028	9.000	9.090	9.060	0.079	0.079

NOTE: Minimum lining thickness is as recommended by the manufacturer. Due to variation in state inspection regulations, the minimum allowable thickness may be different than recommended by the manufacturer.

EXTERIOR

Doors

REMOVAL AND INSTALLATION

Front and Rear

1. Place a jack or stand beneath the door to support its weight.
   NOTE: *Place a rag between the lower edge of the door and jack or stand to prevent damage to painted surface.*
2. Remove door without hinge.
3. Remove the door hinge.
4. Installation is in the reverse order of removal.
   NOTE: *When installing hinge, coat the hinge link with multipurpose grease.*

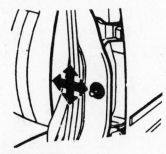

Adjusting door striker

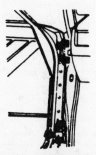

Removing mounting bolts from the door

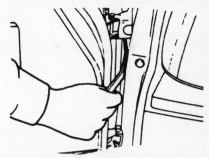

Using special type tool to adjust hinge

ADJUSTMENT

Front and Rear

Proper door alignment can be obtained by adjusting the door hinge and door lock striker. The door hinge and striker can be moved up and down fore and aft in enlarged holes by loosening the attaching bolts.
   NOTE: *The door should be adjusted for an even and parallel fit for the door opening and surrounding body panels.*

Hood

REMOVAL AND INSTALLATION

1. Open the hood and protect the body with covers to protect the painted surfaces.
2. Mark the hood hinge locations on the hood for proper reinstallation.
3. Holding both sides of the hood, unscrew the bolts securing the hinge to the hood. This operation requires a helper.
4. Installation is the reverse of removal.

ALIGNMENT

The hood can be adjusted with bolts attaching the hood to the hood hinges, hood lock mechanism and hood bumpers. Adjust the hood for an even fit between the front fenders.

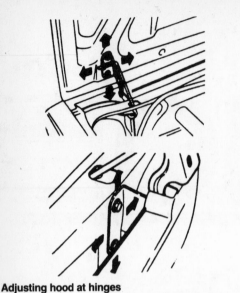

Adjusting hood at hinges

Adjusting hood at bumper rubber

Adjusting hood at lock

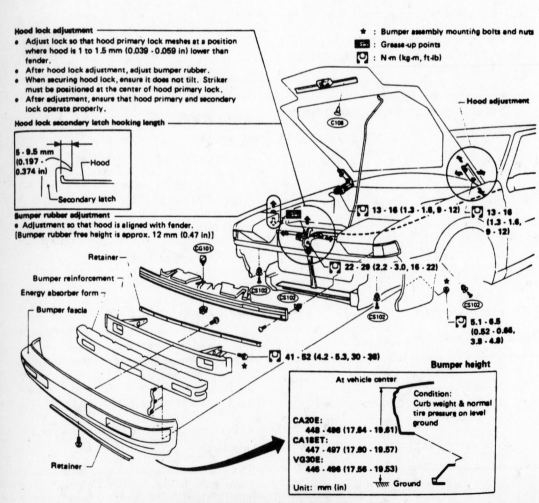

Hood lock adjustment

- Adjust lock so that hood primary lock meshes at a position where hood is 1 to 1.5 mm (0.039 - 0.059 in) lower than fender.
- After hood lock adjustment, adjust bumper rubber.
- When securing hood lock, ensure it does not tilt. Striker must be positioned at the center of hood primary lock.
- After adjustment, ensure that hood primary and secondary lock operate properly.

Hood lock secondary latch hooking length

5 - 9.5 mm
(0.197 - 0.374 in)
—Hood
—Secondary latch

Bumper rubber adjustment

- Adjustment so that hood is aligned with fender. [Bumper rubber free height is approx. 12 mm (0.47 in)]

★ : Bumper assembly mounting bolts and nuts

▨ : Grease-up points

⬚ : N·m (kg·m, ft-lb)

Hood adjustment

13 - 16 (1.3 - 1.6, 9 - 12)

13 - 16 (1.3 - 1.6, 9 - 12)

22 - 29 (2.2 - 3.0, 16 - 22)

5.1 - 6.5 (0.52 - 0.66, 3.8 - 4.8)

Retainer
Bumper reinforcement
Energy absorber form
Bumper fascia

41 - 52 (4.2 - 5.3, 30 - 38)

Retainer

Bumper height

At vehicle center

Condition:
Curb weight & normal tire pressure on level ground

CA20E:
　448 - 498 (17.64 - 19.61)
CA18ET:
　447 - 497 (17.60 - 19.57)
VG30E:
　446 - 496 (17.56 - 19.53)

Unit: mm (in)　Ground

Body front end assembly—1988 200SX model

1. Adjust the hood fore and aft by loosening the bolts attaching the hood to the hinge and repositioning hood.

2. Loosen the hood bumper lock nuts and lower bumpers until they do not contact the front of the hood when the hood is closed.

3. Set the striker at the center of the hood lock, and tighten the hood lock securing bolts temporarily.

4. Raise the two hood bumpers until the hood is flush with the fenders.

5. Tighten the hood lock securing bolts after the proper adjustment has been obtained.

Trunklid
REMOVAL AND INSTALLATION

1. Open the trunk lid and position a cloth or cushion to protect the painted areas.

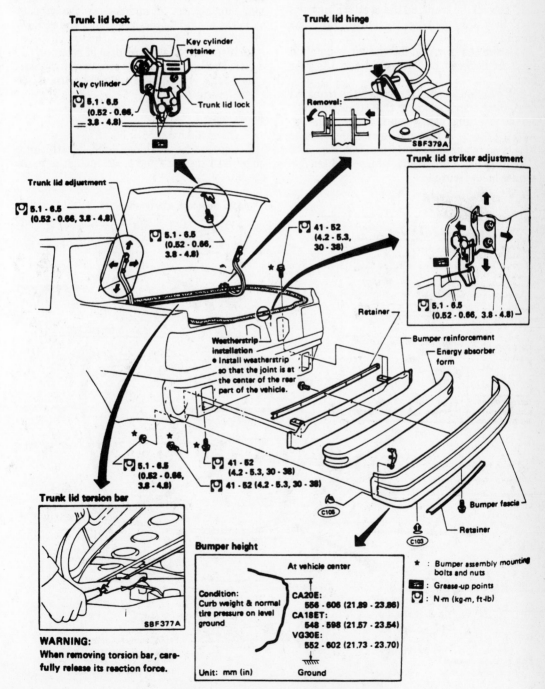

Body rear end assembly—1988 200SX model

2. Mark the trunk lid hinge locations or trunk lid for proper reinstallation.

3. Support the trunk lid by hand and remove the bolts attaching the trunk lid to the hinge. Then remove the trunk lid.

4. Installation is the reverse of removal.

ALIGNMENT

1. Loosen the trunk lid hinge attaching bolts until they are just loose enough to move the trunk lid.

2. Move the trunk lid for and aft to obtain a flush fit between the trunk lid and the rear fender.

3. To obtain a snug fit between the trunk lid and weatherstrip, loosen the trunk lid lock striker attaching bolts enough to move the lid, working the striker up and down and from side to side as required.

4. After the adjustment is made tighten the striker bolts securely.

Hatchback or Tailgate Lid
REMOVAL AND INSTALLATION

1. Open the lid and disconnect the rear defogger harness if so equipped.

2. Mark the hinge locations on the lid for proper relocation.

3. Position rags between the roof and the upper end of the lid to prevent scratching the paint.

4. Support the lid and remove the support bolts the the hinge retaining bolts and remove the lid.

5. Installation is the reverse of removal.

NOTE: *Be careful not to scratch the lift support rods. A scratched rod may cause oil or gas leakaged*

ALIGNMENT

1. Open the hatchback lid.

2. Loosen the lid hinge to body attaching bolts until they are just loose enough to move the lid.

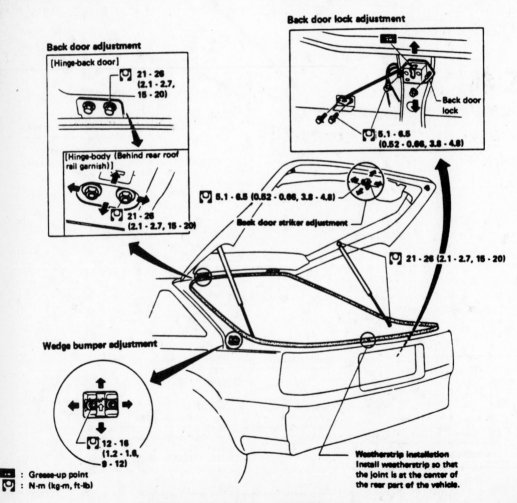

Body rear end assembly—1988 200SX model

1. Lock
2. Bumper rubber
3. Tailgate
4. Tailgate stay
5. Lock cylinder
6. Retaining clip
7. Striker catcher
8. Shim
9. Striker
10. Wedge bumper
11. Back door hinge

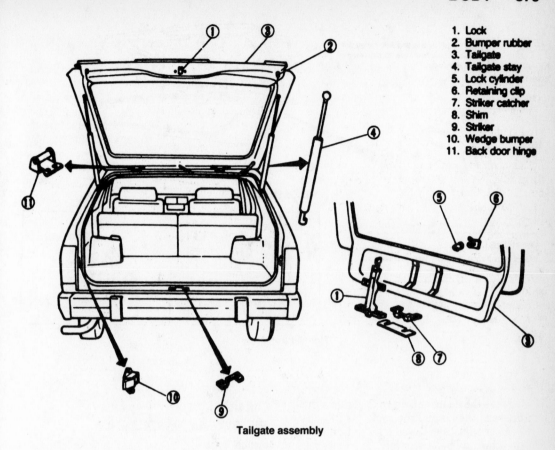

Tailgate assembly

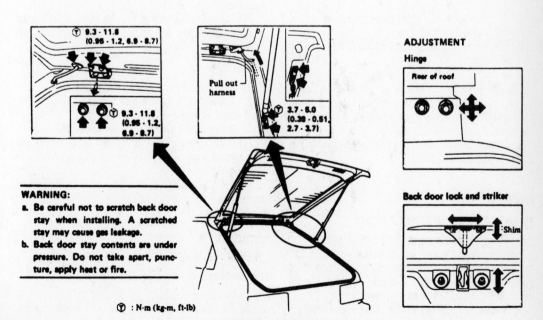

① 9.3 - 11.8
(0.95 - 1.2, 6.9 - 8.7)

① 9.3 - 11.8
(0.95 - 1.2,
6.9 - 8.7)

Pull out
harness

3.7 - 5.0
(0.38 - 0.51,
2.7 - 3.7)

WARNING:
a. Be careful not to scratch back door stay when installing. A scratched stay may cause gas leakage.
b. Back door stay contents are under pressure. Do not take apart, puncture, apply heat or fire.

① : N·m (kg-m, ft-lb)

ADJUSTMENT

Hinge

Rear of roof

Back door lock and striker

Shim

Hatchback assembly

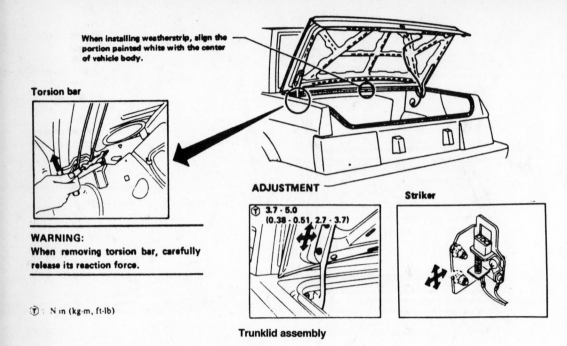

When installing weatherstrip, align the portion painted white with the center of vehicle body.

Torsion bar

WARNING:
When removing torsion bar, carefully release its reaction force.

ⓣ : N·m (kg·m, ft-lb)

ADJUSTMENT

ⓣ 3.7 - 5.0
(0.38 - 0.51, 2.7 - 3.7)

Striker

Trunklid assembly

3. Move the lid up and down to obtain a flush fit between the lid and the roof.

4. After adjustment is completed tighten the hinge attaching bolts securely.

Bumpers

REMOVAL AND INSTALLATION

Front and Rear

1. Disconnect all electrical connectors at bumper assembly.

2. Remove bumper mounting bolts and bumper assembly.

3. Remove shock absorbers from bumper.
CAUTION: *The shock absorber is filled with a high pressure gas and should not be diassembled, drilled or exposed to an open flame.*

4. Install shock absorbers and bumper in reverse order of removal.

Grille

REMOVAL AND INSTALLATION

1. Remove radiator grille bracket bolts.
NOTE: Some early vehicles may use clips to hold the radiator grille assembly in place. The radiator grille assembly is made of plastic; never use excessive force to remove it.

2. Remove radiator grille from the vehicle.

3. To install reverse the removal procedures.

Outside Mirrors

REMOVAL AND INSTALLATION

Manual Type

1. Remove control knob handle.
2. Remove door corner finisher panel.
3. Remove mirror body attaching screws, and then remove mirror body

4. Installation is in the reverse order of removal.
NOTE: *Apply sealer to the rear surface of door corner finish panel during installation to prevent water leak.*

Power Type

1. Remove door corner finisher panel.
2. Remove mirror body attaching screws, and then remove mirror body
3. Disconnect the electrical connection.
NOTE: *It may be necessary to remove the door trim panel to gain access to the electrical connection.*

4. Installation is in the reverse order of removal.

Antenna

REMOVAL AND INSTALLATION

Fender Mounted

1. Remove antenna mounting nut.
2. Disconnect the antenna lead at the radio.
3. Remove antenna from vehicle.

Hood lock adjustment
- Adjust hood so that hood primary lock meshes at position 1 to 1.5 mm (0.039 to 0.059 in) lower than fender.
- After hood lock adjustment, adjust bumper rubber.
- When securing hood lock, ensure it does not tilt. Striker must be positioned at the center of hood primary lock.
- After adjustment, ensure that hood primary and secondary lock operate properly.

Hood lock secondary latch hooking length

More than 5.0 mm (0.197 in)

— Hood

— Secondary latch

Bumper rubber adjustment
- Adjust that hood is aligned with fender. At that time deflection is approx. 0.5 mm (0.020 in).

[Bumper rubber free height is approx. 22.0 mm (0.866 in)]

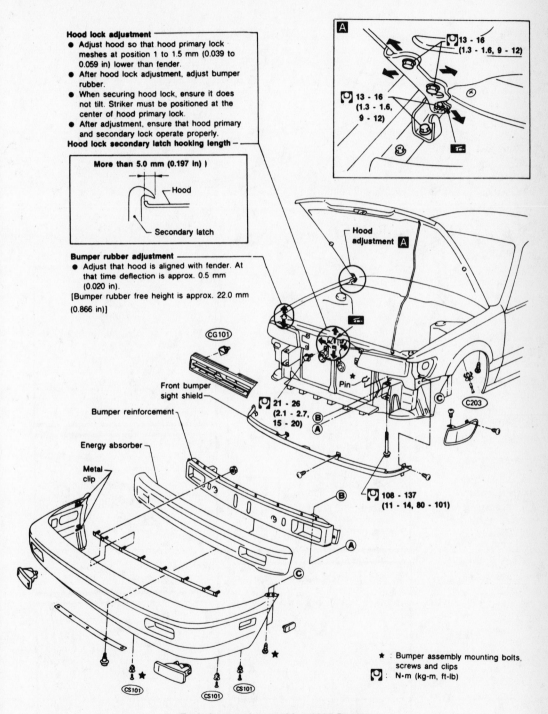

A

13 - 16 (1.3 - 1.6, 9 - 12)

13 - 16 (1.3 - 1.6, 9 - 12)

Hood adjustment A

CG101

Front bumper sight shield

Bumper reinforcement

Energy absorber

Metal clip

Pin

21 - 26 (2.1 - 2.7, 15 - 20)

108 - 137 (11 - 14, 80 - 101)

C203

B
A

B

A

C

CS101   CS101   CS101

★ : Bumper assembly mounting bolts, screws and clips

N·m (kg-m, ft-lb)

Body front end assembly—1992 Stanza

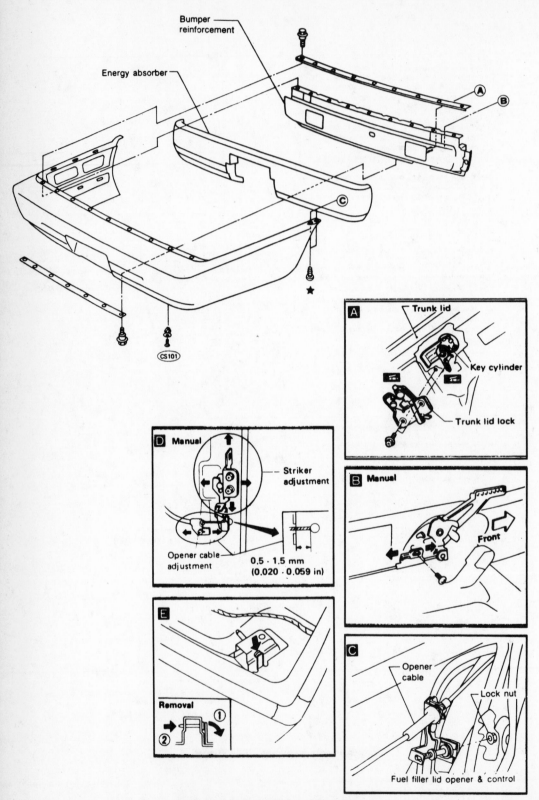

Bumper reinforcement

Energy absorber

Ⓐ
Ⓑ
Ⓒ

CS101

★

A Trunk lid
Key cylinder
Trunk lid lock

D Manual
Striker adjustment
Opener cable adjustment
0.5 - 1.5 mm (0.020 - 0.059 in)

B Manual
Front

E
Removal
①
②

C
Opener cable
Lock nut
Fuel filler lid opener & control

Body front end assembly—1992 Stanza

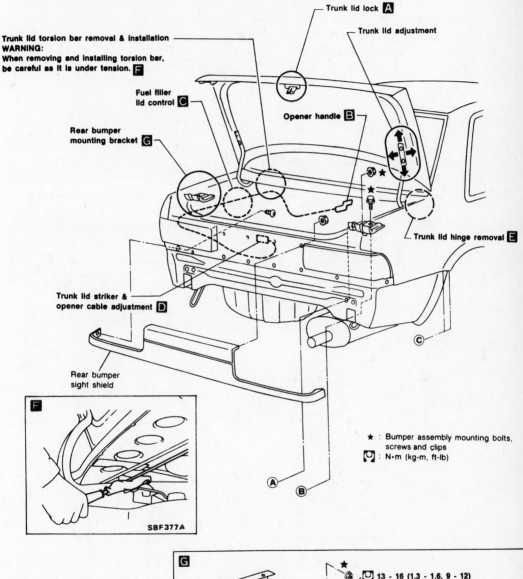

Trunk lid lock **A**

Trunk lid adjustment

Trunk lid torsion bar removal & installation
WARNING:
When removing and installing torsion bar,
be careful as it is under tension. **F**

Fuel filler
lid control **C**

Opener handle **B**

Rear bumper
mounting bracket **G**

Trunk lid hinge removal **E**

Trunk lid striker &
opener cable adjustment **D**

Rear bumper
sight shield

★ : Bumper assembly mounting bolts,
    screws and clips
⊙ : N•m (kg-m, ft-lb)

F

SBF377A

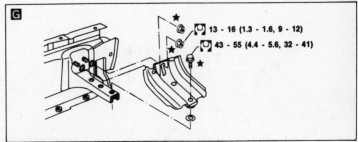

G

⊙ 13 - 16 (1.3 - 1.6, 9 - 12)
⊙ 43 - 55 (4.4 - 5.6, 32 - 41)

Body front end assembly—1992 Stanza

FRONT BUMPER

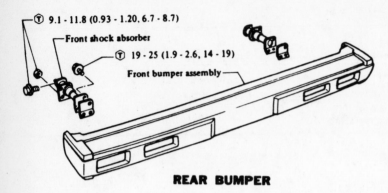

Ⓣ 9.1 - 11.8 (0.93 - 1.20, 6.7 - 8.7)

Front shock absorber

Ⓣ 19 - 25 (1.9 - 2.6, 14 - 19)

Front bumper assembly

Ⓣ : N·m (kg-m, ft-lb)

REAR BUMPER

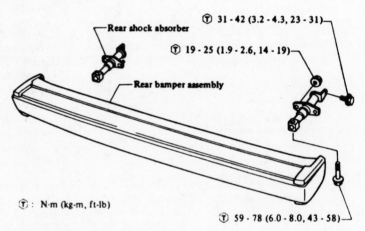

Rear shock absorber

Ⓣ 31 - 42 (3.2 - 4.3, 23 - 31)

Ⓣ 19 - 25 (1.9 - 2.6, 14 - 19)

Rear bumper assembly

Ⓣ : N·m (kg-m, ft-lb)

Ⓣ 59 - 78 (6.0 - 8.0, 43 - 58)

Bumper assembly—early models

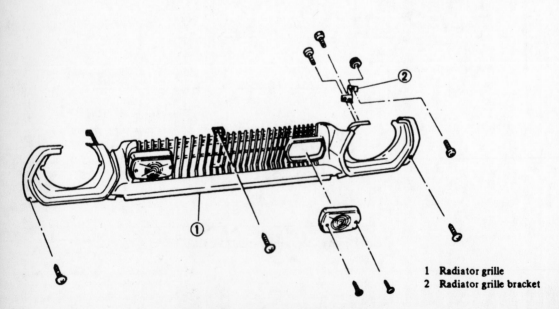

1 Radiator grille
2 Radiator grille bracket

Removing radiator grille retaining screws

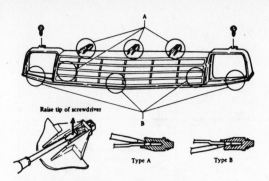

A

B

Raise tip of screwdriver

Type A   Type B

Removing radiator grille retaining clips

4. Installation is in the reverse order of removal.

Antenna Rod (Replacement)
REMOVAL AND INSTALLATION

1. Remove the antenna nut and antenna base.

2. Remove the antenna rod while raising it by operating antenna motor. Turn radio switch from OFF to ON to operate antenna motor.

To install:

3. Lower antenna rod by operating antenna motor.

4. Insert gear section of antenna into place with it facing (see illustration) in the correct position for proper operation.

5. Retract antenna rod completely-attach antenna rod into housing.

6. Install antenna nut and base, check for proper operation.

INTERIOR

Door Panel, Glass and Regulator
REMOVAL AND INSTALLATION
Front and Rear

1. Remove the regulator handle by pushing the set pin spring off.

2. Remove the arm rest, door inside handle escutcheon and door lock.

3. Remove the door finisher and sealing screen.

4. On some models it may be necessary to remove the outer door moulding.

5. Lower the door glass with the regulator handle until the regulator-to-glass attaching bolts appear at the access holes in the door inside panel.

6. Raise the door glass and draw it upwards.

7. Remove the regulator attaching bolts and remove the regulator assembly through the large access hole in ther door panel.

To install:

8. Install the window regulator assembly in the door.

9. Connect all mounting bolts and check for proper operation.

10. Adjust the window if necessary and install the door trim panel.

Clip and Fastener		
• Clips and fasteners in BF section correspond to the following numbers and symbols.		
• Replace any clips and/or fasteners which are damaged during removal or installation.		
Symbol No.	Shapes	Removal & Installation
C101		Removal: Remove by bending up with flat-bladed screwdrivers. SBF256G
C102	SBF114B SBF137B	Removal: Pull up by rotating.

Clip and fasteners

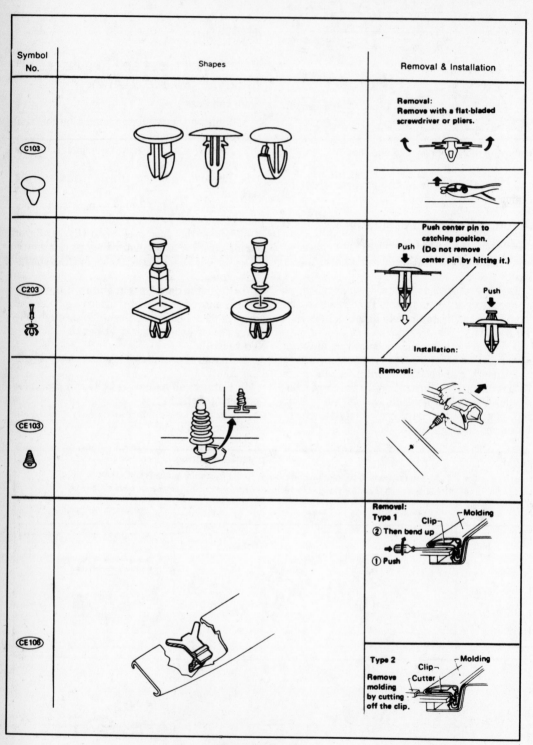

Clip and fasteners

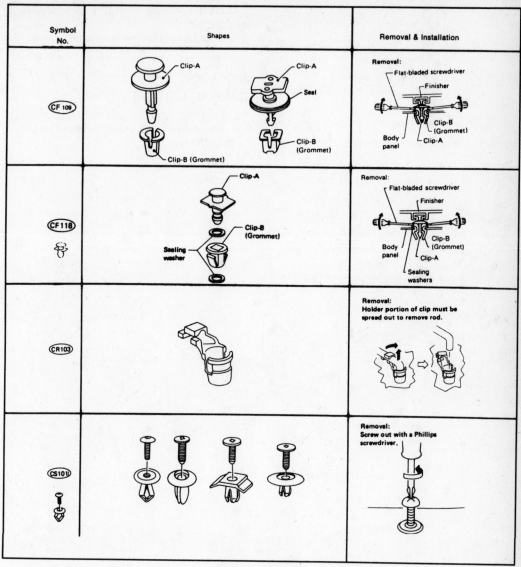

Symbol No.	Shapes	Removal & Installation
CF 109	Clip-A, Clip-A, Seal, Clip-B (Grommet), Clip-B (Grommet)	Removal: Flat-bladed screwdriver, Finisher, Body panel, Clip-B (Grommet), Clip-A
CF 118	Clip-A, Clip-B (Grommet), Sealing washer	Removal: Flat-bladed screwdriver, Finisher, Body panel, Clip-B (Grommet), Clip-A, Sealing washers
CR103		Removal: Holder portion of clip must be spread out to remove rod.
CS101		Removal: Screw out with a Phillips screwdriver.

Clip and fasteners

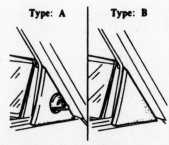

Type: A   Type: B

Two types of door corner finisher panels

Removing mirror mounting screws

Butyl seal

Apply sealer to rear surface of finisher panel

11. Install all the attaching components to the door panel.
12. Install the window regulator handle.

Door Locks

REMOVAL AND INSTALLATION

1. Remove the door panel and sealing screen.
2. Remove the lock cylinder from the rod by turning the clip.

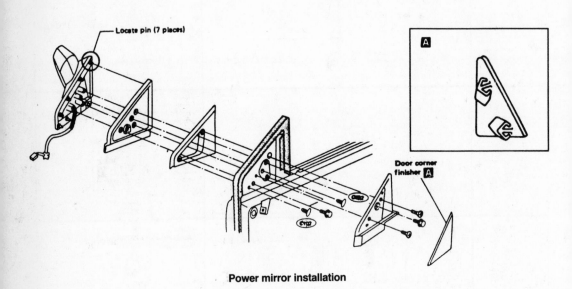

Power mirror installation

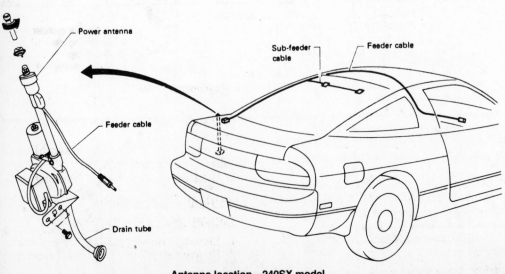

Antenna location—240SX model

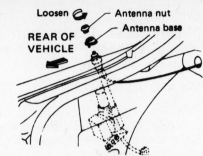

Antenna rod replacement—Step 1

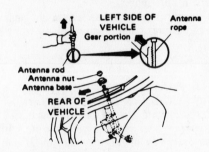

Antenna rod replacement—Step 2

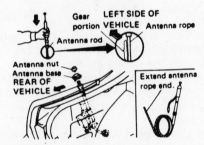

Antenna rod replacement—Step 3

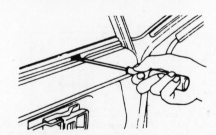

Removing outer door moulding

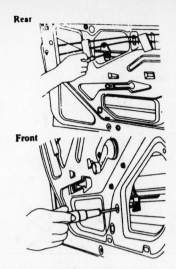

Removing glass attaching bolts

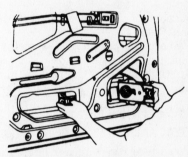

Removing window regulator from the door

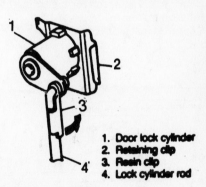

1. Door lock cylinder
2. Retaining clip
3. Resin clip
4. Lock cylinder rod

Lock cylinder assembly

3. Loosen the nuts attaching the outside door handle and remove the outside door handle.

4. Remove the screws retaining the inside door handle and door lock, and remove the door lock assembly from the hole in the inside of the door.

5. Remove the lock cylinder by removing the retaining clip.

To install:

6. Install the lock cylinder and clip to the door.

7. Install the door lock assembly and handles.

8. Install door panel and all attaching parts.

Electrical Window Motor
REMOVAL AND INSTALLATION

1. Remove the door panel and sealing screen.

2. Remove the power widow motor mounting bolts

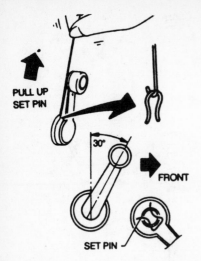

PULL UP
SET PIN

30°

FRONT

SET PIN

Regulator handle and set pin removal and installation

3. Remove all electrical connections and cable connection.

4. Remove the power window motor from the vehicle

5. Installation is in the reverse order of removal.

Inside Rear View Mirror

REMOVAL AND INSTALLATION

1. Remove rear view mirror mounting bolt cover.

2. Remove rear view mirror mounting bolts.

3. Remove mirror.

4. Installation is in the reverse order of removal.

Front Windshield
Rear Window Glass—Coupe/Sedan
Hatch Glass—Liftback
Fixed Side Glass

REMOVAL AND INSTALLATION

The glass assembly installation has to conform to Federal Motor Vehicle Safety Standards. A few special tools are necessary to perform this kind of repair.

1. Remove all external components (wipers, etc.) and all mouldings.

2. Be careful not to scratch/damage glass or body--cut sealant bond using glass removal tools.

3. Remove the glass assembly from the vehicle.

NOTE: *Use genuine Nissan sealant kit or equivalent. Follow instructions furnished with sealant kit. Do not use sealant which is 12 months past its production date. After glass assembly installation DO NOT move the vehicle for a 24 hour period.*

4. Clean all bonding surface thoroughly with proper solvent.

To install:

5. On body side of glass installation, install spacers to panel with double faced tape or equivalent in the correct location.

6. On body side of glass installation, also install upper and side molding fastener in the correct location. Apply primer E to the installation track--allow to dry.

7. On glass, install dam rubber and spacers with double faced tape or equivalent in the cor-

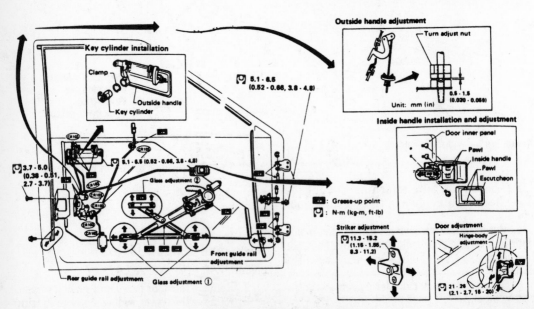

Front door assembly—1988 200SX

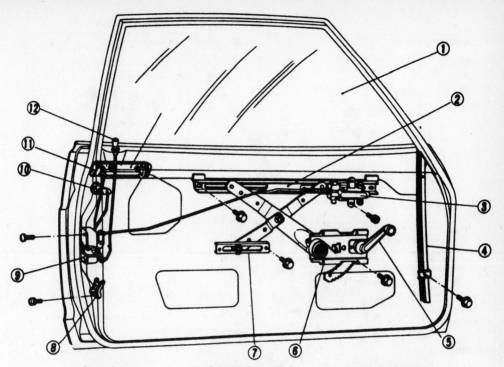

1. Door glass
2. Guide channel A
3. Inside door handle
4. Front lower sash
5. Regulator handle
6. Regulator assembly
7. Guide channel B
8. Glass lower guide
9. Door lock assembly
10. Door lock cylinder
11. Outside door handle
12. Inside door lock knob

Front door assembly—early models

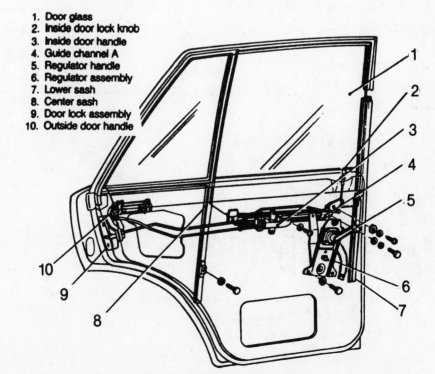

1. Door glass
2. Inside door lock knob
3. Inside door handle
4. Guide channel A
5. Regulator handle
6. Regulator assembly
7. Lower sash
8. Center sash
9. Door lock assembly
10. Outside door handle

Rear door assembly—early models

Ⓖ : LUBRICATION POINT

DOOR GLASS ADJUSTMENT

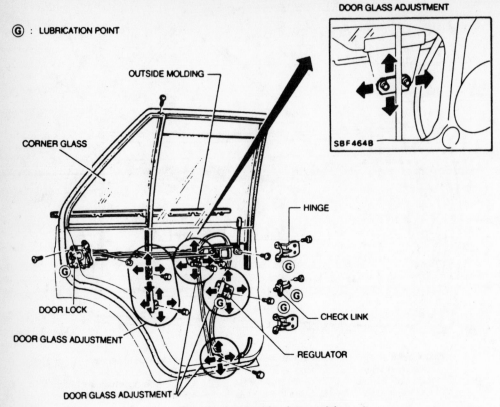

OUTSIDE MOLDING

CORNER GLASS

HINGE

DOOR LOCK

CHECK LINK

DOOR GLASS ADJUSTMENT

REGULATOR

DOOR GLASS ADJUSTMENT

S8F464B

Rear door assembly—late models

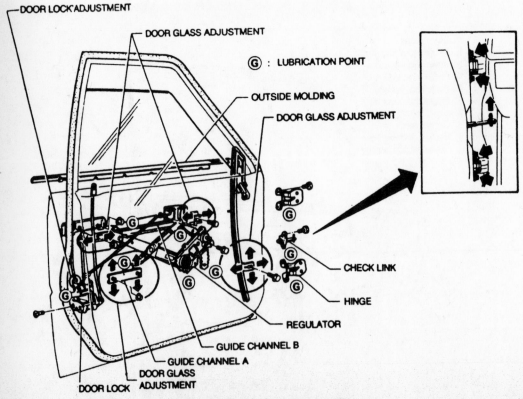

DOOR LOCK ADJUSTMENT

DOOR GLASS ADJUSTMENT

Ⓖ : LUBRICATION POINT

OUTSIDE MOLDING

DOOR GLASS ADJUSTMENT

CHECK LINK

HINGE

REGULATOR

GUIDE CHANNEL B

GUIDE CHANNEL A

DOOR GLASS ADJUSTMENT

DOOR LOCK

Front door assembly—late models

Rear Door

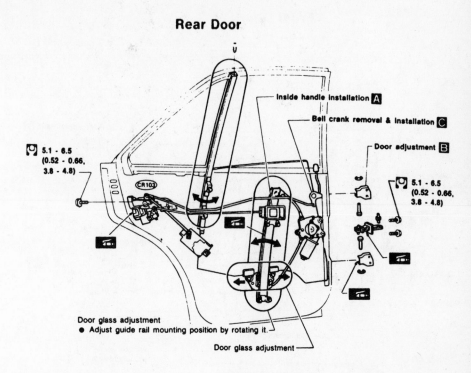

inside handle installation **A**

Bell crank removal & installation **C**

Door adjustment **B**

5.1 - 6.5
(0.52 - 0.66,
3.8 - 4.8)

5.1 - 6.5
(0.52 - 0.66,
3.8 - 4.8)

CR103

Door glass adjustment
● Adjust guide rail mounting position by rotating it.

Door glass adjustment

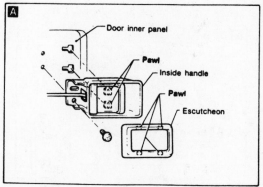

A

Door inner panel

Pawl

Inside handle

Pawl

Escutcheon

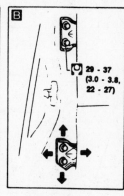

B

29 - 37
(3.0 - 3.8,
22 - 27)

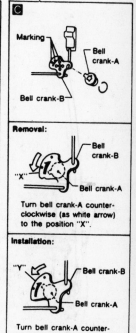

C

Marking

Bell
crank-A

Bell crank-B

Removal:

Bell
crank-B

"X"

Bell crank-A

Turn bell crank-A counterclockwise (as white arrow)
to the position "X".

Installation:

"Y"

Bell crank-B

Bell crank-A

Turn bell crank-A counterclockwise to the position "Y".

Striker adjustment

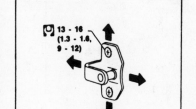

13 - 16
(1.3 - 1.6,
9 - 12)

Rear door assembly—1992 Stanza

Front Door

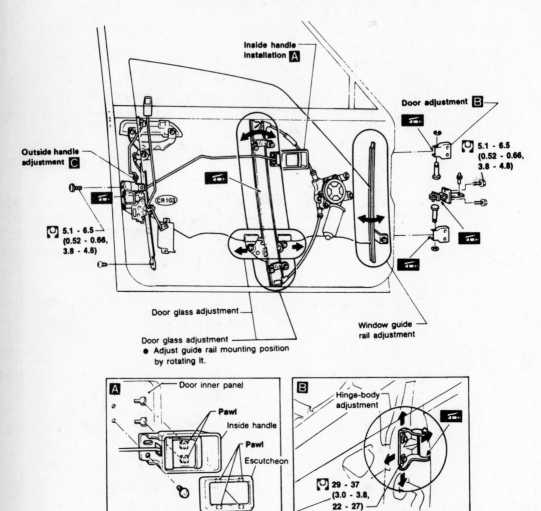

Inside handle installation [A]

Door adjustment [B]

5.1 - 6.5 (0.52 - 0.66, 3.8 - 4.8)

Outside handle adjustment [C]

CR103

5.1 - 6.5 (0.52 - 0.66, 3.8 - 4.8)

Door glass adjustment

Door glass adjustment
- Adjust guide rail mounting position by rotating it.

Window guide rail adjustment

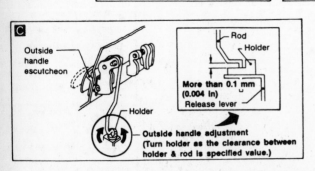

[A] Door inner panel

Pawl

Inside handle

Pawl

Escutcheon

[B] Hinge-body adjustment

29 - 37 (3.0 - 3.8, 22 - 27)

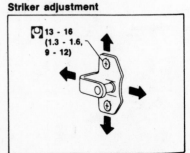

[C] Outside handle escutcheon

Rod

Holder

More than 0.1 mm (0.004 in)

Release lever

Holder

Outside handle adjustment (Turn holder as the clearance between holder & rod is specified value.)

Striker adjustment

13 - 16 (1.3 - 1.6, 9 - 12)

: N·m (kg-m, ft-lb)

Front door assembly—1992 Stanza

CHILTON'S
AUTO BODY REPAIR TIPS

Tools and Materials • Step-by-Step Illustrated Procedures
How To Repair Dents, Scratches and Rust Holes
Spray Painting and Refinishing Tips

With a little practice, basic body repair procedures can be mastered by any do-it-yourself mechanic. The step-by-step repairs shown here can be applied to almost any type of auto body repair.

TOOLS & MATERIALS

You may already have basic tools, such as hammers and electric drills. Other tools unique to body repair — body hammers, grinding attachments, sanding blocks, dent puller, half-round plastic file and plastic spreaders — are relatively inexpensive and can be obtained wherever auto parts or auto body repair parts are sold. Portable air compressors and paint spray guns can be purchased or rented.

Auto Body Repair Kits

The best and most often used products are available to the do-it-yourselfer in kit form, from major manufacturers of auto body repair products. The same manufacturers also merchandise the individual products for use by pros.

Kits are available to make a wide variety of repairs, including holes, dents and scratches and fiberglass, and offer the advantage of buying the materials you'll need for the job. There is little waste or chance of materials going bad from not being used. Many kits may also contain basic body-working tools such as body files, sanding blocks and spreaders. Check the contents of the kit before buying your tools.

BODY REPAIR TIPS

Safety

Many of the products associated with auto body repair and refinishing contain toxic chemicals. Read all labels before opening containers and store them in a safe place and manner.

• Wear eye protection (safety goggles) when using power tools or when performing any operation that involves the removal of any type of material.

• Wear lung protection (disposable mask or respirator) when grinding, sanding or painting.

Sanding

1 Sand off paint before using a dent puller. When using a non-adhesive sanding disc, cover the back of the disc with an overlapping layer or two of masking tape and trim the edges. The disc will last considerably longer.

2 Use the circular motion of the sanding disc to grind *into* the edge of the repair. Grinding or sanding away from the jagged edge will only tear the sandpaper.

3 Use the palm of your hand flat on the panel to detect high and low spots. Do not use your fingertips. Slide your hand slowly back and forth.

WORKING WITH BODY FILLER

Mixing The Filler

Cleanliness and proper mixing and application are extremely important. Use a clean piece of plastic or glass or a disposable artist's palette to mix body filler.

1 Allow plenty of time and follow directions. No useful purpose will be served by adding more hardener to make it cure (set-up) faster. Less hardener means more curing time, but the mixture dries harder; more hardener means less curing time but a softer mixture.

2 Both the hardener and the filler should be thoroughly kneaded or stirred before mixing. Hardener should be a solid paste and dispense like thin toothpaste. Body filler should be smooth, and free of lumps or thick spots.

Getting the proper amount of hardener in the filler is the trickiest part of preparing the filler. Use the same amount of hardener in cold or warm weather. For contour filler (thick coats), a bead of hardener twice the diameter of the filler is about right. There's about a 15% margin on either side, but, if in doubt use less hardener.

3 Mix the body filler and hardener by wiping across the mixing surface, picking the mixture up and wiping it again. Colder weather requires longer mixing times. Do not mix in a circular motion; this will trap air bubbles which will become holes in the cured filler.

Applying The Filler

1 For best results, filler should not be applied over 1/4" thick.

Apply the filler in several coats. Build it up to above the level of the repair surface so that it can be sanded or grated down.

The first coat of filler must be pressed on with a firm wiping motion.

Apply the filler in one direction only. Working the filler back and forth will either pull it off the metal or trap air bubbles.

REPAIRING DENTS

Before you start, take a few minutes to study the damaged area. Try to visualize the shape of the panel before it was damaged. If the damage is on the left fender, look at the right fender and use it as a guide. If there is access to the panel from behind, you can reshape it with a body hammer. If not, you'll have to use a dent puller. Go slowly and work the metal a little at a time. Get the panel as straight as possible before applying filler.

1 This dent is typical of one that can be pulled out or hammered out from behind. Remove the headlight cover, headlight assembly and turn signal housing.

2 Drill a series of holes ½ the size of the end of the dent puller along the stress line. Make some trial pulls and assess the results. If necessary, drill more holes and try again. Do not hurry.

3 If possible, use a body hammer and block to shape the metal back to its original contours. Get the metal back as close to its original shape as possible. Don't depend on body filler to fill dents.

4 Using an 80-grit grinding disc on an electric drill, grind the paint from the surrounding area down to bare metal. Use a new grinding pad to prevent heat buildup that will warp metal.

5 The area should look like this when you're finished grinding. Knock the drill holes in and tape over small openings to keep plastic filler out.

6 Mix the body filler (see Body Repair Tips). Spread the body filler evenly over the entire area (see Body Repair Tips). Be sure to cover the area completely.

7 Let the body filler dry until the surface can just be scratched with your fingernail. Knock the high spots from the body filler with a body file ("Cheesegrater"). Check frequently with the palm of your hand for high and low spots.

8 Check to be sure that trim pieces that will be installed later will fit exactly. Sand the area with 40-grit paper.

9 If you wind up with low spots, you may have to apply another layer of filler.

10 Knock the high spots off with 40-grit paper. When you are satisfied with the contours of the repair, apply a thin coat of filler to cover pin holes and scratches.

11 Block sand the area with 40-grit paper to a smooth finish. Pay particular attention to body lines and ridges that must be well-defined.

12 Sand the area with 400 paper and then finish with a scuff pad. The finished repair is ready for priming and painting (see Painting Tips).

Materials and photos courtesy of Ritt Jones Auto Body, Prospect Park, PA.

REPAIRING RUST HOLES

There are many ways to repair rust holes. The fiberglass cloth kit shown here is one of the most cost efficient for the owner because it provides a strong repair that resists cracking and moisture and is relatively easy to use. It can be used on large and small holes (with or without backing) and can be applied over contoured areas. Remember, however, that short of replacing an entire panel, no repair is a guarantee that the rust will not return.

1 Remove any trim that will be in the way. Clean away all loose debris. Cut away all the rusted metal. But be sure to leave enough metal to retain the contour or body shape.

2 Grind away all traces of rust with a 24-grit grinding disc. Be sure to grind back 3-4 inches from the edge of the hole down to bare metal and be sure all traces of paint, primer and rust are removed.

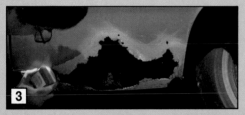

3 Block sand the area with 80 or 100 grit sandpaper to get a clear, shiny surface and feathered paint edge. Tap the edges of the hole inward with a ball peen hammer.

4 If you are going to use release film, cut a piece about 2-3″ larger than the area you have sanded. Place the film over the repair and mark the sanded area on the film. Avoid any unnecessary wrinkling of the film.

5 Cut 2 pieces of fiberglass matte to match the shape of the repair. One piece should be about 1″ smaller than the sanded area and the second piece should be 1″ smaller than the first. Mix enough filler and hardener to saturate the fiberglass material (see Body Repair Tips).

6 Lay the release sheet on a flat surface and spread an even layer of filler, large enough to cover the repair. Lay the smaller piece of fiberglass cloth in the center of the sheet and spread another layer of filler over the fiberglass cloth. Repeat the operation for the larger piece of cloth.

7 Place the repair material over the repair area, with the release film facing outward. Use a spreader and work from the center outward to smooth the material, following the body contours. Be sure to remove all air bubbles.

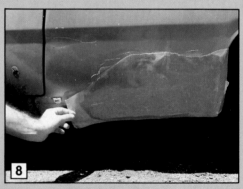

8 Wait until the repair has dried tack-free and peel off the release sheet. The ideal working temperature is 60°-90° F. Cooler or warmer temperatures or high humidity may require additional curing time. Wait longer, if in doubt.

9

9 Sand and feather-edge the entire area. The initial sanding can be done with a sanding disc on an electric drill if care is used. Finish the sanding with a block sander. Low spots can be filled with body filler; this may require several applications.

10

10 When the filler can just be scratched with a fingernail, knock the high spots down with a body file and smooth the entire area with 80-grit. Feather the filled areas into the surrounding areas.

11

11 When the area is sanded smooth, mix some topcoat and hardener and apply it directly with a spreader. This will give a smooth finish and prevent the glass matte from showing through the paint.

12

12 Block sand the topcoat smooth with finishing sandpaper (200 grit), and 400 grit. The repair is ready for masking, priming and painting (see Painting Tips).

Materials and photos courtesy Marson Corporation, Chelsea, Massachusetts

PAINTING TIPS

Preparation

1 SANDING — Use a 400 or 600 grit wet or dry sandpaper. Wet-sand the area with a 1/4 sheet of sandpaper soaked in clean water. Keep the paper wet while sanding. Sand the area until the repaired area tapers into the original finish.

2 CLEANING — Wash the area to be painted thoroughly with water and a clean rag. Rinse it thoroughly and wipe the surface dry until you're sure it's completely free of dirt, dust, fingerprints, wax, detergent or other foreign matter.

3 MASKING — Protect any areas you don't want to overspray by covering them with masking tape and newspaper. Be careful not get fingerprints on the area to be painted.

4 PRIMING — All exposed metal should be primed before painting. Primer protects the metal and provides an excellent surface for paint adhesion. When the primer is dry, wet-sand the area again with 600 grit wet-sandpaper. Clean the area again after sanding.

4

Painting Techniques

Paint applied from either a spray gun or a spray can (for small areas) will provide good results. Experiment on an old piece of metal to get the right combination before you begin painting.

SPRAYING VISCOSITY (SPRAY GUN ONLY) — Paint should be thinned to spraying viscosity according to the directions on the can. Use only the recommended thinner or reducer and the same amount of reduction regardless of temperature.

AIR PRESSURE (SPRAY GUN ONLY) — This is extremely important. Be sure you are using the proper recommended pressure.

TEMPERATURE — The surface to be painted should be approximately the same temperature as the surrounding air. Applying warm paint to a cold surface, or vice versa, will completely upset the paint characteristics.

THICKNESS — Spray with smooth strokes. In general, the thicker the coat of paint, the longer the drying time. Apply several thin coats about 30 seconds apart. The paint should remain wet long enough to flow out and no longer; heavier coats will only produce sags or wrinkles. Spray a light (fog) coat, followed by heavier color coats.

DISTANCE — The ideal spraying distance is 8″-12″ from the gun or can to the surface. Shorter distances will produce ripples, while greater distances will result in orange peel, dry film and poor color match and loss of material due to overspray.

OVERLAPPING — The gun or can should be kept at right angles to the surface at all times. Work to a wet edge at an even speed, using a 50% overlap and direct the center of the spray at the lower or nearest edge of the previous stroke.

RUBBING OUT (BLENDING) FRESH PAINT — Let the paint dry thoroughly. Runs or imperfections can be sanded out, primed and repainted.

Don't be in too big a hurry to remove the masking. This only produces paint ridges. When the finish has dried for at least a week, apply a small amount of fine grade rubbing compound with a clean, wet cloth. Use lots of water and blend the new paint with the surrounding area.

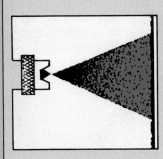

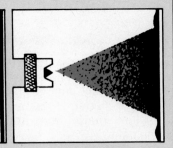

WRONG	CORRECT	WRONG

Thin coat. Stroke too fast, not enough overlap, gun too far away.   *Medium coat. Proper distance, good stroke, proper overlap.*   *Heavy coat. Stroke too slow, too much overlap, gun too close.*

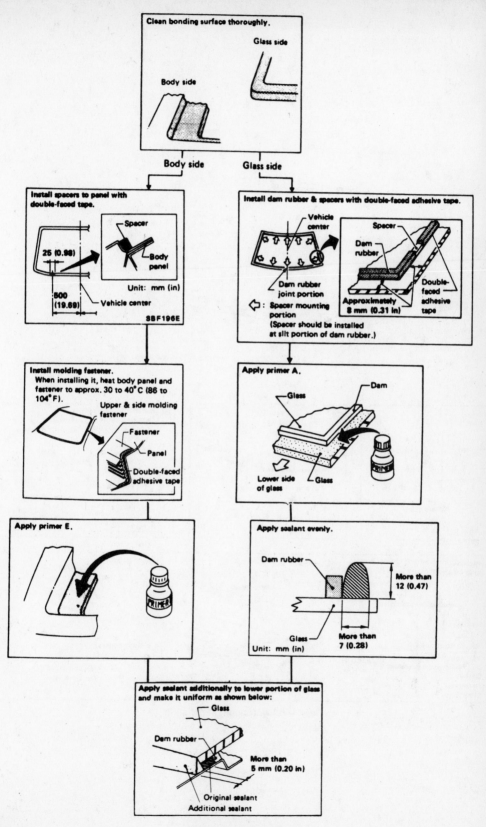

Clean bonding surface thoroughly.

Glass side

Body side

Body side   Glass side

Install spacers to panel with double-faced tape.

Spacer

Body panel

25 (0.98)

500 (19.69)   Vehicle center

Unit: mm (in)

SBF196E

Install dam rubber & spacers with double-faced adhesive tape.

Vehicle center

Spacer

Dam rubber

Double-faced adhesive tape

Dam rubber joint portion

Approximately 8 mm (0.31 in)

⬅ : Spacer mounting portion
(Spacer should be installed at slit portion of dam rubber.)

Install molding fastener.
When installing it, heat body panel and fastener to approx. 30 to 40°C (86 to 104°F).

Upper & side molding fastener

Fastener

Panel

Double-faced adhesive tape

Apply primer A.

Dam

Glass

Lower side of glass   Glass

PRIMER

Apply primer E.

PRIMER

Apply sealant evenly.

Dam rubber

More than 12 (0.47)

Glass

More than 7 (0.28)

Unit: mm (in)

Apply sealant additionally to lower portion of glass and make it uniform as shown below:

Glass

Dam rubber

More than 5 mm (0.20 in)

Original sealant

Additional sealant

Windshield installation

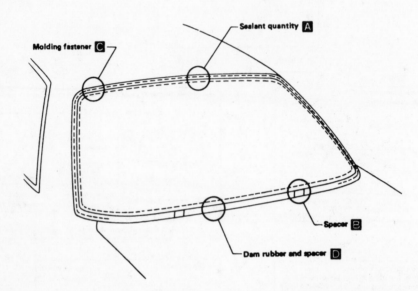

Sealant quantity **A**

Molding fastener **C**

Spacer **B**

Dam rubber and spacer **D**

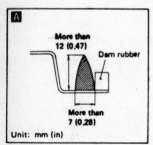

A

More than 12 (0.47)

Dam rubber

More than 7 (0.28)

Unit: mm (in)

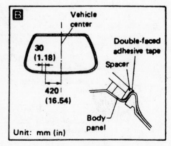

B

Vehicle center

30 (1.18)

420 (16.54)

Double-faced adhesive tape

Spacer

Body panel

Unit: mm (in)

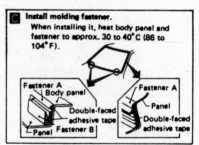

C Install molding fastener.

When installing it, heat body panel and fastener to approx. 30 to 40°C (86 to 104°F).

Fastener A
Body panel
Double-faced adhesive tape
Panel Fastener B

Fastener A
Panel
Double-faced adhesive tape

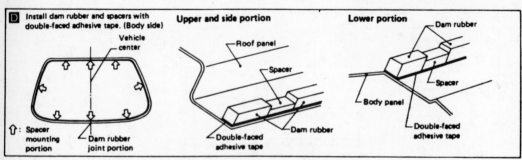

D Install dam rubber and spacers with double-faced adhesive tape. (Body side)

Vehicle center

⇧ : Spacer mounting portion

Dam rubber joint portion

Upper and side portion

Roof panel

Spacer

Double-faced adhesive tape

Dam rubber

Lower portion

Dam rubber

Spacer

Body panel

Double-faced adhesive tape

Back window (coupe) installation

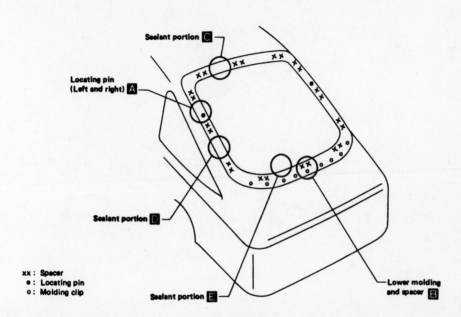

Sealant portion C

Locating pin (Left and right) A

Sealant portion D

Sealant portion E

xx : Spacer
● : Locating pin
○ : Molding clip

Lower molding and spacer B

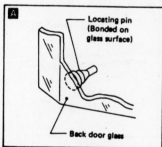

A

Locating pin (Bonded on glass surface)

Back door glass

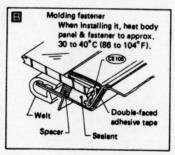

B

Molding fastener
When installing it, heat body panel & fastener to approx. 30 to 40°C (86 to 104°F).

CE106

Welt

Spacer

Sealant

Double-faced adhesive tape

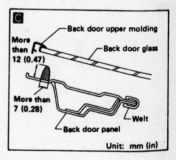

C

More than 12 (0.47)

Back door upper molding

Back door glass

More than 7 (0.28)

Back door panel

Welt

Unit: mm (in)

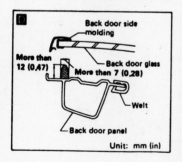

D

Back door side molding

More than 12 (0.47)

Back door glass

More than 7 (0.28)

Welt

Back door panel

Unit: mm (in)

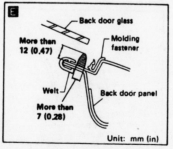

E

Back door glass

More than 12 (0.47)

Molding fastener

Welt

Back door panel

More than 7 (0.28)

Unit: mm (in)

Back window (fastback) installation

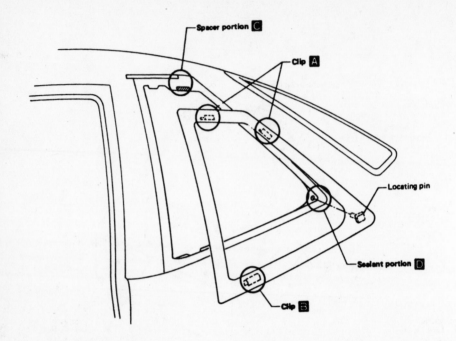

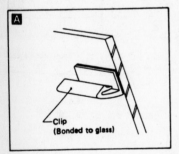

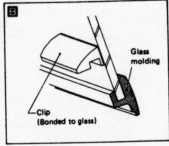

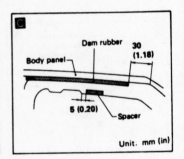

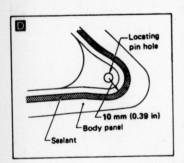

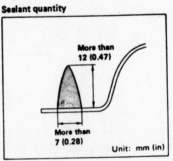

Side window installation

Lumbar support system

Walk-in mechanism

- The walk-in system is non-adjustable.

Walk-in wire

Release wire

N·m (kg-m, ft-lb)

Grease-up point
(Do not apply too much grease as it will drip)

Head rest holder
- Remove holder after rolling back seat back trim.

Nylon housing

13 - 16 (1.3 - 1.6, 9 - 12)

Reclining device

42 - 54
(4.3 - 5.5,
31 - 40)

42 - 54 (4.3 - 5.5, 31 - 40)

21 - 26 (2.1 - 2.7, 15 - 20)

Sliding device

21 - 26
(2.1 - 2.7,
15 - 20)

21 - 26 (2.1 - 2.7, 15 - 20)

13 - 16
(1.3 - 1.6, 9 - 12)

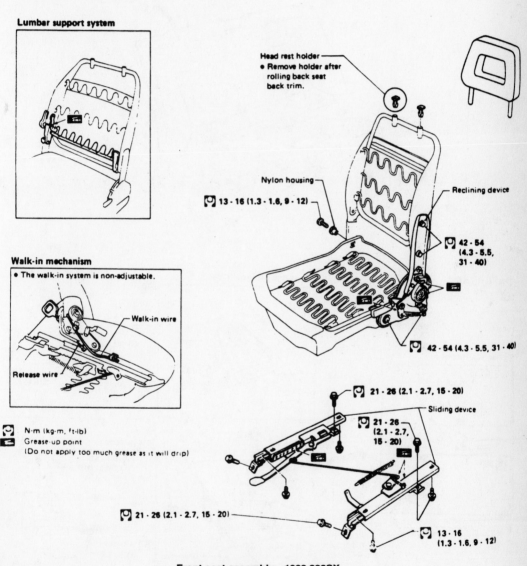

Front seat assembly—1988 200SX

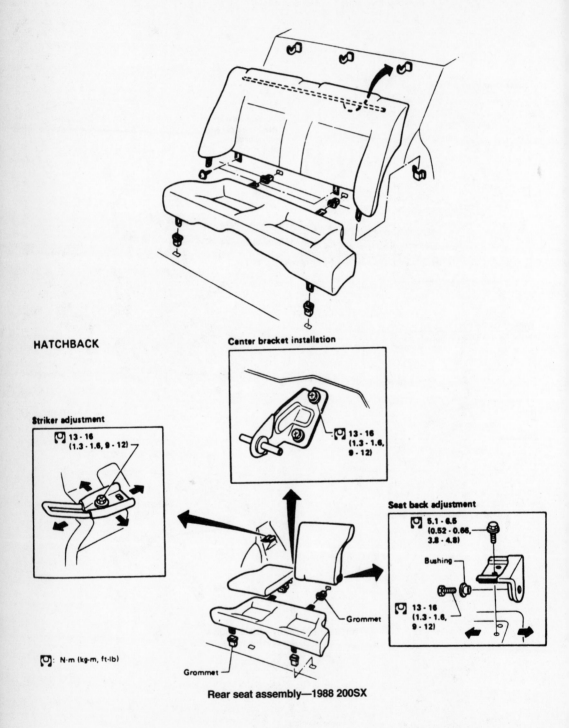

HATCHBACK

Center bracket installation

13 - 16
(1.3 - 1.6,
9 - 12)

Striker adjustment

13 - 16
(1.3 - 1.6, 9 - 12)

Seat back adjustment

5.1 - 6.5
(0.52 - 0.66,
3.8 - 4.8)

Bushing

13 - 16
(1.3 - 1.6,
9 - 12)

Grommet

: N·m (kg-m, ft-lb)

Grommet

Rear seat assembly—1988 200SX

Front Seat

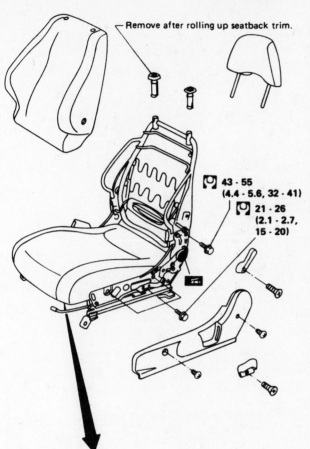

— Remove after rolling up seatback trim.

43 - 55
(4.4 - 5.6, 32 - 41)

21 - 26
(2.1 - 2.7,
15 - 20)

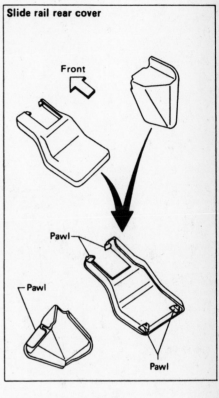

Slide rail rear cover

Front

Pawl

Pawl

Pawl

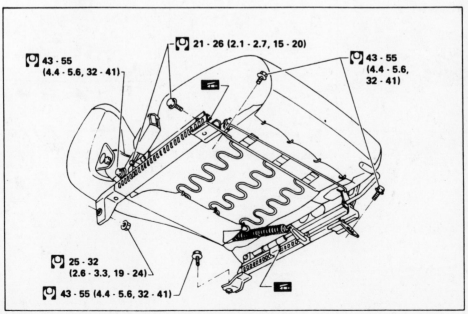

21 - 26 (2.1 - 2.7, 15 - 20)

43 - 55
(4.4 - 5.6, 32 - 41)

43 - 55
(4.4 - 5.6,
32 - 41)

25 - 32
(2.6 - 3.3, 19 - 24)

43 - 55 (4.4 - 5.6, 32 - 41)

: N·m (kg-m, ft-lb)

Front seat assembly—240SX

Rear Seat

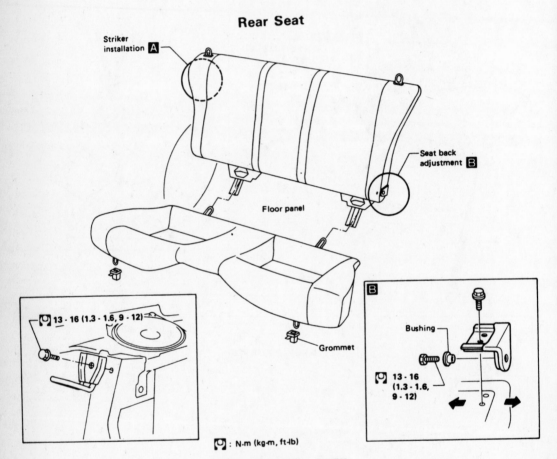

Striker installation **A**

Seat back adjustment **B**

Floor panel

A

13 - 16 (1.3 - 1.6, 9 - 12)

Grommet

B

Bushing

13 - 16
(1.3 - 1.6,
9 - 12)

: N·m (kg·m, ft·lb)

Rear seat assembly—240SX

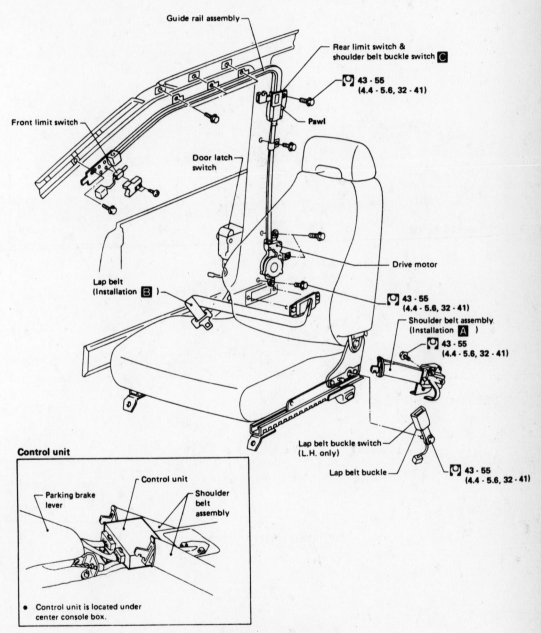

Guide rail assembly

Rear limit switch &
shoulder belt buckle switch **C**

43 - 55
(4.4 - 5.6, 32 - 41)

Front limit switch

Pawl

Door latch
switch

Drive motor

Lap belt
(Installation **B**)

43 - 55
(4.4 - 5.6, 32 - 41)

Shoulder belt assembly
(Installation **A**)

43 - 55
(4.4 - 5.6, 32 - 41)

Lap belt buckle switch
(L.H. only)

Lap belt buckle

43 - 55
(4.4 - 5.6, 32 - 41)

Control unit

Control unit

Parking brake
lever

Shoulder
belt
assembly

● Control unit is located under
center console box.

Automatic seat belt system

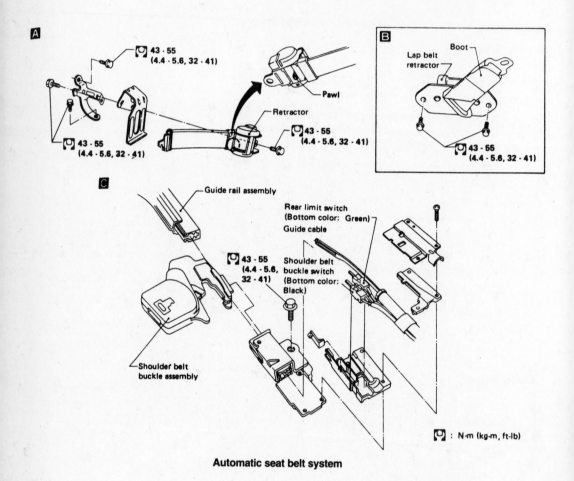

A

43 - 55
(4.4 - 5.6, 32 - 41)

43 - 55
(4.4 - 5.6, 32 - 41)

Pawl

Retractor

43 - 55
(4.4 - 5.6, 32 - 41)

B

Boot

Lap belt
retractor

43 - 55
(4.4 - 5.6, 32 - 41)

C

Guide rail assembly

Rear limit switch
(Bottom color: Green)

Guide cable

43 - 55
(4.4 - 5.6,
32 - 41)

Shoulder belt
buckle switch
(Bottom color:
Black)

Shoulder belt
buckle assembly

: N·m (kg-m, ft-lb)

Automatic seat belt system

Front Seat

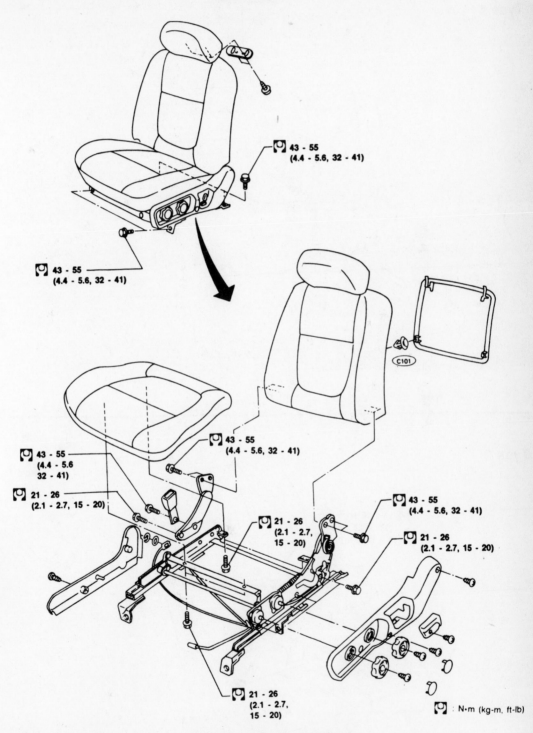

43 - 55
(4.4 - 5.6, 32 - 41)

43 - 55
(4.4 - 5.6, 32 - 41)

C101

43 - 55
(4.4 - 5.6, 32 - 41)

43 - 55
(4.4 - 5.6
32 - 41)

21 - 26
(2.1 - 2.7, 15 - 20)

43 - 55
(4.4 - 5.6, 32 - 41)

21 - 26
(2.1 - 2.7,
15 - 20)

21 - 26
(2.1 - 2.7, 15 - 20)

21 - 26
(2.1 - 2.7,
15 - 20)

: N•m (kg-m, ft-lb)

Front seat assembly—1992 Stanza

Rear Seat

Type 1

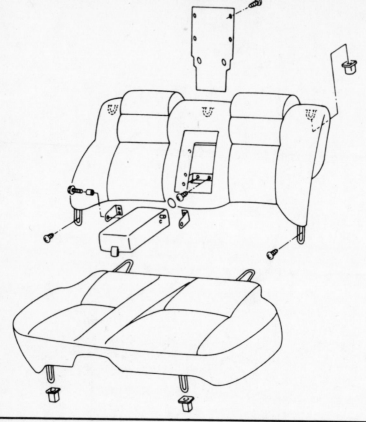

Type 2

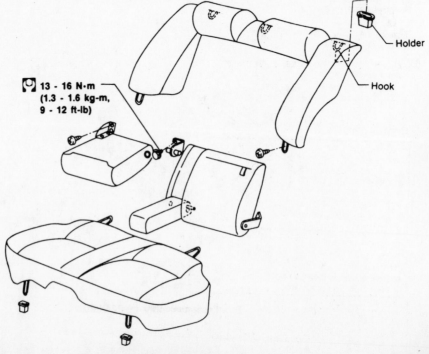

— Holder

— Hook

13 - 16 N·m
(1.3 - 1.6 kg-m,
9 - 12 ft-lb)

Rear seat assembly—1992 Stanza

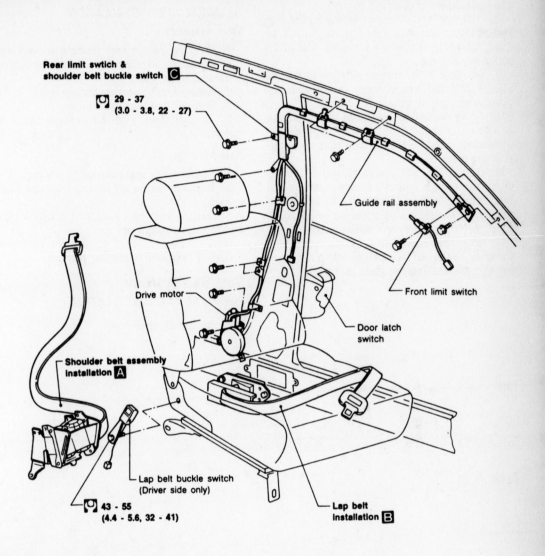

Rear limit swtich &
shoulder belt buckle switch **C**

⬚ 29 - 37
(3.0 - 3.8, 22 - 27)

Guide rail assembly

Front limit switch

Drive motor

Door latch
switch

Shoulder belt assembly
installation **A**

Lap belt buckle switch
(Driver side only)

⬚ 43 - 55
(4.4 - 5.6, 32 - 41)

Lap belt
installation **B**

Control unit

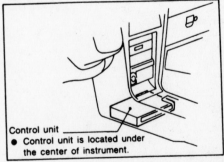

Control unit
● Control unit is located under
the center of instrument.

Automatic seat belt system

rect position and location. Apply primer A to the installation area--allow to dry.

8. On glass, apply sealant evenly in the correct amount and location. The windshield or glass assembly should be installed within 15 minutes after sealant is applied.

9. Set glass in the correct position and press glass lightly and evenly. Apply sealant to lower portion of glass and make it uniform.

10. Apply sealant to upper and side moulding in the correct location. Install mouldings. Mouldings must be installed so that no excessive gap exists.

11. Drying time for sealant to reach the desired hardness is relative to temperature and humidity (as long as 20 days in cold weather)-- the vehicle should not be driven on rough roads until sealant has properly vulcanized.

12. After the finished installation, water test the area. Leaks can be repaired without removing and reinstalling the glass assembly.

Seats

REMOVAL AND INSTALLATION

Front Assembly

NOTE: *On power seat models remove the seat then remove the power seat motor assembly and drive cable.*

1. Remove front seat mounting bolts.
2. Remove front seat assembly.
3. Installation is in the reverse order of removal.

Rear Assembly

1. Remove rear seat cushion mounting bolts.
2. Remove screw attaching luggage floor carpet.
3. Remove rear seat back by tilting forward and pulling straight up.

NOTE: *On hatchback models the rear seat back is removed in similar fashion.*

Seat Belt Systems

REMOVAL AND INSTALLATION

Refer to the illustrations.

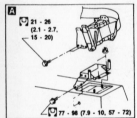

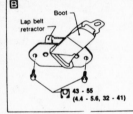

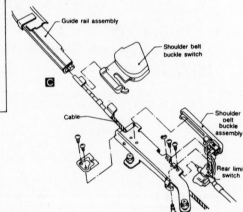

Automatic seat belt system

Mechanic's Data

11

TAX
1":254mm
10.16mm
Liter
Parts
Overhaul

General Conversion Table

Multiply By	To Convert	To	
	LENGTH		
2.54	Inches	Centimeters	.3937
25.4	Inches	Millimeters	.03937
30.48	Feet	Centimeters	.0328
.304	Feet	Meters	3.28
.914	Yards	Meters	1.094
1.609	Miles	Kilometers	.621
	VOLUME		
.473	Pints	Liters	2.11
.946	Quarts	Liters	1.06
3.785	Gallons	Liters	.264
.016	Cubic inches	Liters	61.02
16.39	Cubic inches	Cubic cms.	.061
28.3	Cubic feet	Liters	.0353
	MASS (Weight)		
28.35	Ounces	Grams	.035
.4536	Pounds	Kilograms	2.20
—	To obtain	From	Multiply by

Multiply By	To Convert	To	
	AREA		
.645	Square inches	Square cms.	.155
.836	Square yds.	Square meters	1.196
	FORCE		
4.448	Pounds	Newtons	.225
.138	Ft./lbs.	Kilogram/meters	7.23
1.36	Ft./lbs.	Newton-meters	.737
.112	In./lbs.	Newton-meters	8.844
	PRESSURE		
.068	Psi	Atmospheres	14.7
6.89	Psi	Kilopascals	.145
	OTHER		
1.104	Horsepower (DIN)	Horsepower (SAE)	.9861
.746	Horsepower (SAE)	Kilowatts (KW)	1.34
1.60	Mph	Km/h	.625
.425	Mpg	Km/1	2.35
—	To obtain	From	Multiply by

Tap Drill Sizes

National Coarse or U.S.S.

Screw & Tap Size	Threads Per Inch	Use Drill Number
No. 5	40	39
No. 6	32	36
No. 8	32	29
No. 10	24	25
No. 12	24	17
1/4	20	8
5/16	18	F
3/8	16	5/16
7/16	14	U
1/2	13	27/64
9/16	12	31/64
5/8	11	17/32
3/4	10	21/32
7/8	9	49/64

National Coarse or U.S.S.

Screw & Tap Size	Threads Per Inch	Use Drill Number
1	8	7/8
1 1/8	7	63/64
1 1/4	7	1 7/54
1 1/2	6	1 11/32

National Fine or S.A.E.

Screw & Tap Size	Threads Per Inch	Use Drill Number
No. 5	44	37
No. 6	40	33
No. 8	36	29
No. 10	32	21

National Fine or S.A.E.

Screw & Tap Size	Threads Per Inch	Use Drill Number
No. 12	28	15
1/4	28	3
6/16	24	1
3/8	24	Q
7/16	20	W
1/2	20	29/64
9/16	18	33/64
5/8	18	37/64
3/4	16	11/16
7/8	14	13/16
1 1/8	12	1 3/64
1 1/4	12	1 11/64
1 1/2	12	1 27/64

Drill Sizes In Decimal Equivalents

Inch	Decimal	Wire	mm
1/64	.0156		.39
	.0157		.4
	.0160	78	
	.0165		.42
	.0173		.44
	.0177		.45
	.0180	77	
	.0181		.46
	.0189		.48
	.0197		.5
	.0200	76	
	.0210	75	
	.0217		.55
	.0225	74	
	.0236		.6
	.0240	73	
	.0250	72	
	.0256		.65
	.0260	71	
	.0276		.7
	.0280	70	
	.0292	69	
	.0295		.75
	.0310	68	
1/32	.0312		.79
	.0315		.8
	.0320	67	
	.0330	66	
	.0335		.85
	.0350	65	
	.0354		.9
	.0360	64	
	.0370	63	
	.0374		.95
	.0380	62	
	.0390	61	
	.0394		1.0
	.0400	60	
	.0410	59	
	.0413		1.05
	.0420	58	
	.0430	57	
	.0433		1.1
	.0453		1.15
3/64	.0465	56	
	.0469		1.19
	.0472		1.2
	.0492		1.25
	.0512		1.3
	.0520	55	
	.0531		1.35
	.0550	54	
	.0551		1.4
	.0571		1.45
	.0591		1.5
	.0595	53	
	.0610		1.55
1/16	.0625		1.59
	.0630		1.6
	.0635	52	
	.0650		1.65
	.0669		1.7
	.0670	51	
	.0689		1.75
	.0700	50	
	.0709		1.8
	.0728		1.85

Inch	Decimal	Wire	mm
	.0730	49	
	.0748		1.9
	.0760	48	
	.0768		1.95
5/64	.0781		1.98
	.0785	47	
	.0787		2.0
	.0807		2.05
	.0810	46	
	.0820	45	
	.0827		2.1
	.0846		2.15
	.0860	44	
	.0866		2.2
	.0886		2.25
	.0890	43	
	.0906		2.3
	.0925		2.35
	.0935	42	
3/32	.0938		2.38
	.0945		2.4
	.0960	41	
	.0965		2.45
	.0980	40	
	.0981		2.5
	.0995	39	
	.1015	38	
	.1024		2.6
	.1040	37	
	.1063		2.7
	.1065	36	
	.1083		2.75
7/64	.1094		2.77
	.1100	35	
	.1102		2.8
	.1110	34	
	.1130	33	
	.1142		2.9
	.1160	32	
	.1181		3.0
	.1200	31	
	.1220		3.1
1/8	.1250		3.17
	.1260		3.2
	.1280		3.25
	.1285	30	
	.1299		3.3
	.1339		3.4
	.1360	29	
	.1378		3.5
	.1405	28	
9/64	.1406		3.57
	.1417		3.6
	.1440	27	
	.1457		3.7
	.1470	26	
	.1476		3.75
	.1495	25	
	.1496		3.8
	.1520	24	
	.1535		3.9
	.1540	23	
5/32	.1562		3.96
	.1570	22	
	.1575		4.0
	.1590	21	
	.1610	20	

Inch	Decimal	Wire & Letter	mm
	.1614		4.1
	.1654		4.2
	.1660	19	
	.1673		4.25
	.1693		4.3
	.1695	18	
11/64	.1719		4.36
	.1730	17	
	.1732		4.4
	.1770	16	
	.1772		4.5
	.1800	15	
	.1811		4.6
	.1820	14	
	.1850	13	
	.1850		4.7
	.1870		4.75
3/16	.1875		4.76
	.1890		4.8
	.1890	12	
	.1910	11	
	.1929		4.9
	.1935	10	
	.1960	9	
	.1969		5.0
	.1990	8	
	.2008		5.1
	.2010	7	
13/64	.2031		5.16
	.2040	6	
	.2047		5.2
	.2055	5	
	.2067		5.25
	.2087		5.3
	.2090	4	
	.2126		5.4
	.2130	3	
7/32	.2165		5.5
	.2188		5.55
	.2205		5.6
	.2210	2	
	.2244		5.7
	.2264		5.75
	.2280	1	
	.2283		5.8
	.2323		5.9
	.2340	A	
15/64	.2344		5.95
	.2362		6.0
	.2380	B	
	.2402		6.1
	.2420	C	
	.2441		6.2
	.2460	D	
	.2461		6.25
	.2480		6.3
1/4	.2500	E	6.35
	.2520		6.
	.2559		6.5
	.2570	F	
	.2598		6.6
	.2610	G	
	.2638		6.7
17/64	.2656		6.74
	.2657		6.75
	.2660	H	
	.2677		6.8

Inch	Decimal	Letter	mm
	.2717		6.9
	.2720	I	
	.2756		7.0
	.2770	J	
	.2795		7.1
	.2810	K	
9/32	.2812		7.14
	.2835		7.2
	.2854		7.25
	.2874		7.3
	.2900	L	
	.2913		7.4
	.2950	M	
	.2953		7.5
19/64	.2969		7.54
	.2992		7.6
	.3020	N	
	.3031		7.7
	.3051		7.75
	.3071		7.8
	.3110		7.9
5/16	.3125		7.93
	.3150		8.0
	.3160	O	
	.3189		8.1
	.3228		8.2
	.3230	P	
	.3248		8.25
	.3268		8.3
21/64	.3281		8.33
	.3307		8.4
	.3320	Q	
	.3346		8.5
	.3386		8.6
	.3390	R	
	.3425		8.7
11/32	.3438		8.73
	.3445		8.75
	.3465		8.8
	.3480	S	
	.3504		8.9
	.3543		9.0
	.3580	T	
	.3583		9.1
23/64	.3594		9.12
	.3622		9.2
	.3642		9.25
	.3661		9.3
	.3680	U	
	.3701		9.4
	.3740		9.5
3/8	.3750		9.52
	.3770	V	
	.3780		9.6
	.3819		9.7
	.3839		9.75
	.3858		9.8
	.3860	W	
	.3898		9.9
25/64	.3906		9.92
	.3937		10.0
	.3970	X	
	.4040	Y	
13/32	.4062		10.31
	.4130	Z	
	.4134		10.5
27/64	.4219		10.71

Inch	Decimal	mm
	.4331	11.0
7/16	.4375	11.11
	.4528	11.5
29/64	.4531	11.51
15/32	.4688	11.90
	.4724	12.0
31/64	.4844	12.30
	.4921	12.5
1/2	.5000	12.70
	.5118	13.0
33/64	.5156	13.09
17/32	.5312	13.49
	.5315	13.5
35/64	.5469	13.89
	.5512	14.0
9/16	.5625	14.28
	.5709	14.5
37/64	.5781	14.68
	.5906	15.0
19/32	.5938	15.08
39/64	.6094	15.47
	.6102	15.5
5/8	.6250	15.87
	.6299	16.0
41/64	.6406	16.27
	.6496	16.5
21/32	.6562	16.66
	.6693	17.0
43/64	.6719	17.06
11/16	.6875	17.46
	.6890	17.5
45/64	.7031	17.85
	.7087	18.0
23/32	.7188	18.25
	.7283	18.5
47/64	.7344	18.65
	.7480	19.0
3/4	.7500	19.05
49/64	.7656	19.44
	.7677	19.5
25/32	.7812	19.84
	.7874	20.0
51/64	.7969	20.24
	.8071	20.5
13/16	.8125	20.63
	.8268	21.0
53/64	.8281	21.03
27/32	.8438	21.43
	.8465	21.5
55/64	.8594	21.82
	.8661	22.0
7/8	.8750	22.22
	.8858	22.5
57/64	.8906	22.62
	.9055	23.0
29/32	.9062	23.01
59/64	.9219	23.41
	.9252	23.5
15/16	.9375	23.81
	.9449	24.0
61/64	.9531	24.2
	.9646	24.5
31/32	.9688	24.6
	.9843	25.0
63/64	.9844	25.0
1	1.0000	25.4

GLOSSARY OF TERMS

AIR/FUEL RATIO: The ratio of air to gasoline by weight in the fuel mixture drawn into the engine.

AIR INJECTION: One method of reducing harmful exhaust emissions by injecting air into each of the exhaust ports of an engine. The fresh air entering the hot exhaust manifold causes any remaining fuel to be burned before it can exit the tailpipe.

ALTERNATOR: A device used for converting mechanical energy into electrical energy.

AMMETER: An instrument, calibrated in amperes, used to measure the flow of an electrical current in a circuit. Ammeters are always connected in series with the circuit being tested.

AMPERE: The rate of flow of electrical current present when one volt of electrical pressure is applied against one ohm of electrical resistance.

ANALOG COMPUTER: Any microprocessor that uses similar (analogous) electrical signals to make its calculations.

ARMATURE: A laminated, soft iron core wrapped by a wire that converts electrical energy to mechanical energy as in a motor or relay. When rotated in a magnetic field, it changes mechanical energy into electrical energy as in a generator.

ATMOSPHERIC PRESSURE: The pressure on the Earth's surface caused by the weight of the air in the atmosphere. At sea level, this pressure is 14.7 psi at 32°F (101 kPa at 0°C).

ATOMIZATION: The breaking down of a liquid into a fine mist that can be suspended in air.

AXIAL PLAY: Movement parallel to a shaft or bearing bore.

BACKFIRE: The sudden combustion of gases in the intake or exhaust system that results in a loud explosion.

BACKLASH: The clearance or play between two parts, such as meshed gears.

BACKPRESSURE: Restrictions in the exhaust system that slow the exit of exhaust gases from the combustion chamber.

BAKELITE: A heat resistant, plastic insulator material commonly used in printed circuit boards and transistorized components.

BALL BEARING: A bearing made up of hardened inner and outer races between which hardened steel ball roll.

BALLAST RESISTOR: A resistor in the primary ignition circuit that lowers voltage after the engine is started to reduce wear on ignition components.

BEARING: A friction reducing, supportive device usually located between a stationary part and a moving part.

BIMETAL TEMPERATURE SENSOR: Any sensor or switch made of two dissimilar types of metal that bend when heated or cooled due to the different expansion rates of the alloys. These types of sensors usually function as an on/off switch.

BLOWBY: Combustion gases, composed of water vapor and unburned fuel, that leak past the piston rings into the crankcase during normal engine operation. These gases are removed by the PCV system to prevent the build-up of harmful acids in the crankcase.

BRAKE PAD: A brake shoe and lining assembly used with disc brakes.

BRAKE SHOE: The backing for the brake lining. The term is, however, usually applied to the assembly of the brake backing and lining.

BUSHING: A liner, usually removable, for a bearing; an anti-friction liner used in place of a bearing.

BYPASS: System used to bypass ballast resistor during engine cranking to increase voltage supplied to the coil.

CALIPER: A hydraulically activated device in a disc brake system, which is mounted straddling the brake rotor (disc). The caliper contains at least one piston and two brake pads. Hydraulic pressure on the piston(s) forces the pads against the rotor.

CAMSHAFT: A shaft in the engine on which are the lobes (cams) which operate the valves. The camshaft is driven by the crankshaft, via a belt, chain or gears, at one half the crankshaft speed.

CAPACITOR: A device which stores an electrical charge.

CARBON MONOXIDE (CO): a colorless, odorless gas given off as a normal byproduct of combustion. It is poisonous and extremely dangerous in confined areas, building up slowly to toxic levels without warning if adequate ventilation is not available.

CARBURETOR: A device, usually mounted on the intake manifold of an engine, which mixes the air and fuel in the proper proportion to allow even combustion.

CATALYTIC CONVERTER: A device installed in the exhaust system, like a muffler, that converts harmful byproducts of combustion into carbon dioxide and water vapor by means of a heat-producing chemical reaction.

CENTRIFUGAL ADVANCE: A mechanical method of advancing the spark timing by using flyweights in the distributor that react to centrifugal force generated by the distributor shaft rotation.

CHECK VALVE: Any one-way valve installed to permit the flow of air, fuel or vacuum in one direction only.

CHOKE: A device, usually a moveable valve, placed in the intake path of a carburetor to restrict the flow of air.

CIRCUIT: Any unbroken path through which an electrical current can flow. Also used to describe fuel flow in some instances.

CIRCUIT BREAKER: A switch which protects an electrical circuit from overload by opening the circuit when the current flow exceeds a predetermined level. Some circuit breakers must be reset manually, while other reset automatically.

COIL (IGNITION): A transformer in the ignition circuit which steps of the voltage provided to the spark plugs.

COMBINATION MANIFOLD: An assembly which includes both the intake and exhaust manifolds in one casting.

COMBINATION VALVE: A device used in some fuel systems that routes fuel vapors to a charcoal storage canister instead of venting them into the atmosphere. The valve relieves fuel tank pressure and allows fresh air into the tank as fuel level drops to prevent a vapor lock situation.

COMPRESSION RATIO: The comparison of the total volume of the cylinder and combustion chamber with the piston at BDC and the piston at TDC.

CONDENSER: 1. An electrical device which acts to store an electrical charge, preventing voltage surges.
2. A radiator-like device in the air conditioning system in which refrigerant gas condenses into a liquid, giving off heat.

CONDUCTOR: Any material through which an electrical current can be transmitted easily.

CONTINUITY: Continuous or complete circuit. Can be checked with an ohmmeter.

COUNTERSHAFT: An intermediate shaft which is rotated by a mainshaft and transmits, in turn, that rotation to a working part.

CRANKCASE: The lower part of an engine in which the crankshaft and related parts operate.

CRANKSHAFT: The main driving shaft of an engine which receives reciprocating motion from the pistons and converts it to rotary motion.

CYLINDER: In an engine, the round hole in the engine block in which the piston(s) ride.

CYLINDER BLOCK: The main structural member of an engine in which is found the cylinders, crankshaft and other principal parts.

CYLINDER HEAD: The detachable portion of the engine, fastened, usually, to the top of the cylinder block, containing all or most of the combustion chambers. On overhead valve engines, it contains the valves and their operating parts. On overhead cam engines, it contains the camshaft as well.

DEAD CENTER: The extreme top or bottom of the piston stroke.

DETONATION: An unwanted explosion of the air fuel mixture in the combustion chamber caused by excess heat and compression, advanced timing, or an overly lean mixture. Also referred to as "ping".

DIAPHRAGM: A thin, flexible wall separating two cavities, such as in a vacuum advance unit.

DIESELING: A condition in which hot spots in the combustion chamber cause the engine to run on after the key is turned off.

DIFFERENTIAL: A geared assembly which allows the transmission of motion between drive axles, giving one axle the ability to turn faster than the other.

DIODE: An electrical device that will allow current to flow in one direction only.

DISC BRAKE: A hydraulic braking assembly consisting of a brake disc, or rotor, mounted on an axle, and a caliper assembly containing, usually two brake pads which are activated by hydraulic pressure. The pads are forced against the sides of the disc, creating friction which slows the vehicle.

DISTRIBUTOR: A mechanically driven device on an engine which is responsible for electrically firing the spark plug at a predetermined point of the piston stroke.

DOWEL PIN: A pin, inserted in mating holes in two different parts allowing those parts to maintain a fixed relationship.

DRUM BRAKE: A braking system which consists of two brake shoes and one or two wheel cylinders, mounted on a fixed backing plate, and a brake drum, mounted on an axle, which revolves around the assembly. Hydraulic action applied to the wheel cylinders forces the shoes outward against the drum, creating friction and slowing the vehicle.

DWELL: The rate, measured in degrees of shaft rotation, at which an electrical circuit cycles on and off.

ELECTRONIC CONTROL UNIT (ECU): Ignition module, module, amplifier or igniter. See Module for definition.

ELECTRONIC IGNITION: A system in which the timing and firing of the spark plugs is controlled by an electronic control unit, usually called a module. These systems have not points or condenser.

ENDPLAY: The measured amount of axial movement in a shaft.

ENGINE: A device that converts heat into mechanical energy.

EXHAUST MANIFOLD: A set of cast passages or pipes which conduct exhaust gases from the engine.

FEELER GAUGE: A blade, usually metal, of precisely predetermined thickness, used to measure the clearance between two parts. These blades usually are available in sets of assorted thicknesses.

F-Head: An engine configuration in which the intake valves are in the cylinder head, while the camshaft and exhaust valves are located in the cylinder block. The camshaft operates the intake valves via lifters and pushrods, while it operates the exhaust valves directly.

FIRING ORDER: The order in which combustion occurs in the cylinders of an engine. Also the order in which spark is distributed to the plugs by the distributor.

FLATHEAD: An engine configuration in which the camshaft and all the valves are located in the cylinder block.

FLOODING: The presence of too much fuel in the intake manifold and combustion chamber which prevents the air/fuel mixture from firing, thereby causing a no-start situation.

FLYWHEEL: A disc shaped part bolted to the rear end of the crankshaft. Around the outer perimeter is affixed the ring gear. The starter drive engages the ring gear, turning the flywheel, which rotates the crankshaft, imparting the initial starting motion to the engine.

FOOT POUND (ft.lb. or sometimes, ft. lbs.): The amount of energy or work needed to raise an item weighing one pound, a distance of one foot.

FUSE: A protective device in a circuit which prevents circuit overload by breaking the circuit when a specific amperage is present. The device is constructed around a strip or wire of a lower amperage rating than the circuit it is designed to protect. When an amperage higher than that stamped on the fuse is present in the circuit, the strip or wire melts, opening the circuit.

GEAR RATIO: The ratio between the number of teeth on meshing gears.

GENERATOR: A device which converts mechanical energy into electrical energy.

HEAT RANGE: The measure of a spark plug's ability to dissipate heat from its firing end. The higher the heat range, the hotter the plug fires.

HUB: The center part of a wheel or gear.

HYDROCARBON (HC): Any chemical compound made up of hydrogen and carbon. A major pollutant formed by the engine as a byproduct of combustion.

HYDROMETER: An instrument used to measure the specific gravity of a solution.

INCH POUND (in.lb. or sometimes, in. lbs.): One twelfth of a foot pound.

INDUCTION: A means of transferring electrical energy in the form of a magnetic field. Principle used in the ignition coil to increase voltage.

INJECTION PUMP: A device, usually mechanically operated, which meters and delivers fuel under pressure to the fuel injector.

INJECTOR: A device which receives metered fuel under relatively low pressure and is activated to inject the fuel into the engine under relatively high pressure at a predetermined time.

INPUT SHAFT: The shaft to which torque is applied, usually carrying the driving gear or gears.

INTAKE MANIFOLD: A casting of passages or pipes used to conduct air or a fuel/air mixture to the cylinders.

JOURNAL: The bearing surface within which a shaft operates.

KEY: A small block usually fitted in a notch between a shaft and a hub to prevent slippage of the two parts.

MANIFOLD: A casting of passages or set of pipes which connect the cylinders to an inlet or outlet source.

MANIFOLD VACUUM: Low pressure in an engine intake manifold formed just below the throttle plates. Manifold vacuum is highest at idle and drops under acceleration.

MASTER CYLINDER: The primary fluid pressurizing device in a hydraulic system. In automotive use, it is found in brake and hydraulic clutch systems and is pedal activated, either directly or, in a power brake system, through the power booster.

MODULE: Electronic control unit, amplifier or igniter of solid state or integrated design which controls the current flow in the ignition primary circuit based on input from the pickup coil. When the module opens the primary circuit, the high secondary voltage is induced in the coil.

NEEDLE BEARING: A bearing which consists of a number (usually a large number) of long, thin rollers.

OHM: (Ω) The unit used to measure the resistance of conductor to electrical flow. One ohm is the amount of resistance that limits current flow to one ampere in a circuit with one volt of pressure.

OHMMETER: An instrument used for measuring the resistance, in ohms, in an electrical circuit.

OUTPUT SHAFT: The shaft which transmits torque from a device, such as a transmission.

OVERDRIVE: A gear assembly which produces more shaft revolutions than that transmitted to it.

OVERHEAD CAMSHAFT (OHC): An engine configuration in which the camshaft is mounted on top of the cylinder head and operates the valve either directly or by means of rocker arms.

OVERHEAD VALVE (OHV): An engine configuration in which all of the valves are located in the cylinder head and the camshaft is located in the cylinder block. The camshaft operates the valves via lifters and pushrods.

OXIDES OF NITROGEN (NOx): Chemical compounds of nitrogen produced as a byproduct of combustion. They combine with hydrocarbons to produce smog.

OXYGEN SENSOR: Used with the feedback system to sense the presence of oxygen in the exhaust gas and signal the computer which can reference the voltage signal to an air/fuel ratio.

PINION: The smaller of two meshing gears.

PISTON RING: An open ended ring which fits into a groove on the outer diameter of the piston. Its chief function is to form a seal between the piston and cylinder wall. Most automotive pistons have three rings: two for compression sealing; one for oil sealing.

PRELOAD: A predetermined load placed on a bearing during assembly or by adjustment.

PRIMARY CIRCUIT: Is the low voltage side of the ignition system which consists of the ignition switch, ballast resistor or resistance wire, bypass, coil, electronic control unit and pick-up coil as well as the connecting wires and harnesses.

PRESS FIT: The mating of two parts under pressure, due to the inner diameter of one being smaller than the outer diameter of the other, or vice versa; an interference fit.

RACE: The surface on the inner or outer ring of a bearing on which the balls, needles or rollers move.

REGULATOR: A device which maintains the amperage and/or voltage levels of a circuit at predetermined values.

RELAY: A switch which automatically opens and/or closes a circuit.

RESISTANCE: The opposition to the flow of current through a circuit or electrical device, and is measured in ohms. Resistance is equal to the voltage divided by the amperage.

RESISTOR: A device, usually made of wire, which offers a preset amount of resistance in an electrical circuit.

RING GEAR: The name given to a ring-shaped gear attached to a differential case, or affixed to a flywheel or as part a planetary gear set.

ROLLER BEARING: A bearing made up of hardened inner and outer races between which hardened steel rollers move.

ROTOR: 1. The disc-shaped part of a disc brake assembly, upon which the brake pads bear; also called, brake disc.
2. The device mounted atop the distributor shaft, which passes current to the distributor cap tower contacts.

SECONDARY CIRCUIT: The high voltage side of the ignition system, usually above 20,000 volts. The secondary includes the ignition coil, coil wire, distributor cap and rotor, spark plug wires and spark plugs.

SENDING UNIT: A mechanical, electrical, hydraulic or electromagnetic device which transmits information to a gauge.

SENSOR: Any device designed to measure engine operating conditions or ambient pressures and temperatures. Usually electronic in nature and designed to send a voltage signal to an on-board computer, some sensors may operate as a simple on/off switch or they may provide a variable voltage signal (like a potentiometer) as conditions or measured parameters change.

SHIM: Spacers of precise, predetermined thickness used between parts to establish a proper working relationship.

SLAVE CYLINDER: In automotive use, a device in the hydraulic clutch system which is activated by hydraulic force, disengaging the clutch.

SOLENOID: A coil used to produce a magnetic field, the effect of which is produce work.

SPARK PLUG: A device screwed into the combustion chamber of a spark ignition engine. The basic construction is a conductive core inside of a ceramic insulator, mounted in an outer conductive base. An electrical charge from the spark plug wire travels along the conductive core and jumps a preset air gap to a grounding point or points at the end of the conductive base. The resultant spark ignites the fuel/air mixture in the combustion chamber.

SPLINES: Ridges machined or cast onto the outer diameter of a shaft or inner diameter of a bore to enable parts to mate without rotation.

TACHOMETER: A device used to measure the rotary speed of an engine, shaft, gear, etc., usually in rotations per minute.

THERMOSTAT: A valve, located in the cooling system of an engine, which is closed when cold and opens gradually in response to engine heating, controlling the temperature of the coolant and rate of coolant flow.

TOP DEAD CENTER (TDC): The point at which the piston reaches the top of its travel on the compression stroke.

TORQUE: The twisting force applied to an object.

TORQUE CONVERTER: A turbine used to transmit power from a driving member to a driven member via hydraulic action, providing changes in drive ratio and torque. In automotive use, it links the driveplate at the rear of the engine to the automatic transmission.

TRANSDUCER: A device used to change a force into an electrical signal.

TRANSISTOR: A semi-conductor component which can be actuated by a small voltage to perform an electrical switching function.

TUNE-UP: A regular maintenance function, usually associated with the replacement and adjustment of parts and components in the electrical and fuel systems of a vehicle for the purpose of attaining optimum performance.

TURBOCHARGER: An exhaust driven pump which compresses intake air and forces it into the combustion chambers at higher than atmospheric pressures. The increased air pressure allows more fuel to be burned and results in increased horsepower being produced.

VACUUM ADVANCE: A device which advances the ignition timing in response to increased engine vacuum.

VACUUM GAUGE: An instrument used to measure the presence of vacuum in a chamber.

VALVE: A device which control the pressure, direction of flow or rate of flow of a liquid or gas.

VALVE CLEARANCE: The measured gap between the end of the valve stem and the rocker arm, cam lobe or follower that activates the valve.

VISCOSITY: The rating of a liquid's internal resistance to flow.

VOLTMETER: An instrument used for measuring electrical force in units called volts. Voltmeters are always connected parallel with the circuit being tested.

WHEEL CYLINDER: Found in the automotive drum brake assembly, it is a device, actuated by hydraulic pressure, which, through internal pistons, pushes the brake shoes outward against the drums.

ABBREVIATIONS AND SYMBOLS

A: Ampere

AC: Alternating current

A/C: Air conditioning

A-h: Ampere hour

AT: Automatic transmission

ATDC: After top dead center

μA: Microampere

bbl: Barrel

BDC: Bottom dead center

bhp: Brake horsepower

BTDC: Before top dead center

BTU: British thermal unit

C: Celsius (Centigrade)

CCA: Cold cranking amps

cd: Candela

cm^2: Square centimeter

cm^3, cc: Cubic centimeter

CO: Carbon monoxide

CO_2: Carbon dioxide

cu.in., in^3: Cubic inch

CV: Constant velocity

Cyl.: Cylinder

DC: Direct current

ECM: Electronic control module

EFE: Early fuel evaporation

EFI: Electronic fuel injection

EGR: Exhaust gas recirculation

Exh.: Exhaust

F: Fahrenheit

F: Farad

pF: Picofarad

μF: Microfarad

FI: Fuel injection

ft.lb., ft. lb., ft. lbs.: foot pound(s)

gal: Gallon

g: Gram

HC: Hydrocarbon

HEI: High energy ignition

HO: High output

hp: Horsepower

Hyd.: Hydraulic

Hz: Hertz

ID: Inside diameter

in.lb.; in. lb.; in. lbs: inch pound(s)

Int.: Intake

K: Kelvin

kg: Kilogram

kHz: Kilohertz

km: Kilometer

km/h: Kilometers per hour

$k\Omega$: Kilohm

kPa: Kilopascal

kV: Kilovolt

kW: Kilowatt

l: Liter

l/s: Liters per second

m: Meter

mA: Milliampere

mg: Milligram

mHz: Megahertz

mm: Millimeter

mm^2: Square millimeter

m^3: Cubic meter

MΩ: Megohm

m/s: Meters per second

MT: Manual transmission

mV: Millivolt

μm: Micrometer

N: Newton

N-m: Newton meter

NOx: Nitrous oxide

OD: Outside diameter

OHC: Over head camshaft

OHV: Over head valve

Ω: Ohm

PCV: Positive crankcase ventilation

psi: Pounds per square inch

pts: Pints

qts: Quarts

rpm: Rotations per minute

rps: Rotations per second

R-12: A refrigerant gas (Freon)

SAE: Society of Automotive Engineers

SO$_2$: Sulfur dioxide

T: Ton

t: Megagram

TBI: Throttle Body Injection

TPS: Throttle Position Sensor

V: 1. Volt; 2. Venturi

μV: Microvolt

W: Watt

∞: Infinity

$<$: Less than

$>$: Greater than

Index

Chilton's Repair & Tune-Up Guides

The Complete line covers domestic cars, imports, trucks, vans, RV's and 4-wheel drive vehicles.

RTUG Title	Part No.
AMC 1975-82	7199
Covers all U.S. and Canadian models	
Aspen/Volare 1976-80	6637
Covers all U.S. and Canadian models	
Audi 1970-73	5902
Covers all U.S. and Canadian models.	
Audi 4000/5000 1978-81	7028
Covers all U.S. and Canadian models including turbocharged and diesel engines	
Barracuda/Challenger 1965-72	5807
Covers all U.S. and Canadian models	
Blazer/Jimmy 1969-82	6931
Covers all U.S. and Canadian 2- and 4-wheel drive models, including diesel engines	
BMW 1970-82	6844
Covers U.S. and Canadian models	
Buick/Olds/Pontiac 1975-85	7308
Covers U.S. and Canadian full size rear wheel drive models	
Cadillac 1967-84	7462
Covers all U.S. and Canadian rear wheel drive models	
Camaro 1967-81	6735
Covers all U.S. and Canadian models	
Camaro 1982-85	7317
Covers all U.S. and Canadian models	
Capri 1970-77	6695
Covers all U.S. and Canadian models	
Caravan/Voyager 1984-85	7482
Covers all U.S. and Canadian models	
Century/Regal 1975-85	7307
Covers all U.S. and Canadian rear wheel drive models, including turbocharged engines	
Champ/Arrow/Sapporo 1978-83	7041
Covers all U.S. and Canadian models	
Chevette/1000 1976-86	6836
Covers all U.S. and Canadian models	
Chevrolet 1968-85	7135
Covers all U.S. and Canadian models	
Chevrolet 1968-79 Spanish	7082
Chevrolet/GMC Pick-Ups 1970-82 Spanish	7468
Chevrolet/GMC Pick-Ups and Suburban 1970-86	6936
Covers all U.S. and Canadian 1/2, 3/4 and 1 ton models, including 4-wheel drive and diesel engines	
Chevrolet LUV 1972-81	6815
Covers all U.S. and Canadian models	
Chevrolet Mid-Size 1964-86	6840
Covers all U.S. and Canadian models of 1964-77 Chevelle, Malibu and Malibu SS; 1974-77 Laguna; 1978-85 Malibu; 1970-86 Monte Carlo; 1964-84 El Camino, including diesel engines	
Chevrolet Nova 1986	7658
Covers all U.S. and Canadian models	
Chevy/GMC Vans 1967-84	6930
Covers all U.S. and Canadian models of 1/2, 3/4, and 1 ton vans, cutaways, and motor home chassis, including diesel engines	
Chevy S-10 Blazer/GMC S-15 Jimmy 1982-85	7383
Covers all U.S. and Canadian models	
Chevy S-10/GMC S-15 Pick-Ups 1982-85	7310
Covers all U.S. and Canadian models	
Chevy II/Nova 1962-79	6841
Covers all U.S. and Canadian models	
Chrysler K- and E-Car 1981-85	7163
Covers all U.S. and Canadian front wheel drive models	
Colt/Challenger/Vista/Conquest 1971-85	7037
Covers all U.S. and Canadian models	
Corolla/Carina/Tercel/Starlet 1970-85	7036
Covers all U.S. and Canadian models	
Corona/Cressida/Crown/Mk.II/Camry/Van 1970-84	7044
Covers all U.S. and Canadian models	

RTUG Title	Part No.
Corvair 1960-69	6691
Covers all U.S. and Canadian models	
Corvette 1953-62	6576
Covers all U.S. and Canadian models	
Corvette 1963-84	6843
Covers all U.S. and Canadian models	
Cutlass 1970-85	6933
Covers all U.S. and Canadian models	
Dart/Demon 1968-76	6324
Covers all U.S. and Canadian models	
Datsun 1961-72	5790
Covers all U.S. and Canadian models of Nissan Patrol; 1500, 1600 and 2000 sports cars; Pick-Ups; 410, 411, 510, 1200 and 240Z	
Datsun 1973-80 Spanish	7083
Datsun/Nissan F-10, 310, Stanza, Pulsar 1977-86	7196
Covers all U.S. and Canadian models	
Datsun/Nissan Pick-Ups 1970-84	6816
Covers all U.S and Canadian models	
Datsun/Nissan Z & ZX 1970-86	6932
Covers all U.S. and Canadian models	
Datsun/Nissan 1200, 210, Sentra 1973-86	7197
Covers all U.S. and Canadian models	
Datsun/Nissan 200SX, 510, 610, 710, 810, Maxima 1973-84	7170
Covers all U.S. and Canadian models	
Dodge 1968-77	6554
Covers all U.S. and Canadian models	
Dodge Charger 1967-70	6486
Covers all U.S. and Canadian models	
Dodge/Plymouth Trucks 1967-84	7459
Covers all 1/2, 3/4, and 1 ton 2- and 4-wheel drive U.S. and Canadian models, including diesel engines	
Dodge/Plymouth Vans 1967-84	6934
Covers all 1/2, 3/4, and 1 ton U.S. and Canadian models of vans, cutaways and motor home chassis	
D-50/Arrow Pick-Up 1979-81	7032
Covers all U.S. and Canadian models	
Fairlane/Torino 1962-75	6320
Covers all U.S. and Canadian models	
Fairmont/Zephyr 1978-83	6965
Covers all U.S. and Canadian models	
Fiat 1969-81	7042
Covers all U.S. and Canadian models	
Fiesta 1978-80	6846
Covers all U.S. and Canadian models	
Firebird 1967-81	5996
Covers all U.S. and Canadian models	
Firebird 1982-85	7345
Covers all U.S. and Canadian models	
Ford 1968-79 Spanish	7084
Ford Bronco 1966-83	7140
Covers all U.S. and Canadian models	
Ford Bronco II 1984	7408
Covers all U.S. and Canadian models	
Ford Courier 1972-82	6983
Covers all U.S. and Canadian models	
Ford/Mercury Front Wheel Drive 1981-85	7055
Covers all U.S. and Canadian models Escort, EXP, Tempo, Lynx, LN-7 and Topaz	
Ford/Mercury/Lincoln 1968-85	6842
Covers all U.S. and Canadian models of FORD Country Sedan, Country Squire, Crown Victoria, Custom, Custom 500, Galaxie 500, LTD through 1982, Ranch Wagon, and XL; MERCURY Colony Park, Commuter, Marquis through 1982, Gran Marquis, Monterey and Park Lane; LINCOLN Continental and Towne Car	
Ford/Mercury/Lincoln Mid-Size 1971-85	6696
Covers all U.S. and Canadian models of FORD Elite, 1983-85 LTD, 1977-79 LTD II, Ranchero, Torino, Gran Torino, 1977-85 Thunderbird; MERCURY 1972-85 Cougar,	

continued on next page

RTUG Title	Part No.
1983-85 Marquis, Montego, 1980-85 XR-7; LINCOLN 1982-85 Continental, 1984-85 Mark VII, 1978-80 Versailles	
Ford Pick-Ups 1965-86 Covers all $^1/_2$, $^3/_4$ and 1 ton, 2- and 4-wheel drive U.S. and Canadian pick-up, chassis cab and camper models, including diesel engines	6913
Ford Pick-Ups 1965-82 Spanish	7469
Ford Ranger 1983-84 Covers all U.S. and Canadian models	7338
Ford Vans 1961-86 Covers all U.S. and Canadian $^1/_2$, $^3/_4$ and 1 ton van and cutaway chassis models, including diesel engines	6849
GM A-Body 1982-85 Covers all front wheel drive U.S. and Canadian models of BUICK Century, CHEVROLET Celebrity, OLDSMOBILE Cutlass Ciera and PONTIAC 6000	7309
GM C-Body 1985 Covers all front wheel drive U.S. and Canadian models of BUICK Electra Park Avenue and Electra T-Type, CADILLAC Fleetwood and deVille, OLDSMOBILE 98 Regency and Regency Brougham	7587
GM J-Car 1982-85 Covers all U.S. and Canadian models of BUICK Skyhawk, CHEVROLET Cavalier, CADILLAC Cimarron, OLDSMOBILE Firenza and PONTIAC 2000 and Sunbird	7059
GM N-Body 1985-86 Covers all U.S. and Canadian models of front wheel drive BUICK Somerset and Skylark, OLDSMOBILE Calais, and PONTIAC Grand Am	7657
GM X-Body 1980-85 Covers all U.S. and Canadian models of BUICK Skylark, CHEVROLET Citation, OLDSMOBILE Omega and PONTIAC Phoenix	7049
GM Subcompact 1971-80 Covers all U.S. and Canadian models of BUICK Skyhawk (1975-80), CHEVROLET Vega and Monza, OLDSMOBILE Starfire, and PONTIAC Astre and 1975-80 Sunbird	6935
Granada/Monarch 1975-82 Covers all U.S. and Canadian models	6937
Honda 1973-84 Covers all U.S. and Canadian models	6980
International Scout 1967-73 Covers all U.S. and Canadian models	5912
Jeep 1945-87 Covers all U.S. and Canadian CJ-2A, CJ-3A, CJ-3B, CJ-5, CJ-6, CJ-7, Scrambler and Wrangler models	6817
Jeep Wagoneer, Commando, Cherokee, Truck 1957-86 Covers all U.S. and Canadian models of Wagoneer, Cherokee, Grand Wagoneer, Jeepster, Jeepster Commando, J-100, J-200, J-300, J-10, J20, FC-150 and FC-170	6739
Laser/Daytona 1984-85 Covers all U.S. and Canadian models	7563
Maverick/Comet 1970-77 Covers all U.S. and Canadian models	6634
Mazda 1971-84 Covers all U.S. and Canadian models of RX-2, RX-3, RX-4, 808, 1300, 1600, Cosmo, GLC and 626	6981
Mazda Pick-Ups 1972-86 Covers all U.S. and Canadian models	7659
Mercedes-Benz 1959-70 Covers all U.S. and Canadian models	6065
Mercedes-Benz 1968-73 Covers all U.S. and Canadian models	5907

RTUG Title	Part No.
Mercedes-Benz 1974-84 Covers all U.S. and Canadian models	6809
Mitsubishi, Cordia, Tredia, Starion, Galant 1983-85 Covers all U.S. and Canadian models	7583
MG 1961-81 Covers all U.S. and Canadian models	6780
Mustang/Capri/Merkur 1979-85 Covers all U.S. and Canadian models	6963
Mustang/Cougar 1965-73 Covers all U.S. and Canadian models	6542
Mustang II 1974-78 Covers all U.S. and Canadian models	6812
Omni/Horizon/Rampage 1978-84 Covers all U.S. and Canadian models of DODGE omni, Miser, 024, Charger 2.2; PLYMOUTH Horizon, Miser, TC3, TC3 Tourismo; Rampage	6845
Opel 1971-75 Covers all U.S. and Canadian models	6575
Peugeot 1970-74 Covers all U.S. and Canadian models	5982
Pinto/Bobcat 1971-80 Covers all U.S. and Canadian models	7027
Plymouth 1968-76 Covers all U.S. and Canadian models	6552
Pontiac Fiero 1984-85 Covers all U.S. and Canadian models	7571
Pontiac Mid-Size 1974-83 Covers all U.S. and Canadian models of Ventura, Grand Am, LeMans, Grand LeMans, GTO, Phoenix, and Grand Prix	7346
Porsche 924/928 1976-81	7048
Renault 1975-85 Covers all U.S. and Canadian models	7165
Roadrunner/Satellite/Belvedere/GTX 1968-73 Covers all U.S. and Canadian models	5821
RX-7 1979-81 Covers all U.S. and Canadian models	7031
SAAB 99 1969-75 Covers all U.S. and Canadian models	5988
SAAB 900 1979-85 Covers all U.S. and Canadian models	7572
Snowmobiles 1976-80 Covers Arctic Cat, John Deere, Kawasaki, Polaris, Ski-Doo and Yamaha	6978
Subaru 1970-84 Covers all U.S. and Canadian models	6982
Tempest/GTO/LeMans 1968-73 Covers all U.S. and Canadian models	5905
Toyota 1966-70 Covers all U.S. and Canadian models of Corona, MkII, Corolla, Crown, Land Cruiser, Stout and Hi-Lux	5795
Toyota 1970-79 Spanish	7467
Toyota Celica/Supra 1971-85 Covers all U.S. and Canadian models	7043
Toyota Trucks 1970-85 Covers all U.S. and Canadian models of pick-ups, Land Cruiser and 4Runner	7035
Valiant/Duster 1968-76 Covers all U.S. and Canadian models	6326
Volvo 1956-69 Covers all U.S. and Canadian models	6529
Volvo 1970-83 Covers all U.S. and Canadian models	7040
VW Front Wheel Drive 1974-85 Covers all U.S. and Canadian models	6962
VW 1949-71 Covers all U.S. and Canadian models	5796
VW 1970-79 Spanish	7081
VW 1970-81 Covers all U.S. and Canadian Beetles, Karmann Ghia, Fastback, Squareback, Vans, 411 and 412	6837

Chilton's Repair Manuals are available at your local retailer or by mailing a check or money order for **$15.95** per book plus **$3.50** for 1st book and **$.50** for each additional book to cover postage and handling to:

Chilton Book Company
Dept. DM
Radnor, PA 19089

NOTE: When ordering be sure to include your name & address, book part No. & title.